APARTHEID
AND
EDUCATION

APARTHEID AND EDUCATION

The Education of Black South Africans

Edited by Peter Kallaway

Published in association with
the Education Policy Unit and
Centre for African Studies
(University of Cape Town)

An *Africa Perspective* Project

RAVAN PRESS  JOHANNESBURG

Published by Ravan Press (Pty) Ltd.,
P.O. Box 31134, Braamfontein 2017, South Africa

© Copyright: The contributors
as listed on the contents page of this book

First published 1984
Second impression 1986
Typesetting: Sandy Parker
Cover Design: The Graphic Equalizer
Cover Painting: Ernest Ullmann
(Courtesy Johannesburg Public Library)

ISBN 0 86975 256 1

Printed by Galvin & Sales, Cape Town

To
Our
Children

All royalties from this book will
be used to fund future research
and publications on black
education in South Africa.

Contents

Photographs   *Between pages 48 and 49*
Between pages 114 and 115
On page 126
Between pages 204 and 205
Between pages 268 and 269
Between pages 302 and 303
Between pages 352 and 353

Contributors

Frank Molteno lectures in Sociology at the University of Cape Town.

R Hunt Davis, Jr Director of the Centre of African Studies and Professor of History, University of Florida, Gainesville, Fla., USA.

Penny Enslin lectures in Philosophy of Education at the University of the Witwatersrand, Johannesburg.

Lynn Maree was a lecturer in Education at the London College of Dance and Drama until 1981. She is now an Arts Administrator at Jackson's Lane Community Centre in London and continues to lecture on a part-time basis.

Pam Christie lectured at Kelvin Grove College of Advanced Education, Brisbane, Queensland, Australia; presently at the Department of Education, University of the Witwatersrand.

Colin Collins lectures in Education at the University of Queensland, Brisbane, Australia.

Robert Edgar Assistant Professor in the African Studies and Research Programme, Howard University, Washington, DC.

Adrienne Bird is a mathematics teacher in Hemel Hempstead, England, and has recently completed an MEd degree at the University of Manchester.

Deborah Gaitskell has recently completed her PhD at the School of Oriental and African Studies, London University, and is a tutor in the Extra-Mural Department, London University.

Tom Lodge lectures in the Politics Department, University of the Witwatersrand, Johannesburg.

Rachel Sharp lectures in Education at Macquarie University, Sydney, Australia. She is the author of: *Education and Social Control: A Study of Progressive Primary Education* (with A Green) (London 1978), and *Knowledge, Ideology and the Politics of Schooling: Towards a Marxist Analysis of Education* (London 1980).

Mervyn Hartwig lectures in the Department of History, Macquarie University, Sydney, Australia.

John Davies lectures in the Department of Education, University of Canterbury, Christchurch, New Zealand.

Peter Buckland formerly at the Education Policy Unit, University of Cape Town, now teaching in Bophuthatswana.

Linda Chisholm lectures in the Education Department, University of the Witwatersrand, Johannesburg.

ACKNOWLEDGEMENTS

We wish to thank the following:
The editorial board of *African Studies Review* for permission to republish the article by R Hunt Davis Jr on 'Charles T Loram and the American Model for African Education in South Africa' which originally appeared in *ASR* XIX (2) 1976.

The editorial board of *Comparative Education* for permission to republish the article by Pam Christie and Colin Collins on 'Bantu Education: Apartheid Ideology and Labour Reproduction' which originally appeared in *CE* 18 (1) 1982, and the article by Linda Chisholm, 'Skills Shortage: Black Education in South Africa in the 1980s' which orginally appeared in *CE* 19 (3) 1983, pp 357-371.

The editorial board of *Perspectives in Education* for permission to republish Peter Buckland's article on 'Technicism and de Lange: Reflections on the process of the HSRC Investigation' which orginally appeared in *Perspectives in Education* May 1982, pp 35-51.

EDITOR'S NOTE

I wish to thank my colleagues at the University of the Witwatersrand and the University of Cape Town for their encouragement and critical comment on this project. In particular I am grateful to Prof Ian Phimister for his helpful and detailed assistance with the introduction. Thanks also to Peter Randall for his help with editing, to Mrs King, Gilly Boyce and Anne Brookes for typing, and to Jackie, Julia, Vanessa and Ma for all their patience with hours spent on the project.

Peter Kallaway

It is worth emphasising that in the 1890s (in Britain) many educational reforms were advocated because of anxieties about the possibilities of social and economic disorganization.

David Reeder, 'A Recurring Debate: Education and Industry' in
Dale R *et al* (eds), *Education and the State:* Vol I; *Schooling and the National Interest* (Lewes, 1981), p 182

. . . it can be argued that any society which feels itself threatened from without or enfeebled from within is likely to assert the value of useful knowledge and to stress the extrinsic purposes of education.

ibid p 200

Introduction

An Introduction to the Study of Education for Blacks in South Africa
Peter Kallaway

The need for a political economy of South African education

The schools crisis demands urgent and critical appraisal of the whole enterprise of education in South Africa. Such an investigation requires, first, that education and education policy-making be examined in their own right, within the specific terrains of public and academic debate or administrative policy initiatives, in order to uncover the assumptions which have informed 'common sense' or 'expert' knowledge on these subjects over time. Secondly, and in many senses more problematically, the investigation of educational issues has to be located within the broader context of political, social and economic change if we are to grasp the more general, structural significance of shifts in educational policy. 'The ideological balance within debates about education and the broader ideological struggles in the society at large are inextricably linked, and the crucial relation between schooling and society is often and systematically denied' in public debate; in particular the connections between 'the structure and kinds of education we are said to *need*, and the needs of a capitalist economy in crisis' are often ignored.[1] This collection of papers emphasises the 'dependent' nature of schooling systems, and seeks to stress both their political (ideological and control) functions and their economic role as producers of specific types of 'manpower' relevant to the needs of the dominant systems of production in society. This emphasis is acknowledged without wishing to underplay the 'autonomy of the region' of education itself.[2]

A common assumption underlying the papers in this volume is that any attempt to 'plan' education for the South African future that evades such an explanatory framework, that ignores the unwritten assumptions of past and present education endeavours,

or that fails to locate educational issues within the broader framework of economic and political change runs the risk of naivete and
irrelevance. Worse, it contains the possibility of misleading those
who would undertake the important task of planning for a more
just and equitable educational future.

The focus is on the education of black South Africans, not
because we believe that white education is any less besieged by
problems or that those problems are separate from those
encountered in black education, but simply because the crisis is
most acute in black education. As Penny Enslin points out there
are strong links between the formulation of the policy of Bantu
Education and the general evolution of educational ideas associated
with Christian National Education and Fundamental Pedagogics;
to ignore those links, as many accounts have done, leaves us with a
considerably impoverished view of the evolution of educational
policy since the 1930s.

The issues of educational reform are obviously related to
broader questions affecting the well-being of the politically
rightless people of South Africa and the question of educational
struggle is intimately related to the current crisis in industry (the
so-called 'manpower crisis'). All these aspects highlight the role of
education within the wider context referred to above. Finally,
these papers on black education should be seen against the need
for more critical work to be made accessible to public debate in
order to counter the opinions of the extraordinary variety of self-
appointed experts pronouncing on this topic — often not without
sectional interest — at the present time.

A satisfactory grasp of the current context of black education
and its historical background demands a fuller consideration of all
types of education than will be possible here. The complexities
of the issues relating to missionary and state systems, academic or
vocational/technical curriculums, formal or non-formal schooling,
medical education, and a host of other fields, in addition to their
relations to the area of employment/unemployment, are manifold,
and still in need of detailed research. All that we can do is to offer
a series of pointers to the kind of work that is possible, and the
questions that need to be asked in order to meet the challenge
before us. In that spirit, too, we do not intend to present any
tightly knit theoretical or policy perspective; we are simply not in
a position to offer any blueprint on the basis of our present knowledge. 'Educational policy' or 'educational planning' is, in any
case, a misnomer since such terms imply that there *is* 'One Best
System' for all,[3] ignoring the obvious fact that the very act of
planning and policy-making constitutes a political action which
includes value judgements and statements of interest based on

political or ideological foundations. Educational policies are an aspect of the struggle between different classes in society.

A fundamental assumption of this collection is that such obvious 'truths' are often hidden from those who approach educational systems within the Anglo-American tradition of educational studies, especially 'History of Education' and 'Comparative Education', dominated as they have been by positivism, empiricism, modernisation theory, and the legacy of neo-Classical economics.[4]

Any consideration of South African education has to take account of the conservative nature of the available secondary sources and the current state of educational research which offers a paradigm case of academic colonialism. This work is also often located uncritically within the cruder versions of South African historiography epitomised by the writings of Cory and Theal and is at times blatantly racist.[5]

Even the important work of C T Loram and Edgar Brookes,[6] which had the merit of throwing the spotlight on 'native education' and revealed a detailed acquaintance with the topic, was inspired by a desire to avoid conflict between black and white in the economic and political spheres, rather than by an unequivocal desire to promote the educational interests of black South Africans. The policies they advocated were based upon the conflict-avoidance strategies formulated for schooling in the South during the Reconstruction era and often associated with Booker T Washington at Tuskegee.[7] The fact that there has been no important study of black education in South Africa since their work appeared in the 'twenties and 'thirties is a shocking indictment of educational studies in this country.[8]

A glance at many of the standard texts on the history of South African education reveals a picture of neglect and indifference regarding black education. E G Pells[9] allocated the subject some 22 out of 152 pages (or 15 percent of his text), Ruperti about 12 percent[10] and J C Coetzee 20 percent.[11] Behr represents some improvement, with over 50 percent of his book being devoted to black education (20 percent to African education),[12] and Brian Rose's collection of essays moves conclusively towards a more balanced presentation with more than 75 percent of his section on South Africa being concerned with black education.[13] Of course, these crude figures say nothing about the quality of these contributions, but they do give some indication of emphasis or bias! Norman Atkinson's *Teaching South Africans*[14] represents possibly the only published, coherently integrated history of educational policy for all groups in South Africa, though he too writes from an overtly conservative perspective.

Published work is of course simply a reflection of the state of the art in the area of academic enquiry, and the poverty of educational research in South Africa — especially with regard to black education — is also reflected by the absence of independent research programmes into education even at the present time. Despite the vast outpourings of BEd, MEd, and PhD dissertations on education from South African universities, with some recent important contributions from the USA,[15] only a small proportion has been devoted to black education (see bibliography appended to this collection of essays), and this has been almost exclusively descriptive and empiricist in conception. Liberal writers on the history of education in South Africa have tended to take education policy statements and statements of intent by politicians and officials at face value. For example, the citing of the notorious statements by Dr H F Verwoerd on the nature of Bantu Education have never been matched by detailed research into the nature of the schooling system to ascertain whether these policy statements really did reflect the practice in the schools during the 1950s.

The dominant tradition of educational research seldom, if ever, raises fundamental questions about what schools are for, whose interests they serve, what kinds of knowledge or skills they reproduce or what their relationship is to the labour market. Above all this work is characterised by the fact that it is invariably 'written from a standpoint *internal* to the policy-making process itself' [my emphasis] and that it shares the same assumptions. Few writers or researchers have been able to succeed at the difficult task of emancipating themselves from these presuppositions or transcending the limitations of the administrators and policy-makers adequately to uncover and critically analyse the premises which form the basis of their policies.[16]

The provision of education is, according to this tradition, equated with the expansion of schooling, and it is presented as a process of 'natural' and 'unproblematic' administrative growth (an aspect of the linear process of 'modernisation'), rather than as the outcome of a complex historical process in which each new development is contested by interested parties. The conflicts between family or traditionally-based learning structures, on the one hand, and missionary or state schooling systems, on the other, are ignored; the knowledge embodied in the curriculum is presented as the outcome of a process of simple selection of all 'worthwhile knowledge',[17] rather than as the result of historical struggles over the nature of school knowledge;[18] while conflicts over the form and content of educational policies are masked and the struggles between various interested parties are hidden.[19] The dominant tradition of educational research 'hides from view a whole history of the construction of schooling and encourages a belief in some simple history of educational progress, a history with no costs, no struggles, no ambiguities'.[20] This identification of education with schooling is very conservative in its effects and conceals the power relations embodied in the schooling system, in its political construction, and in the particular mix of initiatives and constraints in society which give rise to educational policy settlements.

Similar problems have emerged in recent attempts to understand the nature of educational policy in Britain (which has always been a model for educational provision and research in South Africa). This has led to a focus on the nature of educational ideology — 'ideologies about education' — by approaching them historically and attempting to understand policies as having determinate (or material) social bases and effects.[21] To put it another way, the desire to gain clarity regarding the nature of educational thinking and practice has led recent writers, in particular those based at the Centre for Contemporary Cultural Studies at the University of Birmingham, and at the Open University, to attempt to relate periods of educational crisis to the political and economic context in which they take place and to examine the contested nature of those crises in order to come to an understanding of the nature of change or conservatism in educational policy.[22]

Part of the explanation for the particular stamp of much conventional writing about the evolution of educational policy is that the dominant tradition of such research presents the 'history of education' as an independent field of enquiry, divorced from the wider political, social and economic context within which policies are formulated.[23] The development of educational policy is described without any attempt to problematise the historical context of which it forms a part.[24] More specifically, that tradition can be said to embody some of the following assumptions:
— that the evolution of schooling systems is an unambiguously 'good thing', a sign of 'progress' and 'civilisation', and that such systems act in the best interests of communities and nations as a whole;
— that the provision of compulsory schooling is the responsibility of a benign and disinterested state which acts in the common and equal interests of all its citizens;
— that educational policy is as a consequence formulated outside the arena of politics by 'experts' (administrators) who are qualified for their role by virtue of their 'neutrality'. They are seen as exemplary products of the schooling system (often ex-teachers, headmasters or inspectors) who by the nature of their training and experience in schooling are deemed to know what is good for everyone else. This explains the dominant research

focus in this tradition on the 'great man' (biographical) approach
or the administrative histories of education;
— that schools are essentially egalitarian institutions which provide
the opportunity for all citizens to fulfil their 'natural' potential.
In other words, those who succeed at school come to believe in
their own superiority, and those who fail demonstrate their
unworthiness or lack of ability, and thereby prove to the world
(and presumably to themselves), that they do not deserve
responsible employment and its 'legitimate' economic rewards;
— that school knowledge is the distilled essence of the collective
wisdom of mankind and that it is as a consequence 'neutral',
'objective' and 'unbiased' — above and outside politics. Any
attempt to inject 'Really Useful Knowledge'[25] into the classroom is therefore seen to be morally indefensible and is liable
to the charge of 'propaganda'.
This collection of essays sets out to challenge many of those
assumptions, and takes for granted the following:
— That in the last analysis educational policies are to be understood with reference to the needs of the productive and political
systems of which they form a part, and by reference to the
conflicts between political, social and economic groupings
in society.
— That the development of schooling systems in the context of the
history of the industrial, capitalist democracies of the West was
an aspect of the struggle between owners and workers — a
struggle which sought to promote the interests of some groups
at the expense of others. Specific forms of those struggles were
also to develop in the context of colonisation and were an
important feature of the relationship between 'the coloniser and
the colonised'.[26] Schools and schooling, on this view, are to be
considered as 'sites of struggle'[27] — the implementation of
schooling systems is to be interpreted as representing a history
of losses and gains for the mass of the people rather than the
unfolding of a scheme for the promotion of the betterment of
society as a whole. The introduction of compulsory schooling in
nineteenth century Britain had, for example, more to do with
the production of skills appropriate to the 'needs' of industry
(manpower), the ideological control of workers, and the
entrenchment of middle-class ideological hegemony, than with
the need to uplift and advance the interests of the working
class. But this process was not simply a question of a neat fit
between capitalist 'needs' and 'educational supply'. Those
policies did not simply evolve in a 'natural' way because they
represented some hypothetical 'need of capital' — they represented part of the organic growth of a political and ideological

struggle, and there is a need to spell out how the mechanisms of conformity (or 'correspondence', to use the term coined by Bowles and Gintes[28]) between education and production were historically constructed and how they operate, while at the same time allowing for the contradictions, discrepancies and internal conflicts between them. The development of educational policy is therefore to be understood within the framework of explanation of the nature of broader periods of crisis and conflict in economy and society.

— That the state is no longer seen as a neutral arbiter between interest groups, ie between various groups of capitalists, or between owners and workers. The state is held to be the vehicle through which those with economic and political power shape public policy in order to establish a rough correspondence between the products of the schools and the kinds of labour required by employers; between the kinds of knowledge taught in the schools and the 'common sense' knowledge of the society at large (ie the screening out of knowledge that might represent a threat to the status quo); between the kinds of discipline required in school and the prerequisites for control in the factory or the society at large. Through these institutions and mechanisms the hegemony of specific sets of dominant ideas and assumptions is secured.[29] This does not imply a simple reductionism — that all educational policies can be attributed to the economic 'needs' of capital — because those 'needs' are often contradictory, or cross-cut by different sets of ideological, social or political factors (eg 'race' in the South African context), but it does imply that the general functions of schools are to be adequately understood only if we give sufficient weight to these aspects of 'policy', and how policy decisions are arrived at historically.

— That far from providing a mechanism of social mobility for the majority of students, schools act to crystallise class divisions and preserve the interests of the middle class. In the 'democracies' of the West, schools certainly did provide mechanisms for social mobility, and as such represented a key aspect of the ideological or legitimating hegemony of the essentially exploitative society of which they formed a part. But the crucial point is that the schools provided mobility for only a relatively small number. The school system therefore represented a kind of lottery for the poor which everyone was forced to play through compulsory education. It was defended in terms of the educational rights of children and of equality of opportunity,[30] and given 'scientific' credibility through such devices as IQ testing.[31] The effect, as Martin Carnoy has pointed out, with specific reference to the

Third World context, is that a large majority of the children of the world 'are brought into schools in order to fail' and to be taught that they are not good enough![32]

Education for Class Domination or Racial Repression?

A particular challenge for those who would explore the nature of black education in South Africa is that they must distinguish analytically between the evolution of schooling for the working classes in advanced capitalist countries and schooling designed for a specifically colonial context. In South Africa blacks are both 'colonised men'[33] and workers in an advanced industrial state with increasingly sophisticated manpower requirements. This gives rise to an important series of contradictions for policy-makers.

There is now, for example, a 'need' for schooling to produce a sufficiently docile, 'colonised' population to prevent the emergence of an outright political challenge to the status quo, yet at the same time there is a demand for appropriate 'manpower' for ever-increasing mechanisation and technological sophistication, with demands for versatile and competent black employees capable of holding their own in the 'open' racial labour market. In other words, there is a need for educational policies which will be seen to meet the general political demand for educational equality and for the provision of an appropriately skilled labour force, while at the same time attempting to meet the needs of control in the apartheid state. In the end this issue, which is intimately bound up with the class/race debate on South Africa,[34] needs to be explored in some depth if the historical background to the evolution of educational policies and the resistance to those policies is to be adequately understood (cf. Hunt Davis, Molteno, Hartwig and Sharp).

In the first place, any attempt to grasp the history and dynamics of education for the indigenous peoples of South Africa must be located within the context of European imperialist expansion and the drawing of most of the world into international capitalist development and underdevelopment during the eighteenth and nineteenth centuries.[35] Such a process, as writers such as Fanon, Memmi, Freire, Carnoy, Lyons and others have shown,[36] was a cultural as well as an economic and political event. The colonised peoples of Southern Africa were not simply conquered in a military sense; did not lose only their political independence; were not simply divorced from an independent economic base; were not just drawn into new systems of social and economic life as urban dwellers or wage labour. Though all these aspects of the process of colonisation have great importance, the key aspect to be noted here is that it also entailed cultural and ideological transformation, in which the schools were major agents.

The schooling of the colonised, whether conducted by missionaries or by agents of the colonial government, was part of the process of colonisation — the co-optation and control of subject groups.

Schools, whether church or state financed, were modelled on the educational systems that had been developed in the industrial countries, and their political motivation should be understood within the context of the spread of mass education in Britain, Europe and North America during comparable phases of capitalist development. Within the colonial context schools became key institutions of control, whereby a new indigenous elite was created to replace the traditional groupings who represented a different cultural and political outlook that was often hostile to the culture and social practices of the conqueror. These elite groups acted as intermediaries between the colonial state and the white colonists, on the one hand, and the mass of the colonised population, on the other. They promoted, by example, the notion of a congruence between the acceptance of 'civilisation' (ie the legitimacy of colonial rule) and the capitalist system that it represented, thereby incorporating the schooled into the elite labour market; they also helped to change social structures to fit in with European concepts of work and interpersonal relationships.[37]

Above all, schools negated the common sense knowledge of the colonised by reinforcing the self-image of incompetence and ignorance for those who did not go to school or those who failed at school. This often also led those who were schooled to despise their own culture and traditions in favour of those of the coloniser or at the very best become ambivalent about their links with the 'traditional' past or social milieu.[38] The process has been described as the creation of a 'culture of silence' — 'where the colonial element in schooling is its attempt to silence, to negate the history of the indigene, to rationalise the irrational and gain acceptance for structures which are oppressive'.[39] Such schooling, even though it served the interests of a small elite (usually the products of the mission schools) who came to benefit from their successes at school, attempted to legitimise the position of those who were worst off economically and to ensure their passive acceptance of the status quo by giving them the hope that through schooling they might in due course also be able to benefit (individually) from the new situation.

These arguments do not seek to underplay the significance or the good intentions of those individuals who promoted the education of black South Africans during the period under review, and it is not our intention to imply that the provision of education simply and unproblematically benefited the colonisers at all times, with no cost being involved. The intention of this collection is in fact to demonstrate quite the opposite — that schools were systematically appropriated by colonised peoples and that they have played an important historical role as sites of struggle in the colonial context.[40] What is asserted is that the educational goals articulated by administrators, academics, teachers and politicians are only to be understood within this ideological context and must not always be taken at face value.

The understanding of schooling as a means of control, co-optation and response in the colonial context is, however, only one aspect of the background to the contruction of educational policies that is in need of explanation. The process of colonisation itself, and the rapid expansion of European and US imperialism in the late nineteenth century, need to be analysed within the framework of the development and expansion of capitalist industrialisation. The evolution of schooling systems in Europe and North America at this time can be adequately interpreted only by asking what work these systems performed for other institutions and interests, and how they were constructed and how they functioned.[41] In a structuralist interpretation, schooling systems are interpreted as mechanisms for the control and repression of the working class and as part of an elaborate design to ensure the reproduction of specific forms of labour and ideological formulations appropriate to the development of industrial or monopoly capitalism.[42] An alternative approach, which complements rather than negates the former, asserts that the forms and nature of such systems need to be examined within specific historical situations, and that general formulations about the intentions of educational policies are of little use unless we examine what they come to mean in practice, against the background of the very real political divisions that emerged in the nineteenth century — in particular, the rise of working class politics and the various reformist policies intended to contain such trends.[43]

On the basis of these important insights into the development of educational policy in the emergent industrial countries, as well as insights developed for the analysis of education in the colonial context, lessons can be learnt about the particular forms of educational policy, and the specific political and economic constraints which provided its parameters in South Africa . . . particularly as the country moved into the phase of industrialisation from the 1880s.

Education and Change: The Nature and Intent of Educational Policies

The history of British education reveals a clear periodisation of policy initiatives. Prior to the middle of the nineteenth century there was little attempt to educate the growing industrial proletariat on the argument that 'a little knowledge is a dangerous thing'. Workers who were required to do simple manual labour on the factory floor were kept in ignorance 'for their own good', lest they become tainted by 'foreign' ideologies that might give them ideas above their station and lead them to put forward 'unreasonable' political demands for social change.[44] Only with dramatic changes in industry and the labour process by the latter part of the century,[45] linked to the decline of a vigorous working class politics, did the opportunity and the necessity arise for an expansion of schooling to correspond with the needs of capitalist development and the need to explore reformist political options.[46]

Reformist policies had a twofold outcome. First, they were intended to provide the basic skills of numeracy and literacy to enable workers to function more adequately and efficiently in the context of advanced techniques of production (mechanisation) and a more complicated division of labour. Secondly, these changes were also politically and economically necessary to entrench middle class knowledge as the only 'legitimate' kind of school knowledge, and thereby counter the influence of the 'Really Useful Knowledge' of the independent working class educational institutions.[47] The policies aimed at a degree of correspondence between the schooling system's demand of the pupil regarding discipline, and the modes of behaviour required of the ideal worker.[48]

There were, therefore, important contradictions in the evolution of those policies — contradictions which provide the researcher with a lever to prise open the nature of the policies being explored via an examination of contemporary public debates and learned discussions. Although the schools might have been designed as mechanisms of control there is little evidence to support the view, often implied in structuralist literature, that they actually always worked in the way intended by their middle class designers. Over time educational institutions took on a dynamic of their own. Members of the working class were able to use them to increase their political strength and promote policies that sought a more equitable distribution of the educational 'goods' of the society. The provision of schooling might be seen as both a mechanism for the provision and reproduction of specific kinds of manpower required by industry, and as a vehicle for the dissemination of ideas that struck at the heart of the political and economic system which had spawned modern schooling; the provision of skills through schooling ironically had the effect of giving workers greater bargaining power vis a vis capital.

Through exploring such ambiguities in the construction and development of schooling systems in advanced capitalist countries, and their influence on the evolving educational systems in the colonial context (which had features of its own), we can come to understand something of the specific forms of schooling that evolved in South Africa at various times. In particular, during periods of crisis, policies which normally went unchallenged became the object of public debate — and at such times we are able more adequately to uncover some of the assumptions that underpinned educational decision-making.

Crises in educational policy — which reflected stresses in the society as a whole — can be identified at times of historical change like the transition from the dominance of mercantile capital to industrial capital during the period between 1880 and the 1920s[49]; or the period of rapid expansion of secondary industry and urbanisation during the 1940s and 1950s.[50] Most significant for an understanding of our current crisis, this perspective would locate education within the broader context of the rise of monopoly capitalism in South Africa during the 1960s and 1970s[51] (see the papers by Molteno, Hartwig and Sharp, Christie and Collins, Davies.) The economic crisis in each of these periods was reflected in politics, with the rise of working class politics a marked feature.

The attempt to locate educational developments within historical contexts will need to uncover the ideologies of education because those taken-for-granted ('common sense') assumptions which underpin public debate and policy-making can be shown 'to conceal or resolve in an idealistic or imaginary way the problematic character of social life' and the evolution of educational policy as an aspect thereof.[52] In the process of presenting a particular social order as 'harmonious' (see especially the remarks below regarding the de Lange Report), 'natural', or in need of rescue from decay or from enemies 'within' or 'without', the particular ideological nature of educational discourse emerges, assisting us to understand the underlying structures of educational policy.[53]

What emerges is the extent to which policies which are defended on grounds of 'scientific expertise' of the various so-called sub-disciplines of education — 'manpower planning', 'educational planning' or 'the economics of education' — are in fact bounded by interest, even if those who make the formulations are oblivious or only partially aware of their ideological character. Accounts of or recommendations for educational policy are usually presented as being in the national interest — for the benefit of all citizens equally — but they can be shown to be ideological to the extent that they serve to secure the position of dominant groups through hiding the true interests which underpin certain forms of educational policy. Conversely, a careful analysis of educational policy formulations and their practical implementation causes crucial aspects of political policy and economic power to be clarified.

An explanation of the manner in which specific groups come to influence educational policy must be sought in an analysis of how these groups come to have their 'point of view' accepted as the 'dominant truth' (even perhaps as 'commonsense') in a particular society.

What is crucial here is the extent to which a particular class or a particular sector of industry (eg 'national capital' vs 'imperial capital')[54] can present its needs as being identical to and compatible with the national interest, and how it comes to have those ideas accepted in society as a whole. In the current crisis in South Africa, 'the national interest' is increasingly defined in economic terms. It is necessary to avoid the simplistic notion that the state is simply 'the executive arm of capital', but where the strategic, political and foreign policies of the state will not be feasible without economic growth such a link assumes greater significance. Therefore international economic competitiveness and sustained economic growth are increasingly equated with political power and preservation of the status quo, and the national interest becomes increasingly defined in terms of capitalist efficiency and profitability.

The 'needs' of industry thus come to exercise a major influence on public policy, and have a direct effect on policies put forward in the face of educational crisis. Public policy comes to be structurally weighted towards capitalist solutions, and whatever else educational policy has to deliver it must certainly aid (or appear to aid) economic growth. Schooling systems, if not schools themselves, must as a consequence be publicly accountable in these terms. It follows that those 'groups that speak from a knowledge of the dilemmas of capitalist management have a particular weight, especially when they can present a global or collective view of managements' problems'.[55] (In South Africa, the Urban Foundation and ASSOCOM may provide examples of such pressure groups, and the recently founded Technical and Vocational Educational Foundation of South Africa (now called The Career Education Foundation of South Africa) can be cited as a specific lobby for education and training policy).[56]

In the light of the significant challenge to the state articulated in the mass struggles of 1976-80, the older and cruder educational policies of the apartheid system are being revised and reformulated. New policies are being explored in an attempt to meet the 'needs' of the post-Soweto situation. The rhetoric of state officials and the Department of Education and Training regarding the new dispensation has concerned arguments about increasing social justice through the greater provision of 'equal education' (whatever that might mean) to the whole population, and the real increases in government spending on black education and training during the 'seventies.[57] Yet the more forceful arguments for an expansion of the quality, quantity and variety of education and training for black South Africans have been put forward by the business community, or that section of it which stresses the manpower requirements of monopoly capital.

As David Reeder has pointed out, such arguments must be understood, at least in part, in terms of the fact that

> ... any society which feels itself threatened from without or enfeebled from within is likely to assert the value of useful knowledge and to stress the importance of the extrinsic purposes of education.[58]

Similar policies were stressed in South Africa in each period of crisis referred to above, and they head the agenda at present. Pressures in favour of vocational education cannot, of course, be explained simply in idealistic terms ('the morality of work' or 'the need for discipline'), or even in purely individualistic economic terms (the need for individuals to secure employment in times of depression). They have to be understood more fundamentally in terms of the imperatives behind structural changes in the nature of production and the labour process under monopoly capital.

The de Lange Commission of 1981 on the *Provision of Education in the RSA*[59] represents an excellent example. Education in South Africa, and in particular the education of black South Africans, is to be *reformed* so that it goes a considerable way towards meeting both the universal condemnation of racist Bantu Education policies, and the specific criticisms of the education system from the business sector on account of its shortcomings in producing adequate supplies of appropriately trained 'manpower' for industry.

'Educational Needs': Reformism and Education

Before undertaking a brief examination of the Report of the de

Lange Committee we need to gain some insights into the general nature of the reformist policies being put forward. Several problems about the notion of reformism in education have recently been raised by the Education Group of the Centre for Contemporary Cultural Studies and by Stuart Hall in his article on 'Schooling, State and Society', which deals with post-World War II education reform in Britain, and I am indebted to them for much of what follows.[60]

They make a distinction between two kinds of educational debate. First, they refer to the simple link between traditional or conservative policy on education and conservative political ideology which supports such a policy as 'defending and reproducing the class nature of the state, and preserving and legitimating existing structures'[61] (eg Conservative Party educational policies in Britain in the pre-World War II period, or the policy of Bantu Education as introduced and defended in the 1950s.) Secondly, they point to the complex problems involved in understanding the nature of educational reformism. The stress is upon arguments in favour of the liberalisation of education, equal rights (the improvement of class/race relations in society), peaceful transition, the survival of the free enterprise system, and questions of 'manpower supply'.[62] There is a stress also on the 'dual repertoire' of education designed to redistribute opportunities to the working class (ie the argument of equity/ equality), and education aimed at recruiting the ablest from all classes (races) for industry (ie the argument for equality of opportunity and/or labour efficiency).[63]

These assumptions need to be rendered problematic if we are to gain an adequate understanding of their implications.

We need to look beyond the rhetoric to the relationship between educational proposals and the political and economic contexts in which they occur. We can come to an adequate grasp of policies only if we are able to demythologise (or 'de-ideologise') their language and assumptions, if we are able to uncover the various interests that lie behind specific reformist initiatives, and if we are able to grasp the contradictions and conflicts which they are intended to deflect.

In essence reformist policies may be defined as strategies designed to change and modify social conditions that have become widely regarded as unjust and unacceptable, but the new formula for 'reform' serves to strengthen and perpetuate the essential power relations (class relations) embodied in the earlier situation while offering considerable improvements in the living circumstances of at least a considerable proportion of the groups for which it is intended.

I propose to examine two key concepts that have provided the focus for wide-ranging debate on reformism in education in South Africa at the present time. As the extract from David Reeder indicates (he is writing about England), there has been an interesting shift in educational currency in recent years. Liberal educationists have always stressed the value of the *intrinsic goals* (or the 'intrinsic good') in education, with the package itself being for the most part taken for granted.[64] The current emphasis by the same intellectual establishment in Britain and South Africa on the need for more vocational or utilitarian education (expressed in the Manpower Services Commission in Britain and the National Manpower Commission or 'Manpower 2000' in South Africa) and the stress on the *extrinsic links* between educational policies and employment, therefore needs explanation.

The strong 'moral' connotations in arguments in favour of vocational education or technical training — especially for the working classes in Britain or for blacks in South Africa — are reminiscent of the policies advocated by the Phelps-Stokes Commissions on African Education and often associated with the work of C T Loram in South Africa during the 'twenties and 'thirties (see paper on him by Davis). The parallels are educationally interesting but they become fully comprehensible only in the light of the sharp changes in the nature of the labour process, economic instability and high unemployment during both periods and the political threat to the South African state that emerged in each period — the threat from the white working class in the second and third decade of this century,[65] and the challenge from the black majority in the years since World War II.[66]

The shift in the dominant liberal position regarding the nature and provision of education for blacks must therefore be seen in its historical context, though it should be added that the current crisis is in some ways different from the earlier one.

The reformists aim to defuse the political situation through granting economic concessions to blacks, allowing them to 'participate more freely in the free enterprise system' through educational advancement. Such a settlement would secure South Africa for capitalism by integrating important groups of blacks (the 'black middle class') more comprehensively into the society. The obvious role of education in creating appropriate social strata and 'manpower', and in legitimating these policies, has therefore become a key political and economic issue for those with influence and power in industry and government.

A further illustration of the ideological nature of educational discourse is found in de Lange's use of concepts such as *needs* and *harmony*. (A similar word much used in official circles is 'normalisation'.) In the language of the current South African educational debate, 'crisis' takes on a particular meaning as the outcome of a lack of 'harmony' in society's educational arrangements. A central tenet of the de Lange Report was that:

> What influence the system for the provision of education has on the country's future, and the strength of that influence, is determined either by how well that system of provision *meets the real needs of the society or by the extent to which it is in disharmony with these needs.*[67]
> [My emphasis.]

In other words, the 'organic' unity or coherence of society — supposedly its 'natural' characteristic — is 'off balance' or in 'disharmony', and there is therefore a need to correct the balance once again to produce 'harmony' (this in a state as 'unnatural' and unjust as South Africa under apartheid!). The implication is that these are purely technical problems, to be sorted out by the 'experts', and not political issues at all. Without entering into an extended critique of structural functionalism, for which there is no place here, what emerges quite clearly from the above is that what are called the 'needs of society' (ie in the national interest), are in fact nothing of the sort. The needs being put forward as 'the real needs of society' are in fact those of a particular system of production at a specific period in its development (see the contributions of Sharp and Hartwig, and Christie and Collins). The 'harmony' that is being sought is not some ideal state of society but a match or correspondence between the products and output of the schooling system and the needs of industry, or more spcifically, the needs of monopoly capital. The satisfaction of *those* needs via a reformist settlement will, it is argued, bring about a more or less enduring set of solutions to the education crisis, and by extension help to reduce the more general crisis in the society, by putting an end to 'destructive conflict' about these issues.

It is obvious that the efficient functioning of monopoly capitalism does not necessarily produce political, economic and educational equity for South Africa's black majority. The provision of a smooth running, administratively well organised, well staffed and well funded schooling system, responding to the needs of industry for *appropriate manpower,* might indeed go some way towards meeting popular demands for education, but it would scarcely provide long-term solutions to the education/employment problem for the whole population.

The conflicts being mediated by reference to the above arguments are not the results of the malfunctioning of a fundamentally egalitarian set of social, political and economic arrangements, they are aspects of the contradictions produced by the particular class imperatives of a system of production at the present time. The state policy of Bantu Education was not an 'irrational' interlude in South politics, as it is sometimes presented in liberal literature, but a reflection of that aspect of policy which attempted to secure the appropriate conditions for the reproduction of capital in general at a particular phase of South Africa's political development under the hegemony of Afrikaner Nationalist ideology in the 1950s and 1960s. With the changing circumstances of the last decade the state has been forced to reconsider that policy in the light of pressure from the dominated classes and from monopoly capital. Yet the state does not directly represent the interests of monopoly capital, nor is it irrevocably tied to the earlier and cruder forms of apartheid still clung to by 'popular' Afrikaner leaders and represented politically by the Herstigte Nasionale Party and the Conservative Party. In attempting to secure the conditions for South Africa's 'survival', the state's essential role of seeking to provide for the survival of capitalism in general once again becomes clear. Its imperatives must, however, be balanced constantly between the political strength of the white and black communities — the former expressed through the ballot box; the latter through a potential to challenge the whole structure of the state itself.

Education as a Site of Struggle

If education is to be considered a site of struggle, policies which are formulated to further the objectives of the ruling party at specific times cannot simply be 'imposed' as if society were a kind of *tabula rasa*. The state does not have the power simply to impose *any* policy without reference to what is possible within a given context (cf the 'art of the possible' argument in politics). This is demonstrated by the fact that educational struggles which have taken place during this century in South Africa have often represented direct attempts by various groups to break with missionary or state schooling and set up alternative schools reflecting their particular interests. This history of educational resistance, so well documented in East Africa,[68] remains largely unwritten in South Africa.

The papers by Robert Edgar, Tom Lodge, Deborah Gaitskell and Adrienne Bird in this collection point to new perspectives in this area, and help us to grasp the significance of education beyond the schools as an important aspect of the unwritten history of South African education. Edgar refers to the neglected field of education within the Independent Church movements, drawing on his work on the charismatic leader Wellington Buthelezi who established a considerable following in the Eastern Cape and the Transkei during the 1920s;[69] Lodge demonstrates the strengths and weaknesses of the African Education Movement as part of the ANC struggles of the 1950s;[70] Gaitskell's account of the Girl Wayfarers' Association examines an important aspect of the history of the women's movement on the Witwatersrand — leisure-time education for young people and the political alternatives that were explored by those who led the movement over a period of more than half a century;[71] and Bird's contribution takes us through the history and metamorphosis of the African Night School Movement on the Witwatersrand, from its origins in the highly successful educational programmes of the Communist Party of South Africa, to its 'reform' under the auspices of the South African Institute of Race Relations from the 1930s.

Each of these case studies underscores the contested nature of the arena of educational struggle. Policies formulated and implemented from the 'fifties onwards have come to be challenged once again since 1976, though Lynn Maree's important article cautions against assuming that an absence of large scale conflict in the intervening period indicated an acceptance of the policies being implemented.[72] The cumulative challenge since 1976 has forced a renegotiation of the terms of the 1950s educational settlement, even within the highly repressive system of apartheid. What is possible for politicians has to be matched against what is at least minimally acceptable to the educational target groups.

The state's interest in gaining sufficient acceptability among blacks for apartheid policies in education is based on its need to avoid having to resort to force at ever more frequent intervals in order to maintain itself. We delude ourselves if we think that educational policies can be formulated in air-conditioned conference rooms (or board-rooms), where academics, statesmen and administrators meet, and simply *imposed* without reference to legitimate community, religious and educational leaders, as well as to students, teachers and parents. This is especially so in the highly charged political atmosphere of South Africa in the 'eighties.

Soweto and the 'Seventies: the Search for Reformist Options

The crisis of the 1976-7 Soweto Riots and the school boycotts of 1980 focused attention on the youth and demonstrated the extent to which educational institutions had become sites of struggle in South Africa. The very institutions designed to propagate 'education for domestication' on the Verwoerdian model, turned out to be trojan horses. The upsurge of student power — probably without historical precedent — linked to heightened community consciousness and worker organisation, and accompanied by a new wave of guerilla incursions, marked the beginning of a new era of resistance to apartheid.

The state's violent reaction to this challenge and the tragic consequences of its brutally repressive measures against school-children were in many ways counter-productive for those in power. The response again highlighted blatant injustices and inequalities and demonstrated the political and economic dangers to the status quo presented by an increasingly hostile international community. In addition, the period of crisis served to demonstrate the political strength of the black majority, particularly those in the urban areas, upon whose labour South Africa's prosperity largely depends and their ability to wring limited reforms from the state during a period of crisis.

As military men frequently pointed out, there was no military solution to South Africa's long-term security problems; if there was to be a serious attempt to check the rapid slide towards conflict and polarisation the government urgently needed to lauch a series of initiatives to secure the loyalty of at least some sections of the black community. Such 'concessions' were also vitally necessary from the point of view of state ideologues in order to give some ammunition to 'overseas friends' who sought to defend the policies of the South African government on the grounds that they were in fact in the best interests of everyone in the country, black as well as white.

In short, the South African government had to find a formula to defuse internal and external threats without destroying its own economic and political foundations — the capitalist system and the system of white privilege that is embodied in the current dispensation.

The response by the Botha government, known by the term 'total strategy', comprises a multi-faceted reformist programme.[73] The design of a new educational system, as embodied in the recommendations of the HSRC (de Lange) investigation into education, is a key aspect of that strategy. In order to grasp its significance at a more general political and economic level it must be seen in a wider context. We need therefore to examine 'total strategy' as set forth in the Wiehahn, Riekert[74] and de Lange Commission Reports (the first two concerned with labour supply and control) if we are to grasp the essential nature of the state's co-ordinated response to changing circumstances.

The task of these various commissions was to devise a series of mechanisms for 'modernising' apartheid in order to make it more acceptable, at least to sections of the South African communities, and also to the international community. The co-ordinated task has been to formulate political and institutional frameworks through which the state could attempt the twin strategies of co-optation and control of the black population. Control could be secured by dividing the working class into 'insiders' — those with the right to live and work in 'white' South Africa — and 'outsiders' — homeland citizens 'needed' in large numbers in the industrial heartland but having no residential rights or security there. Such policies would in addition imply the granting of real economic (and possibly political) advantages to a section of the 'insider' group (the so-called 'black middle class') in return for their support.

The rationale was both political (ie about control and co-optation) and economic (ie about the economic necessity for the survival of the capitalist system in South Africa). Blacks who enjoyed the relative privilege of having the right to live and work in the industrial centres of the country, had very real objective reasons why they should support policies which entrenched their position vis a vis rural blacks who might undercut their economic position if they were allowed unrestricted access to the labour market. The government therefore counted on the economic interests of the urban dwellers (the 'insiders') making it unlikely that they would oppose this aspect of its reform policies too strongly, especially if other tangible concessions, such as a substantially improved schooling system, were granted at the same time. Such reforms would help them to take advantage of the new opportunities for employment that were emerging with the relaxation of the colour bar in industry.

Still at the political level, 'total strategy' works on the assumption that the interests of all urban blacks are not identical. The aim is not simply to create a division between urban and rural blacks, but to encourage the building up of a 'stable middle class', excluding migrants and homeland residents, which would become a buffer between the urban masses and the white political structures. Community Councils (the mouthpieces of the elite); home owner-ship schemes (only possible for those with steady incomes and relatively high wages); the electrification of the major townships (to allow for the more complete incorporation of this group into the consumer society); concessions to black businessmen; massive increases in funds for social services, and the introduction of the 'new education' — these were all aimed at securing that measure of increased social justice for the 'insiders', and deflecting the anger

of urban blacks away from the central government. As Patrick
Lawrence has pithily put it,

> . . . total strategy . . . has two recommendations [for the state]; it
> creates a buffer between the white elite and the relatively impoverished
> black masses, and thereby [translates] the racial struggle between
> white and black into an ideological one between capitalism and
> Marxism.[75]

There are several economic implications of these changes. On the
one hand, there were dramatic developments in the field of labour
organisation during the seventies, with black workers repeatedly
demonstrating their power to wring concessions from management
despite massive intimidation by the state. Industrialists gradually
conceded that the rising wave of industrial unrest had to be met
by means other than outright repression because endless disputes
that led to strike action were too disruptive to production. In
addition, the multi-national corporations operating in South
Africa found themselves under increasing pressure to accept codes
of 'fair labour practices' (eg the Sullivan Code) which included the
granting of union rights to workers and the launching of a variety
of schemes to provide social services, pensions, housing, medical
welfare and opportunities for education and training for black
employees and their families. Such moves were not simply based
on the desire to implement more humanitarian labour practices,
though this may indeed have been a major factor in many
individual cases. They should be seen within the context of
changes in the industrial labour process during the 'seventies.

The crucial links between the political and economic strategies
embodied in 'total strategy' emerge conclusively if we look at the
changing nature of industrial production and the labour process in
South Africa. These changes are partly explicable with reference
to local circumstances, but they are also part of wider changes in
the nature of production under international monopoly capitalism
during this period.[76] The changes were explained by Harry Oppenheimer in a speech to the London Stock Exchange on 18 May
1976:

> The increase in black wages reflects the beginning of a process, still
> actively continuing, of a change-over from a labour-intensive, low-wage,
> low-productivity economic system, typical of industrial development in
> its early stages, to the capital-intensive, high-wage, high-productivity
> system which characterises the advanced industrial countries.[77]

To put it another way, 'modernisation' necessarily means mechanisation and automation, and that inevitably leads to a shortage of 'skilled workers'. As a consequence, so the argument goes, it is necessary (inevitably?) for the labour process to undergo major changes if these shortages are to be met. Older craft skills will have to be fragmented or 'deskilled' if production is to be maintained and industries are to remain internationally competitive.

This 'technicist' explanation from the perspective of management — rooted as it is in the assumptions of neo-classical economics and Taylorism — presents these changes as part of a 'natural' or 'harmonious' order of 'progress' under capitalism — an outcome of the remorseless advance of technology which will, it is implied, benefit all in the long run (See Buckland and Chisholm).

Such an explanation masks the fact that such changes are in the interests of employers. As Athar Hussain points out,

> . . . since there are no restrictions under capitalism to machines performing the work done by artisans or labourers, this lack of restrictions makes it possible and desirable for monopoly capital to take advantage of this freedom to open up scope for manouevre regarding the production of new commodities, the introduction of new methods of production, and the introduction of changes in the labour process.[78]

The introduction of machines can be justified in terms of both greater output (greater efficiency of production) and greater control over labour (efficient labour practices). Mechanisation allows skilled crafts to be 'diluted' (or 'deskilled'), ie broken down into component parts, to be dealt with either by machines or by unskilled or semi-skilled workers who are more cheaply employed and more easily replaced than skilled craftsmen.[79] From this point of view mechanisation in a modern factory often means that skilled craftsmen are displaced by machines, and that the labour requirements then fall in the main into three categories:

(a) a small group, highly skilled and trained in science and technology, who are required for the initial design and production of the automated systems. Under monopoly capitalism this group is almost exclusively physically located in the advanced industrial countries where the 'new technology' is manufactured — in Europe, the USA or Japan, and not in South Africa.

(b) Those required for running these systems. Their training often comprises little more than a good general education with subsequent training in job-specific skills. This category is highly paid. It is of great significance for any consideration of the South African situation because it has until recently been monopolised by whites, but is at the present time the category referred to most often in terms of the manpower 'crisis' or 'bottleneck' with regard to the employment of blacks. There are, it is often argued, at present more job opportunities in this category than there are available persons to fill the vacancies.

(c) the 'operatives' who are mostly unskilled. They are paid low salaries relative to groups (a) and (b), and can be replaced quite easily and therefore have little shop-floor bargaining power.

From the point of view of labour, there is an overall increase in aggregate and structural unemployment. First, there are few jobs as a result of these changes, and therefore overall unemployment increases. Secondly, the kinds of attractive jobs that are available are those for which the unemployed do not have the relevant skills.[80] This issue was captured succinctly in the 1981 Report of the Anglo American Corporation, which referred to the fact that 'the skilled labour shortage coexists with an oversupply of unskilled labour, with unemployment variously estimated at between one and two million workseekers'.[81]

What Wiehahn and Riekert did for the establishment of a reformist initiative in labour relations and for control of the labour supply,[82] de Lange has attempted for education, training and the supply of 'manpower'. Some attention needs to be given to the specific features of the educational climate in which the Commission was appointed.

In the light of the post-1976 situation it would seem that the de Lange Commission was an attempt to rescue a situation of acute crisis in the black schooling system. It was aimed at the resolution of regional crises as well as the general crisis, and any full understanding of its recommendations must be seen within the context of specifically educational debates, as well as being an aspect of the broader reformist initiative being undertaken by the government.

The attempt to enforce Afrikaans as a medium of instruction in the schools of Soweto in 1976 proved to be the last straw in the ongoing crisis of the previous years. The inability of the Bantu Education Department to enforce its regulations on this issue; the intense resistance that resulted from that situation, with demands for educational reform being linked to wider political issues; the physical damage to schools and educational facilities; the rise of a vigorous student politics; the intensity of police activity and the victimisation of students and teachers; the mass resignation of teachers, in particular those in the senior ranks of the profession and those with good qualifications; the administrative collapse demonstrated by the intense recourse to corporal punishment, endless problems about the payment of teachers' salaries, the leaks of examination papers, and extremely high examination failure rates, all added up to a situation in which black schools were simply not functioning. The schools were failing at the level of ideological control; they were not producing appropriate manpower for industry; and above all they were providing a key site for resistance. The schooling crisis was the manpower crisis, and it was a fundamental dimension of the political crisis. By the end of the 'seventies there was wide acceptance by the state and the business community of a degree of urgency in finding solutions to these problems.

Parliamentarians, businessmen and educationists of all shades of political opinion were at least able to agree on the urgency of the questions at issue, even if their analyses of the situation varied widely. Failure to solve these questions would mean for white politicians a failure to adapt in a time of acute crisis; for businessmen it meant declining profitability and greater vulnerability in the steadily declining international economic climate of the late 'seventies; and for educationists it provided an opportunity to assess where they stood and review their contribution to the solution of the crisis.

The Response by the State

The 1979 Education and Training Act[83] marked the government's interim response to the education crisis. The HSRC (de Lange) Report of 1981 was an important milestone because it represents the first significant official document on black education in South Africa since the 1935-6 Inter-Departmental Committee on Native Education (the Welsh Report)[84] and the 1951 Commission on Native Education (the Eiselen Commission Report).[85] The Act and the Report provide a coherent formulation of 'enlightened', 'official' thinking on the subject of educational change at the present time, and thus offer an excellent starting point from which to begin to formulate a critical evaluation of the dominant assumptions of that initiative.

Even before the de Lange Commission reported, the government had made the general intent of its policies quite clear. There was to be a general move towards some form of unitary educational system for all South Africans, but this referred simply to the administrative arrangements regarding curriculum, examinations, teachers' pay scales and finance; there was never at any stage any suggestion that the fundamental tenets of apartheid in education would be breached — state control was to be strengthened where necessary (eg regarding the private schools) and the races were still to go to separate schools and universities.[86] Another important aspect was that the fundamental structure of the apartheid society was never challenged in any way by the 'reforms' — they were intended solely for the inhabitants of 'white' South Africa, which included black 'insiders' (as defined earlier). Homeland citizens/ inhabitants were by definition excluded from the new dispensation because they were now assumed (in terms of the logic of apartheid) to be the responsibility of their own governments — the Transkei, Bophuthatswana, Venda and Ciskei.

The Education and Training Act of 1979 set the tone for these 'reforms' which were subsequently propagandised by the Department of Foreign Affairs and Information on behalf of the Department of Education and Training. An 'Information Newsletter' published as a supplement to *Educamus* in 1980,[87] set out to answer the question: 'What is [sic] the Government and the Department of Education and Training doing to improve education for Blacks?'

The article outlined the following improvements:
— that it was now 'the declared intention of the government to provide equal education, including facilities [sic], to all racial groups', (demonstrated by the fact that the DET's budget had risen from R27 million in 1972 to R250 million in 1981-2)
— that there was increased capital expenditure on black schooling from separate government sources of finance (eg the extensive schools building programme)
— that there had been an expansion of free book facilities
— that compulsory education was in the process of being implemented
— that there had been expansion of pre-primary school facilities
— that teachers' salaries had been considerably increased and conditions of service for black teachers were, it was claimed, identical to those of white teachers
— that the quality of teaching and teacher training was being improved through the provision of new teacher training centres and in-service programmes
— that a massive programme for the expansion of technical education facilities for blacks was under way in the public sector (to complement that in the private sector) with a new range of training facilities being opened for blacks.

Adding some substance to these claims, the chief liaison officer of the DET, Mr G Engelbrecht, announced in September 1981 that

R63 million had been allocated for the building of 2 554 primary and secondary school classrooms and additional buildings for existing colleges in the 1981-2 financial year. According to Mr Engelbrecht, 29 new community and state secondary schools with 616 classrooms were being built at a cost of R25 million and a further R30 million was to be spent on 47 primary schools with 821 classrooms. To this he added that several hundred new libraries, laboratories and centres for practical subjects were being built, along with the extension of facilities for teacher training.[88]

The focus on technical education is significant in the light of what has been said earlier in this regard, and given the pressure being exercised on the state by industry for the expansion of facilities in this direction.[89] At a meeting with black trade unionists in December 1979, the Minister of Manpower Utilisation, Mr Fanie Botha, announced that the government intended to allocate R50 million for the training of black workers.[90] By 1981 sixteen 'technical centres' had been established by the DET in urban townships. 'The purpose of these centres was to introduce black schoolboys to elementary technical training', which would lead to technical high schools where a variety of training skills would be offered. There were at this time twelve technical colleges for blacks in 'white' South Africa and fifteen 'colleges' in the Homelands offering vocational training in such subjects as 'motor mechanics', electrical work and carpentry. The DET plans to erect another twenty six 'technical centres' and another fourteen technical colleges.[91]

By 1981 there were also four technikons in South Africa catering for blacks — at Umlazi, Pietermaritzburg, Pietersburg and Mabopane East, near Pretoria.[92] The new technikon at Mabopane East, which is expected to be one of the biggest educational institutions in South Africa when it is completed, is the showpiece of this policy. Here courses are to be offered in the secretarial and commercial fields, business management, public health, administration, electrical and civil engineering, telecommunication and surveying. The centre is being built at a cost of R80 million and will accommodate five thousand students when complete.[93] According to Mr Winjnbeek, the Director (who also heads the Engineering Department), the establishment of the technikon was the direct result of the increased demand for all kinds of technicians, commercial managers, administrators, para-medical staff, and other professional people.[94]

Another dimension of the state initiative in this area, was the establishment of Vista University, a racially exclusive institution of higher learning for blacks, in the face of strong pressure from the academic and business communities to open the older universities to all races. The bill establishing this institution was rushed through parliament at the end of the 1981 session prior to the tabling of the report of the de Lange Committee — an indication of the government's determination not to allow the pressure for 'liberal' reform to hinder its specific brand of reformism.[95]

The Response of Monopoly Capitalism

Parallel to the state's initiative in the area of educational reform during the 'seventies and early 'eighties, there have been significant moves in the same direction by a number of independent groups. These are either initiated or directly assisted by private enterprise, in particular the large multi-nationals or mining groups, or they are funded through the 'home' governments of those multi-nationals, eg the governments of the USA, West Germany, Netherlands, Switzerland and the United Kingdom. As David B Dlouhy, the Country Officer for South Africa, United States Department of State, pointed out at a Symposium on 'Education Needs of Black South Africans' in June 1981[96] there is at present almost an embarrassment of riches in this area, at least at the formal level. The programmes he mentioned that were at present in operation were:
— the educational arm of the South African Institute of Race Relations, which includes the Education Information Centre, the Winter school (for black matriculants) and the Senior Certificate Tutorial Service
— the Carnegie-financed Council on Black Education and Research, headed by Professor E Mphahlele and Mr F Mazibulo
— the education programme of the new Black Management Forum, which is linked to USSALEP's (United States South Africa Leadership Exchange Programme) Careers Development Project
— the American Chamber of Commerce's PACE Commercial High School in Soweto (see below)
— the St Anthony's EASTER Project funded by the West German Church Aid foundation, Misereor (see below)
— the Educational Opportunities Commission which provides bursaries for blacks to study overseas, especially in the USA, and which is funded by the Ford and Carnegie Foundations through the Institute of International Education
— the National Development and Management Foundation's 'Advancement at Work' programme
— the South African Council for Higher Education (SACHED)
— the KwaZulu Teachers' Training Scheme

— the Careers Research and Information Centre (Cape)
— foundations and trusts such as the Ernest Oppenheimer Memorial Trust and Church Programmes, etc.
— expanding educational support efforts by South African companies (eg Anglo American and De Beer's Chairman's Fund, SA Breweries, Barlow Rand, SASOL, etc.).
— the Urban Foundation.[97]

In 1981 the United States government was operating ten educational, training and assistance programmes for South Africa and Namibia at a cost of $6,7 million.[98] As Dlouhy pointed out, the major change in emphasis in the deployment of these resources since the advent of the Reagan administration is that there has been a shift from the funding of refugee education to educational upgrading within South Africa.

Private sector educational involvement takes three forms, those established and administered by independent trusts (like most of the above), joint ventures with the DET, and those which take the form of 'in-house' training. Amongst the former, there are those like the EASTER Project (Education and Skills Training on the East Rand), which has the object of 'promoting, furthering and providing education and skills training of all persons in all fields and in the interests of the community as a whole.'[99] This is an independent church-initiated trust which combines a night-school programme for adults wishing to obtain literacy training or to improve their formal schooling and a technical training section which offers a variety of courses lasting from a few weeks to six months on an employer 'release' system, with a variety of other projects. It is the only centre of this kind catering for blacks on the major industrial complex of the East Rand at the present time. In order to provide the facilities for the technical training aspect of the programme (leading to NTC (National Training Certificate) and other technical diplomas) the centre has received massive funding from local industry and from foreign sources, in particular Misereor, a Church Aid foundation in West Germany and ITT (International Telephone and Telegraph Corporation of the USA, one of the largest corporations in the world).[100]

The importance of this project lies in the fact that it will in all probability provide a model for many others of its kind over the next few years. Its significance lies in the curious mix of motives behind its conception. On the one hand it is a progressive, church-linked 'community education' project catering for the educationally underprivileged of the East Rand. To this extent it has been possible to promote the project in terms of the current jargon of 'upliftment' or 'enrichment' of educational opportunities. On the

other hand, the success of the project in drawing funding and
support from international and local industry has in no small
part been due to the benefits accruing to employers through a
training scheme of this kind where semi-skilled workers can be
trained for the variety of deskilled jobs being created in industry
in fields such as fitting and turning, woodwork and motor assembly
and maintenance. This curious fit of humanitarian motives and
employer 'needs' is central to an understanding of the ideology
and practice of current education and training schemes of this
kind. Though numbers of individuals do undoubtedly benefit from
such schemes, their overall impact must be judged within the
context of changes in the labour process outlined above if their
economic and political significance is to be grasped.

Also in the category of educational ventures administered by
trusts or foundations, there are formal educational institutions
like PACE College in Soweto and St Barnabas College in Bosmont,
Johannesburg. PACE College (Project for the Advancement of
Community Education) is a commercial college for children and
young adults. The funding for this prestige venture — which had
cost R6 million by the time it opened early in 1982 — came from
the American Chamber of Commerce in South Africa, and 'also
depends on capital from South African companies such as Anglo
American, Anglo Vaal and Barlow Rand and many others, as well
as American companies in South Africa'.[101] The four criteria
which govern the admission of children to the college are as
follows:
— they must be committed to a commercial future (at the age of
   12-14 years?)
— they must have had good primary school records
— pupils must be the 'right age' for Standard 6
— entrance examinations in English and Mathematics must be
   passed.[102]

In theory all students who fulfil these criteria are eligible for
entrance to the college, but the fees of R1 400 p.a. mean for the
most part that only those with well-off parents, or those whose
parents are able to acquire bursaries through employers, have a
real chance in the stakes.

St Barnabas College represents an attempt to create an elite
'formal' private school on a non-racial basis based on the model
of Waterford in Swaziland or Maru-a-pula in Botswana. Despite a
rhetoric of non-racialism the new campus has been built in the
coloured township of Bosmont, presumably in recognition of the
fact that in the current climate few white children are liable to
attend the school. This project has had massive funding from

Anglo American and from overseas aid sources, the new campus having been built at a cost of over R3 million. The venture represents a major shift in the emphasis of private schools away from the 'opening' of established white schools to a few children from the black elite, to 'bringing private schooling to the black community'. Yet once again, fees of R2 000 p.a. ensure that relatively few working class children will be able to benefit from this exciting experiment, despite generous bursaries for the lucky few who do get admitted.[103]

The parameters within which these institutions operate ensure that those who are upgraded are drawn from an elite or relatively privileged group, and that despite the good intentions of the dedicated people who man these projects their overall effect is to bolster the vested interests of the 'new middle class' in the status quo — in line with the general conception of total strategy outlined above.

The second kind of private sector involvement in educational reform is represented by joint ventures with the DET. One of the first large projects of this kind on the Witwatersrand was the Soweto Teacher Training College, built and equipped by Anglo American after 1976, and then handed over to the DET. Since then there have been a large number of similar projects. Jabulani Technical High School, also in Soweto, has recently received grants of over R2 million from the Urban Foundation, Ford (SA), Anglo American, the Old Mutual, Siemens and Philips in order to enable the DET to provide workshops for courses in electronics, motor mechanics, fitting and turning, woodwork, welding, building construction and basic training for some 800 students. The principal, Mr Riekert, maintains that 'no technical school — black or white — will match us as far as specialisation is concerned. Our school will be the most advanced in the country'.[104] Other technical schools that have been funded in a similar manner are the new Buchulof Technical High School at Mdantsane near East London, which the C S Barlow Foundation has built at a cost of R800 000,[105] the C S Barlow Technical Institute in Lebowa, and the New Brighton Technical School in Port Elizabeth.

The third form of educational venture linked to the private sector is that which has come to be known by the title of the 'In-House Training Project'. Most large companies have some form of training programme of this kind at present — to name only a few, Anglo American, Barlow Rand and Barclays Bank. Even state corporations like ESCOM, SASOL and SA Transport Services have launched major training projects for blacks during the last few years.[106] These take the form of 'formal' educational upgrading (assisting employees to improve their basic schooling) and job-related training programmes. Organisations like Chamdor Training Centre[107] in Krugersdorp provide the most up-to-date courses of this kind on behalf of employers.[108]

The de Lange Commission Report: A Critique

The de Lange Report provides the focus for discussions about educational reforms in South Africa. It conforms in many ways to the conventional approach of educational policy documents referred to earlier, and it is instructive from this point of view to read it in conjunction with the influential *Education Sector Policy Paper* published by the World Bank in 1980.[109]

The de Lange Report recognises an educational crisis and addresses itself to finding ways and means of overcoming that crisis, though the nature of the fundamental issues to be confronted remains remarkably vague. The reason why there is an education crisis never becomes clear; why reform should take the particular forms recommended is left, for the most part, unexplained; and the historical origins of the crisis are neglected. The obvious links between the school revolt of 1976-7 and the collapse of the Bantu Education system — a key segment of the overall schooling system in the country and therefore a fundamental aspect in the genesis of the crisis — are never mentioned! The single clue offered to the problem of linking the educational crisis to its political and economic context is the issue of the 'demand' and 'supply' of manpower — the need to restore the 'harmony' between the schooling system and the labour market.

One reason for the neglect of such crucial aspects of the situation is the fact that the document was drawn up by a group of education-ists who agreed to bury their political differences in the interests of providing a solution to South African's educational problems. A common faith in technicist solutions to educational problems made a broad area of agreement possible between them (See Buckland). They also shared broadly idealistic notions about education:
- that it is concerned with the development of the 'humanity' of individuals
- that it is an essential ingredient of 'civilised' life (ie life in capitalist society)
- that it helps the individual to establish his/her own cultural identity
- that it is a necessary aspect of the individual's preparation for adult life and work.

If we put the best possible construction on the Report, we can see a sincere, idealistic, desire to improve the quality of education. There was an acceptance of the 'dual repertoire' of reform which sought to promote equality of opportunity (not equality)[110] in education for all people regardless of race, while at the same time seeking to 'tap the larger pool of ability'[111] in order more efficiently to recruit the ablest of all races and classes for industry thereby ensuring continued economic growth and political stability.

On the basis of the consensus reached it was possible for the commissioners to agree on a number of matters that avoided fundamental political issues:

— there is a crisis in the provision of education in South Africa;
— there is a manpower crisis in South Africa;
— there is a need for a more comprehensive policy of mass schooling, and better quality education for all if those problems are to be solved;
— there is in consequence a need to promote mass literacy and numeracy;
— there is a need for greater diversification of the schooling system, ie a move away from the traditional patterns of formal schooling towards a schooling system that is more versatile and sensitive to the 'needs' of students, employers, and the labour market;
— this education and training should not only be provided for the young, but the idea of continuous education (adult education and non-formal education) is contained in the recommendations;
— there is therefore an urgent need for curriculum reform to fit in with the above requirements;
— there is an obliquely articulated assumption that education policies should be directly linked to economic development, and that such policies should be accountable in terms of 'relevance';
— there is a need to ensure an adequately trained and motivated teaching profession;
— there is a need for the efficient financing and administration of education.

This broad area of consensus represents the strength of the Report, and helps to explain its coherence and sophistication within the limits of the issues it seeks to address.

Yet those strengths must be weighed against the weaknesses of the Report. These stem from its fundamentally reformist bias which explains why it fails to take into consideration fundamental political and economic issues. It also explains the failure of the Report to make any significant impact on the problems it sets out to remedy.

The apolitical veneer of the Report masks its highly ideological nature. The consensus reached reflected the narrowness of the spectrum of opinion represented on the commission. The nature óf the commission and the manner in which it was set up ensured that broad bands of opinion would not be represented, including church and community leaders; students and parents; academics and trade unionists, private schools and industry (with the single exception of Anglo American).

The 'neutrality/objectivity' (or 'scientific nature') of the Report is a reflection of certain types of liberal influence. Just as liberals traditionally view schooling as an ideologically neutral process of acquiring knowledge and skills, with the 'needs of the individual' (as if they were given) at the top of the agenda, so the Report wishes to represent itself as an objective/scientific exercise above the interests of specific parties. Just as there is an ignorance of the role of schooling in 'maintaining the domination of the dominant class and its culture, and the subordination of the subordinate class(es) and their culture'[112] in the liberal view of the school, so in the Report there is a naivete regarding the political context of schooling, its essentially ideological nature, and the parameters of power within which policy recommendations gain acceptance or rejection. It would of course be naive to expect a government commission to address itself to such issues, but a critique of its findings must point to such limitations if we are to find a way forward.

The recommendations of the Commission are framed in the name of the 'National Interest', but can be shown to represent sectional interests. The commissioners do not address themselves to the problematic implications of recommendations which stress utilitarian considerations regarding the links between education and industry. The manpower 'needs' of industry are seen to be quite unproblematically congruent with the education needs or demands of parents, students, communities, or urban or rural populations. Since there is no consideration of any conflict between the 'needs' of the various groups and the 'needs' for social control or economic efficiency, the degree of consensus within the Commission is not surprising.

Since the commissioners failed to take cognisance of arguments about the role of schooling as a mechanism of class domination, they failed to notice that arguments in favour of more 'relevant' or 'vocational' forms of education are not new in the South African context. Such arguments have been a feature of the politics of education in South Africa since the last century[113] and have always been linked to political strategies for more adequate exploitation of available labour or for the avoidance of conflict between the races.[114]

The Report is concerned with the midwifery of a reformist educational strategy aimed at preserving the status quo in South Africa during the 'eighties. It accepts the whole design of 'Grand Apartheid' without comment and its recommendations refer only to 'white' South Africa, ignoring vital questions about education in the homelands and rural areas.

Finally, there is no suggestion in the Report that the commissioners recognised their work to be an aspect of 'Total Strategy'. The related reports on labour supply and control and manpower strategies (the Riekert and Wiehahn Reports) are not mentioned at all. Was that because the authors of the de Lange Report did not recognise the political implications of their work? Or did their own ideologies so colour their deliberations that they failed to see the structural constraints within which they operated? Did they simply comfort themselves in their idealism? Or were they intentionally devious? The ahistorical approach taken by the commissioners was surely not accidental: it enabled them to avoid confronting the structural constraints on change imposed by the apartheid system.

We hope that this collection of essays will help to open up new areas of debate on the great question of our educational future, or at the very least help us to see our present situation of crisis a little more clearly.

Peter Kallaway
University of Cape Town
June 1983

FOOTNOTES

1. Hall, S 'Schooling, State and Society' in R Dale *et al*, (eds) *Education and the State I, Schooling and the National Interest* (Lewes, 1981) p 4.
2. Centre for Contemporary Cultural Studies (CCCS) [Education Group], *Unpopular Education: Schooling and Social Democracy in England since 1944* (London, 1981) Ch. I.
3. The term is taken from the book on American education by Tyack, D B: *The One Best System: A History of American Urban Education* (Cambridge, Mass., 1974).
4. The following works point to the weaknesses of the kinds of scholarship that have tended to dominate in this field: Stedman Jones, G 'History: The Poverty of Empiricism' in R Blackburn, *Ideology in Social Science* (Glasgow, 1976) pp 96-115; Arnove, R F 'Comparative

Education and World-Systems Analysis', *Comp. Educ. Rev.* 24 (1) Feb. 1980 pp 48-62; Taylor, J G *From Modernization to Modes of Production: Critiques of the Sociologies of Development and Underdevelopment* (London, 1979); CCS, (1981); Silver, H 'Aspects of Neglect: The Strange Case of Victorian Popular Education', *Oxford Review of Education* 3 (1) 1977 pp 57-69; Webster, C 'Changing Perspectives in the History of Education', *Oxford Review of Education* 2 (3) 1976 pp 201-213; Stephens, W B 'Recent Trends in the History of Education in England to 1900', *Education Research and Perspectives* 8 (1) June 1981 pp 3-15.

5.   For an excellent critique of South African historiography see: A Atmore and N Westlake 'A Liberal Dilemma: A Critique of the Oxford History of South Africa', in P Kallaway and T Adler (eds) *Contemporary South African Studies: Research Papers I* (Faculty of Education, Univ. of the Witwatersrand, 1978) — first published in *RACE XIV* (2) 1972 pp 107-136.

6.   Loram, C T *Education of the South African Native* (London, 1917); Brookes, E H *Native Education in South Africa* (Pretoria, 1930).

7.   See the article by R Hunt Davis in the collection. Also King, K J *Pan Africanism and Education* (Oxford, 1971), King, K J 'Africa and the Southern States of the USA: Notes on J H Oldham and American Negro Education for Africans' *JAH* X(4) 1969 pp 659-677; Berman, F H 'American Influence on African Education: The Role of the Phelps-Stokes Fund's Educational Commissions', *Comp. Educ. Rev.* XV (2) June 1971; Carnoy, M (ed) *Education as Cultural Imperialism* (New York, 1974) esp. Chap. I.

8.   That is of course not to overlook important contributions by the following authors, but simply to assert that there has been an absence of detailed educational research:
Majeke, N *The Role of the Missionary in Conquest* (Cape Town, 1952); Tabata, I B *Education for Barbarism* (London, 1960); Horrel, M *Bantu Education to 1968* (Johannesburg 1968) and other titles; Troup, F *Forbidden Pastures, Educational Apartheid* (London, 1976-7); Bernstein, H *Schools for Servitude* (London, n.d.); Hirson, B *Year of Fire, Year of Ash* (London, 1979).

9.   Pells, E G *300 Years of Education in South Africa* (Cape Town, 1954). 1st edition published in 1938 under the title *The Story of Education in South Africa*.

10. Ruperti, R M *The Education System in South Africa* (Pretoria, 1976).

11. Coetzee, J Chr. *Onderwys in Suid-Afrika 1652-1960* (Pretoria, 1975).

12. Behr, A L *New Perspectives in South African Education* (Durban, 1980).

13. Rose, B (ed) *Education in Southern Africa* (Johannesburg, 1970).

14. Atkinson, N *Teaching South Africans: A History of Educational Policy in South Africa* (Salisbury, 1978).

15. See HSRC Bibliographies on Educ. Research, etc. Examples of recent theses on Black Education in South African completed at American universities: Shingler, J 'Education and Political Order in South Africa 1902-61' (Ph.D. Yale Univ., 1973); Robertson, I A 'Education in South Africa: A Study of the Influence of Ideology in Educational Practice' (Ph.D. Harvard Univ., 1973); Hunt Davis, R Jr. 'Nineteenth Century African Education in the Cape Colony: A Historical Analysis' (Ph.D. Univ. Wisconsin, 1969); Mbere, A M 'An Analysis of the Association between Bantu Education and Christian Nationalism: A study of the role of ideology in education' (Ed. D. Harvard, 1979). For others see appended bibliography.

16. CCS (1981), p. 13-14.

17. A term made famous by R S Peters. See his *Ethics and Education* (London, 1966).

18. See Young, M F D (ed) *Knowledge and Control* (London, 1971); Young, M F D and G Whitty (eds), *Society, State and Schooling* (Lewes, 1977); Karabel, J and Halsey, A H (eds) *Power and Ideology in Education* (New York, 1977); Sharp, R *Knowledge, Ideology and the Politics of Schooling* (London, 1980).

19. Finn, D, N Grant and R Johnson, 'Social Democracy, Education and the Crisis', CCCS, *On Ideology* (London, 1978), p. 144-5; Dale, R *et al* (eds) *Schooling and Capitalism* (London, 1976); Dale, R *et al* (eds) *Education and the State:* Vol. I, *Schooling and the National Interest* (Lewes, 1981), Vol II, *Politics, Patriarchy and Practice* (Lewes, 1981); Young, M F D and G Whitty (1977); Bowles, S and H Gintis, *Schooling in Capitalist America* (London, 1976).

20. CCCS (1981), p 15.

21. Finn, D *et al.* (1978), p 144.

22. CCCS (1981); CCCS, *On Ideology* (London, 1978); Clarke, J *et al* (eds) *Working Class Culture* (CCCS, London, 1979); and various Open University Coursebooks cited in fn 19.

23. This point is illustrated by the fact that over ten years of revisionist (Neo-Marxist) analysis of the history of Southern Africa has transformed the nature of historical investigation, but it has had no influence on the study of education. This demonstrates once again the isolation of the academic disciplines of education from mainstream sociology, history, economics, etc.

24. Williams, K 'Problematic History', *Economy and Society,* I (4) 1972, pp 425-456; Wolpe, H 'A Comment on "The Poverty of Neo-Marxism" ', *JSAS* 4 (2) April 1978, pp 240-256.

25. Johnson, R ' "Really Useful Knowledge": radical education and working class culture, 1790-1848', in J Clarke *et al* (eds) (1979).

26. The term is taken from the title of the important book by A Memmi, *The Colonizer and the Colonized* (London, 1965). See further comments on this issue below.

27. The term 'sites of struggle' is borrowed from CCCS (1981) p 25. 'Site' is used with intentional ambiguity — 'literally the school down the road' and metaphorically as a particular 'social space'.

28. Bowles, S and H Gintis (1976).

29. Bates, T R 'Gramsci and the Theory of Hegemony', *Journal of the History of Ideas* XXXVI (1975); Althusser, L 'Ideology and Ideological State Apparatuses', in Cosin, B R (ed), *Education: Structure and Society* (Harmondsworth, 1972) pp 242-80; Apple, M W *Ideology and Curriculum* (London 1979); Apple, M W 'Ideology, Reproduction and Educational Reform', *Comp. Educ. Rev.* 22(3) Oct. 1978 pp 367-387; Poulantzas, N *Classes in Contemporary Capitalism* (London, 1975); Shapiro, H Sui 'Education and the State in Capitalist Society: Aspects of the Sociology of Nicos Poulantzas'. *Harvard Educ. Rev.*, 50(3), Aug. 1980, pp 321-331; Bourdieu, P and J C Passeron, *Reproduction in Education, Society and Culture* (London, 1977); MacDonald, M *The Curriculum as Cultural Reproduction* (Milton Keynes, 1977); Barrett, M and P Corrigan, *Ideology and Cultural Production* (London, 1979).

30. Dale, R *Mass Schooling* (Milton Keynes, 1977); King, K *The African Artisan* (London, 1977) esp. Ch. I; See CCCS (1981), p 44 — for a distinction between notions of 'equality' and 'equality of opportunity' in education.

31. Hextall, I and M Sarup, 'School Knowledge, Evaluation and Alienation', in Young and Whitty (1977) pp 151-171.

32. Carnoy, M (1974) p 10.

33. See fn. 26.

34. See Atmore and Westlake (1972); Wolpe, H 'Capitalism and cheap labour-power in South Africa: from segregation to apartheid', *Economy and Society* I (4) 1972 pp 425-456; and 'Industrialism and Race in South Africa', in Zubaida, S (ed) *Race and Racialism* (London, 1970) pp 151-179; Trapido, S 'South Africa in a comparative study of Industrialization', *Journal of Development Studies* 7(3) 1971 pp 300-320.

35. Wallerstein, I *The Modern World System* (New York, 1974); Frank, A G *Dependent Accumulation and Underdevelopment* (New York, 1979); Kay, G *Development and Underdevelopment: A Marxist Analysis* (London, 1975); Amin, S *Unequal Development* (Sussex, 1976); Taylor, J G (1979).

36. Fanon, F *The Wretched of the Earth* (Harmondsworth, 1965); *Black Skins White Masks* (St Albans, 1973); Freire, P *The Pedagogy of the Oppressed* (Harmondsworth, 1972); *Cultural Action for Freedom* (Harmondsworth, 1972); Carnoy, M (1974); Lyons, C *To Wash an Ethiop White: British Ideas About Black African Educability* (New York, 1975); Memmi, A (1965).

37. Carnoy, M (1974) pp 13-20; Fanon, F (1965) and (1973); Memmi, A (1965); Freire, P (1972).

38. Memmi, A (1965).
39. Carnoy, M (1974) p 19.
40. 'The Ambiguity of Dependence' is well illustrated by Shula Marks in an article of that title on John L Dube of Natal (*JSAS* 1(2) April, 1975 pp 162-180) and in Brian Willan's forthcoming biography of Solomon T Plaatjie (Johannesburg, 1984).
41. CCCS (1981) p 17.
42. The most obvious exponent of that perspective was L Althusser (1972).
43. The literature on these changes is uneven, but they are best document-ed in the British and North American context: see Foster, J *Class Struggle and the Industrial Revolution* (London, 1974); Thompson, E P *The Making of the English Working Class* (Harmondsworth, 1968); Johnson, R 'Educational Policy and Social control in early Victorian England', *Past and Present*, 49 (1970) pp 96-119; 'Notes on the schooling of the English working class: 1780-1850' in Dale, R *et al Schooling and Capitalism* (London, 1976); Johnson, R (1979); Simon, B *The Two Nations and Educational Structure 1780-1870* (London, 1974); Katz, M *The Irony of Early School Reforms* (Cambridge, Mass., 1968); Bowles, S and H Gintes (1976).
44. Johnson, R (1976).
45. Braverman, H *Labour and Monopoly Capital* (New York, 1974); Braver-man, H 'The Modern Corporation' and 'Scientific Management' in Dale, R *et al* (1981).
46. See fn. 43; also Corrigan, P *Capitalism, State Formation and Marxist Theory* (London, 1980). A classic statement of this policy was made by Robert Lowe, Viscount Sherbroake, in a speech to the House of Commons on the passing of the Reform Bill on 15 July 1867, when he stated 'I believe it will be absolutely necessary that you should prevail on our future masters to learn their letters' — popularised as 'We must educate our masters'. I am grateful to Dr Ian Phimister for this quote.
47. Johnson, R (1979).
48. Bowles, S and H Gintis (1976).
49. Doxey, G V *The Industrial Colour Bar in South Africa* (Cape Town, 1961); Johnstone, F A *Class, Race and Gold: A study of Class Relations and Racial Discrimination in South Africa* (London, 1976); Davies, R H *Capital, State and White Labour in South Africa 1900-1960: A Historical Materialist Analysis of Class Formation and Class Relations* (Brighton, 1979).
50. O'Meara, D 'The 1946 African Mineworkers' Strike and the Political Economy of South Africa', in Kallaway, P and T Adler (1978) II pp 57-92 (first published in *Journal of Commonwealth and Compar-ative Politics* XIII (2) 1975 pp 146-173; Legassick, M 'Gold, Agriculture, and Secondary Industry in South Africa, 1885-1970: From Periphery to Sub-Metropole as a Forced Labour System', in Palmer, R and N Parsons (eds) *The Roots of Rural Poverty in Central and Southern*

Africa (London, 1977) pp 175-200; Wolpe, H (1972); Lacey, M *Working for Boroko* (Johannesburg 1981).

51. Kaplan, D 'Class conflict, capital accumulation and the state: an historical analysis of the state in twentieth century South Africa', (D. Phil. thesis, University of Sussex, 1977); Seidman, J *Facelift Apartheid: South Africa After Soweto* (London, 1980); Saul, J S and S Gelb, 'The Crisis in South Africa: Class Defence, Class Revolution', *Monthly Review* 33(3) July/August 1981 (Whole edition); French, K *South African Capital Restructuring: Crisis and tendencies* (Johannesburg 1981); Davies, R 'Capital Restructuring and the modification of the racial division of labour in South Africa' *JSAS* 5(2) 1979.

52. CCCS (1981) p 28.

53. Bozzoli, B *The Political Nature of a Ruling Class: Capital and Ideology in South Africa 1890-1933* (London, 1981).

54. Davies, R, D Kaplan, M Morries, D O'Meara, 'Class Struggle and the Periodization of the State in South Africa', *RAPE* 7 (1976) pp 4-30; Clarke, S 'Capital, Fractions of Capital and the State', *Capital and Class* 5 (1978); Bozzoli, B 'Capital and the State in South Africa', *RAPE* 11 (1978) pp 40-50; Innes, D and M Plaut 'Class Struggle and the State', *RAPE* 11 (1978) pp 51-61.

55. CCCS (1981) p 143.

56. Technical and Vocational Education Foundation of SA, Proceedings 1981 Conference: *Technical and Vocational Education in Southern Africa* (Silverton, 1981). Also see P Randall's review of this collection in the *Financial Mail* 21/8/81.

57. Blignaut, S *Statistics on Education in South Africa 1968-79* (Johannesburg, 1981); Roukens de Lange, A *The Dynamics of Upgrading Black Education* (Johannesburg, 1982).

58. Reeder, D 'A Recurring Debate: education and industry', in Dale, R *et al* (1981) p 200. Also see Venn, G 'Man, Education and Work' (1965) in Cosin, B R (1972) pp 97-107; and Denison E F and J P Poullier, 'Education and the Labour Force' *ibid* pp 80-86.

59. Human Sciences Research Council (HSRC), Report of the Main Committee of the HSRC Investigation into Education: *Provision of Education in the RSA* (Pretoria, July, 1981).

60. CCCS (various publications as above) — In particular *Unpopular Education (1981)* and Finn, D *et al* (1978) and Hall, S (1981).

61. Hall, S (1981) pp 4-5.

62. *Ibid*, pp 8-9.

63. *Ibid*, p 15; Finn, D *et al* (1978); CCCS (1981).

64. See fn. 17

65. See fn. 49.

66. Feit, E *South Africa: The Dynamics of the African National Congress* (London, 1962); Gerhart, G M *Black Power in South Africa* (Berkeley, 1978); Luckhardt, K and B Wall, *Organise . . . or Starve: The History of*

the South African Congress of Trade Unions (London, 1980); Kane-Berman, J *SOWETO, Black Revolt, White Reaction* (or *The Method in the Madness*) (Johannesburg and London, 1978); Hirson, B *Year of Fire, Year of Ash* (London, 1979).

67. HSRC (1981) p 20.

68. Anderson, J *The Struggle for the School; the interaction of missionary, colonial government and nationalist enterprise in the development of formal education in Kenya* (London, 1970); Stabler, E *Education since Uhuru* (Middleton, 1969); Ng'eno, J *Education and Political Development in Kenya* (S. Illinois, 1973); Cameron, J and W A Dodd, *Society, School and Progress in Tanzania* (Oxford, 1970); Morrison, D R *Education and Politics in Africa: The Tanzanian Case* (London, 1975).

69. See also Edgar, R 'The fifth seal: Enoch Mgijma, the Israelites and the Bulhoek Massacres, 1921' (Ph.D. dissertation, UCLA, 1977), and 'Garveyism in Africa: Dr Wellington and the "American" movement in the Transkei', *Ufahamu* VI (1) pp 31-57.

70. This article is drawn from Tom Lodge's current work on the history of the ANC. See his book, *Black Politics in South Africa since 1945* (Ravan, Johannesburg, 1983).

71. This article is drawn from Gaitskell, D L 'Female Mission Initiatives: Black and White Women in Three Witwatersrand Churches, 1903-1939' (Ph.D. dissertation. University of London/School of Oriental and African Studies, 1981).

72. This article is drawn from MA dissertation 'What Shall We Tell the Blacks? Bantu Education in South Africa — its problems and possibilities' (MA, University of London/Goldsmiths College, 1976). The research methods used by Ms Maree were novel in the the South African context, and could provide important leads for future work in this area.

73. See Glen Moss 'Total Strategy', *Work in Progress* 11 (February, 1980) pp 1-11; Saul, J S and S Gelb, (1981).

74. Wiehahn Commission: RSA, *Report of the Commission of Inquiry into Labour Legislation* RP 47/1979 (Pretoria); Riekert Commission: RSA *Report of the Commission of Inquiry into Legislation affecting the Utilization of Manpower* RP 32/1979 (Pretoria).

75. *Guardian* 22/11/78.

76. See fn. 45.

77. Harry Oppenheimer, 5th Stock Exchange Chairman's Lecture, London, 18/5/76, cited in Seidman, J (1980) p 12.

78. Hussain, A 'The Economy and the educational system in capitalist societies' (1976) in Dale, R (ed) (1981) I pp 172-4.

79. See *South African Labour Bulletin* 4(7) Nov. 1978 — 'Focus on the Labour Process' — whole edition. In particular see C. Meth's article pp 7-40.

80. Hussain, A (1976/1981) pp 170-71.

81. *Sunday Express* (Business Reporter) 5/7/81.

82. *SALB* 5(2) August 1979 — 'Focus on Wiehahn' — whole edition;
     SALB 5(4) November 1979 — 'Focus on Riekert' — whole edition.
83. NUSAS, *Wiehahn: Exploring the Contradictions* (Cape Town, n.d.)
     No. 90 — 1979.
84. UG 29 — '36.
85. UG 53 — '51.
86. The idea of 'community schools' in the de Lange Report might have
     hinted at non-racialism, but this was never made into a central issue.
     Indeed the recent 'Volkskongres oor Onderwys' (March, 1982) in
     Bloemfontein made it quite clear that separate education for separate
     races was 'non-negotiable' for the vast majority of the supporters of the
     National Party, let alone the Conservative Party or the HNP.
87. 'Education for Blacks in South Africa', Information Newsletter issued
     as a supplement to *EDUCAMUS* October, 1980. Published and dis-
     tributed by the Dept. of Foreign Affairs and Information on behalf
     of the DET (Pretoria) p 4.
88. *Rand Daily Mail* 17/9/81 'Plan for black education to cost R63 million'
     by Sam Maseko (an interview with Mr G Engelbrecht, DET's Chief
     Liason Officer).
89. See fn. 86 and 88.
     This pressure, and the state's reaction to it, is demonstrated by the
     following articles selected from newspapers during the period under
     review:
     — 'Skills Factor: warning minus sign in SA economy' by Chris Freimond
       RDM 6/6/81;
     — 'SA "can't rely on whites only for top personnel" ' — (Report by the
       National Manpower Commission) by Drew Forrest *Star* 4/6/81;
     — 'Manpower now the economic disease — Anglo: Blacks must be
       trained now' *Sunday Express* 5/7/81;
     — 'Accountancy faces collapse due to poor training' by Caroline
       Dempster *Star* 2/4/81;
     — 'Wanted in SA: 700 000 top workers: Train blacks and avert a crisis
       say experts' by David Jackson *Sunday Times* 23/11/80;
     — 'Government to take new look at training issue' by Riaan de Villiers
       RDM 4/6/81;
     — 'Botha [(Fanie), P K] urges more accent on training' by Gerald
       Reilly *RDM* 29/10/81.
90. 'State vows R50 million for Black Training' RDM 9/12/79.
91. 'Plan for black education to cost R63m' by Sam Maseko *RDM* 17/9/81:
     Statement by Mr G J Rousseau, Director General of Education and
     Training reported in *SOWETAN* 17/3/81.
92. 'Why so few apprentices?' by S B Molefe *SOWETAN* 23/3/81.
93. Sam Maseko *RDM* 18/9/81.
94. 'Lectures start at New Mabopane Technikon' by Norman Ngali
     SOWETAN 11/2/81.

95. Vista University; see 'Urban people to benefit from new Black University' *GROWTH* 2(5) May 1982 pp 14-15; 'Township varsity takes off — in borrowed rooms' by Craig Charney *Sunday Express* 28/3/82.

96. Remarks by David B Dlouhy, Country Officer for South Africa, United States Department of State, at the Symposium on Educational Needs of Black South Africans, Wingspread Conference Centre, Racine, Wisconsin, Friday, June 19 1981 (mimeo, 15 p).

97. *Ibid*, p 13.

98. *Ibid*, p 12.

99. 'The EASTER Project: The Second Five Year Development Plan' (Draft) (mimeo, 1981).

100. St Anthony's Adult Education Centre: *BROCHURE* 20 p; 'The Official Opening of the Science Block at St Anthony's (brochure, n.d.) 4 p; Judy Olivier 'St Anthony's: a longing to learn' *Fair Lady,* 29/7/81.

101. 'PACE Towards a brighter future' by Gillian Rennie *Star,* 10/2/82.

102. *Ibid*.

103. Personal communication with members of the St Barnabas staff; Randall, P *Little England on the Veld* (Johannesburg, 1981) pp 6, 95, 129.

104. 'Jabulani Tech. will be very sophisticated' by Len Maseko *SOWETAN* 10/2/81; 'R50 000 for technical training' (Jabulani) by Mokone Molete *RDM* 9/7/81.

105. *People and Profits* June, 1981 p 11.

106. 'SAR to spend R62m on new College for Blacks' by Arnold David *Sunday Express* 25/10/81; 'ESCOM plans to build R40m training centre' by Charlene Beltramo *Star* 17/4/79.

107. 'Chamdor — centre for skills' by Riaan de Villiers *RDM* 16/1/79.

108. It is worth noting that 'liberal' institutions like the University of the Witwatersrand, which sees itself as a bastion of opposition to apartheid, have also been prominent in their participation in the current reformist initiative. A variety of 'enrichment programmes' aimed dominantly at blacks (they were not there before black students began to be admitted to the University in fairly large numbers after 1977) have been launched to ensure that those blacks who do arrive on the campus are able to succeed on a par with whites — 'no dropping of standards' is the watchword! As the University has become drawn into community-related action programmes a variety of other 'upgrading' programmes have also emerged. These include the SOWETO English Language Project (SELP) (aimed at upgrading the English language competence of black teachers). the Anglo Cadet Scheme (aimed at producing black managerial 'manpower' in a highly intensive hothouse atmosphere with the assistance of extravagant funding from business). These projects have spawned whole bureaucratic sub-systems within the University, related directly to the administrative hierarchy rather than the academic departments — an interesting aspect of the internal politics of institutions of this kind in

the current atmosphere of crisis, which would merit further investigation. (See University of the Witwatersrand, *Programmes designed particularly for educationally disadvantaged people* (Johannesburg, 1982).

109. *Education: Sector Policy Paper* (Washington D.C., World Bank, 1980).
110. See fn. 30.
111. Reeder, D (1981) p 180.
112. Hall, S (1981) p 27.
113. See for example: [Stuart, J]. *A Project for the Promotion of education in general as well as for the European as for the Native races of the Colony of Natal, SA* (Pietermaritzburg, 1859).
114. See fn. 7.

Part One: The Origins of Black Education
The Historical Foundations of the Schooling of Black South Africans*
Frank Molteno

Early schooling in colonial 'South Africa'

Formal schools made their appearance in Southern Africa as part
of the new social relations introduced with colonialism. The first
school was opened on 17 April 1658, at the Cape. This was less
than a month after the arrival of the original shipment of 170
slaves. The school was set up specifically for the Dutch East India
Company's slaves and, as far as is known, it took them in
irrespective of their ages. Van Riebeeck was allegedly motivated
by a concern to have something done for the slaves' intellectual
and moral welfare.[1]

From the earliest days of schooling, a distinction has to be
made between the declared aims of schooling and what was and
is intended by those formulating educational policy. Furthermore,
the intentions of policy-makers are not necessarily matched by the
objective consequences of what is implemented in practice. It is
safe to assume that the colonists' real concern was that the slaves
should serve the purpose for which they had been bought, namely
to labour for their masters. They would have been able to do so
more efficiently if they understood the language of their masters.
The relationship between slave and master was a most unequal
one; it was therefore not the master who learned the slaves'
language, but the slaves who had to learn Dutch. Further, the
more total the slaves' subjugation was, the less they would have
resisted the system of forced labour in which they were trapped.
Having been ripped from their homes in West and East Africa and
the East Indies, they had already been removed thousands of miles
from their physical base, but, so long as they still had each other
and their beliefs, their independence was not fully undermined.
Yet, even that minimal ideological base of independence that

* The original version of this chapter appeared as Part I in a thesis entitled *The Schooling
of Black South Africans and the 1980 Cape Town Students' Boycott: A Sociological
Interpretation* (M Soc Sc thesis, University of Cape Town, 1983).

remained would have been removed if the slaves were indoctrinated with their masters' religion. The slaves were driven physically and psychologically into their masters' world. It is in the context just described that the instruction of the younger slaves in the rudiments of the Dutch language and the Christian religion is to be understood.

In a regimented environment where elementary academic matter had to be imbibed by rote and where 'respect' for new 'superiors' and a new authority was beaten in, the slaves were expected to learn obedience and discipline. The colonists presumably hoped that the young slaves, thus schooled, would be easily pressed into positions of servility and become efficient and pliant labourers.

Over and above what it would be reasonable to assume, there is evidence that slaves did not accept their subordinate positions. The resistance displayed by slaves to being students might have reflected, inter alia, resistance to being prepared for such subordinate positions. The student-slaves' most effective mode of resistance was flight. It happened once that the whole school stayed out for five days and went into hiding in a cave near Hout Bay. The teacher was instructed to try and buy their attention by rewarding such interest and diligence as they might show with a tot of rum and two inches of tobacco each. But the slaves' co-operation was not so cheaply bought and they continued to run away until the school was finally forced to close. Thus, from the earliest days of formal education in the sub-continent, the authorities' ability to implement policy was constrained where the form of schooling was rejected.

A second school was established in 1663 to provide primarily for children of the colonists. It opened with twelve of their children, four young slaves and one Khoikhoi child. The first suggestion of segregation in schooling came from within the church in 1676. The recommendation was not expressed in terms of separating children of different colours but rather in terms of the desirability of having a separate school for slaves. In this way the class division between slaves and colonists could be kept adequately clear. In 1685 a separate school was established exclusively for slave children under the age of 12 years. Thereafter, the earlier school, which had been open to all since its founding in 1663, was reserved for colonist and other non-slave children. Children were futher separated into girls and boys for their lessons. In addition to what they learnt at school, the young female slaves were instructed in 'domestic duties' by 'women of standing in the Slave Lodge'.[2] Furthermore, a few young male slaves were selected to be taught trades.

The respective positions of slaves and colonists were reflected in their differential schooling. Malherbe writes,

> While on the one hand, it is due to the strong church (Calvinistic) influence that education often deteriorated into mere formalism, it gave the people, on the other hand, a type of education which was perhaps as well suited to their needs at that time as any we could devise today. It did not cultivate erudition, yet it produced pioneers — men who had to break-in the country. From their earliest youth boys were practised in the use of firearms till they became probably the best marksmen in the world. This type of education helped to preserve them against spiritual as well as physical dangers.[3]

It can be seen how early the character of schooling for supremacy was set. Much later in 1889, the rationale for its character was made explicit by the Cape Superintendent-General of Education, when he described how the government assumed its first duty to be

> to recognise the position of the European colonists as holding the paramount influence, social and political; and to see that the sons and daughters of the colonists . . . should have at least such an education as their peers in Europe enjoy, with such local modifications as will fit them to maintain their unquestioned superiority and supremacy in this land.[4]

One of the DEIC's concerns was to see to it that its men, removed from the bonds of their home institutions, remained united in a common ideology. Religious instruction at school contributed by helping to perpetuate the set of dogmas to which all adhered. This gave rise to excessive formalism, and the teaching of the three Rs tended to be almost incidental to religious instruction. The educationalist M E Martinius, wrote that 'Under such circumstances a man was not likely to make an inspired teacher and the work would be apt to degenerate into a mechanical grind. This the Company overlooked in its desire to spread the doctrines uncorrupted.'[5] Arising from the fear which constantly haunted the colonists that 'false' doctrines might be disseminated, steps were taken at an early date to establish central control over who should be permitted to teach and what should be taught.[6]

It was clearly in the interests of the colonists that a certain minimum of schooling be received by both their own children and the children of those being subordinated to their order. However, in the context of the near bankruptcy and political disintegration of the DEIC, a corrupt and weak Cape Administration, political complications in Europe, an economic depression, and epidemics of smallpox, it is not surprising that formal education was never a policy priority for the Company. Its operations certainly did not depend on it. The colonial authorities did decree in 1682 that all slave children under twelve had to attend school and that older ones had to go for instruction twice a week, but this injuction was for the most part ignored, especially in respect of slave girls, and no attempt was made to enforce it. This was in part because the slave-owners were not prepared to forego the slave children's labour. More importantly, it reflected their fear that any form of education might stimulate slaves to make demands above their station. According to V N Louw, 'the European settler . . . was disturbed at mounting signs of Native restlessness and thoughts of manumission. Ascribing these latter to Western influence, "the civilising efforts of the Company soon dwindled . . . (and) the conscious effort to Christianise . . . died away".'7

Schooling made extremely slow headway in the 17th and 18th centuries. Apart from the schools for slaves belonging to the DEIC, a few elementary schools were established in Cape Town and surrounding villages to provide for colonists' children and to a lesser extent for their household slaves. Ex-slaves who had managed to buy their freedom also often sent their children to such schools. The 18th century also saw the beginnings of missionary education directed at the Khoikhoi people. Thus, for example, in the Moravian Missionary Society's school at Baviaans-kloof (later to become Genadendal), 'The Hottentots were persuaded to forego their nomadic way of life, and made to realise the need for discipline and regular habits.'8 Boys and girls were taught separately and, while the former were trained in certain trades, handicrafts were emphasised for all.

The type of formal education that emerged in Southern Africa was not based in indigenous social structures. It was introduced as part of the process whereby colonialism brought the subcontinent into the emergent world capitalist system. 'As a colonising power, it (the 'British race') has always sought to draw the aboriginal population of its over-the-sea territories into harness . . . the Africans are bending their necks to the life-preserving yoke of labour . . . .'9 P A W Cook, writing in 1949, described education for blacks in South Africa as having been 'for the most part, a purposeful process aiming at the incorporation of dependent peoples into the structures of Western civilisation.'10 It is not that schooling was at every point designed deliberately to promote the new colonial order but its content and consequences were crucially conditioned by this order. Conceptualising the process in terms of culture rather than imperialism, Cook explains how 'the

A rural 'Native' school.
Photograph: Johannesburg Public Library.

A 'Native' primary school near Burgersdorp.
Photograph: Johannesburg Public Library.

Bethelsdorp in the Eastern Cape, one of the earliest mission stations. It was founded by Dr van der Kemp of the London Missionary Society.

The Catholic mission station at Mount Frere in the Transkei. Churches and schools were often located side by side.

missionary came to South Africa to preach the Gospel and to dispel the darkness of the heathen. But he taught elements of the same culture to which the trader, the magistrate, and the farmer belong.'[11]

Black schooling in the 19th century

The major wars, which ended in the Nguni- and Sotho-speaking people of Southern Africa being dispossessed of their land and forced into the colonial order, were waged roughly over the century between 1779 and 1879. It was in 1799 — twenty years after the opening of the latter period — that the first school specifically for Africans was established near what later became King William's Town. Previously, only a handful of Nguni- and Sotho-speakers had had any formal education in colonial schools. From the turn of the century, missions started setting up more such schools, particularly on the fringes of settler penetration. The first school in the Orange Free State was founded in 1823, and the first ones in Natal and what became the Transvaal in 1835 and 1842, respectively. Thus schooling played a part in the process of conquest itself — albeit a relatively minor one — as well as contributing to the social consolidation of conquest and the control of the conquered.

The respective positions of slaves and colonists were reflected in their differential schooling. However, for most of the century formal schooling developed very slowly. The extent of the contribution that schooling was able to make for the settlers was not such as to render it a priority for the colonial government. Nevertheless, as early as 1839, a Department of Education was established in the Cape Colony, and the first Superintendent-General appointed. Thenceforth the mission schools were formally under the jurisdiction of that Department. Some state control was exercised through the grant of funds, which first became available to mission schools in 1841 but, in the main, schooling was left to the churches and missionary societies. Although the latter's financial resources were at times supplemented by contributions from the black communities served by the schools, funds were always very limited. The standard of teaching was low; minimal secondary education was offered and that usually by teacher training institutes. Only a minute fraction of the child population received any schooling at all.

It is suggested that such impact as schooling had in this early period was not achieved through direct contact with a significant proportion of the children of the indigenous millions, as is the case at the present time. Rather the impact was achieved through an 'elite' minority. The process of schooling was indeed a key factor in the creation of such an elite, but that process should not necessarily be seen as the outcome of a specific design. On the contrary, Dr (later Sir) Langham Dale, Superintendent-General of Education in the Cape, explained in 1869, for example, that the aid given to mission schools, insofar as they supplemented the public school system, was 'with a view of bringing elementary instruction within the reach of the mass of the labouring poor, especially those of the coloured races.'

Part of the effect of the emergence of this early schooling was indeed the emergence of a new 'elite' which was from the start potentially at odds with the traditional tribal leadership. With their newly acquired 'knowledge', they represented a threat to the traditional authorities and even a possible challenge to their leadership. As Dale reported in 1891, 'The Kaffirs see in the school the agency that weakens and then effaces all tribal bonds and customs. The levelling tendency of popular instruction is not consistent with their traditions, and the Chiefs specially watch the growth of schools with suspicion.'[13]

Steeped in the conquerors' ways of seeing, converted to their religion, and generally accepting of the new order, the schooled corps could help disseminate a system of ideas, values, loyalties and authorities which were consistent with the colonists' interests and which contradicted, and helped to undermine, the framework that had given the people an independent ideological base in their struggle to retain their land and livelihood. Even a government commission report contains discussion of how 'missionaries' teachings have acted like dynamite on tribal solidarity.'[14] A division was created between Christian converts and adherents to traditional religious beliefs. These are some of the ways in which schooling contributed to weakening the indigenous people's resistance to colonisation and helped to establish them, once conquered, in their new place of subordination.

The year 1854 marked an important point in the development of state interest in, and support for, the schooling of black people. In that year Sir George Grey was appointed as governor of the Cape. He held education to be a prime weapon in the subjugation of the indigenous population. It was as a part of the Cape regime's 'border pacification' policy that he motivated for state subsidisation of the missionaries' education efforts. Thus:

> The plan I propose to pursue with a view to the general adjustment of
> these questions (frontier policy) is, to attempt to gain an influence over
> all the tribes included between the present north-eastern boundary of

this colony and Natal, by employing them upon public works, which will tend to open their country; by establishing institutions for the education of the children, and the relief of their sick; by introducing among them institutions of a civil character suited to their present condition; and by these and other like means to attempt to win them to civilisation and Christianity, and thus to change by degrees our present unconquered and apparently irreclaimable foes into friends who may have common interests with ourselves.[15]

In 1868, Dale was urging that 'the spread of civilisation, by school-instruction and the encouragement of industrial habits among the Natives in the Border districts, is of importance to the political security and social progress of the Colony.'[16] Twenty-three years later he described the black schools as 'hostages for peace' and argued that 'if for that reason only £12 000 a year is given to schools in the Transkei, Tembuland and Griqualand, the amount is well spent; but that is not the only reason — to lift the Aborigines [sic] gradually, as circumstances permit, to the platform of civilised and industrial life is the great object of the educational vote.'[17] In sum, as the Eiselen Commission reported, 'education was regarded as one means among many to be employed in the pacification of the Border.'[18]

The conquered, wrenched from their own material base and traditional social relations, were cast adrift as were the freed slaves. It has been argued that there was greater urgency with regard to the provision of schools after the promulgation of Ordinance 50 in 1820, which gave equal civil rights to the Khoikhoi people, and after the emancipation of slaves in 1833.[19] Almost half a century later, Dale, in an article entitled, 'Technical Instruction and Industrial Training', posed, rhetorically, the question, 'Do you prefer to spend public money on police, prisons and other repressive and protective agencies, or on the workshop and the teachers of handicrafts?'[20] Schooling assisted in incorporating into the new order those set loose from the tribal structures of social control in such a way that they could be disciplined and made to serve the interests of the colonists. Grey saw the integration of the African people into the Cape economy in terms of their becoming 'useful servants, consumer of our goods, contributors to our revenue, in short, a source of strength and wealth to the Colony, such as Providence designed them to be'.[21] The schools helped to make 'useful servants' of them by teaching them the basics of their new masters' language and providing them with the limited vocabulary that would be relevant to their role in the colonial order. They provided them with an elementary level of literacy and trained them in the discipline and skills of manual labour. These servants-to-be were supposed to accept the naturalness of their place of inferiority and to be equipped with an appropriately servile mentality. Dale argued that 'to teach, train and improve the present anomalous part of the community so that their fusion and absorption into the ordinary channels of industry may be steadily consummated is the practical and necessary object of any true method of native education'.[22]

It was not as equal individuals that blacks were brought into the colonial order but as a subordinate category which was integrated economically while kept outside politically and at a distance socially.

Some were schooled into an acceptance of the new 'civilisation', while their expectations of partaking as equals in the fruits of colonial society were suppressed. A few were taken further than the rest to form a small 'educated' class, comprising preachers and teachers, who, schooled in the views and ways of the colonists, could serve as intermediaries between the colonial authorities and the people.

Early responses: resistance and demand

Black resistance to schooling — primarily in the form of outright rejection or avoidance, was considerable for most of the 19th century. For as long as black people managed to remain beyond the reach of the colonial economy — for as long, that is, as the pre-capitalist mode of production remained relatively intact — they would have perceived little, if any, benefit to be derived from schooling and, at the same time, would have resisted sacrificing their children's labour. In 1848, a missionary wrote, in a letter to the High Commissioner at the Cape, 'it is not so difficult to get the church filled with people, as it is, to get the children to school, who are always by cattle herding prevented from it.'[23] A quarter of a century later, *The Kaffir Express* noted, 'The chief objection on the part of heathen parents to sending their boys to school, besides their indifference to education, is that they require them to herd their sheep and cattle.' It mentioned further that girls were 'kept from school for different reasons', but did not elaborate.[24] Dale, in a report drawn up in 1869, observed,

> There is considerable repugnance on the part of heathen Kaffirs to send their children to school.
> Besides feeling that school instruction weakens the hold which native customs and superstitions have over the mind, the Kaffirs say that they are very well content as they are . . . . They want nothing for

themselves, and they wish their children to be as themselves. Each
parent expects his own child to herd his few goats or two or three cows
all day long.[25]

In 1882, the Natal Native Commission recorded its view as follows:
'We think that there is little desire among ordinary Natives for
education, but we do not anticipate that there would be opposition
to schools being placed in Locations.' The Commissioners betrayed
their implicit misgivings, however, through recommendations
contained in the next sentence, thus: 'We should recommend
beginning with tribes known to be favourably disposed; we should
also further propose that schools should be placed in some of the
small tribes, partly because any opposition would be of less
moment, partly because the distances for the children attending
the school would be more manageable.'[26]

Schooling in the 19th Century helped to undermine the unconquered, while incorporating the already conquered into the
structure of settler society. Those parents who sent their children
to school did so to obtain the sort of education which would
provide an entree to the colonial order at a level above the most
menial forms of labour. The education sought was an academic
one and students themselves vigorously opposed its dilution with
manual labour. At Lovedale, for example, 'all native boarders'
were compelled to engage in two hours of 'some kind of work'
every afternoon. In 1872, *The Kaffir Express* admitted that
students entirely rejected this forced labour, characterising it
variously as 'a sore point', 'the bane of their lives' and 'an utter
abhorrence'. The newspaper cited the case of 'one young savage'
who early one morning had run away and subsequently indicated
in a letter written from home that he had done so on account of
the latter imposition.[27] Parents and students voted for an academic
form of education in the only way open to them; with their feet.
Thus, for example, in 1880 *The Christian Express* commented as
follows:

> . . . Roman Catholic missions have been a failure in Africa when they
> attempt to satiate the African craving for education with a few ounces
> of catechism, and communicate nothing to elevate the individual, . . .
> nothing else was to be expected.[28]

A further illustration is taken from the 1892 report of the
commission appointed to enquire into education in the Cape
Colony: 'The heredities of the South African aborigenes [sic] are
not in the direction of a love of bodily toil; consequently schools
which allow the four hours to be occupied with more or less of

dawdling over spelling books or school slates tend to be numerically the strongest.'[29]

In a context of widespread avoidance of 'education' and contact with 'civilisation', the missionaries were not averse to providing the sort of schooling desired so long as it brought children into their schools and thereby aided in the achievement of their primary objective which was to evangelise. It aided the latter in another way too in that it was an appropriate education for preparing children to read the Bible and participate in religious ritual. An academic form of education would, in any case, have been more familiar to missionaries from a European background. Furthermore, it must be added that the missionaries did not always share the interests which were paramount for the colonialists and which might have otherwise oriented their educational objectives. Even though it is safe to assume that the missionaries wished to serve their 'flock' as best they could, the conflict of interests is revealed in the following extract from the *Christian Express:*

> Missionaries are in no sense political agitators. They desire nothing so much as that the relations of the natives toward the Government should be those of perfect loyalty, and they invariably counsel the natives to be law-abiding and peaceful . . . . [30]

Meanwhile, the state's capacity to determine the extent and nature of education in the colony was severely restricted, as is brought out in the following quotation which at the same time illustrates how contested the educational terrain was even in those early days of formal schooling in the subcontinent:

> It may be desirable that education of the right kind should be compulsory for the children of aborigines, but at the present moment the introduction of such a compulsory provision would be inopportune. If the State cannot enforce attendance at school, it can at least define the education for which it is prepared to pay. There should be a definite regulation that one-half of the school time required of those in attendance shall be devoted to such manual training as can best be followed in the locality. The 'literary' instruction sanctioned in native day schools should be purely elementary.[31]

Then again the following appeared in a 1906 issue of *The Christian Express:*

> . . . the Native . . . is too enthusiastic about mere book learning and far too casual with respect to the accumulation of wealth . . . . The way he frequently strips himself to meet his educational expenses is indeed ad-

mirable, but this would be quite unnecessary, were he to pay more attention to developing his means of livelihood. It may be urged that the education he is at present receiving is not one to make money with, and there is a good deal of truth in this, but he has all along shown such a pronounced preference for the European curriculum that it has been deemed impolitic to refuse him. It has rather been hoped that the craze would die a natural death. But it will take long for education . . . entirely to eliminate from his character that conspicuous defect *viz.* his fondness for the royal road, in other words his idea that he is already fitted for various positions at present occupied by white men only. It is true that he is to some extent satisfied with such posts as that of teacher, interpreter, etc., but, except in a few isolated cases, for any occupation involving manual labour he is at present strongly disinclined.[32]

There were few openings in the colonial system for black persons with any degree of schooling, however, and this was the case *a fortiori* for those with a relatively high level of education. According to the Rev. J Mountain, writing in 1884,

> Owing to the colour-prejudice, the only occupations absolutely requiring any education which are now available, or are likely for some years to be available to natives, are those of telegraph messengers, policemen, railway porters, interpreters, school teachers, and ministers of the gospel; and of course the demand from these situations is very limited.[33]

These conditions frustrated certain of the expectations generated by schooling. Giving evidence before the commission on education in the Cape which reported in 1892, no lesser person than G M Theal, the settler historian, put the case for 'industrial' education for black persons. He argued 'that there is a very large number of natives on the frontier who attend these mission schools and are taught to read and write, and they become really unfit for other work, and that class of person is increasing, and they are doing . . . no good to the country.'[34] In a memorandum submitted as evidence to the same commission, the following view was expressed:

> As far as possible, I would at these schools teach every occupation that a servant is required to do in the Colony. Why is it that I have to employ the Red Kaffir boy as my groom and gardener? Simply because he demands half the amount that the educated boy does, he does his work as well, if not better, and is more amenable to discipline. To have 20 000 or 30 000 of this class in the Colony would be a serious matter. The present system of education is not only a waste of money (whether

applied to blacks or whites), but money spent in raising up an army of discontents, who sooner or later would become a serious danger to the country.[35]

Some twenty-three years earlier, Dale — in explaining his inclination 'to discourage the special preparation of a few native lads here and there, at a great expense, and to assist only in the training of a sufficient number of native teachers to occupy the various school stations at the kraals' — reported as follows:

> Native lads have been well educated here, and have completed their course in England, who, on returning to this Colony, find no sphere or occupation but that of teachers, at a salary of about £40 p.a. This is distasteful to most of them; a long period of comparatively easy and refined life at school and at colleges has led them to expect something better. To the educated Kaffir there is no opening; he may be qualified to fill the post of a clerk in a public office or in a mercantile house, but either there is no demand for such persons, or prejudice operates against persons of colour being so employed. To give a high education to Kaffir boys, and then to leave them isolated from their own people in thoughts and habits, and to some extent in language, and without any prospect of useful and settled occupation in another sphere of labour is only to increase the existing temptations of the so-called school Kaffir to fall into the vices of the low Europeans with whom they are brought into contact. We require Native teachers without that over-refinement which elevates the individual too much above his fellows.[36]

While the colonial context may have limited the capacity of schooling to affect individuals' material prospects, it would appear to have provided at least a leadership element with certain linguistic, and other cultural accoutrements, useful in articulating the grievances and demands of their people. With the collapse of military-backed resistance and the concomitant consolidation of conquest, such initiatives had increasingly to be taken on terrain defined by the colonists. It was not, as many have chosen to believe, that education — through exposing black people to new and broader horizons — revealed to them what was wrong with the place to which they were subjected in the colonial order, and unveiled a previously uncontemplated vista of liberty. No vision was needed to conjure up the latter since the experience of liberty was still fresh in people's memories. That people were clear on the former score, independent of any revelatory power which education might have been assumed to possess, was evidenced by more than a century of bitter resistance to their colonisation and subjugation.

It was only as the economic basis for an independent political stand disintegrated with the dissolution of the pre-capitalist mode of production, only as people became impressed by the final failure of their resistance, only as they found their feet anew on terrain which was no longer theirs, and only as the settler authorities demonstrated their power to dictate the terms on which future negotiation might be conducted, that education began to be sought instead of shunned.

Even as early as 1873 a financial appeal by Lovedale College foresaw that, 'Among the natives the tide in favour of education is fast rising, and as they have found their way here, it is a pity to shut the doors against them.'[37] Nine months later it was reported, 'The tide in the direction of education among the native people still keeps steadily rising, and overflows the barrier of fees, which it was thought at one time would seriously check this desire, and limit the numbers of those who might seek entrance here at least.'[38] A further nine months after that it was claimed,

> the tide has set in even among the heathen Kaffirs in favour of education. Many of the mission schools are filled with the children of those who never go to church, and the real difficulty in getting hold of the children in a heathen location does not lie in the unwillingness of the parents, except in some cases in regard to their daughters, but in the natural aversion of the children to the restraint of a school, and that heathen parents cannot be got to compel them.[39]

To conclude, in 1905 the South African Native Affairs Commission reported, 'There is among the people themselves a growing desire for education, which cannot and need not be suppressed.'[40]

The rise of industrial capitalism

Schooling for black people in South Africa made no major advances through most of the early 1800s. Its importance began to increase from the second half of the 19th century. This can be deduced in part from the growth of state interest in 'native education' as well as from the growing numbers in black schools. As the Eiselen Commission was to explain, 'Bantu education as carried on by the missionary bodies became increasingly the care of the government concerned because the Bantu were increasingly affecting the economic and political life of the country.'[41] Thus, in the Cape with the institution of 'Representative Government' in 1854, state money was allocated to the Aborigines (Border) Department for the purpose of subsidising 'missionary institutions

. . . to train Bantu youth in industrial occupations . . . (and) as interpreters, evangelists and schoolmasters . . . . '[42]

In 1863, Dale proposed increased subsidisation such as would encourage the teaching of needlework to girls and carpentry, shoemaking and printing to boys, and would also produce blacksmiths, gardeners and domestic servants.[43] In 1865, legislation was enacted to provide for state aid to three types of schools: public, mission and 'native'. Furthermore, a state inspectorate of education was established. Whereas, in 1865 there were a mere 2 827 African pupils enrolled in schools, by 1885 this enrolment had risen to 15 568, and by 1891 to 25 000.[44] In Natal, a Commission of Inquiry was urging in 1853 that black youths should be apprenticed to white farmers and tradesmen through the resident magistrates and recommended the establishment of government industrial schools in each village. In addition, three years compulsory school attendance was seen as desirable for all children between seven and twelve years of age resident in black locations. As it happened, none of these recommendations was carried out.[45] However, an ordinance published in 1856 made provision for grants-in-aid to mission schools and also permitted the government to establish and maintain public schools. It laid down that the subjects of instruction were to be religious education, 'industrial training' and instruction in the English language.[46] In 1884 black schooling in Natal was made the responsibility of the Council of Education, which had been established in 1877, and placed under separate and specialist officers. Two years later, the first syllabuses for elementary black schools were issued. Hygiene and traditional crafts were emphasised and a fifth of school time was to be spent in manual work which included carpentry for the boys, dressmaking, cooking and laundering for girls, and gardening for both boys and girls.[47] In 1894 the Council of Education was abolished and a sub-department of 'Native Education' under the Superintendent of Education was created. Enrolment in Natal's black schools rose from 145 in 1855 to 10 618 in 1900.[48] State subsidisation of the mission schools for black people started in the Orange Free State and Transvaal in 1878 and 1903, respectively. Although such subsidisation often amounted to little more than occasional grants, it was accompanied by the requirement that mission schools register with the administration. The authorities instituted school inspections, acquired a say in syllabuses and the training of teachers, and increasingly began to make demands on the schools.

These developments coincided with the establishment of capitalist relations of production in agriculture and the mining industry. According to the Eiselen Commission Report the discovery of minerals, the building of railways and the Anglo-Boer War . . . radically transformed the political and economic life of South Africa. The new conditions bred a new emphasis on Native policy and particularly on the view of the state concerning the education of the Bantu. The new mines, railways, farms, cities and industries cried out for labour.[49]

The first half of the 20th century saw a slow but steady increase in black school enrolment and a gradual rise in state expenditure on black schooling. It is clear that the growth of schooling, at any rate that designed for black people, was not initially stimulated by a need for skill training which arose from capitalist production. Generally, the level of skill required was low, and on the farms and mines such skills could most adequately be developed through training on the job. The manual training given at school tended to be manual *labour* rather than training in any specific skills. The racist form taken by class relations in the South African context precluded black workers from developing trade and other higher-level skills. In 1936, the Interdepartmental Committee on Native Education was arguing as follows:

On the one hand . . . any rational system of education should make provision for vocational training leading on to occupations which will give employment and a source of livelihood to a considerable proportion of the population. On the other hand any such policy . . . would in the present structure of South African economic conditions lead to competition of Native tradesmen with European, which is at present prohibited . . . or to a dead-end of unemployment for the Native.

Having regard to the present attitude of the European towards the employment of Natives in industry, where skilled or even semi-skilled labour is used, it seems inevitable that the educationist in South Africa must pursue a 'ca' canny' policy in regard to the training of Native boys and to this extent must turn his back upon sound educational principles.[50]

Schooling and the making of the black working class

It will not be argued that the gradual growth of black schooling from the 1860s through to the mid-20th century was determined by the development of a capitalist mode of production in the region. It is, however, suggested that schooling had some bearing on the way in which capitalist class relations emerged. In general terms, schooling was one minor factor amongst many which went into the making of a black working class. It made, first of all, a limited contribution to the process of proletarianisation itself. It operated in a similar manner to the Christianisation of the indigenous people. The latter was described in 1878 by *The Christian Express*, mouthpiece of the missionaries at Lovedale, in the following remarkably explicit terms:

> This subject of work is a burning one in this country. No complaint is more common . . . from colonists . . . than that there is a great deal of work to be done and few trying to do it.
>
> We want to see the natives become workers . . . . And . . . we believe that Christianity will be a chief cause of their becoming a working people . . . .
>
> . . . how this . . . comes to be is twofold. Christianity creates needs. Generally speaking, every man will work just as much as he requires to do and not more. There will be a constant relation between the time a man works and his necessities . . . . If you want men to work, then, you must get them to need. Create need and you supply stimulus to work; you enlist the worker's own will on the side of labour. Few men anywhere, and certainly no heathen men, ever work for the mere pleasure of working.
>
> 'Now, the speediest way of creating needs among these people is to Christianize them. As they become Christianized, they will want more clothing, better houses, furniture, books, education for the children, and a hundred other things which they do not have now and never have had. And all these things they can get by working, and only by working.
>
> But Christianity also teaches the duty of working, and denounces idleness as a sin.
>
> So to Christianize a Kaffir is the shortest way, and the surest, to make him put his hand steadily and willingly to the work that is waiting to be done. This will make it both his interest and his duty to work, will enlist, besides his bodily appetites, his home affections, his mental powers, and his conscience, on the side of industrious habits.[51]

In 1905, the South African Native Affairs Commission recommended, with a view to driving a greater number of black people into wage labour, inter alia, 'The encouragement of a higher standard among Natives by support given to education with a view to increase their efficiency and wants.'[52] The schooled minority helped to spread ideas and practices which encouraged a layer of the newly colonised to want goods that were obtainable only by means of purchase. Testimony was given to the same Commission regarding education's 'economic effect in raising the standard of material comfort and thus creating wants.'[53] With a steadily declining proportion of the people able to support themselves on the land, let alone produce a surplus which they could market, wage labour became the only means of acquiring the money to satisfy any such 'new needs' as might have been generated. Even longstanding needs such as staple foods, which had previously been met within a pre-capitalist mode of production, had now to be met within the market economy. The above analysis does therefore not attribute any structurally determinant role to either Christianity or schooling.

The making of the black working class involved more than a process whereby people were rendered dependent on wage labour. Some employers of labour began to see schooling as part of a related pocess whereby workers might be made at least minimally amenable to wage labour and increasingly tractable to the new demands of the workplace. They recognised that it might be in their interests to attempt to win from workers some measure of acceptance of the social place towards which conditions propelled them. As one who identified with such interests, Pells argued that it was essential to school the newly proletarianised blacks 'if they are not to be left profoundly dissatisfied and an ever-present menace to society.' He supported his contention by citing the experience of England where he claimed that it had been the provision of universal elementary education which above all else averted a bloody revolution. According to Pells,

> Once the Native is allowed outside of his Reserve . . . we incorporate him into our economic scheme and thus proceed to educate him. But this education by contact with the White man's life and civilisation is unregulated, haphazard . . . . By formal education and instruction . . . we must give him those standards by which we judge good and bad . . . . The Bantu must be educated . . . to have the right sort of 'wants' and to be able to satisfy those 'wants'. Only thus can he become a contented and useful citizen.[54]

Or, as the Interdepartmental Committee on Native Education argued in 1936,

> The Native is becoming Europeanised by more contact . . . . One cannot stop the process . . . . All that can be done . . . is to direct and control the process.
> The problem is, therefore, to devise a type of education which will tide the black man over the period during which his tribal sanctions are weakening, and before he feels the force of the sanctions of European civilisation.[55]

The latter aspect was spelled out still more specifically in 1943 by the Administrator of Natal who was reported as having said that 'the old ways with their folkways, mores and disciplines, which were so characteristic of the behaviour of the Zulus, were passing away and it was therefore incumbent on the Bantu schools to develop in the Zulu young the new controls, disciplines and behaviours of Western civilisation.'[56] And, indeed, from the earliest days of industrial capitalism in South Africa, there was the attempt to drill into black workers an acceptance of their place of inferiority, oppression and exploitation. The report of the Inter-departmental Committee described the view prevalent amongst capitalists that

> we must give the Native an education which will keep him in his place
> — if the Native is to receive any education he should have as his aim the
> idea embodied in Dickens' version of the ancient prayer
>
> Oh, let us love our occupations,
> Bless the squire and his relations
> Live upon our daily rations,
> And always know our proper stations.[57]

The attempt was made to imbue workers with values and attitudes perceived by employers as befitting those in wage labour as well as to teach them the discipline that would be demanded of them as wage labourers. According to the syllabus for Orange Free State primary schools, drawn up in 1945, 'Rightly considered, the ultimate aim of all education and the purpose for which our schools exist, is to provide boys and girls with a training such as will enable them to take their proper place in life when they leave school.'[58]

Expressed quite bluntly by the Native Economic Commission, 1930-32, 'He ("the Native") must learn to school his body to hard work . . . .'[59] In 1903 the Transvaal's first Inspector of Native Education, the Rev. W E C Clarke, had revealed the interest of white employers in black schooling when he stated that the object was to 'Teach the Native to Work.' The report, dealing with the objectives of the new schooling system, put forward the following view:

> No proposal for a plan of native education would be likely to commend itself to the great majority of the people of this country that did not contemplate the ultimate social place of the native as that of an efficient worker . . . . The scheme prescribed makes provision, therefore, in the first place, for the combination of manual training with elementary instruction, and, in the second, for the shaping of that elementary instruction so as to equip the native for a more intelligent comprehension of any industrial work that is set before him.[60]

Such a stance was taken up even in a Catholic weekly, *Um-Afrika*, which, published in Zulu from Marianhill, was obviously directing itself neither at white public opinion nor at the government policy-makers, but at black people. It presumably aimed to elicit their acceptance of the new policies:

> That the African should be given education based on the assumption that one day he shall cease to be an employee of the whiteman is in conflict with the facts. It would be like giving the African an Education with no foundation — a course more dangerous than helpful. That type of Education would make him lose that which he should have derived from his training.[61]

Discussing the recommendations of the South African Native Affairs Commission, 1903-05, concerning black schooling, the Eiselen Commission report pointed out 'how insistently the economic motive was making itself felt: the educated Bantu would be useful in the economic expansion of the country.'[62] In a paper first presented in 1918, the Rev. Albert Leroy posed the question, 'Does it pay to educate the native?' The cleric summarised his conclusions as follows:

> If education induces the best of them to go back and work for the uplift of their people; if the educated native is more temperate, works longer and more steadily than the raw native; if the average educated native is ranked by his employer as varying from good to very good; and from his wages is evidently worth from two to four times as much as the uneducated man — then it seems to us, to use Parliamentary language, 'The answer to the question is in the affirmative'.[63]

Schooling, in general, contributed to separating socially the blacks and whites who economically were increasingly integrated, even though that integration was grossly unequal. Thus, for example, one objective of the Education Act of 1865 was to discourage missions from opening their schools to all, irrespective of colour. This was achieved by permitting state grants to schools which did so to be used only for paying teachers' salaries and leaving the missions responsible for all other expenses. Separate and unequal schooling helped to rigidify racist lines of division which up until the development of capitalist industrialisation had still been somewhat loose. Differential schooling for blacks and whites was aimed at moulding the children for their respective dominant and dominated places. As stated in the report of the 1936 Inter-departmental Committee, 'The education of the white child prepares him for life in a dominant society and the education of the black child for a subordinate society.'[64] The same report explained well, from the standpoint of the white superordinate classes, why the objectives of schooling for whites could not be the same as those of 'native education':

> The two societies do not operate in two water-tight compartments. Geographically they are not segregated and economically they are inter-dependent. These circumstances, however, do not give them equality of opportunity. On the contrary. To frame pious aims, therefore, for Native education, such as 'fullness of life for each and all' . . . is easy, but it is rather futile if not actually misleading. Such an aim can be striven after by education in the European society which is homo-geneous and democractic . . . . But South African society as a whole consisting of Europeans and Natives is not a democratic society.[65]

Referring — although more than a quarter of a century earlier — to a conception of education differentiated in precisely the same racist terms, *The APO* (organ of the African People's Organisation), wrote as follows:

> It means that education is to be of the kind suited to the recipient's station in life. It has not even the merit of that education which is clamoured for by some businessmen for their sons. *Viz* the mercenary man's view [that] education should be directed to giving its recipients the power of getting on in the world, and getting on in the world simply means amassing lucre . . . . But for the blacks' education even that low motive is to be discarded. Their education is to be such as will allow the other fellows, the whites, to get on in the world by trampling on the blacks. There must be no unrest or disappointment felt by the blacks of South Africa. No outlook is to be given to them . . . . They must stay where they are.[66]

From the standpoint of the black subordinate classes, a 1938 issue of *The Territorial Magazine - Ipepa Ndaba Lezifunda* editorialised as follows:

> In a country where there are definitely superior interests, that is the interests of those who form the ruling class, it becomes increasingly difficult even to the extent of embarrassment as to how such interests are to be protected. This is the course which the education of the African has inevitably followed. In educating the African care is being taken that he is given only such education as will fit him for a position which is forever subservient.[67]

Schooling for blacks – necessarily segregated if to be inferior –

provided a schooling in inferiority which helped to prepare black students for the places of inferiority which they would occupy in society.

The content of black schooling

There was a relation — albeit probably not a determinant one — between the form taken by black schooling and the social places for which black youth were generally destined. In a memorandum to the Council of Education, a decade before the turn of the century, an Inspector of Native Education in Natal addressed the question of what the 'scope' of black schooling should be:

> I would define it as being to qualify the native youth for the effective discharge of their probable duties in life. These, for the present generation of school children, are those connected with the stable, kitchen, nursery, wagon or farm.
>
> Whatever may be said . . . in favour of teaching the use of tools . . . the fact remains that a certain amount of preparatory educating of the thinking and observing faculties is necessary.
>
> The inculcation of the habits of industry is a very important part of school work . . . but in a very effective degree it is quite possible without the teaching of any handicraft, and a trade may be taught without making the boy industrious.
>
> There is a great deal of difference between industry and industries; and the former is . . . the more important of the two for this people.[68]

A Select Committee on Native Education, appointed in the Cape in 1908, recommended that the African pupils' language, 'their home conditions, their social and mental environment, their hereditary, tribal or racial instincts, and their future position and work in the country' had to be considered.[69] In 1909, *The APO* commented as follows on 'the peculiar notions' put forward regarding the aims of education by the members of the Cape School Board:

> With them it is not the drawing out of the faculties of the child. It simply means filling his mind with those facts which may be of service to him in fulfilling the work he may be called on to perform; and the filling process of the coloured child's mind is to be carried on in a different building from that in which the white youngster's mind is operated on. If one considers the composition of the Board, he would not be surprised at such views being entertained by some of its unlettered members . . . . They could not find enjoyment in anything beyond the computation of interest or the value of bricks and mortar,

or the addition of columns of figures. All other knowledge is regarded by them as useless lumber. They take the old clerical adages as to the necessity for being 'content with that station wherein it has pleased a kind Providence to place us' as literally true. Any education that would give a being a thought beyond his station in life is accursed in their eyes. It would, if they had their way, consist solely in the inculcation of the divine duty of drudgery. The black people are the descendents of Ham, according to their ideas. They were meant to be 'the hewers of wood and the drawers of water' through all eternity. Their education should therefore be confined to the narrow circle of learning to appreciate the honour they enjoy at the hands of the white, who allows them to live on the face of God's earth.[70]

In 1945, J N le Roux articulated the view in parliament that the schools

should not give the natives an academic education, as some people are prone to do. If we do this we shall later be burdened with a number of academically trained Europeans and non-Europeans, and who is going to do the manual labour in this country? . . . I am in thorough agreement with the view that we should so conduct our schools that the native who attends those schools will know that to a great extent he must be the labourer in the country . . . .[71]

To the extent that 'native education' helped in practice to prepare black children for a place as subordinate workers, it acted in part through deliberate indoctrination with the ideas of the white superordinate classes, in part through the provision of an education which was vastly inferior to that provided for whites, in part through subjecting students to an experience of institutional inferiority, and in part through training them in the discipline and obedience which would be required of them as workers. Thus, for example, the following was written in 1946:

To-day, the system of African education . . . is such as to prepare the African for an inferior type of citizenship. Take history. The history taught in our schools drills into the mind of the African child the idea that in all our fights with the whiteman, the whiteman was in the right and that our forefathers, who fought for their independence and their freedom, were the villains in the whole story.[72]

The Rev. Mr Clarke, in his first and programmatic report cited above, wrote as follows:

Apart from . . . specific subjects I look for substantial results to be produced in the native by the discipline of school life. Habits of obedience and cleanliness and order are what he most wants, and these must be the foundation not only of the usefulness of his school life, but of the life for which the school is but a training.[73]

Rather than a 'bookish' schooling, the 'mechanical arts' were emphasised and students familiarised with manual labour. In 1891, Dale reported as follows:

What the Department wants is to make all the principal day-schools places of manual industry, as well as of book-instruction. It is not expected that all the boys will become expert tradesmen; but it is something to train them to use the spade and the hoe, the plane and the saw, the mason's trowel and the plumb-line.[74]

In reality, according to D D T Jabavu, 'In our schools "manual labour" consists of sweeping yards, repairing roads, cracking stones and so on, and is done by boys only as so much task work enforced by a time-keeper, and under threats of punishment.'[75] Even a government commission report in 1936 had to admit that the 'manual work' in black schools had tended to lapse into 'triviality and mere mechanical drudgery with no educative value'.[76] Characterising it as having had 'no educative value' might have been an implicit reference to what Jabavu had indentified as 'the invariable result' of the imposition of manual labour of the kind described, namely 'that the boys grow to hate all manual work as humiliating, "skulk" from it whenever they can, and ever avoid it at home and in after life'[77] — the very converse, in other words, of the effect which white educationists and employers of labour hoped it would produce.

The scheme for 'native education', which was put forward after Union by the Witwatersrand Council of Education and introduced with a curriculum based thereon in 1915, laid great emphasis on 'training'. This consisted of religious and moral training with the cultivation of such habits as cleanliness, obedience, punctuality, tidiness, orderliness, truthfulness, honesty, respect, courtesy, industry, self-dependence, self-restraint, temperance and chastity, physical training, social training, including ideas of civic duty and acquaintance with the laws specially affecting black people, and industrial training. Schooling also provided, through the 'three Rs', an elementary training in the basic skills of communication and calculation. Most important was a working familiarity with one of the 'official' languages — that is, one of the employers' languages, English or Afrikaans. As Clarke explained, 'The enormous percentage of energy that is at present wasted or lost through the lack of a common medium of communication between white employer and native employee shows the necessity of prescribing for all native schools a knowledge of English as one of the elementary subjects necessary.'[78] Increasing numbers of workers who could read, write and work with figures were being sought on the labour market and the schools were the sole source of supply.

Ideologically and psychologically, schooling helped to mould the young workers-to-be into the dominant social relations. There was an attempt to sever them from their past identity and its base in traditional African culture. The early schools contributed to the students' demoralisation by physically removing them to the world of the white colonists, teaching them to despise their own history and culture, and 'converting' them to the colonists' religion. In place of what was removed, a new world-view and new values were inserted. In this context, the Interdepartmental Committee on Native Education, for instance, regarded religion as 'of paramount importance'. According to its report, 'by religion is not meant merely the learning of the catechism and Bible history, . . . but also those emotional and spiritual experiences which determine a person's ideals and his attitude towards life. Under this category are included also character building, morality and manners . . . .'[79] In religious instruction black students were taught obedience, humility, patience, fear, passivity, and contentment in adversity. There was, however, amongst the indigenous population, even at the time, keen awareness of the subversive implications of their people being schooled in the settlers' religion. To illustrate this the following is extracted from a catalogue of 'Kaffir objections to the Christian religion' described in 1871

. . . the Christian religion deprives his countrymen of their nationality . . . . No sooner does a member of his tribe embrace the Gospel than he conforms to habits and modes of dress which were altogether unknown to his forefathers.

Moreover, when a Kaffir embraces the Gospel, he disowns the authority of his chief, he ceases to be a retainer at 'the great place', he no longer spends his time at court, ready at any moment to go errands . . . for his chief, he ceases to be a Kaffir subject. Every Kaffir who embraces Christianity lessens the power and authority and greatness of his chief. Christianity neither fosters nor encourages a spirit of loyalty to the Kaffir chiefs, but rather the reverse . . . . Any custom . . . which teaches the Kaffir such disloyalty ought never to be accepted by wise men who seek to preserve their country's welfare and the authority of their rulers.

. . . the Gospel has deprived him of his country! . . . Spies they (the missionaries) were, who came to discover the fat of the land. They received grants of land from chiefs for mission stations, but soon they hailed their countrymen who came across the sea in such numbers that the mission station merged into a town . . . . And the unkindest cut of all is that, though robbed of his country, he should yet be urged to accept that which has proved the *greatest foe to the nation!*[80]

Tardiness in the growth of black schooling

In the light of what has been suggested about the relation in which black schooling stood to the development of capitalist class relations up to the mid-20th century, one might ask why the growth of black schooling was so slow. Minimal interest in black schooling was displayed by the state, capitalists or employers in general. Before 1945, black education was seldom debated in the Union parliament.

Except for the Cape provincial administration's commission under Dr W J Viljoen and the Interdepartmental Committee under Welsh (1935-41) — both of which had to report on 'Native Education' — there was little serious state concern with black schooling before the mid-1940s. In 1920 D D T Jabavu contrasted the state of black and white education in the following terms:

> The present condition of Native education . . . is one of chaos . . . . Natives here have a just grievance. They see government spending lavishly in putting up majestic educational edifices for European primary, secondary and university education staffed by highly paid teachers, while they have to be satisfied with having their children taught in mission rooms with walls dilapidated and furniture rough and scanty, teachers recieving miserable pittances, so miserable that a raw illiterate Zulu policeman in Durban today gets better pay than the best paid Zulu school teacher. Provincial grants to Native education are very tiny by comparison with those for white schools and infinitesimal as compared with the enormous revenue derived from Native taxation.[81]

In the mid-1930s, for example, the government was spending more than 40 times as much on education per head of the white population than the African population. In 1940, less than a quarter of the African children between the ages of 6 and 16 were in school. According to Pells,

> In the case of those who did go to school, the time spent and the work done there was so meagre as to amount to no education at all. For over

half of them schooling terminated in the sub-standards. Most of the remaining 40 percent only reached Standard 2. Only a half percent of those who attended school reached Standard 6!

The position by 1940 was that only one in every 1 000 Native children received a fair elementary education! Native education was therefore failing to make the Native literate.[82]

Why was the schooling of black South Africans, on whom the economy rested to such a significant extent, not much more of a priority?

In the period prior to the general penetration of capitalist relations of production, the answer is not difficult to find. Dale, reported on an inspection of schools in 1869 as follows

> The absence of mechanical appliances to develop the resources of the country or to carry on local industries serves as a check to general education, because skilled and intelligent labour is of no higher value than that of the raw, untaught savage. A people without manufacturing industries, living chiefly by agricultural and pastoral pursuits, must remain at a comparatively low standard: the impulse to higher things is wanting, as well as the necessity which ever brings intelligence and enterprise to the front.
>
> The general causes not only lower the value of school instruction, but keep people poor and without the means of lengthening the school-life of their children . . . .[83]

In 1906, *The Christian Express* observed that 'the past figures of Missionary institutions . . . show greatly reduced numbers during bad years (viz years of drought), while numerous letters are received asking for a period of grace with regard to payment of the fees.'[84] Furthermore, schooling of blacks was actively opposed in certain quarters of the settler community and many colonists specifically eschewed the employment of black persons who had had any schooling. Thus, for example, in 1871 *The Kaffir Express* was complaining as follows

> . . . for all except the very rudest kinds of work, such as looking after sheep and oxen, and carrying loads, or leading a team of oxen, the raw Kaffir is immeasurably inferior to the trained native. But the red man is preferred by many, because his ignorance passes for simplicity, and because he has not yet learned the civilised lesson of self-assertion. . . . He is preferred by many because his wants are fewer, because a worse hut will serve him, and coarser rations and lower wages; and because he controls his feelings well.[85]

It must be borne in mind that a society's educative apparatus does not consist solely of schooling. Furthermore, only at a certain stage in the development of a society's capitalist structures does the type of education provided by the school become critical. Before that, while schooling clearly contributes to the educational process, it is but one amongst a number of vehicles for education. In part, this was what the Native Economic Commission, 1930-32, was driving at when it stated that

> for the regeneration of a primitive people there are educational needs which precede ordinary school education. European school education is based on a civilised environment: for a great proportion of the Native population this civilised environment has still to be created. It is an educational task, but it is not solely the task of the ordinary school, although the school can in a measure assist in carrying it out.[86]

The point is illustrated by the following quotation from the Natal Native Commission of 1881-82:

> With reference to Industrial Education, it has to be remembered that there is and has been for many years much of it obtained by the Natives who go to service either at farms or in towns. The former learn to plough and harrow, and to sow crops at proper distances, and to use various tools; the latter are taught orderliness in domestic arrangements and to cook, and in a degree become acquainted with and take part in many of the developments and accompaniments of an advanced civilisation; and it is but fair to the Natives to say that many of them are easily broken in to all this. Still, service of this kind hardly includes instruction in what are ordinarily called trades, such as masonry, carpentry, and iron and leather work.'[87]

The conditions which had led to the introduction of mass schooling in the advanced capitalist societies of England, Europe and the United States of America had not as yet arisen in South Africa. In England and certain European countries, mass schooling developed in substantial part as a response to the social and political problems spawned by the Industrial Revolution. With the breakdown of feudalism went a breakdown of its framework of social control. The context in which the labouring people had 'known their place' was removed and replaced by the relative individual freedom of capitalist democracy. Under these conditions, mass schooling would appear to have played an important role in the reassertion of class control by the newly dominant bourgeoisie and provided a way of reproducing an appropriately socialised labour force. Bowles and Gintis, for example, describe how, in the United States,

The process of capital accumulation drastically changed the structure of society: the role of the family in production was greatly reduced, its role in reproduction was increasingly out of touch with economic reality. A permanent proletariat and an impoverished and, for the most part ethnically distinct, reserve army of the unemployed had been created. Economic inequality had increased. Small manufacturing towns had become urban areas almost overnight. The expansion of capitalist production had at once greatly enhanced the power of the capitalist class and had inexorably generated a condition which challenged their continued domination. With increasing urgency, economic leaders sought a mechanism to ensure political stability and the continued profitablity of their enterprises.[88]

Their thesis is that the mechanism invented to meet these needs was mass schooling. In South Africa, by contrast, the classes in control had achieved their ascendancy by conquest. On that foundation and what it meant for the balance of forces in the ensuing struggle, class control could initially be maintained, mainly through direct repression. This involved the denial of all political rights and the use of state power for the regimentation and physical control of the lives of black people by means of the reserve system, the pass laws, and an encompassing net of repressive legislation. Thus, while schooling might be seen as having been part of the structures of social control, it could in no sense be conceived as having been 'necessary' to the dominant groups under the totalitarian conditions of South African society, given the radically uneven balance of power. Furthermore, where in other capitalist societies, schooling was already important to the process of allocating young persons within the social division of labour, fitting them into the occupational hierarchy of capitalist production, and distributing them into the social hierarchy, in South Africa these functions were partially, if somewhat crudely, served by racist ideology.

Furthermore, there was calculated opposition to the development of black schooling from within the dominant classes on the grounds that it could be politically dangerous and even economically disadvantageous to capitalist interests. Even before the turn of the century, this position was being articulated. Dale was particularly explicit in his report of 1891. There he treated the question of 'diffusing elementary school instruction everywhere among the masses of heathen' as 'a matter of social economy and of political interest'. His argument is significant and warrants quoting at some length:

Whilst the present cautious system is pursued, no social inconvenience or practical danger can result, but if some system of obligatory school-attendance were introduced and thousands of Kaffirs were leaving school year by year with sufficient school-instruction to set them loose from tribal customs and modes of savage life, what would you do with them? What agencies could be devised to direct teeming thousands into the various channels of Colonial industries? Labour, especially agricultural, is wanted; but will the educated Native leave his home and take service, especially in the western districts? If not, the crowding together of educated natives, living without a trade or regular habits of daily employment, must tend to mischief and social disturbances.

The capacity to read and write is not in itself a panacea for the abominations of savageism . . . . Knowledge is power even to them, but it may be a power for ill.

Whether the *festina lente* policy pursued by the Department for the last thirty years in the matter of Native education commends itself favourably to public opinion or not, it has been a safe policy . . .; and it should not be lightly set aside for a showy and popular system to suit the extreme views of philanthropists, or the theories of those who proclaim universal education as the duty of Governments.[89]

In 1936, the Interdepartmental Committee agreed with Edgar Brookes in summing up the general attitude of white South Africa to education of blacks as having, in the past, been 'too humane to prohibit it, . . . too human to encourage it.'[90] Writing later still, Pells found it understandable that neither of the main white political parties had shown any great enthusiasm for the promotion of black education, 'since farmers, mine owners and industrialists view with alarm a process which, as present world experience shows, tends to stimulate the labourers to unreasonable wage demands and uncomfortable social and political aspiration.'[91]

Opposition came also from the white section of the working class since the training of blacks in certain skills threatened the near monopoly on semi-skilled and skilled categories of employment which white workers had won for themselves. Such opposition was already being articulated in the late 1880s. In an article concerning state support of 'native education', *The Christian Express* observed in 1888,

The chief feature of the controversy at present is this — an entire change of the reason why such aid should be withheld. Formerly the Natives got too much school education, and were not taught to use their hands. Now industrial education is in disfavour, because Europeans are not taught the same, and because native industrial work comes into competition with the European artisan.[92]

Schooling as contested terrain

It has been suggested above that the schooling of blacks contributed, albeit in very limited measure, to certain aspects of capitalism's development in South Africa. Yet, the development of education in the forms which it takes under particular historical conditions is not determined mechanically by posited systemic 'needs' nor does it evolve rationally on the basis of what 'logically' might be most functional to capitalist interests: the educational arena is contested terrain. Schooling under capitalism is never just a machine processing the children of the exploited to take their parents' places in the interests of the exploiters. While the political representatives of a class, or of classes in alliance, may be at the state controls, there are limits to what they can manipulate. The limits are set by the level reached in the struggle of the politically, and otherwise, dispossessed, and by the fact that the implementation of policy depends on the collaboration of students and teachers.

Although workers are exploited by employers, it is the wage which they earn through employment that alone gives them access to the means of subsistence which they need for their individual or family survival. It is this — historically transient — mutual dependence that lashes the exploiting and exploited classes together in an antagonistic bond. Schooling, while preparing workers' children for a life of exploitation, as least enhances the individual's chances of finding employment at a rate of remuneration relatively higher than the entirely unschooled can earn.

The latter provides a possible explanation of the popular enthusiasm, even for an inferior education, which gathered momentum from the final quarter of the 19th century. In 1880, *The Christian Express* observed,

> The thirst for education, and the sacrifices we find parents making to gave their sons a good education, are unexampled except in portions of the Home country where education is made the road to success in life — the same use to which the African turns it.[93]

A year later the same newspaper told of a man who had said that he 'just panted' for education for his children, commenting, 'and we are sure that he does not pant alone.' The article continued,

> Behind all this lies another history which we only very partially know, a history of effort and self-denial, chiefly on the part of parents . . . . One young man walks all the way from Natal to get to the school he has set his heart upon, and perhaps we see the whole in his case clearly.

But there are twenty other cases where the real amount and extent of effort is probably even greater, on the part of parents and friends, and there is not seen but a half-hidden fragment of it.[94]

In 1938, *The Territorial Magazine — Ipepa Ndaba Lezifunda* asserted in an editorial,

Education amongst Africans will continue for a long time yet being the standard on which the economic welfare of an individual is judged, and any attempt to deprive him of those opportunities whereby he may attain to such a standard, is murderous . . . . This is the time when they ('Africans') should be gathering their forces against the threatening illiberal clouds.[95]

Another aspect of the context in which to understand this demand for education, which black people have consistently put forward from the earliest years of the 20th century, was the influence of that part of liberal conventional wisdom which had it that change would come 'naturally' when people were educated. As articulated by Dr D G S M'Timkulu, for instance, Africans 'seek for integration into the democratic structure and institutions of the country. To them one of the most effective ways of achieving this is by education — an education essentially no different from, or inferior to, that of other sections of the community.'[96] Or, as spelled out more specifically by Isaac A Mdoda in 1943,

The leadership of any race anywhere in the world today should concentrate on EDUCATION, as its primary factor in preparing it for its new defensive position.

The political position, for the African, is grave. Geographically he has no foothold. He has become the ward of a suspicious, malicious and heartless civilisation . . . he is hemmed in with a limit on his movements. He can go thus far and no farther.

. . . how can he get out of this? It is not by foolishly fighting back, to be clubbed to death economically and politically, but by diplomatically manoeuvring himself out of the situation with credit to himself.

Every African in his sphere must have himself educated to the highest degree, so as to be able to deal with his prejudiced competitor on the spot. Therefore, it is the duty of the African to develop a high state of intelligence superior to his adversary's, and use that education for the means of extricating himself from the hole in which he is placed.[97]

Some black people believed that white workers enjoyed comfortable conditions as a result of their education. Thus, for example,

in a paper presented to the Natal Missionary Conference held in
July 1920, in Durban, D D T Jabavu stated,

> . . . white employees and clerks everywhere are being paid in accordance
> with the times, either as consequence of strikes, threatened strikes, or
> other persuasion. This is all due to the fact that the European, being
> well educated, knows how to speak out his sufferings, plead his case
> intelligently in the press, organise to the point of perfection, enlist
> public opinion in his cause, and finally force the hands of Government.[98]

Furthermore, most black leaders were now being drawn from those
whom schooling had equipped with certain of the skills needed to
lead 'effectively' on the new terrain of political struggle delimited
by the white rulers. Those leaders, in turn, supported an
educational policy which, as described by Shingler, 'accorded with
their political vision by calling for universal compulsory education
on European lines. Such an education would, they believed, enable
African children to enter a common society.' They saw education
'as providing a language of global pre-eminence, as a means of
participating in the structure which had been imposed upon them
and of obtaining familiarity with a literature and ideas, skills and
techniques, which were the source of wealth and power.'[99]

The faith of black people in the potential of education to affect
their life-chances as individuals, and collectively, was challenged
by the harsh realities of racist capitalism. The following is extracted
from a letter to the editor of *The Christian Express,* which was
published under the sub-title, 'Why have you educated me?'

> Of the many promising ('Native') men, thus trained (*viz* for 'industrial'
> purposes), who have gone out into the world to make a living, some can
> be traced who are more or less usefully occupied; but sad to relate, the
> majority are not now engaged in the trades they learned. Many of the
> latter are to be found on the Reef and in other places . . . associating
> with the lowest class.
>   . . . this sad failure, in many cases, is to a large extent attributable to
> the Colour Bar. The Trade Unions in South Africa hold a general
> principle 'employ whites' . . . . There is therefore no opening for a
> Native tradesman.
>   It is useless to send our children to school to learn trades when
> work, the means of livelihood, is denied them . . . we Natives are
> reluctantly compelled to raise our voices in protest against this gross
> injustice.
>   With the present state of unrest among the Native people it would
> not require much to turn the four Provinces of the Union into boisterous
> little 'Balkan States'. Then the real 'Black Problem' would emerge. We

have no desire to appear to threaten; but wise men look facts in the face. Unrest cannot die down while the causes of unrest continue. The Native is loyal but his loyalty is too severely tested when the only answer to his cry for industrial justice is 'Pernicious Agitator'.[100]

Not all black people believed blindly in education. Many had their faith undermined by the conditions referred to above. An alternative attitude to education was suggested by a remarkable editorial in *Inkundla y Bantu* which warrants quotation at length.

Many of us firmly believe that education will solve the European Problem (it is not a Native Problem) in this country. Fort Hare has only to turn out thousands of graduates and lo and behold the European poblem will vanish like darkness at the break of day. Where exactly the magic of education lies is a question we are seldom bothered with. Yet it is absolutely necessary for the development of our people to know the possiblities and limits of education as it is practised today. When we consider that only 30 percent of the Native children of school-going age are at school and that over 50 percent of those are in the Sub-Standards, there is reason to be alarmed at the slow progress of Native Education. Surely it is time that some form of compulsory education was introduced. Such a step would immediately increase the literacy of the Natives, with beneficial results to the development of Bantu literature, which at present is in sore need of a reading public. But reading alone doth not make a full man. Man has to eat to live. It is eating rather than reading matter that is fundamental to the existence of man. Nowadays education has very largely become vocational. It has become a matter of life and death. It is the means whereby human beings may live in comfort and security. With this knowledge let us ask ourselves the question, 'to what extent would intensification of Native education better the economic position of the Natives?' The answer is, 'Very little indeed'. In the first place owing to the poverty of the Natives very few children would receive the benefit of a vocational education. Those lucky enough to go to college would, on completion, find that there were no jobs for them . . . it is fundamental to the policy of cheap Native labour that the Natives should not be admitted to skilled professions. The whole fabric of South Africa's industry rests upon cheap Native labour and vocational education of the Natives meets with strong disapproval and hostile legislation. To be approved by dominant White South Africa Native education must fit the Native ever to become the servant of the white man . . . the Natives must be educated to become good servants of the European.

. . . Native education alone especially as we find it today is not going to solve the European problem. Let our professors and teachers engaged in Native education realise that they are doing a commendable thing

namely, getting a comfortable existence in a hard and cruel world. But
let them have no illusions about being the spearhead of that body of
men who see visions of the Native people taking a respectable place in
the body-politic of South Africa.[101]

In spite of a popularly experienced desire for 'education' and the
marginally better-off positions to which those in school aspired,
significant aspects of the uneven history of black students'
resistance only become intelligible if we examine their opposition
to some of what they were taught, to how they were taught and
the conditions under which they were taught.

Parents, teachers and the black community at large were, at
various points, all involved in this resistance. The history of
such movements has been little researched. Of course, the history
of black students' resistance includes forms which have been
manifested in white schools as well.

There is no implication that the record of resistance presented
here upholds the view that black students were all aware of the
political implications of their schooling. Furthermore, aspects of
what is included as 'resistance' on the part of black students may
be more appropriately conceptualised in some other way, just as
it may be meaningless to conceive of all childish indiscipline as
being resistance to the objectives of schooling.

As described above, resistance to schooling goes back to the
very first formal school: the young slaves, for whom it was intended,
ran away with such frequency that it had to be closed. The earliest
form of resistance to schooling was, indeed, simply keeping clear
of it altogether. In the final quarter of the last century there were
indications of increasing resistance on the part of those in schools.
Diet appears to have been an almost perennial issue at the boarding
establishments. For example, referring to Lovedale in 1876 *The
Christian Express* wrote that 'here as everywhere else, the food
question becomes at times a "vexed question".'[102]

When students were unable to achieve improvement through
negotiation, they would resort to boycotting the food. In 1873, a
section of the students at Lovedale protested against 'Kaffirs and
Fingoes' being 'not treated with the same justice'. The
discrimination was allegedly in favour of the Fingoes. Fifteen
students were expelled. According to a report in *The Kaffir
Express,*

Though 47, who are as truly Kaffirs as the loudest of the complainants,
have declared that no distinction is made, these 15, with a degree of
insolent and infatuated insubordination, persisted in maintaining this
falsehood and in endeavouring to stir up ill-feeling.

Those who were . . . dismissed were requested to stay if they wished, till their friends were communicated with. This offer, with a good deal of strained bravado, they refused to accept . . . . [103]

As a further indication of growing resistance by black students, even before the turn of the century, Lovedale's Report for 1893 identified as 'a pressing serious evil', 'a perceptible increase of wilfulness and self-assertion showing itself in impatience of restraint and sometimes even, as all Institutions can testify, in curious fits of rebellion in numbers.'[104]

The overall picture in the first half of the 20th century was of sporadic collective action restricted to single institutions. Most of the concerted resistance arose in rural secondary schools and teachers' training colleges. Boarders, as opposed to day-students, tended to be in the forefront and the ages of those who played an active role ranged from the mid-teens to the early twenties. The occasion for, if not the 'cause' of, student resistance was generally provided by some immediate issue or set of issues. The most common was the food question. According to a letter written to the Editor of *Inkundla ya Bantu* by 'Once a Student',

The conditions of living in many of our colleges are very poor . . . . Some schools have no proper water system. Nearly in all of them, the diet is bad, being unscientifically weighted with carbohydrates. Now and again you find that the food is poorly cooked and inadequate supervision is exercised on its preparation. Sometimes no proper facilities exist for the cleaning of utensils . . . . I know of quite a famous college where students carry their spoons in their pockets wherever they go.[105]

A month previously the same publication had noted, in an editorial concerned with the frequent occurrences of strikes in African colleges, that 'In the majority of these disturbances, the food question is always associated in one way or the other with the strike.'[106]

Another source of strife was the oppressive authority which staff wielded over students. Punishment constituted a particularly sore issue. To quote an article which appeared in *The Territorial Magazine — Ipepa Ndaba Lezifunda* in 1938,

the relations in schools between the teacher and the taught border on acute antagonism. What progress can be expected where teachers instead of being guardians . . . and legitimate advisers of their students are turned to be tyrants imposing their will, regardless of its being illogic, on the students, failing whose obedience, punishment follows.

The article referred to punishment not only as 'a source of annoyance both to the inflictor and to the person on whom it is inflicted' but also as serving 'to place teacher and student in two diametrically opposed camps.' In addition to the often inappropriate reasons for punishment being administered, the 'kinds of punishment employed . . . enlarge the gulf between teacher and student. The first and commonest is abusive language like 'Silly Asses' and 'Dogs': . . . 'students . . . resent the application of vulgar language to them.' Other forms of punishment mentioned in the article included 'flogging, clapping, kicking' and 'the worst', expulsion.[107]

Related to the latter set of issues was another constituted by the employment of white staff who seemed less than sympathetic to, if concerned at all about, their black wards. The following is extracted from an article written in 1940 by 'Another Victim':

> Native institutions fail in their duty to produce the best trained men and women fit to do their bit. This is attributable to two factors. First that the teaching staff dishing out information to them is composed of a white majority who do not understand the conditions and the background of the African and secondly the Matrons and Lady Superintendents who are supposed to mother the women students are always white ladies . . . . These Matrons, naturally knowing little about the African and caring very little for them act only as policemen to read students' letters and mete out punishment . . . .

The writer's particular grounds for protest on this point are especially noteworthy since they contain an implicit expectation that education could serve black people in the struggle for liberation. The piece proceeds,

> This needs rectifying, the sooner the better, for the good of the African woman who now fails to stand side by side with the African man in the struggle for liberation because she leaves school hopelessly equipped. African progress is hindered by unenlightened womenfolk. A typical example, Boys at Clarkesbury Institution organised a strike fairly successfully, though we are not sure whether they are now provided with better meals, the Girls remained quiet as though all was well; no wonder, poor things, their initiative is thwarted, their creative power is misdirected . . . . '[108]

The lack of students' control over their education, or more specifically, their schools, was also raised as an issue. This is indicated by the following, albeit antagonistic, extract from an article which appeared in a 1945 issue of *The South African Outlook:*

About the end of March we had at one of our Native educational institutions another of those riots that from time to time have so disturbed their life in the past 25 years. It was not marked by much destruction of property . . . but the evidence points to an attempt on the part of some to do grievous bodily injury to at least one member of staff.

Those responsible for the College in question are satisfied that it was an attempt on the part of the students to usurp authority. It seems unthinkable that any body of pupils should have claimed the right to govern, or thought themselves capable of governing, an educational institution in any of its internal affairs or in regard to appointments to the staff, but it is just these unthinkable things that are happening amongst some African students today.[109]

Other issues for students included assaults by white staff on black students and staff, and forced menial labour on farms, roads and school premises. Over the years, students at various institutions organised, protested and demonstrated over such issues. Generally, they undertook more concerted collective action only after they had made representations to the school authorities and after discussions had been conducted. Further action took several forms. Students boycotted the food, chapel and classes. On occasions, they withdrew the menial labour exacted from them. When sufficiently provoked, they confronted the authorities with sticks and stones and set fire to property. The most common collective action became that combination of the latter forms of action in what was known as a 'strike'. Following a 'strike' which had involved violence and destruction by student apprentices at Blythswood Institution on 17 February 1929, *The South African Outlook* commented:

The 'Strike' idea among Native students had its origin in reports brought back from the Rand by Native labourers of the methods followed there and of the reckless violence of the riff-raff of Johannesburg in labour disputes, so it has from the first been conceived of not merely as a quitting of work, but of blows to be 'struck' and damage to be done. As this up to date method of getting grievances righted has in the course of the last ten years or thereabouts been applied at every one of the large Native training institutions . . . as was to be expected, the procedure has become increasingly lawless and dangerous. This last incident at Blythswood, which apparently arose out of nothing more serious than a grievance about bounds . . . outdoes its predecessors in that it seems to have been from the beginning an organised attack upon the staff, with the intent to do them serious, if not fatal injury.[110]

No evidence has been found of students having attempted to broaden their resistance into the community during the period under review. Generally, it remained restricted to the bounds of individual establishments. There appears to have been minimal student involvement in political organisations. However, black students do seem to have been responsive both to the conditions in society at large and particularly to struggles against those conditions. In an editorial arguing that, despite the frequency with which the food question cropped up in student strikes, 'the problem does not start and end with food', *Inkundla ya Bantu* stated, 'The strikes indicate a new sensitiveness to treatment meted out to African students by those schools which have had trouble; a natural reaction when the entire African community has begun to see their problems in the light of their future as full citizens.'[111] The Committee of Inquiry which was appointed by the Lovedale Governing Council to investigate the causes of the student 'strike' at the Institution on 7 August 1946 included in its report the following summary of the grievances which students had aired four days previously at a mass meeting called by the Chairperson of the Students' Representative Council to hear complaints:

(a)   The sugar ration had been cut since the beginning of the session.

(b)   The bread ration had been reduced.

(c)   Shortages in beans and samp.

(d)   The students were not notified of these cuts.

(e)   Failure to implement a promise by the Principal that substitutes would be provided.

(f)   The way in which the food was cooked was not appetising.

(g)   Dirty conditions of the lavatories.

(h)   Closing during certain hours of the woodyard from which hot water was supplied to the students.

(i)   At the Bookstall, Croxley pads were no longer sold to the students.

(j)   That the Principals of the High and Training Schools 'did not respect the senior students, and that the former did not listen to complaints.'

(k)   That the free supply of paper to typewriting students from the High School had been discontinued.

(l)   That members of the Students' Representative Council should have more privileges than the prefects.

(m)   That the Students' representatives should be consulted in cases of expulsion for misconduct.[112]

The Committee's findings, however, were that 'the real causes of the disturbance' were not these grievances but rather were traceable to factors enumerated in its Report as follows:

(i)   General state of unrest throughout the world;

(ii)   Race Consciousness, evident not only in South Africa, but in other parts of the world — in India, Java, the Middle East, and African Colonies and elsewhere;

(iii) The tendency on the part of the students to assert their freedom of action, and the urge to do things for themselves;

(iv)   The Colour Bar and the Economic Disabilities of the African people;

(v)   Resentment of authority and weakening of discipline during the war period and the breakdown of tribal and parental control;

(vi)   Political influences, both within and outside the Institution, political propaganda, the distribution of inflammatory literature, and undesirable contacts during the vacations.[113]

Elaborating on the latter point in its Report, the Committee of Inquiry stated

it should be emphasised that there is a growing middle class comprising the advanced elements of the African people, which is becoming of great political significance, and which has its most active expression in demands for the abolition of laws specifically affecting Africans and for increased representation on public bodies and in the Legislature. Their views are represented by the Native Representative Council, by organisations of considerable influence and by a number of newspapers and political pamphlets and bulletins.

This interest in politics has extended to the schools, and it was stated that even at the High School stage students take a keen interest in the political situation.

Some witnesses suggested that the facts of life were sufficient to influence the minds of the students, while others drew attention to the danger that has arisen from a flood of inflammatory literature, that has found its way among them.[114]

Significantly, the Report also brought out

the fact that the disturbance synchronised with the unrest that ended in a strike of African mine workers on the Witwatersrand Gold Mines on 12 August, 1946. The movement organised by the African Mine Workers Union actually began on 19 May, 1946, and the decision to strike was taken on 4 August. Meanwhile the organisers of the strike were actively engaged in making propaganda, and there is little doubt that the strike bulletins that reached Lovedale during this period and the atmosphere brought back by students, some of whom came from the Reef, after the June-July vacation, contributed to the general dis-affection.[115]

Another source of resistance within the school system was a section of the teaching corps. It is probably impossible ever to determine the extent of attempts by teachers to undermine that system through the content and style of their lessons behind closed classroom doors. Overt resistance on the part of black teachers in the first half of the century was limited in all respects. When they did raise their voices publicly it was most commonly to demand higher salaries and better working conditions for themselves. On 6 May 1944, for example, teachers along the Reef staged a demonstration in support of their demand for improved salaries. Teachers and community members marched through the streets of Johannesburg singing 'Morena Boloka' and bearing banners on which their demands — which included free universal education and more schools — were inscribed. After the demon-stration, a large rally was addressed by numerous leaders of groups and organisations including the President-General of the ANC, Dr A B Xuma, who pledged Congress's support for the teachers and pleaded for unity in their ranks as the only way of struggling through to victory.[116] As a result of concerted agitation around the issue of teachers' pay, a commission was appointed in the Transvaal to investigate the matter.[117] Also in May, 1944, 'Indian' teachers at Sastri College in Durban decided to strike for higher salaries and better working conditions.[118] In June of the same year, a 'mammoth meeting' of the United Cape African Teachers' Association, held over four days at Willowvale in the Transkei, threatened militant action if the Government did not respond to its salary demands.[119] To the extent that teacher resistance was taken further in organised form, this was done mainly by three organisations: the Cape African Teachers' Association (CATA), the Transvaal African Teachers' Association (TATA) and the Teachers' League of South Africa (TLSA), which were all affiliated to the Non-European Unity Movement (NEUM) — the former two via the All African Convention (AAC) and the latter via the Anti-Coloured Affairs department Movement (Anti-CAD) — which, from its inception in 1943, had placed education high amongst its priorities.

Resistance came also from outside the school system, in particular from parents and political organisations. A parents' association was formed in Natal as early as 1939. Another was formed in the Transkei during the 1940s. Parents opposed Native Education in its structure and in its content, in its component parts and in toto. Amongst the resolutions adopted unanimously at the first conference of the Bantu Parents' Assocation in Natal, held on 30 June 1939 in Durban, were the following:

> That this Conference condemns the new method of instruction to Native children, that is the medium of instruction to be Zulu from Std I to Std IV.
>
> The Conference holds that the Official Languages of the Union must for the purposes of Native Education be recognised as the medium of instruction in our Native Schools, and that lessons must be in either or both of the Official Languages.
>
> Zulu to be used in the early stages only as a part subject.
>
> While this Conference is in favour of the Union Government taking over Native Education from the Provincial Administration, it strongly opposes the transfer of Native Education to the Native Affairs Department . . . .
>
> We urge very earnestly on the Minister of Native Affairs (Education) not to establish a precedent that is totally opposed by all parents of Native children.
>
> This Conference would like to see all schools controlled by the Government direct, and that Government Aided Schools be transferred accordingly.[120]

In January 1944, the same body held a meeting in Ladysmith 'with a view to enabling all parents in Natal to present a firm front against Native Education.'[121]

The following is extracted from an article which appeared in a 1943 issue of *Inkundla ya Bantu:*

> This 'Native Education' seems today to mean a special type of inferior education which is meant to lull the Native into the old sleep that has weighed him down for decades already; and to keep the Native lingering in the vestibule of knowledge, wallowing in the quagmire of the slush and ooze of ignorance. Cui bono? The big dog, of course, reaps the benefit thereof.
>
> We must do away with this 'dummy sort' of education. It is as cruel or rather as generous as offering a stone to an unsuspecting ignorant child who craves for bread.[122]

Two months later, the same publication asserted, 'The African does not want Native Education and he is determined to wage a ruthless struggle to give to his child that education which will make him the equal of any other South African, White or Yellow.'[123] Further, it interpreted the appointment of a commission of inquiry into Native Education by the Natal provincial authorities as 'a Government reaction to the fact that Bantu parents in this province have publicly challenged the principle on which Native Education is based — the principle of African development along separate and inferior lines. African parents demand education for full citizenship and not for servitude.'[124]

The 1939 conference of the Natal Bantu Parents' Association expressed its opposition 'to the system of teaching children only over-sea history in the Primary Schools'.[125] In 1946, *Inkundla ya Bantu* took history as an example of what had to be opposed in Native Education on the level of the curriculum, stating, 'Our history, in our schools, seeks to perpetuate this doctrine of White superiority and it is time we raised our voices in protest against it.'[126] In 1946 Professor Z K Matthews wrote in a review of Native Education over the previous 25 years that

> opposition has come in the main from the African people themselves. They have pointed out that there was a danger of their children being given a form of education which might be more of a handicap to them than anything else. They have demanded for their children an education which takes due account of the fact that they are living in the modern world, in an environment which includes both Western and African elements linked together indissolubly. Their view has been that they will not tolerate any course which purports to prepare their children for a purely African environment when they know that such a thing no longer exists in South Africa. Without advocating a slavish following of the curricula requirements of European schools, they have insisted upon the necessity for constructing our curricula in such a way that all children can, in accordance with their varying talents, be led into the common heritage of man in all fields of human knowledge and skill.[127]

Parents and others demanded consistently that the quality of education be improved, that it be offered free, and that it be made compulsory. In 1909, *The APO*, through the columns of its official organ, urged

> further attention being paid to, and fuller provision being made for, the education of the coloured children of the (Cape) colony . . . justice demands it. The coloured ratepayers bear their share of the burden of government, and are justly entitled to fuller facilities for education; and we are convinced that the only solution of the education problem will be found in making primary education free, secular, and compulsory for coloureds as for whites.[128]

Another of the resolutions adopted by the conference of the Bantu Parents' Association mentioned above was as follows: 'The Parents Association requests that schooling of Native children should be free and should be on the same basis as other schools of Non-Europeans made compulsory.'[129] In 1944, *Inkundla ya Bantu* referred to 'the rising tide of African agitation for better Education'. It observed, 'On the education front Africans are gradually marshalling their forces for united action . . . . The struggle for better education and higher salaries is a national affair and part of the national struggle.'[130]

The most fundamental question to be raised by those strictly outside the school system was that of its control. The 1939 conference of the Bantu Parents' Association recorded its conviction that 'the time has come when the Authorities in charge of Native Education should consult the parents of the Bantu children in any change in school syllabus and other changes that vitally concern the Education of the Native children.'[131] In 1944, *Inkundla ya Bantu* asserted 'the eternal right of the African parent to say what form of education shall be given to his child.'[132] Either out of naivete or for polemical purposes, the same publication interpreted the inclusion of Africans in the commissions appointed by the provincial authorities of the Transvaal and Natal to report on black teachers' salaries and Native Education, respectively, as indicating,

> an acceptance (by the Government) of the principle that the black man must have a voice in the making of the laws which affect him, and, therefore, a first assurance that after all the foolish experiments with Native Education, it (Native Education) will cease to be a political instrument used by the Whiteman to curb the free development and training of the African's intellect and therefore an instrument to make the Bantu satisfied with an inferior position in the State.[133]

A few attempts were made to circumvent state control of schooling by setting up independent schools supposedly beyond the reach of state policy. The Second Annual Congress of the Cape Trade Unions held during 1920 in Cape Town resolved 'not to leave the children of the workers in the Cape any longer at the mercy of Capitalist Public Schools, but to get busy in establishing a Labour College in Cape Town, at the earliest possible moment.' The following subjects were proposed:

(1)   History (from the workers' and materialist points of view)
(2)   History and Development of Trade Unionism
(3)   Sociology
(4)   Economics.[134]

Attempts which did come to limited fruition were those of black parents in the Transvaal where by 1948 there were 'shanty' secondary schools, as they were known, in Orlando, Western Native Township, Brakpan, Atteridgeville and Alexandra. Finally, there were occasions when parents attempted to intervene in the school system directly.[135]

The various forms of resistance which had arisen in and around the schools by the time the National Party came into power contained the seeds of what were for the dominant classes ominous potential developments from below.

The introduction and development of Bantu, Coloured and Indian Education

The National Party brought to government a new emphasis on black schooling. In January 1949 a Commission on Native Education under Dr W W M Eiselen was appointed. The Commission reported in 1951 and, pursuant to its recommendations, the Bantu Education Act was passed in 1953. A Commission on Coloured Education was set up in the Cape in 1953 although it was only in 1963 that the Coloured Persons Education Act was passed. This provided for the control of education for children classified Coloured to be transferred from the provinces to a Division of Education within the Department of Coloured Affairs. This transfer of control was effected in the Cape and Transvaal on 1 January 1964, and in Natal and the Orange Free State on 1 April 1964. The last legislative bricks were laid in the wall of segregated schooling by the Indian Education Act of 1965 which similarly provided for the transfer of the control of education for people classified Indian from the provinces to the Department of Indian Affairs. Its provisions were applied throughout Natal and to the Transvaal College of Education for Asiatics as from 1 April 1966, and, a year later, it came into operation in the Transvaal generally. The Act came into operation in the Cape on 1 April 1970.

Opponents of Bantu, Coloured and Indian Education have regarded this system as embodying an entirely new approach to black schooling. They have tended to portray it as the brainchild of Nationalist ideologues who ignored what was functionally required for continued economic growth and deviated from the enlightened direction of Native Education. Such an interpretation, however, is misleading. First of all, it involves a distorted notion of the nature of schooling for blacks in the period prior to the introduction of Bantu, Coloured and Indian Education; secondly, it overlooks what the National Party carried over into Bantu, Coloured and Indian Education from the educational system which it had inherited from previous regimes, the fact being that there were both continuities and discontinuities; and, thirdly, its assumptions about what was functionally required for 'economic growth' are unsubstantiated.

There had never previously been a coherently formulated educational policy integrated into overall state strategy. The Eiselen Commission proposed one. Various changes followed the implementation of the Bantu Education Act. Black schools were taken out of the hands of the church and other non-state bodies and control was centralised in Pretoria. Syllabus revision was centralised. The primary school syllabuses, which were finally enforced in 1956, stressed obedience, communal loyalty, ethnic and national diversity, acceptance of allocated social roles, piety, and identification with rural culture. Teachers were to be rigidly regimented. Schools were as far as possible reorganised on a fragmented sectionalist or 'tribal' basis. They were 'Bantu-ised' in personnel and, to a certain extent, in medium of instruction. Schooling was to contribute to the revival of 'Bantu Culture' and brought into line with 'Bantu Social Institutions'. At post-primary level the schools were as far as possible located away from the urban areas. Community participation was introduced via partially elected committees and boards under the aegis of 'Bantu Authorities'. The provision of elementary schooling was greatly expanded. At the same time, the cost per student was reduced by means of, inter alia, double sessions, employing more under-qualified teachers, paying minimal salaries to black teachers, discriminating even further against women teachers, pegging the amount of the state's financial contribution, extracting more from the African communities themselves, phasing out school feeding services, and abolishing caretakers' posts and making the students responsible for school cleaning. Finally, it became illegal to operate a school not registered with the Department of Bantu Affairs. It is important to ask what developments led to this new state interest in black schooling and what the characteristics of the new response to Bantu, Coloured and Indian Education demonstrated.

One important national development which coincided with the period in which the new regime was fashioning its educational policy was the rise of manufacturing industry. This led to increased demand for workers with some level of literacy and numeracy as well as semi-skilled and skilled workers. In contrast, the growing numbers of black job-seekers with clerical-type skills could not be absorbed within the particular racist structure of employment which prevailed. Yet, the training of any substantial layer of black workers in the skills which were increasingly being sought, could not be undertaken at that time by the National Party government without threatening the white workers' privileged position as a 'labour aristocracy'. It is suggested that part of the aim of Bantu Education was initially to reduce the number of black people with medium-level academic qualifications to that minimum required mainly as teachers and functionaries in the Bantustan bureaucracies. At the same time, it was to increase the number of workers with skills limited to a level which would not threaten the white working class but be sufficiently high for them to move into the growing number of semi-skilled jobs being opened up through the process of deskilling and job fragmentation. Bantu Education was also to begin expanding the number of workers with basic literacy and numeracy.

While not wishing to diminish the significance of what has been put forward so far, it will now be argued that Bantu Education, along with Coloured and Indian Education, was first and foremost part of a broader state reaction to factors other than the 'purely economic' demands of the labour market.

Accelerated capital accumulation — as a result of the expansion of the manufacturing industry and the opening up of new gold fields in the Orange Free State and uranium mines in the West Rand and Klerksdorp areas — meant a growing need for labour. Taxes imposed to push the people off the remnants of their land, combined with an accelerated rate of economic collapse in the reserves, produced an ever increasing flow of black workers to the urban areas. The potential political consequences of the development of a massive oppressed and ultra-exploited black proletariat concentrated around the cities were recognised and feared by the National Party. In the years after World War II the political consciousness of black South Africans was rising rapidly. The spirit of African nationalism was asserting itself with unprecedented force and the call was out for the unity of all oppressed people. Encouraged by the impact that anti-imperialist struggles were having in the colonised countries of Africa and Asia and the success of the people's war in China, a new feeling of solidarity and power was gathering momentum and being expressed in open struggle. The workers in the cities were making increasing use of strike action to advance their demands. The African Miners' Strike of August 1946 was the most notable event of this kind. It was bloodily supressed. In solidarity with the mine workers' stand, the African workers of Johannesburg attempted to organise a general strike. At the same time, resistance to the authorities' rule in the reserves was widespread and determined. The government could not but have recognised these developments as a grave threat to its very economic and political foundations. In October 1946 *The Cape Times* asserted in an editorial that, 'The race problem today is worse than it has ever been throughout our history . . . . Relations between European and Non-European were never nearer breaking-point.'[136]

The National Party saw that the black nationalist movement, in the process of consolidating itself, was either going to become controlled by ·the liberal agents of imperialism, ('anti-apartheid' capitalism) or would accept the leadership of the black fraction of the working class. For the National Party, representing basically the alliance between the white fraction of the working class and domestic agricultural, manufacturing and finance capital, neither could be countenanced. Its leaders realised that merely to continue the repression of revolts and the suppression of political organisation could not in the long run suffice to save the racist structures of exploitation and domination. It was in response to these conditions that a new strategy for education began to take shape.

The underlying strategic conception was based on a belief in the National Party that no political rights could be granted to Africans within a common South African framework without inevitably provoking the demand for full political rights within that common framework and without setting in motion a process over which the government would eventually lose control and which would then result in open civil war or complete capitulation. The government recognised that the granting of any political rights to Africans as national citizens could only foster the further development of African nationalism. The process of withdrawing from Africans such minimal political rights as they had was completed by the Promotion of Bantu Self-Government Act of 1959. In the debate, the Minister of Bantu Administration and Development argued that if the principle of African representation was accepted,

> . . . then the Bantu would have to accept this Parliament as his Parliament, and he would then become involved in a struggle in which he would demand representation in this House on at least the same basis as the White man. That is the trouble which awaits South Africa . . . if there are people who say that the Bantu will always be satisfied to be represented in Parliament by a few people, I say to them that they are living in a fool's paradise. No nation in the world would agree to it, and still much less the proud Bantu.[137]

The more liberal section within the superordinate classes failed to appreciate this. During the House of Assembly debate over the

Transkei Constitution Bill, in 1963, the Leader of the Opposition argued as follows:

> *de Villiers Graaff:* 'They (the Nationalists) believe that there are only two policies in South Africa. The one policy they say is complete separation, and the other policy, they say, is complete integration, complete equality, one man one vote.'
> *A Nationalist interjector:* 'Tell us, how are you going to stop that?'
> *de Villiers Graaff:* 'If the . . . Prime Minister thinks that he can keep the entire mass of the Bantu population living permanently in the Republic which controls our destinies, how can he deny that we (the United Party) can do something much smaller . . . and restrict the representation that we intend to give them in Parliament? Our policy at least has a safety-valve. It gives a degree of representation . . . eight representatives of the Bantu people in Parliament will be far less dangerous than eight sovereign Black states.'[138]

The Nationalists, however, knew from their own history what potential lay in the fusion of working class consciousness and nationalist ideology — it had helped propel their own party into power. They knew that, for their own future, the working class had to be fragmented and the basis of a national (black) consciousness broken. Thus, central to their strategic objectives was the defusion of African nationalism through a systematic attempt to retribalise in such a way that the resultant fragmentation would obstruct the further development of black nationalism. It was primarily for these purposes, and in order to entrench the status of the bulk of the oppressed literally as noncitizens by placing them politically in a sphere completely removed from South African citizenship, that the Bantustans were devised. The political dead-end of the Bantu Authorities was intended to divert African nationalist demands away from the white parliament as the formal seat of political power in South Africa.

The same strategic conception lay beneath Verwoerd's introduction of Bantu Education and provides the key to understanding the critical new dimension in the schooling of black South Africans. The black oppressed had to be put outside the sphere in which the wealth of the land was owned and controlled. In Verwoerd's notorious words:

> There is no place for him in the European community above the level of certain forms of labour . . . for that reason it is of no avail for him to receive a training which has as its aim absorption in the European community, where he cannot be absorbed. Until now he has been subjected to a school system which drew him away from his own

community and misled him by showing him the green pastures of European society in which he was not allowed to graze.[139]

Bantu Education was to prepare young Africans psycho-ideologically for the position in which the Bantustans placed them physically and politically. To that end, Bantu Education, according to Verwoerd, 'should stand with both feet in the reserves and have its roots in the spirit and being of Bantu society . . . . The basis of the provision and organisation of education in a Bantu Community should, where possible, be the tribal organisation.'[140] The Bantu Education Act was passed by parliament two years after the Bantu Authorities Act. Where the latter was intended, inter alia, to create a separate 'Bantu Community', the former was aimed to fit African people into it. The Bantu Authorities were designed for indirect, but rigid, rule through government-recognised (or government-created) chiefs and headmen; it was under the control of these very Bantu Authorities that the Bantu Education Act placed the control of so-called 'community schools'. The emphasis of the Bantu Authorities Act on tribal divisions was reflected in the Bantu Education Act particularly in its provisions concerning language medium and the exclusive tribal composition of schools. At every point, Bantu Education was designed to back up the Bantustans. Where there was a limit to the capacity of Bantustans and 'group areas' to remove all black people all of the time physically from the context in which the wealth of the land was owned and controlled, Bantu, Coloured and Indian Education was designed to help remove them psycho-ideologically and 'resettle' them in their separate 'places' of subordination.

State response to the resurgence of black resistance and the rapid rise of an urban working class was not restricted to the broad political strategy described thus far. New mechanisms of control were introduced and old ones overhauled. Through the Native and Coloured Affairs Departments, the labour bureaux, the pass laws, the location system, group areas, and a web of restrictive legislation, the lives of black people were regimented in almost every aspect. Whereas this regimentation was in the main physical, the systems of Bantu, Coloured and Indian Education were aimed at the mind. The regime recognised that the people's

surest guarantee for ultimate victory in their struggle, and the greatest threat and danger to white exploitation and domination is the political consciousness of the masses of the oppressed people, their contact with current world events and trends in international relationships, their acquaintance with and knowledge of the history of the liberatory movement in other parts of the world, and their unity of purpose with all democrats in this country and abroad — a unity which transcends racial or ethnic differences and strikes at the very foundations of the social, economic, and political structure.'[141]

Bantu, Coloured and Indian Education were designed to control the direction of thought, to delimit the boundaries of knowledge, to restrict lines of communication, and to curtail contact across language barriers. They aimed to dwarf the minds of black children by conditioning them to servitude. Like the segregated and inferior schooling before it, the new system was intended to prepare black children for the subordinated positions that awaited them in such a way that they were appropriately equipped with limited skills as well as ready to resign themselves to their exploitation. White supremacy would be secured if the black product of schooling was 'a person who accepts in full the Nationalist policy of Apartheid, of White domination of the master-servant relationships as between White and Black; a person . . . whose highest aspiration will be to assert the superiority of his own tribe over other tribes . . . a creature whose mind will have been thoroughly regimented into willing acceptance of the status quo.'[142]

The more direct linking of black schooling with the Bantu and Coloured Affairs Departments was designed to achieve a stricter and more rigid, a more efficient and effective, a more completely totalitarian control of student and teacher both in and out of school, than had previously been possible with less direct links through the provincial and church adminstrations. Control seemed clearly to have been the operative objective. As the production of skills was relatively unimportant, 'standards' could safely be sacrificed; this explains how it was possible to increase the numbers in school so greatly with minimal increase in expenditure. The goal was to bring greater numbers of black youth under direct control. Although the system of Bantu, Coloured and Indian Education certainly perpetuated and extended the educational starvation, religious indoctrination, and inferiority of previous black schooling, it was never intended as a simple denial of educational opportunities but represented a more calculated attempt to subvert the political and economic aspirations of Black South Africans. And, as has been seen, it was an attempt tightly articulated with a broader political strategy developed by the political representatives of the superordinate classes to defend their threatened order.

Opposition to Bantu, Coloured and Indian Education

Student resistance during the seven years which elapsed between the National Party's victory at the white polls on 26 May 1948 and the formal introduction of Bantu Education on 1 April 1955 continued in much the same form as before. For instance, in February 1950 forty students of St Matthew's College in the Cape were convicted in the Keiskammahoek Magistrate's Court on charges of public violence. Later in the same year, student 'strikes' — in the form of boycotts — at two institutions in the Transkei, St John's College, Umtata, and the Shawbury Methodist Institute, occurred within six weeks of each other. The latter institution was closed for two days, during June, following the 'strike'. The female students, objecting to the food served, had boycotted the dining-hall. They had gone to a nearby hill where they were joined by their male counterparts. The police had been called and they stood by while 400 students were sent home. In September that year, 200 students were dismissed from Adams College, Natal, for breach of discipline. They had refused to eat their lunch, stayed away from their afternoon classes and refused to attend chapel. They were accused of planning to destroy school property and injure 'loyal' students. In July 1952, 74 students from the Mfundisweni hostels of the Faku Institution, near Flagstaff, were found guilty of violence arising from a 'disturbance' in which the boarding mistress of the girls' dormitory was attacked. The following month, 84 students were arrested for 'rioting' at the Bensonvale Training School near Aliwal North in the Herschel district. All the institution's thatched buildings were burnt down, food supplies were destroyed, and windows were broken. When the police arrived, they were heavily stoned while firing shots into the air. The students were protesting against the dismissal of one of their teachers as well as alleging that there was no co-operation between white and black teachers at the institution. Towards the end of the same year, there was intra-student conflict at Orlando High School after three of its teachers, having been sacked, set up a school of their own. Students 'stoned, stabbed and battered' other students of the school and shots were said to have been fired. On 14 May 1953, 184 students at Bethal Training Institute, near Coligny in the Transvaal, were arrested after they had stoned classrooms and the principal's house, and used gallons of petrol to set fire to them. Their grievances included bad food, weak milk, overcrowding, insanitary conditions, and the fact that one student had been dismissed after allegedly returning drunk from a football-match. Six days later, 42 students at Indaleni Training College, near Richmond in Natal, were arrested after they had burnt down two offices and a classroom.[143]

In October 1953, students at the Healdtown Native Missionary College near Fort Beaufort in the Eastern Cape mobilised around a number of issues which were causing dissatisfaction. They demanded improvement in certain conditions which they claimed were interfering with their studies. They complained that, since the appointment of a new boarding master, the seniors had been deprived of the privilege of electing their prefects. The dignity of the seniors had been further impaired by placing juniors in positions which seniors had previously held. The senior students also objected to the standard of the food, to being compelled to take turns working from 3 am in the bakery, having to wash dishes, being used in the repairing of roads, being debarred from visiting the girls' hostel and being prevented from visiting relatives. The students submitted to the boarding master a written list of suggested improvements but he refused to consider them. Approximately a hundred senior students then embarked on what they called a strike, refusing their meals or even to be seated in the dining hall. After two days of their passive resistance campaign, the College authorities ordered them to leave. Initially the students refused to comply, but when a police detachment, gathered from Cradock, Bedford, Adelaide, Fort Beaufort and Alice, arrived to expel them forcibly, they left without further resistance and boarded trains for their homes in Cape Town, Johannesburg, Port Elizabeth, parts of the Transkei and other centres.[144]

There is no evidence of overt student opposition to the Eiselen Commission's proposals or the Bantu Education Bill. These do not seem to have been at issue even in a 'disturbance' during May 1955 at Xedwaleni Training School which resulted in the expulsion of thirty student leaders. It was teachers who mounted the first concerted resistance and they did so principally through three organisations: the Cape African Teachers' Association (CATA) and the Teachers' League of South Africa (TLSA) — both affiliated to the All African Convention (AAC) — and the Transvaal African Teachers' Association (TATA).[145] Black people in general, however, were from the outset implacably opposed to Bantu Education. Even before its implementation, people perceived Bantu Education as part and parcel of the imposition of passes, Bantustans and the whole repressive apparatus. Resistance to the introduction of Bantu Education was widespread. Even in the remote rural areas it was intense — especially in the Sekhukhuniland and Zeerust regions. In the period of the initial implementation of Bantu Education, parents played a particularly prominent part in the popular opposition mounted against it. Many refused to send their children to Bantu Education schools. In places schools were burned down. Such actions demonstrated dramatically the depth of resentment against Bantu Education in view of the sacrifices black people had generally been willing to make to have their children educated. It can be imagined how those flames devouring the schools might have symbolised for people their consuming desire to rid themselves of the dreaded new system. It was parents, not students, whom the African National Congress (ANC) attempted to mobilise in support of its campaign to resist Bantu Education. The story of the latter campaign has been adequately documented elsewhere and will, therefore, not be repeated here.[146]

Resistance to Bantu Education continued after the collapse of the ANC's campaign and the long-term aim remained to prevent its functioning. However, there was a shift away from any idea that this could be achieved by means of a permanent boycott. Insofar as any general strategy emerged, it was to stay in the schools but refuse to collaborate with the system's methods and objectives. Teachers, by refusing to indoctrinate their students with the ideology of the rulers, aimed to undermine the possibility of schools operating according to the government's design. Parents, by boycotting the Bantu School Boards and Committees, refused to collaborate voluntarily in helping to run a school system that was oppressive. Students in school and university sustained a simmering rebellion, which surfaced variously at different times and in different places. Some examples follow.

The principal of the primary school in Dinokana, Zeerust, came out during 1957 in support of passes for women. According to a report in *Drum,* 'The people went mad. They thought that he was in cahoots with the police and the Commissioner.' They burned down his house and organised a boycott of the school. On the first day of the boycott, only 146 students of the 1200 enrolled at the school attended. The principal informed the Commissioner who relayed the matter to Pretoria. The authorities' reaction was swift and harsh. The following day orders came back from Pretoria for the school to be closed down immediately, the teachers transferred, and the names of the boycotting children taken down and circularised so that they could be prevented from receiving education for the rest of their lives.[147]

Phyllis Ntantala notes that people in the Cape were generally too hostile to Bantu Education to elect School Boards, while many of those appointed to them by the government refused to serve. She records the widespread rejection of ministers of religion who 'broke the people's boycott of the BAD School Boards by agreeing to serve on them'.

Communities which had built and maintained schools and placed them in the hands of the churches, rejected those ministers who, without consulting them, leased such schools to the government. For instance, members of the Peddie community, in the

Eastern Cape, locked up the schools, which they had built with their own money and labour, and told the minister-in-charge to build his own schools if he wished to hire them out to the government. In Port Elizabeth, members of one congregation called upon their minister, who had accepted the chairpersonship of the local Bantu School Board, to resign, reminding him that he depended on them for his livelihood. In Mt. Ayliff, East Griqualand, people burned down the schools they had built rather than lease them to the government, and then told the minister, who had agreed to the lease, to hire out his own schools.[148]

Ntantala also describes the deterioration of conditions in schools after their transference to the BAD. In the boarding schools, maintenance personnel, with the exception of the cooks, were dismissed, and their work given to the students, who had compulsory manual work to do before and after classes every day. According to Ntantala, 'corporal punishment provides the only discipline and a whole "gestapo" system has been introduced, by which — profiting from the poverty of the African people and their desire for education — the authorities are offering scholarships to some students on condition that they spy on their fellows . . . in any one institution there are usually three, four or more of such paid spies.' 'Inevitably,' she continues, 'these boarding schools seethe with student discontent and staff repression.' Ntantala cites several examples thereof. In 1957, a student was shot during a 'disturbance' at the Ndamase Secondary School in Buntingville. The principal admitted in court during the subsequent student trial that he had fired shots to 'frighten' the students. Soon thereafter he shot himself. In the same year, some 30 senior female students at Shawbury in the Transkei were sent home and about 200 male students at St John's College, Umtata, were expelled on the eve of their examinations. In 1958, Adams College, in Natal, sent more than 200 students home. Such was the situation at Lovedale that early in 1959 over 300 students chose to go home.[149]

The connection between the expression of student dissatisfaction in the schools and the demonstration of opposition to the political order outside the schools became overt by 1960. Noting that there had been 'disturbances' at various African schools prior to 1953, Horrell states that 'such disturbances increased in number and in severity' during the following decade.[150] She argues, however, that this cannot be accounted for solely by reference to the introduction of Bantu Education, 'although the dissatisfaction it created among many teachers and parents, and in the controlling mission organisations, naturally permeated to the student bodies.' It appeared to Horrell that 'in recent years normal disciplinary problems have been aggravated by the mounting spirit of unrest among Africans in South Africa.' Numerous factors besides the policy of 'separate development' in education were responsible for this unrest. In this regard, she points out that African students in the higher standards were in general older than students in white schools and were 'likely to be more aware of events outside the school room.' Horrell proceeds to illustrate the coincidence which she identifies between the pattern of student 'disturbances' and 'periods of marked unrest in the country generally.'[151] After the initial wave of resistance around the introduction of the Bantu Education Act, the pattern displays heightened student resistance in the form of 'boycotts or riots' during the period in 1960 when there were mass demonstrations against the pass laws leading to the police killings at Sharpeville and Langa, the declaration of a State of Emergency, and the banning of the ANC and PAC. In 1961 there was a wave of 'disturbances' at African secondary institutions during the period of widespread demonstrations against South Africa becoming a republic, which was also a period of particularly militant mass opposition to the authorities in the Transkei and certain other areas. There were further instances of student 'disturbances' in 1962, which saw the emergence of Poqo and Umkhonto we Sizwe as well as the first cases of sabotage and the Paarl uprising. Another wave in 1963 coincided with increased activity by Poqo and more sabotage.[152]

The Secretary of the Southern Transvaal Region of the South African Institute of Race Relations, Patrick McKenzie, in a 1964 Report on 'Disturbances in African Schools', regarded it as 'significant' that

> the disturbances in the early part of 1963 followed each other in quick succession giving the impression of some connection between them. The troubles at Wilberforce in March 1963 were followed within a few days by those at Lovedale and then Healdtown. Those at the Faku Institution and the Bethal College followed within a few weeks.
>
> I am informed that there was a definite plan behind these disturbances. During discussions that I have had with pupils, some have admitted that the storm centre of the disturbances has been politcal. Most of the disturbances have been sparked off by a genuine complaint and then fanned by a small group within the school, and on occasions there has been additional help (or one might say interference) from outside.

Earlier in his Report, McKenzie states categorically,

> In recent years there has been increased political activity within the

schools. This has been confirmed by all sources as well as by the conviction of pupils by the Courts.[153]

Evidence is for the most part lacking as to whether students were conscious of any connection that there might have been between their own actions and political activity in the broader society. The only directly political issue over which students protested was the establishment of the Republic in 1961 and South Africa's withdrawal from the British Commonwealth. The most common issues concerned food and forms of punishment. There was opposition to corporal punishment but what students objected to most strongly was expulsion, which was used frequently, often for petty transgressions. Also related to the maintenance of discipline was the issue of the police being brought onto the campuses of certain institutions, or, as in one case, a principal's threat to call them in to deal with 'schoolboy agitators'. In another instance, students were incensed by police arriving to search their personal belongings, ostensibly for dangerous weapons; when they resisted, the police removed their trunks and conducted the search at the police station. Students protested over numerous other issues. Hostel facilities were primitive. Many teachers were incompetent. Administration of the schools was poor. Students opposed the enforced introduction of Afrikaans. They resisted the manual work which they were compelled to do and complained that there was too little time to study. They objected to the strict segregation between white and black members of staff and despised the black teachers for being prepared to serve under such conditions. Furthermore, students' complaints were seldom seriously considered and they had no vehicle for the expression of opinion since many student organisations had been suppressed and contact with ex-students was discouraged. Finally there were single-instance issues such as relatives and friends being refused admission to an institution's annual drama night.

Student resistance took various forms, the most frequent being the boycotting of classes and setting fire to classrooms or the principal's office. There were boycotts of chapel, of the dining hall, and of manual work. There were walk-outs and stay-aways. Students sometimes stoned school buildings and on occasion the home of a staff member to whom they objected particularly strongly. In one case, they physically attacked the matron of a girls' hostel.

The reaction of the authorities to student resistance was in most cases repressive. Many hundreds of students were expelled, never to be re-admitted. Of those suspended, some were allowed to apply for re-admission — of those who did, many were refused.

Certain schools were temporarily closed down and the students sent home. Many students were arrested and taken to court on charges of arson, malicious damage to property, public violence, or addressing, holding or being present at, an illegal gathering.[154]

The period 1960-63 was followed by more than a decade of relative quiescence — if only qualified compliance — in the African schools although intermittent instances of student resistance, similar in form to those detailed above, did continue. Resistance to Coloured and Indian Education was given organised expression mainly by the TLSA and a network of Parent-Teacher Associations which had been built up primarily for that purpose. The consensus, however, was that '*teachers should stick at their posts and continue to teach* and refuse to indoctrinate, as . . . required of them. They would not leave voluntarily. They would not sack themselves. They would leave the sacking to the rulers. They themselves would defend true education regardless.'[155] Indeed, some had been sacked already. As early as 1956, officials of the TLSA had been dismissed from teaching for their opposition to segregated schooling. In 1961, 16 officials, executive members and leading speakers in the organisation had been banned under the Riotous Assemblies or Suppression of Communism Acts and, in February 1962, they had been forced to resign as teachers. Many more were to be dismissed in the years that followed. Prior to 1976, very few reports are to be found of overt student resistance in Coloured and Indian schools. Most of the few protests that were reported were over the detention or dismissal of teachers.[156] For the rest, such resistance as there might have been, occurred behind closed classroom doors.

Conclusion

Without having been constricted by any cult of doctrinaire Marxism, this chapter has been informed by historical materialism understood as an approach to analysing particular social processes through uncovering the conditions on which they rest. The development of black schooling has been traced in relation to South Africa's penetration by colonialism and the rise of a racist industrial capitalism. Educational history has been portrayed as the outcome of the interaction between involved parties within a shifting structural setting which conditioned the constitution and actions of such parties as well as the processes in which they participated. Particular attention has been paid to the attitudes of the different parties concerned with black schooling in relation to their respective social locations and concomitant material interests.

Particular attention has been paid also to the changing manifestations of black people's resistance to schooling *per se* and to particular forms of schooling. Overall, the piece represents an exercise in empirical and conceptual reconnaissance of underexplored terrain. It details important information while indicating analytic avenues for further exploration. It is most tentatively that this chapter is offered as a contribution to the re-interpretation of South African educational history.

FOOTNOTES

1. Du Plessis, J *A History of Christian Missions in South Africa* (London, 1911) pp 29-30.
2. Behr, A L and Macmillan R G *Education in South Africa* (Pretoria, 1966) p 311.
3. Malherbe, E G *Education in South Africa.* Volume I: *1652-1922.* (Cape Town, 1925) p 47.
4. Quoted in Wilson, M and Thompson, L M (eds) *The Oxford History of South Africa.* Volume I: *South Africa to 1870* (London, 1969) p 222.
5. Martinius, M E *A Sketch of the Development of Rural Education (European) in the Cape Colony, 1652-1910* (Grahamstown, 1922), cited in Malherbe, E G (1952) p 29.
6. Malherbe, E G (1925) pp 34-35.
7. Louw, V N 'Education for the Bantu: A South African Dilemma' *Comparative Education Review* 2(1) 1958 p 22.
8. Behr, A L and Macmillan, R G (1966) p 314.
9. *Christian Express* XX (256) 2 November 1891, p 1.
10. Cook, P A W 'Non-European Education' in Hellmann, E (ed) *Handbook of Race Relations in South Africa* (Cape Town, 1949) p 348.
11. Cook, P A W (1949) p 348.
12. Quoted in Rose, B and Tunmer, R *Documents in South African Education* (Johannesburg, 1975) p 207.
13. Cape of Good Hope, Appendix I, Volume III to Votes and Proceedings of Parliament for 1892, Report of the Superintendent-General of Education for the year 1891 (G.9-'92) P 11. Quoted in Rose, B and Tunmer, R (1975) p 211.
14. UG 29-1936, Report of the Interdepartmental Committee on Native Education, 1935-36 p 89 para 464.
15. British Parliamentary Papers, Cape of Good Hope. Further papers relative to the state of the Kaffir Tribes presented to both Houses of Parliament, July 1855. Despatch from the Governor, Sir George Grey, to the Colonial Secretary, dated from Cape Town, 22 November 1854, p 38. Quoted in Rose, B and Tunmer, R (1975) p 204.

16. Quoted in UG 29-1936 p 12 para 25.
17. Quoted in UG 29-1936 p 13 para 26.
18. UG 53-1951 Report of the Commission on Native Education, 1949-51 p 39, para 208.
19. Troup, F *Forbidden Pastures: Education Under Apartheid* (London, 1976) p 9.
20. *Christian Express* XXI (260) 1 March 1892, pp 45-46.
21. Quoted in Majeka, N *The Role of the Missionaries in Conquest* (Cape Town, 1952) p 66.
22. *Christian Express* XXI (260) 1 March 1892, p 46.
23. Quoted in Du Toit, A E *The Earliest South African Documents on the Education and Civilisation of the Bantu* (Pretoria, 1963) p 41.
24. *Kaffir Express* IV (45) 1 June 1874, p 1.
25. Cape of Good Hope, Appendix I to Votes and Proceedings of Parliament for 1869, Report of an Inspection of Schools in the Middle and Eastern Districts by the Superintendent-General of Education during the months of March, April, May and June, 1869 (G. 31-'69) pp 3-6. Quoted in Rose, B and Tunmer, R (1975) p 208.
26. Natal Native Commission, 1881-82, p 11. Quoted in Rose, B and Tunmer, R (1975) p 210.
27. *Kaffir Express* II (26) 1 November 1872, pp 1-2.
28. *Christian Express* X (115) 1 April 1880, p 2.
29. Cape of Good Hope, Third and final report of a commission appointed to enquire into and report upon certain matters connected with the educational system in the Colony, 1892 (G. 3-'92) p 32. Quoted in Rose, B and Tunmer, R (1975) p 216.
30. *Christian Express* X (112) 1 January 1880, p1.
31. G. 3-'92. Quoted in Rose, B and Tunmer, R (1975) p 217.
32. *Christian Express* XXXVI (427) 1 May 1906, p 125.
33. *Christian Express* XIV (165) 1 April 1884, pp 60-61.
34. G. 3-'92. Evidence of G M Theal. Quoted in Rose, B and Tunmer, R (1975) p 214.
35. G. 3-'92. Memorandum by Mr Levey. Quoted in Rose, B and Tunmer, R (1975) p 215.
36. G. 31-'69. Quoted in Rose, B and Tunmer, R (1975) p 208.
37. *Kaffir Express* III (28) 2 January 1873, p 2.
38. *Kaffir Express* III (36) 6 September 1873, p 1.
39. *Kaffir Express* IV (45) 1 June 1874, p 1.
40. South African Native Affairs Commission, 1903-05. Quoted in Rose, B and Tunmer, R (1975) p 223.
41. UG 53-1951 p 34 para 169.
42. Quoted in Rose, B and Tunmer, R (1975) p 206.
43. Rose, B and Tunmer, R (1975) p 207.
44. Cook, P A W (1949) p 351.
45. UG 29-1936 p 19 para 61.

46.   UG 29-1936 p 19 para 64.
47.   Horrell, M, *African Education: Some Origins and Development until 1953.* (Johannesburg, 1963) p 19.
48.   Cook, P A W (1949) p 352.
49.   UG 53-1951 pp 39-40 para 210.
50.   UG 29-1936 p 114 para's 575-576.
51.   *Christian Express* VIII (95) 1 August 1878 pp 1-2.
52.   Quoted in UG 53-1951 p 40 para 212.
53.   Quoted in UG 53-1951 p 40 para 211.
54.   Pells, E G *300 Years of Education in South Africa* (Cape Town, 1956) p 152.
55.   UG 29/1936 p 89 para 465.
56.   *Inkundla ya Bantu* 6 (66) 30 September 1943 p 8.
57.   UG 29-1936 pp 86-87 para 453.
58.   Quoted in UG 53-1951 p 83 para 470.
59.   UG 22-1932. Report, Native Economic Commission, 1930-32 p 12 para 77.
60.   Transvaal Education Department, Report for school year January-December 1903 pp 62-63. Quoted in Rose, B and Tunmer, R (1975) p 220.
61.   Quoted, in translation, in *Inkundla ya Bantu* 7 (92) 18 December 1944 p 3.
62.   UG 53-1951 p 40 para 213.
63.   Le Roy, A E 'Does it Pay to Educate the Native?' *Report of the Sixteenth Annual Meeting of the South African Association for the Advancement of Science, 8-13 July 1918* (Cape Town, 1919) p 18.
64.   UG 29-1936 p 87 para 458.
65.   UG 29-1936 p 88 para 459.
66.   *APO* 17 July 1909.
67.   *Territorial Magazine — Ipepa Ndaba Lezifunda* I (4) 15 July 1938.
68.   *Christian Express* XX (237) 1 April 1890 pp 51-52.
69.   Horrell, M (1963) p 14.
70.   *APO* 19 June 1909.
71.   Hansard 1945 col 4528.
72.   *Inkundla ya Bantu* IX (119) May 1946 p 2.
73.   Transvaal Education Department, Report for school year January-December 1903 pp 62-63. Quoted in Rose, B and Tunmer, R (1975) p220.
74.   G. 9-'92 pp 11-12. Quoted in Rose, B and Tunmer, R (1975) p 212.
75.   Jabavu, D D T *The Black Problem: Papers and Addressess on Various Native Problems* (Lovedale, 1921) p 95.
76.   UG 29-1936 p 92 para 475.
77.   Jabavu, D D T (1921) p 95.
78.   Transvaal Education Department, Report for School year January-December 1903 p 63. Quoted in Rose, B and Tunmer, R (1975) p 220.

79. UG 29-1936 p 90 para 469.
80. *Kaffir Express* 1 (6) 3 March 1871 pp 2-3.
81. Jabavu, D D T (1921) pp 12-13.
82. Pells, E G (1956) p 140.
83. G 31-'69 pp 3-6. Quoted in Rose, B and Tunmer, R (1975) p 208.
84. *Christian Express* XXXVI (427) 1 May 1906 p 125.
85. *Kaffir Express* I (4) 4 January 1871 p 1.
86. UG 22-1932 p 91 para 627.
87. Natal Native Commission, 1881-2 p 11. Quoted in Rose, B and Tunmer, R (1975) p 211.
88. Bowles, S and Gintis, H *Schooling in Capitalist America: Educational Reform and the Contradictions of Economic Life* (New York, 1977) p 159.
89. G. 9-'92 pp 11-12 Quoted in Rose, B and Tunmer, R (1975) pp 211-212.
90. UG 29-1936, p 87 para 453.
91. Pells, E G (1956) p 146.
92. *Christian Express* XVIII (210) 2 January 1888 p 1.
93. *Christian Express* X (115) 1 April 1880 p 2.
94. *Christian Express* XX (248) 2 March 1891 p 1.
95. *Territorial Magazine — Ipepa Ndaba Lezifunda* 1 (4) 15 July 1938.
96. Quoted in Herbstein, D *White Man, We Want to Talk to You* (Harmondsworth, 1978) pp 85-86.
97. *Inkundla ya Bantu* 6 (69) 30 December 1943 p 1.
98. Jabavu, D D T (1921) p 2.
99. Shingler, J D *Education and Political Order in South Africa, 1902-1961* (PhD Thesis, Yale Univeristy) p 54.
100. *Christian Express* LI (610) 1 September 1921 p 146.
101. *Ikundla ya Bantu* 4 (42) September 1941 p 2.
102. *Christian Express* VI (70) 1 July 1876 pp 2-3.
103. *Kaffir Express* IV (40) 6 January 1874 p 7.
104. *Christian Express* XXIV (281) 1 January 1894 p 3.
105. *Ikundla ya Bantu* 8 (102) 30 June 1945 pp 2-3.
106. *Ikundla ya Bantu* 8 (101) 31 May 1945 p 2.
107. *Territorial Magazine — Ipepa Ndaba Nezifunda* I (9) December 1938 pp 6-7.
108. *Ikundla ya Bantu* 3 (28) July 1940 p 2.
109. *South African Outlook* 75 (889) 1 May 1945 p 70.
110. *South African Outlook* 59 (694) 1 March 1929 pp 41-42.
111. *Ikundla ya Bantu* 8 (101) 31 May 1945 p 2.
112. As reproduced in *South African Outlook* 77 (909) 1 January 1947 p 6.
113. As reproduced in *South African Outlook* 77 (909) 1 January 1947 p 13.
114. As reproduced in *South African Outlook* 77 (909) 1 January 1947 p 12.

115. As reproduced in *South African Outlook* 77 (909) 1 January 1947 p 12.

116. *Ikundla ya Bantu* 7 (78) 17 May 1944 p 5.

117. *Ikundla ya Bantu* 7 (80) 17 June 1944 p 3.

118. *Ikundla ya Bantu* 7 (79) 31 May 1944 p 3.

119. *Ikundla ya Bantu* 7 (82) 17 July 1944 p 3.

120. *Territorial Magazine — Ipepa Ndaba Lezifunda* 2 (18) September 1939 p 3.

121. *Ikundla ya Bantu* 6 (71) 31 January 1944 p 3.

122. *Ikundla ya Bantu* 6 (68) 30 November 1943 p 5.

123. *Ikundla ya Bantu* 6 (71) 31 January 1944 p 3.

124. *Ikundla ya Bantu* 7 (80) 17 June 1944 p 3.

125. *Territorial Magazine — Ipepa Ndaba Lezifunda* 2 (18) September 1939 p 3.

126. *Ikundla ya Bantu* IX (119) May 1946 p 2.

127. *South African Outlook* 76 (905) 2 September 1946 p 140.

128. *APO* 3 July 1909.

129. *Ikundla ya Bantu* 2 (18) September 1939 p 3.

130. *Ikundla ya Bantu* 7 (80) 17 June 1944 p 4.

131. *Territorial Magazine — Ipepa Ndaba Lezifunda* 2 (18) September 1939 p 3.

132. *Ikundla ya Bantu* 6 (71) 31 January 1944 p 3.

133. *Ikundla ya Bantu* 7 (80) 17 June 1944 p 3.

134. *Bolshevik* 1 (8) May 1920 p 7.

135. See Lodge, T elsewhere in this volume.

136. *Cape Times* 17 October 1946.

137. Hansard 1959 para 6009.

138. Hansard 1963 para's 2265 and 2272.

139. Verwoerd, H F *Bantu Education: Policy for the Immediate Future* (Pretoria, 1954) p 24.

140. Verwoerd, H F (1954) p 23.

141. Quoted in Feit, E *African Opposition in South Africa: The Failure of Passive Resistance* (Stanford, 1967) pp 150-151.

142. Quoted in Feit, E (1967) p 151.

143. *Drum* July 1953.

144. *Rand Daily Mail* 30 October 1953.

145. See Lodge, T elsewhere in this volume, and Stradling, W '1948-1976: The Background. A Review of the Struggle against BAD-CAD-IAD Schooling' *Educational Journal* XLVIII (3) October-November 1976 pp 5-10.

146. See Feit, E (1967); Karis, T, Carter, G M and Gerhart, G M *From Protest to Challenge: A Documentary History of African Politics in South Africa, 1882-1964.* Volume 3: *Challenge and Violence, 1953-1964* (Stanford, 1977) and Lodge, elsewhere in this volume, as well as Tillema, R G 'Apartheid in South African Education' (PhD Thesis,

University of Wisconsin, 1974) and Hirson, B *Year of Fire, Year of Ash. The Soweto Revolt: Roots of a Revolution?* (London, 1979).

147. *Drum* July 1957.
148. Ntantala, P 'The Abyss of Bantu Education' *Africa South* 4 (2) January-March 1960 p 45.
149. Ntantala, P (1960) p 44.
150. Horrell, M *A Decade of Bantu Education* (Johannesburg, 1964) p 86.
151. Horrell, M (1964) p 87.
152. Horrell, M (1964) pp 87-89.
153. RR 19/64. Report on Disturbances in African Schools by the Regional Secretary (Patrick McKenzie), SAIRR (Southern Transvaal Region).
154. RR 19/64; Horrell, M (1964) pp 86-89; SAIRR, *Survey of Race Relations in South Africa* (1959-60, 1961, 1962, 1963); *Cape Times* 1 June 1960, 9 June 1960, 18 August 1960, 31 August 1960; *Bantu World* 13 June 1961; *Contact* 1 June 1961, 29 June 1961, 27 July 1961, 24 August 1961, 21 September 1961, 26 July 1962.
155. Stradling,W (1976) p 7.
156. Eg *Argus* 24 July 1963, 4 April 1968, 30 May 1968, 3 June 1968, 4 June 1968.

Charles T Loram and the American Model for African Education in South Africa*

R Hunt Davis Jr

Between the two world wars, a principal theme underlying African education was a belief that the black school system of the American South constituted a suitable model for Africa. This belief was prevalent throughout the continent (especially in the English-ruled colonies and Liberia) but nowhere was it stronger than in South Africa, due mainly to its unique position of having a large settler population that was steadily augmenting its political sovereignty. White South Africans could readily view their position as akin to that of white southerners in the United States, while Africans could easily draw parallels between their situation and that of black Americans. Certain individuals, institutions and organisations in the United States believed that American answers to problems of race relations (which encompassed education) were applicable to other countries. They were thus ready to aid South Africans in transferring and adapting a generalised American model of black schooling.

In fact, more than one model of black American education existed for South Africans. Africans saw a progressive education system that emphasised black initiative and educational advancement. For example, while only 25 percent of their own children attended school and 88 percent of their community were illiterate, 70 percent of black American children of school age were in school, and black illiteracy had dropped from 90 percent in 1866 to 23 percent in 1926.[1] White South Africans (those not totally

* This article was originally presented as a paper at the Eighteenth Annual Meeting of the African Studies Association in San Francisco, 29 October — 1 November 1975. Research was made possible by a Younger Humanist Fellowship from the National Endowment for the Humanities, a Grant-in-Aid from the American Council of Learned Societies and a Summer Grant from the University of Florida Humanities Council.

opposed to some form of schooling for Africans) saw a system that seemed to train blacks sufficiently for life in a modern society yet served to limit any challenge they might pose to white control. As one white visitor to the United States noted, 'the education of American blacks was aimed at helping them . . . to attain better methods for doing the daily tasks in respect of which intelligent guidance can greatly improve their lot and simplifying the whole of the . . . (Negro) problem.'[2] Charles T Loram was the principal figure amongst those who wanted to educate Africans within a framework tailored to the needs of the colonial system. He found in the United States educational theories and practices that provided guidance for developing schools which would inculcate African subservience to and acceptance of white authority.

Before examining Loram's links with American education, his educational philosophy and his involvement in the construction and utilisation of an American model for African education in South Africa, it will be helpful to study briefly his views on the African's proper place within South African society. Loram was, in the South Africa of the 1920s and 1930s, a liberal. White liberals constituted a generally optimistic minority who believed that a policy of gradualism would win over the white majority to toleration for the principle and practice of equal rights for all 'civilised' persons.[3] Loram's principal concern was with African welfare. As he said, 'Let me do what good I can for the black folk . . . .'[4] Doing good on behalf of Africans also meant opposing the repression they experienced, but not the system that imposed the repression.[5] The extent and the limitations of his liberalism are readily apparent in Loram's criticism of Minister of Justice Oswald Pirow's unprovoked use of force against Durban Africans in 1929:

> The weakness of his whole position and that of the Govt. [sic] and white man generally is that he will put the blame on the Communists while the real reasons for discontent are (i) the very real grievances under which Natives live (ii) the 'headiness' which follows as a result of education.[6]

In short, Africans suffered from genuine social and economic disabilities, but were as yet immature in their stage of civilisation. They were in the process of development, but remained a subject race in need of betterment. Therefore, whites had to decide what was best for Africans.[7] The task of liberals was to pressure the authorities into making the correct decisions on matters affecting African welfare. Loram's ideal was 'That there should be a reasonable outlet for the educated Native to earn an honest living, to dwell under decent conditions and to have some voice in the management of his affairs'.[8]

Links with the United States

Loram was born in South Africa in 1879. He began his career as an educator as an assistant inspector of schools in Natal after returning home from Cambridge University in 1906. The Natal education department was mainly concerned with white schools, but there was also a steady growth of African schools under the department's supervision. Loram's work brought him into direct contact with the problems of African education, in which he became increasingly interested. African education was then almost synonymous with missionary education, and the most influential missionary group in terms of education was the American Zulu Mission.[9] Loram was thus able to observe educational methods that drew heavily on the American experience with black schooling in the southern states. Maurice S Evans, then Natal's leading so-called 'expert on the Native problem', also influenced Loram to look toward the United States for answers to problems of African education. In 1912 Evans had travelled extensively in the American South to study its race relations from the perspective of a resident of another country with similar problems. The result was a book entitled *Black and White in the Southern States (1915)*, which in its concluding chapter specified the lessons that South Africa could learn from the United States.[10] By 1914 when Loram took leave of absence to pursue graduate work at Teachers' College, Columbia University, he had already apparently developed an interest in studying the education of black Americans.

Loram went to Teachers' College on a scholarship from the Union government to study educational administration; much of his first year's study was taken up with courses in this field. From the start, however, he was interested in studying black schooling to learn which of its aspects were applicable to South Africa. Within a few weeks of his arrival, he was writing to Booker T Washington that his chief interest was in African education and that he was anxious to observe what Washington had accomplished at Tuskegee.[11] A few months later he wrote again: 'I am taking advantage of my stay in this country to attempt to convince my fellow whites in South Africa that the example of the United States proves that with proper training and eduation the negro can be made a valuable asset to any country'.[12] Loram later visited Tuskegee, in addition to Hampton Institute, Virginia Union University, and a number of smaller black schools in Alabama,

Maryland, and Virginia in connection with his doctoral research.[13] The ensuing dissertation, 'The Education of the South African Native' (later published as a book with the same title), posited the relevance of black American education to African education in South Africa as one of its basic premises.

Shortly after his return to his position with the Natal education department, Loram won promotion to the newly created post of chief inspector of native education. Two years later, in 1920, he took indefinite leave of absence to accept a position on the newly formed Union Native Affairs Commission. He served with the Commission until 1930, adding to his stature as South Africa's leading white authority on African education. This led to his becoming a member of the first Phelps-Stokes African Education Commission when it visited South Africa and Rhodesia in 1921. His membership of the commission re-established his links with the United States — it also pulled him into the orbit of the Phelps-Stokes Fund, and later the Carnegie Corporation. Both organisations had major philanthropic interests in Africa, the former being especially involved in education. Several years later, Loram was to write Anson Phelps-Stokes (the Fund's president) that his contact with Thomas Jesse Jones, the Fund's educational director and head of the education commission, had altered the course of his life.[14] Certainly his ties with the Fund projected him into the international arena. For instance, he served as a member of the second Phelps-Stokes African Education Commission in 1924, played a leading role in the 1926 Le Zoute (Belgium) Conference on the Christian Mission in Africa, was a visiting professor at the 1929 summer session of Teachers' College and was one of the leading candidates in 1929 for the principalship of Hampton. Loram also became the chief adviser on African affairs to the Phelps-Stokes Fund and the Carnegie Corporation. These foundations in turn placed great value on his 'unusual ability and devotion to native welfare'.[15] In short, Loram joined Jones and J H Oldham of the International Missionary Council to form a triumvirate on education in Africa.[16]

Early in 1930, Prime Minister Hertzog dropped Loram from the Native Affairs Commission after he had served on it since its inception in 1920. He then returned to the Natal education department as superintendent of education. For a Nationalist government that had won the 1929 election outright (after having shared power with the Labour Party since 1924) on the basis of an alleged 'Black Peril', Loram's interest in expanding African education and his concern for African social and economic conditions placed him increasingly at odds with the leadership of the ruling party. Furthermore, Nationalist politicians viewed his position as a representative of the Phelps-Stokes Fund and the Carnegie Corporation with distrust and misgiving.[17] Loram stated his own views of his dismissal in a letter to Keppel of the Carnegie Corporation:

> It is enough to say that I am the victim of a political intrigue and that the change is due 1/2 to dislike of my opposition to the Nationalist Govt's Native proposals, 1/4 to the desire of Natal to get me to clear up its educational mess and 1/4 to my association with overseas (American) bodies which are 'interfering' (save the mark!) in what our bucolic Govt. regards as domestic matters.[18]

Events in South Africa were making Loram increasingly frustrated, as he saw what he regarded as his constructive role in influencing so-called native affairs coming to an end. He had also become a 'philo-American' and was preparing to emigrate to the United States where Yale had offered him a post.[19]

Loram joined the Yale faculty in 1931 as Sterling Professor of Education and remained there until his death in 1940. By the time he moved to New Haven, he had come to believe he could accomplish more on behalf of Africans from the United States than by continuing to live and work in South Africa. Yale offered Loram the opportunity to train officials, missionaries and Africans for educational work among 'retarded peoples'.[20] Although his interests broadened to include programmes such as Yale-in-China conferences on 'Education in Pacific Areas' and 'The North American Indian Today', his primary interests lay with African and American race relations. Loram's teaching emphasised education in Africa and the American South, as did his work in organising the 1935 Jeanes Conference in Salisbury, Southern Rhodesia, and the 1937 seminar on 'The Education of the American Negroes and the African Natives'.[21] He also continued his work with the Phelps-Stokes Fund and the Carnegie Corporation.

Educational Philosophy

Loram's close ties with the United States infused his educational philosophy with a large component of American-derived ideas. However, much of his thinking on African education directly related to his membership of a settler minority. Furthermore, there had been all along a cross-fertilisation of educational theory and practice for black Americans and the subject peoples of the British Empire. Thus, although the ideas that Loram espoused on African education were most prominent in the United States, they also had roots in South African and British colonial thought and practice.

Two premises underlay Loram's thinking on African education. The first, which has already been discussed, was that whites would continue to rule and Africans would continue to be ruled. Africans could at best aspire to become 'junior partners in the firm'.[22] While in his later years he saw a need to place Africans in positions of real responsibility in their own affairs, this did not represent an alteration of his views regarding the majority.[23] The second basic premise was that Africans were a rural people and that their future lay in the countryside. This premise rested on several assumptions: agriculture was a natural way of life for Africans; social adjustment or the avoidance of race friction between blacks and whites demanded that most Africans remain in the rural areas; South Africa's future development depended heavily on agriculture, and Africans could best contribute to the country's welfare through improved farming of their own smallholdings or by working on white-owned farms; cities were largely the preserve of whites; urban life debased and demoralised the vast majority of Africans who migrated to town; white dependence on and contact with Africans could result in social degradation for whites.[24] African education, therefore, should be geared toward entrenching white control and a rural-oriented way of life.

These premises were the base for three principal themes that ran through Loram's philosophy of African education: adaptation, 'education for life', and the relevance of black American education to African schooling.[25] The third theme needs no additional elaboration except to note that the type of black education that Loram admired in the United States stemmed from premises similar to his own. It also provided the model of a fully developed application of the two central concepts of adaptation and 'education for life'.[26] What then constituted these two closely related concepts?

The fundamental problem with the existing system of African education was, asserted Loram and like-minded critics, that it was 'very much a bookish affair and almost entirely tinged with the white man's outlook'.[27] It was too academic and too little related to the everyday needs of the African people.[28] Schools for Africans should adapt to their needs, which Loram defined according to two sets of criteria. One set was related to the needs of supposedly backward, primitive, and retarded peoples who were just emerging from barbarism — in contrast to Europeans who (so the claim went) were the heirs to two thousand years of civilisation.[29] Under such circumstances, Loram asked rhetorically: 'Which is really more important in the African villages today — practical hygiene or the ability to read? Elementary agriculture or geography? Wise recreation or arithmetic?'[30] The second set of criteria concerned the needs of Africans as determined by South Africa's ruling white minority. While whites also defined the first set of criteria, it differed from the second in that the needs of Africans and not those of Europeans supposedly formed the deciding factor. According to the second set, literary instruction produced white collar workers, but whites had reserved this occupational category for themselves. Africans were to perform manual and agricultural work. If race enmity were to be avoided, their schooling had to be adapted to these ends.[31]

Adaptation was clearly linked to the second theme, that of 'education for life'. Adapted education would prepare Africans for the life they were to lead. Loram assumed that it was natural for whites to decide the type of life that blacks were to lead; but again, two somewhat contradictory views emerge from what Loram had to say. On the one hand, he posited the image of educated Africans returning to their own land, drawn there by reasonably secure land tenure and the promise of earning a progressive livelihood in agriculture through their own industry and enterprise. Such a mode of existence had the dual advantage of being in keeping with the Africans' supposed nature and view of life and of not thrusting them into competition with Europeans.[32] Although small-scale African farming would contribute indirectly to European welfare through its contribution to the overall South African economy, Africans would be the chief beneficiaries. Not so with the alternative view which held that Africans were more clearly to serve European interests. As Loram noted in 1921, 90 percent of the students leaving African schools would earn their living with their hands, and the majority of male pupils would either work their own land or that of a European employer.[33]

Adaptation and 'education for life' dictated an African curriculum 'based upon the particular instincts, capacities, interests, past and present experiences, and probable future of the pupils for whom . . . (it was) intended'.[34] As a member of the Native Affairs Commission, Loram outlined an African education policy that incorporated these objectives: the principal aim should be to make elementary education accessible to every African child; the emphasis at the elementary level should be on 'character training, habits of industry, use and appreciation of the vernacular, health and hygiene, agriculture and other practical subjects'; a limited number of students should attend approved teacher training institutions; men should train as farm demonstrators and women as home demonstrators at special schools set up for this purpose; a

Mission school. *Photograph: Johannesburg Public Library.*

St Matthew's College, Eastern Cape, in 1966. This was one of the prestige schools. *Photograph: Johannesburg Public Library.*

Craft training at Lovedale, 1930s.
Photograph: Johannesburg Public Library.

Training woodwork teachers for 'Native' schools. Pax Training Institution near
Pietersburg, Northern Transvaal. *Photograph: Johannesburg Public Library.*

limited number of African high schools should (a) offer vocational training for positions such as that of secretary to a chief or civil service in the African reserves, and (b) prepare students for admission to the South African Native College at Fort Hare (n.d.). While chief inspector of native education in Natal, Loram had already revised the syllabuses of that province's African secondary schools. This included dropping subjects such as algebra, geometry, and translation, since they supposedly had no definite or practical bearing on African life; adding physiology, hygiene, nature study and similar subjects, which had a practical and demonstrable value; emphasising agriculture and manual work through courses such as agriculture, woodworking, needlework, and domestic science.[35] Loram considered college level training necessary for a few students who would contribute to the uplift of their own people: 'The South African Native question must, to a large extent, be solved by the Natives themselves through the efforts of their leaders.' Fort Hare was to provide this training, though Loram wished to reverse its emphasis on an academic curriculum to the exclusion of other and more practical aspects. Commercial and industrial training would have the further merit of attracting wider European support. To those whites who opposed educating Africans at the college level, Loram warned that if South Africa did not provide such training at home, where it could be kept under proper supervision, Africans would go overseas to attend college. They would thus be outside the control of the South African educational system.[36]

Loram's philosophy of African education, from its full formulation while he was a graduate student at Teachers' College until his death in 1940, remained fairly consistent in its acceptance of the two basic premises of continued white rule and a rural orientation for Africans and its stress upon the three themes of adaptation, education for life, and the relevance to Africa of black schooling in the American South. The appearance in 1926 of Thomas Jesse Jones's *Four Essentials of Education*, however, provided Loram with a new framework for expressing his philosophy.[37] The four essentials (sometimes referred to as fundamentals or simples) were sanitation and health, agriculture and simple industy, the decencies and safeties of the home, and healthful recreation. Loram praised the four essentials for what they pinpointed as vital in African education:

> These essentials . . . seem so obvious that one might think they have always been stressed in the curricula of Native Schools, but a weekly time table which gives two hours for geography but only half an hour to hygiene, which has no periods for gardening or agriculture and

makes no provision other than needlework for the special needs of
the girls, is not adequately helping the puplils to adapt themselves to
their environment.[38]

Futhermore, the four essentials — along with two which Loram
sometimes added, religion and relationships towards other groups
— formed the basis for implementing the supposedly dominant
new education trend among so-called indigenous peoples. This
trend consisted of combining valuable aspects of traditional
cultures with those of the intrusive Western culture in order to
develop schooling adapted to the life of indigenous (ie non-Western)
peoples. The core of the instructional process would then rest on
these four or six essentials. Their nature made the school's social
significance its most prominent aspect.[39] In short, Jones's four
essentials led Loram to promote the school as an instrument for
social transformation in terms of community development. Not
only was education to be adapted to the special needs of Africans,
but its purpose was also to link schoolwork with the home
activities of the pupils and their families.[40] Community-centred
schools, in turn, rested on the four essentials.

An American-Derived Model for African Education

'The point of attack on the evils of African life' was to be the
village schools scattered throughout the rual areas. Education
would become a community matter with the school focusing on
the everyday problems of villagers: health, family life, agriculture,
industry, recreation, and religion.[41] Loram turned to the United
States for a model to accomplish these ends. He found one in the
system of Jeanes visiting teachers. With this discovery, he became
an avid advocate of 'Jeanesising' African education — not only in
South Africa, but throughout much of the continent.[42]

The Jeanes scheme (named after Anna T Jeanes, who had
donated the money to pay for the teachers) originated in Virginia
in 1908 with the employment of Virginia E Randolph as a supervising teacher for rural schools. Her task was to put new life into
these schools by helping the teachers augment the traditional
three Rs with so-called practical work. Generally, rural teachers
had not received training in 'industrial' work, nor were funds
available to provide such training for the thousands of teachers in
the small rural black schools of the South. Private philanthropy,
however, could support visiting teachers who would have the
training necessary to aid local teachers in making their schools
centres for community betterment. The Jeanes teachers also hàd

to change the attitude of both teachers and parents. Instead of the school being thought of in terms of books and symbols, it was crucial to have the local community view education in terms of successful living and the performance of everyday tasks in the home and on the farm.[43]

By the mid-1920s, the Jeanes teachers were increasingly becoming supervisors of teaching, as the condition of rural black communities began to change and as federally-funded extension workers became active in rural communities. Loram viewed the earlier period of Jeanes work as more closely approximating South African conditions. He saw the needed functions of supervisors in African schools as being the same as those reported for the first Jeanes teachers:

> The Jeanes teacher teaches in the various rural schools simple industrial work, helps the regular teacher with her work, raises money for the extension of school terms, the erection of new buildings, the improvement of buildings and grounds, the supplementing of teachers' salaries and the purchase of school materials, helps the women of the community to can and sew, holds teachers' meetings, distributes supplies, and in general does anything to promote the welfare of the Negro people and especially of the Negro schools of the county in which she works.[44]

Despite the basic similarities in functions, however, there were several features that differentiated the proposed Jeanes teachers in South Africa from those in the southern United States. For one thing, although the Jeanes teachers in the South were under contract to local school boards, their salaries came from the Jeanes Fund. In South Africa, the provincial governments paid the salaries of all the supervisory personnel in education. Secondly, the American Jeanes teachers were all black women, as were most of the teachers in the rural schools. In South Africa, on the other hand, most of the African teachers were males. Loram thought that it would be a breach of etiquette for women to assume positions of authority over men — most African Jeanes teachers would have to be men. Finally, in the United States it had not been necessary to establish specialised institutions for training Jeanes teachers: a sufficient pool of experienced teachers existed. This was not the case in either South Africa or the British colonies. An adequate supply of African Jeanes teachers demanded specialised training institutions.[45]

In 1926, Loram proposed twenty-one places in British-controlled Africa, the Belgian Congo, and Portuguese east and west Africa which seemed feasible locations for Jeanes training institutions.

One was already in existence in Kabete, Kenya. Four would be in the Union of South Africa, located at Lovedale (Cape Province), Amanzimtoti (Natal), Nongoma (Zululand), and Lemana (Transvaal). Additional southern African sites included two in Southern Rhodesia, and one each in South West Africa, Basutoland, Bechuanaland, Angola, Mozambique, Nyasaland and Northern Rhodesia. All five locations where Loram thought Jeanes programmes could begin within one year were in southern Africa, two within the Union. In most instances, established institutions would simply add Jeanes training to their existing educational programmes.[46] Loram thought that he had found 'the ideal school and the model for African education' along Jeanes lines at Penn School, South California.[47] He visited the island school in October 1926: 'I had not been there very long before I saw that this was the school which, more than any other I had seen, exemplified my ideal for African education, with the school as the centre and chief factor of village development.'[48]

Penn School became Loram's specific model for Jeanesising African education, because its curriculum embodied the four essentials of Thomas Jesse Jones.[49] He viewed it both as a potential training centre for black and white educators from Africa and as the prototype which, with the necessary modifications, could be reproduced at African institutions. With the backing of the Phelps-Stokes Fund and the Carnegie Corporation, Loram set out to implement a system of Jeanes visiting teachers in southern Africa. His specific use of Penn consisted of sending in 1927 two experienced Natal African women teachers to be on its staff for a year to learn Penn's methods; attempting to initiate Jeanes training programmes at selected African educational institutions in South Africa and in neighbouring countries; having white educators, government officials, missionaries, and later his graduate students at Yale (including some Africans) visit Penn to observe its educational techniques; distributing literature about Penn to persons (mostly whites) involved in African education; placing articles about the school in South African newspapers and periodicals. These ventures had a limited and uneven success. The two women became dissatisfied with Penn and left for study first at Tuskegee and then elsewhere in the United States, breaking with Loram in the process. Despite the availability of £5 000 from the Carnegie Corporation for a Jeanes school in South Africa, Loram was unable to raise matching funds from the Union government or the provincial administrations, so there never was a Jeanes training centre in South Africa. In 1929 and 1930, however, new Jeanes schools did begin in Southern Rhodesia (two schools), Northern Rhodesia (also two) and Nyasaland; schools later developed in Portuguese East Africa and Zanzibar. The distribution of literature served to acquaint leaders in African education and other concerned officials with Penn School, as did the visits to the school itself. As a result, the Penn approach to education became fashionable within African education circles in southern and east Africa.[50]

Loram's greatest success with the Jeanes concept (especially within South Africa) lay in fostering its approval among African educators, particularly among whites. Two other programmes (in addition to the distribution of literature and visits to Penn) contributed to spreading the Jeanes idea. The first was a set of three Jeanes Vocation Courses that Loram conducted in South Africa in 1928, 1930 and 1931, with funding support from the Carnegie Corporation. Loram regarded those attending the courses as the cream of the African school teaching force. The 1928 course, for instance, enrolled forty whites, including one superintendent of education, and seventy-nine Africans from all the South African provinces except the Cape, the High Commission Territories, and Rhodesia.[51] The courses actively promoted the educational ideas of Thomas Jesse Jones and the example of the Jeanes visiting teachers in the United States:

> The chief point emphasised in the lectures was the significance of the school as a social centre for the development of the Native peoples. This is of permanent importance in Native education where the school is often the only sign of civilisation in the whole district. In these lectures, the school was not regarded merely as a place where Native children were instructed for so many hours a day, but also as the centre of the spiritual, mental, physical, and material welfare of the pupils.[52]

The second programme was the Inter-Territorial Jeanes Conference held in Salisbury, Southern Rhodesia, from 27 May to 7 June 1935. Its purpose was to evaluate the progress of the Jeanes experiment in Kenya and in the Rhodesias and Nyasaland. Special problems, such as the language medium of instruction, educational financing, and planning for the future direction of African schooling, were also on the agenda.[53] Those who attended included a large number of white educators and missionaries from southern and east Africa and Jeanes teachers from Southern Rhodesia. Aside from a principal of a Bechuanaland training institution and two teachers from Northern Rhodesia, no Africans from outside Southern Rhodesia attended.[54] Community work, teacher training, the model African village and its activities, religious education, and recreation were among the topics of discussion. There were also visits to the nearby Domboshawa Jeanes school and the Salisbury

African location, and the governor hosted an unsegregated reception. In general, the participants convinced each other of the utility of their work.[55] Loram left the conference convinced that 'the experimental stage has been passed and that missionaries and governments alike are "sold" on the Jeanes ideas'.[56] His decade-long effort had not resulted in Jeanes schools in South Africa or the High Commission Territories, but several were thriving to the north. Furthermore, a large number of educators espoused the Jeanes concept.

An Assessment

Charles T Loram's efforts at utilising an American-derived model of black education for African schools in South Africa and elsewhere on the continent were important for several reasons.[57] For one thing, they demonstrated the strong appeal that American educational theories and practices had in Africa. Nor was this appeal limited simply to black education. Loram, for instance, had originally gone to Teachers' College to study education administration and two of his fellow students were Afrikaners named Marquard and De Villiers.[58] American theories and practices had the greatest significance in black education. Loram's reputation as the leading authority on African education was indicative of the far-reaching impact of the American example.[59] In an era when whites controlled the education of Africans and therefore made the crucial policy decisions, Loram's espousal of American solutions for the issues facing African education carried considerable influence over a large area of the continent. In turn, the support that the philanthropic foundations and leading American educators provided Loram testified to the interest in the United States in exporting American thinking on black education to Africa. Secondly, the particular American model that Loram and others of like mind selected is of importance. Black education in the United States was not a monolith, despite efforts to make it so, eg the 1913-1916 survey of Negro education financed by the Phelps-Stokes Fund.[60] Howard, Fisk and other universities offered black Americans advanced academic and professional training. Loram believed, however, that 'the need for such institutions has not yet made itself felt in South Africa'. He further asserted that 'we should take cognisance of the danger (so apparent in India and Egypt) of educating any number of individuals beyond the requirements of their race.' Nor, except for the small South African Native College at Fort Hare, was training needed even at the level offered by Hampton and Tuskegee.[61]

Instead, institutions along the simple lines of Penn School would adequately fill most of the needs for some form of advanced training among Africans. All that the mass of Africans required was an elementary education geared to everyday needs. Jeanes visiting teachers would meet this need.

Loram's choice of an American model reflected his views (and the views of others in the United States and South Africa) about the Africans' proper position in society. 'I have always been a segregationist', he wrote a colleague in 1924.[62] The education of Africans was for Loram not an end in itself, but a means to maintain a segregated society. A lack of schools would create discontent among Africans and threaten the status quo, but so would an education that raised African expectations beyond a certain level. Schools, then, were key weapons in the 'battle of race adjustment' that was taking place in South Africa.[63] Racial strife was against the best interests of the white community in South Africa and of the colonial governments to the north. Loram spoke of going round with an oil can and reducing race friction wherever he could. Schools run along Penn/Jeanes lines constituted part of the oil that would reduce the friction and thus make the white minority in South Africa more secure. Africans would supposedly be satisfied, for their leaders would be involved in social service to their own people and the masses could see improvements in the conditions of their everyday life; whites, if they understood the purpose behind such schooling, would not need to fear an African challenge to their continued domination. This form of education also supposedly supplied whites with the type of labour they needed.

From Loram's perspective, both blacks and whites were the beneficiaries of an American-derived education. His concern with Africans' welfare was sincere. He truly believed that he was a 'friend of the Native' — but to paraphrase W E B Du Bois's assessment of the Phelps-Stokes Fund,[65] Loram found it much easier to work for the African than with him. The reason was that Loram was working on behalf of Africans primarily in the interest of whites, and he found an American model of education for Africans well-suited to his purposes.

FOOTNOTES

1. Huss, B *Agricultural Economics among American Negroes* (n.p. 1931) p 2.
2. Holloway, J E *American Negroes and South African Bantu* (Pretoria,

Carnegie Corporation Visitors' Grants Committee, 1933) p 16.

3. Robertson, J *Liberalism in South Africa, 1948-1963* (Oxford, 1971) pp 6-7. Liberalism was closely associated with the Cape, and Cape Liberalism has served to define liberalism in South Africa a as whole. Recent studies such as Lewsen, P 'The Cape Liberal Tradition — Myth or Reality?' *RACE* 13 July 1971 pp 65-80; *John X Merriman: Paradoxical South African Statesman* (Johannesburg 1982); and Trapido, S 'Liberalism in the Cape in the 19th and 20th Centuries' in *The Societies of Southern Africa in the 19th and 20th Centuries* 4 (London ICS, 1974) have provided a better understanding of the nature of liberalism in the Cape. Loram's Natal origins would suggest a somewhat different background for his liberal beliefs, but the necessary research has not been done on the elements of liberalism outside the Cape that contributed to South African liberalism in the period after Union.

4. Carnegie Corporation of New York Files, New York (hereafter cited as CCNY), Loram to Keppel, 24 October 1928: Folder Loram 1927-1928 (F P Keppel was the president of the corporation).

5. For example, Loram thought that it was a grave mistake for the Joint Council movement (with which he was intimately connected) to become involved in political matters (CCNY, Loram to Keppel, 8 February 1929: Folder Loram 1929).

6. CCNY, Loram to Keppel, 19 November 1929: Folder Loram 1929.

7. CCNY, Loram to Keppel, 29 May 1928: Folder Loram 1927-1928; Loram, C T 'Address . . . on the Occasion of a Dinner given in his honour by the Phelps-Stokes Fund' (New York, Phelps-Stokes Fund, 1926) p 3.

8. Loram, C T 'The Phelps-Stokes Education Commission in South Africa' *International Review of Missions* 10 (October 1921) p 505. For an elaboration of the nature of Loram's liberalism see Heyman, R D 'C T Loram: A South African Liberal in Race Relations' *International Journal of African Historical Studies* 5 (1) 1972 pp 41-50.

9. Province of Natal, Department of Education *Report of the Superintendent of Education for the Year 1914* (Pietermarizburg, 1915) notes that all but one of the African schools in Natal belonged to the missionary societies. For the educational work of the American Zulu Mission, which was part of the American Board of Commissioners for Foreign Missions, see Du Plessis, J *A History of Christian Missions in South Africa* (London, 1911) pp 304-305 and Marks, S 'The Ambiguities of Dependence: John L Dube of Natal' JSAS 1 (1972) pp 162-80.

10. For Loram's indebtedness to Evans, see Loram, C T *The Education of the South African Native* (London, 1917) p XII.

11. Booker T Washington Papers, MSS Division, Library of Congress, Washington, D.C. (hereafter referred to as BTW), Loram to Washington, 28 September 1914; Box 508.

12. BTW, Loram to Washington, 27 December 1914; Box 523.

13. Loram C T (1917) p XI; Loram visited Tuskegee in August, 1915, but its principal was absent at that time; BTW, Loram to Emmet J Scott, 22 August 1915; Box 532.

14. Anson Phelps-Stokes Family Papers, Sterling Memorial Library, Yale University, New Haven, Conn. (hereafter cited as APS) Loram to Stokes, 15 November 1926; Box 31, Folder 510.

15. APS, Jones to Stokes, 18 April 1924; Box 27, Folder 510; for fuller details on Loram's relationship with the Phelps-Stokes Fund, see Berman, E H 'Education in Africa and America: A History of the Phelps-Stokes Fund, 1911 — 1945' (Ed.D. dissertation, Columbia University 1970) pp 230-259; for his connection with the Carnergie Corporation, see Heyman, R D 'The Role of the Carnegie Corporation in African Education, 1925 — 1960' (Ed.D. dissertation, Columbia University 1970) pp 91-118.

16. King, K J *Pan Africanism and Education: A study of Race Philanthropy and Education in the Southern States of America and East Africa* (Oxford 1971) p 52.

17. Ilcyman, R D (1972) pp 44-46.

18. CCNY, 6 January 1930: Folder Loram '30.

19. APS, Loram to Stokes, 5 August 1939 and 22 May 1932; Box 75, Folders: 1236-37.

20. APS, Loram to Stokes, 4 March 1931; Box 75, Folder 1236.

21. For Loram's work at Yale, see reports of the Department of Race Relations for 1938 and 1939. (CCNY: Primitive Peoples, Education of . . . through 1939); announcement of Yale University, Fourth Summer Seminar in Education, 1934. (APS: Box 75, Folder 1238). A programme for the Jeanes Conference and a list of those invited to participate in CCNY (Folder: Jeanes Conference); and outline for the 1937 seminar, jointly sponsored by Yale, the University of North Carolina, and Hampton Institute, can be found in CCNY (Folder: North Carolina, University of: Seminar on Education and Race Relations).

22. APS, Stokes to Keppel, 21 June 1928; Box 28, Folder 465. Stokes was referring to an address that Loram had delivered which contained this phrase. He noted that 'It is most encouraging to find that the *Natal Witness* commending so highly his idea of the Native African as a 'junior partner' in the firm' [sic] .

23. APS, 'The Loram News No. 6', Summer 1936; Box 75, Folder 1238.

24. Loram, C T (1917) pp 5-17, 234-38; (1921) pp 502-3; (1926) pp 6-7; 'Education in the Union'. (CT Loram Papers Typescript of paper. 1930(b); Box 1, Folder 26).

25. King, K J (1971) pp 252-59 lists these as three of the major themes in African and Afro-American education during the half century after 1881.

26. Loram, C T 'The Education of Indigenous Peoples' (C T Loram Papers, Sterling Memorial Library, Yale University New Haven, Conn., Type-

script of paper (1931) Box 1, Folder 28) p 7, notes how 'the stimulating experimental pedagogy of the United States and its remarkable success in the development of education among the Negroes' had struck the 'keynote of the adaptation of education to meet the needs of the people to be taught'.

27.   Loram, C T, 'Native Education in South Africa: The Community Outlook' (CCNY files, Typescript report (1930(a)) Folder: Loram 1930.

28.   APS, 'The Loram News No 6'.

29.   Loram, C T (1917) p 74. Terms such as 'backward', 'primitive' and 'retarded' in reference to Africans and their culture appear throughout Loram's writings.

30.   Loram, C T 'A National System of Native Education in South Africa' *SAJS* 26 (Dec. 1929) p 7.

31.   Loram, C T (1917) p 125 (1930(b)).

32.   Loram, C T (1917) pp 234-38.

33.   Loram, C T (1921) pp 502-503.

34.   Loram, C T (1917) p 93.

35.   Province of Natal, *Report of the Superintendent of Education for the Year 1918* (Pietermaritzburg, 1919) p 46.

36.   Loram, C T (1917) pp 296-312.

37.   Loram and Jones spent considerable time together in 1926.

38.   Loram, C T (1929).

39.   Loram, C T (1930).

40.   Loram, C T (1930(a)).

41.   Loram, C T (1926) p 7; APS 'The Loram News No 6'.

42.   See King, K J (1971) pp 150-76 for fuller discussion of efforts to transform African schools along Jeanes lines.

43.   Davis, J *The Jeanes Visiting Teachers* (New York: Carnegie Corporation 1936); Loram, C T 'The Jeanes Teachers in the United States' (C T Loram Papers. Typescript of paper 1933; Box 1 Folder 38).

44.   Loram, C T (1933) p 5.

45.   Loram, C T (1933) pp 5-7; (1926) pp 7-8.

46.   Loram, C T (1926) p 8.

47.   Loram, C T (1926) p 4.

48.   Loram, C T *Adaptation of the Penn School Methods to Education in South Africa* (New York, Phelps-Stokes Fund, 1927) p 3. Loram had visited the US in 1926 with the specific intent of returning to Africa 'with something very concrete to do in the matter of agricultural development, training Jeanes supervisors, medical provision and the establishment of interracial groups, with the financial support they need' (APS, Loram to Stokes, 23 July 1926; Box 31, Folder 510).

49.   Jones wrote to Rossa B Cooley, principal of Penn School, that her book *Homes of the Freed* ran parallel to his own *Four Essentials of Education*. 'You have put in terms of life what I have been compelled

to put in words or principles'. (Penn School Papers, Jones to Cooley, 22 December 1926; Box, 5 Folder 44).

50. For further details, see Davis, R Hunt Jr., Davis R H 'Producing the 'Good African' South Carolina's Penn School as a guide to African Education in South Africa', in Mugomba A T and Nyaggah, (eds) *Independence without Freedom: The Political Economy of Colonial Education in Southern Africa* (Santa Barbara, 1980) pp 83-112.

51. CCNY, Loram to Keppel and Bertram, 3 July 1928; Folder: Loram 1928 − 1928.

52. Loram, C T (1930(a)) p 3; see also Loram to Dear Sir/Madam, n d: Folder: Loram 1930.

53. CCNY, Loram to Keppel, 10 March 1933; Folder: Jeanes Conference. For further information, see Loram to Keppel, 11 October 1932 (CC: Folder Loram 1932 − 1933), Loram to Jowitt, 24 June 1934 and Loram to Keppel, 23 June 1935 (CC: Folder Jeanes Conference). H Howitt held the position of director of native development in Southern Rhodesia and was the conference secretary; Loram was its principal organiser and chairman.

54. CCNY, list of Jeanes Conference participants: Folder: Jeanes Conference.

55. CCNY, Jeanes Conference Programme: Folder: Jeanes Conference; APS, 'The Loram News No 6'.

56. CCNY, Loram to Keppel, 23 June 1935; Folder: Loram 1934 −1940.

57. In this assessment I have omitted consideration of Loram's impact on present-day Bantu Education in South Africa. Obvious parallels exist between his basic premises and those of the Bantu Education theorists. Whether or not Dr W W M Eiselen and others responsible for constructing the Bantu Education scheme drew on any of Loram's ideas remains a matter for further research.

58. This, at least, was the opinion of Thomas Jesse Jones, *Education in East Africa* (New York: Phelps-Stokes Fund, 1925) p XXI who in turn was considered by many to be America's leading authority on black education. Jones first gained national prominence as a director of the US Bureau of Education's 1913 − 1916 survey of black schools.

59. Berman, E H (1970) pp 39-99; King, K J (1971) pp 31-43.

60. Loram, C T (1917) pp 310-13. During the 1920s Hampton and Tuskegee added the type of academic courses that Loram envisaged would make them fully satisfactory models for Fort Hare.

61. APS, Loram to Malcolm, 15 November 1924, enclosed in Loram to Stokes, 18 November 1924; Box 31, Folder 509. D McK Malcolm held the position of chief inspector of native education in the Natal Education Department Loram (1917 pp 17-25) put forward the segregationist solution to the so-called native problem along with the solutions offered by what he terms 'the repressionists' and 'the equalists'.

62. APS, Loram to Stokes, 31 January 1924; Box 31, Folder 509.

63.   APS, Loram to Stokes, 10 January 1929; Box 31, Folder 512.
64.   Du Bois, W E B 'Negro Education' in *The Crisis* XV (February 1913)
      p 177 cited by King, K J (1971) p 57.

Demonstration of physical drill under a Jeanes teacher.
Photograph: Johannesburg Public Library.
See p. 116.

The Administration and Financing of African Education in South Africa 1910-1953
R Hunt Davis Jr

The twin issues of the administration and financing of African education in South Africa during the first four decades of Union served to highlight the still somewhat ambivalent position of Africans prior to the Nationalist victory of 1948. Africans lived in a segregated state in which the white group was steadily consolidating its authority in all spheres. They witnessed an accelerating erosion of their position, marked by the passage of such discriminatory legislation as the Natives Land Act (1913), the Colour Bar Act (1926) and the Hertzog Bills (1936). There were influential voices calling for their education to be integrated with other elements of South African 'native policy' to achieve a systematic approach toward Africans. Yet, until the passage of the Bantu Education Act in 1953, African school education remained under the control of the provincial administrations rather than becoming a central government concern. To this extent at least, Africans were in a position similar to whites. Furthermore, for a brief period from 1945 to 1953 the financing of African education came from the same sources (the Consolidated Revenue Fund) as that for whites. This change in financing was one of several ameliorative steps taken by the Smuts government in its last years, a process that concluded with the moderate proposals of the Fagan Commission in 1948.

Prior to 1953 Africans were not treated fully as colonial subjects when it came to the administration and financing of their schools but rather as a highly disadvantaged group of second-class citizens. It was possible for 'the few' at least, as opposed to 'the many' (to borrow Basil Davidson's categorisation)[1] to seek an education that would lead to their assimilation into the modern sector of South African society. This, at least, was the theory under which much of their education operated. Beneath the surface of the inherited system of segregated schools, however, there waged a fierce debate about their administration. Though initially the issue was not deemed to merit the attention that would produce national legislation, it did presage the arguments that would find favour with the Nationalist Party after 1948 and lead to the passage of the Bantu Education Act in 1953. The argument was essentially between those who viewed African education in the context of other educational issues and those who thought of it as an element of 'native policy', to be treated on such grounds. To come more fully to terms with these issues, this paper will first describe the administration and financing of African education from 1910 to 1953 and then examine the accompanying debate.

The Administration of African Education — An Overview at the National Level

Under the Act of Union (1910) education, except for higher education, was designated a provincial matter for five years. After this period Parliament could decide on other arrangements for the control of schooling. On the other hand the administration of 'native affairs' fell under the heading of national concerns, although the initial arrangements placed African education in the context of education. Thus, its administration remained a provincial respons- ibility.[2] Basically this situation remained until 1953 when the passage of the Bantu Education Act transferred the control of African schooling to the Union Department of Native Affairs.

The matter was not quite so straightforward however. For one thing, within the provincial context Africans attended segregated and sadly under-funded schools often run under a different set of regulations from white schools. Secondly, the Union govern- ment soon took an indirect hand in determining African educational policy when, in 1920, it established the Union Native Affairs Commission. This was especially true while Charles T Loram was a member of the Commission during its first decade, for he was South Africa's leading 'expert' on African education.[3] The Union government's role increased considerably with the creation of the Union Advisory Board on Native education in 1945. Its purpose was to advise 'the Union Government and the Administration of the Provinces in matters relating to Native education and the maintenance, extension and improvement of educational facilities for Natives.'[4]

The Union Advisory Board on Native education was part of a general reorganisation of the financing of African education which involved a shift from a special fund financed from the general tax on Africans to the budget of the Department of Education which itself came under the Revenue Fund. Of further significance was the fact that two of the Board's eleven members were Africans, Professor Z K Matthews a promiment member of the African National Congress from Fort Hare, and Dr James S Moroka, who was to serve as president-general of the African National Congress from 1949 to 1952. (Alternative members were Mr P Mosaka and Professor D D T Jabavu). Until 1953 the Board strongly influenced the direction of African education, particularly in finance.

The Union government had direct influence in financing of African education. This was to be the principal focal point of legislation until Parliament completely revamped African education through the Bantu Education Act. At the time of Union, each of the four provinces was entirely responsible for funding African schools from its own tax revenues. In 1922, however, Parliament enacted the Financial Relations Fourth Extension Act, No 5 of 1922, which removed the power for direct taxation of Africans from the provinces and vested it solely in the Union government. This legislation was in response to the Transvaal Provincial Council's decision to levy a direct education tax on Africans. The Act also required provincial councils to fund African education at a level not less proportionately than the entire education budget for the 1921-22 fiscal year. Under this provision of Act No 5 provincial expenditure worked out at £340 000. More than two-thirds of this amount came from the Cape Province's expenditure on African Schools (see Table I). Furthermore the Act empowered the Union government to make additional grants to the provinces for the extension and improvement of African education. The provincial councils interpreted this clause to mean that any expenditures on African schools beyond the 1921-22 level was the responsibility of the national government.[5]

Following on the heels of the 1922 legislation came the Natives Taxation and Development Act, No 41 of 1925. In addition to imposing a new and uniform tax on the Union's African population, the Act established a special development account which among other things was to finance African education out of the account's General Fund. Companion legislation relieved the provinces of expending any of their own tax revenues on African education. It also transferred £340 000 from the Union's general revenue fund plus one fifth of the African General Tax (amounting initially to £240 000) to the General Fund for purposes of African education and other activities supportive of African welfare.[6]

Over the years, additional legislation increased the portion of the General Tax paid into the Native Development Fund, until the Finance Act of 1943 made the whole of the General Tax payable to the redesignated South African Native Trust Fund. Four-fifths of this sum was designated for education.[7] The growing value of the General Tax increased further the amount of funds expended on African schools, but growth in enrolment (from 183 862 in 1925 to 604 063 in 1945)[8] outstripped the growth in funds. As a result the financing of African education remained in a constant state of crisis. The government sought to resolve this chaotic state of affairs with the passage of legislation in 1945 (Act No 29) which transferred the funding of African education entirely to the Consolidated Revenue Fund. The 1945 legislation produced a sharp increase in the level of funding, from £2 055 798 in 1944 to £7 856 194 in 1953-54.[9]

A new direction emerged in African education with Act No. 29 of 1945. Now, more than ever before, the schooling of Africans constituted a Union responsibility. But it was not the Department of Native Affairs which assumed control as many of the advocates of Union responsibility had sought. Instead, it was the Department of Education. Furthermore, Africans as the poorest segment of the population would no longer have to carry the financial burden for their schooling through whatever taxes they paid. Their education had become the responsibility of the state. The Bantu Education Act (1953) reversed the situation once again. In addition to its transfer of administrative responsiblity from the Union and Provincial departments of education to the Union Department of Native Affairs, the Act returned to the funding principle of 1925. Specifically, the Union government provided a fixed subsidy of £6 500 00 per annum and a further allocation of four-fifths of the African General Tax. As the Ministers of Native Affairs and Finance both clearly stated, Africans would have to pay for their further development from their own resources.[10]

Provincial Administration

The nature of African school administration varied considerably from province to province, especially during the early part of the period from 1910 to 1953. The one consistent factor was that African schools were segregated from those for whites. Furthermore, individual schools were generally under the charge of the various missionary societies. The principal exception to this practice was Natal, where in 1918 the provincial administration established state-run schools for Africans. By 1937 there were 92 such institutions with 12 977 students. By way of contrast, government-aided schools, almost all of which were mission-run, numbered 627 with 67 897 students.[11] Thus, even in Natal, most

Africans attending school did so under missionary auspices. The other provinces funnelled all of their financial support for African education into state-aided schools under private — that is, almost entirely mission — control.

The Cape Province, which had the longest tradition of significant support for African education, had the most developed system of African schools as the basic educational statistics clearly illustrate. In 1920-21, for instance, the Cape, with 34,9 percent of the Union's total African population, accounted for 76,5 percent of government support for African education or 60,9 percent of the total of African students enrolled. The Transvaal, on the other hand, with only a slightly smaller African population (31,8 percent of total), expended only 11,6 percent of government aid on African schools and enrolled only 16,0 percent of the total number of students (see Table II). Union government financing after 1925, and especially after 1945, however, had the effect of eliminating much of this great disparity between the four provinces. By 1953, the Transvaal had a larger African population than the Cape (40,7 percent of the country's total, as compared to 29,1 percent), and the Cape's commanding lead in various areas of education had been sharply reduced. It now accounted for only 36,2 percent of the total primary and secondary enrolment and 37,9 percent of the total expenditure. The Transvaal, with its large male migrant labour population, had 33,4 percent of the total number of African students in its schools and expended 30,6 percent of government funds. The remaining two provinces had a close correlation between their African population and the number of schools and students and the level of expenditure. (See Table III).

With the exception of the Transvaal, the provinces had by 1924 established within their departments of education separate sub-departments for African schools under the direction of chief inspectors of native education. The Transvaal did not take such a step until 1935, although it did have separate inspectors for African schools as early as 1920. In addition to these separate administrative sub-structures, there existed advisory boards on African education. The purpose of the boards was to provide advice on African educational issues to the appropriate provincial school administrators. Their membership generally comprised white missionary officials who, for the most part, were acquainted with the conditions of African schooling. In some instances, a limited number of Africans, usually with close church ties, were also members of the boards.[12]

The development of separate administrative sub-structures for African schools was associated with a general effort after World War I to 'reform' African education. In the Cape Province, for example, the chief inspectorate of African education resulted from a recommendation by the 1919 provincial commission on African education. This commission also produced recommendations which led to provincial legislative and administrative action to consolidate provincial ordinances pertaining to African schooling, to differentiate between the white and African primary school curriculum, and to provide free primary education for African and white children. In the Orange Free State, the first Organising Inspector of Native Education took office in 1924. According to one report, he found 'conditions which can only be described as chaotic.'[13] The organising inspector was soon to issue a separate African primary education syllabus following the lead of the Cape and Natal. Despite the discussion of a differentiated syllabus for African schools, however, in none of the provinces did the African curriculum diverge very much from that for whites, except for the language of instruction at the lower level. It was not until 1953, with the passage of the Bantu Education Act, that African students began to pursue a course of studies that was sharply differentiated from that of their white counterparts.

At the local level the vast majority of African schools were under mission control while at the same time receiving state aid. With the exception of the Cape which had African ministers running many schools, this meant that the managers of the individual schools were whites. Some schools had local committees, but those were strictly advisory in nature. One important exception to this pattern was Natal's system of government African schools, while the Transvaal had community schools unconnected with any missions and managed by the education department inspectors. The role of the provincial departments of education lay primarily with the professional supervision and inspection of government and government-aided schools. A staff of white school inspectors carried out these functions. In the Cape, African schools were under the same inspectors as 'European' and Coloured schools, but they reported on African schools to the chief inspector for African education. The other three provinces had separate inspectors for African schools, though they had initiated this practice at different dates. Beginning about 1924, the provinces also all began to employ African school supervisors to work under the direction of the inspectors. With the partial exception of the Cape, then, the administration of African schools was almost exclusively in white hands, though the teachers at the primary level and to some extent at the secondary level were usually Africans.

The Debate Over the Administration of African Schools

Behind the facade of an African school system that saw little administrative change for nearly a quarter of a century after the 'reforms' centering on 1920, there was an ongoing debate about the administration of African education which foreshadowed the arguments presented before the 1949-51 Eiselen Commission that led to the Bantu Education Act.[14]

Basically the debate was between the assimilationists and the segregationists.[15] There were many participants in the debate but the 1919 Cape Native Education Commission, in the conclusion to its report, and Charles Templeman Loram provide representative statements of the two positions. The Cape Commission argued that African schools should be administered by departments of education:

> There is a consensus of opinion amongst Natives, which the Commission believes to be well grounded, against any change likely to cut them off from the main course of educational development in the country.[16]

Loram, on the other hand, argued in favor of placing African education under the administrative control of a Union Department of Native Education. His position rested on two premises: whites would rule and Africans would be ruled: Africans were a rural people and their future lay in the countryside. He concluded that Africans needed an education differentiated from that for whites and therefore that their school system should be administered separately from that for whites.[17]

Despite their sharply divergent views on the nature and control of African education, the assimilationists and segregationists were united on one issue — the existing system of African education was generally in an unsatisfactory state. Africans speaking out on educational issues also were in agreement with the white educators on this point. As the 1935-36 Interdepartmental Committee on Native Education commented after hearing extensive evidence from advocates of both the assimilationist and segregationist positions: 'No more compelling fact has emerged from the evidence than the general conviction that the status quo is untenable'.[18]

While the Revenue Act of 1925 was a partial victory for the segregationists, the assimilationists seemed to come out on top with the passage of the 1945 legislation. Their 'victory', however, was short-lived, for in 1953 the Bantu Education Act firmly entrenched segregation as the guiding principle for the administration and financing of African schools in South Africa. Despite some modification in the area of finance, the situation remains much the same at the present time.

Conclusion

Having examined the administration and financing of African education over the period 1910-1953, we need to place the educational issues in their wider political and economic context. In other words, how is one best to interpret the significance of the administrative history of African education during the first four and a half decades of Union?

One approach is simply to take the assimilationist-segregationist debate on its own merits and interpret it as a manifestation of the wider liberal-conservative debate over the role of Africans in South African society. At one point, historians tended to equate the liberal-conservative dichotomy with an English-Afrikaner dichotomy. This was true, at least, of the so-called liberal school of South African historiography. More recently, however, scholars have searched for, and found, roots of the present apartheid policy among the English-speaking white South African community as well as among Afrikaners. As John Shingler has observed, 'In the early years of the 20th century British and South African politicians created a structure of racial domination based on doctrines of segregation and White supremacy.'[19]

Shingler goes on to stress the important role that educational policies played in forging the South African political order:

> The superior status of the Whites was sustained in turn by the skills which their position enabled them to acquire . . . . The subordination of the Blacks was reinforced and complemented by their education, parsimonious financial support, the refusal to make education compulsory even in the cities and circumscribed curricula, all combined to limit Black participation in society.
>
> The educational policies and ideas of Union were thus . . . directed . . . to the reinforcement of an overall structure of differentiation and domination.[20]

Shingler clearly establishes educational issues as essentially political in nature. But there is another important dimension to the debate on African education — the economic one. As Martin Legassick has recently noted, the change in the direction of African education that took place with the Bantu Education Act more or less coincided with the transformation of the South African economy from one based primarily on mining and agriculture to one that increasingly relied on manufacturing.

Mining and farming, Legassick argues, require basically an unskilled, and an uneducated, African labour force. Hence the state did not have any particular imperative to intervene very much in the process of educating Africans. What schooling there was could be left largely in the hands of missionaries, where it had been from the start, even if the missionaries could be somewhat irritating with their mildly assimilationist tendencies. Since the 1950s, however, state policy has increasingly had to meet the needs and demands of a manufacturing industry. According to Legassick:

> For this reason the state also assumed control from 1953 of the black educational system which had previously been in the hands of missionaries. A new curriculum was devised with two purposes. First, to provide for the mass of Africans the minimum of educational skills necessary for participation in semi-skilled positions in the forced labour economy. Secondly, to attempt to train a small African elite who would seek their economic and political outlets not within the central white-controlled state but in the 'homelands'.[21]

Education policy can be linked not only to the forging of South Africa's political order but to its economic order as well. Bantu Education, and the prolonged debate which led up to it, fitted in with the state's overall programme of establishing increased political and economic control over the African population as it worked both to perpetuate and modernise the segregationist structures of social control. The historical study of African educational administration in South Africa needs to be undertaken in the context of both the wider political issues and the wider economic issues impinging upon Africans within the social order.

Table I

Provincial Expenditure
on African Education
under the terms of Act No 5 of 1922.

Cape Province	£240 000
Natal	49 000
Transvaal	46 000
Orange Free State	5 000
Union Total	£340 000

Table II
Basic Statistics for African Education 1920

Province	African Population[1]		Schools		Teachers		Enrolment		Expenditure		Per Pupil Expenditure		
	No.	%	No.	%	No.	%	No.	%	£	%	£	s.	d.
Cape	1 639 634	34,9	1602	59	3412	63,5	110 519	60,9	257 853	76,5	2	6	3
Natal	1 139 804	24,3	468	17,5	700	13,0	25 579	14,1	36 195	10,7	1	8	3
Transvaal	1 495 869	31,8	409	15,3	891	16,6	28 953	16,0	39 054	11,6	1	6	6
OFS	421 978	9,0	200[2]	7,5	3742	10,0	16 433	9,1	4 000	1,2		4	4
Union	4 697 285	100,0	2679	99,9	5377	100[1]	181 484	100,1	337 102	100,0			

Notes: 1 Based on the 1921 census
         2 Figures are for 1925; 1920 figures are not available

Source: Union of South Africa *Report of the Interdepartmental Committee on Native Education* [U G No. 29/1936]
         (Pretoria Government Printer, 1936) pp 18, 22, 27, 35.

Table III

Basic Statistics for African Education, 1953

Province	African Population[1]		African Schools		Ave. Enrolment (elem. & sec.)		Expenditure	
	No.	%	No.	%	No.	%	£	%
Cape	2 492 021	29,1	2407	43,0	311 873	36,2	2604	37,9
Natal	1 810 102	21,2	1145	20,4	176,697	20,5	1547	22,5
Transvaal	3 480 077	40,7	1446	25,8	288 257	33,4	2106	30,6
OFS	774 190	9,0	604	10,8	85 543	9,9	625	9,1
Union	8 556 390	100,0	5602	100,0	862 370	100,0	6882	100,1

Notes: 　1　Based on 1951 Census

Source: 　Official Yearbook of the Union of South Africa No. 28-1954-55 Pretoria: Government Printer, 1955/56 pp 250-52, 685.

FOOTNOTES

1.   Davidson, B *Let Freedom Come: Africa in Modern History* (Boston, 1978) pp 148-9.

2.   Union of South Africa — Official *Report of the Interdepartmental Committee on Native Education* UG 29-1936 (Pretoria, 1936) p 52.

3.   Davis, R Hunt Jr. 'Charles T Loram and an American Model for African Education in South Africa' *African Studies Review* XIX (2) September 1976 pp 97-99 (reprinted in this volume).

4.   Union of South Africa — Official *Annual Report for 1946 of the Union Advisory Board on Native Education* (Pretoria, 1947) p 1.

5.   UG 29-1936 pp 44-45; *Educational Facilities for the Bantu in South Africa* Native Affairs Paper XV (Department of Education, Arts and Science, January 1950) p 9.

6.   UG 29-1936 pp 45-46.

7.   South Africa (1947) p 1.

8.   South Africa (1947) p 4.

9.   Davis, R Hunt Jr. *Bantu Education and the Education of Africans in South Africa* (Athens, Ohio, 1972) p 37-9; Horrell, M *African Education: Some Origins and Development Until 1953* (Johannesburg SAIRR, 1963) p 33.

10.   Davis (1972) p 48-49.

11.   Province of Natal *Report of the Education Commission 1937* (Pietermaritzburg, 1938) p 92.

12.   UG 29-1936 Chapters 1-2.

13.   *Ibid.* p 32.

14.   South Africa *Commission of Native Education, Report of:* (The Eiselen Commission) UG 53-1951 (Pretoria, 1952).

15.   Shingler, J D 'Education and the Political Order in South Africa, 1902-61' (Ph.D. dissertation, Yale University, 1973) pp 65-70.

16.   Cape Province *Report of Commission of Native Education* included in *Report of the Superintendent-General of Education* for 1919 (Cape Town, 1920) p 62.

17.   Loram, C T *The Education of the South African Native* (London, 1917).

18.   UG 29-1936 p 52.

19.   Shingler, J D (1973) p 291; also see Welsh, D *The Roots of Segregation: Native Policy in Colonial Natal 1845-1910* (Cape Town, 1971).

20.   Shingler, J D (1973) pp 291-2, 294.

21.   Legassick, M 'Gold, Agriculture and Secondary Industry in South Africa 1885-1970; From Periphery to Sub-Metropole as a Forced Labour System' in Palmer, R and N Parsons (eds) *The Roots of Rural Poverty in Central and Southern Africa* (London, 1977) p 192.

Part Two: Apartheid and Education
The Role of Fundamental Pedagogics in the Formulation of Educational Policy in South Africa
Penny Enslin

Louis Althusser's 'Ideology and Ideological State Apparatuses'[1] offers penetrating insights which illuminate education in South Africa. Althusser's analysis, while not theoretically unproblematic, clarifies the dominant position of the educational ideological apparatus, including the most obvious examples of schools and universities, in the reproduction of the ruling ideology, and thus of the relations of production in capitalist social formations. And his observation that the Ideological State Apparatuses are frequently the site of class struggle 'because the resistance of the exploited classes is able to find means and occasions to express itself there'[2] finds a striking example in the prominence of educational issues in the disturbances of 1976 and the boycotts of 1980.

Althusser's observations on how Ideological State Apparatuses function can be used to illuminate the function of Fundamental Pedagogics,[3] currently a powerful doctrine in educational theory at several Afrikaans-medium universities. I propose to use Althusser's insights to analyse the role of Fundamental Pedagogics in reproducing the ruling ideology in South Africa. I shall begin by commenting on Christian National Education, which is an aspect of the ruling ideology. Then, after examining the foundations of the more recent doctrine of Fundamental Pedagogics as a view of philosophy of education, I shall discuss the role of Fundamental Pedagogics in reproducing the ruling ideology.

I

The Christian National Education Policy[4] of 1948 (subsequently referred to as 'the policy') purports to be a policy for white Afrikaans-speaking children, but it has had far-reaching consequences for the education of all children in South Africa. However, much of the critical response to the policy since its publication in 1948 has taken the form of rejection on the grounds that it is narrow and chauvinistic, and likely to lead to Christian-National indoctrination of white English-speaking pupils in state schools. But the policy as a whole, including the sections devoted specifically to black education, clearly needs to be understood as a statement of those aspects of the dominant ideology which find expression in the apparatus of Bantu Education.[5]

According to CNE policy, education for blacks should have the following features:

— it should be in the mother tongue;
— it should not be funded at the expense of white education;
— it should, by implication, not prepare blacks for equal participation in economic and social life;
— it should preserve the 'cultural identity' of the black community (although it will nonetheless consist in leading 'the native' to acceptance of Christian and National principles);
— it must of necessity be organised and administered by whites.

The final point reflects a significant paternalistic element in the policy. This is particularly evident in articles 14 and 15, entitled 'Coloured Teaching and Education' and 'African (Bantu) Teaching and Education' respectively. Black education is the responsibility of 'white South Africa', or more specifically of 'the Boer nation as the senior white trustee of the native', who is in a state of 'cultural infancy'. A 'subordinate part of the vocation and task of the Afrikaner' is to 'Christianise the non-white races of our fatherland'. It is the 'sacred obligation' of the Afrikaner to base black education on Christian National principles. Thus, revealingly, 'We believe that only when the coloured man has been Christianised can he and will he be secure against his own heathen and all kinds of foreign ideologies which promise him sham happiness, but in the long run will make him unsatisfied and unhappy'.

The CNE policy is explicitly a statement of the beliefs ('We believe' appears frequently) which purport to constitute the life-and world-view of the *Afrikanervolk*. But there seems to be a curious contradiction between the relativist view which sees each group as having its own beliefs about education, and the argument that Afrikaners have a special responsibility as trustees of black education. This apparent contradiction reflects an essential element of the ideology of which the policy is an expression — the racial superiority of whites.

The notion of racial superiority is essential to the function of an ideology like CNE. The Bantu Education apparatus functions to reproduce the relations of production necessary for the continued exploitation of blacks in South Africa. That blacks, in their state of 'cultural infancy', need the guidance of the superior white culture, is to be learned in schools. Black children are thus to learn submission to the rules of the established order. Furthermore, the reproduction of the relations of production takes place alongside the learning of what Althusser calls 'know-how' or 'techniques and knowledges'. Here Bantu Education contributes to the reproduction of the forces of production by aiming to reproduce suitably unskilled or semi-skilled black labour power appropriate to the division of labour in South Africa and to the accompanying exploitation of black workers.

The CNE policy as an expression of some aspects of the dominant ideology can be seen to serve the purpose of justifying a separate and inferior schooling system for blacks. Since 1948 it has been an obvious candidate for critical scrutiny by educational theorists. The responses of Fundamental Pedagogicians to the issues and problems raised by the policy are therefore of considerable significance.

II

Fundamental Pedagogics, a more recent development than CNE, purports to be an approach to educational theory, rather than a statement of popular belief. Although CNE has certainly not been rejected in favour of Fundamental Pedagogics, it is true to say that it has been replaced by Fundamental Pedagogics as the centre of attention in certain academic circles in South Africa. The development of Fundamental Pedagogics can be traced historically from the publication of C J Langeveld's *Beknopte Theoretische Pedagogiek* in Holland in 1944. The first publication in the field in South Africa was C K Oberholzer's *Inleiding in die Prinsipiële Opvoedkunde*, which appeared in 1954.

Practised mainly at the University of South Africa and the University of Pretoria, 'Pedagogics' or 'theory of education' comprises various part-disciplines, for example psycho-pedagogics and socio-pedagogics. One of these part-disciplines is Fundamental Pedagogics, sometimes translated as 'philosophy of education', which forms the epistemological grounding for the other part-disciplines. The various part-disciplines, including Fundamental Pedagogics, follow 'the scientific method', said to be the only authentic method of studying education, by using the phenomenological method'.[6] Use of this method enables the Fundamental Pedagogician to learn to know the phenomenon of education by undertaking 'radical reflection' on the educational situation or occurrence. The essence of the educational situation is then described in terms of pedagogic categories, and corresponding criteria derived from them.[7] This science, in the view, for example, of Landman and Gous,[8] is free of both metaphysics and dogmatics. Making what appears to be a similar point, Gunter[9] emphasises the importance of practising Pedagogics as a science, in preference to what he calls 'the ideological approach' to educational theory. This emphasis on the notion of Fundamental Pedagogics as a science is the key to identifying both the central problem in Fundamental Pedagogics as a theory of education, and the nature of its relationship with CNE.

In their textbook, *Fundamental Pedagogics*,[10] Viljoen and Pienaar distinguish three stages or moments in scientific research

> the *pre-scientific* (pre-reflective) life-world in which the original phenomena reveal themselves, and which rouse the wonderment of the scientist,
> the *scientific* reflection on the phenomenon and the universal, verifiable logically systemised body of knowledge offered by such reflection and
> the *post-scientific* meaningful implementation of this body of knowledge in society.[11]

This distinction between the pre-scientific and the scientific stages and the scientific and post-scientific stages, is seen to be of crucial importance. Central to this distinction is the exclusion of values from the scientific stage, by contrast with the other two stages, where values or life-views play a prominent role. Fundamental Pedagogicians are careful to stress that values are very important in relation to education — but in education as practice, as against education as theory, the latter being a strictly scientific pursuit. While the practice of education is conducted by the pegagogue or educator, the pedagogician or educationist as scientist is concerned with education as theory.[12]

Viljoen and Pienaar describe the work of the pedagogue or educator

> Education is a particular occurrence in accordance with accepted values and norms of the educator and eventually also of the group to which he belongs. He is engaged in accompanying the child on the way to self-realisation, but this realisation must be in accordance with the demands of the community and in compliance with the philosophy of life of the group to which he belongs. In this way the South African child has to be educated according to Christian National principles.[13]

The crucial stage or distinguishing factor in the scientific method followed by the pedagogician appears to be the epoché or bracketing — the provisional suspension by the scientist of her extrinsic aims and her beliefs, values or world-view. Thus science presupposes a 'viewless view'. The only scientifically accountable point of departure is the 'pedagogic phenomenon' as it appears in the 'empirical life-world'. And the findings of the scientist are universally valid, as against the particular view of life which characterises the attitudes and actions in practice of the pedagogue or educator.

However, Viljoen and Pienaar do argue that there is a need for a link between the scientific and the post-scientific stages. They suggest that at the post-scientific stage the scientist 'may choose to implant the new knowledge he has gained back into the life-world of everyday, and by so doing enrich the culture of the group to which he belongs as well as that of society as a whole'.[14] That is, by formulating criteria in terms of which everyday practice may be assessed, the pedagogician must try to make her findings 'serviceable' to her people and thus to humanity in general. In this way pedagogics can 'lay the foundation' of various systems of education which reflect different life- and world-views, including the Christian National system. But,

> The meaning he [the scientist] gives to the findings he has come to, the way he interprets his discoveries with a view to implementing his knowledge towards the welfare of his people, will reveal the order of values within that particular community.[15]

III

Having outlined the view of educational theory as 'science' held by Fundamental Pedagogicians, I will now show how Fundamental Pedagogics is related to CNE and thus how this notion of 'science' plays its role in the educational ISA in South Africa.

The relationship between *science* and *values* in Fundamental Pedagogics can be summed up as follows. Firstly, it is held that educational theory as a science is and must strive to be value-neutral. Secondly, values (including, I presume, what might be called moral and political values)[16] play a crucial role at the pre- and post-scientific stages, which must reflect the order of values of the particular community in question. Thirdly, science has a role to play at the post-scientific moment of education by providing criteria for evaluating the authenticity of educational practice.[17] But this application of scientific findings, in forming the foundation for educational practice, will reflect the order of values of the community.

Two essential features of Fundamental Pedagogics emerge here. The first is that the values which operate at the pre- and post-scientific stages, and also where the link is made between science and educational practice, are accepted as given and not to be questioned. The second significant feature is that it is categorically not part of the task of educational theory, seen as the science of Pedagogics, to consider values at all. There is therefore ultimately (although to its credit Fundamental Pedagogics does recognise the importance of values in education, albeit at a non-theoretical level) no possibility of recognising the obvious fact to which this collection of papers attests. This is that questions of value — centrally, political questions — are fundamental to, and inextricably involved in, an adequate theoretical understanding of education in South Africa. In the end one is left asking what the purpose of the scientific stage can be if it cannot examine critically the vital question of the values in operation at the pre- and post-scientific stages, in the South African case the highly controversial CNE policy.

This question brings to light an essential function of Fundamental Pedagogics, and the nature of its relationship to CNE. While it is claimed that the science of Fundamental Pedagogics can offer us a means of establishing 'universally valid' knowledge about education, instead of 'ideology', 'metaphysics' and 'dogmatics', as philosophy of education used to do, the consequence of the practice of this science is to legitimate the CNE ideology. This Fundamental Pedagogics does by endorsing CNE and the values it espouses as the accepted policy on education, and by excluding the questioning of CNE as a legitimate theoretical activity. Thus, the red herring of Fundamental Pedagogics makes its contribution to the reproduction of the dominant ideology.

Educational theory, as taught at the English-medium universities in South Africa, may well to some extent contribute to the reproduction of the ruling ideology. In this paper I do not undertake to investigate this question. Nevertheless, there would clearly be grounds for arguing that educational theory as practised and taught in these institutions, drawing on both marxist and 'liberal' traditions (especially as 'liberal' educational theory moves further away from the positivist influences which had tended to stifle it), allows for and encourages criticism of the dominant ideology, a possibility excluded by Fundamental Pedagogics.

Althusser helps us to understand further the role in the educational ISA of the university departments of education which practise Fundamental Pedagogics. He writes of ideology:

... all ideology represents in its necessarily imaginary distortion not the existing relations of production (and the other relations that derive from them), but above all the (imaginary) relationship of individuals to the relations of production and the relations that derive from them. What is represented in ideology is therefore not the system of the real relations which govern the existence of individuals, but the imaginary relation of those individuals to the real relations in which they live.[18]

The imaginary distortion in the case of Fundamental Pedagogics lies in its endorsement of the distortion of the real relations between the 'superior' ruling class and the 'inferior' black culture in South Africa as represented in CNE, the real relations of exploitation being concealed, where the ideology is effective, from both exploiters and exploited. Fundamental Pedagogics contributes further to the reproduction of this distortion by preventing its exposure through criticism of CNE. And this it achieves by distorting the relationship between moral and political issues and education.

Althusser shows how an ideology has a material existence in an apparatus and its practices. In the institutions or apparatuses which practise Fundamental Pedagogics the reproduction of the ideology of CNE occurs through practices like the following:

— Students of education are provided, by means of the syllabuses, prescribed readings and examinations in Fundamental Pedagogics, with the ideology which suits the roles which they will have to fulfil as teachers, bureaucrats and professional ideologists.

— The nature of research conducted in the institutions in question is determined by the ideology of CNE and by the role of Fundamental Pedagogics in the reproduction of this ideology. Such research, which excludes issues and analyses which might threaten the official ideology, can at best make only a limited contribution to issues of theoretical relevance to education.

— The structuring and staffing of departments of education is determined by the structuring of Pedagogics into its part-disciplines, which reflect, of course, the epistemological presuppositions of Fundamental Pedagogics.

Ironically, instead of a theory which could, as promised, provide a means of breaking away from ideology, in Fundamental Pedagogics we have, in Althusserian terms, ideological practice masquerading as theoretical practice. In spite of the problems in Althusser's analysis,[19] his distinction between ideological practice and theoretical practice is illuminating here. Ideological practice may be contrasted with scientific practice in that it 'reflects many "interests" other than those of reason',[20] that is, extra-theoretical interests like, for example, political interests. So, unlike scientific practice, ideological practice cannot provide us with adequate instruments of knowledge. In other words, in Fundamental Pedagogics we have ideology rather than science, because the practice of Fundamental Pedagogics is determined by the interests which it serves. The epistemological break from ideology to science is prevented because adequate instruments of knowledge are excluded from Fundamental Pedagogics by the very way in which this pseudo-science is formulated.

FOOTNOTES

1. Althusser, Louis 'Ideology and Ideological State Apparatuses' in B Cosin (ed) *Education: Structure and Society* (Harmondsworth, 1972).
2. Althusser, p 225.
3. For a broader critique of Fundamental Pedagogics, see P Beard and W Morrow (eds) *Problems of Pedagogics* (Durban and Pretoria, 1981).
4. Federasie van Afrikaanse Kultuurvereenigings, *Christelike-Nasionale Onderwysbeleid* (Instituut vir Christelike-Nasionale Onderwys, Johannesburg, 1948).
5. The authorities now prefer the term 'education and training' to 'Bantu Education'. Some argue that the old Verwoerdian vision of black education has been abandoned; see for example 'Education Dept. attacks reports' *Rand Daily Mail,* 27 November 1980. As blacks are still schooled in a segregated system, inferior in many ways to that provided for whites, 'Bantu Education' remains an appropriate term to use in discussing black education.
6. Fidéla Fouché in 'Pedagogics: the Mystification of Education and of Phenomenology' *The Journal of Education* University of Natal, Vol. 10, 1978, challenges the claim of Fundamental Pedagogics to identify its method and aim with phenomenology.
7. For example, the category of authority, whose criteria are obedience and achievement.
8. Landman, W A and Gous, S J *Inleiding tot die Fundamentele Pedagogik* (Johannesburg, 1969) p 40.
9. Gunter, C F C *Aspects of Educational Theory* (Stellenbosch/Grahamstown, 1974) p 2.
10. Viljoen, T A and Pienaar, J J *Fundamental Pedagogics* (Durban and Pretoria, 1971).
11. Viljoen and Pienaar (1971), p 10.
12. It is suggested that Fundamental Pedagogics as a science *is* practical insofar as it is a human activity. Nonetheless this seems a strikingly

simplistic view of the relationship between theory and practice, one which could be criticised from a variety of different points of view. Althusser, for example, emphasises that science (or theory) is as much a form of practice as economic practice, for example, each being a mode of production.

13. Viljoen and Pienaar (1971), p 95.
14. Viljoen and Pienaar (1971), p 10.
15. Viljoen and Pienaar (1971), p 10.
16. I am aware that notions of moral and political values can be seen as problematic in a discussion which makes use of marxian tools of analysis.
17. This is where, presumably, the perplexing idea of planting new knowledge back into the world is assumed to make sense to the Fundamental Pedagogician.
18. Althusser, L (1972), p 266.
19. See for example Louis Dupré 'Marx's Critique of Culture and its Interpretations' *The Review of Metaphysics* September 1980; and Norman Geras 'Althusser's Marxism: An Account and Assessment' in *New Left Review Western Marxism; a Critical Reader* (London, 1978).
20. Louis Althusser and Etienne Balibar *Reading Capital* trans. Ben Brewster (London, 1970) p 58.

The Hearts and Minds of the People
Lynn Maree

> I require a new suit and go to the tailor who has just made an excellent
> garment for a friend of mine. I ask him to make exactly the same suit
> for me. Do I now expect him to give me an identical twin garment or
> would he even think of making an exact replica of the former suit?
> Certainly not. What he will do is to take all my measurements most
> carefully to produce a suit, looking exactly like the other but built up
> in an entirely different way and made to fit me and me only. What is
> true of a suit of clothes is true of education. If it is to be the genuine
> thing it has to be fashioned and cut to my measurements, that is to say,
> it must take cognisance of my peculiar circumstances, my home life,
> my mother-tongue and my social environment in general and it must be
> tailored to these measurements. Otherwise it hangs on me like a strange
> garment. It does not really belong to me, it makes me uncomfortable
> and selfconscious, it may even make me appear ridiculous. In short, it
> does not suit me and tends to be an impediment rather than an asset.[1]

Whose ends are being served when each black South African
school pupil is neatly clad in the 'suit tailored to his/her measure-
ments'? When is education 'the genuine thing'? Incoming governments, like Castro's in Cuba, and freedom movements, like Frelimo
before it came to power in Mozambique, looked at the education
systems they inherited, the languages they are taught in, the values
carried with them, the world-view embodied in them, and have
tried to make decisions and changes within their power which
seem more clearly to 'fit' their political purposes — which might
be creating new or reinstating old value systems, responding to
new economic realities, and so on.

When the National Party came to power in 1948, it aimed at
taking control of the education of South African blacks by removing
it from the hands of the missionary societies and the churches. No

one in South Africa was in any doubt as to the reasons. They were made plain in Parliament: they took note of the 'social environment in general' of black South Africans, defined as rural, tribal and unskilled, and they said 'and so shall it remain'. Dr H F Verwoerd made it clear that his intentions were ideological, his aim to preserve the status quo and prevent black agitation. Mission education, for those who received it, was providing a base of confidence — unintentionally, it would appear — for political demands, which were unacceptable to the Nationalist and Afrikaner sense of what was right. Government thinking was that control of the system of schooling, control of teacher-training, the removal of liberal influences, could so shape black people's consciousness that they might accept a white ruling class view of what the world was like, and of their fitting and comfortable place within it.

In recent years the South African government has had many more educationally and, in some senses, politically, respectable justifications for its education policies. Governments the world over have — at any rate in theory — seen the need to make their education systems more relevant to their specific cultural and economic circumstances; for changing the medium of instruction, the history syllabus, the choice of literature; for preparing people for an agricultural future, or even an egalitarian one. A book prepared for the South African Department of Information and distributed to schools in London and elsewhere in England had this to say on separate education systems:

> The school belongs to the community, serves the community, is staffed by teachers from the community and is concerned with the welfare of the particular people it serves. From the earliest mission days it has been accepted that the diversity of the peoples of South Africa, with their various languages and cultures and their geographical dispersion, requires schools specifically designed to serve these disparate peoples according to their needs and circumstances. In the 1920s the Phelps-Stokes Commission, of which the famous West African Dr Aggrey was a member, stated that while educational aims were the same the world over, the needs of the African people were such that special adaptations were necessary, that there must be appreciation of the pupil's mind and character, and also of the community from which the pupil has come.[2]

Educational theorists, particularly in the sixties and seventies, talked about the need to start 'where the child is'. If we teach what is too alien, there will be no accommodation and assimilation; if we do not understand the culture of the children we are teaching, what we teach will be ignored or misunderstood, and we will misread any signals the children may give; if we do not start in the mother-tongue the child will make a much slower adjustment to school and will fall behind; the child is not an empty vessel waiting to be filled with neutral knowledge — the teacher's role is to provide a stimulating and unthreatening environment in which the child's potential can develop. All this progressive, child-centred theory is echoed in the rhetoric used by apologists for Bantu Education. Dr Eiselen, having exhausted his analogy of the suit, went on to say:

> There are no different sets of educational principles, no principles of Bantu Education, or Afrikaans education. The same principles of education apply to us all, but their conscientious translation into practice demands a different approach according to the circumstances of every community.[3]

The ideological intentions become masked; the system appears to be but another version of contemporary principles of community need and child-centredness. I do not intend to spend time analysing Bantu Education in terms of these principles, but rather to regard any adherence to them as purely rhetorical. I am interested in examining the outcomes of the original intentions. Is the 'Bantu child' content to be a Bantu child? Is he happy to stay in his own 'green pastures'? Does he feel comfortable and at ease in his 'hand-tailored' suit? Has their education so tribalised blacks in long-established urban areas like Soweto that they have come to see themselves as citizens of somewhere else, of legitimated home-lands, as units of labour who 'live' and have rights in another 'country', as people with a proud 'pot-making' past, put on the road to civilisation by the whites?

These ideas constitute a very concrete set of understandings about being black in South Africa. The research on which this paper is based also set out to discover whether the architects of Bantu Education had succeeded in establishing what Bourdieu calls 'systems of thought'.[4] Did the teachings of school, supported by informal education, come to set the parameters within which any thinking, any accepting or even opposing, could take place; did they define students' understanding of concepts like knowledge, success, worth, work, democracy, the economy? Did school and what they learned there encourage any 'spontaneous' consent 'to the general direction imposed on social life by the dominant group' (in this case the white ruling class)? Had the rulers of South Africa succeeded in obtaining what Gramsci called 'hegemony'?

In order to begin to hypothesise, very tentatively, about these questions, I spent some time in April 1975 in black secondary schools, mainly in Soweto. I sat in on lessons, predominantly History and Social Studies, observing and recording the relationship of both teachers and pupils to the content of their schooling. And I asked one class (indirectly, through their teacher) to write an essay entitled 'What I think South Africa will be like in Fifty Years Time' (cf. Danziger, 1963).[5] My work was only in urban areas and only in secondary schools, and only on a small case-study scale. So I do not know how children in rural areas, and in 'homeland' areas, react. I do not know how children who receive only a primary education react, *and* my Soweto material is pre-1976, and out of date.

Textbooks

The lessons observed were organised fairly religiously round text-books. So I examined those History and Social Studies textbooks I could obtain. Writing textbooks was clearly the business of many white officials involved in Bantu Education: there were many Social Studies textbooks all covering similar ground. The schools I visited were short of textbooks, and uncertain about which to use. Rumour had it that you could pass history only if you used the textbook written by the particular inspector who had been appointed examiner that year, and no-one seemed to know who this was.

The way South African history is treated by South African historians and teachers is well documented. I found all the myths dealt with by Marianne Cornevin[6] — the empty land theory, blood-thirsty savages civilised and well-treated by whites, etc. 'We notice therefore that a very large portion of South Africa fell into the hands of the Europeans by virtue of first occupation, conquest or purchase . . . . '[7] But an educational philosophy which is meant to make people proud of their tribal past sits oddly with these myths and the authors find themselves occasionally adrift:

> Basket-making and mat-making were also important occupations of the Bantu and they knew the art of making beautiful clay pots generally used for household purposes. The Bantu certainly had a rich and highly developed culture.[8]

They hover between pointing out how reluctant blacks were to leave their homelands (hence the need to import Indian workers) and how they flooded into the towns where their 'moral standard assumed a low level'[9] and the building of railways 'provided employment for thousands of Bantu'.[10]

There is throughout a tone of inevitability. Events happen because it is in the natural order of things that they should.

> There are many different nations in South Africa. All these people have their own language and traditions. It is natural that these people will be proud of that which is their own. They will also want their own country where they can decide on their future. In South Africa these different people have been given their own Homelands with their own governments to decide on their own matters.[11]

They are virtually never the result of action on the part of anyone — statements are constantly in the passive tense. If there are any 'actors' then they are white. Dingiswayo had creative military ideas only *after* he had spent some time at the Cape.[12] Positivism rules. The text says that the most important result of Ordinance 50 was 'that a new nation came into being. Instead of Hottentots, they became the Free Coloureds'.[13] And the question asked in Revision at the end of the chapter is 'What was the most important result of Ordinance 50?'

Blacks are depicted as useful labour, dishonest bargainers, foolish farmers, or homeland citizens — where the proposed future is constantly transmuted into the traditional and immutable past/present.

> Of which homeland will you become a citizen? What language is your mother-tongue? How well do you use it? Each citizen must carry out his duty to defend his . . . . Mention the names of the Budget Committee of your homeland. What is meant when we say that certain things are characteristic of a nation?
>
> In Soweto, people of the same ethnic group live, as far as possible, in the same residential areas. Why?[14]

There is no mention of black resistance, black political activity, leadership, nor of the illegality of any of this. History is always about nation-building — not, for example, about conflicts of interests within societies.

The Teachers

The secondary teachers I met ranged from mission-educated, middle-aged men and women, to new graduates from places like Turfloop, the University of the North, and young and unqualified enthusiasts. After the introduction of Bantu Education, a purge of many teachers was carried out. Baruch Hirson[15] indicates that even those teachers who had conformed and never dared criticise were arbitrarily replaced under the new dispensation after 1956. I do not have a large enough sample, nor enough background about the teachers I met, to speculate on how their own education affected their practice as teachers. I watched some lessons on English poetry and grammar which were examples merely of classroom knowledge, having no links with anything else at all. The teachers were instilling something the book said the children had to be taught. And I watched some lessons on South African geography which gave factual statistics like rainfall (though how the map of South Africa is drawn in a geography lesson has obvious extra-school significance). I read a Domestic Science textbook which listed as one of the housewife's weekly tasks the instruction of the maid. But the history classes I saw, however far removed from South Africa the subject was, showed again and again the tendency to forge links with the real world, as it was experienced by the teachers and the students.

For instance, one teacher was detailing the action taken by the Dutch East India Company to avoid bankruptcy. One of the recommendations was that salt pans should be sold by auction. The teacher was anxious to ensure that the pupils understood what selling by auction involved:

> Remember when — but it was a long time ago — I wonder if you saw it — it was during those times when you owed some rent to the municipality. The municipality would send his policeman and take everything you possess in your house.

He went on to dramatise the auctioning of someone's household possessions. This teacher in particular seemed to draw quite unconsciously on the known world in order to assist his pupils' understanding. These were the analogies which were closest to hand.

Another means by which the Dutch East India Company intended to offset its losses was the collection of taxes.

> . . . you meet a policeman and he makes you pay now. I did it in '73. I had my pass here and I was coming from school. They asked me 'Where's your pass?' and there was a school stamp. You know there are so many stamps in a pass-book. There's that other stamp and that other one. So he asked me 'Did you pay your tax?' I said, 'No, there's a school stamp — some stamp there.' So the policeman said, 'No, you should have paid'. I say, 'No, I am a student.' He says, 'No, we are here to arrest people like you. May I handcuff you, sir?' I said, 'But sir, it's a long weekend and I want to go to Durban' (class laughs). He said,

'Come along with me' and ultimately I had to pay R2.50 right there.

The 'Causes of the French Revolution' were begun in one senior lesson I observed. The teacher seemed to know that he was making topical points when he drew analogies or made general statements. Pupils had defined 'political' as 'It's when you're against the government'. The teacher explained that 'political' meant 'a relationship between citizens and their rulers', and went on to say:

> Sometimes it happens this way, that the king there is a ruler and the people are satisfied with his government. Well, he will go on ruling because all are happy. (He said later that, in the past, the power of the chiefs had resided in their ability to do what the people wanted.) Sometimes the ruler may be oppressing these people — passing the laws which are bringing them down and make them uncomfortable and their life becomes miserable. In which case, here, there are two things which can happen. One will be — perhaps citizens may try to endure it for a time and go about if they can see how best they can get along . . . another one may be that the citizens may come to the point where they can no longer take it or if they wanted they can say so far and not further and so they take up arms and they fight against their ruler. In this case, we speak about a revolution, a change brought about by the fact that these people were — were not satisfied with the government.

In his lesson on Charles X of France, he said, 'People defend a country only if they have rights', and suggested that France was not completely democratic because the large majority of labourers were excluded. The only way to get the vote was to become rich, but because labourers were underpaid, this was impossible. When discussing legal equality, he pointed out that this did not pertain in South Africa — whites were not subject to pass laws, nor any form of influx control.

There was often an assumption of shared memory on the part of the teacher:

> Now those Coloureds we generally find in Western Native Township — you remember when Western Native Township were being forced out of the area over to Meadowlands, some people wouldn't part with their houses, probably in view of — you know — being familiar with the place, so they decided rather than leave Western Native Township they would rather change their identity and become Coloureds. Whereas, we knew them, some of them were our neighbours, they were quite black, and automatically they became Coloureds.

Slavery was touched on by two teachers. One offered to lend his copy of *Uncle Tom's Cabin* to the class, and explained that *he* would never be an Uncle Tom and rescue his master, and another accounted for the importation of slaves to the Cape by suggesting that the Xhosa were too proud to be enslaved.

In terms of the teaching of the History syllabus, it seemed that in some cases, the Civics sections were simply omitted, on the grounds that not everything in a long syllabus could be covered. I would suggest that this had two causes: dislike of what was written in the textbook, and unease as to how to teach it to students who would ridicule. A young teacher said, 'How do you teach history, particularly South African history, to a class of Black Power students? They don't want historical objectivity'. An older teacher whom I observed read earnestly from the textbook and then allowed questions to interrupt her reading. That way, *she* had not raised any thorny issues.

The Students

On one or two occasions I was questioned by the students, either about myself or about South Africa. For instance, 'If you are a South African, why do you live in Britain?' and 'If a black country invades South Africa, which side should we fight on?' and 'How must we answer questions in the exam? For example, if we are talking about the Eastern Frontier must we say Boers and Kaffirs, rather than blacks and whites, so they don't think we are politically minded?' It was as though I was being tested, there was no pupil-teacher deference, and the questions came from a high degree of awareness of current events. In a lesson on the French Revolution, the teacher was asked, 'How can the rich have no power? Were palace servants paid? Couldn't the king imprison the thinkers? From which estate came the soldiers?'

Comments were made about the difference between European and South African history as experienced through the textbooks. South African history was 'less exciting', 'more boring', 'not true', 'done' in primary school and therefore 'finished'. I would argue that these dissatisfactions arise because of the bland, settled tone of the textbooks when talking of South Africa. The French Revolution on the other hand speaks of a world in which changes were made by the people, real changes by oppressed people. The version of their own past which they are given is not their version.

When it came to thinking about the future, which is what the essay-writing exercise was about, the writers (it must be remembered this was in 1975) were overwhelmingly optimistic about the position of blacks.

I am definitely sure that there would not be friction between Whites and Blacks with the abolition of segregation policies. Everything will run as smoothly as before. A sense of responsibility shall prevail on every individual to take care of the next man's property.

There was a total rejection of a 'homelands' future; that was not how they envisaged the situation fifty years hence. It would be peaceful, there was enough in South Africa for everyone's needs so there would be no poverty, all children would be in the same schools, able to live in the 'posh' suburbs, with equal job opportunities and equal salaries.

The government will be of mixed races. There will not be many education departments, there will be the same education for all races and no racial discrimination. People will have the right job they would like to have if they are qualified. There will be no job reservation and the people of South Africa will use the same entrance and the same lift. All in all petty apartheid will come to an end.

The society envisaged was always a meritocratic one, never socialist. Ezekiel Mphahlele's point about the world being experienced through one's blackness seemed to predominate and leave no room for a class analysis. 'The much dreaded black participating in anything will turn to the much liked black participating.'

On the whole there was little account of the process which would bring these changes about — but then the essay title had only required the future vision. Some saw pressure from black Africa; some saw a liberalisation on the part of the whites; one said, 'Riots are going to occur. We are now going to event things for ourselves'.

The tone on the whole was factual and detached, even when fairly bitter. One told the story of a man kicked to death by the police, the cause of death being given as congenital syphilis, but the author was distanced from the event. 'Blacks do not benefit; instead they are economically exploited, politically dominated, physically oppressed and socially humiliated.' 'The object of this pass system is to channel African labour to the white man's mines, factories, farms and kitchens.' There were some references to Nelson Mandela and to political prisoners in general.

Conclusion

My field-work methodology was influenced by that sociology of education which argues that it is important to examine the lived experience of the classroom, and the actual context of the lesson — the shared construction of reality. So, in some senses, I was concentrating on the micro-level.

Bowles and Gintis[16] argue that the social relations of the school correspond to and are largely determined by the social relations of the workplace, and thereby tend to minimise the ideological and political significance of educational policy and practice. From the limited scope of my research, I suggest that in the actual content of ideas and attitudes, schooling outcomes are not determined primarily by policy-makers, nor in any simple way by the needs of the South African capitalist economy. The mediation of the black teachers in the classroom and the reality of oppression generally had affected the way the students knew both their past and their future. Their consciousness was not predominantly tribal, their aspirations were contrary to Dr Verwoerd's expressed intention of an acceptance that 'equality with Europeans is not for them; there is no place for him in the European community above the level of certain forms of labour'.[17]

On the basis of a very tiny research project, undertaken before Soweto became world news and the black school children of South Africa were shot for their opposition to their education system and their oppression, it would seem that Bantu Education had not succeeded in turning their eyes away from forbidden green pastures: the experience of life in Soweto, the reading of newspapers, and possibly a sense of a history of opposition, were together stronger than the textbooks and the segregated structure of their schools.

But the wider parameters of thought and ways of understanding had been influenced. The essays reflected a certain passivity — the government would build the houses. 'In Parliament every person will be represented by somebody they have chosen, not any man the state thinks will do in representing such a nation. In so doing everybody will be satisfied with the government. Since someone he has chosen will be representing him.'

Schools are very powerful institutions, though they do not act in isolation. Schooling encourages passivity, removes responsibility for learning from the learner, legitimises what schools teach over other knowledge. My research did not touch on 'know-how' knowledge where perhaps acceptance of a world 'out there' is greatest. The division of labour carves out pre-existing identities, reality is organised and controlled in specific ways. Schools demand respect for hierarchy and authority. In a lesson on *Animal Farm*, a teacher used the analogy of a football team to show that there was always a need for a leader. Schools also grade and define worth. It was finally a desire to write their examinations and pass into the next year that brought most children back to school in 1977. The whole system of grading contains a rhetoric of equality and objective trial-by-merit. And it was not the schools that were burnt, though it was on the issue of the use of Afrikaans as a medium of instruction in school that opposition had originally been centred.

It is possible in the secondary school to become critically aware of being manipulated, and therefore to be fairly cynical about what is taught. Black children of secondary age in urban areas are aware of their exploited position and the education system does not succeed in winning acceptance of it. They do not feel that all is fair and that they ought to be grateful. But their schooling aids in blurring their class position. Jarvis[18] argues that even in Tanzania, the messages of the hidden curriculum make it difficult for socialist definitions of knowledge and worth to be generated. Clearly the state sees some value in maintaining the education system — it could have closed the schools down in the face of fierce boycotts.

Now, as more students take their matriculation exams through 'cram' colleges, they may lose even the self-awareness that a segregated, clearly inferior system gave them, taught by people who in the main shared their experiences.

Demands for integration, or for the abolition of Bantu Education (by whatever name), may only be asking for more of the same one-dimensional way of seeing the world, and for fewer radical ways of visualising the future, as may the spread of computer-based learning and the growing emphasis on 'training' and skill acquisition.

Mtshali writes in *The Detribalised* of a man who skipped school, who can barely write, who reads about murder, rape and robbery in the newspaper:

> He knows
> he must carry a pass
> he don't care for politics
> he don't go to church
> he knows Sobukwe
> he knows Mandela
> They're in Robben Island.
> 'So what? That's not my business!'

Opponents of Bantu Education, since its inception, have seen its segregated and inferior nature as the evil. The demand is *always* for integration and equality of opportunity. Somehow then it will be fair and objective; scientific methods of measurement will find the bright child of whatever colour, and conversely failure will be located in the child who fails. It is crucial to recognise that it will still be black children who will fail in such a system in South Africa. The 'Bantu Education' nature of black schooling can be said to have obscured the power of the institution of schooling itself for social control and hegemony under capitalism.

FOOTNOTES

1. Eiselen, W M M 'The standard of English and Afrikaans in our Bantu Schools', *Bantu Education Journal*, 23 March 1971.
2. *Stepping into the Future*, Erudita Publications, 1976, p 77.
3. Eiselen, (1971).
4. Bourdieu, P and J C Passeron, *Reproduction in Education, Society and Culture* (London, Sage, 1977). This paper is based on research completed in 1975 by Lynn Maree for a MA dissertation 'What shall we tell the Blacks? Bantu Education in South Africa — its problems and possibilities.' (MA University of London, Goldsmiths College, 1976).
5. Danziger, K 'Ideology and Utopia in South Africa: A Methodological Contribution to the Sociology of Knowledge', in *British Journal of Sociology*, vol XIV, No 1, March 1963.
6. Cornevin, M *Apartheid: Power and Historical Falsification* (UNESCO, Paris, 1980).
7. Van der Merwe et al, *Social Studies Forms 2 and 3*, (Bona Press, 1973), p 163.
8. Grové, Le Roux and Dugard, *Revised Social Studies Form 1*, (Via Afrika Ltd, n d).
9. Van der Merwe, (1973) p 138.
10. *Ibid.*
11. Schoeman, J and Prior, D *New Structure, Social Studies Std 5* (De Jager-Haum, 1975) p 98.
12. Van der Merwe, (1973) p 112.
13. Hurry et al, *Social Studies: Form II Structure*, (Via Afrika Ltd, n d).
14. Hurry, *op cit.*
15. Hirson, B *Year of Fire, Year of Ash* (Zed Press, 1979) p 62.
16. Bowles, S and Gintis, H *Schooling in Capitalist America* (RKP, 1977).
17. Dr H F Verwoerd, Minister of Native Affairs, speaking in the Senate 7.6.1954.
18. Jarvis, J *Aspects of Education and Development with special reference to Tanzania and Malawi*, (MA Thesis, University of London 1973).

Bantu Education: Apartheid Ideology and Labour Reproduction

Pam Christie & Colin Collins

Liberal historians view 1948 as a crucial year in the history of South Africa and, more especially, in the history of its black people. In that year the Nationalist government came into power with a political policy of apartheid, or the enforced segregation of black and white people into different areas.

Liberal opinion holds that in the pursuance of apartheid a new ideology was introduced into the black schooling system. In January 1949, the Nationalist government, believing that schooling was an essential means in bringing about apartheid, set up a Commission on Native Education under the chairmanship of Dr W W M Eiselen. The main terms of reference, these historians usually point out, were

> the formulation of the principles and aims of education for Natives as an independent race, in which their past and present, their inherent racial qualities, their distinctive characteristics and aptitudes, and their needs under ever-changing social conditions are taken into consideration.

The Eiselen Commission reported in 1951. In the main, it considered that black education should be an integral part of a carefully planned policy of segregated socio-economic development for the black people. Above all, it emphasised the functional value of the school as an institution for the transmission and development of black cultural heritage.

Subsequent to this report the Bantu Education Act was introduced giving wide powers to the Minister of Native Affairs, then Dr H F Verwoerd, to bring into effect the major recommendations of the Eiselen Commission. Black education was to be directed to black — not white — needs; it was to be centrally controlled and financed under the Minister, syllabuses were to be adapted to the black way of life and black languages introduced into all black schools. Most importantly, however, the control of black schools was to be taken away slowly from the missionary bodies who were running the vast majority of black schools at that time and placed under the Native Affairs Department. This latter factor is of crucial importance to liberal historians. The struggle is viewed in the following terms.

On the one side is the Nationalist Party which represents, in the main, the Afrikaner people. Because of their frontier background, they are not only isolationist but also racially prejudiced against the blacks. Their view of themselves is of a pure race which needs to maintain its purity by racial segregation. The policy of apartheid is geared towards establishing their own identity and removing other groups either geographically or culturally from them. To that effect, they need to control other groups. A reinforcing mechanism to the apartheid creed is the Calvinist religion in its most severe form, adding the divine touch of predestination of the chosen people to Afrikaner cultural identity.

With such a creed, the liberal analysis goes, it is not suprising that the control of black schooling would be viewed as a main purveyor of ideology wherein, it is argued, the blacks would be taught not merely the value of their own tribal cultures but that such cultures were of lower order and that, in general, the blacks should learn how to prepare themselves for a realistic place in white-dominated society, namely (at that point in time) to be 'hewers of wood and drawers of water'. To this purpose, the Nationalist government set out what was allegedly the greatest piece of ideological manipulation of the young since Hitler.

In terms of this analysis, the move to Bantu Education was opposed by the English-speakers in general, and more particularly by the English-speaking missionaries who controlled and owned the black schools (despite the government subsidies that they received, mostly by way of teachers' salaries). Teachers in these schools, it is stated, subscribed — despite being segregated — to an integrationist view of society. The English-speaking churches opted for equality of opportunity in education, attempted to 'raise' blacks to 'European' standards, taught blacks the dignity of all humans and their right to equal treatment in a country that was theirs just as much as it was, by conquest, the possession of whites.

However, this ideology of Christian integration by education into a communal society was directly subverted by the advent of the Nationalist Government in 1948 and by the gradual implementation of the Bantu Education Act of 1953. The effects were far-reaching. Of 7 000 schools, over 5 000 had been missionary-run prior to Bantu Education. By 1959, virtually all black schools except the 700 Catholic schools had been brought under the central control of the Native Affairs Department. Finance had been pegged to a set figure. All teachers were being trained in government training colleges and all syllabuses were to be those emanating from the government and imbued with the ideas of racial inferiority. The Christian ideals of an egalitarian and communal society, in which everyone aspired to a universalist culture which was both western and Christian, were struck a severe blow.

The conflict is thus viewed as a clash between two ideologies: apartheid with is concomitant notions of *baasskap* (dominance) on the one side and the liberal ideal of integration on the other. For apartheid followers, it is alleged, Bantu Education signifies education for subservience and cultural domination precisely by imposing outmoded tribal customs, languages and government on to unwilling blacks. Blacks must learn their tribal place in white-dominated society. To that effect, schooling must be centrally controlled. Opposing apartheid is the tradition of academic excellence, of equality of opportunity and multiplex education control in a religiously pluralist but socially integrated — as ideal — society.

There is however an alternative mode of analysis that can be used to understand the South African situation in general and its educational system in particular. The preferred analysis is a marxist one, which tends to ask different questions, views other aspects of reality as problematic, and ultimately interprets data somewhat differently. Marxists argue that the system can be fully comprehended only if analysis is situated within the broad set of economic interests underlying the present structure, ie class analysis. One Marxist dismissal of the liberal thesis is set in the following terms:

> The cornerstone of liberal analysis of South Africa is a distinction between 'political' and 'economic' systems as discrete, independent units. In Horwitz's phrase, racial oppression is a 'political factor' whose 'increasingly monolithic character justified its description as an ideology'. This political factor 'became the determining agency of inter-action and major theme in the country's economic history'. The key independent variable is thus the racial ideology of the state (the political factor) itself outside of, but productive of distortions within, an otherwise rational colour-blind capitalist economy.[1]

Class analysis suggests that a consideration of broad economic interests indicates better the real contradictions in South African society. Wolpe and others maintain that the real contradiction is not simply between the white racists and the black oppressed; but rather, the contradiction is between white capitalists and black proletariat, at least since the 1950s. The history of South Africa is thus better analysed in terms of a coercive labour-repressive form of economy.

> Since the establishment of the Union of South Africa (to go back no further), the state has been utilised at all times to serve and develop the capitalist mode of production. Viewed from this standpoint, racist ideology and policy and the state not only appear as the means for the reproduction of segregation and racial discrimination generally, but also as what they really are, the means for the production of a particular mode of production.[2]

In simple terms, the argument of the class approach is that whites are oppressing blacks not merely because they are racists (which they may well be) but because they need them as non-competitive cheap labour.

In applying such a Marxist methodology to the schooling of blacks in South Africa, a first proposition would be that the inter-relationship between state policy and economic realities (the capitalist accumulation process) should be analysed. In this paper, we shall attempt to outline a Marxist framework for considering Bantu Education before looking in more detail at the introduction of the system and at its principal features.

Central to the consideration of schooling in a capitalist state is a theory of the reproduction of labour. It is important to state at the outset that such a theory does not necessarily imply economic reductionism. This would be to overlook the fact that capital is a social relation, and that ideological and political structures and processess, as well as class struggle, are part of the accumulation process, and of its reproduction.

Similarly, the reproduction process cannot be deterministically assumed. Capitalist reproduction is not inevitable; linked as it is with the relationship between capital and labour, and with economic, political, and ideological processes, it is essentially a process of struggle, taking specific forms in particular historical conjunctures. The reproduction of the relations of production involves contradictions and conflicts, and is not unproblematic.

The reproduction of the capitalist class relationship, and hence of labour power, is essential to the capitalist accumulation process. The reproduction of agents, as capitalists and as workers, needs to be secured for the continued functioning of capitalism. Not only do workers need to be adequately trained and skilled, they need also to have the appropriate work ethic, attitudes, and willingness to participate in capitalist exchange relations. The state has played a significant role in the reproduction of labour suited to the needs of capital in general.

The principal, but by no means the only, institution in which the production and reproduction of labour power takes place, is the school. In the pre-capitalist mode of production, and in the early stages of capitalist development, labour reproduction has been ensured in the family and other institutions, and in appropriate workplaces. With the development of capitalism and the increase of its labour needs, schools have become the principal focus of the labour reproduction process, and have come increasingly to be the preserve of the state.

Again, however, a mechanistic approach to the state and the reproduction of labour through schooling is not implied. Firstly, the relationship between the state and schooling should not be treated as an over-simplified correspondence in which the labour needs of the accumulation process are unproblematically met by the institutions serving those needs. Just as the capitalist state ensures the maintenance of capitalism in general, so with the reproduction of labour, the state's function is to ensure the maintenance of capitalist class relations in general, rather than meeting the specific labour needs of particular capitalist interests. An approach to schooling in a capitalist state which attempts to trace changes in schooling directly back to changes in the labour needs of particular capitalist groups, may be attempting a correspondence which, in its over-simplicity, reduces institutional changes to mechanistic responses. The same problem occurs with attempts to pattern a temporal correspondence between capitalist needs and schooling.

An over-simple correspondence theory underestimates the complexity of the institutional forms of capitalist society, of which schools are one, and the fact that these areas are sites of struggle and contradiction, rather than mechanistic response to capitalist demands.

Black Education in the 1930s and 1940s

In concentrating particularly on the segregationist and unequal dimensions of the system, it is not uncommon for liberal accounts of Bantu Education to go back no further than National Party policy to explain these features. This is however to ignore the unity of the 1930s and 1940s as a whole. Not only were segregationist and unequal educational structures and supporting ideology firmly entrenched before 1948; in addition, the measures introduced in 1953 were to a large degree a particular response to the needs of capitalist accumulation in the period as a whole.

As has been demonstrated elsewhere,[3] segregationist schooling patterns were not introduced in 1948; they had already been established by the 1930s, and throughout the 1930s and 1940s operated to reproduce racial inequality, even in the period of mission school predominance. This becomes apparent when examining schooling provisions for blacks in the 1930s and 1940s.

Looking in more detail at black schooling provisions, it is apparent that there was virtually no standardisation of administrative arrangements before Bantu Education. Most of the schools operated under church or mission auspices, but there were also state schools and community or tribal schools. While the provinces were legally responsible for the control of black education, responsibility for funding resided in the central government. The funding arrangements of the 1925 Act persisted until 1945: state expenditure was fixed, supplemented by a proportion of the direct taxes paid by blacks. This proportion was increased a number of times between 1925 and 1945. Nevertheless, the principal feature of the funding arrangements throughout this period was their inadequacy. Compared with white education, the per capita expenditure on blacks remained low throughout the period, as the following Table I shows.[4]

Table I
Per capita expenditure on
schooling 1930-45

Date	Whites	Blacks
1930	£22.12.10	£2.02.08
1935	£23.17.02	£1.18.06
1940	£25.14.02	£2.04.04
1945	£38.05.10	£3.17.10

Not only was expenditure on black and white vastly different; throughout the period the relative difference remained virtually unaltered. As a result, educational provisions for blacks were far from adequate. There was a shortage of teachers, many of whom were poorly qualified, or not qualified at all. School facilities were limited: buildings were usually rudimentary and inadequate, and there were shortages of furniture, books, and other equipment.

Turning to school enrolments, the figures for the 1930s and

1940s show a slow but steady increase in the numbers of blacks attending school.

Table II[5]
Enrolments of black students 1930-45

Year	Number of black students	Percentage of black population receiving education
1930	284 250	4,9%
1935	351 908	5,5%
1940	464 024	6,6%
1945	587 586	7,7%

In spite of the increased overall attendance, schooling remained concentrated at the lower levels. In 1945, 76 percent of blacks at school were in the first four years of schooling, and only 3,4 percent were in post-primary classes.

In explaining the low percentages of blacks attending schools, it is important to remember that schooling is not the only educational apparatus in society. After conquest, African social structures were largely maintained, with the 1913 Land Act, labour bureaux, pass laws, and coercion providing a migrant labour supply needed primarily by mines. Thus labour was reproduced primarily by institutions other than schooling structures. The migrant labour/reserves base of the black workers meant that many blacks were not integrated fully in the capitalist economy, and consequently schooling was less important.

Moreover, South African capitalism has been characterised by extreme forms of extra-economic coercion of the labour force. Repressive measures operated alongside ideological apparatuses such as the school to ensure the subordination of colour-castes. The denial of political rights, together with repressive measures such as reserves and pass laws, served to ensure the reproduction of relations of subordination, thus fulfilling functions assumed primarily by ideological apparatuses such as schools in certain other capitalist social formations.

Segregation in South Africa has involved attempts to regulate and control class status on the base of racial characteristics, using both ideological and repressive means. To the extent that blacks did attend school, segregated schools affirmed the division between colour castes, with different systems preparing blacks and whites for their respective sub- and super-ordinate positions. Unlike schooling in bourgeois democratic states, where children may be differently prepared for respective class positions within a single schooling system, South Africa operated different schooling systems to reproduce social relations.[6] This was reinforced by the concentration of blacks at lower levels of schooling, where the education they received would ensure their position as working class.

For those blacks who did attend schools, the overtly ideological dimensions of schooling were aimed specifically at the reproduction of the sort of workers demanded by the capitalist system. As regards skills, schooling was geared to instruction in basic communication, literacy and numeracy. Familiarity with one of the official languages, English or Afrikaans — the languages of the employers — was an important part of the curriculum. As well as this, schooling for blacks was based overtly on religious and moral training, with values such as cleanliness, punctuality, honesty, respect, courtesy, etc being explicitly articulated as aims of the system.

Looking at these features of black schooling, it would be tempting to formulate a correspondence model between the needs of capital and schooling provisions, a move cautioned against earlier. In stating that black schools function to reproduce the sort of workers desired by capitalism in general, a mechanistic model is not being proposed. Administrative disorganisation, the extent of missionary control, shortages of funding, and general deficiencies of the system, point to possibilities of contradiction and dysfunction. It is in the general functioning of schooling and other educational provisions (in the broad sense) that the reproductive needs of capital in general can be said to be met by the schooling system.

That there was at least some degree of concern about the provisions for black schooling well before 1950 is indicated by the establishment of an Interdepartmental Committee on Native Education (the Welsh Commission) which reported in 1936. The principal concern of the Committee was whether or not the state should assume responsibility for the administration and financing of black education. The recommendations of the Interdepartmental Committee that the state should intervene in these areas were not in fact adopted. Nevertheless, the report of the Committee provides valuable documentation of the ideology surrounding black education before 1953.

Considering the aims of black education from the standpoint of the average white South African, the Committee identified lack of support on the issue of state provision of black schools:

From the evidence before the Committee it seems clear that there still exists opposition to the education of the Native on the grounds that (a) it makes him lazy and unfit for manual work; (b) it makes him 'cheeky' and less docile as a servant; and (c) it estranges him from his own people and often leads him to despise his own culture.[7]

Implicit in these segregationist-based comments is concern that blacks be no more than workers, and the assumption that appropriate work attitudes would be acquired outside the schools. It would seem that whites had little confidence in the ability of schools to reproduce black labour in the form they desired; it is possible that they themselves, believing in the ideology of mobility through education, feared that schooling would operate in the same way for blacks, and thus impede the continuous provision of the lowest level of workers.

Concern with social relations of dominance and subordination is also reflected in what the Interdepartmental Committee took to be the thinking of white South Africans:

Some (of the witnesses to the Committee) maintain that there is no difference in the ultimate aim of education, whether you are educating black people or white people. But the two social orders, for which education is preparing white and black, are not identical and will for a long time to come remain essentially different.

It is not that the aim is the same and that only the methods to be used are different. The ends themselves are different in the two cases. The education of the white child prepares him for life in a dominant society and the education of the black child for a subordinate society. There are for the white child no limits in or out of school. For the black child there *are* limits which affect him chiefly out of school. It is no use shutting our eyes to that fact and ostrichlike positing aims for Native education which the very circumstances of South Africa make impossible to realise, merely because these aims are laudable and we should like them to apply to the black people as well. Limits are there which form part of the whole social and economic structure of the country, and it serves no good purpose to act as if they did not exist.[8]

Statements such as these are clear evidence against any suggestions that segregationist and unequal schooling provisions were introduced as part of the apartheid racist ideology. As the 1936 Committee verifies, they were part of the social and economic structure long before apartheid. The role assigned to schooling in preparing colour-castes for sub- and super-ordinate positions is stated quite unambiguously: schooling provisions would reflect the dominant and subordinate colour-caste divisions and prepare people for them.

By the end of the 1940s, the segregation system as a whole was facing a general crisis, which, as will be indicated, had effects on schooling. In outline, the main features of this crisis were as follows: firstly, the underdevelopment of the black reserves, generating rural unrest; secondly, the protracted class struggle accompanying the development of capitalist agriculture by whites, bringing with it an acute rural labour shortage; and thirdly, the unprecedented growth of secondary industry after 1933, which, in 1943, surpassed the mining sector.

These three processes resulted in the growth of a large black urban proletariat, almost exclusively migrant in mining, but becoming non-migrant in commerce and industry. Between 1921 and 1946, the urban black population trebled; and by 1946, almost one in four blacks was living in urban areas. The decline in the reserve supplement was coupled with low wages in the capitalist mode of production. Rural impoverishment and intense urban poverty were characteristic conditions of black labour.

Rural unrest and labour shortages were accompanied by a high degree of labour unrest in the urban areas as well. Although black workers did not have institutionalised bargaining rights, trade unionism grew, both in size and militancy, as did the black nationalist movement. Very significantly, the class struggle was not only concerned with wages and working conditions, but also called into question the whole system of capitalist exploitation and its segregationist structures. There was considerable industrial unrest, culminating in the 1946 Mineworkers Strike, which was ruthlessly suppressed.

Given the role of schooling in the reproduction of labour, and without resorting to a reductionist argument, it is not unexpected that these changes in the conditions of black labour and its reproduction — both urban and rural — would result in some response in the area of schooling. Apart from the crisis in rural labour shortages, the urbanisation and proletarianisation of large numbers of blacks produced a greater need for schooling for blacks. Urbanisation meant the need to incorporate into capitalist social relations people who were no longer participating in tribal structures and forms of social control. The form of education most widely used in the capitalist mode — namely schooling — was one means of facilitating this incorporation. Equally importantly, as indicated earlier, schooling plays a key role in the process of the formation of the working class. Not only would blacks learn the skills necessary for participation in the capitalist mode of production; they would also acquire, through the particular form of schooling provided for blacks, an ideological orientation geared towards appropriate work attitudes such as diligence and punctuality, the operation of the colour-caste system, and their subordinate position in the social relations of dominance and subordination in South Africa. In 1936, before the urbanisation and greater participation of blacks in the capitalist mode of production, it was possible to regard schooling as a hindrance to labour reproduction; by the 1940s this was no longer the case.

As has been argued, features such as segregation and subordination were already present in the schooling provisions for blacks in the 1930s and before. The existing system was, however, inadequate, in terms of organisation and funding, to cope with the demands generated by the changed social relations and labour unrest. In 1945 the state moved to change the funding provisions for black schooling so as to allow for an expansion of the existing system. This was one response — however inadequate — to the demands on schooling. Bantu Education was another — more throughgoing — response.

Bantu Education in the 1950s

So far, the essential points of continuity between Bantu Education and the provisions for the education of blacks which went before it have been stressed, locating both in a theory of the reproduction of labour needed for the capitalist accumulation process. We now propose to look in more detail at the Bantu Education system as a particular solution to the demands on schooling generated by the capitalist accumulation process, and, where relevant, to show its points of difference from the previous provisions.

The victory of the National Party in 1948 meant the ascendance to political power of a combination of white workers, petit bourgeoisie, and farmers, bound together by an Afrikaner nationalist ideology. The principal differences between the National Party and its predecessors centred around the issue of urban black labour. The United Party, supported by manufacturing and diverse mining capital, appeared to be moving towards the phasing out of migrant labour and allowing certain blacks to settle in urban areas, while still maintaining labour bureaux, pass laws, and a policy of segregation to secure cheap black labour. The National Party, in contrast, stressed the homeland base and the extension of migrant labour, with the pass system and labour bureaux being extended as extra-economic coercive methods to control labour and maintain its supply at a cheap level. As Legassick points out:

Both arguments, it must be stressed, were primarily concerned with the interests of capital and continued capital accumulation from an extra-economically coerced labour force; their differences were over the character, and to some extent the intensity, of such extra-economic coercion.[9]

In addition, the National Party propounded a strongly segregationist ideology based, in the 1950s, on cultural differences and racial inferiority. The specificities of this ideology in education can clearly be seen in official state discourse on black education, as well as in the provisions adopted for black schooling.

The principal effect of the Bantu Education Act of 1953 — and in this respect it was certainly a break with past practices — was that black education was brought under state control. Although this measure had been suggested by the 1936 Interdepartmental Committee, it was not adopted by the previous government. The Eiselen Commission Report stressed that a planned, centrally controlled schooling system for blacks should be an important element in the overall development of South Africa, and in particular, in ensuring its labour needs. The provisions of the Bantu Education Act leave little doubt that central control was to be the springboard for educational policies to contribute towards the reproduction of black labour in a stable form.

The Bantu Education Act stipulated that all black schools would have to be registered with the government, and that registration would be at the discretion of the Minister. This measure enabled the government to close any educational programmes which did not support its aims. The administrative differences characteristic of black schooling in the previous decades were to be replaced by a uniform system. Three types of schools could operate: community schools; government schools; and private, state-aided schools, including mission schools. Schools falling into the last category could only operate with government permission, after consultation with the black communities concerned.

In 1955 the state enacted legislation to restrict the operation of mission schools even further, with the result that mission education reduced dramatically, to be replaced by state schools. Whereas in 1953 there were over 5 000 state-aided mission schools, by 1965 there were 509 out of a total of 7 222 black schools.

The Act gave wide powers to the Minister of Bantu Education, including control over teachers, syllabuses, and 'any other matter relating to the establishment, maintenance, management and control over government Bantu schools'. The Act made provision for community participation in the running of schools through school boards and committees, but clearly power and control were to be firmly in state hands.

State control extended into other areas of black schooling as well. Measures taken in 1955 brought night schools and part-time classes for blacks under state control, bringing about the closure of almost all night schools in the years that followed. It is estimated that enrolment in night schools was 12 000 in 1953-54,[10] thus the closure of these schools meant a significant drop in the number of blacks obtaining schooling. In effect, the state showed itself prepared to reduce schooling provisions rather than to allow them to operate outside its control: institutions not certain of promoting state interests were not to be allowed to operate.

This policy of control extended to universities as well. The 1959 Extension of Universities Act effectively closed white universities to black students and began the establishment of separate tertiary institutions for blacks. One reason for this was undoubtedly to extend state control: those blacks who proceeded to tertiary institutions, thus forming a black elite, were to be trained in institutions in which the state could control both administrative structures and curriculums.

This extension of state measures to bring education under its direction was part of a wider system of extending state control, which included strengthening and increasing repressive mechanisms such as labour bureaux, pass laws, and restrictions on urbanisation. Whereas these last measures were largely geared towards physical coercion, schooling was a less repressive means of working towards the reproduction of labour in a stable form. State control over schooling meant that schooling could be used to support other state policies, and in particular the homeland or Bantustan policy. As well as serving hegemonic functions, control facilitated schooling being more specifically geared to fulfilling the labour needs of capital in general, both in respect of skills, and of attitudes and values appropriate to capitalist social relations.

The homelands or Bantustan policy was an important part of the National Party's plan for South African development, and its accompanying ideology. The 1959 Promotion of Bantu Self-Government Act provided for the establishment of separate black governments in the geographically fragmented homelands, under the influence of the all-white South African government. Tied in with the National Party's stress on the extension of migrant labour, labour bureaux and other extra-economic coercive methods to control labour, the homeland policy would reduce the numbers of permanently settled blacks in urban areas, and provide an alternative basis for the supply and control of black labour. Both politically and economically, homelands would provide a focus for black aspirations outside a common framework, and would thus contribute to continued domination by whites. In the homelands a combination of tribal with bureaucratic authority structures would help to retribalise, and thus further fragment, black consciousness. Though this homeland policy did not develop fully until the 1960s and later, it had always been an important part of apartheid ideology in embryonic form, as the role ascribed to reserves evidences.

The homeland policy depended on the existence of a black elite and bureaucracy in the homelands who would both support these structures ideologically and also provide the means for their operation. One of the functions of Bantu Education was to contribute to the homeland policy in both of these ways.

Ideologically, Bantu Education clearly envisaged the separation of whites and blacks in political and economic structures, and promoted this ideology through schooling. Pre-dating the Promotion of Bantu Self-Government Act of 1959, which planned the setting up of homeland governments, the Bantu Education Act promoted the notion of political, cultural, and economic segregation in broad terms. Verwoerd's notorious comments as Minister of Native Affairs in 1954 indicate a clear link between schooling and the reserves:

More institutions for advanced education in urban areas are not desired. Deliberate attempts will be made to keep institutions for advanced education away from the urban environment and to establish them as far as possible in the Native reserves. It is the policy of my department that education would have its roots entirely in the Native areas and the Native environment and Native community. There Bantu education must be able to give itself complete expression and there it will perform its real service. The Bantu must be guided to serve his own community in all respects.

There is no place for him in the European community above the level of certain forms of labour. Within his own community, however, all doors are open. For that reason it is of no avail for him to receive a training which has as its aim absorption in the European community, where he cannot be absorbed. Until now he has been subjected to a school system which drew him away from his own community and misled him by showing him the green pastures of European society in which he was not allowed to graze. This attitude is not only uneconomic because money is spent for an education which has no specific aim but it is also dishonest to continue it. It is abundantly clear that unplanned education creates many problems, disrupting the community life of the Bantu and endangering the community life of the Europeans.[11]

The Eiselen Commission perceived the two-way relationship between schooling and reserves as follows:

> The reserves, being areas in which Bantu culture functions most completely, have a special task to perform in the furtherance of the development of Bantu culture and schools. Many educated Bantu feel that the reserves are fast becoming economic and cultural slums; places to be avoided by the educated and enterprising.
>
> Your Commission feels that special steps should be taken to facilitate and encourage the evolution of a progressive, modern and selfrespecting Bantu order of life. Cosmopolitan areas in industrial centres where people of many languages and customs are herded together, provide particularly difficult conditions for the orderly and progressive development of the Bantu cultures. But if the reserves are to play their part they must be developed so that there can be a harmony between the schools and the way of life of the people; a way of life which will give scope for the expression of talent and ambition. The best schools in the world cannot keep people in an area if there is no opportunity for satisfying their desires and ambitions. On the other hand, if the reserves can be developed economically and culturally, those who come to labour centres will have a background sufficiently rich and respected to prevent their demoralisation.[12]

In line with this policy, outlined in 1953 but only developed in the 1960s, was the move to concentrate secondary schools as far as possible in the reserves. This would remove blacks who were in secondary schooling from urban areas and locate them in the area where the state wished them to be. Similarly the provisions in the Bantu Education system for separation in schools along tribal lines, and the language teaching provisions, bolstered the retribalisation which was part of the homeland policy.

The establishment of black tertiary institutions (tribal colleges) in reserves together with the restrictions on attendance of blacks at white universities, also supported the homeland policy. Blacks attending these colleges were to be encouraged to use their skills in the homelands to enable these areas to function administratively and economically. And this, as we have indicated, would contribute towards the state formation which the National Party envisaged and was attempting to achieve.

Another central feature of Bantu Education was its hegemonic function. As mentioned earlier there were segregationist, colour-caste and unequal social relations in the pre-apartheid period, and the mid-1940s witnessed a general crisis in the accumulation process, centred partly on labour disruption. One of the aims of Bantu Education was to facilitate the reproduction of the relations of production in a docile form, so that these relations would appear natural and based on common sense. Stressing cultural differences between white and black, and the development of a separate black community, in which black aspirations could be realised, the Bantu Education system would thus to able to prepare Blacks to accept differences as part of the unchallenged order. The following statement from the Eiselen Commission is a clear example of the use of cultural difference to establish the need for separation:

> The Bantu child comes to school with a basic physical and psychological endowment which differs so slightly, if at all, from that of the European child, that no special provision has to be made in education theory or basic aims . . . . But education practice must recognise that it has to deal with a Bantu child ie a child trained and conditioned in Bantu culture, endowed with a knowledge of a Bantu language and imbued with values, interests and behaviour patterns learned at the knee of a Bantu mother. These facts must dictate to a very large extent the content and methods of his early education.
>
> The schools must also give due regard to the fact that out of school hours the young Bantu child develops and lives in a Bantu community, and when he reaches maturity he will be concerned with sharing and developing the life and culture of that community.[13]

Again, Voerwoerd's Senate speech, quoted earlier, provides evidence of hegemonic design. Within the schools, state control over teachers and curriculum would serve as a basis for hegemonic interests. This becomes clearer when the relationship between Bantu Education and the reproduction of labour is examined more closely.

The reproduction of labour is a two-fold process, involving on the one hand the reproduction of attitudes and values appropriate to the social relations of production, and willingness to participate in capitalist exchange relationships; and on the other hand, involving the reproduction of appropriate skills.

With regard to the reproduction of appropriate attitudes, values, etc, the Eiselen Commission makes an explicit link between schooling and work. Along with religious knowledge, hygiene, and literacy in one black and at least one white language, it sets out the following functions of schooling:

> Social patterns and values which make a man a good member of his community, a good parent and a useful member of his society. (He should, for example, possess such qualities as punctuality, initiative, self-confidence, sense of duty, persistence, sociability, mannerliness,

neatness, reliability, power to concentrate, etc.)[14]

Explicit references to education and the social relations of production are also contained in the following excerpts from parliamentary speeches by prominent Nationalist politicians, prior to Bantu Education:

> As has been correctly stated here, education is the key to the creation of the proper relationship between European and non-European in South Africa . . . . Put native education on a sound basis and half the racial questions are solved . . . . I say that there should be reform of the whole educational system and it must be based on the culture and background and the whole life of the native himself in his tribe . . . . This whole (present) policy is also a danger for our Western civilisation.

and:

> We should not give the natives an academic education, as some people are too prone to do. If we do this we shall later be burdened with a number of academically trained Europeans and non-Europeans, and who is going to do the manual labour in the country? . . . . I am in thorough agreement with the view that we should so conduct our schools that the native who attends those schools will know that to a great extent he must be the labourer in the country.[15]

Again, it may be over-hasty to infer that because these were attitudes expressed by members of the ruling group, they would necessarily be reflected in the schooling practices of Bantu Education. Nevertheless, their hegemonic functions and the intention that they should be part of schooling for blacks is clear. Moreover it is possible to relate these statements to actual Bantu Education practices which would prepare blacks for their position as workers, and thus reproduce the social relations of capitalism on colour-caste lines.

Bantu Education was clearly aimed at extending the mass base of schooling at the lower levels. Not only was this envisaged by the Eiselen Commission: in addition, both the schooling structures and enrolment figures provide empirical evidence.

The Bantu Education schooling structure provided for lower-primary schools (Grades 1-4), higher-primary schools (Grades 5-8), and a series of post-primary schools. In the lower-primary schools, the curriculum would be not unlike that of the 1930s and 1940s — based on functional levels of communication, literacy and numeracy, and an introduction to either English or Afrikaans. Promotion would be automatic, thus increasing the possibility that children who started school would complete the first four years.

After four years of automatic promotion, there would be a test 'in order to determine whether (pupils) have made sufficient progress to be able to benefit by the following course', that is, should move on to higher-primary school. At this point many blacks would leave school.

In terms of curriculum, higher-primary schools were designed to continue the work of lower-primary schools, increasing the subjects to be studied (one of them being 'Gardening and Agriculture') and extending proficiency in English or Afrikaans. Higher-primary schools provided both academic and vocational courses, the academic group spending two-thirds of this time on academic subjects and one-third on vocational, with the ratios being reversed for the vocational group.

Students who succeeded in higher-primary schools could move to post-primary schools. The purpose of these schools was functionally stated: 'to provide the types of educated Bantu necessary for the development of Bantu society'. For academic schools, the curriculum was similar to, but not identical with, white secondary schools.

To supplement enrolment figures in primary schools, the so-called 'double sessions' and 'platoon system' were introduced to provide for the use of schooling facilities by two groups each day. This increased school enrolments, but at the expense of quality. Not only were facilities strained; in addition the school day was shortened by approximately one-third.

Considering enrolment figures alongside school structure, a pattern of labour reproduction emerges. Table III provides a break-down of black school enrolment for 1950-60.[16] Looking at these figures, there is no doubt that the introduction of Bantu Education increased black school attendance, indicating to some degree the expansion of schooling demanded by the increased numbers of blacks participating in the urban capitalist mode of production. However, the percentage distributions across the grades are almost static, indicating that efforts were not being put into redressing the imbalanced distribution in lower-primary schools. On this pattern of distribution it is obvious that most schooled blacks would be prepared for subordinate positions in the work force. This is substantiated by a close look at the provision of teachers and at aspects of the curriculum of the lower-primary schools.

Before Bantu Education was introduced, black schools were ill-staffed and teacher qualifications were generally low. Mission schools in particular relied on white teachers as an important

Table III
Black pupil enrolment by years

	1950	1955	1960
Substd. A & B	350 640	466 527	665 655
Standard			
1	114 729	151 144	238 146
2	82 847	113 449	188 668
3	67 154	90 948	138 495
4	48 211	66 101	97 437
5	34 087	47 353	70 012
6	25 325	34 667	53 833
Form			
1		16 122	21 310
2	17 162	9 879	14 105
3	4 873	6 915	9 607
4	840	1 393	1 741
5	439	674	835
Unclassified	719	552	164
Totals	747 026	1 005 774	1 500 008

Expressed in percentage distributions, these figures become[17]

	1950	1955	1960
Substandard A to standard 2	73,5	72,7	72,8
Stds 3-6	23,4	23,8	24,0
Forms 1-5	3,1	3,5	3,2
Substandards only	46,9	46,4	44,4
Forms 4 and 5 only	0,171	0,206	0,172

source of staffing. In his Senate speech, Verwoerd indicated that it would be state policy to phase out white teachers in black schools (part of his hegemonic, separate-cultures strategy), and also to replace men teachers with women teachers in lower-primary schools, which would bring about 'a considerable saving of funds'. These staffing changes, together with the expansion of lower-primary schools, meant that additional provision had to be made for training of black teachers. To boost the number of teachers available for primary schools, a three-year post Form 1 certificate and a three-year post Form 3 certificate were introduced. Overall there was a marked deterioration in the qualification levels of teachers under Bantu Education. Together with an increase in teachers without matriculation, came a significant reduction of professionally qualified teachers with university degrees, in comparison with the pre-1953 period. This would no doubt affect the quality of education offered, especially when compared with whites. But the policy achieved its aims in increasing the numbers of black teachers trained to fill the primary schools, which was the critical area of expansion.

Turning briefly to pupil-teacher ratios, figures show an increasing shortage of black teachers to fill the needs of the system:

1946	42,3 pupils per teacher
1959	51,1 pupils per teacher
1960	54,7 pupils per teacher

These figures include primary, secondary, vocational and teacher-training institutions, thus obscuring high numbers in the more crowded levels of the system.

In a situation of poorly qualified teachers, lack of facilities, and a system of automatic promotion, it is not likely that academic standards would be high. And, although the purpose of language instruction was undoubtedly to facilitate communication in the language of the employer, it is unlikely that such a rudimentary exposure would result in mastery, and this in itself would perpetuate the ideology of inferiority, and the social relations of domination and subordination. On the other hand, four years of schooling would certainly perform the function of preparing blacks to participate in capitalist social relations. This elementary level of literacy would, for example, enable blacks to participate in such bureaucratic practices as filling in basic forms, reading basic instructions, and so on, as well as to locate their position in the hierarchy of social relations. And those blacks who managed to succeed in schooling would form an elite, to be catered for in separate institutions right up to tribal colleges, where the ideology of the state would be promoted.

It is tempting to see the introduction of Bantu Education, and its emphasis on vocational training, in terms of the greater skill requirements demanded by the participation of blacks in industry on skilled and semi-skilled levels. This argument would be supported by the emphasis which the Eiselen Commission put on the importance of vocational training, geared specifically to the needs of the economy. In the Eiselen recommendations, it was suggested that vocational schools be established for a range of training, depending on 'actual and potential avenues of employment'. In line with the Eiselen recommendations, higher-primary and secondary schools in the Bantu Education system had vocational components, and provisions for both academic and vocational courses of study.

It should be remembered, however, that skills training is more likely to occur on the job than in the schooling system, particularly for the levels of skill in which most blacks were involved. Moreover the rhetoric of vocational education was not supported by the practices of Bantu Education in the 1950s. With the introduction of the Bantu Education system, came the requirement for separate facilities for blacks, forcing blacks to leave white training colleges without the provision of alternative facilities. This is indicated by the following Table IV.[18]

Table IV
Enrolment in Technical and Vocational
Education

Year	No. of institutions		No. of students	
	Whites	'Non-Whites'	Whites	'Non-Whites'
1953	82	54	10 716	13 842
1954	88	21	11 814	3 981

During the 1950s, technical and vocational training for blacks was virtually non-existent. It was only in the period of economic growth in the 1960s that this sector of education expanded.

Another point of importance in Bantu Education — a break with immediate past practices — was its funding provisions. The Bantu Education Act broke with the 1945 funding measures, fixing the state's contribution to Bantu Education, and providing for blacks to contribute to the financing of their own schooling. Initially four-fifths of the direct taxes paid by blacks were channelled into the Bantu Education account. This proportion was later increased. When this funding proved inadequate, black parents had to contribute to the cost of erecting buildings and paying additional teachers. The account was also augmented by government loans. Black children were required to make a compulsory contribution to their schools, as well as to pay for their own textbooks and stationery (which was not required of white children).

The following Table V on per capita expenditure on black education illustrates a number of important trends.[19]

Table V
Per Capita Expenditure on African Education

Year	Expenditure (SA Rands) (in thousands)	Enrolment (in thousands)	Cost per pupil (SA Rands)
1930	1 235	282	4,2
1935	1 382	348	4,2
1940	2 030	465	4,2
1945	5 724	589	7,3
1950	11 635	749	9,7
1954	16 210	942	8,7
1955	15 879	1 014	7,7
1956	17 467	1 103	7,6
1957	18 225	1 259	6,8
1958	18 184	1 345	6,1
1959	20 223	1 409	6,1
1960	19 662	1 506	5,6

Firstly, expenditure on black education was greatly increased after the introduction of Bantu Education: the total expenditure of 1953-54 was nearly four times that of 1945. Clearly the establishment of the system — including its expansion, and separate facilities — was not to be achieved without expenditure. Nevertheless, expenditure did not increase greatly during the decade, and increased enrolment meant that expenditure did not keep up with expansion. During the same period, however, the per capita expenditure on whites increased, as is shown in Table VI.[20]

It is self-evident that the quality of schooling provided for blacks could not equal that provided for whites. From a liberal standpoint, the state's funding policy is criticised for making the poorest section of the community pay for its own social services. As Horrel states: 'As should have been obvious to all the legislators . . . this method of financing Bantu Education inevitably curtailed development . . . .'[21]

But analysing the system on the basis of a theory of labour reproduction, the discrepancy is not unexpected. Bantu Education is geared towards the reproduction of labour as required by the needs of capitalist accumulation in general: it is a mass-based system, geared towards schooling on the lower levels, quite unlike its white counterpart. Rather than judging it in terms of equality with white education, it is more useful to understand the part it plays in the reproduction of unequal social relations which were part of the particular form of the capitalist accumulation process in South Africa at that time.

Table VI
Per capita expenditure on education
(SA Rands)

Year	Blacks	Whites
1945	7,78	76,58
1953	17,08	127,84
1960	12,46	144,57
	(Republic)	(Cape)

Expressed as ratios, these figures become:

Year	Blacks	Whites
1945	1	9,84
1953	1	7,48
1960	1	11,60

In the liberal interpretation of black schooling and the 1953 Bantu Education Act, the crisis was viewed as an exclusively ideological struggle between liberalism and racialism with the Christian missionaries allegedly wanting to produce scholars with a good 'academic' background, of sound character, and with the ability to take their place as Christian gentlefolk in a communal society. The Nationalists are seen as emphasising an inferior and somewhat more 'vocational' education for the purpose of producing inferior non-threatening and tribalistic Africans. They do so, it is said, because they are racially prejudiced against blacks.

The Marxist view sees a continuing thread in African schooling. This does not imply that black schooling would be perceived as always fulfilling a single purpose; it must be recognised that different needs operate at different times, and that there are contradictions within schooling systems, and conflict between various groups demanding different kinds of education. Nonetheless the central continuing feature remains, namely that schooling for the indigenous people of South Africa is in the main for the purpose of reproducing a certain kind of labour, as required by the particular form taken by the accumulation process at a particular time.

1948 brought a change in the ruling class grouping which in 1949 set about creating a social formation more consonant with their needs. Apartheid was the mask and Bantu Education was their best means for reproducing labour in the form they desired. The Nationalist government did introduce new curriculums, new financing and new methods of control into African schooling, but in the interests of their socio-economic needs and not because they were racialist. The historically changing reproduction of labour is the thread which holds together all African schooling policies in South Africa where from the beginning the early white settlers set up a labour-exploitative state.

FOOTNOTES

1. O'Meara, D 'Class and Nationalism in African Resistance: Secondary Industrialisation and the Development of a Mass Movement in South Africa 1930-1950' (M.A. dissertation — Sussex University 1973).
2. Wolpe, H 'Capitalism and Cheap Labour Power in South Africa: From Segregation to Apartheid' *Economy and Society* 1 (4) 1972 p 425.
3. Collins, C B 'Black Schooling in South Africa' *Africa Perspective* 17 1980 p 4-16.
4. Horrel, M *Bantu Education to 1968* (Johannesburg, SAIRR, 1968) p 23.
5. *Ibid.*
6. Molteno, F 'The Schooling of Black South Africans: An Historical Overview' (Unpublished mimeograph, University of Cape Town, 1980) p 17.
7. Rose, B and Tunmer, R (eds), *Documents in South African Education* (Johannesburg, 1975) p 232.
8. *Ibid,* p 233.
9. Legassick, M 'South Africa: Capital Accumulation and Violence' *Economy and Society* 3(3) August 1974 p 227.
10. *A Survev of Race Relations in South Africa 1953-4* (Johannesburg, SAIRR, 1954) p 112, see also article by A Bird in this collection.
11. Verwoerd, H F Speech to the Senate 7.6.1954.
12. Union of South Africa — Official, *Report of the Native Education Commission 1949-51 (The Eiselen Report)* UG53-1951 (Pretoria, 1951).
13. The Eiselen Report, 1951.
14. *Ibid.*
15. *Ibid.*
16. Horrell. M (1968) pp 51-2.
17. *Ibid,* p 52-3.
18. *Union Statistics for Fifty Years 1910-1960* (Pretoria 1960) p E.
19. Malherbe, E G *Education in South Africa II* (Cape Town 1977) p 745-6.
20. *Ibid,* p 39.
21. *Ibid,* p 142.

Part Three: Education Beyond the Schools
African Educational Protest in South Africa: The American School Movement in the Transkei in the 1920s
Robert Edgar

A leading catalyst of African protest in the 1970s against the system of apartheid was student opposition to Bantu education. Momentous boycotts like those in Soweto in 1976 and Cape Town in 1980 triggered student actions in other parts of the country and rekindled a spirit of resistance throughout the African community.[1] African educational protest is not a recent phenomenon: there is a rich history over many decades of sustained African opposition to inequalities in the educational system.[2] This article deals with a protest of the 1920s, the American School Movement in the Transkei, which saw Africans founding and running alternative schools separate from and in opposition to mission and government institutions.

The American School Movement was inextricably bound up with a major protest movement in the Transkei called the Wellington movement. We need to place it in the context of the larger movement and to understand the role of its controversial leader, Elias Wellington Butelezi.[3] Butelezi was born at Emtonjaneni near Melmoth, Natal, about 1895. He was educated up to Standard IV at Mapumulo Training College, a Lutheran mission school, and eventually found his way to Lovedale Institution in 1921 for a year of schooling. Thereafter he earned his living as a salesman for the African Life Assurance Society, an agent for Hobbs' hair grower, a clerk for a labour recruiting firm, Reynolds Ltd., and as a herbalist in Basutoland and Griqualand East in the mid-1920s.

Also in the mid-1920s Butelezi assumed a new identity, that of Dr Butler Hansford Wellington, an American medical doctor. In this role, he began operating as a representative of Marcus Garvey's Universal Negro Improvement Association (UNIA), an American-inspired organisation which had taken root in South Africa shortly after the first World War. Garveyite disciples had established bases in industrial centres like Cape Town, Kimberley and Johannesburg and had gradually spread Garvey's ideas to the rural areas through returning migrants or by word of mouth and rumour and by intermediaries like Wellington.

The essence of Garveyism was its call for the upliftment and liberation of black peoples throughout the world; it stressed the renaissance and reassertion of black culture and values, the material advancement of blacks, and the unity of black peoples of Africa and the Diaspora. That, too, was the thrust of the message that Wellington brought to receptive African audiences — except for one critical departure. Drawing upon a belief that had spread throughout South Africa (and other parts of Africa) in the postwar period, Wellington prophesied that black Americans were coming soon to free South Africa from its European oppressors. On an appointed day these liberators would arrive in airplanes and cast down fiery balls of charcoal on all Europeans and African non-believers; Europeans would be driven out of South Africa and the material wealth of the country would be handed over to Africans. Followers of Wellington (or 'Americans' as they were called) would be spared if they painted their houses black and killed all their pigs. On several occasions Wellington predicted dates for the arrival of the Americans, but his liberators never materialised.

Nevertheless, at the height of his popularity, Wellington's message attracted thousands to his banner. They joined for a variety of reasons: to demand relief from increased taxes, antagonism towards state intervention in African agriculture and resentment over government meddling in local political affairs, the decline and near collapse of peasant agriculture, and prolonged drought. Many had turned unsuccessfully on previous occasions to other forms of protest in seeking a reversal of their fortunes.[4] But at this stage all were united in their belief that Wellington's promise of salvation and immediate deliverance from oppressive conditions was the only alternative.

While his flamboyant personality and his message of the Afro-American liberator are the most dramatic and conspicious ingredients of Wellington's movement, they should not be allowed to overshadow other elements which sustained it long after its millennial phase dissipated. At the heart of Wellingtonism was a rejection of all institutions which served as instruments of European domination, so Wellington and his assistants set out to counter them by establishing organisations free of European control. One example was chapters of Garvey's UNIA; another was a church; and a third was the American school.

That Wellington should found both an independent church and school was a logical step: in other parts of Africa the independent church movement often spawned alternative schools antithetical to mission schools.[5] The questioning of mission Christianity did not stop with religious doctrines or church hierarchy, but encompassed educational instruction as well. Like his counterparts elsewhere, Wellington argued that the mission schools were imposing alien cultural values and ideologies on African children, divorcing them from traditional beliefs and conditioning them to accept subservient positions in a European-dominated system. Wellington proposed that to break this monopoly Africans should establish and control their own schools and churches so that their children could be brought up in institutions which reflected and preserved African values. Teachers and the curriculum were to be under the control of the people, not foreign agents.[6]

Wellington elaborated on his educational philosophy in some of his speeches. The following selections illuminate his thinking, which, in many ways, prefigured contemporary Black Consciousness pronouncements.

When are you going to have churches, schools, Ministers and teachers of your own, why are you calling your churches, Wesleyan, Church of England, Church of Scotland, they believe in Jesus Christ painted white and made to look like an European, I can also paint my Jesus Christ black to suit all natives of Africa. Build yourself as a nation and don't expect the white people to do it for you.[7]

In schools you are taught to say Boss to any white man young or big all the same. Your names are Jim, John, George, Jack, etc. You go to Church but they won't mix with you. In the House of Assembly you'll find all white men and no black man and a black man is there represented by white men, where's justice in it.[8]

The white people have done their best for you, they have civilised and educated you, they have completed the work they intended to do for you. There are many learned men amongst the black people in this Country and there are some of them here. I can mention Dr Rubasana and Professor Jabavu, they are learned men, do they get the respect from the white people, when an inspector of Schools is wanted, a Dutch fellow will be picked out who has passed the 6th Standard, he will be an Inspector for our native schools, some of our black students would be better for the work than the Dutch fellow.[9]

Despite a lack of money, buildings and trained teachers, Wellington achieved a measure of success in establishing his schools. When his movement was at its peak in the late 1920s thousands of students deserted the missions for the American schools.[10] In 1930 he claimed that he had opened 181 schools and 200 churches.[11] Many were concentrated in the northeastern districts of the Transkei and Griqualand East where Wellington had personally operated, but there were few areas of the region which were left untouched.

Although at one point Wellington advocated that his followers should claim the already existing mission school buildings as their own since they had paid subscriptions towards their erection, most of the American schools were housed in the homes of supporters and went under a variety of names such as St. Booker Washington, St. Mount Garvey's, Mount Justice, Willbewill, Hellhillgate, Mount Prejudice, and Atlanta, Georgia. Wellington himself founded his own school, St. Booker Washington Memorial Industrial Liberty College, near Edendale, Natal.

Some former mission teachers offered their services to the American schools, but most of the teachers had had little formal education themselves and were called upon to teach classes beyond their own educational levels. For that reason, the missions still had ultimate control over students since they controlled admissions to higher standards in their own schools.

The curriculum of the American schools conformed to that taught in the mission schools; it differed principally in ideological content. Religious and political instruction were an integral part, and lessons were designed to promote African values. One missionary reported that the Americans were teaching in their schools and churches ' . . . that the people must not pray to the God of Abraham, Isaac and Jacob, because they were white people, but they should pray to the God of Mtirara, or Langalibalele or any of the prominent Africans.'[12]

Predictably, the missionaries were vehemently opposed to Wellington and his American schools. Mission journals were punctuated with denunciations of the Wellington movement, calling it 'sinister' and a 'league of evil workers'. Some individuals called on the government to use force to shut down the American schools, but the prevalent attitude was to let popular enthusiasm run its course and to wait for the students to return on their own. Most eventually did so although some of the American schools survived through the 1930s. Wellington was not treated with the same restraint. His presence in the Transkei was so threatening to the authorities that they banished him from the territory in March 1927.[13]

His expulsion did not prevent the establishment of more American schools. Their continued popularity depended more on local factors and leadership than on Wellington's presence. The American school was heir to a long-standing dissatisfaction with mission education, so it was left primarily to Wellington's lieutenants to catalyse and channel existing discontent for their own purposes. In some areas, they were able to build on protest which had already been directed at the mission schools. An example of this was Herschel district in the Eastern Cape, which had long been a storm centre of anti-government activity.[14] After the first World War, African protest had escalated and was aimed at a variety of targets. For instance, in the early 1920s, Africans had directed their ire at trading stations which they boycotted in an attempt to force lower prices.[15]

School boycotts came several years later and were directed by a local organisation, *Mafela Ndawo Enyes* (we will all die fighting together). *Mafela* was led by a deposed headman, Makobeni Mehlomakulu, and was originally created to fight against government administrative measures such as the Native Taxation Act of 1925, which dramatically increased taxes, and the registration of lands, which people perceived as a means by the government of establishing the unpopular *Bunga* (the Transkei advisory council) in their district. *Mafela* seems to have turned its attention to boycotting schools in late 1925; its target was to force the dismissal of schoolteachers who were accused of being sympathetic to government legislation and to be subverting the minds of schoolchildren.

The boycott achieved success in keeping children away from schools. Women who had played a prominent role in earlier protests were also at the forefront, surrounding schools and refusing to allow children to attend. In several cases bands of protesters physically threatened teachers and, as a result, in October 1927, 27 women were sentenced to two months in jail for forcibly closing down schools. Their sentencing caused such an uproar in the courtroom that armed police had to be brought in to restore order.

According to the South African authorities, it was after the boycott had peaked that Wellington appeared in the district in late 1926 and reinfused enthusiasm into the protest. He was able to hold only a few meetings in Herschel district before the local authorities banished him. He returned once more in December 1926 but was again ordered to leave. Despite his fleeting stay, his continued presence in the region (for he established a base at Tylden and repeatedly held meetings on the Herschel border) was enough to inject new energy into the school boycott and lay the foundation for American schools.

Most American schools operated for only a few years before

inadequate funds and lack of qualified teachers forced them to close. All in all, they had limited success in deflecting the entrenchment of mission and government-controlled education, but it is noteworthy that for a brief period they mounted a major challenge to European control over African education and they remain one of the few serious attempts to create an African-run system of education in South Africa.

It is instructive to compare features of the American school movement with those of educational protest a half century later. The primary focus of both protests was on inequities in education for blacks and whites and the indoctrination inherent in a white-controlled system. Moreover, both found it impossible to keep the question of educational protest separate from more general protests against the whole system of white rule. Nevertheless the protests of the 1920s and the 1970s differ in several crucial respects. First the American schools were directed by community organisations, while the actions of the 1970s were marked by an absence of coordinated community participation and leadership. In the 1970s, students were in the forefront of leadership, while in the 1920s, parents, most with little or no formal education, played instrumental roles. Finally the American school leaders did attempt to establish an educational system independent of white institutions; that option is rarely given serious consideration today. That there have been these changes in the form and content of educational protest over the last fifty years is a measure of the entrenchment of state education and the extent to which government policies have undermined the cohesiveness of African communities, but the very fact that educational protest has not diminished but intensified underscores the resilience of African communities in continuing to resist white domination.

FOOTNOTES

1. Recent studies on the Soweto protests include Baruch Hirson *Year of Fire, Year of Ash. The Soweto Revolt: Roots of a Revolution?* (London, Zed Press, 1979) and Alan Brooks and Jeremy Brickhill *Whirlwind before the storm: The origins and development of the uprising in Soweto and the rest of South Africa from June to December, 1976* (London, International Defence and Aid Fund, 1980).

2. For a brief survey of educational protest, see 'History Lesson' *Sunday Post* (Johannesburg, 4 May 1980) p 9 and F Molteno in this volume.

3. For a fuller treatment of the Wellington movement, see my 'Garveyism in Africa: Dr Wellington and the "American" movement in the Transkei'

Ufahamu VI (1) 31-57.

4. An overview of African protest in the region is found in William Beinart and Colin Bundy 'State intervention and rural resistance: The Transkei, 1900-1965' in Martin Klein (ed) *Peasants in Africa* (Beverly Hills, Sage Publications, 1980) pp 271-315.

5. Additional discussions of independent churches and schools are contained in F B Welbourn *East African Rebels* (London, 1961); John Anderson *The Struggle for the School* (Nairobi, 1970); Harold Turner 'African Independent Churches and Education' *Journal of Modern African Studies* XIII (2) pp 295-309; T O Ranger 'African attempts to control education in East and Central Africa, 1900-1939' *Past and Present* XXXII (1965) pp 57-85.

6. For a brief period Wellington established links with the Old Apostolic Church headquartered in Johannesburg. He was commissioned as a Bishop and authorised to establish branches, but shortly after Wellington fell from grace with the South African government the church expelled him.

7. 1/ELN (East London) v. 86, part 1. Report of an ICU meeting by the CID, South African Police, East London, January 21, 1929 (Cape Archives, Cape Town). At a meeting in Herschel district Wellington was quoted as saying 'If at my death I go to heaven and find a white man there I shall take my hat and go out at once and even if I go to hell and there come across a white man that hell won't contain me.' 2/SPT (Sterkspruit) v. 16. Report by Native Constable Sigenu to Magistrate, Herschel, 15 August, 1928, (Cape Archives, Cape Town).

8. 2/SPT v. 16, 15 August, 1928.

9. 1/ELN v. 86 part 1, 4 April, 1929.

10. Some of these secessions are enumerated in *46th Annual Report of the Missionary Society of the Wesleyan Missionary Society of the Transkeian Missionary Conference, 1928*, 5-9; *Illustrated Report for 1927 of our African Missions* (London, Cowley Fathers, 1927) 38; *Missionary Reports, Society for the Propagation of the Gospel (1927)* Section 30.

11. 1/MCR (Maclear) 4/1/8 (Cape Archives).

12. *47th Annual Report (for year 1928) of the South African Missionary Society*, 27.

13. This was not Wellington's first or his last run-in with the authorities. Not too many years after his banishment from the Transkei a criminal record sheet on Wellington detailed that he had been arrested 18 times in a number of towns on charges of violating the Medical and Pharmacy Act (practising as a doctor without a licence), theft, illegal possession of liquor, contempt of court, contravening pass laws, unlawful possession of a revolver, and ignoring various motor ordinances.

14. For an analysis of the economic situation in Herschel district, see Colin Bundy 'The Herschel Peasantry: a case study' in *The Rise and Fall of*

      the South African Peasantry (University of California Press, 1979) pp 146-165.

15.   Details of African protest in the Herschel district in the post World War I period are contained in 2/SPT v. 16.

The Adult Night School Movements for Blacks on the Witwatersrand 1920-1980
Adrienne Bird

The development of black adult night schools on the Witwatersrand from the early part of this century illustrates the relationship between educational needs and programmes and wider political and ideological considerations.

During the first half of this century the Communist Party developed a challenge to the ruling racist ideology and initiated extensive trade union action in an attempt to give a structure to black resistance in South Africa. It later also co-operated with African nationalist movements to broaden the area of attack.

And it was the Communist Party which initiated the first effective night school movement — effective primarily in that those that passed through it were not simply given the tools with which to better survive in the existing society. As will be shown, the CP night schools trained many who were later to lead the black resistance movements.

Section one of this paper will deal with the rise of a radical adult education movement; section two will consider the liberal response; section three will look at the intensification of repressive action in the fifties and sixties, and the final section will consider the situation that evolved in the seventies.

The Radical Tradition

Formal educational institutions are primary structures for the perpetuation of ideologies sympathetic to the *status quo,* or at least able to be contained by it. Ideological forces which seek to subvert and radically transform the structures of society do nevertheless survive so long as the reality they see, and seek to transform, corresponds sufficiently closely to the experience of certain sections of the population. While these forces may be denied influence in the formal educational structures, they may seek to establish alternative educational structures within which to articulate their philosophy.

In South Africa there was undeniably a mass basis among blacks for such alternative ideologies. For many years after the martial superiority of the colonial powers had been established, no real attempt was made by the state to gain ideological control over 'the natives'. The army of missionaries operating at the time did more than their share but they never reached more than a tiny minority.[1] Depending rather on its repressive apparatuses — army, police and legal machinery — the state forced the blacks off their land to mine gold and diamonds and later, at the time of World War I, to work within the growing number of secondary industries where conditions were poor and wages low.

This urbanisation/industrialisation process did not immediately affect the demand for education from black adults. Initially much of the upper-grade, skilled artisan work was reserved for whites, some of whom already had the know-how, while others were trained on the job or in state-financed technical colleges. Furthermore white workers were united in traditional craft unions and were able to maintain their position of strength and the high wages that went with it.[2]

However, as industrialisation progressed and secondary industry emerged, fragmentation of skilled work occurred creating opportunities for black workers. Also a limited number of white collar jobs (eg teachers, clerks, interpreters) were opened to blacks. This led to increased demands for education, which was an advantage in obtaining this more lucrative employment. Later it also became an advantage in bargaining for better wages. This was one of the major reasons given to the Eiselen Commission why differentiated education for blacks and whites was undesirable:

> The Bantu feel that if they do not follow the same curricula and pass the same examinations they cannot obtain certificates of equal pay, and the possession of the same qualifications is held to be a powerful instrument in pressing for improved financial treatment.[3]

However, this demand was not met, leaving the frustrated expectations of an increasingly militant section of the proletariat, who sought alternative means to improve their wages and conditions.

The Communists

In 1915 the International Socialist League (ISL) was formed by certain left-wing socialist members of the South African Labour Party, who opposed the Labour Party's support for what they saw as an imperialist war. In 1921 the ISL was reconstituted to form the Communist Party of South Africa, which affiliated to the Third International.

The activities of the ISL were initially directed towards the skilled white workers. However, within the ISL there were men, in particular Sidney Bunting, David Jones and later Edward Roux, who argued that a major section of the working class was being ignored, namely the African workers, and they strove to organise among this group. In 1919 Bunting and other ISL and African National Congress (ANC) men were arrested in connection with the 'night-soil workers' (sanitation collectors) strike.

Even at this stage, this organisational work included the setting up of a night school.

Roux, later to become the central figure in night school activity, wrote of these years:

> Bunting and Jones continued to have difficulties, not only with the police, but also with their fellow members of the International Socialist League, many of whom doubted the wisdom of this approach to the black workers. But the two intransigents were not discouraged . . . Jones started night classes for Africans, teaching them to read and write. He got them to write on their slates: 'Workers of the world unite. You have nothing to lose but your chains and a world to win.' But few natives actually joined the League, they felt uncomfortable and shy at white meetings.[4]

This is the first reference to any night school activity on the part of what was to be the Communist Party. The organisation of night schools was to play an important role in the CP's attempts to recruit and train black working class leaders.

The question of the CP's relationship to black workers was thrown into stark relief in 1922 when white mine workers went out on strike. The strike was against the threat of undercutting by cheap black labour. The Chamber of Mines intended to increase the ratio of black miners to white supervisors. Within the CP, one faction, led by W H Andrews, maintained that the main emphasis should still be given to the white workers, while the opposing faction in the party, led by Bunting, favoured an Africanisation policy.

At the 1924 Party Conference Africanisation won the day when the Conference rejected a motion that a fresh approach be made to the Labour Party for affiliation. This new direction — 'the turn to the masses' — had to meet unique organisational problems. Firstly when organising Africans they could not draw on any prior trade union tradition. Secondly, many of the men who came to town to find work had little or no formal schooling and little formal knowledge of the capitalist structures under which they were working.

Following the 1924 conference which launched trade union activities for Africans, party schools were established under the general direction of the veteran Communist T W Thibedi, who launched a drive against illiteracy.[5] It seems that Thibedi with his 'natural genius for getting people together'[6] became responsible for the school, but he later moved into trade union organisation. Such a school was increasingly viable by the late twenties as greater numbers of Africans were becoming permanently urbanised and performing work of a more skilled nature.[7] While organising a Bakers' Union for non-Europeans in 1928, Thibedi met Moses Kotane, who subsequently joined the CP and attended the night school, which had been taken over by Charles Baker (an ex-Roman Catholic priest turned atheist). Moses Kotane was to become the general secretary of the CP and an executive member of the ANC. Kotane believed that the early night schools had been a formative influence for him and had been responsible for his own political initiation.[8]

Moses Kotane was not the only leader to have been recruited into and trained by the CP night school, which in the late 1920s boasted 80 regular students.[9] Among the pupils were leading ICU and Party organisers: Stanley Silwane, Thomas Mbeki, Tantsi, Johannes Nkosi and Gana Makabeni.[10]

Johannes Nkosi was to become the first African Communist martyr when he was shot while addressing a meeting during an anti-pass campaign in 1930 in Durban. Gana Makabeni became the secretary of the strong Clothing Workers' Union in 1928, a post he held for many years. The other names mentioned have also left their mark in the history of the struggle against oppression and exploitation.

The law was frequently used against the Communists in an attempt to frustrate their efforts. In the late twenties when the Hertzog Bills[11] were being debated and feeling among blacks was running high, the Party school was accused of promoting racial hatred and was taken to court. The account given by Roux of the trial illustrates the constraints under which they were forced to work:

> Meanwhile in Johannesburg the prosecutions of communists continued. Nzula had given up his post as headmaster of a Native school at Evaton and has come to Johannesburg, where he was helping Baker with the

night school. In February (1929) he had delivered a lecture to the scholars on 'Hertzog's Native Bills'. On the evidence of the inevitable Native police spies, two of whom had joined the school, Nzula was charged and found guilty of 'inciting hostility' between the races. Baker appeared as witness for the defence. He contradicted the evidence of the two detectives who alleged that Nzula had used the words 'hate the enemy' and 'fight the white man'. The trial was held two months after the lecture, one of the detective spies admitted that he could not understand English very well and neither had made notes at the time. The defence maintained that Baker's evidence should be accepted by the court. The magistrate, however, preferred to believe the Crown witnesses. Nzula was sentenced to a month's imprisonment with hard labour, or a fine of R10.[12]

Direct state harassment was not the only difficulty under which the Communist Party night school suffered. Poor physical conditions and the pass laws contributed to their difficulties:

(The night school) was held on the ground floor of what was actually a slum tenement. There were few desks so that pupils sat on benches or on the floor. There were no blackboards so comrades blackened the walls. The nearby rooms were occupied by poor-white down-and-outs, by prostitutes and methylated-spirit drinkers. Lessons would be interrupted by loud stamping from the floor above or by drunkards who forced their way in. We taught reading, writing and simple arithmetic and held occasional lectures and debates on general topics of working class interest. The teachers, as before, were enthusiastic white comrades. We were not expert in teaching, but we improved as we went along. And our pupils were hungry for knowledge . . . .

Night passes were a great nuisance. Every African, if he wishes to avoid arrest after 9 pm, must carry a special night pass written and signed by his employer. Many white employers were not at all willing to sign passes for attendance at night school, especially a communist night school, so that teachers had to write out these passes themselves.

This was a laborious and time-wasting business. Later we had forms printed on which only the bearer's name, the date and a signature had to be written.[13]

The early successes of the Party and its night school were short-lived. In the late twenties and the early thirties the Party was split and weakened by conflicts revolving around the bolshevisation policy. Many stalwarts, including Bunting, were expelled at this stage for 'right deviations'.

The effect of this 'purge' served not only to weaken the leadership but also to diminish the grassroot support which the Party had enjoyed up to this time. Evidence suggests that the Party school dwindled, but did not altogether cease to function over the period of crisis.[14] Certainly a school existed during the war, for reference is made to a school conducted by the Central Branch of the Communist Party in Johannesburg in 1946, teaching 'English, Arithmetic and History' to an average of forty pupils.[15] But the lack of evidence over this period implies a changed role for the Party school, more simply educational than training for leadership within the organisation.

Roux himself, deeply disillusioned over Bunting's expulsion, went to Cape Town and started an educational newspaper in co-operation with Motane. It was written in Basic 'Ogden' English. (He apparently sent material to Prof Ogden in Cambridge for correction). This newspaper had as its motto 'Paper for Bantu Education and Development — There is no knowledge which white men have which black men cannot have as well'.[16] This publication went under the title of *Umvekele — Theba (The African Defender)*. In 1938 Roux broke his ties with the Communists and thereafter worked only part-time at the new night school which had been started by an organisation known as the People's Club.[17] This subsequently developed into the Cape Town liberal night school movement, offering formal examination courses. It is interesting to note how that those who later initiated other night schools in Johannesburg still looked to Roux as having started the movement.[18]

Other radical groups

Within the radical tradition there were other groups besides the Communists who were involved in education at different times in South African history. However, records of their activities are sparse. Oral evidence suggests that classes were held by the ICU and the trade unions organised both by the 'Trotskyite' Max Gordon and later by the South African Congress of Trade Unions (SACTU).[19] Fanny Klenerman, a trade unionist in the twenties and thirties, has given the following account of her own involvement in the ICU's school and that conducted under the auspices of Max Gordon's unions:

> I did a lot of work, I worked in Max Gordon's organisation the Joint Committee of African Trade Unions, I taught at his schools'.[20]

The scale of the latter activity for the ICU can be gauged from the fact that Fanny Klenerman had to hire three buses to take the group on an educational excursion. These activities were, however, shortlived. For the ICU collapsed in the late twenties due to poor organisation and leadership problems, and the night school organised by Max Gordon's unions seems to have disappeared after his internment at the beginning of the war.

All these radical organisations were concerned with political education. They worked under difficult conditions. They distanced themselves absolutely from the formal channels of education. Their aim in general was to train leaders and allow as many as possible to understand the structure that oppressed them. Their success in the twenties can be gauged by the relatively large number of leaders who emerged after attending the night schools. Education for the radicals had to be part of an active struggle. The internal and external events which eventually weakened the movements should not eclipse their achievements.

Liberal Response to the Demand for Education

There was initially no major departure from the radical tradition by the liberals during the 1930s. In fact, in many instances, those involved in the later tradition were sympathetic to the communists or were even card-carrying members of the Party.[21] The fact that Roux was virtually the founding figure of the liberal tradition underlines this point. But in spite of these sympathies, a definite shift in emphasis can be discerned. Learners were no longer viewed as potential leaders but as individuals needing skills with which to operate within the given social structure. A more formal school-type education was taught to more adequately equip learners for employment. The Cape Town night school in 1939, 'in response to persistent demands', added a Junior Certificate class which 'soon became the largest in the school'.[22] But even these more limited activities fell outside the apartheid framework and were ultimately stopped by the Nationalist Party government.

The African College and the Mayibuye Night Schools

Against a background of anti-fascism in 1938 the African College was started by a group of students from the University of the Witwatersrand in Johannesburg. Within two years another school had also opened.[23] The latter school was the first of many to become known as a Mayibuye School[24] and in addition to university students had school teachers on the staff.

The aims of both schools at this early stage were similar. Those of the African College are reproduced below:

a. Teaching of . . . English, arithmetic, civics and Government — with special emphasis on the native laws and geography, with proposed extension to include Hygiene and Debating and Speaking for the higher classes . . . .
b. To impart useful knowledge adapted to the needs of the pupils.
c. Emphasis on imparting as much general knowledge as possible to help the pupils adapt to and understand their present cultural environment.
d. Solution of special problems and difficulties brought by the pupils or known to be common to the Bantu.
e. Encouragement of free expression and discussion by the pupils to reveal and clarify their difficulties and attack superstition and prejudice through discussion and explanation from both sides. In the course of these discussions, the pupils will be able to see European approaches and attitudes more clearly when these stand out in contrast to their own.[25]

This is clearly a liberal programme, suggesting that the environment is given and the pupils must 'adapt' to it, and revealing a belief that the traditional culture is inferior and must be transcended in order to 'adapt' to modern or 'European' ways. Together these endorse a liberal reformist and not a revolutionary programme. A corollary to this was a belief in a politically neutral education. This is illustrated through a story told by one of the teachers at the African College who started teaching civics to some of the higher classes, but was only allowed to continue this practice once she had reassured the Teachers' Council (a body composed of all who taught at the school) that she was simply describing the laws, was in fact working from her own university lecture notes, and was in no way making judgements about them.[26]

Trade unions were not seen by those in the African College or in the Mayibuye school as a threat. In fact the schools attempted to encourage trade unionists to send their members for elementary education, and it seems that some did attend, although no students were asked to state allegiances, just as the teachers were expected to remain silent on politics.[27]

Unlike those run by the Communists these schools emphasised skill development rather than collective organisation. The arguments of the night schools in support of this approach were in line with the Van Eck Commission of 1946 (a government commission which called for greater mechanisation, the rationalisation of industry and more efficient use of African labour in skilled positions). A policy document of the night schools argued that:

> . . . the present method of paying low wages to inefficient employees is very wasteful. It raised the cost of production, decreased the value as a market of large sections of the community and leads to wastage of labour power.[28]

The night schools in fact wished to extend their activities to include vocational training[29] — a strategy which would supposedly strengthen the bargaining position of blacks. In the end the schools did not themselves initiate such training, but they were instrumental in 1943 in persuading the Technical College to open a 'department for Non-European adults'.[30] Similar projects were subsequently begun in other Reef towns. These ran successfully until 1955 when, presumably as a consequence of the regulation requirements of the Bantu Education Act of 1953, they were forced to discontinue this service.[31]

As with the communists, these schools had to contend with the difficulties of the Pass Laws and poor physical conditions.[32]

Nevertheless, owing to the influx of pupils ('at one time some eighty teachers, each with a dozen or so pupils around a table'),[33] teachers opened new schools in whatever premises they could find. Finally, their accommodation problems were solved when the Rand School Board made available to them the premises of a day 'coloured' school, and subsequently a second school was also used.

While overall attendance grew, individual students were unable to attend regularly for a range of reasons which are similar to those which obtain today: unemployment and insecurity of tenure of employment; the shift system; long hours of work (particularly affecting female domestic workers); difficult weather conditions and sickness; high cost and difficulties of transport; long hours without food; and low income with its attendant evils and domestic difficulties.[34]

In spite of these difficulties, the African College students were actually involved in the direct running of their school. Monthly meetings of the pupils' council were held to discuss matters relating to the school and to formulate suggestions and criticisms of the teaching, books, etc.[35]

Through teachers at the Mayibuye schools, the Transvaal Teachers' Association (TTA) became interested in the work of the night schools. In March 1942, they were sufficiently persuaded by the arguments in favour of the schools to agree to sponsor their efforts. As a result

the whole aspect of work was changed — viz, while carrying on with the
work at existing schools an attempt was now made to co-ordinate the
activities of all night schools with the object of getting financial support
from the Government or Province.[36]

This was possible in the war years as there was a general government concern to enhance the education, and hence the skill, of
blacks to meet the requirements of the war economy, which in
turn required rationalisation of education and implied upward
mobility for blacks. Smuts, the then Prime Minister, is quoted
as saying 'segregation has fallen on evil days'. There was even some
relaxation of the pass laws at this time, and talk of recognising
African trade unions.[37]

Due to war-time conditions in general, and in particular due to
lack of transport and teaching personnel, two Mayibuye night
schools had to close. The remaining schools were thus increasingly
interested in formal ties of co-operation and co-ordination. In the
mid-forties the Johannesburg Central Committee for Non-European
Continuation Classes was formed, and became known as the J4C's.
Besides the Mayibuye schools, other organisations were represented,
the most important of which was the South African Institute of
Race Relations (SAIRR).

The importance of the SAIRR lay in the fact that it represented,
and had done since 1929, the mainline liberal tradition of South
Africa. Originally it had supported a separatist policy broadly
along racial lines, but in the face of the political and economic
pressures of the war years the SAIRR became the most outspoken
protagonist of the necessity for integration. The general economic
climate has already been described, but to illustrate that the
SAIRR in particular was consciously responding to these changes
the following extract from a 1947 conference on Adult Education
is given:

> While an appeal must be based on justice and Christian principle, what
> the European group must also be asked is: Can South Africa, in the face
> of present and future developments on this Continent and overseas
> afford *economically* to carry this burden of illiteracy . . . ? South
> Africa has been urged to develop secondary industries in order to offset
> a possible decline in gold production but the post-war world is going to
> see intense economic competition for markets and South Africa is
> already heavily handicapped.[38] [emphasis in original]

Politically, the war against fascism in the name of democracy led
to an upsurge of mass popular activity at this time,[39] and the
influence of left-wing ideas posed a real challenge to the traditional

ideologies of segregation and minority control. In order to neutralise these tendencies, the liberals called for integration. That this was in response to militant activity can be gauged from a statement by Mr Quintin Whyte, the then director of SAIRR:

> The soldiers, who have visited other lands and have imbibed new ideas, will return with a new conception of human dignity and with a new perspective of a land where the majority of them have not the elementary rights of citizenship. Such material, more conscious of its deprivations than of its own limitations, is ready for the hands of the agitator . . . . These unhappy and distressing conditions have been aggravated by the fact that the great mass of non-Europeans is illiterate; that is to say, they cannot express themselves and cannot be communicated with through the written word. They cannot read public notices affecting themselves, and they are dependent upon what they hear for an understanding of matters that often affect them in vital and intimate ways. They are thus easy prey to foolish or unscrupulous would-be leaders who give their own stupid or malicious interpretation of the motives and actions of Government and other authorities.[40]

A deputation from J4C's was sent to the Johannesburg Municipality in 1945 to request financial support. Mr J D Rheinallt Jones, director of SAIRR, was the primary spokesperson. An application was made for a full-time organiser's salary. To follow up the discussion, Rheinallt Jones wrote to Mr Venables of the Johannesburg non-European Affairs Department on 20 August 1945 making the following recommendations on behalf of the whole deputation:

> . . . I ask you to consider favourably the following possible forms of help to the night schools:
> A, 1. The formation of a Committee under the auspices of an approved body to supervise those night schools which are prepared to come under the Committee, *provided that they are in no way connected with any political group or used for political purposes.*
> 2. The provision of a grant for Adult Education to enable the Committee to appoint a full-time organiser who will not only supervise the schools coming under the Committee, but also make a survey of the needs and of all existing facilities.[41] [my emphasis]

Although the Mayibuye schools and SAIRR stood on the same platform in this exercise, a distinction between the two needs to be drawn.

The former did not seem to fear the left in the same way as the latter. In a separate memorandum to Mr Venables, Mr Fanaroff of the TTA stressed the urgency of the need for education but made no allusion to a threat from subversive elements. Some of the teachers in the early schools were known to be Communist sympathisers, but in the post-war anti-communist climate their silence in the face of the SAIRR's 'agitator' statements can be understood.

The J4C's application for municipal finance was successful and in 1947 they received £3 400 which gave the 19 night schools a far sounder financial basis. This fund also enabled them to employ African teachers at a small fee to take over some of the work done by the less satisfactory volunteers.

In 1944, the Minister of Education, responding to the general climate, had set up a Commission of Enquiry into Adult Education, which had included an investigation of African adults' basic education in its terms of reference.[42] As a result of the report, published in 1946, the Minister appointed a National Advisory Board 'to consider applications for monetary aid from local voluntary organisations.'[43] But in another respect the Report reflected developments which had already been started independently by the SAIRR, for it recommended:

> that experiments be made by the research section of the National Council for Adult Education with a view to ascertaining what will be the best method and technique for a large-scale combating of illiteracy.[44]

The South African Institute of Race Relations' Project

The stated aim of SAIRR's project, begun in 1945, was 'to provide material and work out methods and techniques of teaching and of training teachers for making adult non-Europeans literate.'[45]

This research had in fact been initiated in the thirties by Eddie Roux and had been continued by Mrs Rheinallt Jones. But in 1946, Mrs Maida Whyte, wife of Quintin Whyte, the director of the SAIRR, was given the go-ahead to work full-time on this project. She worked primarily on the Laubach literacy method which had been developed in the Philippines by Dr Laubach, a missionary. The slogan under which the literacy method was carried was 'Each one teach one and win one for Christ'.[46] Clearly this was fundamentally different from the radical education of the twenties, both in content (religious rather than political) and in the methodology (individual rather than collective). Mrs Whyte adopted the method to teach literacy in the South African vernaculars and in English and Afrikaans. Her work was heralded as a major step towards overcoming the problem that had beset literacy efforts until that time. The government gave recognition to her work by subsidising it.[47]

The Institute itself did not run courses. In 1958, at the end of a five-year experimental period, the following description of their activities was given in a special report:

> We help sponsors to train teachers and see their classes initiated. Classes range from domestic ones for two or three learners, to large ones as run on mine compounds and in Durban Night Schools. There are well over 100 classes using our methods running under all conditions throughout the country. Concentration is on mines and in Durban Night Schools. No class is initiated without the approval of the Union Education Department.[45]

It should be noted that this type of activity followed the spirit as well as the letter of the law, in a way that the other schools did not. Any organisation which contained unknown elements, such as volunteer teachers with left-wing leanings, could have been viewed as a potential breeding ground for 'agitators'. By working with state approval and through employers, for example the mining houses, the SAIRR dispelled all such fears. Herein lay the reason why in the long term the Mayibuye schools were closed by the state and why the Race Relations initiative flourished.

However, it took nearly a decade before state controls were implemented and in the intervening years the Mayibuye night schools flourished. In 1947 there were 19 schools attached to J4C's and by 1957 there were 32 with a total enrolment of 3 000 taught by 160 teachers, many of whom were paid Africans.[49] Even when the subsidies were withdrawn in the early sixties the schools continued to survive on fees alone.

The liberal response in the realm of education has been shown to have taken two distinct forms, which may be termed national and regional. The SAIRR, representing the former, argued from general principles, and having on this level justified the need for literacy, proceeded to develop the expertise which would enable them to attack illiteracy on a national level. The latter form, which was represented by regional endeavours in Johannesburg and Cape Town, was more concerned to build up from small beginnings. This group did not address itself directly to national policy decisions and found that it was less antagonistic to other efforts being made, whether by radical political groups or traditionalist African teachers. Both groups gained impetus from

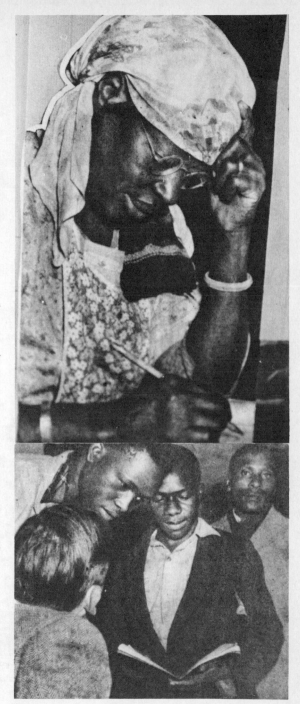

African Night Schools in Cape Town in the Fifties.

Photographs: Johannesburg Public Library.

Fort Hare staff and students, circa 1920.
Photograph: Johannesburg Public Library.

Fort Hare graduation photograph, 1954.
Photograph: Johannesburg Public Library.

the economic trend which had begun during the war, but only the SAIRR felt that any liberalisation had to exclude more radical groups.

As will be shown in the next section, the only strategy which survived the onslaught of apartheid was that of the liberals.

The State Attacks

The Afrikaner Nationalist Party came to power in 1948. In 1950 the Suppression of Communism Act was passed, and as was noted at the time 'anyone who demanded equality with Europeans was a Communist' and many people were prosecuted under the Act.[50] However, protest was not silenced. The fifties were characterised by much activity on the part of the ANC and the Indian Congress. Resistance took the form of a defiance campaign rather than dialogue, which had been tried ineffectually since 1912.

The strength of the state in the fifties was such that it did not bend in the face of this attack. As Dave Lewis[51] points out, this did not mean that the state was all powerful, for it did not outlaw the ANC at this time in spite of the threat which it posed. Rather the state used this period to enact the legislation and establish the machinery needed for the full implementation of apartheid. One of the earliest pieces of legislation passed was the 1953 Bantu Education Act.[52] This Act sought to bring all education for blacks under the control of the central government. The means used was to insist that all educational undertakings be registered and in order for registration to be granted certain conditions had to be met, which were only clarified for the night schools in 1957. Before this time, however, many of the left-wing volunteers in the schools had withdrawn their help in the face of the Bantu Education Act, stating that they did not want to be party to such a system. But the movement continued to grow. Dr Franz Auerbach represented the view of those who remained in the movement. 'It was more important to educate people than to salve your conscience.'[53]

In 1955 the Native Affairs Department took over the administration of grants for African adult education, and insisted that all classes should register irrepective of whether or not they were subsidised. The actual numbers involved at this time are summarised below.[54]

African Adult Education: 1955

Centre	Controlled by	No of Teachers			Enrolment	No of
		Total	Afr.	White		Schools
Johannesburg	J4Cs	160	100	60	3 000	32
Cape Town	Cape Non-European Night School Assoc.	214	12	200	1 200	12
Cape Town	Cape Education Department	—	—	—	303	5
Durban	Durban City Council	—	—	—	3 500	25
Pietermaritzburg	Pietermaritzburg City Council	—	—	—	1 500	5

Schools were also being conducted in Pretoria, Port Elizabeth, East London and elsewhere by various church groups, although exact details of these are difficult to find (see above).

In 1957 a crisis came with the publication of Government Notice 1414, entitled 'Regulations for Night Schools and Continuatión Classes for Bantu Pupils in European areas'.[55] A night school was defined as 'a Bantu School for pupils above the age of sixteen who are bona fide employees and who receive primary education'.[56] The definition of continuation classes differed only in so far as the education provided was at secondary level. These definitions automatically excluded young people, the unemployed and those employed in the informal sector. Also it linked the type of education to be provided with that given to children in the formal sector. All such schools or classes were compelled to register before 1 January 1958, or else be closed. In European areas applications for registration had to be accompanied by permits from the Group Areas Board.

These schools were to be conducted only during normal school terms and were to be held in official school buildings unless permission to the contrary was given by the Director of Bantu Education. All teachers' appointments were made subject to the Director's approval which could be withdrawn at 24 hour's notice without any reason being given. Furthermore schools had to be open to departmental inspection at all times. In 'white' areas registration had to be renewed annually, and in all areas except 'Bantu reserves' no pupil could be admitted unless he or she was both over 16 and able to prove that he/she was resident in the area of employment. As regards control in 'European' areas the Notice said:

> 3, 1. Any night school or continuation class in a European area shall
> . . . be controlled and administered as a private school by the
> proprietor or his representative who shall be a European.

2. Where the Director (of Bantu Education) . . . deems it necessary an advisory board shall be appointed to assist the manager in an advisory capacity (which shall consist of Europeans only).[57]

In the African urban residential areas or African rural areas schools could be conducted only by African school boards or committees. Private organisations conducting such classes were required to hand over control and all their assets and liabilities by 1 January 1958.

As a consequence of the difficulties, both financial and administrative, arising from the new measures, all the Durban night schools were closed. The Cape non-European Night Schools Association was forced to hand over four schools to African school committees, and to conduct the remainder without subsidy. Eight schools in Pretoria were closed due to transport problems. The adults who attended, primarily those in domestic service, often found it impractical to attend classes in the townships. Many other schools are also reported to have closed at this time and the remaining schools in Pretoria, Port Elizabeth and East London were eventually handed over to the Department of Bantu Education.[58]

The 1957 measure made J4C's continued existence as a co-ordinating body impossible as each school had to be controlled by its own white manager or African school board. The spirit of co-operation was lost as it was usually impossible to get sympathetic people to act as nominal managers in municipal areas or compounds and it was certainly difficult to influence school boards. About ten of the original schools continued, mainly in the industrial areas, but they lacked cohesion and the sense of a movement was broken.[59]

Those schools which survived were in fact granted Group Areas permits and official registration in 1958, but for seven years after that, although annual applications for registration were submitted in terms of the regulations, no replies were received. In the interim those schools receiving subsidies found that the amount granted steadily decreased, and by 1963/4 the subsidies dried up altogether.[60]

An amendment to the 1957 Government Notice was gazetted in 1962 (5/1/62).[61] This was in essence no different to its predecessor, except that in addition to the official documents required from the Group Areas Board, the owner of the building in which the school was conducted was required to endorse the application and a locality sketch of all the buildings in the block was to be provided. A list of all the owners of property in the immediate vicinity was required to accompany the application.

This was a prohibitive task, given the usual hostility of white property owners who were afraid they would infringe one of the multitude of Group Areas regulations.

The degree to which these two decrees were successful in stifling the night schools can be gauged by statistics given by the Minister of Bantu Education in the House of Assembly in 1962.[62] In that year there were 33 night schools and 19 continuation classes in South Africa with a combined enrolment of 2 218. Before the new system was introduced there had been over ten thousand students all over the country.

Although, as has been stated, annual applications had been made to the Department for registration and Group Area Permits, no replies at all were received until 1966. A letter received by Dr Auerbach (acting manager of one of the original J4C schools) was typical of those sent throughout the country:

> Ministerial approval in terms of section 9(7) (e) of the Bantu (Urban Areas) Consolidation Act, 1945 (Act No 25 of 1945) is hereby conveyed for the conducting of the above mentioned school (Mayibuye Bantu Evening School) until the 31st December, 1967.
>
> Kindly note that any application for the extension of the above mentioned period will not be entertained under any circumstances,
>
> Yours faithfully
> Bantu Affairs Commissioner, JHB (Dated 29-7-66)[63]

And thus ended the possibility of any night school movement in the 'white' areas of South Africa. As has already been noted schools in the black areas were not made illegal in the same way, but they did suffer as the school boards to which they were tied had little interest and no experience in night schools, and were in any case taken up with their own day-school work.

Beyond publically expressing their condemnation of the measure in the press,[64] the organisers could do nothing and there was certainly no organisational basis on which the adults who had attended could react — as the real 'movement' had been broken in 1958 and by this time the schools were in any case isolated units.

The reason for the government's actions can be understood only by looking at the wider context. These were not isolated acts of malice — South Africa of the sixties was very different to South Africa of the forties. The power bloc was significantly more stable, and the foundations of a stable economy were well laid in the post-war boom. From that position of strength the legislation of the fifties was enforced and apartheid was made a reality. For example, a degree of independence was afforded to the first

'Bantu Homeland', the Transkei. By the same token, resistance was ruthlessly suppressed, most drastically by the killing of pass law protesters at Sharpeville in 1960.

Throughout this period the literacy and language work of the Institute of Race Relations continued. By 1956 they judged that they had amassed sufficient expertise and equipment, both in the teaching of vernacular literacy and offering courses in the two official languages, to graduate into a full-time independent activity. On 1 October 1956, encouraged by the recommendations of the Eiselen Report and the Tomlinson Report,[65] an interim committee was set up to establish 'Bureaux of Literacy and Literature'. The aims of the Bureaux were defined as follows:

> To foster literacy by training personnel in the techniques which had and were being evolved to make adults literate in the shortest possible time, to provide the basic literature required for this, and, primarily through missionary societies and other bodies, to foster the distribution of Christian and other healthy and useful literature.[66]

Once the Bureau was initiated it applied for registration as an 'Association not for Gain', under Section 21 of the Companies Act. After a long delay, this was granted in 1964.

When the government ceased to subsidise night schools in the sixties the Bureau was affected as well. In an effort to solve its financial difficulties it embarked on a campaign to increase literacy work in mine compounds. The mining houses responded favourably to the drive, and gave a per capita grant to the Bureau to train teachers to teach in the compounds. This involved a large number of people and to the present day constitutes the largest source of income for the Bureau.[67]

There were both social and economic reasons why mining houses in particular, and other industrial and commercial concerns more generally, were prepared to concern themselves with literacy. On the social level literacy work, which is commonly understood to include courses in the official language, was seen as a way to improve relations between black miners and white supervisors in the workplace. This was possibly based on an assumption that lack of communication was what caused labour unrest rather than starvation wages or dangerous working conditions. On the economic level, it became increasingly possible over time and within the limits of the colour bar to advance blacks to more responsible positions.

But in order to facilitate this mobility a certain minimal education was required. Another possible factor, both political and economic, was a desire to provide social welfare services to the men who lived in bachelor compounds for nine months of the year and who were understandably restless.[68]

The carefully orchestrated attacks made by the state on the night school movement were, it has been argued, part of a total strategy to implement apartheid. The Mayibuye movement was broken because it depended on independent urban-based organisation, whereas the Bureau prospered because it operated through employers and promoted a religious view of the word.

Literacy in the Seventies

For literacy and language teaching movements, 1967 marked both an end and a beginning. The tradition of a tightly organised, urban-based movement was broken. In its place there developed, on the one hand, several organisations modelled on the Bureau of Literacy and Literature, and on the other, attempts by radical black students to set up community learning groups. The first of these were organised from above, primarily through employers, and allowed for only limited initiative on the part of would-be learners. The latter were short-lived attempts to once again unite language with broader political issues — related though to the broad aims of Black Consciousness rather than those of any particular party. Again, these developments must be seen against the political and economic changes of the times.

During the sixties the economy expanded at an unprecedented rate.[69] This was due not only to gold mining, but also to the broadening base and increasing sophistication of South African industrialisation. But few of the advantages reached blacks, for whom the average per capita share of the GNP was 1, as against 14,5 of the whites.[70] During this period inflation spiralled and black wages fell even further behind those of other race groups. In response, there was a wave of strikes between October 1972 and January 1974 involving tens of thousands of black workers.[71] These resulted in substantial wage increases in many sectors of industry.

Employers, faced with more expensive labour, attempted to cut costs by retrenching workers and demanding higher productivity from those who remained. Recessive economic trends contributed to a critical shortage in certain categories of jobs (skilled work was still reserved mainly for whites) and rising rates of unemployment in general. One reason for the shortage of white skilled labour was the drying up of the supply of under-employed whites who could be transferred from unskilled to skilled or supervisory work. Furthermore, the traditional source of recruitment of white labour, namely, from other countries, was not sufficient to meet demand. This helped to promote the belief that greater stress needed to be placed on internal labour supplies, as did the fact that 'white collar' occupations were expected to grow from 16 percent of the labour force in 1970 to over 20 percent.[72] Even Afrikaans businessmen, who during the sixties had sheltered under the apartheid umbrella, were joining the chorus for a liberalisation of labour laws. The President of the Johannesburg *Handelsinstituut* told the Johannesburg *Afrikaanse-Sakekamer* in 1971 that African labour would have to be used more productively and that more effort was needed to ensure adequate levels of education for blacks.[73]

Politically, a taut calm had been achieved in South Africa in the mid-sixties by repressive means. However, in the late sixties, after nearly a decade of quiet, black resistance emerged in the form of the Black Consciousness Movement. The movement began in 1968 on the campuses of the black universities under the auspices of the South African Students' Organisation (SASO).[74] The object was to foster pride in and community awareness of black capabilities and achievements. This, it was argued, was an essential preliminary if blacks and whites were eventually to come together on a basis of equality. In 1972 the Black People's Convention (BPC) was inaugurated, in an attempt to broaden the base of Black Consciousness.

While this movement was growing, very important changes were taking place just beyond South Africa's northern borders in Mozambique, Angola and Zimbabwe, where armed resistance to the white colonial powers had emerged. Prior to 1974 South Africa had a buffer-zone between itself and black African states. But in April 1974 the situation was dramatically changed when Portugal was forced to surrender her colonies to the liberation movements she had been fighting for nearly two decades. This was a dual blow for the South Africa state. It lost its stable borders and was at the same time faced with internal repercussions. The lessons were not lost within the country on young blacks who identified with the national liberation struggles.

These then were some of the political forces which influenced the June 1976 student protest throughout the country, which, although triggered off by the Afrikaans language issue in schools, soon became a generalised expression of opposition to apartheid.

SASO

In the climate of radicalism which grew up in the black universities, much debate focused on broadening the appeal of Black Consciousness. Around 1970, Rev. Colin Collins of the radical University Christian Movement (UCM) began receiving and circulating the works of Paulo Freire, which were just emerging in English translation, to black students. The ideas excited the students who felt they had suffered from the 'banking' type of education which Freire described and the material offered concrete alternatives. Freire's work was banned in South Africa but over 500 copies were made and circulated. A few courses which aimed to inform fellow black students of Freire's ideas were run informally at the black universities and some students became involved in compiling community surveys to clarify critical areas for later discussion.[75]

As a result some literacy (vernacular) teaching was done in centres throughout the country but in a dispersed fashion with no reliable records now available of the extent of this work. As with earlier radical programmes, this work was linked to a wider programme, in this case community health centres and other self-help projects under the auspices of the Black Community Programmes (BCP).

This work did not continue. Due to SASO's involvement in the Soweto'76 demonstrations, SASO, BPC, BCP and other related organisations were banned on 19 October 1977 and many of those who had been involved were detained by Security Police, the most famous being Steve Biko, who subsequently died in police detention.

'Bureau-Type' Literacy and Language Programmes

Responding primarily to the economic pressures a completely separate set of literacy organisations developed modelled on the Bureau of Literacy and Literature. At the centre of this response was the view that literacy and language training 'should be instituted, because the pay-off would be much quicker than waiting for school children to grow up.'[76]

Reaction against labour militancy was also influential in stimulating this initiative as can be deduced from the aims of 'Communication in Industry'. This organisation, started in 1969 in Pietermaritzburg, was concerned to promote good labour relations by teaching black workers — through the medium of English

1. To understand what is said to them in the work situation
2. To make their wants known
3. To read simple instructions and reports

4. To write simple sentences.[77]

The methods of teaching adopted by Communication in Industry were based on those evolved in the 'English Through Activity' (ETA) method 'walks, games, rhymes, tours of the factory area, stories and plays as teaching devices'.[78] Similar methods were developed for South African black primary schools. They were recently evaluated by J V Rodseth for the Institute for the Study of English in Africa. He concluded:

> These points help to isolate a fallacy upon which ETA appears in part to be based. This is that pupils should be involved *physically* in language-learning activities. Physical involvement is of course no guarantee that mental involvement will exist. Many 'chanting-and-doing' exercises are echoic and call for an extremely small degree of mental concentration.[79]

Yet in spite of this apparent fallacy, the method and the organisation which sells it, have expanded rapidly. By 1974, 165 instructors had been trained, mainly in Natal where the first centre was established. Today the list of firms using ETA is much longer.

Operation Upgrade of Southern Africa (Upgrade)

The third major literacy organisation functioning at present in South Africa is Operation Upgrade of Southern Africa (Upgrade) which, like the Bureau, uses the Laubach method but in a different form.

The project was pioneered in 1966 when Dr F Laubach himself worked for a while in Durban with a local organiser. Although religious in orientation, Upgrade was responsive to the economic climate as is seen in frequent statements of Mr D'Oliveira, the Director.[80] More interesting is the degree to which Upgrade acquired government legitimacy by accepting and working within apartheid structures. This is illustrated from the organisation's official magazine:

> Because the Government has come to realise the need for intelligent manpower on a national basis, and because of its need to make Bantustans viable, it has given tremendous support to Operation Upgrade. The Minister of the Interior, Mr Theo Gerdener, is the organisation's patron.[81]

Over the years the relationship between Upgrade and the state has grown to a point where Upgrade can be seen as *the* literacy and language organisation which meets state-perceived needs. Most recently this has been shown by the fact that Upgrade, rather than any of the other organisations, was requested to teach teachers for the government Adult Education Centres throughout the country[82] (the formation of these centres is discussed below).

The method itself is based on the stimulus-response/Skinnerian behavourist theory of learning. Lessons are characterised by chiming responses to visual stimuli. Some preliminary evaluation[83] suggests that the popularity of this approach is based on the degree of assistance (total) given to the teachers and learners by means of manuals and charts — no real preparation is required once one has learnt the set moves. The theory of learning on which this method is based has now been widely criticised, although the actual effect of this still needs careful evaluation.

Other Programmes

In the climate of political and economic upheaval in 1976, the Anglo American Corporation, the biggest gold producer in South Africa, allocated R700 000 for the development of its own English language course. This relatively huge budget was granted when the government started making substantial moves in regard to the dismantling of significant job-reservation restrictions.[84]

The course, designed by Dr Ken Baucom, was planned in such a way as to include information needed on the mines, such as what procedures to adopt for dealing with grievances. More general topics like safety procedures and the types of protective clothing available were written into the course at every stage, as were production home truths, eg 'I must not be late', and censures like 'he is a lazy worker'.[85] The course television-based, is essentially programmed instruction. The materials are self-contained and the teachers need merely to manipulate the technology and read instructions from a manual. The mines train their own teachers on short in-service training sessions. The teachers themselves come from that group of employees who have at least a matriculation certificate. They are paid overtime for their services. The students, black miners, volunteer to join the group, which is conducted in their own time on mine premises.

Contrasting with this highly structured approach is the approach of 'Learn and Teach' (L&T). The organisations already described depend primarily, although not exclusively, on employers to initiate literacy classes. In contrast, L&T, which started as a small pilot project in 1974, placed the emphasis on the community to initiate the classes.[86] This difference in orientation and emphasis is not merely theoretical but can be seen both in the material that is provided (these are primarily compilation of learner writings about their experiences) and the method of learning used (discussion-based).

The State's Response

The state's response to the crisis of the seventies was to scrutinise almost every aspect of the life of urban blacks, including education and employment. One particularly important piece of legislation was the 1976 Bantu Employees' In-service Training Act (Act No 86, 1976) which aimed to encourage the formation of training establishments at the place of work by offering substantial tax incentives to employers.

Literacy (including the official langauges) was seen to have an important preparatory role in relation to the above scheme. The *Bantu Education Journal* of November 1975 stated:

> There is no need to labour the point that (illiteracy) . . . is one of the main brakes on personal, social and economic development. It has been spotlighted in the last two years as industry has endeavoured to upgrade the black worker: the man with the industrial skill has not always had the communication skills to function at a higher level . . . . Whatever the reason, we have to do here with a handicap which prevents the full realisation of his potential.[87]

In 1975 the Department created a new section dealing with adult education, concentrating on literacy and night schools. A steering committee consisting of three members was given the task of 'determining what is already being done and how instruction can be properly planned, controlled and financed.'[88] In particular, 'the Human Sciences Research Council was approached for assistance with regard to the evaluation of literacy programmes.'[89]

While the question of method was still under consideration the Department went ahead with planning 'Adult Education Centres', all situated in industrial centres. By the end of 1977 twenty centres were operating throughout the country, offering courses at the primary level, and also secondary courses leading to form III and form V certificates. The Department also began certain in-service teacher training refresher courses. A total of 6 068 adults were being taught at the lower level, while the majority were receiving instruction at the higher levels, altogether these centres were catering for 15 580 learners in 1977.[90]

At the primary or elementary level literacy is taught. Initially Operation Upgrade was invited to train teachers for these courses, and this practice has continued.[91] However, the Department (now re-labelled the Department of Education and Training) has also initiated its own courses which are still in the experimental stage.

Further indications of state involvement in basic adult education have appeared in the Bantu Education Annual Report. For example, in 1976:

> Existing regulations governing State centres, night schools and continuation classes are being revised at present with a view to adaptation to the present stage of development of adult education.[92]

In the remainder of the report proposed changes were given. The most immediate difference from earlier regulations was the raising of the minimum age for enrolment from 16 to 18. This is significant in terms of student militancy — the Department was clearly determined that these centres should not become an alternative for radical students expelled from regular day schools. Further it made it clear that the Department was in no way changing its fundamental belief in 'separate development' — the requirement that any person who wished to enrol should either be fully and legally employed or, if female, have full residence rights, was in no way changed. This was underlined by the fact that 'homeland' centres were to be encouraged. One major departure was the setting up of a local 'Governing Council and a Student Liaison Committee at each of the State Centres'[93] — control was no longer simply to be left to inexperienced school boards.

Other statements made by government policy-makers suggest that the changes will go further. When opening a conference convened by the Human Sciences Research Council for all persons involved in literacy and language teaching in 1978, the Minister of Education and Training said:

> . . . the adult literacy programmes should fit in with the existing school programmes on the one hand, and programmes for continuing the education on the other hand. Any literacy programme which is divorced from the normal school system can only lead to frustration.'[94]

He then went on to explain that any literacy group wishing to obtain registration in order to continue functioning would have to furnish proof that it did not deviate from this 'school' principle. Once this proof had been given they would be allowed to function 'subject to certain conditions laid down by the Department'. But any expansion of this work would again have to be referred to the

Department before it could be instituted. In essence therefore it can be seen that what appeared to apply to state centres is to be a national policy.

More disturbing though is what the Minister had to say about methodologies:

> However, there is a further important task, which should receive urgent attention. During the course of this conference, various teachers will elaborate on the literacy work they are doing. I accept that literacy programmes can vary in their methods and aims, but I think that we can ill afford an expansion in the range of programmed techniques offered by so many different parties It is in this regard that one hopes that the assistance of the Human Sciences Research Council as an independent research organisation will act as a type of clearing house which will evaluate the techniques used and that the Human Sciences Research Council will help to determine the norms to be set for success to be achieved in the literacy programme . . . . It is doubtful whether a single type of literacy programme will meet the needs of the various interests within the community. The Department may have to accept responsibility for developing a literacy programe which could serve as the basis for further study.[95]

Interestingly, these statements have not in fact inhibited research, which has been started (in 1980) at the University of Natal, Durban, and at the University of the Witwatersrand, Johannesburg, in response to the very great demands being expressed. No doubt the situation will be clarified once legislation is passed and implemented. But some significant compromises have been made, for example the state has accepted the need to support adult education financially.

Whether this is at the cost of such freedoms as existed before, for example in methodological research and development, remains to be seen. Certainly the state has made it clear that it will not countenance such radical options as were provided by SASO. There seems therefore to be both a liberalisation and a renewed element of control in these recent moves. This strategy can be called 'state-sponsored liberalisation', and has been evident in other areas as well. For example, in legislation convening black trade unions.

In general terms it is not difficult to understand this policy of state sponsored liberalisation. For the country is facing sanctions from the West, and has insecure borders with neighbouring countries. In the government's terms, if there is a realistic chance of survival, it is based on being able to maintain stability internally. Every possible area of conflict is being brought under state control. 'Deviants' are ruthlessly dealt with. Success however, also depends on maintaining a healthy self-reliant economy, hence, the pursuit of policies which aim at allowing blacks to fill skilled labour shortages. A by-product of this will supposedly be the emergence of an increasingly large group of blacks with a vested interest in the status quo. But the contradiction of having economic power with little or no political power remains.

FOOTNOTES

1. Report of the Commission on Native Education 1949 — 1951 (Eiselen Report), Pretoria UG No. 53/1951, (Pretoria 1951) p 35.
2. Johnstone, F *Race, Class and Gold* (London, 1976).
3. Eiselen Report, 1951, paragraph 235, p 43.
4. Roux, E *Time longer than Rope* (Winsconsin, 1948) pp 131-2.
5. Discussed in Lerumo, A *Fifty fighting years* (London, 1971) p 58.
6. Roux, E and R *Rebel Pity* (London, 1970) p 66.
7. Lewis J, 'The New Unionism: Industrialisation and Industrial Unions in S A, 1925-1930' in Webster, E (ed) *Essays in Southern African Labour History* (Johannesburg, 1978).
8. Discussed in a letter dated 31 March 1956, quoted in Bunting B, *Moses Kotane* (London, 1975) p 44.
9. Roux (1948), p 163.
10. Discussed in Simons, H J and R E, *Class and Colour in South Africa 1850-1950* (Middlesex, England 1969) p 376.
11. These related to legislation, proposed by Hertzog, which aimed to divest Africans of all political rights, even those few they had enjoyed in the Cape since 1854, and to restrict for all time the amount of land available to blacks to 13 percent. These Bills were finally passed in 1936.
12. Roux (1948), p 225.
13. Roux (1970), pp 67-8.
14. Roux (1948), p 346.
15. 'Memorandum submitted to the Municipality of Johannesburg' by I Fanaroff and N D Lester from the Witwatersrand Federation for Non-European Adult Education (1946) Document: Rheinallt Jones Collection. University of the Witwatersrand Library, AD 483 B50 (a), p 3.
16. See Roux (1970), pp 141-2. Also see issues March 1937, p 1 and October/November 1937 p 5.
17. Roux, E 'Adult Education for Africans in Cape Town', Document in Rheinallt Jones Collection, AD 843 B 82 (a) undated) p1.
18. Interview with F Auberbach, July 1978 (cf 21 below) Johannesburg.

19. Interview by E Webster and J Lewis with F Klenerman, 23/6/78.
20. Interview F Klenerman.
21. Interview with Dr F Auerbach of the Transvaal Teachers' Association July 1978, Johannesburg, teacher in Mayibuye School 1948-52 Director of J4C 1952-67.
22. Roux, 'Adult Education for Africans in Cape Town', p 1.
23. Lewin, J 'Night Schools in Johannesburg' in *Books for Africa* (London) January 1943, 9 (1), p 8.
24. The name 'Mayibuye' was taken from the slogan of the ANC, and literally meant 'Let it come back' — 'it' meaning Africa. Roux while working in Cape Town made up a song, together with J N Tantsi, of the ANC, song to the tune of Clementine: (in translation)
    Let it come back! (Mayibuye)   Let it return, let it return
    We brown people bless Africa   Let Africa return to us!
    Which was taken from our fathers   Down with passes
25. Document: 'Night Schools for Adult Africans: History of African College and Mayibuye Night Schools' in Rheinallt Jones Collection, AD 343, B 82 (a), Misc. 73/41 p 4-5.
26. Interview with Maida Lipshutz, ex-teacher at African College (London September 1978).
27. Interview with Maida Lipshutz.
28. Document: 'Night Schools for Adult Africa' p 11.
29. See 'Memorandum to the Municipality of Johannesburg' (1946) pp 4-5.
30. See 'Night School for Natives 1938-47' p 2. For extent of this activity see Eiselen Report, paragraph 345 p 66.
31. Horrell, M *Bantu Education to 1968* (Johannesburg 1968) p 112.
32. See 'Night School for Natives 1938-1947' p 1.
33. See 'Night School for Adult Africans' p 1.
34. Document: 'Memorandum to be submitted to the Adult Education Commission by the Federal Committee for African Adult Education' Rheinallt Jones Collection B54(b), 1944 p 6.
35. Lewin (1943) p 9.
36. See 'Night School for Natives 1938-1947' p 2.
37. Legassick, M 'Legislation, Ideology and Economy in post- 1948 South Africa' *Journal of Southern African Studies* 1 (1) October 1974 p 8.
38. Document: 'Adult Education: What is it?' from SAIRR conference in Cape Town, January 1947, Rheinallt Jones Collection AD 843 B82 (a), p 3.
39. For a full discussion see Lewis D 'African Trade Unions and the South African State 1947-1953' unpublished paper University of Cape Town also O'Meara, D 'The 1946 African Mine Workers Strike and the Political Economy of South Africa' *The Journal of Commonwealth and Comparative Politics,* XIII (2) July 1975.
40. Document: 'Adult Education for Non-Europeans' by Quintin Whyte,

SAIRR document RR 35/46, p 6.

41. Document in Rheinallt Jones Collection, AD 483 B50 (a).

42. Report of the Committee of Enquiry into Union Adult Education (L.C. 5258) (1946).

43. Eiselen Report, paragraph 368, 370.

44. Eiselen Report, paragraph 80, p 40.

45. Whyte, M 'Report in Brief in respect of 5 years experiment in Literacy 1.4.47 − 30.3.52', SAIRR 326: 374 (68) Box 25 (A), p 1.

46. Laubach, F & R: *Toward World Literacy, the Each One Teach One Way* (Syracuse University Press, 1961).

47. Eiselen Report, Annexure, P, 'Bantu Adult Education', paragraph 5, p 213, also paragraph 371, p 68.

48. Whyte 'Report in Brief', p 2.

49. Interview with F Auerbach, 7 July 1978.

50. Mokgatle, N *The Autobiography of an Unknown South African* (Hirst and Co, London 1971) p 285.

51. Lewis D, 'African Trade Unions and the South African State: 1947-53' (mimeograph) Cape Town.

52. Act No 47 of 1953, Statutes of the Union of South Africa (Cape Town 1953).

53. Interview with F Auerbach.

54. Compiled from information given by Auerbach interview and also Horrel (1968) p 19.

55. G N No 1414, 13 September 1957 in *Bantu Education Journal* (Pretoria, November 1957).

56. G N No 1414, *ibid* definitions 1.

57. G N No 1414, section 3(1) and (2), in *ibid* p 450.

58. *A Survey of Race Relations: 1957-58,* SAIRR (Johannesburg, 1958) p 206.

59. Interview with F Auerbach.

60. Horrell (1968) p 112 and interview with F Auerbach.

61. Government Gazette Extraordinary (Regulation Gazette 1654) (Pretoria, 5 January 1962) R26.

62. *A Survey of Race Relations* SAIRR (Johannesburg 1963) p 187.

63. In the possession of Dr F Auerbach. Kindly show to the author.

64. Interview with M Lipshutz, also see *The Cape Argus* 3.10.1967, p 2.

65. Eg Eiselen Report, Annex P p 213, Tomlinson Report (U.G. 61-1955).

66. Horrell (1968) pp 119-120.

67. A total of 22 000 out of 36 000 claimed learners were miners according to a document entitled: 'The Bureau of Literacy and Literature: Aims and Scope of Present Activities' (Johannesburg, 14 April 1977) p 2.

68. The provision of social services for compound dwelling miners, in the form of language classes, was given by Dr Ken Baucom (then of the Anglo American Corporation English teaching project (July 1978)) as one reason for developing their project.

69. Discussed in Johnson R W *How Long will South Africa Survive?* (London, 1977) pp 26-45.
70. Johnson (1977) p 84.
71. Johnson (1977) p 86.
72. *A Survey of Race Relations, 1972* SAIRR (Johannesburg 1973) p 261.
   A Survey of Race Relations, 1977 SAIRR (Johannesburg 1978) p 229.
73. *A Survey of Race Relations 1970* SAIRR (Johannesburg 1971) p 245.
74. *Ibid.*
75. Biko, S *I write what I like* (The Bowerdean Press, London 1978).
76. *A Survey of Race Relations* SAIRR (Johannesburg, 1977) p 230.
77. Communication in Industry 'Communication in Industry: The Arnold Varty technique of English Teaching'. (Pietermaritzburg, undated) p 1.
78. *Ibid*, p 10.
79. Rodseth, V *The Molteno Report*, (Grahamstown, 1978) p 43.
80. Operation Upgrade 1972 *Upgrade Magazine*, (Johannesburg), p 1.
81. *Ibid*, p 10.
82. *Post Transvaal*, 7 July 1978.
83. Bird, A *Learn and Teach, an evaluation*, 1980 (mimeo).
84. Interview with K Baucom, 22 July 1978.
85. Baucom, K *CCTV English Course*, (Johannesburg, Anglo American Corporation, 1977).
86. Environmental Aid Development Agency 'Learn and Teach' in *Link*, No 6, Feb 1978 pp 16-22.
87. *Bantu Education Journal*, Pretoria, November 1975, p 3.
88. Bantu Education Department, *1976 Annual Report*, Pretoria (R P 36/1976) p 4.
89. Bantu Education Department *1977 Annual Report*, Pretoria (R P 27/1977) p 75.
90. *Bantu Education Journal* April 1978, pp 30-31.
91. *Post Transvaal*, 6 July 1978.
92. Bantu Education Department, *1977 Annual Report*, Pretoria, (R P 27/1977) p 75.
93. *Ibid*, p 77.
94. Cruywagen W — Transcript of speech by Minister of Education and Training at conference convened by HSRC, 11 July 1978, (unpublished).
95. *Ibid.*

Upward All and Play the Game:
The Girl Wayfarers' Association in the Transvaal 1925-1975
Deborah Gaitskell

Introduction: Supplements to Mission Education

Schools were from the outset an inevitable adjunct of virtually all Protestant mission work in Africa, because Bible study demanded literacy. Most African education in South Africa, though increasingly dependent on state funds for teacher training and salaries, remained in missionary hands until 1953, but it began to lose its direct role in Christian conversion quite early on as Africans, forced to look for labour with white employers, perceived the usefulness of English and arithmetic. Scholars acquired an often nominal Christianity and it was hoped that they would retain their links with the Christian community and become full church members. While some African parents and teachers chafed under church control for the couple of decades prior to the assumption of full state control of education, it was in these years particularly, under the state's special 'Native' school inspectorate, that mission education became increasingly sophisticated, secularised, standardised and professionalised, to the concern of the more evangelistically minded. 'Were they not giving education and economic and social factors more attention than evangelisation?' Rev James Dexter Taylor asked the General Missionary Conference in 1925. 'Is it not true that even in our schools the least definite, most haphazard part of education is the training in religion and morals?' In the mid-thirties, it was no less evident that 'the aridity of religious education in the schools caused great anxiety'; worship and religious instruction were deemed inadequate and unreal, sterile in influencing personal and community life. Some observers pointed to the secularising effect of Western civilisation, while others blamed the school-teachers, 'the poverty of whose spiritual and mental equipment was deplored'.[1]

Partly in order to counter this religious deterioration, there emerged on the Reef and in other mission areas two important supplements to the influence of the school: Sunday schools and Christian youth movements. The former were, like their predecessors in Britain and America, co-educational, the latter separated the sexes, but in both Sunday schools and the youth movement for girls, women missionaries often had a dominant role, and almost always a woman involved in the one was also a leader in the other. Both types of youth work used more informal and pleasurable methods to impart or reiterate Christian teaching; the uniformed youth movements also offered healthy recreation and useful skills. With day schools, they formed three mutually reinforcing educational agencies, the youth movements occupying the centre of the spectrum — more recreational than school, less purely religious than Sunday school.

It is noteworthy that it was generally black school teachers who provided the leadership of these supplementary agencies, under white supervision. Out of 1 729 African teachers in govern-ment-aided schools in the Transvaal in 1937, 648 taught in Sunday schools, that is, 37,5 percent of the total number of teachers, while 849, of whom 363 were women, helped with youth move-ments. This was virtually half the total.[2] For a significant number of African teachers, then, involvement in either or both mission organisations was an important dimension of their employment in education. This blurring of secular and religious teaching functions went back a generation or two. The fact that a third of the Transvaal teachers were also active as pastors, preachers and evangelists, provides a reminder that in the early days of mission education, before the real development of the teaching profession for Africans, the roles of catechist and school-teacher were filled by the same person. Denominational schools in late Victorian Britain commonly required their employees to teach in the Sunday school too;[3] Transvaal teachers, by contrast, appear to have given their time voluntarily to these extra-curricular activities, though probably both pupils and mission authorities informally pressured them into involvement at times. These organisations were also part of the school staff's own background: 65,8 percent of student teachers in the Transvaal in 1935 attended Sunday school, a significant majority even though well below the national average of 82,5 percent.[4] Finally, many of the teachers were very young, which would facilitate easier relationships with children and youth: half the staff in Transvaal schools in 1937 were under twenty-nine years old.[5]

By and large too, recruitment to Sunday schools and Christian youth movements came through the schools. Contemporary social commentators remarked on the ample provision of leisure activities for African school children, especially by comparison with the non-schoolgoing majority which churches and social agencies hardly reached.[6] The advantages to leaders were obvious: day school children would come to the mission's supplementary activities with some Bible knowledge, reading ability and habit of discipline, while the English learnt in school simplified communication. Urban missionaries not proficient in vernaculars relied on Africans to teach the younger children who were less fluent in English. It seems likely that even within that group of pupils, it was those who stayed on to the higher standards who were largely drawn into the auxiliary organisations, for they became more favourably disposed towards school than were the short attenders who encountered in the substandards the least qualified teachers.[7] At the culmination of their primary schooling, over half of the Transvaal Std VI pupils in 1935 attended Sunday school; the proportion among girls was even higher, at nearly two-thirds.[8] Thus a minority of African children received through these new institutions an intensified exposure to Christian social and spiritual education, as the influence of the school was supplemented weekly, first by the Sunday school and later by Pathfinders for boys and Wayfarers and Sunbeams for girls.

The supplements to mission education were adopted at a time of great educational expansion, which undoubtedly put the social and spiritual influence of the school under particular strain, while simultaneously highlighting the needs of youth. Whereas in 1921 an estimated 9,1 percent of the Transvaal school-age African population were at school, 16,1 percent were in 1936. The number of pupils in aided schools more than doubled in each of the two decades prior to P A W Cook's detailed investigation:[9]

Number of Aided Schools and Scholars, Transvaal

Year	Schools	Scholars
1917	330	21 421
1927	407	47 632
1937	807	105 054

By the late thirties, there was a schooling crisis: facilities could not keep pace with the 'constant clamour for more schools, more teachers, more money and higher classes'.[10]

This increase in the school population after the First World War was even more noticeable on the Reef, where a much higher percentage of African children — at least a quarter — were in school. Mission work there went through successive stages corresponding to the demographic shifts in the African population. Churches concentrated initially on male converts, then, as more African women came to the Witwatersrand after the Boer War, female prayer unions were formed. Subsequently, recalled Winifred Grant, wife of the prominent Reef Methodist minister E W Grant, 'almost before one was aware of it' the children were there 'in great numbers, crowded together in the yards and slums of downtown Johannesburg' and new initiatives were necessary to cater for them.[11] Between 1921 and 1936 the number of African children under fifteen on the Witwatersrand increased fivefold, from some 16 000 to nearly 80 000.[12] About a third were in school in 1937, for the 1930s saw enrolments shoot up.[13]

Whereas in the Transvaal as a whole the Lutherans undoubtedly dominated mission education, for 30,8 percent of African schools belonged to the Berlin and Hermannsburg Missions,[14] on the Reef a trio of British and American Protestant missions led the field until the mid-1930s. By then, Roman Catholic numbers in school outstripped the American Board's, but the Methodists and Anglicans combined still had more pupils than all the other missions together.[15] This mission trio of Anglicans, Methodists and American Board was not only central to early Wayfarer fortunes on the Reef and in the Transvaal, but also exercised the greatest influence in Witwatersrand Sunday school work. The American Board taught 850 children in nine Sunday schools by 1939. This represented about one-third of the pupils in their ten Reef day schools.[16] Anglican women missionaries were responsible by 1939 for at least 3 600 children in Sunday schools, representing just over half of the number in day school.[17] The Methodists taught over 2 000 in their Sunday Schools throughout the 1930s. Concern that this represented only one-third of day school attendance may have prompted the great boost to enrolment in 1940, when numbers passed 4 000, two thirds of the day figures.[18]

Reef Methodist Sunday schools differed significantly from those of the other two churches in their higher level of male and, especially at first, white leadership. Rev E W Grant from 1926 headed an African Sunday school movement which deliberately set out to be inter-racial, having sixty-two whites working alongside fifty-nine African teachers at its height in 1932.[19] He saw the joint spiritual venture in Sunday schools as 'a far more promising solution to the "native problem" than any political one could be'. It might mean 'the suppression and ultimate elimination of mutual distrust between the races of the land' because

in their most impressionable years, and during critical days in this country, great numbers of native children are gaining their ideas of the qualities of the white race, of the mission and purpose of Christianity, of the Master Himself, from intimate contact with a virile, courageous, and joyous type of Christian disciple.[20]

The outstanding female-led institutional example of this white inter-racial mediation in the 1920s, Dorothy Maud's Anglican settlement venture in Sophiatown from 1928, was explicitly named The House of Peace (in Zulu, Ekutuleni) and did its peacemaking primarily among children, using girls' and boys' clubs in addition to Sunday schools and youth movements.[21] It is important to remember that white missionaries did not teach Africans in Transvaal day schools. Outside the few boarding schools, their educational contacts were limited to intermittent supervisory visits, though the administrative responsibilities could be extensive in the way of departmental returns, collecting fees, paying salaries and seeing to buildings and equipment. This made additional forms of interracial activity all the more urgent, particularly in the political climate of the Reef from the mid-1920s, when the Communist Party, the African National Congress and the mushrooming Industrial and Commercial Workers' Union all had their headquarters in Johannesburg. Whether for moral or political reasons (in some cases, I would argue, on social and spiritual grounds), white contacts with black children fared better than attempts with adult Africans. Just as Clara Bridgman considered that the 'line of least resistance seemed to be with the children' rather than their mothers in the Doornfontein 'dens of drink and vice', so Dorothy Maud found the children of Sophiatown less suspicious than their elders, more responsive to the white women living in their midst.[22]

Scholars have recently shown interest in British Sunday schools, whether as vehicles of 'religious terrorism' extolling industry and obedience 'to discipline the new child labour force in the factories', or as popular, authentic working class creations, significantly boosting educational self-improvement by their pre-1850 literacy training.[23] In view of this debate, but also considering their symbiotic relationship with secular schooling and their cultural and political overtones, African Sunday schools in South Africa merit further investigation. Their educational relevance cannot be seen only in religious terms.

Wayfarers and Pathfinders were the second supplement to mission schooling evolved in the inter-war period. Youth movements have been identified as a key development by South Africa's veteran educational researcher, although Malherbe says nothing of their adoption among groups other than white:

> Though they were of an extra-curricular nature, the emergence of youth movements such as the Boy Scouts, Girl Guides and Voortrekkers was probably the most significant growth point in the field of education of young adolescents in South Africa during the last half-century.[24]

His brief account effectively discusses Scouts only, however. Similarly, Springhall's illuminating analysis of British youth movements from the 1880s into the 1930s, concentrates on those for boys.[25] But the Christian movement developed for African girls in South Africa merits a consideration which goes beyond an attempt to redress this neglect of adolescent female socialisation, necessary though that is — research into the race- and sex-specific education of African girls is minimal, apart from Jacklyn Cock's stimulating foray.[26]

Youth movements were a more prominent part of female extra-curricular education than of male. Wayfaring, with its 30 000 members throughout Southern African in 1935, commanded double the following among African girls compared with the Pathfinder Movement among boys.[27] 63 percent of women teachers took part in youth movements, compared with only 42 percent of men in Transvaal schools, so again the relatively greater weight was on the female side.[28] The Transvaal Wayfarers are of additional interest because they held back from absorption into the worldwide Guide movement in the 1930s and continue to exist today as a separate African youth organisation, claiming 80 000 members in 1975, their fiftieth anniversary year. While initially drawing on the same pool of Reef missionary and liberal leadership, Wayfarers outlasted several other contemporaneous examples of inter-racial, extra-curricular, broadly educational co-operation. The character of the movement and the shifts in its ethos and activities also provide important examples of the vitality and persistence over the last half century of the ambiguous notion of racially differentiated education. Finally, the 'progressive' aspirations of a movement taking 'Upward' as its slogan, alert us to another of the cultural agencies for Christian upliftment and respectable self-improvement which contributed to social differentiation in the African community. Indeed, Wayfaring might, at times and at its most extreme, be seen as part of the 'cultural colonisation' of the African inter-war generation for which Black Consciousness has indicted liberals and missionaries.

The Origin of Wayfarers

The establishment in October 1925 of the Girl Wayfarers' Association can be traced to three main influences: the example of the Boy Scouts and Girl Guides; the growing concern of missions with youth and leisure; and ideas of educational 'adaptation' in vogue in the 1920s. Each will be considered in turn.

The Girl Guide movement was launched in 1909, and by the end of the 1920s had over half a million members in Britain alone.[29] The aims were as follows:

> To develop good citizenship among girls, by forming their character; to train them in habits of observation, obedience, and self-reliance; to inculcate loyalty and thoughtfulness for others; to teach them services useful to the public and handicrafts useful to themselves; to promote their physical development; and to render them capable of keeping good homes and of bringing up children in the right way.
>
> The method of training is to give to the girls healthy activities which, while giving them pleasure, will afford them a course of education outside the school along four principal lines:
> Character and Intelligence, through the Guide Law and Promise, the Patrol system, woodcraft, games, etc.
> Skill and handicraft, encouraged by badges for proficiency.
> Service for others and citizenship, through daily good turns, organised public service, etc.
> Health and Hygiene, through open-air life, camping, physical exercises, games, etc.[30]

In South Africa, Guiding started as early as 1910. Within a decade, it had made great advances in all four provinces among white girls. The inclusion of African girls was then discussed, but shelved in 1925 on the grounds that it was premature.[31]

As the growth of the Sunday school movement in the 1920s demonstrated, that decade saw a new missionary focus on youth on the Reef, a focus to which growing numbers of children, the secularisation of the teaching profession, the concern for white safety and the need to Christianise the next generation all contributed. As women missionaries made contact with schoolgirls in their regular, supervisory needlework classes and again in the Sunday school, they became convinced that some sort of additional organisation was needed, a youth movement offering the benefits of Guiding. Such a movement would 'help in the adjustment to civilised conditions of these girls, and be for their spiritual, moral and physical well-being'; it 'would teach the right use of leisure, give wholesome discipline through teamwork and games, and inculcate loyalty to authority and the idea of sisterhood for service.'[32]

Girls elsewhere in the country were showing interest in joining the Guides, the demand being described as 'acute' among coloured girls in the Cape peninsula. Various imitations sprang up: the African Methodist Episcopal Church started a group in Cape Town called 'African Guides' which held some parades and 'was photographed for a Southern States magazine'; the Cape Girls Pathfinder Society borrowed the name of the mission adaptation of Scouts; Lovedale's 'Sunshine Girls' sounded like a music-hall act; the 'Lightfinders' surfaced on the Reef in 1924. In early 1925 a Transvaal Council was formed with Mrs Rheinallt Jones as Superintendent, Mrs Ray Phillips of the American Board as Treasurer, and Caro Happer, an Anglican woman missionary, as Secretary to the Lightfinders. Wayfarers was an amalgamation, performed later that year, of Lightfinders and Girl Pathfinders.[33]

As Mrs Jones was to be the driving force in Transvaal Wayfarers until her death in 1944, she needs some introduction, and her active co-operation with and leadership of what was really a mission-centred enterprise merits explanation. Edith Barton, born in Yorkshire in 1882, had been a Student Christian Movement member and a Student Volunteer (for missionary service) in her university days in Leeds, where she took an MSc and education diploma. She came out to South Africa in 1905 to teach, heading a girls' teacher training school of the Paris Mission in Basutoland for a while, before returning to Cape Town, where she married J D Rheinallt Jones, a Welsh minister's son, in 1910. Her encouragement of coloured women teachers in gatherings for study and service there, the foundations of the later YWCA coloured branch, was an early indication of the direction of her lifelong interests: working with the black women and girls of South Africa for their advancement. In 1924 (by which time the Joneses had moved to Johannesburg and become involved in the Joint Council movement) Rheinallt Jones, Secretary to the Witwatersrand Council of Education, became Chairman of the Transvaal Pathfinders. The formation of the Pathfinder Advisory Council that year under the auspices of the Scouts (who similarly insisted on racially separate movements at this stage) must have stimulated Mrs Jones in her endeavours for a girls' movement.[34] This was just one of an astonishingly wide range of social service projects to which she devoted her considerable energy.

The attraction for missions of a form of Guiding needs, secondly, to be set in the context of a decade in which leading urban missionaries, backed up by liberals and financed at times by commerce and industry, devoted a great deal of attention to 'constructive recreation' for the African. This was what Ray Phillips, its chief exponent, called 'moralising the leisure time of natives in city and country alike', on the principle that 'whoever captures the leisure time of the people gets the people in the long run.'[35] Initially interest was shown in the adult African male. Phillips's film shows in the mine compounds, his football clubs, and his provision for the educated elite through the debates and social facilities of the Bantu Men's Social Centre,[36] were meant to keep the African from both the Devil and the Communist agitator, who were assumed to be equally eager to find work for idle hands. J D Taylor, Phillips's superintendent after 1928, underlined the social and political relevance of 'constructive recreation' in a blatant appeal to white self-interest:

> Proper and adequate provision for Native recreation would mean better workers, keener mentally and physically, better citizens, less likely to be criminals, better neighbours, less likely to be anti-white, more likely to possess a true sense of community values.[37]

But the mission interest in recreation was also part of a new broader approach to conversion. The Christian youth movements came to be seen as an important element in the permeation of African life by that social Christianity which was deemed by 'progressive' missionaries at the end of the twenties to offer the best chance of winning Africans for the Gospel. This was a viewpoint voiced not only by the social activists themselves. Rev Crabtree of the Primitive Methodists, lamenting the defection to the Communists of Albert Nzula, their Aliwal evangelist's son who had condemned Jesus's 'slave morality', mused:

> one comes more and more to see that it is not by preaching alone that the native is to be saved. We must ... permeate his whole life with the spirit of Jesus. And that means play-centres, school, work, better housing, organisations such as Wayfarers and Pathfinders, health work, and a hundred other agencies.

Taylor wrote in similar vein in the *South African Outlook:*

> Is not the old type of evangelism ineffective in the present day conditions? . . . . Does not our preaching cover a very limited area of life? Does not our redemption fail to give the Christian control over his environment and to deepen and sweeten the channels of his community life?
>
> I venture to suggest that the most effective evangelism for today will be done through Community Service Leagues, Pathfinder and Wayfarer movements and similar efforts unless these are allowed to become separated from the Church instead of centering around it.[38]

As soon as Phillips came to Johannesburg in late 1918, he started an African Pathfinder troop, then equipped a modern supervised playground in Doornfontein (1919-24), and initiated football and hockey leagues for school children.[39] Both he and Grant helped to lead the Pathfinder movement on the Reef, Grant going on to become District Superintendent in the Eastern Cape. It was little surprise then that the wives of both these missionaries, already running Sunday schools, became prominent in the Wayfarer movement, Dora Phillips giving over thirty years' service to the Association. Phillips was especially exercised by the problem of the negative morality missions had brought to rural Christians. For younger people, the life of church members, with its restrained propriety and hymn singing, appeared intolerably dull and staid by comparison with the liveliness of heathen dancing, singing, clapping and beer drinking.[40] A more positive alternative had to be provided or the church would lose the children. And so Wayfaring was described by a woman missionary as supplying

> 'the fun of the Fair' to our Christian girls whom we have cut off from all the fun and excitement of heathen life. We don't want them to dance and yell and sing as the heathen girls do, and if we put nothing in the place of that, we have the danger of the empty house into which the seven devils enter.[41]

On the Reef missionaries faced a different counter-attraction for Christian girls — commercialised dances and later the popular Marabi.[42] It is significant that when Wayfarers began, games and singing formed an important part of their work. A Games leaflet was issued to leaders early on, and English country dancing attempted to substitute for African, in recognition of the appeal of rhythm and movement to girls.

The reference above to the perils of the 'empty house' touches on a final facet of the concern for Christianised recreation: it was seen as a solution to the problem of social disintegration and the destruction of traditional life. Allusions to the breakdown of tribal sanctions, parental authority and sexual mores became almost the cliches of white urban Christian lament in the inter-war decades. The burden of expectations vested in mission youth movements comes through in Schapera's comment to the New Education Fellowship conference in 1934:

> The degeneration of the sexual life; the loss of parental control; the decay of family and tribal education and discipline; the growth of irresponsibility and licence: these call for the development of positive forces and organised activities such as are provided by the Pathfinder

and Wayfarer movements.[43]

In the case of black urban adolescents in the thirties, organised recreation was combating two specific bogeys produced by this disintegration — male juvenile delinquency and female pre-marital pregnancy, rather than the political discontent of their elders in the twenties.

The third influence on Wayfarers, that of 'adaptation', was initially forced on the movement by default by the rebuff from the Girl Guide Association: if African girls could not belong to a branch of the world-wide movement, they would have to have their own version, with their own uniforms, rules, promises, tests and awards. But as the Association evolved, it came to have certain dimensions which aligned it with the philosophy of Thomas Jesse Jones, C T Loram and the Phelps-Stokes education commissions of the early 1920s. 'Anxiety about social disintegration, a frankly racist view of African capacities, and an effort to make education functional in a colonial economy' is how one recent author summarises the dominant strands of this ideology.[44] 'Adaptation' went hand in hand with 'co-operation' (indeed, E W Smith comments that these were the two watchwords of the 1926 Internation Missionary Conference at Le Zoute[45]) although it was axiomatic that in joint inter-racial ventures, whites were to have the guiding role of the older brother or sister. Wayfaring was not mooted as an all-African movement, like Jabavu's Pioneers in the Eastern Cape: white leadership coupled with the training of African deputies was the agreed model.

Jesse Jones sought to apply to African as to Negro education two general principles: adaptation (to people's instincts, experience and future) and community consciousness. These values 'could best be embodied in schools through emphasis on what Jones called the "Simples" of health, home life training, industry (including agriculture), and recreation.'[46] The embodiment of these very values in the Girl Wayfarers' Association is most striking. The recreational stress on games and singing has already been referred to,[47] while the other three elements — health, home life training and industry — correspond neatly with three of the categories of proficiency badges towards which the girls could work, as outlined in the Association's first handbook. These were entitled the Home Way, the Health Way and the Hand Way. (Guide badges were grouped, by contrast, under the four divisions stressed in all their work — Character and Intelligence, Handicrafts and Professions, Service, and Physical Development and Strength.[48]) The fourth, the High Way, which included an interpreter's test, and badges for nature and traffic knowledge, was less directly in this tradition. A fifth group of badges, the Heart Way, relating to Bible knowledge, was added round 1932, and provides a necessary reminder of the unique Christian emphasis of the movement. Nevertheless, the close correspondence with Jones's 'Simples' cannot be coincidental. It is regrettable that the early days of the movement are so little documented (Mrs Jones's correspondence on Wayfarers appears to have nothing preserved prior to 1934.) Despite Rose Kerr's assertion that the Wayfarer handbook was drawn up by two Guide Commissioners,[49] it does not seem fanciful to detect Loram's guiding hand or the Rheinallt Jones's imbibing of the key notions of Jesse Jones.

It is not without interest or relevance that it was Loram who called and chaired the October 1925 conference which made a South African organisation of the two movements for girls then existing in the Cape and the Transvaal. 'Some day I shall tell you', wrote Loram to Jesse Jones in late August 1925 (no record survives, unfortunately, to indicate he ever did!) 'how I butted in to save several good women from forgetting that they were Christians. Jealousy and other less noble qualities showed themselves as they so often will. However we are now at peace. I have found the ideal Secretary.' On 11 October he reported

> The culmination of our planning for the Native Girl Guides is coming when we meet tomorrow at Bloemfontein. I am to preside at a National Conference which I have called at the request of the acting and warring factions. Mrs R Jones will be there. I hope that I can keep her in order. It will be a ticklish meeting. Hold your thumbs up for me.[50]

Loram was a close friend of the Rheinallt Joneses,[51] a member since its inception in 1920 of the permanent Native Affairs Commission, and South Africa's most prominent educationist, whose work, *The Education of the South African Native* (1917) had won him participation in the Phelps-Stokes Commissions to South, West, and later, East Africa.[52] His book argued forcefully for a differentiated and rurally rooted education for Africans in a segregationist South Africa in which they were bound to have a subordinate role, precisely the sort of approach which Jesse Jones could endorse.

Kenneth King has very skilfully demonstrated the ambiguities and ambivalences of 'adaptation', which 'attracted support from racists as easily as from progressive educators'. For Oldham of the International Missionary Council, it was an education term, for Norman Leys 'a thinly disguised formula for political inferiority', while W E B du Bois protested that the 'Phelps-Stokes Fund was making Africa safe for white folks'. Indeed, in African colonies with substantial white settler populations, 'Tuskegeeism', with its aim of creating a gradualist, contented, rurally-based African leadership, implied containing African political advance while enhancing its value to the economy.[53]

The Girl Wayfarers' Association was not free of such ambiguities either. Community consciousness and practical skills and knowledge were to be allied with loyalty and discipline; badges could be won for what were clearly skills inappropriate even to an 'adapted' village home and more likely to be used in domestic service.[54] Leadership and uplifting initiative of a specific sort were to be fostered, within a framework of happy partnership with and ultimate deference to white superintendents.

In sum, then, the Girl Wayfarers' Association, like uniformed youth movements in Britain, grew out of a specific social context which meant that it did not exist simply to provide girls with the benefits of Christian character-training and enjoyable pastimes and skills. It was also intended to be a facet of the urban Christian social work of the 1920s, led by whites, to supplement evangelism and provide a counter-attraction to rural heathen or degraded or commercial urban leisure pursuits. This social work hoped to help Africans adjust to changed conditions, both for their own good and that of the whites, for by keeping the channels of communication and co-operation open through such seemingly insignificant joint ventures as youth movements, such social work kept society orderly and whites in charge.

The Nature and Appeal of Wayfaring

The 1925 conference in Bloemfontein created a Union-wide Girl Wayfarers' Association, but the two strongholds, the Cape and the Transvaal, were represented by provincial committees supervising work in the north and the south. Although the OFS, Natal and Basutoland subsequently got their own committees, the two largest provinces continued to provide the numerical weight in the movement.[55]

For the first year, leaders worked from a roneod handbook,[56] but by the end of 1926 a printed one appeared.[57] This handbook is a fascinating document, providing a detailed exposition of the movement's goals and methods at that stage. The Association aimed

> primarily to help girls of the non-European races of South Africa to become better Christians by training them in habits of truthfulness, obedience, industry and courtesy; teaching them services and handcrafts

useful to others as well as to themselves; promoting their physical development; making them good homemakers and capable of bringing up good children.

Significance might be attributed to its omission of the Guide aims (see beginning of previous section) of developing powers of observation and self-reliance, and its addition of truthfulness and industry! It also substituted 'better Christians' as its all-inclusive objective for the 'good citizenship' of Guiding. This Christian emphasis is one of the marks distinguishing Wayfaring from Guiding. A girl guide simply promises to do her duty to God, a promise which need not exclude Hindus or Jews, for example. With regard to method, the handbook reminded Wayfarer leaders that the whole movement was

> based on the idea of training character by play and voluntary activities, and not by ordinary school methods, and therefore the weekly meetings should be varied, and should include plenty of games, indoor and outdoor, while singing, story-telling, make-believe and simple acting may all be used.[58]

The Girl Wayfarers' Association consisted of a number of local detachments, each under a Leader helped by one or more Sub-Leaders. The key unit was the Group of six to eight girls, led by a Grouper, with perhaps five groups forming a detachment. Before she could be enrolled, a girl had to attend for at least six weeks to prove her keenness, and pass a test of her knowledge and understanding of the four Wayfarer Laws and the Health Laws. These laws reflected the twin concerns with character and health training:

1. A Wayfarer does her duty to God.
2. A Wayfarer helps others.
3. A Wayfarer is a friend to animals.
4. A Wayfarer always does her best in work and play.
                    and
   Be clean
   Eat suitable food
   Wash with plenty of water
   Wear light clean clothes[59]

'Ceremonial', it was asserted, 'makes a great appeal to most girls. It is therefore the policy of the Girl Wayfarers to use it as much as possible.' Enrolling ceremonies were outlined, with their form of words accompanying the entry of the new girl into the circle of members, who agreed to receive her as a comrade; she would shake hands all round and the enrolment concluded with the Wayfarer prayer. She could then wear uniform: a badge with a flame emblem and, unless she could not afford it, a brown dress with matching hat.[60]

The four Main Ways which followed this First Step were voluntary, but girls were to be encouraged to take the proficiency tests, rewarded with badges of different colours. It was clearly the badges for the Home Way which one woman missionary (who later supported the move to Guides) 'always had in the back of my mind . . . were really teaching them to be a good domestic or something like that, not a leader', a charge an opposing missionary strenuously denied.[61] For the cookery badges, the girl had to lay the table and prepare either twelve different dishes, or twenty for the advanced one. The laundry badges involved washing and ironing three (for the second stage five) different items of clothing each representing a different type of fabric. It was the Housework section of the Home Way, above all, that brought out the contradictions of the Jesse Jones approach, for the skills rewarded appeared increasingly likely to be of use to a white employer rather than enriching the community life of a 'good' village African. For the first stage, the Wayfarer was to polish silver, clean the kitchen and the stove, and light the fire. For the second, she had to be able to dust furniture, books and ornaments, clean windows, get rid of vermin, and turn out a sitting room, while the third was awarded if she could do the daily work necessary in a bedroom, answer the door and where possible the telephone, take messages and wait at table.[62] (But it should be noted in fairness that British Guiding had Domestic Service and Laundress badges too.)[63] The Hand Way, with badges for sewing, knitting, crochet, embroidery and handwork (like making mats and toys), was more likely, one would think, to be both of use and enjoyable to the girls, and built on skills already encountered by many in day school sewing classes.

Whatever the intentions of the framers of the Home Way, it appears that, initially at least, the Health Way was the most attractive to members; in preparation for the Home Nursing and First Aid badges, quite detailed instruction was given in caring for patients, using splints and bandages and coping with burns, faints and accidents.[64] The prestige of nursing as a career for African girls was being entrenched in these years, as a perusal of Skota's *African Yearly Register*, with its sublime photo-portraits of young African nurses, or of the black petit bourgeois press, confirms. It was thought that the Wayfarer movement definitely encouraged that trend towards taking up nursing,[65] the most popular future occupation with Transvaal African Std VI girls in 1935.[66]

Branches for younger girls between eight and thirteen, soon called Sunbeams, were also being established and the Handbook outlined their regulations too. Enrolment was more dependent than for Wayfarers on religious knowledge on the one hand, and on the other, demonstrating physical and manual dexterity. The little girl had to know the Lord's Prayer and the Junior Wayfarer's special prayer, as well as their laws: 'A Junior Wayfarer says her prayers every day. A Junior Wayfarer is truthful, obedient, clean and cheerful.'[67] Six weeks regular attendance with clean hands and face, tidy hair and no pins fastening her clothes was a further prerequisite. Finally, she had to be able to skip, with three fancy steps, and run in and out three times with others without missing her turn, and do two of three 'craft' activities: bead-threading, making a basket or mat, or sewing on buttons. The blue uniform was not compulsory. The various tests, again with colour badge rewards, suggested for the juniors — modelling, writing, sewing, crochet, handwork, washing, housework, basket-making, gardening, toy-making, knitting, and Scripture repetition — were similar, though of course simpler, to those for older girls, but were not organised into the division of the different 'Ways'.[68]

An enrolment ceremony for Sunbeams suggested a few years later and clearly modelled on the Brownies', conveys something of the cheerful team spirit the movement hoped, in a rather 'precious' fashion, to inculcate: when 'Mother Sun' asks the Sunbeams gathering round her, 'Who are you little people?' their reply includes the lines:

> We're the Sunbeams, here's our aim
> Upward all and play the game . . .
> We're the bright and shining 'Rays'
> Lighting up the rainy days.[69]

('Upward' was of course the Wayfaring motto, while the phrase 'play the game', an exhortation borrowed from the Guide movement, recalls that whole British public school 'vocabulary of morality' drawn from the playing field, where games instilled a code of decency as well as developing physical courage, team spirit and leadership ability.)[70]

The initial response to the movement throughout the Transvaal was encouraging, indicating, the Wayfarer Council there felt sure, 'the need there was for a Christian Social Organisation of this kind'. Within two years there were just under two thousand girls involved, with support concentrated in the north and east and on the Reef, areas of extensive African settlement. Already over four hundred proficiency badges had been earned, the most popular being those in Home Nursing, Hygiene and First Aid, 'though Interpreting attracts many diligent workers, and the Cookery and Needlework badges have been taken by many groups'. Most detachments had attempted some sort of social service too, such as visiting or helping in African hospitals. At this stage, in line with 'co-operation' philosophy, the leaders were white women (though African women could qualify after getting twelve badges and spending a year as a sub-leader) and the sub-leaders usually African teachers or nurses. By 1927 two training schools for the forty sub-leaders had been held since, despite the 'domestic servant' slur, Wayfarers clearly aimed to foster at least some African women's leadership potential. Two other persisting features of the movement had made their appearance in these early years: 'reviews', that is, large gatherings of uniformed detachments ceremonially inspected by a notable dignitary (Lady Baden Powell herself in 1926), and camps for which the two country areas 'were very enthusiastic.'[71]

No trace has come to light of anything in Wayfaring like the interesting links between the British army and the Boy Scouts, nor would one expect it in the same way of a girls' movement; but even in Britain in the 1920s, youth movements had to adapt to the anti-military temper of the day to stay popular. It would be interesting to know whether other African adults agreed with Archibald M'belle of Herschel that 'the idea of our girls donning military uniforms, drilling and parading them in the streets, and sending them out camping, is objectionable'. Individual officials hastened to assure him in the columns of *Umteteli* that militarism was not their intention, and that Wayfaring's promoters believed, 'no less ardently than himself, that the place of Native womenfolk is in the home'. Furthermore, Mrs Jones commented mildly,

> Singing, drill and games will be encouraged (but not in the streets) and I cannot help feeling that nicely brought up Native girls will be happier and more wisely employed in their spare time in such pursuits than in lonely rooms or aimless wanderings in the streets.

Nevertheless, M'belle criticised their 'mock militarism' again three years later, in a further complaint about its social dangers and undermining of parental authority.[72] Ray Phillips was able to induce favourable verdicts on the mission youth movements from Reef African adults: 'Should be encouraged to the utmost' and 'Useful organisation to enforce discipline in young folks'.[73] But these somewhat bland comments cannot be said to be particularly revealing of the attitude of African parents to their children's membership of the Wayfarer and Pathfinder movements.

We have equally little individual documentary record of the African girls' attitude to the movement, though further oral research could help here.

An essay by a Methodist Wayfarer in the mid-1930s reflects the attraction exerted by the public and visible lure of dress and crowds; her striking moral earnestness recalls the breast-beating style of Evangelical conversion accounts:

> When first I had not joined the Wayfarer Movement I led a very peculiar and extraordinary life, selfish, disobedient, lazy, unpunctual and untruthful. When Wayfaring spirit crept into me, I was first attracted by the brown uniform and parades, which often took place. I wished to be in the crowd, also to be admired in brown, though I did not know what it meant. [After learning the Laws parrot-fashion, she was suprised when her enrolment was delayed because she punched a girl who mocked her, and was punished for being late at school.] I was so careful never to be misled by any of the former deeds for fear I would be delayed from my uniform . . . . Wayfaring has created in me a better life and uplifted me, from what I was.[74]

In view of the example of by then well-established uniformed women's prayer societies, it was probably not wishful thinking for a woman missionary to suggest that, for some girls at least, the donning of a uniform immediately created a standard of morals.[75] The uniforms *were* clearly a drawcard perhaps all the more because schools generally did not have uniforms. It availed nothing to protest their relative unimportance. 'We always tell them that they need not have their uniform', said Dorothy Maud 'and need not get them in a hurry, but they do love their uniforms and they look after them well.[76]

The Venda schoolgirl who, in the 1950s, wrote about her child-hood for Blacking,[77] must have been a typical Wayfarer recruit: it was not by chance that the Association's motto was 'Upward'. She was bright in class and won over to all the aspiring and self-improving enthusiasms which mission education sought to impart: knitting to earn pocket money; ambitious for higher education and a nursing career so that she would be able to save money; delighting in her school choir's competitive exploits and athletic prowess — 'Our school is indeed very civilised'. She was quick to learn her Wayfarer Laws (but recalls them incorrectly!). She remembered songs and games learnt, and commented on the 'really smart' uniform. Her memories also point up what must have been an all too common gap between the intentions of the movement and the actual features enjoyed by the girls. The most 'wonderful' part of the 'splendid game' in which her own school was involved at a rally was the fact that 'our European' had been clever enough to think of a play including food, which was clearly to her its outstanding feature; any deeper meaning to be attached to the five buttered loaves of brown bread used for portraying Jesus's feeding of the 5 000 gets no mention.[78]

Some Reef Missions and Wayfarers

As has already been shown, the women missionaries on the Reef were involved with the Wayfarers Association from its inception, although undoubtedly Mrs Edith Rheinallt Jones, while not a mission employee, was the movement's mainspring. In 1925 under Mrs Jones's superintendence, Dora Phillips acted as Treasurer and Caro Happer, of the Anglicans, as Secretary. By 1931, Mrs E W Grant was National Secretary for the movement under Mrs Patrick Duncan (wife of a politician) as Central President, while Ruth Allcock, the daughter of the Transvaal Methodist Chairman, was Secretary for the Transvaal.[79] American Board, Anglican and Methodist missionary women thus took leading official positions in the Transvaal movement, and theirs were the most numerous and energetic detachments on the Reef. All missions active in the Transvaal joined in Wayfaring as the thirties progressed, however: in a list of thirteen European superintendents from that period, only four were not identified as missionaries; of these, Mrs Franz and Mrs Hartshorne were the wives of leading education official.[80]

Miss Happer's verdict in 1927 was that the Anglican girls welcomed the movement, 'for it has brought so much brightness and help into their lives.' It was only the necessity for white detachment leaders that was holding her back from enrolling all the girls who were showing interest.

> The meetings start off with prayer followed by an instruction and some motherly advice; we then settle down to some work for a while always ending up with some exciting team games which all the girls enter into most heartily. It is with great joy that one sees them dispersing off to their homes with happy smiling faces, a most cheering sight I can assure you.[81]

The movement was still very short of white helpers in 1931, when Mary Phillips was Leader of eighteen 'English Church' detachments, mostly attached to a school or church along the sixty miles of Reef. She had only two white co-workers, each in charge of a detachment. No African sub-leaders on the Reef had yet been promoted to Leader, but they took much of the responsibility and carried on the 'work 'splendidly with very few exceptions'. Mrs Phillips would visit between once a month and once a term. Her affection for the Sunbeams is patent: they tried very hard to say their Law in English, 'and the result is sometimes very amusing, it is really a great effort, but then great is the triumph when it is accomplished.' As for bead-threading, 'the perseverance with which even the smallest thread their own needles is amazing!'[82]

It is salutary, lest one should be tempted to overstress the instrumentality of Wayfarers, to read Mary Phillips's lyrical account of a great joint African youth rally on the occasion of another visit by the Baden Powells. She was clearly caught up in the elevated spirit of earnest aspiration and youthful enthusiasm. After the singing of 'Onward Christian Soldiers', itself an interesting reminder of that whole milieu of nineteenth century Christian militarism[84] in which the first uniformed church youth movements were born,

> the Chief Pathfinder spoke in clear tones to the Chief Scout and said 'Sir, you see before you Young Africa' — one felt it was just worth every ounce of keen-ness and perseverance one could muster to help along this young Africa which is keen, so keen, to think rightly and to serve God with the devotion of which he is capable.
>
> 'Upward' shout the Wayfarers, echoed by the Sunbeams, 'Forward' shout the Pathfinders — and together we press along the Road, adding to our numbers as we go and trying to keep our faces to the goal towards which we strive.[84]

By the end of 1932, Mary Phillips was running twenty-three Wayfarer detachments. The training of the sub-leaders was regarded as work of special value; no doubt, as they were mostly teachers, the movement had served indirectly to combat the problem of the declining sense of the teacher's vocation. When Frances Chilton succeeded as Wayfarer and Sunday school organiser the following year, she found that Wayfarers filled a great need, particularly in the country districts (where the Reef Anglican missionaries always had a few church congregations on farms) which were short of amusements for children. Thus the movement was showing encouraging growth by 1935. Wayfaring was a prominent feature of the work for children carried on at Ekutuleni too, and by 1934 some 250 girls formed ten detachments in Sophiatown.[85]

The teachers and girls were very enthusiastic when the American Board in 1926 started detachments in areas where Sunday and day schools had preceded them and on which they drew. Missionary Alice Weir and a lady teacher who helped with Sunday school gave afternoon classes in cookery, bed-making and other domestic skills. Wayfaring was described as helping the African girls — the order chosen may be significant — 'to make good servants, House-wives and Mothers who will understand how to take care of their children'. (Miss Weir's position in 1919-20 as first superintendent of the Helping Hand Club, the ABM hostel and informal employ-ment agency for servant girls,[86] no doubt helped form her view of the future ahead of black female adolescents). They joined in provincial and national activities: in June 1931, for example, when over 2 000 Wayfarers were inspected by Lady Baden Powell, and in a conference that year for forty to fifty leaders from all over South Africa.[87] By 1934, Mrs Phillips, in addition to acting as Provincial Treasurer, ran Wayfarer and Sunbeam groups in all three ABM schools in Brakpan, Doornfontein and Western Native Township. Ray Phillips commented genially from personal experience on the absorbing enthusiasm of the women leaders of the movement: 'Husbands of the ladies concerned complain that they hear nothing else in their homes but "Wayfarers, Way-farers!" '[88]

The first Wayfarer constitution was hammered out, at least according to E W Grant's recollection, on the Grants' type-writer,[89] and Mrs Grant started the first Methodist Wayfarer detachment on the Reef, subsequently becoming National Secretary. By 1929, there were three detachments meeting at the Wesleyan Men's Institute, as well as nine along the Witwatersrand, under the charge of the new lady worker from Britain, Florence Brown. This meant 'individual knowledge of about 250 keen and intelligent girls, with all the opportunities of shaping their character which this splendid movement affords.' Considerable work had been done in visiting the girls' homes.[90] By March 1930, the Methodists had 450 Wayfarers and 600 Sunbeams altogether in the Transvaal, so the Reef membership was just under half the total. There were about 1 500 Wayfarers and 600 Sunbeams of all denominations in the province at that stage.[91]

Miss Brown became a lifelong devotee of the Wayfarer movement, and was still on the white advisory committee nearly fifty years later, her enthusiasm for it unquenched. In addition to her sixteen years as a Methodist worker, she spent over a decade as full-time Organising Secretary for Wayfarers and could be seen as Mrs Jones's successor in keeping the movement alive. In the thirties she organised economical training weekends for Wayfarer Groupers in Methodist school buildings. At such sub-leaders' camps, the young teachers would be taught first aid, nature, country dancing, games and singing, all for use in their detach-ments.[92] Affection for the children came without effort: 'I just used to love those Sunbeams' she recalled, while an African Biblewoman commented admiringly after a special meeting where Miss Brown conducted the Albert Street Wayfarers and Sunbeams in Negro spirituals, that she had been 'training them with ease, for she has the love for them'.[93]

Increasingly, big rallies played a valuable part in inspiring members with the joy of feeling they belonged to a larger movement, while probably reinforcing respect for the notables in authority whom rallies were meant to impress. In such a gathering at Kilnerton in 1932, the Wayfarers were inspected and addressed by the Governor General, Lord Clarendon. A Reef Methodist Wayfarer Rally was held in November 1933 at the Men's Institute with a programme 'made up of Action Songs, Fancy Drills, First Aid Display by Wayfarers, and Songs, Games and Dances by Sunbeams.' In keeping with the employment difficulties of the time, the Central President stressed in her talk to the girls 'the need for thoroughness and reliability', a clear case of Wayfaring encouraging industry and diligence: 'Men and women who sought work and found it were those who paid attention to detail; those who were successful in keeping work were those who gave of their best.'[94] Despite pacificatory remarks to the likes of M'belle, the movement did parade girls though the street *and* in male company. In April 1934, 300 Pathfinders and 300 Wayfarers from Methodist Reef detachments met at the Men's Institute and marched through the city centre for their first joint service in the Methodist Central Hall, attracting the crowd as they went: 'Flags and banners set what was already a magnet for curiosity ablaze with interest and appeal.' The following year, the Pathfinder bands and the 'flags flying' again made the march through Johannnesburg the outstanding feature of the day.[95] Miss Brown did not neglect the country members either. On a 650 mile trip with the Rev and Mrs Robinson in 1936, she visited 11 detachments, enrolled 180 Wayfarers and 67 Sunbeams and 7 officers, and returned to Johannesburg 'greatly inspired, and with a deeper knowledge of what Wayfaring and Pathfinding means to country children'.[96]

The Transvaal Wayfarer Rejection of Guides

In 1925 the South African Girl Guide Association refused to allow African girls to join as full members on an equal footing. This was repeated in 1929 on the grounds that it would mean the end of the movement altogether for the whites, as had happened to the Boys Brigade in Cape Town: once opened to coloureds, 'within a year there was not a white boy left in'. 'As you know', explained

Lady Baden Powell, deferring to current racism, 'our policy is one of complete sisterhood and it would not be possible to lay down defining laws within the Movement which would secure the complete safety of the white girls and the peace of mind of their parents.'97 By the early 1930s the Wayfarers had spread to all four provinces of the Union and beyond to Basutoland, Bechuanaland and Northern and Southern Rhodesia, and had 24 000 members. On the basis of their geographical spread beyond the boundaries of any one Girl Guide council, and of the equal rights of African girls to Guiding's benefits, the Wayfarers requested recognition by the World Headquarters as Guiding for non-Europeans. They were always turned down and told to apply through the South African headquarters. In 1932 the latter asked them to form a Joint Council to discuss matters of common interest and the possible inclusion of the Wayfarers.98

In January 1934, after negotiations had been in train some time, the Guides gave the Wayfarers a definite invitation to join as a separate branch in the same way, as it was later somewhat unfortunately phrased by a British official, 'as, for instance, our Extension Branch, which deals with Guides who are crippled, or blind, or deaf.'99 At the time it was thought that all the Wayfarer leaders were unanimously in favour, for a separate branch in which they could maintain their own Christian identity had been the GWA's desire. 'Imagine our amazement and disappointment,' complained an indignant Eastern Cape Wayfarer Superintendent, 'when we learnt that the Transvaal had refused the invitation and asked for further delay of years before considering any proposal of amalgamation!!' After further conferences — first of Wayfarer heads and then with Guide leaders in August 1934 at Bloemfontein, when the Transvaal remained unwilling —

We then found out the reason, ie that Sir Herbert Stanley is going to hold a Conference in Salisbury, S Rhodesia, next June at which among other things youth movements are to be discussed, and Mrs Rheinallt Jones is anxious to start a youth movement for Africans only from Cape to Cairo: and if that is not raising a colour bar I don't know what is?

Anyhow the Guides will not wait any longer for our answer, so it has to be settled in January, and if we refuse they are going to start non-European work themselves! It is an extraordinary situation, but I hope that all will end well, for I believe that the majority will vote for fusion.100

Mrs Jones's objections to incorporation in the Guide movement were crystallising round the very issue of 'adaptation' which had been a foundation principle of Wayfaring. She wanted a Wayfarer Association as a separate Guide Association represented on a Joint Council with the South African and Southern Rhodesian Girl Guide Commissioners; although this would presuppose a colour bar, it would in her view be less objectionable than segregated branches of one interlocking association. She felt that under such a plan European ideas and methods would permeate the general conduct of the Association: she firmly believed 'that the whole conception of Guides for Africa should be coloured by non-European needs'.[101] Although one could of course counter-argue that the Wayfarer movement was not so much coloured by 'non-European needs' as by white conceptions of those needs, Guide records show that her fears of white, non-mission Guide domination were not unfounded. In June 1935 the Chief Commissioner for South Africa told a special meeting that the Wayfarers 'were not to be real guides as they were not ready', and more help could be given 'by bringing them in as a branch than by having them on parallel lines as we would then have more control. They would not be on the same social standing . . . . The great fear in Johannesburg is that there will be combined companies and camps. To this the answer is definitely "NO".'[102]

At the 'very muddled' August 1934 meeting, where the Wayfarer Council simply shelved any new decision, it appeared to Mrs Jones that the Cape favoured joining the Guides, but with safeguards, Natal was rather indifferent, Bechuanaland would prefer delay, and the OFS, Basutoland and Transvaal were against the plan, 'at any rate now'. However within her Transvaal ranks, she had opponents in the Anglican women of Ekutuleni mission in Sophiatown, who favoured the Section plan. Dorothy Maud 'spoke several times, and at some length', saying 'plainly in open Council that she would resign if this arrangement were not accepted'. By September Mrs Jones had made up her mind that the plan would not 'give adequate possibilities for the expression of African interpretation of world wide Guide principles' and should be refused for the moment as it would be wrong, she told Miss Maud as they exchanged some frank correspondence, 'to make a rushed decision from a mistaken idea of politeness'. Mrs Jones protested that 'It has been my duty as superintendent to try and dispel ignorance and prejudice — not to put forward my own views.' The integrity of Wayfaring did not matter in itself. 'What does matter is that the emerging African girls should have the best and most characteristic means of expressing themselves for peace and goodwill and uplift in fellowship with girls of other races all over the world.'[103]

The fact that Dorothy Maud and her associates later destroyed correspondence about this conflict, misguidedly reluctant to perpetuate unpleasantness, makes balanced reconstruction difficult.[104] Mrs Jones characterised these missionaries 'who have been very anxious for immediate Guide inclusion of any kind' as

> Guide workers of some standing,[105] who are working with groups of urbanised and detribalised girls with whom they feel ordinary Guide methods would be successful; whose girls have constantly seen European Guides and been attracted by the uniform; whose girls belong to a particularly race conscious and 'difficult' district. But these conditions are rare and I cannot sacrifice the need of the great body of my girls to that of a small group.

She also doubted whether such urbanised girls would settle for anything less than wearing the Guide uniform like the white girls; a 'Wayfarer Guide' branch would not make them happy.[106]

As a result, the Transvaal Council in November 1934 tried to have it both ways, to ward off the resignation of members who, Mrs Jones feared, 'would have proclaimed, through the Press, presumably with the support of the two Native women present, that we had insisted on the retention of a Colour Bar . . . though I have always protested against this untrue way of stating the position.' The offer from the Guides was accepted in principle, Mrs Jones fearing that they might not make it again, but the Council 'not convinced that this is the wisest method of inclusion' begged 'that other methods may still be considered', such as a parallel movement, especially as further light might be thrown on the matter by discussions with the Indians and coloureds, and by the proposed youth conference in Salisbury. Mrs Jones had a battery of reasons for opposing the Section plan: Wayfarers were not ready for the move; they should be trained not on conventional Guide lines but more in keeping with African needs; it was unsuitable to have black and white in the same organisation, as closer association would only generate friction (a familiar refrain in more recent days), and needed to be preceded by far more welfare work (to modify attitudes no doubt).[107]

It appears as though Mrs Jones and her husband were giving thought at this time — and the impatience of the Guides disrupted their plans — to a further adaptation of the two youth movements they led (he as Chief Pathfinder for South Africa, she as Wayfarer Superintendent for the Transvaal), possibly in the direction of a better substitute for traditional initiation. With their wide subcontinental overview, their passion for inter-territorial and not merely inter-provincial organisation, their links with missionary and welfare leaders, especially since Jones had become director of the South African Institute of Race Relations (SAIRR), they wanted to inaugurate a more educationally ambitious, geographically comprehensive youth movement adapted to African needs. Mrs Jones had hopes, for instance, of a full-day meeting in February 1935 'to give long consideration to the problems of the initiation schools and the Wayfarer replacement of their teaching.'[108] The claim had been made from time to time prior to this that Pathfinders and Wayfarers filled the gap in discipline and training left by the abandonment of tribal circumcision or initiation schools, or that the Christian movements could be shaped 'into something closely akin to age-sets but without some of the heathen presuppositions of the system'.[109] Certainly it was hoped that Wayfaring would combat the problem of widespread premarital pregnancy among Christian African girls, just as traditional forms of initiation were credited with preserving female chastity.[110]

In February 1935 Rheinallt Jones, as SAIRR Secretary, sent out a letter notifying educational officials and youth movement leaders throughout the subcontinent (even as far afield as the Sudan) of a conference he was convening under the Institute's auspices on 'Youth Movements in Africa', to be held in Salisbury on 8 and 10 June 1935 immediately following the Inter-Teritorial Conference on Jeanes Training. Of all the movements in East, Central and Southern Africa trying to meet the moral and psychological needs of youth 'bewildered by the loss of traditional forms of group discipline and social control', he wrote, the most significant were 'the tendencies to revival in the indigenous forms of youth organisation'. The Joneses had been involved, just prior to his planning of the youth conference, in discussions proposing the absorption of Pathfinders into the regimental or *ibutho* system being reintroduced by the Swazi Paramount.[111] This clearly reinforced their predisposition in favour of adaptation. As Jones explained in a memorandum to the conference, they had become aware that, despite the encouraging response to European innovations in youth movements, they were teaching only a fraction of African youth, who progressively withdrew from the interests and activities of the vast bulk. On the other hand, the age-grade system still had extensive influence. The African boy must be adjusted to his own environment, and even European adaptations of British youth movements would have to be considerably modified if they were to be incorporated in African life. But just as in Swaziland the Christian Africans became heated at this liberal zeal and wanted rather to protect their children from the undesirable features of the *ibutho* system, so at the youth conference, as Jones and Franz enthused about the value of African proverbs, old ritual songs and indigenous arts and crafts,

J R Rathebe of the Bantu Men's Social Centre made a pertinent comment. The African had followed his masters, who were now saying he should go back to pick up the things he had dropped. 'But the African himself must be allowed to do this himself when he feels the need for it.'[112]

Even though it seemed six months too late, the June conference adopted resolutions clearly in line with Mrs Jones's stand on the Wayfarer/Guide issue: it was against racial discrimination in any youth movement, though full membership 'should not necessarily involve uniformity of methods'; concurrent organisations in the same movement could ultimately converge. In fact, she had already been overtaken by events.

In January 1935 in Cape Town, after further Joint and Wayfarer Central Council meetings, the Branch scheme was accepted by majority vote (11 to 2), a decision Mrs Jones predictably called 'premature if not definitely unwise'.[113] The GWA was to cease to exist, though Wayfarer enrolments could go on until 1945, but the preparation and enrolment of the new Wayfarer Guides was to be complete by 1950. However, apart from 'a minority' in the Anglican mission, all the key missions in the Transvaal entirely disapproved of the plan. It is hard to know now how much they were encouraged in this by Mrs Jones and how much their continued opposition was a result of their own conservatism. Loyalty to Mrs Jones was certainly strong: to some, it was Miss Maud who was 'mean' and had gone 'behind Mrs Jones's back' to the Guides.[114] In February, Mrs Jones was hoping that the movement could hold together with, if necessary, the absorption of the dissident minority in the Guides.[115]

As a result, the Transvaal Council continued with its policy of saying, 'Yes, but . . . .' It passed a resolution regretting that more weight had not been given to Transvaal views, as they had about half the number of Wayfarers, but feeling compelled to accept the decision, though on the distinct understanding that no detachment in the Transvaal would pass over to Guides before January 1940. The DRC mission promptly resigned to organise its own girls' youth movement in the Transvaal and OFS, and the German missions started consulations with them. Subsequently, the Transvaal Council asked the Guides to postpone further steps until another Joint Council meeting, as they could not agree on the rights of African officers to equal status with whites.[116]

A year later, on 11 January 1936, the North's misgivings notwithstanding, the Branch plan was finally ratified, while the Baden Powells were touring Africa before attending a huge Scout jamboree in South Africa. Lady Olave recalled it as 'one of the most thrilling, history-making moments.'[117] But when she came to the Reef at the end of the month, despite a full-page spread in the press entitled ' "Lend a Hand and Play the Game" The Spirit of Girl Guides', with cheering photographs of Guides making fires, bandaging arms and doing semaphore,[118] there was no mention of the amalgamation. This was an indication of the opposition within the white movement and the fears of white prejudice. The Guides protested later that there was 'actually nothing to conceal' — it was parents who 'precipitated' matters by rushing into print. One 'Interested Father' set the cat among the pigeons by urging the parents of Guides to think about the ramifications of the Guide promise to be a sister to every other Guide: would it now extend in racially mixed training camps 'to the joint use of tents, beds, cooking utensils and bathing pools?' While another felt that the Guides should have reassured the public that 'there would never be any question of Guides and Wayfarers coming into contact, or operating together under any circumstances'. Then the Guides' Divisional Commissioner for the Transvaal and four of her Commissioners resigned, claiming amalgamation would harm working-class white Guides whose mothers could no longer maintain 'the prestige of her children' over fellow slum children who were black, once the Guide movement removed the social barrier. But of course mixed companies were not contemplated. As Lady Baden Powell saw it,

> the occupants of the two houses continue to carry on their own activities within their four walls as heretofore, each naturally keeping their own identity, uniform and phraseology. But a bridge has been thrown across at the top storey, so that there may be friendly and helpful co-operation between the grown-up leaders at the top.[119]

The matter was far from settled within the Wayfarer movement either. First, the Transvaal Wayfarer Council called a joint meeting of all missions concerned to make a final, last ditch plea to the Girl Guides not to insist on terms which would cause dissension. This was prompted by the quite different terms the Pathfinder movement had just accepted from the Scouts, giving them self-government and complete Scout status as a parallel independent section of the movement. Mrs Jones naturally hoped for equally favourable terms, even though incorporation appeared a fait accompli. Though the Ekutuleni members and the Girl Guide Commissioner did not object at the meeting, they subsequently left the Council, deeming 'the suggestion of reconsideration as disloyal.' Mrs Jones saw the question of control as the issue at this stage. The DRC and the Lutherans wanted the final constitution and methods to be in the hands of a Council properly representing the missions, so that 'such missions as wish could go very slowly in making changes; such as wish can move more quickly, but all could go on together in Christian unity in the work of building up the character of our girls.'[120] In a sense then, rather than be party to dissension in the hitherto happy country districts, Mrs Jones was sheltering the conservative, slow-moving missions from the more Westernising, and potentially racially equalising, influences they feared were embodied in Guiding. Personal pride cannot have been entirely absent. Having 'ruled supreme' for a decade 'in the affairs of her beloved Wayfarers',[121] the strong-willed Mrs Jones presumably did not relish the prospect of losing control of a large, comprehensive movement.

Thus by the beginning of 1937, the Transvaal Wayfarer Council was reconstituted and the DRC joined the other missions again.[122] Although only the Ekutuleni Anglican workers had stood out against this wavering about and final rejection of Guide incorporation, when it became clear that a Wayfarer schism was inevitable the Bishops of Johannesburg and Pretoria decided to advise all Anglican Wayfarer detachments in their dioceses to join the Wayfarer Guide movement, allying themselves with the Cape and Natal in acceptance of the Guide offer.[123] The Protestant mission establishment elsewhere in South Africa registered its disapproval of Mrs Jones's obdurance, the *South African Outlook* berating the Transvaal Wayfarers for their undemocratic disregard for a majority decision 'reached in a constitutional manner'.[124]

The upshot of the years of negotiation and counter-suggestion between 1932 and 1936 was that Transvaal Anglican African girls became Guides and all the other missions in the province (ABM, Berlin, Hermannsburg, Swiss, Congregational, Methodist, Presbyterian and Roman Catholic) remained in a much larger, distinct movement for African girls that claimed to be more suited to their needs and allowed more flexibility to individual missions.

Mrs Jones had argued that because there were so many Wayfarers in the Transvaal, the movement there should have a greater say nationally. That numerical superiority continued. The Transvaal Girl Wayfarers claimed they had 18 000 girls under their care in mid-1937.[125] In 1938, their rivals returned 7 460 Wayfarer Guides (including those not yet enrolled) for all of South Africa including the Protectorates, and 5 810 Sunbeam Brownies. For 1939, when only the enrolled were counted, there were respectively 5 460 and 3 907 in the whole Union, with only just over a thousand altogether in the Transvaal.[126] That year, by contrast Mrs Jones flaunted over 22 000 members and 500 officers, and rejoiced that 'Wayfarers are absolutely booming. If I had more time, I could enrol a new detachment every day for a whole year. We just cannot cope with the demand.'[127]

The GWA after 1936

An important result of the split was that, with the Reef Anglicans leading those who 'went Guides', Wayfaring became more than ever a movement with its numerical strength in the rural Transvaal; it also used the vernaculars more than Guides, and with time came to have more Africans in the higher ranks. Its stance remained more explicitly Christian. Its main drawback, perhaps, continued to be that it was so intimately linked with the mission schools, which often provided the detachment meeting place, that Wayfaring tended to be looked down on by the older teenage girls once they had left school,[128] and, like other social activities of the missions, it reinforced the concentrated attention given to the schoolchild to the neglect of the unschooled or the recent school-leaver. The further stage of the movement, Torchbearers, intro-duced in the 1930s for this older teenage group, never mustered a large membership and was more oriented towards service than recreation.

There were about one thousand Girl Wayfarers in Johannesburg in 1938, and Dora Phillips and Florence Brown remained senior officers. To Mrs Jones it was a very sore point at this stage that the Municipality helped to finance the Anglican Wayfarer Guides while she had to scratch for funds to pay for badges, supervisional expenses, grants to detachments for handwork or First Aid materials, the training of officers, training camps for girls and occasional rallies.[129] She did not stint in her routine work for the organisation, despite her greatly increased commitments once her husband had become a Senator. She continued writing to African women leaders in country places to praise and encourage them,[130] thanking those who helped at training courses for leaders; keeping track of the minutiae of office record cards of the girls' names, badges and general progress; visiting schools, and despatching certificates, enrolment cards and badges to leaders.[131] Mrs Jones was a very energetic woman of great initiative; one woman missionary's chief recollection of her was that she was never tired![132]

She does appear to have had an unflagging personal interest in the African women leaders with whom she worked in the movement. It was Edith Jones's funeral service in 1944, where all races crowded to honour her memory, that Alan Paton later described as the 'deep experience' which had emancipated him and made him 'militantly non-racial'. He drove her on some

Wayfarer visits early on in the War: he relates admiringly how this plain, heavy woman in late middle age, despite a bad heart, travelled into remote country areas to visit detachments and encourage and instruct their leaders. Paton remembered most vividly the 'spiritual intoxication' of a Vendaland Wayfarer leader: 'You must bring her again,' she said. 'When she comes she makes things new.' It was the easy familiarity and affectionate friendship between the women which particularly impressed Paton.[133]

Ideologically, perhaps partly pressured to justify their holding out against Guides, the GWA seemed to stress its 'adaptation' approach even more at this time. It was attempting, the Association stated in late 1941, 'to meet the special needs of those who, with an ancestral heritage from tribal Africa, seek to blend the best from that ancestral heritage with the new life which the coming of Christianity has opened to them.'[134] Mrs Jones appears to have got her wish for 'experiments in the replacements of heathen initiations for girls by modern health and social teaching' in mid-1942. She arranged a one week course under GWA auspices at Donald Fraser Hospital, Sibasa, in the Northern Transvaal; Dr and Mrs Aitken were to direct the programme, for which Mrs Jones was responsible, and she planned to send two young African women, a BA graduate and a social work student, to help in instruction. This opportunity had arisen from a discussion of the relation between Wayfaring and initiation schools at a joint officer training course in Venda-land in May 1941. As in Masasi, the aim was to provide a substitute institution for Christian girls, not indigenise a Christian movement in order to attract heathens. 'There is no reason why our girls should not be as proud of the Church membership and Wayfarer training as of the old Initiation School mark.' A married white Wayfarer leader organised it in the end as the Christian African mothers felt unable to. The girls were secluded by a bush fence and did their own cooking. The mothers came for part of each day and to all classes. Simple instruction was given in anatomy and physiology, the main facts about sex and childbirth, cooking, the housewife's duties and the care of children. The course aimed to save the girls from the 'degrading teaching' of the traditional *domba* ceremonies for which the Venda area is famed, and to enable them to withstand temptation (ie to unchastity, a perennial mission concern about adolescent females).[135]

It is worth noting that a young Venda schoolgirl, writing a decade later of the Sunbeam laws, called them *milayo,* the word used for the phrases taught at the traditional initiation school and in effect the certificate of identity, the proof of one's attendance there. Possibly, then, by the 1950s it was not far-fetched to consider Wayfaring a kind of parallel to initiation, although its deficiencies might be indicated by the fact that this same girl decided at nineteen, rather late, to go to the traditional puberty school after all![136]

Mrs Phillips and Miss Brown, the leading figures in Reef Wayfarers at the end of the thirties, stayed with the movement far beyond that time. Mrs Phillips had been in America on furlough at the height of the incorporation controversy, but was soon giving the teachers training days, after which they 'went away full of enthusiasm and pep'.[137] GWA Vice-President and Reef Superintendent in the late 1940s, Dora Phillips, headed the Association as President from 1952 until her retirement to the United States in 1957, when she was made Honorary Life President, which gave her thirty-three years in the movement from its inception.

Florence Brown's connection was possibly even more significant. By 1941 she supervised about 900 girls from Delmas to Randfontein. 'All day and every day,' Mrs Jones said at a fund-raising garden party, 'including most Saturdays and Sundays, Miss Brown is working among these girls, teaching sewing, visiting detachments, training leaders, holding weekend camps, Sunday services and enrolments.'[138] Wider co-operation with other districts and denominations was not neglected. In 1940-1, the Witwatersrand and Pretoria Divisional Superintendents, namely Mrs Phillips, Miss Brown, Mrs G H Franz and Miss D Cartwright,[139] were reported as having been 'indefatigable' in organising district rallies and competitions (sometimes with many hundreds present), officer training camps and days, and special services on Wayfarer Sunday.[140] By 1943, Florence Brown supervised 1 150 girls in sixteen detachments each of Wayfarers and Sunbeams, but 44 African officers who were also school teachers did the work, while Miss Brown herself conducted 146 meetings that year. From 1944 she was assisted full-time by Julia Maaga, a former teacher. There were 1 600 girls under their care for whom there were never enough Wayfarer camps.[141]

Although Miss Brown retired as Methodist mission worker and Wayfarer Reef Divisional Superintendent in 1946, receiving a 'remarkable manifestation of esteem and affection',[142] she was back as full-time Organising Secretary to the Girl Wayfarers Association from 1948-60 driving thousands of miles annually to visit and encourage isolated detachments.[143] The movement, which had languished somewhat because of the war, Mrs Jones's death, and the lack of visits to the Northern Transvaal, began to expand vigorously. By 1956, several thousand Wayfarers and Sunbeams were being enrolled each year and the estimated number attending meetings each week was given as 36 000.[144] In 1960 the

Council gave long-service certificates to sixty Section Leaders and Superintendents who had had twenty-five years or more in the movement,[145] for it was an association that elicited lifelong loyalty from many of its leaders. There are one or two at the head of the movement even today who joined as schoolgirls in the late twenties or early thirties.

Had the nature of the movement changed? Wayfaring after the Second World War still awaits detailed examination, but it does appear as though the rural and traditional received more emphasis, even apart from the initiation substitution. Immediately post-war it was reported that Wayfarer activities varied 'a good deal with the localities and their native crafts':

> In addition to child care, the elements of hygiene, first aid and sewing, which are common to most detachments, there are practised in various areas, clay pot making, calabash mending, bead-work, the making of meal baskets and mats, plastering of mud houses and court-yards — the smoothing being done with river-worn stone — weaving, toy making, mending of clothes and the using up of orange pockets, oddments of sheepskin and other material. In both town and country they use the songs and hymns for which they show such aptitude, and games, so helpful in the promotion of the team spirit.[146]

A quarterly bulletin sent to detachment leaders offered ideas for songs, games, stories, drill, recipes and health hints. The Divisional Superintendents were still whites, although in the Districts African women leaders were slightly in the majority. The approval and co-operation of the Education Department was important to the movement — the wife of the Senior Native Education Officer, Franz, was an office bearer.

In the early 1950s, annual reports stressed the GWA's ideals of self-help and voluntary service and its concern to decrease its isolation from the parents' communities. Consequently, a Home-builders section was formed in 1955, for older women, often the mothers of Wayfarers. Worry about lower moral standards continued and papers on sex education were prepared for leaders.[147] By 1955 many camps, rallies and training days were being held in thirty centres, while the marked expansion towards the end of the decade was shown by the more than 600 centres which had one or more detachments.[148] The close ties with day schooling persisted: while the specific Christian slant lost its prominence with the end of mission dominance of both the movement and education, the GWA was still seen in the sixties as helping with activities which supplemented classroom training, and the ever-increasing number of African women helpers were still mostly teachers.[149]

By the end of the 1960s, when the diminishing interest of whites in the movement was explained by the death or retirement of a great many pioneers in the field, government policy decreed that the GWA should pass into African control. The first African Organising Secretary, Mrs Harriet Monimodi (enrolled 1927), had been appointed in 1964. African office bearers under Mrs M G Demas as President took over from 1973, with a white advisory committee and under a constitution approved by the Department of Bantu Administration and Development, who were then giving an annual grant of R1 200. By then, even the Divisional Superintendents were African — appointed in 1962, 1970 and 1972 — but their lengthy loyalty no less than the movement's lengthy control by whites is illustrated in the fact that they had been enrolled respectively in 1927, 1928 and 1938. Mrs Jane Segale succeeded as Organising Secretary in 1975, when the Girl Wayfarers' Association was half a century old.[150]

Conclusion

In reviewing fifty years of the Transvaal Girl Wayfarers' Association, this article has concentrated particularly on its formative first two decades. This was when white women missionaries under the prominent liberal, Mrs Edith Rheinallt Jones, created and perpetuated a version of Girl Guides specially adapted to enrich the leisure-time of African girls, in an era of decreasing spiritual influence for the day school.

At the local level, Wayfarer leaders were black school-teachers, with two-thirds of Transvaal women staff involved in youth movements in the 1930s. How should the role of these African agents be evaluated? Ray Phillips described teachers as 'strategically placed for rendering heroic service' in the application of the social gospel to their fellow Africans. 'Unquestionably these organisations are responsible for the marked improvement to our schools in discipline and in moral tone,' asserted Mrs Bridgman in the late 1920s.[151] A radically different viewpoint comes from later researchers. Legassick sees black teachers as part of a 'colonised' elite, along with clergymen, lawyers and others whom white liberals had 'assiduously fostered' in the inter-war period. As a group, they were meant to serve the function of 'social control of the remainder of the African population' though they had the potential for resisting this role.[152] Shula Marks writes of the 'psychological conversion if not psychological colonisation' of the John Dube generation, which accepted mission ideology with its belief in advance through education, working with sympathetic whites and adopting Christian values.[153] The ambiguities of the teachers' situation and of the Wayfarer movement itself should not be underplayed. Organisations like Wayfarers increased the social distance between certain school children, themselves a minority of a minority, and the mass of the African population. The black leaders were an elite anyhow. Cook, after detailed statistical analysis of paternal occupations, concluded that 'a very large proportion of student teachers' were drawn 'from a small economically privileged class'.[154] Teachers passed on, through Wayfarers, the aspirations towards self-improvement and upward mobility which their own social position embodied. Twenty years after its establishment, the GWA could confidently claim that 'a measure of discipline, and habits of industry, co-operation and courtesy are being steadily inculcated by the Movement'.[155]

'Adaptation,' so stubbornly fought for by Edith Jones, was similarly an ambivalent concept. White Guides looked down on Wayfaring as having lower standards in its simplification and modification of Guiding for black girls, while it appears as though, by the thirties, the Anglican African girls in Sophiatown similarly thought it an inferior version of the world movement. On the other hand, the Anglican Reef Wayfarer Superintendent, though she felt compelled to give in to her compatriots' stand, was 'all against' the move to Guides: she considered that African girls were not hankering after anything else and Wayfaring 'fitted them better'. In her view, it was more difficult to fulfil the aims of the movement once the Anglicans had been incorporated into the Guide movement, as the white Guide Commissioners were not as conscientious about visiting their members as missionaries had been.[156] The affection, interest and enthusiasm of white Wayfarer leaders is well documented, and the persistence of a separate association may well have ensured its members more attention.

The sex-specific impact of this supplement to mission education also demands consideration. The 'vocational, domestic and sub-servient' stress of nineteenth-century schooling of African girls[157] can be detected in Wayfaring, with its conscious attempt to adapt Guiding to Africans; its stress on supposedly female skills like knitting, sewing and child-care; its badges for cooking, laundry and housework, such as might equip a domestic servant. At the same time, however, it encouraged intellectual development through rudimentary nursing training and the imparting of, for instance, interpreting skills and Scriptural knowledge. The GWA also trained African women leaders: by 1964, over three thousand headed Wayfarer detachments. Numerous African women, that year's report commented, 'in responsible positions today received their early training in this movement'.[158] As far more girls than boys were involved in Christian youth movements, which was possibly true also of Sunday school,[159] the beginnings of the importance which religion had in many African women's lives may have to be sought in this formative school period. That would make Wayfaring one of the roots of that female numerical dominance of the black mission churches which was well established throughout South Africa by the 1950s.

Finally, the enjoyment of games and songs and adolescent female sociability which Wayfaring signified to so many of its members should not be lost sight of. A girl might be involved on into womanhood, in which case the movement's explicit and unstated purposes would presumably have some impact; but she might belong only for a year. The slogan 'Upward' encouraged aspirations towards leadership and competence, while inevitably distancing Wayfarers from others. The exhortation to 'play the game' perhaps encouraged members to 'do the decent thing' in co-operating with whites and submitting to authority; the subtlety of cultural influence must be granted. But probably for many African girls the only game they were playing which mattered was the literal, energetic team one.

FOOTNOTES

I gratefully acknowledge financial support for my research from the Central Research Fund of London University and the International Federation of University Women.

1. *The Evangelisation of South Africa, being the report of the Sixth General Missionary Conference of South Africa* (Cape Town, 1925) p 23; E G Malherbe (ed) *Education Adaptations in a Changing Society* (Cape Town, 1937) p 495.
2. Cook, P A W *The Transvaal Native Teacher* (Pretoria, 1939) pp 77-8. That Cook specifically investigated these extra-curricular responsibilities of teachers, confirms their prominence and salience to contemporary observers. There were 2 082 government-paid teachers that year. Cook obtained a 73 percent return on his questionnaire (1 522) and had additional information about privately-paid teachers. His excellent research is a mine of information which should be more widely known and used.
3. Chadwick, O *The Victorian Church* Part II (London, 1970) p 259.
4. Cook, P A W *The Native Student Teacher* (Pretoria, 1940) p 51.
5. Cook, *Transvaal Teacher* (1939), *op cit*, p 48.

6.   Phillips, R *The Bantu in the City* (Lovedale, 1938) pp 292,310; E Hellmann, *Problems of Urban Bantu Youth* (Johannesburg, 1940) p 44.

7.   Hellman (1940) p 69. Over half of Transvaal school children were in sub-standards and the later drop-out rate was very high.

8.   Cook, P A W *The Native Std VI Pupil* (Pretoria, 1939) p 79.

9.   Cook *Transvaal Teacher*, 1939, pp 8, 9.

10. *Ibid*, p 11.

11. *Transvaal Methodist (T M)* March 1930.

12. Union of South Africa *Third Census . . . 1921, Part VIII. Non-European Races* (Pretoria, 1924), Table 7, and *Sixth Census . . . 5th May, 1936. Ages and Marital Condition of the Bantu Population*, Table 3.

13. Phillips (1938) pp 152-3.

14. Cook *Transvaal Teacher* (1939) ix.

15. Phillips (1938) p 154.

16. There were 2 500 pupils in their ten day schools. School of Oriental and African Studies (SOAS) Microfilm, Phillips News, 3 July 1939.

17. *The Watchman*, August 1937, records 2 000 Sunday scholars in 1937, excluding those in the Sophiatown and Orlando missions. These had 1 600 by 1939 out of 2 490 in day school. Day pupils on the rest of the Reef numbered 4 628. *Ekutuleni Annual Report*, 1939, and S Carter, *Diocese of Johannesburg: Anglican Primary Schools Witwatersrand Area 1939 Review.*

18. *T M*, Sept 1939 and Feb 1940. 25 day schools then had 6 807 scholars while 52 Sunday schools had 4 273, so the overlap between the two constituencies may not have been complete.

19. *T M*, Feb 1932.

20. *T M*, Nov 1926.

21. See Paton, A *Apartheid and the Archbishop* (Cape Town, 1973) pp 123-7, and A Ashley, *Peace-Making in South Africa: The Life and Work of Dorothy Maud* (Bognor Regis, 1980); D Gaitsekll, 'Female Mission Initiatives: Black and White Women in Three Witwatersrand Churches, 1909-1939', Ph.D. London University, 1981.

22. Archives of American Board of Commissioners for Foreign Missions, Harvard, ABC: 15.4 v.29, Annual Report Transvaal 1913. SOAS, M4581, D Maud to Native Economic Commission (NEC) p 7617.

23. Compare J O Foster, *Class Struggle and the Industrial Revolution* London, 1974) p 28, and E P Thompson, *The Making of the English Working Class* (Harmondsworth, rev. ed 1968), pp 412-415, with T W Laqueur, *Religion and Respectability: Sunday Schools and Working Class Culture 1780-1850* (New Haven and London, 1976) xi-xii, p 239.

24. Malherbe, E G *Education in South African, Vol II, 1923-75* (Cape Town, 1977) p 399.

25. Springhall, J *Youth, Empire and Society: British Youth Movements*

1883-1940 (London, 1977).

26. Cock, J *Maids and Madams* (Johannesburg, 1980) ch 8 'Education for Domesticity'.

27. Witwatersrand University Library (WUL) AD843, B25.1, 'Pathfinder Movement', 'The Wayfarer Movement'.

28. Cook *Transvaal Teacher* (1939) p 78. Three-quarters of the teachers were male, *ibid* p 28, unlike Natal with its female majority , so women teachers perhaps had greater individual responsibility.

29. Springhall (1977) pp 131-2. British membership was 518 826 in 1929. See *The World Assocation of Girl Guides and Girl Scouts Fourth Biennial Report 1 July 1934 to 30 June 1936* p 129.

30. Girl Guide Association (GGA) *First Steps in Guiding* (Glasgow, 1921) p 50.

31. Kerr, R (comp) *The Story of a Million Girls, Guiding and Girl Scouting Round the World* (London, 1936) pp 58-70; A Liddell *The First Fifty Years* (London, 1960) pp 17, 24-27. These give 1924 as the date for the rebuff but Institute of Commonwealth Studies (ICS) London Mf JC 13/37 'Marion' Institute to Rheinallt Jones 16 Feb. 1925 notes that the Girl Guide Headquarters Executive was shortly to meet to consider opening its ranks to Non-European girls. This would account for the formation of Wayfarers later that year, once it was clear there was nothing to be gained from the Guides for the time being.

32. International Missionary Council (IMC) Papers, SOAS, 1229, File 'Wayfarers and Pathfinders', 'The Girl Wayfarers Association in South Africa' (n d). Unless otherwise indicated, all material used here from Box 1229 is from this file.

33. IMC 1229 'Girl Wayfarers Association in Africa, 1927'. Also Archives of United Society for the Propagation of the Gospel (USPG) London, Committee for Women's Work, Letters Received Africa, C Happer to A Saunders, 20 May 1925.

34. Information on Mrs Jones from unheaded account of her life in WUL, J D Rheinallt Jones Collection, A 394, D1.

35. Phillips, R *The Bantu are Coming* (London, 1930) pp 58, 128.

36. *Ibid.* pp 42-6, 116-122. Also J D Taylor, 'The Rand as a Mission Field' *International Review of Missions (IRM)* XV (60) October 1926.

37. *Report of the European-Bantu Conference . . . Cape Town . . . 1929* (Lovedale) pp 194-6.

38. *Advance* Nov 1929 p 203. Taylor, J D 'The Social Motive in Evangelism' *South African Outlook* Dec 1933 pp 239-40.

39. Phillips (1930) pp 100, 103. Also SOAS MF 'Phillips News' 17 Feb 1919 and 18 June 1921.

40. He brings out the contrast from an incident in Zululand in *Bantu are Coming* pp 93-4.

41. Forrest, L M 'Evangelism and the Bantu Girl' *Report of Proceedings of Eighth General Missionary Conference of South Africa* (Lovedale,

          1932) p 140.
42.   See Dikobe, M *The Marabi Dance* (London, 1973).
43.   Malherbe, E G (1937) p 409.
44.   Strayer, R W *The Making of Mission Communities in East Africa:
      Anglicans and Africans in Colonial Kenya, 1875-1935* (London, 1978)
      p 93.
45.   Smith, E W *The Christian Mission in Africa* (London, 1926) p 92.
46.   King, K J *Pan-Africanism and Education* (Oxford, 1971) p 97.
47.   And note the approval for Johannesburg missionary provision of
      'healthy recreation' and the detail on Bridgman, Phillips, the BMSC and
      the Helping Hand Club in T Jesse Jones *Education in Africa* (New
      York, 1921) pp 37, 215-6.
48.   GGA *Girl Guide Badges and How to Win Them* (Glasgow, 1920) p 45.
49.   Kerr, R (1936) p 71.
50.   IMC 1229 File 'S.A. Native Affairs Dr C T Loram' Loram to T Jesse
      Jones 26 August 1925 and 11 October 1925.
51.   See Brookes, E H 'J D and Edith Rheinallt Jones' in R M de Villiers
      (ed) *Better Than They Knew* (Cape Town, 1972) p 140.
52.   King, K J (1971) pp 52-6.
53.   *Ibid.* pp 7, 49, 122, 145-6.
54.   See discussion in next section.
55.   IMC 1229 'G W A Eastern Province News Letter' (1931).
56.   IMC 1229 'Girl Wayfarers Association in Africa'.
57.   IMC 1229 *Girl Wayfarers Association. Handbook of Rules and Organis-
      ation. Revised November, 1926* (Lovedale, n d) (hereafter *Handbook).*
58.   *Handbook,* p 6.
59.   The Law is a simplification of the ten laws of the Guide promise.
60.   *Handbook* pp 1, 3, 9-10.
61.   Interviews, Clare Lawrance, 31 August 1977, and Frances Chilton,
      26 February 1978.
62.   *Handbook* p 12.
63.   *Girl Guide Badges* pp 189, 307.
64.   *Handbook* pp 16-17.
65.   SOAS M4581, Evidence of D Maud to NEC p 7614.
66.   Cook *Std VI Pupil* (1939), p 97. 40,75 percent wanted to be nurses. For
      South Africa as a whole, teaching was the first choice of girls.
67.   A few years later 'A Sunbeam thinks of others before herself' was
      added, and 'tries to serve God by being [truthful etc]' inserted in the
      second law.
68.   *Handbook* pp 5-7.
69.   IMC 1229 'G W A Eastern Province News Letter' (1931) from Miss
      A M E Exley.
70.   See Mangan, J A 'Play Up and Play the Game: Victorian and Edwardian
      Public School Vocabularies of Morality' *British Journal of Educational
      Studies* XXIII 3 October 1975.

71. This paragraph based on IMC 1229 'Wayfarers Association of South Africa. Report of Transvaal Council' (1927).

72. Letters in *Umteteli wa Bantu:* from M'belle 23 May 1925, 23 June 1928; from Iris Northam for Organising Secretary GWA, Cape Town, and Edith Jones 20 and 6 June 1925.

73. Phillips (1938) p 301. Although the people of Rooiyard were antagonistic towards whites, the children spoke with gratitude of the time spent with Pathfinders and Wayfarers. E Hellman, 'Native Life in a Johannesburg Slum Yard' *Africa* VIII Jan 1935 p 61.

74. *T M* Feb 1935.

75. Forrest 'Evangelism and the Bantu Girl' p 139.

76. SOAS M4581 p 7613.

77. Blacking, J B *Black Background: The Childhood of a South African Girl* (New York, 1964).

78. *Ibid.* pp 101-7 'Wayfaring at Our School'. The second law especially is strangely recalled: 'A Sunbeam loves to help others, and must help herself. For ever and ever. Amen.'

79. IMC 1229 'Wayfarers Association of South Africa. Report of Transvaal Council' and 'G W A Eastern Province News Letter'.

80. See 'Girl Wayfarers' Association 1925-1975' (Mimeo).

81. USPG Report from C C Happer 14 Dec 1927.

82. USPG Report from M Phillips, 29 Jan 1932 (filed 1931).

83. Anderson, O 'The growth of Christian militarism in mid-Victorian Britain' *English Historical Review* LXXXVI Jan 1971.

84. USPG Report from M Phillips, 29 Jan 1932.

85. *SWM* (Society of Women Missionaries) *Journal* April 1935 p 27. *Ekutuleni Annual Reports* 1933, 1934.

86. On the Club and similar ventures, see D. Gaitskell, ' "Christian Compounds for Girls": Church Hostels for African Women in Johannesburg, 1907-1970' *Journal of Southern African Studies (JSAS)* 6, 2, Oct 1979.

87. ABC: 15.5 v.5 Miss Weir to Miss Emerson 25 June 1926. ABC: 15.4 v.39 Transvaal Report 192607. ABC: 15.4 v.41 Weir to Emerson 4 Jan 1927 and '1931 Annual Report A B M Children's Work in Johannesburg and Reef Locations'.

88. ABC: 15.4 v.43, R Phillips's Annual Report *Bantu are Coming* p 103.

89. Rhodes University, Cory Pamphlets 4, Grant, E W 'A Missionary Looks Back' p 7.

90. *Tvl Meth Directory* 1930-31 pp 38-9.

91. *T M*, March 1930.

92. Interviews F Brown, 6 and 25 October 1977. *T M*, May 1935.

93. *T M* May and October 1933.

94. *Ibid.* Nov 1933, Jan 1934.

95. *Ibid.* June 1934, June 1935.

96. *Ibid.* Oct 1936.

97. IMC 1229 *The Pathfinder* Oct 1934 and copy of letter from Lady Baden Powell 9 Dec 1929.

98. WUL, South African Institute of Race Relations, Rheinalt Jones Collection, Mrs Jones to Rev E Carter. Unless otherwise indicated, all Mrs Jones's correspondence in this and the following section, comes from this source. Also see M Brandel, 'African Women's Needs' (1955, Ts in SAIRR Library, Johannesburg) p 456.

99. IMC 1229 Lettice Hill, Sec to the Overseas Dept, GGA, to Miss Betty Gibson 22 Oct 1937.

100. IMC 1229 Miss Exley to Miss Gibson 27 Nov 1934.

101. Mrs Jones to Miss Rudd 21 Feb 1934, and to Mrs Duncan 11 Sept 1934.

102. WUL, A394/C43, Minutes of Special Meeting 19 June 1935 in K Hill to J D Rheinallt Jones, 11 June 1948 enclosing Extracts from the Minutes of Headquarter Council Meetings of the Girl Guide Association (South Africa).

103. Mrs Jones to Mrs Duncan 11 Sept 1934 and to D Maud 12 Sept 16 and 23 Oct 1934.

104. Interview, Clare Lawrance, 31 Aug 1977. The views of African sub-leaders are also lacking, but could perhaps be reconstructed by means of oral research.

105. Clare Lawrance at Ekutuleni, for instance, had a London Guider diploma and had worked with Guides in the West Indies.

106. Mrs Jones to Dame Katherine Furse (head of the Guide World Bureau and Dorothy Maud's aunt, which no doubt reinforced Maud's preference for Guides) 24 July 1935. In 1927 Dorothy Maud first encountered the resentment of young African women teachers in Johannesburg city centre who helped lead a Wayfarer detachment. 'The group of five were well-educated and chic, dressed beautifully and full of the nationalism that one reads about.' Ashley *Peace-Making* pp 24-5.

107. Mrs Jones to Mrs G H Franz 19 Nov 1934 and to Mrs H Gibson 10 Dec 1934.

108. Mrs Jones to Mrs J Reyneke 13 Nov 1934.

109. See H P Junod 'Anthropology and Mission Education' *IRM* XXIV, 94 April 1935 p 221; *Umteteli*, 9 June 1928; SOAS M4581 evidence of J D R Jones to NEC p 9032; Mrs Jones in *Report of the National European-Bantu Conference 1929* (Lovedale) p 207; Phillips (1930) p 106; 'Do Native Customs Prepare for Pathfinding?' *South African Outlook* Jan 1935 pp 19-20.

110. See Gaitskell,D ' " Waiting for purity": prayer unions, African mothers and adolescent daughters 1912-1940', in S Marks and R Rathbone (eds) *Industrialisation and Social Change in South Africa* (London, 1982) esp. p 346.

111. WUL, AD843, B25.1 for invitations and 'Minutes of a meeting of the Committee appointed by the Board of Advice on Native Education to

consider the possible amalgamation of the Ibutho and Pathfinder Systems'.

112. WUL, AD843, B25.6, 'Youth Conference. The Use of Indigenous Age-Grade Organisations. The Swazi Ibutho'; B25.1, Proceedings of the First Conference on Youth Movements in Africa.

113. Mrs Jones to Mrs Saul Solomon, 14 Feb 1935.

114. Interview, F Brown, 25 Oct 1977.

115. Mrs Jones to G H Franz, 19 Feb 1935.

116. Mrs Jones to Dame Furse 24 July 1935. Perhaps it was the prospect of this equal status that caused the DRC to resign.

117. Baden-Powell, O *Window on my Heart* (London, 1973) p 171.

118. *Rand Daily Mail (RDM)* 31 Jan 1936.

119. 'Natives Can Be Girl Guides' *RDM* 6 Feb 1936; 'Guides and Wayfarers Commissioners Resign' and 'No "Split" in Guide Association' *RDM* 7 Feb 1936, 'Guide Movement Facing Crisis' *RDM* 8 Feb 1936.

120. Mrs Jones to Rev E Carter, 10 Nov 1936.

121. Brookes 'J D and Edith Rheinallt Jones' p 155.

122. Mrs Jones to Mrs J Reynecke, 8 Feb 1937.

123. Parker, W (Bishop of Pretoria) 'Wayfarers in the Transvaal' *South African Outlook* Nov 1937 p 265.

124. 'Transvaal Girl Wayfarers Association' *South African Outlook* Oct 1937 p 221.

125. *Ibid.*

126. GGA, *Directory of the British Isles, Overseas Dominions and Colonies, and Foreign Lands 1940 also Report for 1939* (London) pp 9-19.

127. Mrs Jones to Secretary, SA Townships, Mining and Finance Corporation 25 April 1939 and to Miss M Wrong 30 June 1939.

128. Brandel 'African Women's Needs' pp 467-8 and ff.

129. Mrs Jones to G Ballenden, 26 July 1938 and 7 July 1939. Grants of £50 from the Pretoria City Council and £25 from the NRC Deferred Pay Interest Fund were secured, and by the end of the 1940s the GWA was getting substantial grants from the Union Dept of Social Welfare and the Johannesburg Municipality.

130. See eg Mrs Jones to Mrs Makgala, 16 April 1941.

131. See Mrs Jones's letters on a wide range of such matters in early 1941 and account in WUL, A394, D1, of how, at the time of her death, there were 40 000 cards with every Wayfarer's name, details of service, and badges.

132. Interview, F Chilton 26 Feb 1978.

133. 'A Deep Experience' in A Paton *The Long View* ed by E Callan (London, 1968) pp 54-9.

134. IMC 1229 'Girl Wayfarers Association: Sixteen Years of Wayfaring' (November 1941).

135. *Ibid.* and Note by Mrs Jones to the Adviser, SAIRR, 11 June 1942. Also R D Aitken, *Who Is My Neighbour? The Story of a Mission*

Hospital in South Africa (Lovedale, 1944) pp 53-4.
136. Blacking J B (1964) pp 9, 188-9.
137. ABC:15.4 v.47a, Mrs Phillips to Miss Emerson, 2 Feb 1938.
138. *T M* June 1941.
139. Mrs Franz's husband was Chief Inspector for Native Education in the Transvaal while Miss Cartwright headed the Domestic Science School at Kilnerton.
140. IMC 1229 'Girl Wayfarers Association. Sixteen Years of Wayfaring'.
141. Transvaal Methodist Synod Minutes 'Witwatersrand Methodist Native Mission, Report of Social Worker Miss Florence Brown, July 1943'. Report in Synod Minutes 1944.
142. *T M* June 1946.
143. Girl Wayfarers' Association. *Annual Report January 1947 to December 1948.*
144. *Ibid.* 1956.
145. *Ibid.* 1960.
146. *Ibid.* 1946.
147. *Ibid.* 1951-5.
148. *Ibid.* 1955, 1958.
149. *Ibid.* 1965, 1968.
150. This paragraph based on 'Girl Wayfarers Association 1925-1975' (mimeo).
151. Phillips (1930) p 104; *The Realignment of Native Life on a Christian Basis being the Report of the Seventh General Missionary Conference* (Lovedale, 1928) p 66.
152. Legassick, M 'Legislation, Ideology and Economy in Post-1948 South Africa' *JSAS* 1, 1, Oct 1974 p 22.
153. Marks, S 'The Ambiguities of Dependence: John Dube of Natal' *JSAS* 1 (2) April 1975 pp 173, 180.
154. The fathers were teachers, ministers, clerks, artisans, traders etc Cook, *Student Teacher* p 45.
155. *Annual Report* 1945-6.
156. Interview, F Chilton, 26 Feb 1978. There is probably scope for further investigation of developments in the Guide movement once Africans joined.
157. Cock, J (1980) p 305.
158. *Annual Report* 1964.
159. See footnote 8. On African women's religious activity in the fifties, see M Brandel-Syrier, *Black Women in Search of God* (London, 1962).

The Parents' School Boycott: Eastern Cape and East Rand Townships, 1955

Tom Lodge

In 1955, the South African government assumed control over black education. The Bantu Education Act transferred administrative responsibility for black education from the provincial authorities to a Government Department. The content of the syllabus, the employment of teachers, the admission of pupils — all previously matters over which schools themselves had a degree of autonomy in decision-making — were now subject to central authority.

The Bantu Education Act was vigorously opposed in the South African press, various public forums and by some white and many black opposition politicians. The opposition was ineffective in altering government policy and in many areas did not succeed in arousing much popular participation. In this paper we will be looking at those instances in which opposition to Bantu Education *did* transform itself into a popular movement. This was particularly the case in the East Rand townships as well as, to a lesser extent, the Eastern Cape urban centres and black rural communities. In tracing the local antecedents and history of this movement it is hoped the paper will provide understanding of broader traditions of popular resistance in these places, as well as an appreciation of why these were stronger in some centres rather than in others. So, first of all, this is an essay on local history, with an especial concern for documenting some of the popular movements of the East Rand, a region hitherto unexplored by most researchers. Secondly, the intention is to situate education and popular desire to participate in it and have some control over it, as one of a range of issues which in the post-war period in South Africa struck a particular resonance with poor people; an issue which together with such concerns as the cost of transport, the price of food, the availability of housing, and freedom of movement, lay at the heart of mass political responses in those years.

I

Before 1955 most African schooling was run by missionary
societies. Schools could qualify for state financial aid if they
registered with the Provincial Education Department. Registration
required conforming to syllabuses laid down by the Department
but the day-to-day administration of the school was in the hands
of a school manager or superintendent, himself usually a white
missionary. Schools which did not receive a government subsidy
determined their own syllabuses and trained their own teachers.
As well as mission schools, in the Transvaal there were 600
community schools, which had been built from funds supplied by
the local community and matching government grants. In such
cases control was in the hands of a superintendent employed by
the province and advised by an elected parents' school committee.
School syllabuses· varied between provinces but were all specially
written for African primary school children though secondary
school pupils followed the same curriculum as their white peers.[1]
   Though the system included some justly prestigious schools, it
had serious shortcomings. Being atrociously paid, teaching was not
an attractive profession and many teachers were under-qualified.
Mission control could be heavy-handed and paternalistic and
resentment of it (especially at rural boarding institutions) would
often overboil in fierce and destructive riots.[2] There was a vast
imbalance in the number of primary and secondary schools. Until
1945 the system was seriously underfinanced as expenditure
depended on the level of African taxation revenues. Finally,
wartime industrialisation and its corollary, urbanisation, had
contributed to fresh pressures on the education system. By 1953
African school enrolment had risen by 300 000 or 50 percent
since the war. Classrooms were crowded, teachers overworked, and
parents desperate to get their children into schools filled beyond
capacity. The need for some form of public intervention was
beyond dispute. The African National Congress's (ANC) 'African
claims' in 1943 had called for free compulsory education provided
by the state,[3] and in the Transvaal by 1949, 800 of the 2 000
mission schools, in response to the feelings of African parents, had
been placed under direct departmental control.[4] Black communities themselves were willing to make considerable sacrifices,
raising the money for extra teachers' salaries, classroom buildings
and equipment, as well as establishing their own independent
schools. 'Shanty' secondary schools existed in 1948 in Orlando,

Western Native Township, Brakpan and Atteridgeville.[5] In Alexandra, an independent primary school, Haile Selassie School,
founded in 1950, was to play a significant role in the 1955 boycott.[6]
The Nationalist Government accepted the need for intervention,
though its first concern was not so much with meeting African
educational needs, but rather in attempting to control the social
consequences of educational expansion. Consequently its concern
was to restructure rather than reform the system. Growing
numbers of literate job-seekers with basic clerical skills were being
thrown into an employment market increasingly reluctant to
absorb them. Crude sociological considerations were foremost
in the minds of the policymakers. In the words of Verwoerd,
Minister of Native Affairs:

> . . . good racial relations are spoilt when the correct education is not
> given. Above all, good racial relations cannot exist when the education
> is given under the control of people who create wrong expectations on
> the part of the Native himself, if such people believe in a policy of
> equality, if, let me say, for example, a communist gives this training to
> Natives.[7]

It is doubtful that many missionaries had quite such egalitarian
beliefs as Verwoerd was to attribute to them and certainly few
were communists; and the government was to underestimate
considerably the difficulties of instilling an ideology of subordination. Official thinking on African education was tendentious, naive,
and brutally simple. In 1949 the Eiselen Commission was set up to
produce a blueprint for 'Education for Natives as a Separate Race'.
Its report was published in 1951. Its 'guiding principles' included
the reconstruction and adaptation to modern requirements of
'Bantu Culture', the centralisation of control, the harmony of
schools and 'Bantu Social Institutions', increased use of African
languages and personnel, increased community involvement in
education through parents' committees, efficient use of funds, and
an increased expenditure on mass education. Black social
expectations were to be orientated to the reserves ('there is no
place for him in the European community above the level of
certain forms of labour').[8] Community participation in partly
elected committees and boards would serve to legitimise the
system as well as giving neo-traditional 'Bantu Authorities' tighter
control. Central dictation of syllabuses would ensure the
production of skills appropriate to a subordinate role in the
economy:

> A beginning (at the end of Standard II) should be made with the

teaching of at least one official language on a purely utilitarian basis, i.e. as a medium of oral expression of thought to be used in contacts with the European sector of the population. Manipulative skills should be developed and where possible an interest in the soil and in the observation of natural phenomena stimulated.[9]

Cost per pupil would be lowered and expansion facilitated by the use of shorter daily sessions, the employment of underqualified female assistants, and the pegging of the state financial contribution (the balance to be drawn from African taxation). As much as possible, post-primary schools were to be sited 'away from an urban environment' in the reserves.

In 1953 the Bantu Education Act was passed transferring direct control of education from the provinces to the Native Affairs Department. All schools had to be registered, all state-aided schools had to be staffed by government-trained teachers, and all would have to use official syllabuses. Mission schools from 1957 could continue only if they registered — they would receive no subsidy. Syllabuses for primary schools outlined in 1954, though in operation only from 1956, stressed obedience, communal loyalty, ethnic and national diversity, the acceptance of allocated social roles, piety, and identification with rural culture.[10]

Superficially, the new order had some features which may have appeared attractive to some African parents. Access to education was to become a little easier and school boards and communities provided an illusion of local accountability. But to parents whose children were already at school (as opposed to those whose children were not) Bantu Education promised obvious disadvantages. These included the insistence on primary school children learning the fundamentals of both official languages, making it less easy to acquire proficiency in the one, English, which was a minimum requirement for most white-collar employment. Shortening of primary school hours made life more difficult for working mothers, as did the closing down of nursery schools. School boards and committees were at best only partly elected — nominated members were likely to be unpopular (and in rural areas were compliant servants of local authorities). Fierce competition for elected places on such committees[11] probably testified more to parental anxiety than to approval of the system. The rural and 'tribal' bias of proposed syllabuses would have been especially objectionable to parents in long-established urban communities. The linking of education with 'development' ensured its unpopularity with societies resisting government land 're-habilitation' and 'stabilisation' schemes. Less apparent at the scheme's inception was that the system was going to impose

A Soweto school in the 1950s.
Photograph: Johannesburg Public Library.

Day School, Alexandra Township, Johannesburg, 1957.
Painting by E Ullmann: Johannesburg Public Library.

Day school, Alexandra Township, 1957 (detail).
Painting by E Ullmann: Johannesburg Public Library.

increasing financial obligations on African communities. For example, a two shilling monthly education levy was implemented on urban households,[12] while teacher/pupil ratios would increase,[13] per capita expenditure would decrease,[14] school meals services would be shut down and the abolition of caretakers' posts would make pupils responsible for school cleaning.[15] For an under-privileged society in which access to education provided the most common means of social mobility for one's children these were serious blows.

II

Popular involvement in educational issues considerably predated opposition to Bantu Education. In its most positive form there was the establishment on local African initiatives of schools entirely independent of external administration or finance. The shanty school movement of the Recf townships mentioned above is an example of this. Popular concern could take the form of resistance: for example in 1944 the Amalgamated Mission School in Brakpan was boycotted by the parents of some of its 900 African pupils. Mothers picketed the school's entrance and persuaded children to return home in protest against the dismissal by the Education Department of a politically active school teacher (see below).[16] This was not a unique incident. In 1952 a parents' protest committee organised a boycott of Orlando High School after three teachers, who had publicly opposed the Eiselen recommendations, were sacked (see below). The parents established a 'people's school' for boycotters. The protest committee was headed by the Chairman of the local ANC branch, I.M. Maseko, and apparently gained wide local support. Less than a third of the pupils attended school in the two month long boycott. Parental indignation in this case was intensified by the venality of the local superintendent.[17] Political groups sometimes attempted to enhance their following through sharing popular educational concerns. The South African Communist Party's night school programme was a good example of this. Less well known was the ANC Youth League's establishment of a 'shanty school' in Newclare to cater for children who had been refused admission at local schools through lack of accommodation[18] or the League's projected 1949 night school and literacy campaign.[19] There is evidence that, in urban African communities at least, education was an issue evoking common interest and, at times, anxiety.

Not surprisingly, the earliest concerted resistance to Bantu Education proposals came from that group most directly affected and most sensitive to their implications — the teachers. Bantu Education, because of the 'Africanisation' of lower reaches of the inspectorate and the expansion of schools, did offer to teachers a slight improvement in promotion possibilities. However, in many other respects the profession was to be degraded. Teachers would have to work a double session day with larger classes, employment qualifications would be lowered, salaries (it was made quite clear) would remain at their existing (and inadequate) levels, and teachers would be reduced to the level of state employees.[20] They would also be directly subordinated to the sometimes uneducated members of school boards which had the power to recommend their dismissal.[21] Verwoerd made little effort to conceal official hostility to the profession:

> The Bantu teacher must be integrated as an active agent in the process of the development of the Bantu community. He must learn not to feel above his community, with a consequent desire to become integrated into the life of the European community. He becomes frustrated and rebellious when this does take place, and he tries to make his community dissatisfied because of such misdirected ambitions which are alien to his people.[22]

Teachers' opposition to Bantu Education came mainly from two sources: the Cape and Transvaal African Teachers' Associations (CATA and TATA).[23] Let us examine developments in the Cape first. Of all the different teachers' organisations CATA was the earliest to become politicised. In the Cape the Non-European Unity Movement, founded in 1943 and drawn principally from 'coloured' teachers, from its inception took an interest in educational issues. It and a sister organisation, the Teachers' League of South Africa, were both affiliated to the All African Convention (AAC), an organisation which had been transformed in the early 1940s by the departure from it of the ANC and the infusion into its leadership of a number of Marxist intellectuals. The AAC had originally been founded as a response to the Hertzogite 1936 franchise and land legislation and Marxists within its leadership differed from the more orthodox South African Communists in their preoccupation with agrarian issues. The AAC consequently attempted to build a following among peasants in the Transkei and Ciskei (areas then rather neglected by other national organisations) through its immediate constituency, the teachers in the dense network of mission schools long established in the region. CATA affiliated to the AAC in 1948 and helped organise peasant resistance to the rehabilitation scheme.[24] The Transkeian teachers' faction of the AAC (W.M. Tsotsi, L.H. Sihlali,

A.K. Manglu, M. Mbalo, Z. Mzimba, L. Mkentane, N. Honono *et al)* were later to break away from their more theoretically purist Cape Town colleagues because they favoured redistribution of land on an individual private basis to the peasantry.[25]

The first serious instance of conflict between CATA and the educational authorities was in 1950 when CATA, together with the AAC, attacked new provincial regulations aimed at easing over-crowding by imposing a quota system on schools, effectively excluding 30 000 pupils in the Eastern Cape.[26] In 1952 CATA's annual conference condemned the Eiselen regulations, calling on its members to 'organise the people and explain to them the recommendations of the report,' and the following year, in defiance of warnings from the authorities, 200 teachers met at Queenstown to discuss ways of resisting Bantu Education. This had been preceded by a well attended public meeting in Langa, Cape Town, called jointly by CATA and the Vigilance Association to protest against the proposed legislation.[27] CATA's attempts to mobilise public opinion were unusual for an African professional body. They were obviously influential; the authorities' alarm at the teachers' agitation against land rehabilitation led to the closure of a school near East London in December 1953.[28] The following year, spurred by the introduction of double sessions in the Cape, CATA's annual conference called upon 'teachers and parents to do everything in their power to oppose the Herrenvolk schemes for their enslavement' (without being very explicit as to what exactly should be done). The state responded to this opposition by with-drawing recognition from CATA and bestowing it on the newly established and supportive Cape African Teachers' Union (a similar process took place in the Transvaal) and having isolated the militants, ensuring their dismissal through the rural school boards[29] (which were largely composed of Bantu Authorities personnel and their supporters) as well as redundancy through especially strict application of higher teacher/pupil ratios.[30]

The militant stance of Cape teachers and the severity of depart-mental response should be understood in the context of the much wider struggle against land rehabilitation and the reorganisation of local government under Bantu Authorities, which took an except-ionally intense form in the Transkei and Ciskei.[31] Interestingly, teachers were not the only people to link Bantu Education with Bantu Authorities and rural 'development' programmes. In Cildara in the Ciskei, the local Masizakite (acceptance) Association arranged a school competition to popularise Bantu Authorities and promote the substitution of academic by manual subjects.[32]

It should be noted that teachers in rural communities during the 1950s were potentially natural leaders of opposition to authority.

First of all they were educated people in societies which placed a high premium on education.[33] Secondly, they were people with no formal power as well as being badly paid; there was little to set them apart from the rest of the community. Thirdly, the Bantu Authority and School Board systems, with their elevation to greater power of traditionalist (and hence often illiterate) leaders, confronted teachers with a direct threat to their security and status. When teachers were politically motivated, they could be a very important element in rural opposition movements and it is no coincidence that the Bantu Education boycott movement (see below) had its most significant rural impact in the Eastern Cape and adjoining reserves.

The Transvaal African Teachers' Association (TATA) in contrast to CATA was a principally urban-based organisation. African teachers on the Witwatersrand had been especially sharply affected by wartime price rises (TATA's journal, *The Good Shepherd,* complained in 1942 that Johannesburg domestic servants could earn more than a female teacher) and in 1944 teachers had demonstrated for higher salaries in the streets of Johannesburg.[34] Through its partly successful salaries campaign, TATA became a dominant, and in some cases a politicising, force among Transvaal African teachers.

By the end of the decade some of TATA's leaders were tending to identify with the militant assertion taking place in African politics at the time. A 1949 *Good Shepherd* editorial, taking its cue from Z.K. Matthews, called for the formation of an 'African Association' 'for the purpose of keeping our heroes remembered.'[35] One year later TATA's Rand District Conference was addressed by G.M. Pitje of the ANC Youth League (ANCYL) who informed his audience that:

God placed Africans in Africa, Europeans in Europe, Asiatics in Asia.[36]

Pitje was in 1954 to become editor of *The Good Shepherd.* The ANCYL's Africanism, though, was only one of several influences affecting the political outlook of Transvaal teachers. Es'kia Mphahlele attributes to the AAC considerably more appeal at the time. Young intellectuals and junior teachers in the Orlando branch of TATA also tried to persuade their branch to take some stand in respect of the May Day strike the ANC and the Communist Party were organising in protest against the Suppression of Communism Act.[37]

However, unlike its sister organisation in the Cape, TATA was never to link educational issues with broader concerns and was to resist calls by some of its members for a similar political affiliation to CATA's.[38] It was, though, forthright in its condemnation of Bantu Education, its journal summing up the purpose of the scheme quite succinctly:

> It (the Government commission) wants to find out how it can give the African the training necessary to make him an efficient worker, without giving him any real education, for the simple reason that it would be dangerous if the oppressed sector of the population were sufficiently advanced to fight for their freedom.[39]

A group of Orlando teachers, who were elected in 1951 to leading positions on the TATA Executive, began to campaign quite effectively along the Reef, organising meetings of teachers and parents to explain and condemn the findings of the Eiselen Commission. Matters came to a head when the Transvaal Chief Inspector of Education was heckled at a prize-giving ceremony. The principal reported the teachers he suspected of organising the students to the Department and they were later sacked. The success of the subsequent boycott (mentioned above) is testimony to their effectiveness in arousing parental concern at the threatened changes.[40] From 1952 TATA began organising anti-Bantu Education teachers' conferences in Johannesburg and the East Rand and attempted to set up or revitalise Parent/Teacher Associations, so as to lend some popular weight to resistance to Bantu Education. However, progress was slow — by late 1954 these had been formed only in Johannesburg's South West Townships, Lady Selbourne and the East Rand.[41] At least one of the Parent/Teacher Associations demonstrated the trend of local feeling when, in February 1954, 500 people at a Moroka-Jabavu PTA meeting called for a boycott of schools in the near future.[42]

Compared to Cape teachers, the opposition to the Act demonstrated by Transvaal teachers was less widespread. Relatively few Transvaal teachers suffered dismissal from their jobs as the consequence of criticism of the authorities. Unlike their Cape colleagues, Transvaal teachers were subjected from 1950 to a strict provincial prohibition on political activity. Nor did the ANC (unlike the Cape-based organisation) interest itself in the preoccupations of teachers in the early 1950s.[43] Nevertheless in the links they did establish with parents through the Association in Johannesburg and the East Rand, their activity forms an important part of the backdrop to the communal boycott of schools that took place in those areas and to which we now turn.

The conception and preparation of the ANC's campaign to resist Bantu Education has been the subject of one monograph as well as receiving detailed treatment in Karis and Carter's

documentary collection.[44] The ANC's approach to the issue was
to be characterised by uncertainty and disagreement between
different sections of the leadership and between leaders and rank
and file. The decision to oppose Bantu Education was taken
shortly after the passage of the Act, when the ANC in May 1954
announced the launching of a 'Resist Apartheid Campaign' which
included the Bantu Education Act amongst its six issues.[45]
Concrete plans for resistance only emerged at the ANC annual
conference held in December 1954 in Durban. Here the National
Executive recommended the withdrawal of children from schools
for a week. At the same time, the Executive noted in its report
that 'progress on Bantu Education was very slow in all provinces'.[46]
However, the conference itself over-ruled the Executive, resolving
in favour of an indefinite boycott, timed to begin on 1 April (the
date of the administrative transfer of schools). It was decided that
local organisation for the boycott should be in the hands of the
Women's and Youth Leagues.

Preparations in the Transvaal began quite buoyantly with the
Youth League organising a meeting in early January in Sophiatown, which called for 1 000 volunteer teachers to provide alternative educational facilities. At the same time the Transvaal Youth
League established a number of local 'anti-Bantu Education
committees'.[47] By February, though, the initial caution of national
leaders was beginning to reassert itself. A National Executive
Committee meeting held in Durban on 5 March at Chief Luthuli's
and Z.K. Matthews' instigation, agreed to postpone the boycott
to an unspecified later date. Those who favoured this course were
influenced by reports of the intimidation of teachers by the
authorities, the announcement that the new syllabus would not be
implemented until 1956 and the fact that 1 April was in any case
during Easter recess. They also felt preparations to be inadequate.[48] Such apprehensions were not limited to the more conservative leaders; the left wing pro-Congress journal *Fighting
Talk* pointed out in March: 'to imagine that the ANC has yet the
power to bring about such a boycott in a few months would be
totally unreal.' Instead of beginning the school boycott in April,
the National Executive decided that the ANC should take on the
more modest task of mounting a boycott of school boards and
committee elections.

This decision prompted open dissension. A special conference
held again in Sophiatown the following week reaffirmed the
December decision. The Transvaal Youth League enjoyed the
support of the Johannesburg based members of the National
Executive Committee (including Oliver Tambo) and to prevent a
serious breach from taking place yet another conference was

arranged. This was held in Port Elizabeth on 9 and 10 April, the weekend before schools were due to open.[49]

The 700 delegates from all four organisations of the Congress Alliance, as well as two delegates from the Liberal Party, eventually decided on a compromise. In principle, it was agreed, government schools should be boycotted indefinitely. The date for the initiation of this boycott should be left to the National Executive to decide. If any area had completed its preparations (including the provision of alternative facilities) before that date then, with the permission of the National Executive, it could begin its local boycott. Meanwhile the ANC was to discourage participation in school committees and boards. The National Executive would establish a National Educational Council which would make provision for a network of cultural clubs providing informal education.[50] The mood of a majority of the delegates was in favour of immediate action; a proposal to limit the boycott for a trial period to the Port Elizabeth area was decisively rejected.[51]

The underlying tensions within Congress reflected in these hesitations and compromises are not a major theme in this paper. In brief, they were caused by isolation of some members of the leadership from more activist branches as a result of bureaucratic inefficiency; the presence on the National Executive of men who belonged to an older and less militant generation of African politicians; provincial and ideological rivalries; class considerations; and well-founded apprehensions concerning Congress's organisational vigour.[52] They have been discussed extensively elsewhere. In this paper our concern is to examine the local response to the ANC's boycott appeal and the reasons for its peculiar strength in certain areas. First, we will consider the area in which the boycott movement was to have its greatest impact: the townships along the Reef.[53]

Reports of fairly energetic Youth League campaigning on the issue begin to occur several months before April, this being especially the case in the Western Areas (Sophiatown, Newclare, and Western Native Township) which were threatened by the government's removal scheme. Despite regular rallies and street corner meetings, local politicians appeared to be a little disappointed by public response. One spokesman pointed out at a Sophiatown meeting on 2 January: 'It is a pity that I see very little youth here, as they are the people directly affected [by Bantu Education].'[54] One month later there seems to have been little improvement: P.Q. Vundla, regional chairman, complained: 'Your organisation (the ANCYL) is very important indeed; but it should be much stronger in this area.'[55] However lack of interest amongst many young people did not appear to dampen the confidence of the organisers in Western Native Township:

> From 1 April is the time we must sit down and work and have our own
> schools. We have got well educated people like Dr Matthews, Mr Robert
> Resha, Mr P.Q. Vundla and Dr Conco to draft the syllabuses for the
> children.[56]

Outside the Western Areas, the most active centre appeared to be
Benoni and here there were indications from early on that the
movement would receive substantial popular support. For example,
in February *Bantu World* reported 'growing feeling in Benoni
against the Bantu Education Act'. A teacher was threatened at a
women's prayer meeting and people were contributing generously
to the Branch Chairman's fund raising appeal.[57] Another encouraging sign was the apparent popular antipathy to the new school
committees which were being established under the Act: in early
March noisy parents' meetings considered these in Roodepoort,
Moroka, Jabavu and Sophiatown.[58] In Alexandra too there
seemed to be plenty of enthusiasm, though here the branch was
divided between those who accepted the need for alliance with
non-African political groupings and the Africanists. The latter
were led by the soon to be expelled branch chairman, the flamboyant, bearded Josias Madzunya, who used to address his audience
as 'fellow slaves of Africa'. On Bantu Education the Africanist
leader proclaimed 'they want to teach them that white people
originated in Africa.'[59] Among Madzunya's opponents on the
branch executive was J.J. Hadebe, a former teacher who was
going to play an important role in the boycott movement later on.
 With all this activity it is not surprising that the National
Executive decision in early March to postpone the boycott aroused
considerable local discontent. On 13 March speakers at a meeting
in Orlando proposed there should be established two ANC branches
at Orlando — one in opposition to that which obeyed leadership
directives. The former squatter leader, Schreiner Baduza (not a
Congress member), said: 'If I was a member of the Youth League I
would say the leaders of the ANC are sellouts, and otherwise I
would say "let us do away with Congress." ' Another speaker
concluded: 'Congress here is nothing. I am sure that the ANC
members will do nothing about Bantu Education.'[60] In the case of
Orlando he may have had a point — the branch was riddled by
factional disputes and tended to be dominated by Africanists
totally at odds with provincial and national leaders.
 Elsewhere on the Rand branches ignored the National Executive's postponement decision. In Benoni the ANC resolved to
boycott as had been decided though amending the date for the

inception of the boycott to Tuesday, 12 April, the first day of school after the Easter holidays.[61] The meeting was addressed by both Robert Resha, national leader of the Youth League, and its Transvaal president, H.G. Makgoethi. A week later a well attended gathering in Lady Selbourne pledged its support for the boycott.[62] By the end of the month Transvaal Youth League and even some of the older leaders were in open rebellion against the National Executive. A 'Save our Children' conference in Orlando came out in favour of the boycott and several prominent individuals including P.Q. Vundla and Bob Ngwendu (Transvaal ANC executive member) promised to withdraw their own children from school.[63]

As we have seen, this rank and file feeling forced the national leaders to reconsider and the Port Elizabeth conference gave a qualified assent to those areas which favoured an immediate withdrawal of school children, subject to National Executive approval in the case of each local movement. By this stage however, branches were acting autonomously of any higher authority. On Tuesday 12 April, children were withdrawn or stayed away from schools in Benoni, Germiston (and Katlehong), Brakpan and Alexandra. In Benoni, Youth League volunteers and mothers visited the ten primary schools in the Old Location and ordered all the children home.[64] In Germiston, events were more dramatic with ANC Youth League volunteers marching through the location streets at 3.30 am shouting slogans and calling on children not to go to school. All school children remained at home until the Congress branch announced that it had opened an 'independent school', rounded up the children and took them there.[65] In Katlehong, the new Germiston township, five miles away, 22 women were arrested after police stopped them from taking children out of school. There the local effectiveness of the boycott was to be enhanced as the result of the location's superintendent advising people to keep their children from school the following morning.[66] In Alexandra, the ANC branch canvassed houses through the night of the 11th — half the township's school children stayed at home. In the case of Alexandra the provincial ANC president, E.P. Moretsele, attributed the main responsibility for the boycott to parents rather than the ANC.[67] The ANC was apparently anxious to dissociate itself from some rough behaviour, blaming intimidation of school children on 'Tsotsis'.[68]

In the days which followed the boycott movement was to widen considerably. By Wednesday 3 000 Brakpan children were out of school — the highest figure for any single location. Parents marched with children in a Germiston procession. All Benoni and Germiston schools were empty and in Katlehong Township only 70 out of the 1 000 odd pupils at a community school attended.[69]

On Thursday the Minister of Native Affairs announced that any school children still absent by 25 April would receive no further education. The same day a march by women and children in Benoni was broken up by police. By the following Monday the boycott movement had penetrated Johannesburg with six primary schools in Western Native Township and Newclare abandoned by their 3 500 pupils after visits from Youth League youths and women.[70] The marches and processions continued more or less daily in the affected locations and became increasingly violent in nature. By the end of the week two unsuccessful attempts at arson had been staged against school buildings in Benoni and near Katlehong. On Friday the total number of children out of school exceeded 10 000 and the boycott, still strong in the original centres, had spread to Moroka/Jabavu schools in Soweto and to Sophiatown (though here disaffected parents sent their children, with apparent ANC approval, to the newly established unregistered church school run by Anglican missionaries). Over the weekend, though, threats by authority were having an effect: in Western Native Township 1 000 parents resolved to return their children before Verwoerd's deadline. P.Q. Vundla, the most prominent local ANC leader, supported their decision — an action which was to earn him a beating up by youth leaders and, later, expulsion from the ANC.

Notwithstanding Verwoerd's ultimatum, as well as conservative criticism from African politicians and the *Bantu World*, the third week of the boycott began with nearly 7 000 school children absent and hence banned from further schooling. The most resilient boycott centres were Johannesburg's Western Native Township and Brakpan, where loudspeaker vans successfully exhorted parents to keep their children at home and where a teacher's house was set alight.[71] One thousand three hundred children were expelled in Brakpan and 2 000 were reported to be still out of school by the beginning of June in the Western Areas.[72] In several townships schools were closed down permanently and the 116 redundant teachers sacked.[73]

The National Organisation's reaction to these events was somewhat sluggish. The Transvaal-based Working Committee congratulated the boycotters in a circular dated 23 April and called for an intensification of the boycott for the next week.[74] However, unanimity within the National Executive was achieved only a month later, on 21 May, when an ambitious three phase campaign was announced. The boycott could no longer depend on 'haphazard and spasmodic efforts whose origin is unknown.' Phase one would involve an educative campaign, phase two, withdrawal of children in areas of readiness where alternative facilities had been prepared, and finally total non-cooperation with all activities directly or indirectly connected with Bantu Education.[75]

A serious effort was made to improve 'alternative education' facilities with the establishment of the African Educational Movement at a meeting in Johannesburg on 23 May attended by churches, ANC and Congress of Democrat representatives. The AEM however, only began operating from the end of June[76] and meanwhile local Congress organisers ran illegal 'independent schools' in some of the centres — two accommodating 300 children were broken up by police in Alexandra in June.[77] Notwithstanding the courage and commitment of local activists, Congress branches were scarcely equipped to provide facilities for thousands of small children. Organisers would make brave promises about Congress running private schools[78] but some parents in other townships were beginning to consider other options. In some areas the position of anti-boycotters was strengthened by the lack of solid support branches received from leadership. A Brakpan school committee member informed the press:

> When the boycott started we called on the ANC members to tell us what the position was. We asked them what alternative plans there were for the children. They said there were none and they had no instructions from Head Office about that yet. In the meantime nothing would be done.[79]

In most of the affected locations local parent organisations tried to establish schools independently of ANC/AEM initiatives. In the Western Areas by August 1955 the Matlehomola Private School had 950 children (almost half the children affected by the bans). ANC officials had sounded out the school's secretary on the possibility of their serving on the school's committee. They had been told that before they could stand for election 'they must confess to their followers that they have changed and that they support the present system.'[80] AEM records mention independent schools in Orlando and Sophiatown, apparently not antagonistic to the ANC.[81] In Brakpan a school was opened in September 1955 by the Brakpan Civic Protection Society (a group which grew out of the Brakpan School Committee mentioned above). There was stiff opposition from the ANC. The school was attended by only 230 pupils (in contrast to the local ANC Cultural Club which attracted about 800 boycotters)[82] and many parents would have been unable to afford high fees. In Germiston there is no evidence of hostility between the ANC branch and any parents. Perhaps this was because here the ANC had succeeded in establishing, despite police interference, a proper school. The 380 children were taught by trained teachers who were Congress members and possibly because of this the school decided to legalise its status by applying for registration. Registration was refused on the grounds of a technicality but it was suspected the Department regarded it as a 'protest school'. The school reopened as a cultural club — within the limits of the law so long as no formal education was provided.[83] Similarly, there are no indications of a rift in Alexandra but here it was the dissident Africanists who were involved in a community school: the Haile Selassie School which had existed over the previous 5 years increased its enrolment by nearly 1 000 children. The AEM organiser (probably Hadebe) mentioned in a report difficulties between him and the school because of the involvement of an H S Madzunya (Josias?) 'reluctant to work with a committee which has on it Europeans, Coloureds and Indians.' The report also mentions a 'dissatisfied element' amongst Haile Selassie's pupils and friction between parents and the school. This could not have been very large; the local cultural club formed partly from disenchanted Haile Selassie children had only 200 members. Like the Germiston school, Haile Selassie failed in its bid for registration.[84]

How genuinely popular was the boycott movement in its local centres? Were the Congress branches reflecting local feeling or trying to dictate parental response to Bantu Education? This is difficult to assess as the available evidence is thin and patchy. The press (uniformly hostile to the boycott from its inception) reported the progress of various deputations from the affected locations which pleaded with the Department for the admission of the expelled children (this was eventually granted over a two year period). But such groups need not have been very representative of the whole community. Apart from the reports concerning tsotsis in Alexandra and an allegation from an obviously partisan Brakpan School committee member there were few accusations of intimidation of parents. The tension which appears to have developed in certain areas between the ANC and boycotters' parents might not have existed at the inception of the boycott: it was probably a result of worries over the quality of alternative educational options offered by the ANC as well as the increasing isolation of the movement. It seems a little unlikely that branches on their own initiative, with no encouragement from higher authority, would have imposed an unpopular policy on their own local constituency. Most telling of all, there are no signs of any apparent decline in ANC support on the East Rand. For example, in Natalspruit and Benoni, in the 1956 elections, the ANC won control of the location advisory boards.[85] In Brakpan, the Civic Protection Society, the main local critic of the school boycott, showed its true colours when in March 1956 it opposed a well supported bus boycott led by the ANC and the Vigilance Committee. Obviously the society's leaders were well insulated from the concerns of the former inhabitants of the location.[86]

The other area in which the boycott had a certain impact was in the Eastern Cape — like the East Rand, an area in which Congress had a strong following in the urban locations and townships. Here again the boycott movement appeared to suffer from a lack of central direction (the Cape-based members of the National Executive were in any case unenthusiastic) and in general was much weaker than on the East Rand. Reports of preparations are sparse: a March meeting in Korsten (Port Elizabeth's oldest location) attended by 3 000 parents called for action on 1 April in conformity with the December ANC resolution[87] and no less than six electoral meetings were held in Grahamstown by the authorities, all of which failed to persuade parents to choose a school committee. Their unwillingness was attributed to Congress influence.[88] In the event, despite local rank and file feeling in favour of the boycott (evident at the Port Elizabeth conference in April) children all attended school on 12 April. The next reported activity was in May when Port Elizabeth's New Brighton branch called for a regional boycott of schools from the 23rd. East London's ANC denied any knowledge of this decision. Apparently there had been leadership difficulties which left the local branch in total disarray.[89] In any case in East London some ANC members had accepted positions on the new school committees.[90]

The Port Elizabeth boycott only slowly gathered impetus from the 23rd. There was a significant police presence that day and many parents escorted their children to school. Parental fears were probably aroused by Verwoerd's threat of instant dismissal of any school children who participated which precluded even a symbolic limited withdrawal. Despite a house-to-house canvass the day before there were no pickets outside schools.[91]

Despite this unpromising start the movement was slowly to gather strength, particularly in the small rural towns and villages around Port Elizabeth.[92] *The Evening Post* reported a fairly effective primary school boycott in Kirkwood, the centre of a closely settled citrus farming area.[93] ANC influence in this area may have been linked to the local strength of the Food and Canning Workers Union.

In Port Elizabeth and Uitenhage a second boycott attempt was made in July despite considerable opposition from sections of the location community. Clashes between police and some parents on the one hand and pickets of young men on the other occurred in both centres on the 18th, but despite these difficulties at the end

of the first week in August Congress claimed that 1 700 children
were staying away from Port Elizabeth schools.[94] Altogether the
Eastern Cape boycott was to involve, according to the AEM, over
2 500 children from Uitenhage, New Brighton, Korsten, Kirkwood,
Missionvale, Kleinvee, Kleinschool and Walmer location.[95]

It was a surprisingly light response when one remembers that
the Eastern Cape was the region most affected by the Defiance
Campaign and an area in which the ANC and the Trade Union
movement were comparatively strong, with links between the two
well developed. Part of the explanation lies in the deep cleavages
between grass roots membership and a very cautious leadership
still steeped in the pre-1950 liberal tradition in African politics
rather than the style which now prevailed in the Transvaal. T.E.
Tshunungwa, the ANC's 'national organiser' in a revealing letter to
Oliver Tambo wrote:

> Well my duty here (in the Eastern Cape) is to toe the line in the best
> interests of the organisation and to strictly confine the disputes and the
> differences to the officials and the organisation only and that masses
> should never know it was a mistake to carry out the boycott.[96]

Joe Matthews of the Youth League, writing to Walter Sisulu, later
that year, accused the Cape leaders of 'passivity', complaining that
he was 'really fed up with the whole leadership.'[97]

The most sustained local reaction to Bantu Education in this
area was to be encountered in the reserves, already as we noted the
scene of some agitation by All African Convention affiliates. The
AAC opposed the school boycott as 'adventurist' (after all, had it
been effective, many of the members would be without jobs) and
confined its campaigning to opposing school committees and
boards. Opposition to these institutions and nominations to them
is reported to have taken place in Tsolo and Butterworth in the
Transkei in early 1955 and in the Ciskei villages at intervals
between 1955 and 1958. The committees and boards were linked
with the issue of increased taxation: at Butterworth officials were
asked:

> Where are the monies to come from which school committees are to
> handle? Seeing that this is a government affair, why are the people
> going to be taxed?[98]

In Glen Grey, it was reported that at 11 out of 24 villages represented at a meeting in early 1955 between headmen and
magistrates, school committees could not be established because
of local opposition.[99]

Besides widespread passive opposition and suspicion, there were a few instances of more active revolt. The Police Commissioner's report for 1955 mentions arson of school buildings in Peddie.[100] In September of that year 50 men entered a school in Mgwalane, Peddie, dismissed the children, locked the building and removed the keys.[101]

There were therefore indications of considerable anxiety and tension — provoked by state intervention in Eastern Cape Schools — which might have been more effectively exploited by determined political organisation. In rural areas more oppressive local government, growing taxation and increasingly generalised economic hardship were powerful and explosive factors. Had rural and urban movements been more closely articulated, the challenge to authority might have been formidable. The situation might have been exploited by a revolutionary movement, but in the mid-1950s neither Congress nor the Convention could be so described. By the end of the decade local Congress leaders themselves were participating in the new system, energetically contesting and winning school board elections despite official ANC disapproval. Boycotts often involve the renunciation of power: the boards and committees had real if limited powers. Christopher Gell, reporting from Port Elizabeth in 1955, mentions African members of school boards influencing appointments in the direction of relatives and friends.[102] Men and women struggling to survive economically and provide a better world for their children are not necessarily revolutionaries. The pressures arising from everyday life need to be countered by inspired and powerful political leadership if they are to be disregarded.

What Congress did try and provide was some kind of alternative to Bantu Education and its efforts in this direction deserve consideration if only for their persistence. As we have seen, in the wake of the boycott affected branches tried to establish 'independent schools'. By June, the African Education Movement chaired by Trevor Huddleston and with energetic support from Johannesburg's Congress of Democrats activists, was beginning to assist these ventures. The formal aims of the AEM were threefold: the establishment of private schools; the assistance of cultural clubs for those boycotters whose parents could not afford private school fees, and a home education programme. In practice the cultural clubs became the AEM's main preoccupation. These, for legal reasons, were conducted on an informal basis. The children would be taught, through a programme of songs, stories and games, the rudiments of mathematics, geography, history and general knowledge. Club leaders, supported financially by the modest fees that were charged, would be provided by the AEM with cyclostyled teaching material, encouragement, and a training programme.

Given the limitations of what could be achieved, the clubs were in some centres surprisingly well attended — Brakpan being the outstanding example where a year after the boycott began, the club still had over 700 members and leaders were paid up to £16 a month from local resources.[103] One of these was a fully qualified teacher, who had resigned his post to join the club, bringing his pupils with him.[104] Problems mentioned in a memorandum by the AEM's full-time organiser, J.J. Hadebe, included the poor qualifications of club leaders — only a minority it seems were trained teachers (and in any case informal educational techniques require specialised expertise) — shortage of leaders, insufficient money to pay them and a lack of facilities and equipment. Clubs were often held in the open.[105] The material provided by the AEM was well prepared and imaginative, emphasising a tactful and sensitive approach to certain topics:

> The Freedom Charter — to be taught to the children as they understand it. Care to be taken not to offend parents, the Charter not to be imposed on the people. The importance is not the name but the ideas embodied in it. The Freedom Charter to be the basis for our education.[106]

The AEM's approach involved a reversal of normal South African educational conventions; considerable demands were placed on future club leaders:

> Trust the children — let them take responsibility for themselves.[107]

Even in terms of formal criteria, the clubs could be successful. Some of their members wrote and passed Standard VI examinations, and in Benoni and Brakpan as late as 1956 they were even winning recruits from government schools.[108] The AEM and the cultural clubs were a brave experiment but their significance became increasingly symbolic as numbers dwindled and children were reabsorbed into government schools. Nevertheless they represented the first sustained effort by Congress members to attempt to flesh out in educational terms an alternative world view: something that had been called for often in political rhetoric but seldom attempted before.

Opposition to Bantu Education, though widespread, only developed into open political rebellion in a few areas. In fact most of the opposition movements of the 1950s were geographically isolated and sporadic: amongst a fearfully poor and politically rightless population a peculiar combination of factors had to be present before anger could be translated into active defiance. What follows concentrates on isolating those factors which help to explain why this happened in the East Rand townships.

III

The driving force of South Africa's industrial revolution was located in the East Rand townships. Gold mining operations began in the 1880s, and the presence in the Transvaal of large coal and iron deposits led to the establishment in Benoni of the first steel works in the Union. By the end of the First World War engineering was beginning to be the most important local industry and this trend was strengthened during the 1930s, with an influx of foreign firms, and in the 1940s when wartime import substitution policies gave rise to another spurt of industrialisation. By 1947 Benoni was the union's centre of heavy industry, it and its neighbouring town Boksburg making up South Africa's most densely industrialised area. To the west, Germiston grew in importance, first as a mining centre, then as the main railway junction on the Reef and centre for lighter industries — 400 of which were established in the period 1917 to 1957.[109]

The relatively early establishment of secondary industry in this area had important social consequences. The towns became important employment centres for black workers and early centres of black urbanisation: with the exception of Nancefield (in what is today Soweto) Benoni's African location with its 9 600 inhabitants was by 1929 the biggest on the Rand.[110] Secondary industry required a relatively skilled and permanent workforce — the men and women who lived in the locations of the East Rand were by the 1950s members of a long established proletariat. Nevertheless these were small towns and at a municipal level the major political force was not the industrialists and businessmen who predominated in the affairs of the nearby metropolis, Johannesburg, but rather white workers. Given their constituency, Labour and Nationalist town councils of the 1930s and the 1940s were reluctant to embark on ambitious programmes of public works and African locations on the East Rand were notoriously horrible. In some, squalid living conditions were exacerbated by the uneven application of the provisions of the Urban Areas Act. Areas of municipal neglect tended to coincide with inefficient or negligible control. Benoni's location was to develop into a refuge for people driven out of other Reef towns by the enforcement of the Act.[111] These places were always the object of public in-

dignation as a war-time sanitation official pointed out in Benoni:
'the conditions under which the Natives are living are vile'[112] and
as recently as 1981 a *Star* report had this to say of Germiston's old
location:

> Fetid rivers of liquid filth run down the side of each dirt road, collecting
> in noxious pools of swirling scum. Peeling and rusting corrugated iron
> plastered walls form shelters for humiliated families.[113]

Nor was the disgust limited to external observers. In Benoni, for
example, an African Housing and Rates Board existed from 1945
and squatter movements were to unilaterally occupy buildings and
land kept empty by the council.[114]

The chances of escape from the poverty-stricken despair of the
locations through individual enterprise and initiative were just that
much more limited in the East Rand than in, for example,
Johannesburg. The small towns did not supply the same degree of
administrative or commercial white collar employment: local lack
of demand for well educated blacks was reflected in the lack of
single secondary schools in the area until the 1960s.[115] Despite the
frequent employment of women in the food and textile industries
(for which the East Rand was an important centre), household
incomes were well below Johannesburg's.[116]

The 1950s were an important transitionary phase for these
communities. For in this decade the African populations of
Germiston, Benoni and Brakpan were to be subjected to the full
thrust of Afrikaner and Nationalist social engineering. Vast
geometrically planned and tightly administered 'model' townships
were erected — in each case at a considerable distance from the
city centre — and slowly location inhabitants were screened and
sorted and resettled according to the dictates of Verwoerdian
dogma. Germiston, with its Katlehong township, and Benoni,
with Daveyton, in 1949 and 1950 were among the first municipal-
ities in the Union to comply with the Group Areas Act. In terms
of living space, housing standards and sanitation, the new townships may have represented an improvement on the old locations
— but to some groups within the community they would have
appeared threatening[117] and the fashion in which these changes
were implemented evoked widespread resentment.[118] The removals
tended to speed up a process of social differentiation within the
local communities. The new townships being isolated from city
centres provided improved business opportunities for African
traders and with their own administrations created a certain
amount of clerical employment. This and their geographical features
tended to make it less easy for political leaders to evoke a united

communal response to a particular issue. The strength of political movements of the 1950s in the old locations of the East Rand was no accident. With the onset of the removals (a process which lasted more than a decade) the old locations became even more neglected[119] and their inhabitants increasingly insecure about their future.

IV

The socio-economic history of the East Rand is, for an important part, the history of African working class communities characterised by the depth of their proletarian experience, a measure of poverty unusual even among urban black South African people, and because of their relative smallness and the importance of industrial employment among their male and female members, a high degree of social solidarity. With these points in mind, it is easier to understand the political radicalism which took root in the East Rand locations during the 1940s and the 1950s. The strength of the 1955 boycott is better understood if it is put in the context of political and trade union responses in the preceding years.

The most active and militant political force on the East Rand during the 1940s was the Communist Party of South Africa, which seems to have won considerable support with its involvement in small local disputes, usually arising out of day-to-day difficulties of economic survival. The issues could include municipal prohibition of female hawkers (Benoni, November 1943);[120] police violence against location inhabitants (Brakpan, December 1943);[121] intimidation of rent defaulters (Brakpan, March 1944);[122] location conditions and the behaviour of the location superintendent (Brakpan, August 1944);[123] dismissal of teachers (Boksburg and Brakpan, March to November 1944);[124] housing shortages (Benoni, June 1945 to September 1947);[125] brewing (Springs, July 1945);[126] bus services (Brakpan, April 1946);[127] food shortages (Brakpan, May 1946);[128] or municipal extension of passes to women (Brakpan, July 1946).[129]

Let us look more closely at Communist Party involvement in local issues in the town where there seems to have been most activity, Brakpan. Though of the East Rand townships by no means the worst in terms of overcrowding or living conditions,[130] the small location community (5 000 in 1939)[131] seems to have been in a state of constant ferment in the 1940s. Brakpan was exceptional on the East Rand in the 1940s in having a Nationalist town council and provisions for control of its African population seem to have been distinguished by their rigour. The City of

Johannesburg's 1939 *Survey of Reef Locations* makes especial mention of recent increases in the size of the Brakpan municipal police force, erection of fencing and a clamp-down on illicit brewing.

During the 1940s, Brakpan's Native Affairs Department was headed by a Dr Language, whose other claim to fame was as the leading theoretician and 'native expert' of the Ossewa Brandwag. (The OB appears to have had quite a following on the East Rand, doubtless enhanced by the blowing up of Benoni's post office in 1942 by some of its local enthusiasts).[132] Even by the standards of his calling, Language seems to have been a formidably intolerant and unpleasant man. His term of office began with the re-organisation of local influx control into the location, raising of lodgers' fees, and harassment of minor rent defaulters. Matters came to a head between the council and the location community when, on Language's initiative, the council successfully arranged the dismissal from his teaching post and Brakpan's Amalgamated Mission School of an important local politician, David Bopape.[133]

Bopape was one of the most energetic and active of the grass roots Congress leaders of those years. Initially drawn into politics by his involvement in the TATA salary campaign of 1940-41, he became a founder member of the Youth League, and was by 1943, a forceful and effective spokesman for the Brakpan African community. He does not appear to have shared the normal Youth League antipathy to communists, perhaps because, unlike many young Congress intellectuals, he was himself involved in bread and butter political issues, and by 1946 is thought to have actually joined the South African Communist Party, while retaining an important position in the Transvaal ANC.[134] Bopape's activities appeared to have gained him a large personal following, for his dismissal was to provoke a school boycott affecting 2 000 children and a one day stay-at-home of the location's 7 000 workers on 10 August 1944.[135] Bopape had apparently angered Language by his campaigning for better living conditions in the location and the issue of his dismissal was to fuse with a range of grievances, which included the housing shortage, inadequate and expensive transport, low pay for municipal workers, high municipal rents, no running water within the location and Language's racism.[136]

The action of Brakpan's parents inspired a similar protest the following year in Boksburg after teachers' dismissals there. In this case parents organised under the slogan 'African Education run by Africans' and their case was taken up by TATA, which had already begun to establish Parent/Teacher Associations in the East Rand. The existence of these may have something to do with the effectiveness of both these and later school boycotts.[137]

The communal support for Bopape did not succeed in gaining his reinstatement (despite initial promises by the Brakpan Council) and discontent within the location continued to simmer. In May 1945 the Council announced that it was going to use beer hall profits for general street cleaning, refusing at the same time to grant the Advisory Board extensions to its powers which would have included some say in location revenue expenditure. Three months later a fresh permit system was introduced and a wave of arrests of illegal location residents took place. In all these local disputes, the Communist Party's local spokesman played a prominent part, and in their African language newspaper *Inkululeko,* reported these extensively. In its sensitive approach to local issues and its down-playing of more remote and abstract political problems, it seems to have gained a real popularity. A former Youth leader and Brakpan resident remembers:

> The ANC missed out a great deal (in the 1940s) because it would not interest itself in the little things that bug the people . . . the popularity of the Communist Party in places like Brakpan was because they took up such things.[138]

The December 1945 Advisory Board elections illustrated the effectiveness of the approach. Communist candidates stood and were elected in Springs, Brakpan, Benoni and Nigel. The newly elected Brakpan Board went on to win a significant victory by organising a bus boycott which successfully reversed a Council decision to relocate the bus terminal to a longer distance from the location boundary.[139]

Brakpan's African community was administered unusually heavy-handedly. For example, the municipality was the first on the Reef to consider enforcing a registration system on African women.[140] The role of an exceptional individual like Bopape was obviously important in consolidating the local representation of Communists. But the latter's performance here was not untypical of their activity on the East Rand as a whole; the Benoni squatters' movement was given energetic leadership by the local Communist Party branch which held mass meetings, encouraged occupation of empty premises and organised the biggest political demonstration in Benoni's history when in 1945 several hundred people marched through the city centre bearing placards saying 'We are homeless'; 'We are starving'; 'Slums cause crime'; and 'We sleep in tents this winter.'[141]

The Communists established a tradition of involvement in local socio-economic issues that was taken up by later nationalist politicians. Communists were also important in the work place struggles that took place during the 1940s on the East Rand. Their role in the 1946 African Mineworkers' strike is well known, though the effect on location residents of the brutal treatment of miners who marched out of their compounds into the East Rand towns has yet to be considered. Communists had a role in the organisation of the African Iron and Steelworkers' Union, which with the Food and Canning Workers' Union were to form the two strongest regional affiliates to, first, the Council for Non-European Trade Unions, and later the South African Congress of Trade Unions.

The East Reef in the mid 1950s, then, was an area in which a tradition of radical politics had existed for a comparatively long time within its black communities, a tradition which was characterised by sensitivity to parochial concerns and successful intervention in them by African nationalist and socialist politicians. With this background, it becomes easier to understand why the parents within these communities responded in the way they did to the call for a boycott of schools in 1955. The boycott should be seen as flowing out of a well established momentum by poor people to retain some control over their lives.

FOOTNOTES

1.   Muriel Horrell, *African Education: Some Origins and Development until 1953,* South African Institute of Race Relations (hereafter SAIRR) (Johannesburg, 1963), pp. 35-41.

2.   See Baruch Hirson, *Year of Fire, Year of Ash* (London, 1979), pp. 20-34, for examples.

3.   Gwendoline Garter and Thomas Karis (eds.) *From Protest to Challenge,* Volume II (Stanford 1975), p. 217.

4.   Horrell, *op. cit.,* p. 37.

5.   *The Good Shepherd,* March 1948, p. 27.

6.   *Drum,* June 1955.

7.   Quoted in E. Murphy, *Bantu Education in South Africa,* PhD Dissertation. University of Connecticut, 1973, p. 118.

8.   Brian Rose and Richard Tunmer, *Documents in South African Education* (Johannesburg, 1975), p. 266.

9.   *Ibid,* p. 254.

10. Murphy, *op. cit.,* p. 199.

11. Mia Brandel-Syrier, *Reeftown Elite* (London, 1971), p. 38.

12. Federal Council of African Teachers' Memorandum to Department of Native Affairs, April 1956, SAIRR Library, Box File 26A. A new school built in Tyutyu near King William's Town cost the location's inhabitants £411 — two thirds of the total. *The Torch,* 11 November 1958.

13. R. Hunt Davis Jr., *Bantu Education and the Education of Africans in South Africa* (Ohio, 1973), p. 46.

14. Murphy, *op. cit.*, p. 121.

15. Federal Council of African Teachers' Memorandum to Department of Native Affairs.

16. *Imvo Zabantsundu* (King William's Town), 12 August 1944.

17. Reports of this boycott appear in *The Torch*, 26 August 1952 and 4 November 1952 and *The Spark*, 5 September 1952.

18. Report of proceedings at ANCYL meeting, Newclare, 5 December 1948, SAIRR papers, AD 1189, Unsorted ANCYL papers.

19. Agenda, Bloemfontein Youth Conference, SAIRR papers, AD 1189, Unsorted ANCYL papers.

20. Misconduct which could justify the dismissal of a teacher could include political activity and any public opposition to any state agency. Murphy, *op. cit.*, p. 165. In fact the Transvaal Province had already made this a regulation in 1950. See *The Voice of Orlando* (South West Townships), May 1950.

21. Leo Kuper, *An African Bourgeoisie* (New Haven, 1965), p. 184.

22. Rose and Tunmer, *op. cit.*, p. 262.

23. Organised opposition from Natal teachers developed later: perhaps partly because of the absence of political organisations prepared to involve themselves in educational issues and also, possibly, because in Natal direct state control of schools, in contrast to other provinces, was common before the passage of the Act. See Kuper, *op. cit.*, pp. 187-190 and Horrell, *op. cit.*, p. 36.

24. See for example: 'Tsolo people will not suffer oppression', *The Torch*, 29 January 1952, p. 2.

25. The best history of the evolution of the AAC and associated bodies is a University of Cape Town sociology B A Honours dissertation by R. Gentle (no title available) from which many of these details are drawn. *The Torch* contains useful information as does the breakaway faction's *Ikwezi Lomso*, Queenstown.

26. *The Torch*, 26 December 1950.

27. Leo Sihlali, 'Bantu Education and the African Teacher' in *Africa South*, I, I (October — December 1956). See also *The Torch*, 10 November 1953 and 22 December 1953.

28. Sihlali, *op. cit.*

29. *The Torch*, 24 December 1957.

30. *Ibid*, 3 December 1957.

31. The history of resistance in these areas to various government land schemes should be linked with the especially overcrowded conditions characterising these areas as early as the 1940s. See *Report of the Witwatersrand Mine Natives' Wages Commission*, UG 21 1944, pp. 10-12.

32. *The Torch*, 4 November 1958.

33. Ciskeian school attendance figures, for example, were the best in the

country. See *Ciskeian General Council Proceedings* (King William's Town), 1954, p. 18.

34. *The Good Shepherd*, March 1942 and November 1946.
35. *Ibid*, May 1950.
36. *The Voice of Orlando*, April 1950.
37. *Ibid*, May 1950.
38. *The Good Shepherd*, March — June 1950.
39. *Ibid*, January 1950.
40. Interview with Professor Es'kia Mphahlele, Johannesburg 1980. See also *The Torch*, 5 August 1952 and 26 August 1952.
41. *The Torch*, 3 August 1954.
42. *Ibid*, 2 March 1954.
43. Professor Mphahlele remembers approaching ANC activists in 1952 and attempting to discuss Bantu Education with them but failing to elicit much interest. The ANC, at the time, had all its energy caught up in the organisation of the Defiance Campaign. There were relatively few teachers in the higher echelons of the ANC and those teachers which remained in Congress after 1952 tended to be Africanist-inclined (e.g. Zeph Mothopeng, A.P. Mda, Godfrey Pitje, Peter Raboroko, Robert Sobukwe, Potlake Leballo. and Tsepo Letlaka).
44. Edward Feit, *African Opposition in South Africa* (Stanford, 1967), and Gwendoline Carter, Gail Gerhart and Thomas Karis (eds.) *From Protest to Challenge*, Volume III (Stanford, 1975).
45. Hirson, *op. cit.*, p. 47.
46. Annual Report of the National Executive Committee to 42nd annual ANC conference, 16-19 April 1954, p. 10, SAIRR papers, AD 1189, ANC III. Brakpan must have been atypical: here energetic campaigning against Bantu Education began as early as June 1954, according to a report in *Advance*, 1 July 1954.
47. Feit, *op. cit.*, p. 164.
48. See Carter, Gerhart and Karis, *op. cit.*, pp. 31-32.
49. *Ibid*, pp. 32-33.
50. Legal advice submitted to the conference by the Liberal Party lawyer J. Gibson made it clear that the law would not tolerate any formal education outside that provided by the schools registered with the new department.
51. Information on this conference drawn from: Carter, Gerhart and Karis, *op. cit.*, p. 33; Ts. memo. by Congress of Democrats delegation, Federation of South African Women papers, CIII (4) (IV) 15 10 55; Ts. memo by Liberal Party delegation, Margaret Ballinger papers, File B 2 14 1.
52. This has been exhaustively discussed in both Feit, *op. cit.*, and Carter, Gerhart and Karis, *op. cit.*
53. The earliest Congress campaigning appears to have been in Brakpan. See reference 46.

54. *Treason Trial Record* (Original copy held by the South African Institute of Race Relations), p. 2265.
55. *Ibid*, p. 7485.
56. *Ibid*, p. 2266.
57. *Bantu World*, 26 February 1955.
58. *Ibid*, 12 March 1955.
59. *Treason Trial Record*, p. 2472.
60. *Ibid*, p. 2438.
61. *Ibid*, p. 2450.
62. *Bantu World*, 26 March 1955.
63. 'The Girl Who Will Not Go to School Again', *Drum*, April 1955.
64. *Bantu World*, 16 April 1955 and *Cape Argus*, 13 April 1955.
65. *Bantu World*, 16 April 1955.
66. *The Torch*, 19 April 1955 and *Treason Trial Record*, p. 2413.
67. *The Star* (Johannesburg), 12 April 1955.
68. *Treason Trial Record*, p. 2413.
69. *Cape Argus*, 12 April 1955 and *The Torch*, 26 April 1955.
70. *The Star*, 18 April 1955.
71. *Rand Daily Mail*, 26 April 1955.
72. *Bantu World*, 11 June 1955 and 27 August 1955.
73. *The Star*, 4 May 1955 and *Pretoria News*, 29 April 1955.
74. Carter, Gerhart and Karis, *op. cit.*, p. 33.
75. Feit, *op. cit.*, p. 183.
76. Cyclostyled letter on origins of the AEM, Federation of South African Women papers, CIII (2).
77. *Bantu World*, 25 June 1955.
78. Germiston meeting reported in *Rand Daily Mail* (Johannesburg), 2 May 1955.
79. *Bantu World*, 7 May 1955.
80. *Bantu World*, 10 September 1955.
81. Pencilled memo. on the cultural clubs, SAIRR papers, AD 1189, ANC IV.
82. Trevor Huddleston, *Naught for your Comfort* (London, 1956), p. 174.
83. See *The Torch*, 5 July 1955 and 5 June 1956, and *AEM News*, 1, 1 June 1956, p. 4.
84. See report in *Drum*, June 1955; pencilled memo. on cultural clubs, SAIRR papers, AD 1189, ANC IV; *Bantu World*, 10 December 1955 and 17 December 1955.
85. *Bantu World*, 8 December 1956.
86. *Bantu World*, 25 June 1956.
87. *Eastern Province Herald*, 15 March 1955.
88. *Ibid*, 7 April 1955.
89. *Daily Despatch*, 15 May 1955.
90. *The Torch*, 24 April 1955.
91. *Evening Post*, 23 May 1955.

92. Helen Joseph (interviewed by the author in January 1981) recalled that local enthusiasm for the boycott was very evident in smaller centres when she visited the Eastern Cape in June 1955.

93. *Evening Post,* 25 May 1955.

94. *Evening Post,* 19 July 1955 and *The Torch,* 26 July 1955.

95. *AEM News,* I, 1 June 1956.

96. Quoted in Feit, *op. cit.,* p. 184.

97. Carter, Gerhart and Karis, *op. cit.,* p. 34.

98. *The Torch,* 15 February 1955.

99. *The Torch,* 5 April 1955.

100. Union of South Africa, *Annual Report of the Commissioner of the South African Police,* 1955, Pretoria, UG 52/1956, p. 5.

101. *Cape Times,* 21 September 1955 and *New Age,* 10 November 1955.

102. *African X-Ray Report,* October 1955, p. 12.

103. Pencilled memo on cultural clubs, SAIRR papers, AD 1189, ANC IV.

104. *Counter-Attack,* 2, II, March 1956.

105. Pencilled memo on cultural clubs.

106. Handwritten note on political instruction, Federation of South African Women papers, CIII 3.

107. Federation of South African Women papers, CIII, 4 X 9 13 56.

108. *Counter-Attack,* 2, 11 March 1956.

109. See Chapter 7 of D. Humphriss, *Benoni, Son of my Sorrow* (Benoni, 1968) and City of Germiston, *Official Guide,* 1957.

110. Humphriss, *op. cit.,* p. 99.

111. *Ibid,* p. 99.

112. *Ibid,* p. 97.

113. *The Star,* 26 January 1981.

114. Humphriss, *op. cit.,* pp. 113-116.

115. Muir and Tunmer, 'African desire for education in South Africa', *Comparative Education,* ix, 3 October 1965.

116. *Ibid.*

117. See T. Lodge, *Black Resistance Politics in South Africa,* 1945-1981 (London, forthcoming), chapter 4.

118. Ethnic grouping policies were universally disliked by urban Africans. Both Humphriss and Brandel-Syrier *(op. cit.,* p. 8) mention resistance to the removals but more research is needed to uncover the details.

119. See for example: 'Benoni hit by glaring class-room shortage', *Imvo Zabantusundu,* 2 December 1961.

120. *Inkululeko,* 9 November 1943.

121. *Ibid,* 4 December 1943.

122. *Ibid,* 4 March 1944.

123. *Ibid,* 14 August 1944.

124. *Ibid,* 24 November 1944.

125. *Ibid,* 9 June 1945, September 1947; Humphriss, *op, cit.,* p. 184.

126. *Inkululeko,* 28 July 1945.

127. *Ibid*, 4 April 1946.
128. *Ibid*, 15 May 1946.
129. *Ibid*, 1 July 1946.
130. That distinction belongs to Benoni. For a brief review of location housing statistics see: City of Johannesburg, Non-European and Native Affairs Department, *Survey of Reef Locations*, May 1939.
131. *Ibid*.
132. Humphriss, *op. cit.*, p. 85.
133. *Inkululeko*, 4 March 1944 and 24 November 1944.
134. A brief biography appears in Carter, Gerhart and Karis (eds.) *From Protest to Challenge*, Volume IV, p. 10.
135. *Inkululeko*, 18 April 1944.
136. *Ibid*, 4 October 1944.
137. *Ibid*, 10 May 1945.
138. Author's interview with Dr Nthato Motlana, Soweto, January 1981.
139. *Inkululeko*, 7 April 1946.
140. *Ibid*, 1 July 1946.
141. Humphriss, *op. cit.*, p. 184, and *Inkululeko*, 9 June 1945.

Part Four: The Current Crisis
The State and the Reproduction of Labour Power in South Africa
Mervyn Hartwig & Rachel Sharp

Introduction

This chapter seeks to elaborate a framework for comprehending the role of the state in the accumulation process in the Republic of South Africa since the early 1960s. Since the course of this process is structured by the particular way in which South Africa has been inserted into the world capitalist system, and by the political and ideological mechanisms through which this was achieved, it is necessary, as a preliminary step, to elaborate the particular way in which capitalist development in South Africa was initiated and guaranteed in the specific conditions encountered during its history.[1] The argument centres around the need to locate at all times the specific analysis of South African capitalism and its trajectory within the context of the various phases of the world capitalist accumulation process, rather than within an idealist and descriptive account of its racist ideology.[2]

The Historical Background — An Overview
Merchant Capital and Modes of Production: From the Sixteenth to the late Nineteenth Century

A fundamental premise of this chapter is that the most adequate conceptual framework for grasping the main developments in South African history since the sixteenth century (and earlier) is provided by Marxist theory of the structure, internal dynamics and articulation of modes of production. Such a framework best captures long-term regularities and transformations in human history in general, but has particular applicability to South Africa, where many of the great epochs and transitions in human history from pre-class to class society, from slavery to feudalism, to capitalism — have been telescoped into a few recent centuries. When Europeans first arrived, three main sub-types of the primitive communist mode of production (hunting-gathering, pastoral nomadic and lineage) were articulated in two complex social formations. The hunting-gathering mode was organised under the dominance of the pastoral nomadic mode in much of the present Cape Province, and of the lineage mode in Natal, the Orange Free State, the Transvaal and, together with the pastoral nomadic mode, the Eastern Cape. While early forms of exploitation and political coercion existed, the social formations were pre-class and pre-state in that, with the possible exception of the northern Sotho-Tswana, the people had nowhere split up into a class of labourers separated from ownership of the means of production and a class of non-labourers which controlled the means of production and appropriated surplus labour. Nor had there developed a set of political institutions relatively exclusive to the ruling group which were not directly accessible to the people.[3]

From the sixteenth century these social formations were increasingly brought into a relationship with others, in particular with feudal and capitalist Europe, via a world commodity market created by European-based merchant capital. The new relationship, mediated by merchant capital, first as the predominant form of capital and then as emissary of the capitalist mode of production, entailed swift collapse for the herder/hunter social formation. Merchant capital survived in a reconstituted and attenuated form until the twentieth century. The outcome of that interaction can be explained only in terms of differences in the internal structure of the various modes of ownership of wealth and effectiveness of redistributive mechanisms, in the size of the workforce they could support, and the development of the division of labour. Merchant capital also spawned, or helped to give rise to, modes that had never before existed in South Africa — slave, feudal, tributary — and it had the contradictory effect of preparing the way in some respects for the development of the capitalist mode of production itself. At the same time it gave rise to the dominance of relations of production in many areas that would act as a barrier to later capitalist development.

That the relationship was mediated at first by merchant, not productive or industrial, capital, and further, by merchant capital before it became the agent of productive capital, or of capitalism as a mode of production, is of great importance, for where merchant capital is the predominant form of capital it has a dynamic of its own.[4] It is the oldest and historically most general form of capital, far older than capitalism itself, which is a qualitatively new mode of production, the first in history to revolutionise the productivity of labour continually through improvements in technology. For the first time in history, production has become generalised competitive production for a market, and the capacity to labour itself has become a commodity. Capitalism in that sense developed only in the seventeenth century, whereas merchant capital has flourished wherever trade and money have extensively developed, in ancient Greece, for example, or Asia. While the creation of a world market by European-based merchant capital in the sixteenth century both preceded and was a necessary precondition for the transition from feudalism to capitalism in parts of Western Europe in the two following centuries, that transition was decisively effected, not by the market itself, but by the transformation, through class struggle, of feudal relations of production in the countryside.[5]

Though the agrarian class structure of the United Provinces was embryonically capitalist by the time the Dutch established a refreshment station for passing ships at the Cape in 1652, merchant capital, which had developed in its modern form in relation to needs structured by feudal class relations, remained the predominant form of European capital in the seventeenth and eighteenth centuries and was not to become subordinated to the requirements of capitalist production until well into the nineteenth.

Unlike productive or industrial capital, merchant capital is restricted to the sphere of trade or exchange and must buy cheap and sell dear (or engage in outright plunder) in order to accumulate. It mediates *between* the various branches of production and modes of production, taking a share via unequal exchange (or plunder) of the surplus created by the direct producers and penning it up in the sphere of exchange. Because of this, and because it therefore becomes concentrated in state supported monopolies, its impact on pre-capitalist social formations is ambiguous and contradictory. It simultaneously encourages and inhibits the development or expansion of commodity production. Its overall tendency, since it always drains surplus labour from the sphere of production and does not plough it back, is to dissolve pre-capitalist modes, but it cannot of itself call forth a capitalist mode to replace them. At the Cape during the period of Dutch East India Company rule, by encouraging the sale of surplus livestock for provisioning ships, it set in train a process of rapid disintegration of the pastoral nomadic mode, in which livestock, unlike land, was owned on an individual and family basis and constituted the fundamental source of wealth. At the same time it inhibited the development of production on a capitalist basis.

Where it could not meet its requirements by trade, it tended to encourage or allow plunder and conquest. And since trade, plunder and conquest and their associated effects (notably disease) tended to destroy the societies which were meeting its requirements, and since some of the foodstuffs it required (notably grain, fruit and vegetables) were not in any case produced locally, it encouraged the development of production on the basis of slavery.[6]

By the end of the period of Dutch rule (1806), most of the original 'Khoisan' (herder/hunter) social formation had been destroyed and the surviving peoples dispossessed of their land and reduced for the most part to a condition of de facto slavery alongside nearly 30 000 imported slaves. Together they constituted the bulk of the labour force in expanding state-promoted and white-owned agricultural and pastoral industries, and they predominated in urban crafts and household service. There had clearly emerged in South Africa a social formation dominated by slavery as a mode of production and likely to generate the ideology and politics of a slave society. However, because there were significant divisions and conflicts within the master class, between company officials and burghers, and between the agricultural and commercial Southwest as against the predominantly pastoral North and East, with internal trade and credit coming increasingly under the control of a growing merchant landholding class in the Southwest, it was never able to extend its hegemony over the colony to the extent that the slave owners of the southern United States did. Nonetheless, the new contradictory class relations both between masters and slaves and between pastoral Boers and their dependent workers generated a prevalent ideology of paternalism which masked and legitimated their exploitative nature. Such an ideology, which is dominant in most pre-capitalist class societies, often incorporates a notion of the congenital inferiority of the subordinate class, and conversely of the superiority of the superordinate class, even where no observable physical differences exist, as in feudal Europe, for example. Where they do, and especially where they broadly coincide with race divisions, as in seventeenth and eighteenth century Cape society, the notion is incorporated more comprehensively.[7]

After the second British occupation of the Cape in 1806 merchant capital, progressively assuming the form of banking capital, remained dominant in the colonised areas of South Africa until the 'mining revolution' of the final quarter of the century. Later, it became increasingly subordinated to the interests of triumphant industrial capital (in its 'competitive' or commodity-exporting phase), and hence of the British state, in the procurement of foodstuffs, raw materials, and markets. The dynamic of merchant capital was thus decisively altered. The dominance of slave relations of reproduction which it had earlier produced now had to be swept aside and an attempt made to restructure African societies to meet the expanding reproductive needs of the capitalist mode. A 'far more radical colonialism' was accordingly inaugurated as the British state launched a 'battery of measures . . . to bring the Cape into line with the requirements of early nineteenth-century British capitalism'.[8] These included strengthening the military apparatus of the colony and military action to protect and extend its frontiers, abolition of the slave trade (1807) and of the institution of slavery (1833) and enforcement of a partial transition to wage labour, progressive removal of mercantile restrictions on trade, promotion of immigration (partly in the interest of social control at home), fostering of missionary endeavour, and encouraging production of raw materials and foodstuffs by a peasantry as well as on a capitalist basis in parts of the Cape and the new colony of Natal. In the eastern Cape and Natal, Africans were increasingly drawn into a feudal rent relationship with merchant landholders, and indentured Indians and Tsongans from Delagoa Bay were brought out to labour in a capitalist agricultural sector producing sugar. Both the colonial and the post-colonial state presided over the elaboration of a racial division of labour within, and coercive forms of control over, a nascent working class.

The new colonialism both strengthened the position of merchant capital and ensured British control over it, with the result that the local merchant landholding class could be relied upon to secure Britain's interests in the area during most of the period under review.[9]

Developments had meanwhile occurred within Afrikaner and African society which ensured that any transition to the dominance of the capitalist mode of production in the interior would necessarily be abrupt and revolutionary. The 'Great Trek', which resulted in the establishment of the formally independent Afrikaner republics of the Orange Free State and the South African Republic (Transvaal) in the 1850s, was undertaken largely to escape from dependence on mercantile interests and from the ideology and politics of industrial capitalism. It was, in part, an attempt to preserve and develop a pastoral, hunting and herding way of life based on captive (slave) and tributary labour obtained largely by means of the commando.[10] This was made possible by two factors. Firstly, the stronger military apparatus of the Cape under the British made breaches in the westernmost defences of the lineage social formation which had blocked settler expansion for some fifty years. Secondly, an ongoing revolutionary process of class and state formation in African society had given rise to tributary ('Asiatic') modes of production. These were characterised by communal production and the absence of private property in land, and by elaborate militarised state apparatuses which exercised overall control of the process of reproduction and production and maintained surplus labour appropriation from the homestead. This took the form of tribute to the ruling class in labour, produce and captives, but was not independent of the state machine. What had happened in essence was that the chiefly group within the lineage mode had constituted itself a class and founded expansionary states without destroying many of the characteristic forms, and the kinship ideology, of the lineage mode. This process seems to have been set in train largely by two interrelated factors: population pressure on deteriorating resources and the advantages of larger and more complex social systems in improving their exploitation of the environment. The reinforcement and extension of the chiefly group's control over the distribution and accumulation of goods through monopolisation of profits deriving from an increase in trade occasioned by the penetration of merchant capital in draining off part of the surplus without transforming the forces of production probably contributed to population pressure indirectly as well as directly. It rendered it more imperative and tempting for the chiefly class to take a greater share of the surplus for itself and for the expansion of the state.[11]

The *difaqane* or *mfecane*, as this process of class and state formation was known, facilitated Afrikaner expansion by occasioning major tensions and disruptions in African society. The British annexation of Natal in 1843, also made possible by the *mfecane*, deprived the trekkers of the possibility of realising their goal of forging independent commercial links with the outside world. In addition to difficulties they were experiencing in controlling and extracting a surplus from resurgent African society, it induced them to try their fortunes on the highveld.

Until the 1860s neither Afrikaner republics nor African states in the interior possessed much cohesion, as Afrikaner factions joined with African factions against rival alliances, and all competed for captives, booty, tributary groups, hunting resources and trade.[12] While increasingly powerful state systems did emerge from this process, all inevitably became enmeshed in varying degree in a commercial network emanating from the Cape and Natal. When its hold was threatened in 1877 by a general crisis in the Transvaal state, brought on by expansionist tendencies, administrative inefficiency, the reluctance of its prosperous ruling class to contribute adequately to its coffers, and the constant need for military expenditure occasioned by the growing strength of African rivals Britain made an armed intervention in the area, only to withdraw in 1881 when the mercantile hegemony seemed again assured. In the late nineteenth century, as earlier in parts of Natal and the eastern Cape, there was a transition to predominantly feudal relations of production in the republics, a transition which could not occur in any of the African states because of the absence of private property in land. Ownership of the land became ever more concentrated owing to the state's need to use land to pay officials for their services, back the currency, and raise loans. Land values rose, too, as local and absentee owners became attracted to the idea of extracting rent from efficient African (and Afrikaner) peasant producers in the form of cash, produce or labour services. There was, however, one important difference to the feudalism in the Cape and Natal. Those states were fairly amenable to the requirements of industrial capital and its agent and were not likely to be reluctant to intervene to structure class relations to that end: in the republics the feudal mode was capped at the political level with formally sovereign and increasingly powerful feudal states inimical to the development of capitalism.[13]

Thus on the eve of the era of imperialist penetration of South Africa, when the export of capital rather than commodities would require the creation of a massive proletariat for the development of large-scale indigenous capitalist production, the articulation of modes of production mediated by merchant capital had had an extraordinarily complex, contradictory and uneven outcome. There was now a far greater diversity of modes than at the beginning of the mercantile era: hunter-gathering in marginal areas, lineage, tributary, feudal, capitalist, with slavery persisting as one form of labour among others in the interior. None, however, was dominant throughout the social formation, and, indeed, in important respects there still existed not one but several formations. While production and consumption within all the modes had in the nineteenth century increasingly been directed towards the reproductive requirements of industrial capitalism in the metropolis, this had been a very uneven process, far more advanced in the Cape than in Natal, and in Natal than in the northern republics and the African states, where the various modes were integrated into the mechanism of reproduction of feudal and tributary modes respectively. The merchant landholding class, which had strong links with metropolitan capital, was the most powerful local class. It had located the various social formations within an overall framework of dependence, but the power of that class was challenged regionally by feudal and chiefly ruling classes. A

Primary school, Orlando Township, Soweto, on a smoggy winter morning.
Photograph: P Kallaway.

SCHOOL IN MOFOLO NORTH.
SKOOL IN MOFOLO NOORD.

School in Mofolo North, Soweto.
Contrast the typical Bantu Education architectural design with that depicted
on the following page.　*Photograph: Johannesburg Public Library.*

Progress High School is one of the prestige state schools built in Soweto since 1976. It is in the style of modern white schools in South Africa and is situated near to the new prestige suburb of Selection Park. The school had a white headmaster and deputy-head in 1982, a novel phenomenon for Soweto schools.

Photographs: P Kallaway.

limited process of primitive accumulation had been set in train both in African and Afrikaner society. One of the consequences of this development was the divorce of direct producers from the soil. While there were significant pockets of agrarian capitalism in the Cape and Natal, non-capitalist relations of production were most prevalent in the greater part of the countryside. Penetration under the dominance of merchant capital, first as the predominant form of capital and then as agent of industrial capital, had thus introduced and reinforced modes of production that would act as a barrier to capitalist development. These would have to be transformed in an era of imperialist penetration, and in the interior their transformation would meet with determined resistance not only from the direct producers themselves, but from entrenched ruling classes. Owing to the different structures of the feudal and the tributary social formations, however, the transition to capitalist agrarian relations would be more readily accomplished in the former — with fateful consequences for the making of the South African working class.

Imperial Capital and the Dominance of the Capitalist Mode of Production: From the Late Nineteenth Century to Sharpeville

(a) The first phase of imperialist penetration, c. 1880s to 1930s: 'capitalist revolution from above and without' and the making of a divided working class.

With the transition from 'competitive' to monopoly capitalism or imperialism in the metropoles, and the discovery of diamonds and gold in South Africa, there was a consequent shift of the economic centre of gravity to the interior with particular emphasis on the Transvaal. As a consequence, Britain's strategy of relying on commercial hegemony to secure her interests in the area became unviable. Massive investment of finance capital in long range gold-mining programmes, spurred by an unprecedented demand for gold to underpin the currencies of the major capitalist economies, and the prospect of high rates of profit, both necessitated and helped to effect 'capitalist revolution from above and without'.[14]
    Conditions were thereby created for the dominance of the capitalist mode of production in South Africa — not in the sense that capitalist relations of production immediately became the most prevalent but in the sense that state policies were geared into the reproductive requirements of productive capital invested locally. These were above all in mining, but also increasingly in agriculture and in secondary industry as it developed. The 'dull

compulsion' of the law of value now began to make itself felt throughout the social formation. The trajectory of major changes was henceforth determined chiefly by the outcome of class struggle between capital and labour (white and black, settled and migrant) over the rate of surplus value and the conditions of its extraction.

The investment of finance capital in less developed social formations in the age of imperialism has typically produced a number of common results. While offering many advantages (a low organic composition of capital, for example, and potentially abundant supplies of low-cost labour power) such social formations have also presented formidable barriers to investment, in particular because of the existence of non-capitalist modes of production with entrenched ruling classes, which previous phases of capital penetration had helped to call into being or reinforce. Since finance capital, unlike merchant capital, seeks to maximise profits by involving itself directly in production, it requires the establishment of capitalist production units and the creation of a low-wage proletariat. While the existence of non-capitalist modes provides the indispensable basis for the creation of such a proletariat, prising direct producers loose from the means of production and the control of ruling classes requires the establishment of a colonial state to impose taxation, appropriate land and exert various other forms of coercion. Moreover, the securing of the extended reproduction of capitalism within such non-capitalist modes requires the promotion of the political dominance of local classes favouring this outcome. The resultant state, whether colonial or post-colonial, therefore normally assumes an imperial, non-incorporationist form in which the exploited and dominated classes are denied the classic liberal rights: freedom of association, universal suffrage, formal equality before the law within a single legal system and compulsory education. Short of launching a major colonial war, imperialism is often unable to destroy completely the previously dominant mode of production and the political power of its ruling class, and this places severe limitations on the development of capitalism, particularly in the agrarian sector. The internal development of capitalism is also necessarily restricted and distorted by the reproductive requirements of industrial capitalism itself. In general, extension of capitalist relations into various sectors only occurs when they are crucial for the reproduction of industrial capitalism (until the 1930s and 1940s, capital-intensive raw materials and agricultural cash-crop export sectors) or when they do not compete with imports from the industrial metropoles (import substitution, which offers severely limited possibilities).[15]

While export of finance capital to South Africa produced many features conforming to this general pattern, a number of unusual circumstances resulted in some important differences. While the state assumed a 'normal' non-incorporationist, imperial, form with respect to the great bulk of the working and rural classes (ie Africans in particular), the pre-existing settler community was accorded the classic bourgeois rights. That is, a *racially exclusive* bourgeois democracy was founded[16] — *exclusive* of non-whites (the token political representation of Africans and Coloureds in the Cape was eliminated in 1936 and 1956) and inclusive of whites. That representation became more comprehensive during the 20th Century. White trade unions soon came to be officially recognised, white workers were incorporated into a compulsory industrial relations system in the 1920s to the exclusion of blacks, and white women were enfranchised in 1930. Further, all major sectors of the economy were capitalist by the 1920s — not only mining and a small manufacturing sector, but agriculture in the white-owned countryside (more than 80 percent of the total area).[17] While the South African economy was never more than semi-peripheral within the context of the World Capitalist System, all major sections of capital, international as well as national, had come to favour the promotion of industrialisation, differing only over its form and rate.[18] By the early 1930s, the basis for significant industrial development had been laid. From the perspective of a theory of imperialism and its effects, it is not the denial of bourgeois rights to blacks that requires explaining but their existence and persistence for whites of all classes. Also of importance is the removal of various obstacles to capitalist development in agriculture and manufacturing.

An explanation for the above is to be sought above all in the peculiar importance of gold to finance capital and the demand of the mining industry for a massive supply of cheap labour. These demands arose partly because the nature of the gold mining process entailed that costs other than labour were high. An understanding of the labour issue also entails an examination of the different structures of the feudal and the lineage and tributary modes of production.

It is important, too, to note that some of the surplus created in the mining industry was used to promote capitalist agriculture and manufacturing. The first circumstance — the demand for cheap labour — produced imperial military intervention which swept aside barriers to capitalist development presented by the feudal mode of production in the Afrikaner Republics and by the African lineage and tributary modes. Following conquest, they were 'reconstructed', the former in such a way as to promote a transition to capitalist agriculture, a process that led to complete proletarianisation of the majority of Afrikaners; the latter so as to provide the basis for a cheap and controlled migrant labour force, thus resulting in incomplete proletarianisation of an African working class. The main reasons for this differential outcome, this 'fatal dichotomy'[19] which was the root cause of the making of a divided working class, are to be sought in the different structures of the modes: the existence within feudalism of large privately owned estates which could be transformed 'from above' into capitalist production units; and communal ownership of land and redistributive kinship networks within the African modes, which could provide the foundation of a typical migrant labour system based on the continued local production of a share in the cost of reproducing labour power.[20]

The destruction of the regional power of the feudal ruling class and the subordination of African societies to the capitalist mode of production in terms of the reproduction of labour power rather than of production of commodities, entailed the weakening of significant non-capitalist dominant classes and their political incorporation as part of a new collaborating class. In other words, the locally dominant classes were now exclusively 'white' and either bourgeois or incipiently bourgeois, thus favouring the maintenance and extension of capitalist social relations. When a unified state was created in 1910 to guarantee the conditions for continued capital accumulation, including above all the operation and maintenance of the system of cheap African labour (which came to be known as Segregation), formal state power could be entrusted to these classes since they would favour imperial capital's continuing hegemony. Indeed, such an arrangement had to be secured in order to place the internal reproduction of capitalism on a secure basis. These classes alone could marshall political support for the continued dominance of the capitalist mode of production and promote commitment to its superiority as a form of production in the ideologies that structure everyday life. Because they were bourgeois, and because of the prior existence of bourgeois democratic forms in the Cape and Natal, the state necessarily assumed a bourgeois democratic form. But, unlike earlier forms of bourgeois 'democracy', such political incorporation was not in respect of the dominant classes alone. Maintenance of the system of cheap black labour, which supplied the great bulk of the workforce, made it necessary to seek support for the form of state among all sections of the white population. The early militancy of the white working class (especially in mining), arising from the importation of skilled class-conscious workers from Europe and from their extreme 'structural insecurity' owing to their complete proletarianisation and the constant threat that capital would replace them with cheap black labour, made a strategy of incorporating them doubly expedient.[21] Moreover, given that the bourgeois democratic state necessarily presents itself as representing and embodying the unity of the people/nation whilst simultaneously fostering a notion of the equality and individuality of every citizen, it was a strategy with considerable prospect of success in a situation where the concept of the 'white race' facing a common 'black enemy' could be appealed to as an organising principle to bridge the rift between Afrikaner and English-speaking settlers.[22]

The destruction of feudalism and the formal possession of state power by locally dominant capitalist classes, their bargaining power vis-a-vis imperial capital strengthened by their crucial role in supplying the mass of labour power so cheaply; and their control over the actual labour process in the burgeoning capitalist sectors, goes some way towards explaining the relatively early and successful capitalist penetration of the agrarian sector and the development of manufacturing capacity. State power was used to divert some of the huge surplus, derived from the production with low-cost labour of large quantities of internationally saleable commodities (diamonds and gold), into the promotion of capitalist agriculture and industry. But by and large this did not occur in a way inimicable to the interests of international finance capital in the context of the local balance of class power and conditions of class struggle. Capitalisation of agriculture, stimulated initially by the emergence of the mining industry, a lucrative internal market, and by the use of state power to eliminate competition from efficient African peasant rivals, had the advantage not only of securing the political support for this form of state from large landholders but also ensured the 'freeing' of African labour for the mines and cheapening the means of subsistence of the workforce both locally and, through generation of export capacity, in the metropolis. And the development of local capacity to manufacture basic consumer goods and essential mining inputs was rendered inperative by the interruption of supplies during the South African War and World War I. Significant sections of mining capital itself early diversified into manufacturing, initially into mining supplies. Industrial development also served to contain the class struggle of increasing numbers of proletarianised whites whom mining capital refused to employ owing to the 'high' value of their labour power and whose militancy threatened to trigger revolutionary struggle among African workers. Such development was promoted by the state, partly to head off a potential threat to the continued existence of the capital relation. But above all, manufacturing too benefited from the system of cheap labour and the 'fatal dichotomy' created in the first instance to serve the interests of the mining industry.[23]

The capitalist class, the most significant section of which was international, pre-empted the possibility of a general alliance between black and white workers and inflicted a major defeat on the white working class in 1922. This was achieved by taking advantage of an already elaborated racial division of labour (in which the exploitative colour bar of capital must be seen as historically and analytically prior to the employment colour bars of the white workers); by constantly going on the offensive to keep overall labour costs down, especially in mining; and by replacing high-cost skilled white labour with low-cost semi-skilled black labour.

Many white workers then put their faith electorally in the Nationalist and Labour Parties which came to office in the Pact government of 1924-1933. Nonetheless, the state then proceeded to pre-empt the renewed danger of an alliance between black and white workers by further elaborating the racial division of labour in mining, the state sector and manufacturing and by co-opting white workers into a compulsory industrial relations system which exluded blacks. At the same time capital slashed white wages in manufacturing and mining and went on replacing (relatively, as the economy expanded) white male workers with ultra-cheap black, and white female, workers in manufacturing). The resulting surge of organisation and militancy on the part of a minority of the white working class (most had had the autonomy of their organisations completely undermined) who sought to make common cause with an increasingly well-organised and militant black working class, was met by a state campaign of terror and crushed by 1932, thereby creating the conditions for the higher exploitation of all sections of the working class and for sustained economic growth after 1933, especially in manufacturing.[24]

Black workers had been 'forced into temporary submission, while those elements among the white workers who had looked to the strength of the black working class for support in their struggle against capital turned their attentions back to the prospect of winning advantages for themselves within the industrial relations structures laid down by the state.'[25]

(b) The second phase of imperialist penetration, 1930s to Sharpeville: the transition to 'Apartheid'

The transition to Apartheid is best explained in terms of a general crisis in the system of controlled cheap labour in the 1940s, brought on by three interrelated processes. First, the under-development of the Reserves and hence the generation of wide-spread unrest and revolt within them sparked off by resistance to various 'betterment' and 'rehabilitation' schemes (reallocation of land, restrictions on the amount of land each peasant could plough and the number of cattle he could graze, enforced rotational grazing and fallowing of land, etc) which were promulgated by the state in an effort to shore up the declining Reserve supplement.[26]

Second, a developing crisis within capitalist agriculture in the 1930s and 1940s which triggered off protracted class struggle between capitalist farmers and their labour tenants. Farmers responded to the crisis by reducing the amount of land available to labour tenants and drastically curtailing their grazing rights, whilst simultaneously holding their wages constant. Labour tenants responded with massive urban migration, which now supplied more town labour than the Reserves under conditions in which the counterpart of the Reserve supplement had been significantly eroded. The result, within capitalist agriculture, was an acute labour shortage and the political mobilisation of farmers to resolve it by creating a full-time settled workforce.[27]

Thirdly, there was unprecedented industrial expansion after 1933, with the contribution of manufacturing to GNP surpassing that of a rapidly expanding mining industry in 1943. (It had surpassed that of agriculture in 1930). Growth was just as sustained during the period 1933-1939 as it was during World War II. Its essential precondition, thus, was the defeat inflicted on the black and militant white section of the working class referred to earlier. It took the form almost exclusively of import substitution, necessitated during both world wars and occurring behind moderate tariff barriers in the period 1919-1939. The continued diversification of mining capital (by the Anglo-American Corporation in particular) into industries which could supply it with cheap and reliable mining materials, played a significant role. Since all major sections of capital had come to favour some form of industrialisation by the mid-twenties, the state also played a key role, partly by erecting selective tariffs but more importantly by supplying infrastructures and establishing industries too large or initially unprofitable for private capital. Production got under way in ISCOR in 1934, and in the early forties, when gold-mining seemed to have a limited future. The Smuts government also embarked on a policy of systematically encouraging secondary industry, laying particular stress on its rationalisation by encouraging mechanisation and changes in the labour process (the replacement of skilled artisans by semi-skilled operatives). These changes were encouraged in order to increase the productivity of labour by moving the racial division of labour upwards while at the same time keeping down overall labour costs.[28]

All three processes led to the growth of a large urban black proletariat, predominantly non-migrant in industry and commerce but still exclusively migrant (and increasingly drawn from outside South Africa) in mining. In either case, the rural supplement now meant very little, and life in shanty-town and compound was miserable. The resulting surge of black trade union activity and militancy produced significant gains in real wages for industrial workers, especially after 1940, but these must be offset against the decline of the rural supplement. The struggle was by no means merely economistic. A growing proletarian consciousness increasingly called into question capitalist exploitation itself, especially insofar as it was based on a racially defined cheap labour force. It culminated in 1946 in a mineworkers' strike which demanded in effect an end to the migrant labour system and which was ruthlessly suppressed by the state when it threatened to escalate into a general strike of black workers.[29]

In sum:

> The path of capitalist development in South Africa generated both rural impoverishment and intense urban poverty as the decreasing amount of necessary product provided by Reserve production [and by its counterpart in the white-claimed countryside] was not replaced by significantly higher wages in the capitalist mode. Capitalist development thus generated conflict not only over wages but over all facets of urban and rural life. This structurally induced conflict centred on cheap labour, bringing into question the structure of the system of exploitation. These conflicts came to a head in the period 1942-6, when the problems of political control over urban Africans became acute, culminating in the 1946 strike with the use of massive repression to stifle the challenge. All sections of the dominant classes had then to develop new responses to this conflict.[30]

One response was provided by an ascendant Afrikaner nationalism, which must be seen as 'the historically specific . . . reaction of particular class forces to the pressures of capitalist development.'[31] While the Nationalist Party had been based historically on class alliances between the Afrikaner petit bourgeoisie and capitalist farmers in the Cape and the poorer section of farmers in the North, in both of which the petit bourgeoisie played a subordinate role, it was the petit bourgeoisie, particularly as organised in the secret, extra-parliamentary, northern-dominated *Broederbond,* who came to occupy a class vanguard position in the nationalist movement in the thirties and forties. They were instrumental in mobilising the support that resulted in a Nationalist electoral victory in 1948.

Articulating a 'populist' and anti-'imperialist' ideology which reflected the structural insecurity of the petit bourgeoisie, stressing the dangers of class divisions, the virtues of individual entrepreneurship and hard work, and the need to mobilise savings and political support in order to create a 'people's capitalism', the *Broederbond* and its front organisations explicitly set out in 1936 to wean the Afrikaner workers from the politics of class to the politics of the *volk*. By exploiting the craft/semi-skilled conflict within the white trade-union movement and pointing to the 'dangers' of class mobilisation in a situation in which the African working class was strong and militant, it achieved a considerable measure of success, especially on the Rand. In 1948 the Nationalist Party won six mining seats for the first time from the Labour Party. This put it into office with an overall majority of five.[32]

While the Nationalist Party has consolidated itself in office since then, there seems little warrant for the liberal view that 1948 constitutes a key point of transition, the primacy of politics over economics, the point at which backward-looking (even 'anti-capitalist') Afrikaners seized control of the state and used it to dam up the modernising and integrative tendencies of the economy. Apart from its arbitrary conceptual divorce between 'politics' and the 'economy', such a view ignores the fact that the financial institutions founded by the petit bourgeoisie to mobilise savings and formulate economic policy inevitably came to be dominated by Afrikaner capitalists. More importantly, it ignores the fact that, in the fifties, the Nationalist government pursued in most essentials the strategy elaborated by its predecessor. In particular, it continued to pay systematic attention to planned development of the (capitalist) economy. While real white wages rose in the fifties as whites moved up in the division of labour and the Nationalists consolidated their electoral base, black wages fell, and the productivity of labour increased at an annual rate of 2,2 percent. This did not, however, create the conditions for sustained economic growth in the 'fifties: the rate of growth declined from 7 percent in 1947/8 to 4,6 percent in 1951-1955 to 3,8 percent in 1956-1960; there was a serious recession during 1958-1961. Among the reasons for this were a high level of imports owing to pent up consumer demand and a need to replace worn out production capacity after the War; a decline in foreign investment in the mid-fifties, brought on by labour unrest and a mass political challenge to the segregationist form of state, which was only partly offset by state loans from abroad; and the fact that much state and private capital went into *development* in mining, in

ISCOR and in new parastatals producing oil from coal (SASOL) and fertilisers (FOSCOR). The result was that real fixed investment rose at a higher rate than the GNP. Thus, while there was a crisis of capital accumulation during the decade, and the economy remained heavily dependent on the export sectors of mining and agriculture, the foundations for more spectacular growth in the sixties had been laid.[33]

What differences there were between the Nationalists and their predecessors centred chiefly on the role of blacks in secondary industry, with the Nationalists placing greater emphasis on migrant labour and all that entailed in terms of social welfare and control, and the United Party, with the support of significant sections of manufacturing and diversified mining capital, favouring a limited incorporationist strategy.[34] Little store should be set by these differences, however, since what the state actually does, as opposed to what political parties say they are going to do, depends upon the requirements of the accumulation process, including the necessity to contain class struggle. Certainly, given the existence of segregationist structures and in particular the racial division of labour, and given the balance of class forces, in particular a structurally insecure white petit bourgeoisie and working class, any thoroughgoing incorporation of the black working class was not a viable option for capital in 1948.

The fifties saw the development of broad-based class struggle by black workers and petit bourgeoisie and a small radical section of the white petit bourgeoisie. While the defeat of 1946 had led to the temporary demise of African trade unions, the liberal promise of slow African advance within the system had come to look increasingly hollow for the petit bourgeois leadership in the ANC and other nationalist organisations. The stage had thus been set, especially when the rate of economic growth slowed down, for the merging of most elements of the African opposition (petit bourgeois and proletarian) into a movement articulating a much more radical nationalist ideology.[35]

Its demands ranged across increased wages, abolition of the pass laws, and political representation, to national liberation, and the new tactic of the mass political strike ('stay-at-home') was devised and put into practice, along with passive resistance. It was met with ruthless repression from the outset, and the movement remained divided and confused concerning its aims and strategy ('Africanists' versus 'Charterists') for much of the decade. The shootings at Sharpeville in 1960, coinciding with the trough of the recession, touched off a wave of strikes, riots and demonstrations which were systematically suppressed. The more radical leadership then embarked upon a suicidal campaign of sabotage. This brought a ferocious response from the state which eliminated, incarcerated or exiled the whole of the movement's established leadership by 1963, thereby laying the foundations for a sustained phase of 'stability' and capital accumulation.[36] It was only then that Apartheid was systematically implemented, as the elaboration and perfection of segregationist instruments for maintaining a cheap and controlled labour force, and a high rate of exploitation, under conditions of increasing capital intensification and changes in the character of the reserve army of labour.[37]

The State and the Reproduction of Labour Power in the Sixties and Seventies

The Sixties: The Expansion of Manufacturing Production

During the sixties there was a further consolidation and expansion of the manufacturing sector accompanied by significant changes in the pattern of employment of both white and black workers. Between 1963 and 1969 manufacturing increased its contribution to the GNP from 20,8 to 23,4 percent, whilst the shares of agriculture and mining, the main sources of foreign exchange earnings, declined from 28,3 to 21,2 percent. Table 1 shows the shifts in employment in the three sectors between 1960 and 1970.

Table 1 — Shifts in the Distribution of Productive Workers

	1960		1970	
	Black	White	Black	White
Agriculture	1 437 900	118 487	2 260 386	91 813
Mining	548 000	61 599	609 000	62 677
Manufacturing	308 332	213 680	2 513 000	281 603

38

The table shows that the increasing proportion of black workers was particularly significant in manufacturing. The large increase in the number of black workers employed in agriculture reflects not an expansion of agriculture's contribution to the GNP but the relocation of surplus blacks into the homelands, a phenomenon which will be discussed below. The proportions and numbers of females in the African labour force also increased.

Manufacturing experienced an exceptionally high rate of growth from 1963 to 1970, averaging 8 percent increase per year. The expansion was due more to an increase in the absolute numbers employed, however, than to any marked increase in productivity per worker. Between 1963 and 1970, employment rose by 53 percent, whilst production increased by 72 percent. The growth was particularly rapid in the engineering, metals and mineral products branches which comprised 39 percent of manufacturing output by 1964. Pulp, paper, military hardware, electronics and chemicals also increased their share of manufacturing output. Such a high rate of growth was financed, largely, by foreign capital inflows, inflationary financing, and the redistribution of surplus value from mining and agriculture, illustrating the increasing inter-penetration of capital occurring during this decade. Wages rose steadily at the same rate for both white and black employees, but the gap between white and black average earnings therefore widened considerably. The decade was also marked by an increasing concentration and centralisation of capital. The total number of manufacturing firms increased by over 1 000 to 13 121 in 1970 but the average number of employees per firm increased from 70 to 83. Such crude figures, however, mask a high level of industrial concentration. Table 2 shows the percentage of total turnover in different branches of economic activity accounted for by the largest firms.

Table 2 — Percentage of total turnover in different branches of economic activity in South Africa: 1972

Percentage of largest firms	Manufacturing		Wholesale & Retail		Construction	
	No. of firms	% of turnover	No. of firms	% of turnover	No. of firms	% of turnover
10	1 210	75,7	5 360	77,0	785	74,6
25	3 026	90,3	13 404	87,8	1 961	87,9
50	6 053	97,5	26 809	95,5	3 923	96,0

39

Manufacturing was characterised, on the one hand, by a large number of relatively small, uncompetitive enterprises, using out-moded technologies and employing low levels of skill, enabled to survive by tariff barriers and ample supplies of cheap labour; on the other hand, 10 percent of the largest firms accounted for 72 percent of turnover, 65 percent of employment and 80,2 percent of fixed assets. Regional concentration of industrial production was also high. In addition, over 40 percent of the 100 largest firms were foreign owned or foreign controlled.[40]

Accurate figures concerning the degree of foreign control over domestic manufacturing production are unavailable. Legassick (1974) has described the Afrikanse Handelsinstituut's figure of 80 percent as possibly an exaggeration. Similar difficulties arise when trying to assess the significance of Afrikaner capital. The *Official Yearbook of South Africa* for 1978 estimates that it had grown from 3 percent in 1939 to 11 percent by 1965, dropping, however, to 9 percent by 1977. The growth of Afrikaner control over commerce, however, was more rapid: 3 percent in 1939 compared with 30 percent in 1977.

Fixed capital investment increased rapidly during this decade, reflecting the increase in the organic composition of capital. Fixed investment comprised 20 percent of GDP in 1960 and had risen to 26 percent by the mid 1970s. The largest capitals and the parastatals were responsible for a disproportionate share of capital investment, relying to a great extent on imported technology. Capital goods comprised 30 percent of total imports in 1957 but this proportion had risen to 45 percent by 1970. The organic composition of capital was lower in mining and agriculture. Both sectors imported only a relatively small proportion of their capital goods requirements, relying to a large extent on domestic production.

A high proportion of manufacturing production was still import substitution. Department I (ie the local manufacture of machines for use in productive processes) was comparatively underdeveloped although during this decade some expansion took place, largely by the parastatals as part of a long term strategy by the state to achieve economic self-sufficiency.[41]

The rapid expansion of manufacturing was paralleled by an increase in manufacturers' share of exports. It had reached 21,2 percent by 1966 and grew further to 27 percent in 1973. Despite this, however, maufacturing remained a net consumer of foreign exchange largely due to the high level of imports of machinery required for its own expansion. By 1964, 70 percent of all fixed investment in the manufacturing sector comprised imported capital goods. Thus, South Africa in the 1960s remained a typical semiperipheral economy. Food and minerals were the chief earners of foreign currency, but there was an increase in the export of processed and semi-processed agricultural and mineral products. Together these comprised nearly 80 percent of all South African exports. Her biggest trading partners were the EEC, and Britain, Japan and the USA, to which she exported mainly food and minerals in their raw or processed state, and from whom she derived her imports of capital and consumer goods. Africa was the main consumer of her exported finished products but for political and economic reasons, the prospects of further penetration of African markets to any great degree were not good, despite the optimism expressed in the Reynders Report.

As the decade proceeded, South Africa's reliance on the export of food and minerals, both subject to potentially severe fluctuations in prices, became more problematic as the degree of technological dependence accelerated. Between 1963 and 1971, for example, the value of imports had grown by 150 percent, whilst that of exports, excluding gold, had increased by only 50 percent.[42] Consequently, severe pressure began to reveal itself in the balance of payments, despite the continued high receipts from the sale of gold. This imbalance between the value of imports and exports, however, is only the surface manifestation of a more profound set of circumstances and pressures which produce impediments to the accumulation process in South Africa.[43]

Barriers to the Accumulation Process

Peripheral capitalist economies are affected by the trends in the global pattern of accumulation and are peculiarly vulnerable to the cyclical upturns and downturns in the expanded reproduction of capital on a world scale. Nevertheless, disregarding the effect of the onset of a world recession in the capitalist system of production and trading relationships which began to manifest itself in the late sixties, the South African capitalist economy by that time was already confronting major impediments to a further development of the productive forces and the expanded reproduction of capitalist social relationships. Import substitution industrialisation, characteristic of peripheral capitalism, inevitably comes up against the problem of its own saturated markets. Further expansion requires an internationalisation of the circuits of production, distribution and exchange, an option which is only feasible for the strongest and most efficently competitive fractions of capital. Despite the theory of comparative advantage, the prospects for export-led recovery strategies are dim because other peripheral economies are simultaneously experiencing the same problems. Further penetration into African or other peripheral economies by South African manufacturing exports confronts the barrier of their own import-substitution industrialisation and low purchasing power, whilst the lower level of technological advancement compared with that of the metropolitan economies renders any large-scale penetration of the latter's manufacturing markets almost impossible. Moreover, the acceleration of mechanisation as manufacturing capital, encouraged by the state, attempts to enhance its international competitiveness through restructuring of the labour process, itself aggravates the drain on foreign exchange because of the increased capital imports that an increase in the organic composition of capital requires. South Africa has achieved metropolitan status only with respect to Department I in mining technology. Given the rapidity of the advance in the computer-chip industry in Japan, the USA and to a lesser extent Western Europe, an industry which is fundamental to much of the new and higher forms of technology now being developed, the possibilities for South African capital to break into these areas of production and exchange are limited. Consequently the import of such technology puts pressure on the balance of payments which only a huge and regular inflow of foreign capital can offset. Such inflows, however, are especially vulnerable to the internal political climate which, in much of Southern Africa, including the Republic, deteriorated during the late 60s and 70s. South African capitalist development, necessarily structured and regulated, as we have seen, through the framework and institutions of Segregation and Apartheid, is peculiarly vulnerable to internal class conflicts. Thus the contradictions of earlier modes of orchestrating the articulation between different modes of production, and of regulating the relationship between capital and labour, produce more intense contradiction in subsequent phases of the accumulation process.[44]

The conditions of accumulation of total social capital have required increasingly repressive forms of extra-economic coercion by both individual competing capitals and the state. The pressures to contain and to control the class struggle within the limits of capitalist class relations are rendered increasingly difficult as the accumulation process proceeds, whilst the costs of doing so cause an unhealthy drain on surplus-value. In an accumulation crisis, this surplus-value is sorely required for other purposes, such as research and development, which might, in the long term, promote the necessary expansion of Department I production. More specifically, the shortages of skilled labour caused by the rapid expansion of manufacturing employment and the unavailability of white skilled and supervisory manpower, has proved a barrier to the further development of the productive forces. This shortage of white labour was itself the result of past job reservation legislation necessary to incorporate and placate the white working class in earlier phases of the class struggle. Whilst capitalist rationality, conceived in purely economic terms, requires job reservation regulations to be breached, the mechanisms for so doing run the gauntlet of potential opposition from white trade unions which have provided political support for the Nationalist party in articulating its apartheid policy.

In summary, the particular way in which South African capitalism has been inserted into the international capitalist system as a supplier of food and minerals, and the money-commodity, gold, and as an importer of manufactured products, together with the unique and peculiar social and political forms which were necessary within the South African conjuncture to secure the general conditions for capital accumulation, combine to render capitalism in South Africa peculiarly vulnerable to a world accumulation crisis.

The South African State and Capital Accumulation in the Sixties

(a) Direct State Intervention in the Sphere of Production

The state, as the political form of the domination of capital in general, responded to these structural contradictions in the accumulation process to safeguard the possibilities of extended reproduction and the maintenance of capitalist social relations. Given the recognised need to expand secondary industrialisation, the state was responsible for a high proportion of capital investment directed both at developing the necessary infrastructure (power, water, transport and communications) and at direct investment in the manufacturing sector through the various parastatals, often in joint projects with private capital. The strategy of the state during the 1960s was directed at a long-term policy of economic autarchy thereby broadening the industrial base and facilitating the development of manufacturing production in both capital and intermediate goods. Whilst, as has been argued above, these sectors are still relatively underdeveloped compared with the situation in advanced metropolitan economies, a high level of research and development support was initiated. This adds relatively little to GNP in the short term but has some prospect of long term viability. In addition, the establishment of the Economic Advisory Council in 1961, together with a range of other planning and development bodies, illustrates the extent to which the South African state is intervening in the sphere of production and exchange and orchestrating the relations between the various fractions of capital whose interests varyingly converge and diverge.[45]

(b) The State and the Restructuring of Manufacture

Through a variety of fiscal incentives, and other schemes, the state has tried to encourage the trend towards a rising organic composition of capital through mechanisation, reorganisation and rationalisation of the labour process to enhance capital's national and international competitiveness. It successfully encouraged the inflow of foreign capital through tax incentives and changes in the system of exchange controls. Furthermore, in its endeavours to improve South Africa's trading position and encourage foreign capital, it lowered tariff barriers during the sixties and early seventies and moved towards a more selective system of import controls, in line with GATT policy. By the early seventies and in line with the Reynders Report, it initiated an export drive with generous tax incentives to exporting industries.

Such measures combined to produce a significant degree of both expansion and rationalisation, but had the consequence of leading, on the one hand, to an acute shortage of skilled and supervisory manpower, and on the other, to the generation of increasingly politically problematic levels of black structural unemployment, despite the overall increase in the absolute numbers of blacks employed.

Table 3 — Migration to and from South Africa

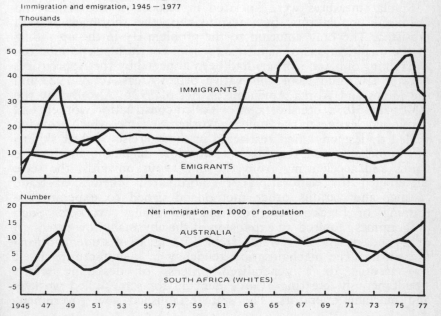

(c) The State and the Reproduction of Skilled Labour Power

Earlier it was argued that the institutions and forms of segregation and apartheid had produced a situation whereby most categories of skilled and supervisory labour were reserved for whites. Despite the state's successful attempt to encourage immigration in the sixties, the net inflow was nowhere near sufficient to meet the shortages of skilled labour power which were developing. Table 3 shows the extent of immigration (and also how migration is affected by the prevailing political climate).

The sixties saw the establishment of two new universities for whites (Port Elizabeth and Rand Afrikaans Universities) and the designation of four Colleges of Advanced Technical Education (Technikons) for whites in 1968. A number of apprenticeship schools were upgraded into technical colleges, and a range of technical institutes established in continuation centres. This stress on vocational and technical education, which was accompanied by similar trends in the schooling system, was paralleled by a proliferation of private and government training schemes. By the 1970s a streamlining of the whole tertiary sector was in train with the Van Wyk de Vries Commission on universities advocating a greater flexibility between the various institutions and encouraging a greater inter-flow of students and more uniformity of qualifications.

Similar measures were initiated in respect of the Asian and Coloured populations, but despite this, the shortages of skill persisted. The only solution to the problem lay in the upgrading of the qualifications of significant sections of the black population.

Training of black workers had been impeded by the Apprentices Acts of 1922 and 1944, the Native Urban Areas Act of 1923 and the Mines and Works Amendment Act of 1926. Already, by the 1940s and 50s, acute shortages of skilled construction workers had developed, leading to the Building Workers Schemes which provided skilled tradesmen, albeit restricted in the exercise of their skill to the homelands and the black townships. Beginning in the late fifties and accelerating from the mid-1960s onwards, the state encouraged the elaboration of co-ordinated schemes of trade testing, and various other methods designed to expedite the training of black operatives and semi-skilled workers. Such programmes required an expansion of the abysmally low provision of secondary schooling which trebled its intake of students during the sixties. The mechanisation tendency in manufacturing itself was leading to a generalised process of deskilling whilst simultaneously creating a large demand for semi-skilled workers and machine operators. The state established new government training schemes in the homelands, the border areas and some urban centres, provided incentives for employers or groups of employers to establish private subsidised training schemes, and set up Training Centres and ad hoc Training Schools, offering, for example, 10-week crash courses to meet the demand for semi-skilled workers. Early in the seventies a number of multi-purpose Manual Training Centres were established in the main townships and in the homelands. As the official government handbook describes them:

> It is not intended that these practical courses should replace or attempt to compete with the existing trade or technical schools which serve a different purpose. What is aimed at rather is a general industrial orientation or 'readiness' that will equip the young man to find his feet more quickly in an industrial society so that he can make better and more immediate use of work opportunities (p 49).

It would be hard to find a more apt characterisation of the kind of work opportunities available in an era of deskilling.

Over and above the demand for semi-skilled operatives, there existed a need for more highly trained manpower. A College of Advanced Technical Education has been built in KwaZulu with the help of a big 'donation' from a large corporation, whilst a number of additional secondary technical schools have been established in the homelands, again with buildings financed by funds from private capital. Whilst the vocational training of girls is less well developed, a number of training courses have been established. As the official government handbook puts it:

> The majority of these courses serve a dual purpose: they prepare the girls for their future task as home-makers and also train them for work opportunities, particularly in the clothing industry.

Such developments are, of course, framed within the parameters of the ideology of Bantu Education, elaborated by the Eiselen Commission of 1949–1951 which led to the controversial Bantu Education Act of 1953. Likewise, the three black universities of Fort Hare, Zululand and The North, established by the Extension of Universities Act of 1959 and the Universities of Bophuthatswana, Transkei and Venda, are all located within the homelands in line with the basic assumptions of the Bantustan policy. Together they train the highest level of black manpower which the capitalist mode of production in South Africa both permits and requires.

Despite these developments, often initiated and encouraged by the state, the shortages of skilled manpower persist.[47] The barriers to the further training of blacks are mainly political rather than economic or legal, a situation which will be further discussed below. The state has, however, endeavoured to break down job reservation schemes when the needs of capital require it. It has, for example, established a framework and machinery for dealing with the opposition of white trade unions, and has shown a willingness to orchestrate the reorganisation of jobs where white workers retain their supervisory functions, overseeing blacks who perform fragmented semi-skilled tasks at lower rates of pay. More-over, in government enterprises, a number of training schemes for apprentices have been established specifically for blacks, as in the railways and post office.

The rise in the organic composition of capital thus creates a demand for new forms of skilled and semi-skilled labour. Accompanying this trend, however, is the structural generation of unemployment for those whose skills are being replaced or who lack any skill at all.

(d) The State and the Control of Structural Unemployment

Whilst it is difficult to ascertain accurate figures for black unemployment, it has been estimated that even before the manufacturing boom commenced, black unemployment was about 9 percent. By the end of the sixties, it had probably doubled. With a black population growth of more than 3 percent per year, and the generation of surplus labour through technological development, a very high proportion of blacks entering the employment market remain unemployed.[48] Structural unemployment particularly impinges upon those under thirty and is especially high for females and matriculated blacks who lack technical qualifications. This situation is aggravated by the declining subsistence sector in the homelands. The Tomlinson Commission of 1956 had already exposed the appalling poverty, unemployment and under-employment in those areas. During the 1960s further changes in class relations in the homelands, often encouraged by state policy, accelerated the process of primitive accumulation through increasing the concentration of landholdings. This led to the unemployment of a vast number of blacks whose prospects of employment either in the homelands, the border areas or in the urban townships were almost nil.[49] Transkei unemployment had reached more than 22 percent, for example, by 1968, and has doubtless accelerated since then.

The potential for accentuated class conflict and political mobilisation among a black population already subject to a repressive system of labour control is self-evident. As structural unemployment among the blacks accelerated so pressures were generated for the state. It needed to safeguard the reproduction of labour power consistent with the continuation of capitalist class rule and to step up the mechanisms for regulating the flow of cheap labour into the capitalist employment market, whilst simultaneously controlling and containing those whom the capitalist mode of production had no prospect of absorbing.[50]

The State's Articulation of a More Repressive System of Labour Control

Although the broad outlines of the Bantustan policy had been implicit in the Nationalist Party's ideology of apartheid before 1940, the specific elaboration of its details developed pragmatically as a response to both economic necessity and the political and ideological implications and repercussions of the accumulation process. Overt class struggle, or the desire to prevent it, figures prominently in the trajectory of the history of apartheid. The defeat of the black working class struggles in the fifties, culminating in the massacre at Sharpeville and subsequent developments, necessitated a further elaboration and acceleration of the policy of separate development. This necessity was reinforced by the growth of structural unemployment in the sixties, discussed above.

This policy has three central elements. Firstly, the homelands were to be developed both politically and economically as the arena where Bantu political aspirations could be expressed through a combination of traditional and representative forms ultimately leading to self-government as envisaged by the Promotion of Bantu Self Government Act of 1959. By the Bantu Homelands Citizenship Act of 1970 and subsequent developments the long-term goal eventually became multi-national development and full political independence. This policy necessitated the establishment of a tame black elite and a supporting middle class, hence the establishment of a high proportion of South Africa's black secondary and all its black tertiary education in the homelands by the mid-60s. Schools for the sons of chiefs to train a subservient black ruling elite were established in 1960. It also required the export of capital through the state from white South Africa to the homelands in order to make provision for the necessary economic and social infrastructure to fulfil the needs of capital — ie, the reproduction of cheap labour power in a politically docile form.

Bantu health and welfare facilities were to be provided primarily in the homelands, as also post-elementary education. The 'successful' implementation of such a policy, of course, required considerable economic development in the homelands to absorb the surplus population, but despite the preparedness of the state and the various homeland governments to provide the necessary infrastructure, derived in the main from the taxation of the African petit bourgeoisie, little success has been gained in attracting either foreign capital investment or encouraging the geographical relocation of manufacturing production from the white areas of South Africa.[51]

The state initiated an industrial decentralisation policy in the early 1960s to encourage labour-intensive industrial expansion in the border areas around the homelands and on the edges of the main urban concentrations in 'white' South Africa, but this too has not been very productive in job creation. Between the mid-1960s and 70s, it has been estimated that only 2 200 new jobs have been created every year.[52] The Planning and Resources Act of 1967 gave the Minister of Planning power to control the allocation of all resources to industry, including the distribution and control of labour supply, but those aspects of the act designed to encourage jobs in the border areas have been less successful than those designed to facilitate the export of unemployed[53] and surplus blacks from the white areas back into the homeland.[54]

The second attribute of the policy of separate development concerns the migrant labour policy. The aim was to reduce the number of permanently settled blacks in urban areas, and for capital to rely instead on an elaborated system of migrant labour focused on single workers whose wives and families were to be sustained in the homelands which, in addition, would provide the focus for political aspirations and national identification. Capital would recruit such workers on a yearly basis, as and when required, under a rigid contract-labour system from labour bureaux in the homelands, thus facilitating the state's orchestration of labour supply and labour control. This policy was stepped up in the late sixties; a high proportion of labour contracts had to be negotiated in the homeland labour bureaux and permanent settlement rights for blacks in the urban areas were substantially reduced.

The third, and related, aspect of the Bantustan policy concerns the physical removal of those affected by structural unemployment from white areas, along with any other undesirable elements, and their forcible transportation back into the reserves.[55] The pass system and other measures of influx control are intimately related to all aspects of the homelands policy, as is the lack of opportunity for secondary and higher education in the urban townships. In 1969, for example, 28 percent of all schools for blacks in South Africa were located in the homelands. This percentage had risen to 54 percent by 1972. It has been estimated that some 2 million blacks and half a million Asians and Coloureds, many of whom have no identification with the homelands and have lived all their lives in urban townships like Soweto, were forcibly uprooted and relocated into townships in the homelands between 1960 and 1970; the removal of at least a further 4 million was projected in the seventies.[56] The lack of widespread organised political opposition during the sixties has to be understood in the context of an accentuation and elaboration of the system of extra-economic coercion by the state concerning which the defence budget increases in the 1960s and 1970s is only an indicator.

Table 4 — South African's Defence Expenditure

Financial Year	Funds voted	% of State Expenditure	% of GNP
1971/2	R 316 500 000	12,2	2,2
1972/3	335 336 000	11,8	2,1
1973/4	472 022 000	13,5	2,5
1974/5	692 000 000	16,4	3,2
1975/6	948 000 000	18,5	3,7
1976/7	1 350 000 000	15,0	4,1
1977/8	1 700 000 000	19,0	5,1
1978/9	2 040 000 000	15,0	5,5
	(approx)	(approx)	(approx)

57

Given accelerating structural unemployment and the build-up of decades of class antagonism and frustration within the black population, the capitalist state, in order to sustain and guarantee the social, political and ideological preconditions for continued capital accumulation, has had to resort to increasingly repressive legislative and physically coercive methods of social control.

Simultaneously, the ideology articulated to legitimate separate development has undergone some significant shifts. In the 1940s and 1950s, whilst stress was laid on the inherent cultural differences between black and white, the implicit assumption of the inferiority of 'the Bantu' was plain. He or she was not only different but inherently incapable of participating fully in the structures and institutions of white (capitalist) society on a basis of equality. By the early seventies, however, 'the Bantu' was both different and equal, his or her equality of opportunity, however, to be realised within the institutional forms of multi-national development, albeit articulated and economically interdependent with 'white' South Africa.[58]

> South Africa's objective is self-determination by all its peoples. This
> simply cannot be achieved by forcing all the national identities within
> the country's borders into a single integrated unit, to be governed on
> the basis of one-man, one-vote. The white nation, for one, would
> lose its identity and would, in effect, revert to the colonial status it has
> long since outgrown . . . . A policy designed to avoid group conflicts
> cannot be said to run counter to civilised conceptions of human rights,
> dignities and freedom, irrespective of race, colour or creed. On the
> contrary, the government's fundamental aim with self-determination
> for all the country's peoples is the elimination of the domination of one
> group by another. The very purpose is to facilitate the development of
> each people into a self-governing national entity, co-operating with
> others in the political and economic spheres in a manner mutually
> agreed upon.[59]

Thus, the reality of capitalist class domination is obscured.

The World Recession in the 1970s and the Contradictions of Capitalist Production in South Africa

The beginning of the seventies saw the onset of a world recession,
the surface manifestations of which were the crisis in the world
monetary system, rising levels of unemployment and inflation
in the metropolitan economies, accentuation of class struggles
both nationally and internationally, and the oil crisis. This situation
brought about a further deterioration internally within the South
African economy. The high inflow of foreign capital characteristic
of the sixties began to drop off, accelerating the balance of
payments difficulties. The rand was devalued in order to promote
exports but, given the continuing high rate of imports of capital
goods, indispensable, as has been argued above, to improve the
competitiveness of South African manufacturing, the increased
costs of imports offset any increase in exports which arose. The
domestic rate of inflation was somewhat higher than her major
trading partners. The annual increase in GNP fell sharply, particularly affected by a slackening in the manufacturing sector.
Despite the continuing shortages of skilled labour, unemployment
among the non-white groups began to rise rapidly. For the first
time since the early sixties, unemployment among whites began to
surface. The effects of the crisis in the world accumulation process
were aggravating, and combining with, the already deteriorating
conditions of the South African economy.

It is thus hardly surprising that the seventies have been characterised by a resurgence of overt class struggle among the non-white population. The repressive system of labour control, extended and further elaborated in the growth conditions of the sixties, may have contained the accentuating class contradictions, but are rendered vulnerable in less favourable economic circumstances. In 1972 and 1973 there were widespread strikes and labour unrest among African workers, brought on by high price rises and excessively low wages. Despite the fact that concessions in the form of higher wages were granted and the state moved strongly against those involved, unrest continued throughout 1974, and more sporadically in 1975. More than 200 African workers died in the course of the troubles, and many more were injured, including a large number who were involved in disturbances in the mines.[60]

The large number of strikes and stoppages and days lost through strikes reflect the extent of the opposition to exploitation among the African proletariat despite the 'illegality' of work stoppages.

Table 5 — Non-White Work Stoppages

Year	No. of work stoppages	No. of shifts lost	No. of employees involved
1971	69	3 316	4 196
1972	71	13 774	8 814
1973	370	229 136	98 029
1974	384	98 395	58 975
1975	274	18 559	23 103

61

Partly as a result of these industrial disputes, and the continuing shortages of skilled and semi-skilled labour, wages of blacks began to rise rapidly from 1972, especially in the mines where labour shortages were becoming critical due to the rapid decline in the number of foreign migrant labourers who were prepared to work in the exploitative conditions in the mines and live in the prison-like mining compounds. The Anglo American corporation broke the longstanding agreement with the Chamber of Mines and offered higher wages in order to attract more labour and other mines were forced to follow suit;[62] but still the shortages persisted. Meanwhile unemployment among blacks continued to rise, coupled with an even more zealous response by the state to deal with it through the methods discussed in earlier sections.

Widespread malaise and frustration were accompanied by renewed attempts at African political organisation. The success of the anti-imperialist revolutions in Angola and Mozambique together with the widespread guerrilla activity in Rhodesia and Namibia had important implications in South Africa itself. The Black Consciousness movement provided a focus for much of the discontent.[63]

Baruch Hirson has criticised the Black Consciousness movement for its petit bourgeois ideology and its lack of concern for struggles developing among the black working class. Despite this, however, it was a significant factor in the 1976 student troubles in Soweto which sparked off widespread disturbances spreading throughout the country. Initially a protest against the compulsory implementation of Afrikaans as a medium of instruction in the school system, it developed into a broader based protest not only against the iniquities of the Bantu Education system but against all the repressive institutions of the apartheid policy, ie against the very structures developed to sustain the capitalist accumulation process itself. Whilst led by school students, and starting with school stay-at-homes and public demonstrations, it was accompanied by widespread labour unrest penetrating even into the homelands. The violence of the state's response, resulting in hundreds killed, and thousands detained, many of them school children, illustrates the extent to which ideological mediation and economic concession have failed to produce the conditions necessary for the reproduction of labour power in a docile form for capitalism in South Africa.[64] The internal class struggle, aggravated by the crisis in the world accumulation process, had reached the stage where it could be contained within the limits of capitalist class relationships only by tear gas, batons and guns. Thus the contradictions of capitalist development in South Africa are reproduced in a higher form. The 1976 disturbances were followed by a massive exodus of foreign capital which persisted for some years. The state's defence budget has risen by about 20 percent per year, a high proportion of which is devoted to internal security — ie the containment of the class struggles; GNP has been rising at a much lower rate than previously.

There is a deep underlying crisis of accumulation in the manufacturing sector symbolised by serious under-utilisation of industrial capacity. Inflation remains high, exports are not rising rapidly enough. Structural unemployment among blacks in white South Africa (excluding the homelands) is estimated to be as high as 24 percent. Meanwhile the international recession deepens, thus accentuating the potential for domestic economic recession characteristic of a peripheral economy.

The Dilemma Confronting the South African State

In order to guarantee the conditions for continued capital accumulation in South Africa, the interests of capital in general require the state to embark upon a somewhat altered course designed to bring about some limited incorporation of the black proletariat within the institutions which legitimate bourgeois society. Recent liberal commentators on South African state policy have heralded the end of apartheid, thereby 'validating' liberal theory which enunciates the long-term incompatibility between racism and capitalism and the former's eventual demise to be replaced by the ideology and practice of formal equality of opportunity. The argument elaborated in this paper throws doubt on any such proposition. Apartheid was necessary, given the specific conditions of capitalist development in South Africa and the course of the class struggle. The contradictions within the capital relation now require, however, a restructuring and modification of those institutions regulating the production, distribution and control of African labour power to conform with capital's ends. Through a policy of limited economic and political concessions to the African proletariat, and a strategy designed to separate the African petit bourgeoisie ideologically from the masses, the state is attempting to create in a restructured form the economic, political and ideological conditions for a renewed phase of expanded reproduction. This 'total strategy' requires some considerable reconstitution of the ideology which, since the Second World War, has legitimated the domination of social relations by capital and permitted the appropriation of the surplus product. The following elements of state strategy can be cited: firstly, the recognition system of industrial arbitration procedures alongside those already established for white unions (Wiehahn 1979). Such a strategy was already being initiated for the unrecognised but legal black trade unions in the sixties but is now being further elaborated. By bringing African workers further into the state system of labour representation it is hoped to ensure that African workers' demands become economistic and reformist. As Hemson puts it, bourgeois ideology has to have a material basis in order to be implanted in the subject's consciousness. Secondly, increased 'rights' are to be granted to blacks permanently settled in 'white' South Africa (Riekert 1979): rights of limited home ownership by non-transferable leasehold; some relaxation of the pass laws; opportunities to take apprenticeship training; more trading and entrepreneurial rights to operate in the urban townships, etc. Thirdly, 'free' and compulsory schooling is being phased in, more opportunities for secondary and technical education in areas other than the homelands, and a change in the name of the ministry responsible from Bantu Education, with all that this symbolises, to Education and Training. Fourthly, all remaining job reservation agreements are to be abolished (with concessions to buy off the white workers). Fifthly, big rises in the salaries of black teachers and other petit bourgeois black workers are being granted to bring them closer to those prevailing among whites in similar occupations. Sixthly, abolition of the Immorality Act is projected. Seventhly, redistribution of some surplus value collected through rates and taxation to the urban townships to build up the social infrastructure, extend electrification and provide more housing. Eighthly, an acceleration of the 'independence' strategy for the other homelands, together with some minor redistribution of land to enlarge and unify some of those currently divided. Finally, some limited constitutional changes, especially affecting the Asian and Coloured communities.

Such concessions are too little, and probably too late. There is little evidence so far that the state intends to reverse its policy to relocate structural unemployment into the homelands or to abandon influx controls. It is attempting to change course in a very different set of circumstances from those which existed when an earlier choice between a policy of limited incorporation and thoroughgoing apartheid seemed to present itself. In the wake of the high growth period of the sixties, the South African economy now has deep underlying structural problems. The bourgeois state faces the problem of retaining its mass base of political support and organising the various supporting classes and class fractions in a context where their objective and subjectively perceived class interests are being undermined. For the blacks, with structural unemployment increasing and low wages confronting an inflation between 12 percent and 15 percent, it is only a matter of time before a new outbreak of disturbances occurs. The costs of providing an adequate infrastructure of health, welfare, education and unemployment support for blacks, including those in the homelands, are far in excess of what the state, forced by the accumulation crisis into a policy of austerity, can provide. Even were there to be an upsurge in the world capitalist accumulation process, the particular mode of South Africa's insertion into the international division of labour means that South Africa's economy could pick up but without any marked effect on the high level of structural unemployment among blacks. Despite the increase in surplus value accruing from the rocketing of gold prices between 1979 and 1981 the financial demands on the state emanating both from her attempt to become economically self-sufficient — for example, in oil derived from coal — together with the massive defence expenditure required both by guerrilla activity in Southern Africa and the threat of insurgency in South Africa itself, will preclude the granting of the level of economic concessions to the black Africans which the situation currently requires. In any case, there is a strong speculative element in the price of gold which renders any long-term reliance on gold revenues unwise. The mini-boom occasioned by high gold prices in no way overcomes the fundamental vulnerability of the economy.

The pressures by South Africa on the Rhodesian state prior to Lancaster House, to grant concessions to the blacks and resolve the conflict there, together with her activities in Namibia and the surrounding black states, reflect the extent to which she fears the eventual outbreak of widespread nationalist black guerrilla activity within the borders of the South African social formation itself. The policy towards the blacks aimed at a limited incorporation strategy will inevitably have to be coupled with increased repression to contain the class struggle within the parameters imposed by capital.

A further and more significant issue for the nature of the bourgeois democratic state in South Africa emanates from the effects of the accumulation crisis on the white population. The weaker and more backward sections of national capital are hard hit by the recession. Over 3 000 businesses have gone bankrupt or have been subject to takeover bids since the late sixties. The restructuring of capital, and the concentration and centralisation tendencies inherent in the accumulation process lead to a devalorisation of inefficient capital with significant employment and political implications. Labour intensive industry is particularly hard hit.

However, it is the position of the white working class which may well produce a political crisis within the state, posing threats to the stable system of political representation. The hostile reaction of many white unions to the Wiehahn proposals reflect real threats to their living standards. Since the early seventies, real wages of whites have hardly risen at all, compared with the large increases received by blacks, and Table 6 illustrates.

Table 6 — Percentage Increase in Real Disposable Income 1972-77

	1972	1973	1974	1975	1976	1977
Whites	+ 1,2	-0,8	+ 1,9	+ 1,7	-1,6	+ 1,3
Blacks	+ 4,3	+ 3,5	+ 7,7	+11,4	+ 6,6	+ 11,9

With the high rates of inflation of the 1970s and the changes in direct taxation, the standard of living of the white working class has deteriorated. Whilst, in 1968, 75 percent of national income accrued to whites, by 1974 it had been reduced to 70 percent and is now even lower. Given the large differences, however, which persist between black and white incomes, there is a real fear, not without foundation, on the part of the white working class that white labour will be replaced by cheaper black labour. The breaching and projected abolition of job reservation regulations have meant that blacks have experienced higher possibilities for upward social mobility than have whites. Moreover, the transformations in the labour process and the de facto changes in the job colour bar initiated in the sixties, have led to some white workers, skilled and unskilled, being left behind. There has thus been a blurring of the racial division of labour at the margins which has added to the feeling of insecurity among whites. Furthermore, whereas in the sixties there was virtually full employment, the seventies saw a big increase in the level of unemployment among whites, affecting professional, semi-professional, administrative and clerical workers, and some in the manual strata — despite shortages of skilled workers. This situation is likely to further deteriorate as the effects of computerised technology begin to be felt in the retail, commercial and public service sectors where a high proportion of whites have traditionally been employed. The re-organisation and rationalisation of work under capitalism and the deskilling consequent upon changes in the labour process recognises no colour bar. This process accelerates during periods of capitalist crisis as employers attempt to save labour costs and enhance the efficiency and productivity of a reduced number of workers. Although the levels of white unemployment in South Africa are still very low by comparison with those prevailing in other semi-peripheral economies, nevertheless they are beginning to affect graduates from the schooling system from all socio-economic groups.

The political implications of these trends are, potentially, of great significance. A policy of limited incorporation of the blacks can only add to the generalised feelings of insecurity and loss of socio-economic status among the white working class and the old and the new petit bourgeoisie. Given the strength of racist ideology among these groups, racism which is not only directed against blacks but also has anti-semitic aspects, directed towards the strongest sections of mining, commercial and industrial capital which are thought to be controlled by Jews, a basis exists for political mobilisation by extreme right-wing political organisations which may well cause a realignment of the traditional bourgeois parties and a transformation of their mass base. The large electoral gains of the Herstigte Nasionale Party in the by-elections of 1979 and the rise of the Conservative Party are significant omens of possible future trends. The HNP is opposed to large monopolies, and advocates an extreme racist line of 'total' separation of the 'races' with no concession to any policy of incorporation. It has been especially successful in mining constituencies. Moreover, in the Transvaal, a Youth Preparedness Programme has recently been instituted as part of the Transvaal Education Department's secondary education provision. This programme bears a striking resemblance to the Hitler Youth Movement with its concern for 'love of the fatherland', living space, political and racial indoctrination, and military training in Veldskools.

However, it is within the Nationalist Party itself that the most interesting conflict among whites is occurring. A major struggle is developing between the *verkramptes* and the *verligtes* regarding future political strategy. The policies discussed earlier go totally against the views of the conservative hardliners who wish to see no concessions to the blacks and want a continuation of all the old petty apartheid policies, including mixed marriage prohibition, segregated facilities, a ban on African unionisation, the main-tenance of job reservation, etc. The class basis of the *verkramptes* and the *verligtes* differs. The latter probably represent the most progressive sectors of capital, both national and international, and the new petit bourgeoisie, whereas the former articulate the perceived interests of the rural sector, sections of the old petit bourgeoisie and the white working class. Already the shifts and changes in state policy in the past two years have revealed the difficulty the *verligtes* are experiencing in convincing the party of the correctness of their strategy. The move to extend and consolidate one of the homelands, for example, announced in 1979, came up against fierce opposition from the *verkramptes* and many of the proposals initiated by the government have not yet been implemented by the state because of party opposition. This centred around the person of Dr Treurnicht the former effective leader of the party in the Transvaal, the traditional home of the *verkrampte* ethos, and now leader of the breakaway Con-servative Party. The liberal press has debated the possible need for a benevolent despotism, a 'de Gaulle' solution. If the long tail of the Nationalists cannot be persuaded to support the 'enlightened' policies of the *verligtes,* capital may have a need to suspend democratic processes in South Africa. As the South African *Sunday Times* puts it, South Africa is 'heading for a state of emergency'. In other words, if (white) voters oppose the necessary internal 'reforms', if democracy gets in the way of the only option for capital (given the present state of class consciousness among the urban blacks) ie a policy of limited incorporation, then some other way of safeguarding the political rule of capital will have to be found. Mulder and Vorster's re-emergence on the political scene in support of *verkrampte* policies is significant, and is only the surface manifestation of a struggle going on in most areas of civil society: in the Afrikaner Universities, churches, trade unions, the apparatuses of the state, and the media. Of particular interest is the extent of *verkramptheid* in the army. While significant sections of the army leadership are in favour of the current government's strategy, it is likely that *verkrampte* attitudes are far more general in the lower echelons, given the latter's class origins.[66] In addition, the military imperatives generated by the war against the guerrillas will not necessarily permit a continuation of a 'bourgeois democracy', western style. In March 1977, General Malan stated that there were conflicting requirements between a 'total strategy' and 'the democratic system of government'. This view was subsequently endorsed by Mr Botha in a speech to Parliament. At around the same time a 'Senior Nationalist MP' was quoted as having told the *Sunday Express* newspaper that 'the government would not be able to meet future demands without giving the heads of the defence force a definite say in the decision-making process in the country, and that South Africa may ultimately be ruled by a civilian-military junta.'[67]

Such an eventuality should not be ruled out. With the steadily increasing level of guerilla activity in the Transvaal and the number of incidents of sabotage and 'terrorism' reported in the South African press in recent years which, given South Africa's censorship laws, are likely to be a considerable under-estimate, the preconditions exist for further polarisation within the white community between those who favour a tough line and those seeking a 'political' solution. The full extent of white opposition to the latter will become clearer as the government seeks support for its new constitutional plans.

Another factor impinging on the struggle between the *verkramptes* and the *verligtes* is the deteriorating international situation and the resurgence of cold war tactics vis a vis the Soviet Union. The *verkramptes* have received a big boost from the aftermath of the Afghanistan invasion. The Soviet Union has consistently supported the armed guerilla struggle in Southern Africa and is seen to be South Africa's prime enemy.[68] The ascendancy of the hawks in the United States, symbolised by Reagan's success in the Presidential elections, led to a relaxation of the pressure on South Africa to adopt a more 'liberal' approach. Greater 'realism' vis a vis Soviet world-wide intentions is being urged even by some who were previously adopting a softer line. Such shifts in perspective have to be interpreted against the background of the severity of the crisis in the advanced capitalist economies, discussed earlier, and the resurgence of rearmament which has been the traditional route taken by the capitalist class out of an accumulation crisis. The weak diplomatic response to South Africa's continued violation of international borders through military incursions into Angola, Mozambique and Lesotho has to be seen in the context of growing fears of Soviet dominance in areas crucial to the maintenance and preservation of capitalist enterprise.

The central problem for bourgeois class relations in South Africa, however, is the organisation of the mass support for the traditional mode of political representation. That mass support among the white population cannot necessarily be guaranteed, given the state of the class struggle and the peculiar problems confronted by the accumulation process in a peripheral economy. The extreme forms of racism which have been required to cement the elaborate system of labour control and reproduction in the conditions obtaining in South Africa in the long run produce the conditions which threaten the capital relation and undermine the necessary class alliances which capitalist class rule requires.

FOOTNOTES

1. Clarke, S 'Capital, fractions of capital and the state: neo-marxist analysis of the South African state,' *Capital and Class* 5 1978.

2. Holloway, J and Picciotto, S *Capital and State: A Marxist Debate* (London 1977); Jessop, B *Theories of the Capitalist State: A Critique* (London, 1981).

3. Hartwig, M 'Merchant capital and modes of production: South Africa from the sixteenth to the late nineteenth century.' (Unpublished paper presented to SAANZ Conference. Christchurch, NZ, 1981.)

4. Marx, K *Capital* Vol III (Progress Publishers, Moscow, 1959); Kay, G *Development and Underdevelopment: A Marxist Analysis* (London, 1975); Taylor, J G *From Modernization to Modes of Production* (London, 1979).

5. Dobb, M *Studies in the Development of Capitalism* (London, 1967); Brenner, R 'Agrarian class structure and economic development in pre-industrial Europe', *Past and Present* 70, 1976; Brenner, R 'The origins of capitalist development: a critique of neo-Smithian Marxism' *New Left Review* 104, 1977.

6. Hartwig, M (1981).

7. Elphick, R *Kraal and Castle: Khoikhoi and the Founding of White*

South Africa (New Haven and London, 1977); Elphick, R and H Giliomee (eds) *The Shaping of South African Society 1652-1820* (Cape Town and London, 1979); Genovese, E D *The Political Economy of Slavery: Studies in the Economy and Society of the Slave South* (New York, 1965); Hartwig, M (1981); Marks, S 'Khoisan resistance to the Dutch in the seventeenth and eighteenth centuries' *Journal of African History* 13(1) 1972 pp 55-80; Marks, S 'Southern Africa and Madagascar' in R Gray (ed) *The Cambridge History of Africa* 4, (Cambridge, 1975); Marks, S and A Atmore, 'Introduction' in S Marks and A Atmore (eds) *Economy and Society in Pre-Industrial South Africa* (London, 1980).

8.   Marks, S and A Atmore (1980) p 5, 22.

9.   Bundy, C 'The Abolition of the Masters and Servants Act' *SALB* 2:(1) (1975); and *The Rise and Fall of the South African Peasantry* (London 1979); Hartwig, M (1981); Legassick, M 'South Africa: forced labour industrialisation, and racial differentiation' in R Harris, (ed) *The Political Economy of Africa* (New York, 1975); Marks, S 'Natal, the Zulu royal family and the ideology of segregation' *JSAS* 4(2); Marks, S and Atmore, A (1980); Slater, H 'Land, labour and capital in Natal: the Natal Land and Colonisation Company, 1860-1948' *JAH* 16(2).

10.   Trapido, S 'Aspects of the transition from slavery to serfdom: the South African Republic 1842-1902' in *Collected Seminar Papers on the Societies of Southern Africa in the 19th and 20th Centuries* 6 (London, 9CS, 1976) and 'Landlord and tenant in a colonial economy: The Transvaal 1880-1910' *JSAS* 5(1) 1978; cf Hartz, L *Founding of New Societies* (New York, 1964); Genovese, E D (1965) and *The World the Slaveholders Made* (New York, 1969).

11.   Bonner, P *Kings, Commoners and Concessionaires: The evolution and dissolution of the nineteenth-century Swazi state* (Johannesburg, 1983); Guy, J *The Destruction of the Zulu Kingdom* (Johannesburg, 1979); 'Biological factors in the rise of Shaka and the Zulu Kingdom' in Marks, S and A Atmore (1980) pp 102-119, Parsons, N 'The economic history of Khama's country in Botswana, 1844-1930' in R Palmer and N Parsons (eds) *The Roots of Rural Poverty in Central and Southern Africa* (London, 1977); Gluckman, M 'The rise of the Zulu Empire', *Scientific American* 202.

12.   Bonner, P 'Factions and fissions: Transvaal/Swazi politics in the mid-nineteenth century' *JAH* 19(2) 1978; Legassick, M 'The frontier tradition in South African historiography' in Marks, S and A Atmore (1980) pp 44-79; Wagner, R 'Zoutpansberg: the dynamics of a hunting frontier 1846-1867' in Marks, S and A Atmore (1980) pp 313-349.

13.   Trapido, S (1976), (1978) and 'Reflections on land, office and wealth in the South African Republic, 1850-1900' in Marks, S and A Atmore (1980) pp 350-368; Wagner, R (1980); Keegan, R 'The restructuring of

agrarian class relations in a colonial economy: The Orange River Colony, 1902-1910' *JSAS* 5(2) 1979.

14. Legassick, M 'Legislation, ideology and economy in post 1948 South Africa' *JSAS* 1(1) 1974, pp 5-35.

15. Taylor, J G (1979); Mandel, E *Late Capitalism* (London, 1974); Bozzoli, B 'Capital and state in South Africa', *Review of African Political Economy* 11 (1978) pp 40-50; Innes, D 'The Mining industry in the context of South Africa's economic development, 1910-1940' *Collected Seminar Papers on the Societies of Southern Africa in the 19th and 20th Centuries* 7 (London, ICS, 1976).

16. Kaplan, D 'The South African state: the origins of a racially exclusive democracy' *Insurgent Sociologist* 10(2) 1980.

17. Morris, M L 'The development of capitalism in South African agriculture: class struggle in the countryside' *Economy and Society* 5(3) 1976, pp 292-343.

18. Innes, D (1976).

19. Marks, S and A Atmore (1980) p 36.

20. Guy, J *The Destruction of the Zulu Kingdom* (London, 1979) and 'The destruction and reconstruction of Zulu society', unpublished paper presented to conference on *Class Formation, Culture and Consciousness: The Making of Modern South Africa*, University of London Centre for International and Area Studies, January 1980; Marks, S and S Trapido 'Lord Milner and The South Africa State' *History Workshop* 8 (1979) pp 50-80; Mendelsohn, R 'Blainey and the Jameson Raid: the debate renewed' *Collected Seminar Papers on the Societies of Southern Africa in the 19th and 20th Centuries,* 8 (London, ICS, 1977); Trapido, S (1976); Wolpe, H 'Capitalism and cheap labour power in South Africa: from Segregation to Apartheid' *Economy and Society* 1(4) 1972, pp 425-56.

21. Johnstone, F A *Class, Race and Gold: A study of Class Relations and Racial Discrimination in South Africa* (London, 1976) p 57.

22. Davies, R *Capital, State and White Labour in South Africa 1900-1960: An Historical Materialist Analysis of Class Formation and Class Relations* (Brighton, 1979); Kaplan, D (1980); Legassick, M 'South Africa: capital accumulation and violence' *Economy and Society* 3(3) 1974, pp 253-91.

23. Beinefeld, M and D Innes 'Capital Accumulation and South Africa' *RAPE* 7, 1976; Davies, R (1979).

24. Innes, D and M Plaut 'Class struggle and the state, *RAPE* 11, 1978, pp 51-61; Davies, R (1979); Lewis, J 'The new unionism: industrialisation and industrial unions in South Africa, 1925-1930' in E Webster (ed) *Essays in Southern Africa Labour History* (Johannesburg, 1978); Johnston (1976).

25. Innes, D and M Plaut M (1978) p 59.

26. Bundy, C (1979); Beinart, W and C Bundy 'State intervention and

rural resistance: The Transkeian territories, c 1900-1960' paper presented to Peasant Seminar, Centre of International and Area Studies, London University, 1978; Hirson, B 'Rural revolt in South Africa, 1937-1951', paper presented to the ICS Seminar on the Societies of Southern Africa in the 19th and 20th Centuries, London, 1977.

27. Morris, M (1976).

28. Legassick, M 'Legislation, ideology and economy in post 1948 South Africa' *JSAS* 1(1) 1974, pp 5-35; Davis (1979); Innes, D (1976).

29. O'Meara, D 'The 1949 Mineworkers' Strike and the political economy of South Africa' *The Journal of Commonwealth and Comparative Politics* 13(2), 1975, pp 146-173; Hemson, D 'Dock workers, labour circulation and strikes in Durban, 1940-1959' *JSAS* 4(1) 1977, pp 88-124.

30. O'Meara, D (1975) p 152.

31. O'Meara, D 'The Afrikaner Broederbond 1927-1948: class vanguard of Afrikaner nationalism' *JSAS* 3(2) 1977, p 158; and *Volkskapitalisme: Class, Capital and Ideology in the development of Afrikaner Nationalism 1934-1948* (Johannesburg, 1983).

32. Davies, R (1979); Kaplan, D (1980); Morris, M (1976); O'Meara, D (1983); O'Meara, D (1975), (1977), 'Analysing Afrikaner Nationalism: The "Christian-National' assault on white trade unionism in South Africa, 1934-1948' *African Affairs* 77(306) 1978, pp 45-72; Moodie, T D *The Rise of Afrikanerdom: Power, Apartheid and the Afrikaner Civil Religion* (Berkeley, 1973); Stultz, N M *Afrikaner Politics in South Africa 1934-1948* (Berkeley, 1975).

33. Legassick, M 'Legislation' (1974); Davies, R (1979).

34. Legassick, M 'Legislation' (1974).

35. O'Meara, D (1975); Lodge, T *Black Politics in South Africa* (London, 1983).

36. Johnson, R W *How Long Will South Africa Survive?* (London, 1977).

37. Legassick, M and Wolpe, H 'The Bantustans and capital accumulation in South Africa' *RAPE* 7 (1976) p 103.

38. Source: South African Economic Development Plan, 1974-1979.

39. Source: Du Plessis, P G 'Concentration of economic power in the South African manufacturing industry' *SAJE* 46 1978 (based on 1972 data).

40. Legassick, M and Hemson, D *Foreign Investment and the Reproduction of Racial Capitalism in South Africa:* (London, 1976); Rogers, B 'Apartheid for profit', *Business and Society Review* Fall 1976; First, R J Steel and C Gurney *The South African Connection: Western Investment in Apartheid* (Harmondsworth, 1973).

41. Melba, H 'Staatskapitalismus in Sudafrika' *Zeitschrift fur Politic und Obonomie in der Dritter Welt* 1(1) 1980.

42. Innes, D 'The role of foreign trade in industrial development' in J Suckling, R Weiss and D Innes, *The Economic Factor: Foreign Investment in South Africa* (Study Project Paper No 5-9, Africa Problems

Trust: Uppsala, 1975).

43. Beinefeld, M and D Innes (1976); Legassick, M and D Innes 'Capital restructuring and apartheid: a critique of "Constructive Engagement", *African Affairs* 76 (305) 1977; Davies, R, 'Capital restructuring and the modification of the racial division of labour in South Africa' *JSAS* 5(2) 1979 (b); Clarke, S (1978).

44. Davies, R (1979); Wolpe, H (1972); Legassick, M (1974).

45. Melba, H (1980).

46. Source: *Official Yearbook of South Africa* 1978, p 293.

47. Hindson, D 'Conditions of labour supply and employment of African workers in urban based industries in South Africa' in *Workshop on Unemployment and Labour Reallocation* (Development Studies Research Group, Department of Economics, University of Natal, Pietermaritzburg 1977); Davies, J 'Capital, state and educational reform in South Africa', unpublished paper presented to the African Studies Association of Australia, Sydney, 1981 (published in revised form in this volume).

48. Wolpe, H (1972); Simkins, C E W and D G Clarke *Structural Unemployment in Southern Africa* (Durban, 1978); Knight, J B 'Is South Africa running out of unskilled labour?' in F Wilson, A Kooy and D Hendrie (eds), *Farm Labour in South Africa* (Cape Town, 1977); Van der Merwe, P J 'Black employment problems in South Africa', *Volkskas Finance and Trade Review* 12(4) 1976; Maree, J 'The dimensions and causes of unemployment in South Africa' *SALB* 4(4) 1978.

49. Legassick, M and H Wolpe (1976); Innes, D and D O'Meara 'Class Formation and Ideology: The Transkei region' *RAPE* 7 1976.

50. Knight, J B (1977).

51. Emy, H V 'Stability and Viability in Contemporary South African Politics' *Australian Journal of Politics and History* 18(1) 1972, pp 18-33.

52. Bell, T *Industrial Decentralization in South Africa* (Cape Town, 1973); Gottschalk, K 'Industrial Decentralization, jobs and wages' *SALB* 3(5) 1977.

53. Rogerson, C M 'Industrialisation of the Bantu Homelands', *Geography* (GB) 59(3), 1974, pp 260-64.

54. Legassick, M (1974).

55. Baldwin, A 'Mass Removals and separate development' *JSAS* 4(2) 1978.

56. Kane-Berman, J *Soweto: Black Revolt, White Reaction* (Johannesburg, 1979); Callinicos, A and V Rogers *South Africa after Soweto* (London 1980).

57. Source: *South African Yearbook* 1978.

58. Gann, L and P Duignan *Why South Africa Will Survive* (London 1980); Balusten, R 'Foreign Investment in Black Homelands of South Africa' *African Affairs* 75 (299) 1976.

59. *Official Yearbook of South Africa*, 1978, p 208.

60.   Hemson, D 'Trade unionism and the struggle for liberation in South Africa' *Capital and Class* 6 (1978).

61.   Source: *Official Yearbook of South Africa* 1978.

62.   Stahl, C 'Recent changes in the demand for foreign African labour in South Africa and future prospects', unpublished paper presented to the African Studies Association of Australia, Canberra, 1979.

63.   Hirson, B *Year of Fire, Year of Ash: The Soweto Revolt, Roots of a Revolution* (London, 1979); Gerhard, G M *Black Power in South Africa* (Berkeley 1979).

64.   Kane-Berman (1979); Davies, J (1981).

65.   Source: *South African Reserve Bank: Report* 1979.

66.   Gann, L and P Duignan (1980).

67.   International Defence and Aid Fund: *The Apartheid War Machine — The Strength and Deployment of South Africa's Armed Forces* (London, 1980).

68.   Gann, L and P Duignan (1980).

Capital, State and Educational Reform in South Africa
John Davies

In the years after the Soweto uprising of 1976, the apartheid state adopted the so-called 'total strategy'. Launched officially in 1979 as a means of countering the 'total onslaught' being directed against South Africa, this strategy coupled military measures aimed at ensuring a better defence capability with a programme of social reform, which, the state asserted, would result in a transformation of the apartheid system in order to satisfy black aspirations. An integral component of the social design was educational reform, and in particular the promise of a new and dramatically improved education 'dispensation' for black schoolchildren and students. After several years of operation and of failure to produce a new educational dawn for blacks, the question of educational reform invites critical evaluation.

The objectives of this paper are four-fold: (i) to locate the roots of the impetus for educational reform; (ii) to subject the central aims of this reform to critical examination; (iii) to assess post-Soweto educational policy in the light of these aims; and (iv) to discuss the policy's likely future course. In so doing, a focus is adopted which draws attention firstly to the influential role played by capital within the broad movement towards educational reform, and secondly, to the relationship between the state and capital with respect to the issue of educational change.

As already indicated, educational reform in South Africa is one aspect of a co-ordinated strategy. For this reason, and also in view of the fact that no major educational reform can be understood independently of the broader question of social change, an examination in some detail of the nature of the 'total strategy' social reform programme forms the necessary starting point for an analysis of educational developments.

The Social Background to Educational Reform

The origins of reform lie in a complex conjunction of problems with which the state was confronted. The forms these problems took included economic recession; a new pattern of militant industrial unrest among blacks that began with the Natal strikes of 1973; heightened military anxiety after the collapse of the Portuguese African empire; and fears for political instability due to the demonstration of mass-resistance to apartheid in Soweto which, although suppressed, led to world-wide condemnation of apartheid, a marked decline in foreign investment in South Africa, and to renewed demands for the use of economic sanctions against South Africa. Initially, the state reacted to these challenges solely by deploying its repressive apparatus. A more 'constructive' response evolved only slowly, and was prompted by an initiative taken by capital.

In the aftermath of the Soweto uprising, major organs of the bourgeoisie — such as the Chamber of Mines, the Association of Chambers of Commerce, and the Federated Chamber of Industries — began to beat the drum of reform with renewed vigour. This drum had been sounded during the political and economic dislocations surrounding the Sharpeville massacre of 1960, but had grown fainter following the subsequent conditions of political stability and economic recovery.[1] There were elements to the more recent crisis, however, which required a more persistent approach by capital in its pursuit of certain changes to the apartheid system.

Over the years capital has, it is true, derived enormous benefits from the close relationship between capitalism and apartheid, and between it and earlier forms of segregation. The racial division of labour has been conducive to high rates of exploitation, while the repressive capacities of the apartheid state have been indispensable in containing class struggle and in ensuring political stability. Nevertheless, the marriage of capitalism and the racial system contains a fundamental contradiction relating to capital's natural tendency to treat all labour-power as a pure commodity; the particular dis-economy inherent in the privileged and protected positions enjoyed by the white wage-earning classes, and the monopoly of those classes over the skilled labour pool based on the job colour-bar regulations, became of increasing concern to capital.

The question of shortages in this skilled white labour pool constitutes the basic focus of an important article by Robert Davies on the structural crisis confronting capital in South Africa. According to Davies, shortages had been a matter of concern to capital since the 1960s, but the problem was offset by means of job-redefinition or 'floating the colour-bar'. However, by the mid-1970s the shortage had become acute: the transition to monopoly capitalism required accelerating capital-intensification to make South African manufacturing more competitive internationally, and this intensified the demand for certain categories of highly skilled labour-power — a demand which could not be met because of restrictions on the use of black labour. Under conditions of internal and international recession, capital is seen to have no other choice but to raise its organic composition. Consequently, more corrective measures were needed than a mere increase in the rate of job-redefinition; modifications to the racial division of labour itself as well as the removal of job colour-bar legislation became crucial to restore profitability.[2]

In arriving at this view of the matter, Davies is evidently impressed in part by the statistics used, the claims made, and the agitation mounted by functionaries of capital. Other commentators, however, are less impressed. Charles Meth, for example, is one who has heard the 'skill shortage melody . . . played too often' in the past by capital to be anything other than sceptical about this recent agitation.[3] Eddie Webster, for his part, recognises the gravity of the situation for capital, but makes the important point that one should distinguish between skill shortages 'as such', and skill shortages 'at a certain price' to capital resulting from capital's inability to employ lower-priced black labour-power.[4]

The view taken here with regard to the question (which has considerable implications for educational reform because of restrictions on the training of blacks) is that the problem did become more acute in both a shortage and a price sense, but that capital's reform initiative was motivated by additional considerations. The most important of these were (i) the mass-resistance demonstrated in Soweto, which was not only anti-apartheid but apparently anti-capitalist as well, and involved an (unsuccessful) attempt by students to link up with the increasingly militant black proletariat; (ii) the international economic repercussions following the uprising, which resulted in a marked decline in foreign investment capital. What seemed to capital to be at stake at that point was the preservation of the system of capitalist production itself (to be fair to Davies, it ought to be said that he makes the same points;[5] but he is so concerned to locate his analysis in a specific problem at the point of production that he accords insufficient weight to the other political and economic developments mentioned); (iii) what also needs to be highlighted is the ideological dimension, stamped by the inherent need of South African capital to obscure not only the exploitative relations of production, but also the complicit nature of its relations with an overtly repressive racist system.

For some time capital has been waging an ideological campaign designed to distance itself from apartheid by asserting the incompatibility of capitalism and apartheid, and in fact the 'skill shortage melody' is an important aspect of this activity. The failure of Soweto students (and of many leading members of the Soweto community) to make this distinction (indeed, they were convinced of a growing coincidence between race and class) under-lined the ineffectivity of the ideological venture among the targeted groups themselves, viz the aspirant and extant black petty bourgeoisie. Capital's resolve to redouble its ideological efforts both at home and abroad was strengthened because much of the international criticism following the Soweto uprising was directed against its role within racist South Africa.

The concerns that gave rise to reform were addressed in a set of proposals communicated to the state. These called for the removal of statutory racial restrictions on labour mobility and training, as well as for additional social improvements — all of which would stimulate the economy and produce an enlarged black urban 'middle class', which would in turn be supportive of the 'free enterprise system' and a testament to its inherent promise. The intention behind these proposals, as a communique to Prime Minister John Vorster makes clear, was to rescue only the most skilled and relatively privileged sections of the black population from the deprivations and humiliations of the past, so that they might serve as a counter-revolutionary buffer between continued white domination and black subordination.[6]

The character of these reformist moves reflected the fundamental dilemma facing capital: on the one hand, it was confronted with the necessity to project itself as a constructive force for liberal-isation, combined with its ambition to moderate the most obviously repressive features of the racial hierarchy in order to secure conditions more favourable to capital accumulation. On the other hand, it was beset by an over-riding fear of industrial and political turmoil which meant continuing dependence on the apartheid state because of the latter's monopoly over centralised political coercion. It was this latter horn of the dilemma which imposed limitations on both the scope of capital's vision of reform and the lengths to which it was prepared to go in its advocacy for reform vis-a-vis the state.

The state, for its part, had been far less apprehensive in its reaction to the Soweto uprising. It had reasoned correctly that, at least for the near future, it possessed the capabilities to suppress black resistance. Nonetheless, the state had since 1973 become increasingly aware of the economic and political problems arising from the unwavering continuation of apartheid in its traditional form, and accordingly had begun, especially after 1976, to introduce some adjustments. The reform process was still painfully slow from capital's point of view until 1979, when, at a summit conference in Johannesburg, capital and state reached an accommodation on reform.[7] This accord also had the backing of military strategists, who believed that their counter-insurgency measures could not succeed so long as a vast majority of the population remained alienated.

Thereafter, the state began espousing the merits of Friedmanite 'free enterprise', and its solutions to the country's problems through an economic growth policy that would transform race relations. Beyond this rhetoric, however, the accord amounted to a neo-apartheid strategy for reconstructing the system in order to improve its economic efficiency and to strengthen the ruling white power bloc. This entailed the introduction of some modifications to the racial division of labour, both in order to create greater labour mobility and thereby reduce the constraints on capital, and as a core tactic of a 'hearts and minds' co-optation campaign aimed at granting material, but not political, concessions to favoured urban blacks (the objective here being their separation from the black masses, who in turn would be subjected to increasing controls as a necessary condition for the exercise in conciliation).[8]

Despite the apparent confidence with which the state took up the cause of reformism, its fundamental problem remained: how to pursue policies that would lead to the 'embourgeoisement' of urban blacks, however limited, without thereby activating serious class conflict among whites. Major sections of the white wage-earning and petty bourgeois classes supported the state precisely because of its traditional apartheid policies which offered significant material benefits as well as ideological reinforcement of their position. A need to remain responsive to their interest (given increased rumblings of discontent within their ranks) in order to avoid undermining its own legitimacy, coupled with a continuing conflict within the ruling National Party and the state apparatuses themselves over the course adopted, all bore on the capacity of the state to set upon a reformist course. Consequently, reformism emerged hesitantly and replete with contradictions. Even during 1979-80, the period of greatest thrust, it was far from proceeding in a straight line.

By 1981, the strategy was in extreme difficulty. On the one hand it had failed to impress the targeted black groups; on the other it had produced a vehement white anti-reformist challenge from the right.[9] To the intense dismay of capital, the state deemed it prudent to beat a tactical retreat from reformism in the face of the election of that year. The loss of votes to the right in that election and the more recent divisions within the National Party have given the state more grounds for introspection.

The Origins and Aims of Educational Reform

A major impetus for the 'total strategy' has been seen to arise out of the events surrounding the Soweto uprising. The educational aspect of this strategy acquired a particular sense of urgency because the initial mass agitation by fifteen thousand youngsters was directed specifically against 'Bantu Education', which had been a source of outrage and a target for criticism within the black community since its inception in 1953 as an undisguised institutional attempt by the state to prepare black children for a totally subordinate role in society.[10]

The brutality of the state's response to the demonstration left several hundred children dead, but opposition to educational apartheid continued until the end of 1977 in the form of school boycotts which spread to many parts of the country and to 'coloured' schools.[11] These events put the question of education reform on the immediate agenda.

The challenge of the students to Bantu Education was taken further and given more coherent form by newly radicalised leaders of the black community, who pressed the regime for the following major changes: the repeal of the Bantu Education Act; the establishment of a single national Department of Education; equal per capita expenditures on the education of all children; equal school facilities; free and compulsory education for black children; equal salaries for teachers; and open universities.[12] A favourable response to at least a number of these demands was forthcoming from capital's representatives, who had already begun to set in motion certain schemes of their own to effect change. The general concerns motivating the reformist direction taken by capital have already been referred to; it remains to give them a specific education focus.

Behind the reform initiative in education was the need to tackle the skilled labour crisis, which was seen as a major educational problem because of restrictions on the training of blacks due to the structure of the educational system. With regard to the training aspect of schooling, Bantu Education had been established to provide blacks with schooling sufficient only for employment at the unskilled and semi-skilled levels. Limited higher level training, in line with the apartheid policy of linking black aspirations to the 'homelands', was concentrated on the bantustans where most of the black secondary schools and all of the black universities were located. Although this policy had generally suited the needs of capitalist production at the time, and though the former was in considerable measure determined by the latter, it became less functional under conditions of increased capital-intensification, precipitating moves by capital to ease the restrictions on the education of highly trained black 'manpower'.

This is not just a recent concern, and it is instructive to digress briefly here to examine the way in which the skill-shortage argument has been advanced over the years in a literature purporting to explain the relationship between education and economic growth in South Africa.

The first major study in this genre, by Nathan Hurwitz, was published in 1964. It was sharply critical of Bantu Education for curtailing the flow of vitally needed skilled and professional manpower, and thereby impeding economic growth.[13] A second study that sought to underline the contradiction seen to exist between the national economic interest and the state's irrational pursuit of racial policies in education (the proof of which lay in the restrictions placed on the educational advancement of badly needed able black youngsters) was reflected in two reports published in 1966 by the self-styled 1961 Education Panel.[14] The reports asserted that the skilled labour stock would shortly be exhausted, and among the measures called for to avoid this situation were free and compulsory primary education for blacks, as well as an advanced stream within Bantu Education to confer education of the very highest quality on suitable candidates.[15]

A consistent critic of the state's educational policy, and especially of its approach to educated Bantu manpower, was E G Malherbe, whose general critique of policy is embodied in an enormous (800 page) investigation of South African education,[16] which appeared in 1977 and coincided with the increased attention then being given by capital to educational reform issues. In support of the now familiar charge that educational apartheid acted as a brake on economic development because of its manifest inability to promote black talent, Malherbe charged that such short-sighted prejudice had contributed in no small measure to the current economic crisis. At the level of policy, Malherbe supported a programme designed to avert economic disaster by making far more effective use of the nation's intellectual resources. This was to be achieved through the introduction of schemes aimed at increasing the flow of educated black personnel into the high professional, managerial and entrepreneurial levels of the work force. In pursuit of this reform, Malherbe aligned himself with those 'top businessmen' who were demanding 'a drastic revision of the racially exclusive employment policies'.[17]

What is of further significance about Malherbe's work is an additional perspective which he brings to the subject of skill-shortages. For Malherbe, white education, especially in the Afrikaans-speaking sector, was bedevilled by inefficiency and low standards. The high proportion of finance devoted to the education of whites was regarded as providing a poor rate of return because of its extreme scarcity value.[18]

Although this literature had another purpose, to which reference will be made below, it certainly was the case that changes in the accumulation process were compelling capital to consider alterations to the education system. It was necessary for education to respond more efficiently to meet the new skill requirements of the workplace. This required adjustments to ensure a relatively higher level of skill among black students. But much more was required of a reorganised educational system than an improvement in its technical functions.

A further pressure behind capital's reappraisal of existing educational policy was the need to contain black working class militancy and restiveness among the vast ranks of the urban unemployed, particularly unemployed youths. Even before 1976, black schools were experiencing considerable difficulty in instilling the appropriate discipline and subordination needed in the future labour force and reserve army of labour. The Soweto uprising made the task of working out more effective mechanisms of socialisation within education — including measures for co-optation — imperative if widespread dissent was to be disarmed.

Reference has already been made to the anti-capitalist stance adopted by the student protesters at Soweto, but although there is no doubt that capitalism and apartheid were linked together as twin agents of exploitation in the minds of some students,[19] this hostility to capitalism should not be exaggerated. A number of accounts of the uprising make it clear that the demonstration was closely linked with the exclusivist Black Consciousness movement, directed by leaders who lacked a developed class consciousness, and aimed overwhelmingly against apartheid in education.[20] Yet from the point of view of capital, there was sufficient awareness among the students of the relationship of race to class for an attempt to have been made to forge a closer association with the black working class; and it was precisely because the uprising itself was a 'petit bourgeois concern', inspired by the petit bourgeois Black Consciousness movement, that it proved so unnerving to capital. Obviously an educational system that alienated and radicalised so many youngsters, and especially capital's 'natural' supporters within the black student elite, was in considerable need of overhaul. Furthermore, something had to be done educationally in order to overcome the image of South Africa abroad as a society that could respond to genuine educational grievances only by indiscriminately killing its schoolchildren.

Consequently, the media of capital began to propagate a new education era. New policies were called for that would eliminate Bantu Education in favour of a free and compulsory system, within which the principles of equal opportunity, equal standards and freedom of association would be enshrined.[21] Behind these lofty statements of principle the intention has been not to abolish massive discrimination in education but to obscure its operation by giving new policies a more class-differentiating twist. The object of the exercise has been to reduce the racial component of education's contribution to the reproduction of the social division of labour, but on a selective basis only. This task has been couched in the demand for a more rigorous implementation of mental-manual differentiation, to be effected (and legitimised) by such practices as increased specialisation and vocationalism, and the development of an achievement ethos. In reality, 'differentiation' would be administered only to that minority of blacks accorded some kind of permanent status within 'white' urban areas. The ultimate division of this already exclusive grouping would result in the 'mentally superior' students — the future 'middle class' — beng granted access to 'open' elite private schools and universities where they would complete their education.

This intention, to use education for the purpose of incorporation, was not something new to the post-Soweto period; it was the other side of the 'education and economic growth' literature. This literature's castigation of 'Bantu Education' was another example of the effort to distance capitalism from apartheid at the level of ideology whilst the groundwork for co-optation via education was being laid.

The financial costs of this new operation would be met in part by pruning expenditure on the bloated and unproductive white educational system, which was likewise in urgent need of the purgative of 'differentiation'. Once this reformist outline had been shaped, the next and more difficult task became to secure its acceptance and execution by the state. Reference has already been made to the dilemma facing capital in its dealings with the state on the whole question of reformism and this helps to explain the (at least initial) caution of capital's approach on the specific issue of educational change.

It appears that the state had for some time recognised the need for education to reflect more accurately the changing requirements of capital accumulation. Per capita educational expenditures had been slightly improved since the late 1960s, and the introduction of a number of industrial training programmes in some black schools, as well as the establishment of a number of state training schools from 1973 onwards, were undoubtedly linked to the growing demand for trained labour.[22]

These adjustments were inadequate from capital's viewpoint, and its pressure for more significant alterations increased considerably after 1976. At first the state was reluctant to meet the new demands, partly because it did not share the extreme anxieties of capital over the Soweto uprising and remained wedded to Bantu Education in its traditional form. Furthermore, Bantu Education embodied the material and ideological interests of important sections of the supportive white classes. They relied on traditional educational policy to limit the opportunities of blacks to acquire skills, to inculcate in blacks a belief in their own inferiority, and thereby to help preserve and strengthen the dominant position of whites in South African society. Consequently they were hostile to any form of black advancement through educational institutions. It was this pressure that served as a constant reminder to the state that it could not adjust the traditional mechanisms of social reproduction within the education system without incurring considerable political risk. Yet it could not ignore a combination of circumstances and conflicts which not only limited the capacity of Bantu Education to train skilled and disciplined black youngsters, but also activated ideologies of resistance amongst black students in school (and in the universities, which had become centres of disruption as well). Clearly then, some reorganisation was necessary. The alternative to cracking children's heads, which enraged capital and provoked international condemnation, appeared to lie in more discreet forms of educational control combined with educational concessions to favoured black youngsters, consonant with the broad co-optation policy.

Post-Soweto Educational Policy

A thorough re-evaluation of educational policy took some time to be worked through, and in the immediate aftermath of the uprising only faltering attempts at educational change resulted. The state's overriding aim until the end of 1977 was to batten down the hatches on continuing student protest which reached its post-Soweto peak in October of that year when the number of black pupils absent from school for political reasons reached 196 000.[23]

State repression took the form of expulsions, school closures, arrests of students and teachers, and, finally, the banning of eighteen black consciousness groups including the Association for the Educational and Cultural Advancement of the African People of South Africa, the South African Students Movement (SASM) and the South African Students Organisation (SASO).[24] These actions brought the mass stage of resistance to Bantu Education to a temporary halt, although the majority of secondary schools in Soweto remained closed throughout 1978.

The limited improvements simultaneously taking place included the immediate repeal of the regulation requiring the compulsory introduction of Afrikaans as a third language of instruction in black schools, and the scrapping of the hated label Department of Bantu Education in favour of Department of Education and Training. More positively, but clearly with co-optation and the solving of accumulation problems in mind, the salaries of qualified black teachers were raised, as was expenditure on black education, and more industrial training introduced into black schools.

By the end of 1978, the state was establishing a new trend of conciliation and the Minister of Education and Training announced his intention of introducing new and significant legislation. Accordingly, an Education and Training Bill was released early in 1979 and passed with minor amendments later that year. The Bill was designed to replace the Bantu Education Act of 1953 and the Bantu Special Education Act of 1964. The essential provisions of the Bill were as follows:

(1) Educational policy to be decided by the Minister of Education and Training after consultation with the Advisory Council of Education which would comprise 20 members appointed by the Minister.

(2) That education should have a Christian character.

(3) That the principle of mother-tongue instruction be observed.

(4) That it is the aim to introduce compulsory education in all areas with the co-operation of the parents, but with penalties to be imposed on parents who do not co-operate.

(5) That recognition be given to the active involvement of the parents and communities.

(6) That school health services be introduced.

(7) That provision be made for the Minister to establish or dis-establish schools, that power to appoint, promote and discharge teachers be vested in him, and that penalties for teacher misconduct be laid out.

(8) That provision be made for the establishment of a Teachers' Council for blacks and all teachers to be required to register

with this council.[25]

In response to the Bill, some black educational groups, such as the African Teachers' Association (ATASA) and the Transvaal United Teachers' Association (TUATA), expressed cautious approval of certain provisions, but all black organisations rejected the continuing categorisation of education on a racial basis and the retention of a separate department of black education.[26] Indeed, it could be argued that 'separate development' had been strengthened by the provision allowing the formation of a Teachers' Council for blacks to run parallel to the SA Teachers' Council for Whites. Major concern was also voiced about the centralisation of power in the hands of the Minister and about the punitive clauses of the Bill regarding teacher misconduct. In the opinion of the secretary-general of the South African Council of Churches, Bishop Desmond Tutu: 'The Bill to my mind emphasises control. It is as if we are dealing with a dangerous animal — how to keep it caged'.[27] Bitter disappointment was also expressed about the lack of commitment to a more equitable distribution of educational resources. As the South African Institute of Race Relations noted, for the commitment to the introduction of compulsory education to be meaningful, the clause should also stipulate that education should be free.[28]

The reaction of capital to the new Bill was mixed. From the moment of announcement of the Bill in draft form, the modifications to 'Bantu Education' seen to be entailed in the proposed legislation met with its approval. At the same time there was consternation because the Bill did not go far enough to satisfy the aspirations of 'moderate' groups such as ATASA who wanted a single national education department.[29] The major concern of the political arm of English-speaking capital, the Progressive Federal Party, was that the draft Bill was insufficient as a means of defusing mass discontent over education. In opening the parliamentary debate on the Bill, the party's spokesman on education, Alex Boraine, warned the state:

> But if it is true that black education has to bear the brunt of black opposition to government policy, then it is equally true that black education holds in its hands one of the crucial keys to the resolution of the conflict by peaceful means.[30]

During the second reading debate on the Bill, the PFP, while praising certain provisions, declined to support the Bill as a whole because it perpetuated a racially differentiated educational system.[31]

Lovedale Institution, circa 1902: It was often stated that 'mission natives' received school education and no training for work. Lovedale provided a model for educational adaptation. All students were required to do two hours of manual labour daily. Here they muster in companies, each under a 'native captain', to carry out their tasks.

Photograph from Picturesque South Africa (D Edwards & Co, 44 Shortmarket St, Cape Town, 1902).

A model colony: central portion of the East London Kaffir Location, circa 1904. The planning of the social context of life for blacks went far beyond the schools. *Photograph: Star Weekly Edition 16/1/1904.*

It was because educational reform was regarded by capital as an important means of forestalling revolution and because of a strong suspicion that the state was an unreliable reformist vehicle that capital was prompted to initiate some educational measures of its own. Limited moves by capital in the direction of educational improvements for blacks can actually be traced back to the early 1970s when the giant Anglo American Corporation offered a substantial donation to a Soweto secondary school and *The Star* newspaper launched TEACH to collect money for schools in Soweto.[32] But it was unquestionably the Soweto crisis that spawned a more resolute approach to educational objectives.

In November 1976, two of South Africa's major capitalists, Harry Oppenheimer of Anglo American and Anton Rupert of the Rembrandt Group, launched the Urban Foundation with the backing of every major corporation in South Africa. The declared aim of this organisation was to 'improve the quality of life of the urban citizen' through projects relating to employment, education, housing and health, which were to be determined by the requirements of the black communities themselves.[33] In addition, the Foundation's executive director, ex-Justice J H Steyn, spoke of the avowed intention of the founding fathers for the organisation to serve as a 'catalyst for change towards the establishment of a just society'.[34] In discussions with those corporate interests from whom the Urban Foundation had solicited support, however, the origins and aims of the Foundation were presented in a quite different light. Addressing himself to the implications of the Soweto uprising, Steyn had, on appointment, referred to the growing recognition on the part of the business community of the 'gravity and urgency of our situation not only so far as the maintenance of the free enterprise system is concerned, but in regard to the survival of everything we hold dear.'[35] And, referring to the primary objective of the Foundation, the *Cape Argus* commented that it was the sound strategy of facilitating the emergence of a substantial middle class which would embrace the free enterprise system and work for its preservation.[36]

The 'real' purposes of the Urban Foundation appear to be three-fold. Firstly, it has an organisational role which is designed to mobilise large-scale capital in defence of its interests at a time of apparent crisis. In terms of education, this entailed a call to capital to adopt a more emphatic approach to educational issues and to assume greater responsibility within the area of black education and training.

Secondly, it has an ideological purpose aimed at encouraging the adoption of free enterprise values within the black urban communities as a counter to the growth of socialism. This has meant presenting such values as a force for positive de-racial change and fostering the image of capital as the enemy of racial ascription and the champion of a colour-blind meritocracy. Fundamental to the playing of this ideological role has been the necessity to break with the traditional ideology of 'Bantu Education' and to replace it with the doctrine of equality of educational opportunity as a means of fostering the belief that positions under a free enterprise system are determined by the educational achievements of individuals and not by imputed racial characteristics. Consequently, the concept of equality of educational opportunity, together with that of equality of access to the economic system, became the central themes of countless Urban Foundation speeches to prominent members of the black community and to students.[37]

The third purpose embodies what *Work in Progress* has called a material role: the attempt to create an urban black middle class which will act as a supportive buffer between capital and the black working class and give concrete expression to the ideological aim.[38] Increasingly, these material activities of the Foundation were to be concentrated on education and, by September of 1979, 44 percent of the Foundation's total expenditure had been spent on educational projects, the largest of which was the establishment of the Jabulani Technical Centre in Soweto.[39] In addition, the Anglo American Corporation embarked on a number of educational advancement programmes, including an adult education centre for its black employees, and announced plans for the establishment of an undergraduate cadet scheme for potential black managers.

Regarding the reception of these educational projects among urban blacks, the approach of the Urban Foundation appeared to make some headway among educational groups like ATASA who were willing to consider collaboration, but they had been rejected outright from the very beginning by SASO who accused the Foundation of trying to 'sabotage the goals of black liberation'.[40] Indeed, by September 1979 the general credibility of the Urban Foundation among blacks remained low. This was due in large measure to the refusal of the Foundation to deviate from what was acceptable to the state. It accepted constraints on its supposedly reforming role to the extent of clearing all major educational projects beforehand with the Department of Education and Training. The inability of the Urban Foundation to pursue change without state approval, coupled with its increasing preoccupation with educational solutions to urban problems, brings to mind a conclusion reached by Tom Christoffel regarding the Good Society reforms of the 1960s in the United States:

The reformers had to make the reform fit the proportions of what was politically feasible, they had to define a solution modest enough to pass political inspection, but significant enough to look like a solution . . . . Consequently, educational reform was put forward as a safe solution to the problem.[41]

The acceptable level of capitalist involvement in reformist-type projects began to rise significantly after the state-capital summit meeting on 22 November 1979. Of further encouragement to capital was the state announcement, in June 1980, of the establishment of a commission of inquiry into all aspects of education, to be undertaken by the Human Sciences Research Council under the chairmanship of J P de Lange, rector of the Rand Afrikaans University. The commission was given the responsibility of making recommendations to the Cabinet within 12 months regarding:

(1) Principal guidelines for a practicable educational policy, so that —
     (a) The optimum potential of all inhabitants be realised.
     (b) The economic growth of the country be promoted.
     (c) The quality of life of all inhabitants be improved.
(2) The organisational and control structure, as well as the financing of education.
(3) The consultative and decision-making mechanisms in education.
(4) An infrastructure for education that would fulfil the manpower needs of the country.
(5) A programme whereby equality in education for all population groups can be attained.[42]

These recommendations appeared to have been lifted straight off the pages of capital's own book of reform and industrialists began to speak of a new and distinctly appreciative official climate within which the role of capital in educative matters could become more assertive.[43] Indeed, it was necessary for both capital and the state to pursue educational reform more purposefully, given the implications arising from two other important state commissions of enquiry, which also enjoyed the support of capital as significant in the struggle to secure co-optation and to remove the obstacles to capitalist development. The first of these was the Wiehahn Commission on industrial relations, which recommended the removal of the industrial colour bar from the statute books; if implemented, this would make the skilled labour power shortage largely a problem of educational deficiencies. The second, the Riekert Commission, was specifically mandated to look into the proper utilisation of 'manpower' in the urban areas. Its recommendations pointed to the necessity for improved training facilities for blacks and to the importance of the state educational bureaucracies in implementing labour training policies.[44]

Yet, by the end of 1980, capital was displaying signs of distinct impatience with the slow pace of industrial and educational reforms. Once again, labour process problems and an outbreak of mass discontent over education were principal causes of disaffection.

During that year, the economy had unexpectedly entered a boom phase based on a sharp rise in the price of gold. This created an even greater demand for skilled labour-power which could not be met because the state had yet to overcome the legacy of 'Bantu Education' whose dead hand was now, in capital's view, preventing capitalist expansion. A report by the University of Pretoria's Bureau for Economic Policy and Analysis estimated that a yearly increase of 3,2 percent in the skilled labour force was needed to secure a growth rate of 5 percent and that, since more than half of this increase needed to be drawn from the ranks of blacks, a major uplifting of state expenditure on black education was required. The Bureau noted that if expenditure parity between blacks and whites had been sought in 1978, the total estimated current expenditure by the state would have had to have been R3000 million — nearly three times the actual amount spent.[45] Despite promises from the Director-General of Education and Training that the 1981 budget would significantly push up state spending on black education, and despite a commitment from the Minister of National Education to erase the backlog in black education, criticism of state inactivity continued to mount.[46]

Dissatisfaction with the state was also expressed over its failure to create an improved educational environment, the lack of which gave rise to a new wave of student boycotts. The end of the 1980 academic year saw 60 000 mainly 'coloured' pupils in the Cape striking for a non-racial educational system and for free and compulsory education.[47] Reacting with customary brutality, the state closed the schools and called in the riot police who fired on protesters, arrested hundreds of their leaders, and placed them in detention, all of which left a pall of bitterness behind. Ironically, the boycotts had broken out at a time when the Cillie Commission Report into the causes of the Soweto uprising was being tabled in Parliament. *Die Vaderland* had summed up the report as a 'story of regimentation and discrimination . . . anyone who reads the report and tries to oppose reforms is both blind and deaf.'[48]

What was particularly unsettling about this volatile situation in the Cape, to the PFP in particular, was that the mass of protesters were 'coloured' students, the supposedly 'natural' allies of white South Africa. There was a danger now that the boycotts would give rise to a new generation of radical 'coloured' youths in addition to the politicised young African generation. Furthermore, there was disturbing evidence that the students had situated their protest within a context of broad political struggle by becoming involved in a series of political actions such as the red meat boycott, the Free Mandela Campaign, and rent strikes.[49] As one student statement put their position:

> We must see how . . . short-term demands are linked up with the political and economic system of this country. We must see how the fail-pass rate in schools is linked up with the labour supply for the capitalist system.[50]

In an effort to avoid further black community involvement in the rising tide of militancy, and to get the boycotting students back to school, the PFP began an initiative to resolve the crisis by organising a high-level meeting between Cabinet Ministers and 'black moderates'.[51]

The protagonists did, in fact, move away from confrontation, and the boycotts had mostly ended by the beginning of the 1981 academic year. To prevent a recurrence of the crisis, the state brought forth the now familiar carrot-and-stick strategy. The protesters returned to school to find new regulations giving the educational authorities power to 'summarily expel' any pupil who 'intentionally or negligently' violated any terms of the Education and Training Act, damaged property of the school, or took part in any boycott or riot.[52]

Conciliation took the form of an official announcement promising compulsory education to 38 selected urban school districts applicable to pupils entering the first year of schooling. The measure was acclaimed by the state as a major step towards fulfilment of official pledges to the black community to equalise education between the races,[53] and was welcomed by the PFP as a praiseworthy effort.[54] Many blacks, on the other hand, perceived a more sinister purpose behind this new dispensation; that of a political tool to be used against school boycotts, since trouble-free areas could be given educational preference over troublesome localities. Furthermore, as penalties were to be imposed for non-attendance at school, the onus for getting children to school, and thereby containing student unrest, was being shifted from the authorities to the parents.[55]

The compulsory education scheme was consistent with the state's own conception of co-optation, as were a number of other measures adopted at this time. These included plans for a university to be built in Soweto and for two additional campuses to be attached to the black University of the North and situated in the 'independent states' of QwaQwa and Venda. These strictly segregationist proposals were not compatible with capital's conception of necessary change which had recently been outlined in Harry Oppenheimer's annual chairman's statement to the Anglo American Corporation. Oppenheimer emphasised that 'Bantu Education', as the centrepiece of black resentment of apartheid, had to be broken with in favour of a national free and compulsory system of education that opened its uppermost levels — the universities, technical institutes and training colleges — to students of all races.[56] It was evident that the state could not or would not bring itself to withdraw from racial structures despite having repeatedly to defend itself against continued references by blacks to the infamous 'Bantu Education' speech by Verwoerd in 1954, in which he had warned blacks that their education would never allow them to rise above the level of labourers within white South Africa.[57]

The response of the state to the educational recommendations of the Wiehahn and Riekert Commissions also fell within this pattern of allowing some concessions only within a traditional framework. The Wiehahn Commission had created the expectation that blacks would be granted full artisan status by means of apprentice training in open institutes, but the state, while conceding the need for improved training, proposed that it be confined to racially separate facilities, because in the opinion of the Minister of Education and Training experience had shown that 'different race groups achieve much more at their own institutions.'[58] Similarly, the state reacted to recommendations by Riekert for greatly improved technical education for the black labour force with proposals to build a number of new but separate technical institutes for blacks in 'white areas'.[59]

The state's ideological apparatus continued to pump out the message that economic growth was being subverted by chronic skill shortages which necessitated educational reform, but capital was now questioning the strength of the state's commitment to 'free enterprise' solutions. The first impulse of the Anglo American Corporation was to lay the blame for state indecision on education at the door of the bureacracy which was seen as inert.[60] And there was no doubt that the old Department of 'Bantu Education' had, as R W Johnson has pointed out, 'last got any clear ideological instruction from Verwoerd' and was now in a state of 'ideological confusion and uncertainty'.[61]

Of greater significance at a time when a general election was pending was that this confusion was widely manifest within the ranks of the state's traditional supporters to the extent that thousands of them were abandoning the governing party for the reactionary embrace of the *Herstigte Nasionale Party* (HNP). To combat the increasing threat from its right, it was necessary for the state to shed its reformist image for at least the duration of the election campaign. This in turn provoked wails of consternation from the English-speaking media which, since the time of the state-capital summit had been egging on the state to greater reformist efforts.[62]

This political development compelled capital to intensify its own sponsorship of educational reform. Consequently, the Urban Foundation produced a major position statement committing itself to faster social change and Anglo American sought to reinforce its cadet-training scheme for potential black managers. Other corporate interests too began to involve themselves in black advancement programmes including an initiative taken by the American Chamber of Commerce in South Africa, who founded the first private black commercial school in the country. Named Pace, it was designed to enrol 600 of Soweto's most talented teenagers. Given the reaction of the prominent journalist and critic of Bantu Education, Percy Q>Quboza, to the new school as the 'realisation of a dream',[63] this was for capital an encouraging testament to the potentiality of co-optation.

In the final analysis, the corporations could proceed only so far since they were unwilling to outlay massive expenditures on educational projects and required the state to bear the cost of reform. As a result, their attention became focused on the investigation of education taking place under the auspices of the HSRC.

The actual deliberations of this commission had got off to a faltering start when several educational organisations, including the Soweto Committee of Ten, refused to participate because of grave doubts about the impartiality of a body so closely associated with the state and whose main committee was so replete with establishment figures. The most comprehensive criticism of the commission and its objectives came from the non-racial National Education Union of South Africa (NEUSA), which rejected the commission on the following grounds: (1) the demands of black students were by now so well established that the commission must therefore be a 'stalling tactic' aimed at defusing conflict and providing some relief to industry by 'tinkering' with the education system; (2) the totally unrepresentative nature of the main committee which contained neither popularly recognised community leaders nor students; (3) the function of the commission was to align educational policy with the aims of total strategy, and to divide black people by means of bestowing concession on the middle class and exercising repressive control over the working people.[64]

Shortly after the publication of the NEUSA critique, the twelve guiding principles of the HSRC Commission, formulated by a special work committee, were leaked to the press. These principles indicated that no far-reaching break with tradition was as yet being contemplated within the commission.[65]

The responses solicited from some of the 'interested parties' to these principles were presumably of a sufficiently critical nature to provoke a re-appraisal within the main committee of the commission. The final Report, when tabled in Parliament in October 1981, indicated a significant departure from the original guidelines. The Report recommended the establishment of a single Ministry of Education and the introduction of compulsory and free education. It upholds the principles of equal educational opportunities and equal standards; it rejects differentiation on a racial basis; and it comes down in favour of free association in education.[66]

The business community, the PFP and the English-language newspapers not suprisingly took the Report to their collective bosom. The Federated Chamber of Industries gave the Report its blessing,[67] and the PFP's Alex Boraine described it as the 'true voice of South Africa' and a 'vindication' of his party's policy.[68] In the opinion of *The Star,* the Report heralded a 'revolution in education',[69] while Ivor Wilkins, political correspondent of *The Sunday Times,* called it a 'detailed route-map to show the way from Verwoerdian concepts of education to a new dispensation'.[70]

A thorough examination of the Report in the light of an understanding of the social milieu in which it was formulated reveals, however, that the Report amounts to considerably less than is claimed. The changes to education which are envisaged fall pitifully short of instituting a new and revolutionary educational dispensation for the black population as a whole. The suggestion of a 'route map' thereto is either a cynical deception or at best a delusion. For example, priority is given to a single Ministry of Education — a call which, according to Martin Feinstein, 'a host of free enterprise barons were falling over themselves to echo' [71] On this question, *The Star* acknowledged the need for one Ministry, but then gave the game away with the qualification: 'even if they have to have separate departments below that'.[72]

Upon close scrutiny, the actual implications of the basic principles enunciated are so ambiguous or qualified as to be virtually useless as prescriptions in any genuine struggle against inequalities and discrimination in education. The principle of 'equal opportunities' is given pride of place in the Report. In its authors' attempt to define this concept, we are informed that what is really meant is 'education of equal quality', which 'cannot be interpreted as equal share' but must be viewed as 'rightful share' or more specifically, 'equality-in-the-light-of-justice'.[73] Since the Report lacks any clear definition of social justice, this becomes meaningless.

The implications which follow on from the acceptance of the principle of 'compulsory and free education' provide other telling examples. These principles, we are told, are meant to apply only to basic literacy,[74] while 'compulsory education' must not be confused with 'compulsory school attendance'. The former can be completed on a part-time basis in vocationally-oriented courses within non-formal education.[75] As for 'free' education, since it is 'educationally unsound for education to be altogether free', parents and communities would have to contribute financially.[76] In fact, for the main committee, the whole concept of parity of expenditure is to be determined by 'financially realistic norms'.

The loftily stated principles are obviously aimed at placating popular black opinion and offered doubtless for international consumption. At the same time, the contents of the Report unmistakably signal that a process of real restructuring is being urged on the state. Significantly, that function of education which is accorded primary attention (thereby fulfilling the conditions of the Commission's mandate) is education as an agent of economic growth. New policies are recommended that will provide 'manpower' with the necessary level of skill and an appropriate 'value-system'.[77] Indeed, the Report's most trenchant criticism of the exsiting system of education (black *and* white) focuses not on oppression, but on its failure to effect a satisfactory integration between education and 'working life'. The fundamental flaw of current educational policy is seen to be its misplaced preoccupation with 'academic education' and consequent neglect of preparatory courses for practical vocations. Thus, in an attack on white education, current policy is castigated for its extravagance and its overblown 'academic ethos' that results in far too many whites entering the labour force 'without adequate vocational qualifications, skills or appropriate value-systems'. By 'inappropriate value-systems' is meant a marked tendency 'to look down on manual work'.[78]

This is reminiscent of the 'education for economic growth' literature referred to earlier, and the purpose is the same — namely to prepare the ground ideologically for capital-inspired reformism. Hence, the remedy for the educational malaise proposed in the

Report consists of massive doses of vocational guidance and technical education, in order to orientate 'prospective workers' into what is euphemistically called the 'complexities of the occupational world'.[79] In short, the cure envisaged is the rigorous application of those most classic and most explicit of all educational instruments in order to prepare youngsters to accept later the capitalist relations within the labour process.

In addition, within the strategy to 'satisfy manpower needs more readily', a pronounced emphasis is placed on non-formal (adult) educational schemes.[80] The immediate origins of this projected programme appear to lie in the 'solution' to the 'urban problem' devised by the Urban Foundation. As Tony Morphet and Clive Millar have written:

> No wonder the searching eyes of the main committee had lit upon non-formal education. Just as the concerned eyes of the British power establishment reflecting on the increasingly angry faces and voices of working men after 1867 and again 1906 and 1919 and 1945 had found again and again that adult education provided a wonderfully simple, cheap, flexible, and penetrative tool for diffusing ambitions and purposes not their own.[81]

The exploration of this new form of organisation signals the main committee's concern not only to tighten the link between education and industry, but also to serve capital's direct involvement in the process. As Principle 7 of the Report declares on non-formal education: 'the private sector and the state shall have shared responsibility'.[82]

Turning to the crucial ideological underpinnings of the Report as a whole, we find that the implicit claim that a process of genuine and comprehensive transformation is being prescribed sets out from the assumption that education will be based on 'non-racial differentiation'. Hence, entry into what the Report calls the 'elite group' will be determined by meritocratic mechanisms of selection.[83] The typical method employed by meritocratic ideologists to mask the inherent elitism of this doctrine is to characterise it as an 'open society' doctrine. It is therefore hardly surprising that the principle which has most captured the imagination of those who welcomed the Report enthusiastically is that of 'open' education.[84] Upon closer examination, however, this notion of (racially) integrated education turns out to be a highly exclusive one, seen to embrace only the private schools and universities (and possibly the technikons) — the latter being the only ones which would operate under the banner of 'free association'.[85] As far as schooling is concerned (the Report does not deal with higher education in any detail), it is therefore only those black pupils within the elite private schools who will enjoy relative shelter from the oppressive winds of apartheid; and it is from this narrow base that the future black 'elite' will be recruited. This pocket of educational privilege is earmarked to receive the benefits of discriminatory resource-allocation in the form of direct state subsidies equivalent to those given to state schools.[86]

Taken as a whole, the HSRC Report reflects too wide a range of opinion — some of it manifestly contradictory — to be viewed simply as a systematic and explicit formulation of the reformist position. Nevertheless, its definition of educational crisis as lack of management, the orgy of 'manpower' planning proposed, and the primary importance attached to the incorporation of an elite are all entirely consistent with the conventional wisdom of reformism.

The reaction of the state to the Report was predictable. It attempted to distance itself from the more 'controversial' recommendations by reaffirming its stand on educational reform (ie, reformism within the parameters of separate development only), while at the same time delaying its official response. This was symptomatic of the prevailing indecision amongst its strategists. From this and other indications of vacillation (particularly the inability to press forward on the recommendations of the Wiehahn and Riekert Commissions) it is clear that the 'urban' thrust of the 'total strategy' has become a crawl.

Another indication of the serious difficulties faced by the state's crisis-resolution strategy was its increased use of naked coercion by means of banning orders and detention without trial. Repression has, of course, always been the other side of the 'total strategy', but the original intention was to shield favoured urban blacks from its harsher effects while subjecting them to the more subtle controls of co-optation. Now it is the 'chosen' themselves, including their student leadership, who are also exposed to the full force of the repressive onslaught.[87] This 'tough line' is no doubt designed to impress white reactionaries, but the ad hoc compromises which the State is limited to producing at the policy level are not succeeding in placating either those reactionaries or the state's reformist critics.

Indeed, the champions of 'freedom of educational association' have been outraged by the state's reaction to the HSRC Report,[88] and by several other actual or proposed pieces of educational legislation. These include the proposal to establish Vista University for blacks; a Bill imposing a quota system for black students at 'white' universities and technikons; and the Financial Relations Bill which provides for the re-classification as black of any white private school which admits a majority of black pupils. These developments have been viewed as violating the principle of 'open' education proclaimed in the HSRC Report, and as running counter to the basic thrust of two hitherto confidential Reports (those of the Retief Committee and the National Manpower Commission) which, it is claimed, favour a much more tolerant ministerial approach to the question of black access to certain educational institutions.[89]

The exasperation felt by capital over the state's equivocations was forcefully expressed at a second state-capital summit held in Cape Town during November 1981. The critical attitude was in marked contrast to the spirit of accord that characterised the first summit.[90] In the opinion of Herman Giliomee, businessmen now have serious reservations about the state's commitment to the alliance forged to tackle the 'urban problem' and to 'ensure the long-term future of capitalism'.[91]

It would be over-simplification, however, to view capital as united over, and determined upon, a bold reformist push, or, alternatively, to view the state as immobilised, as is consistently maintained in the English-language newspapers. The attempt by capital to distance itself ideologically from the state has, after all, a long historical pedigree. Several prominent industrialists have been chiding the business community for being fearful of accepting the full implications of, and being reluctant to engage actively in, concrete reformist strategies.[92]

As for the state, notwithstanding its lack of reformist achievements to date, it has not closed the chapter on reformism. In the area of education it continues to make sporadic adjustments of a co-optive nature, and there is some recent evidence that not all of these are exclusively along segregated lines. The much-criticised Financial Relations Bill, for example. makes possible the re-classification of white private schools which admit blacks, but at the same time it has been welcomed by the representatives of the private school movement for giving legal sanction to a hitherto illegal trend.[93] Moreover, and this is one of the most significant political developments, the 'Botha men' have been working aggressively — if not always successfully — to accumulate executive power that could possibly be used against anti-reformists within and without Parliament. The establishment of the President's Council has been viewed as a major step in the direction of a so-called *verligte* dictatorship.[94] It is of note that the 1982 'power-sharing' Report of this Council has called for a non-parliamentary executive powerful enough to push urgently needed political reforms.[95]

Reformism: Its Likely Course

The future of reformism ultimately depends on the outcome of the related conflicts within the social formation which were identified and investigated earlier. Since these conflicts are unlikely to diminish in intensity, the need for crisis-resolution appears to be a permanent imperative. What is certain is that, to date, the 'total strategy' has been an inadequate response to the challenges being faced by capital. Capital restructuring problems remain; black trade unions continue to swell; and the internal activities of the liberation groups have been intensified.

On the education front, the demand for highly-trained black labour-power remains high, and student dissent within and without educational institutions is endemic. Unmistakable signs of continued student militancy are an increased level of support for the ANC within schools and universities, and the greater belligerence and more socialist outlook of new black student organisations such as COSAS (Congress of South African Students) and AZASO (Azanian Students Organisation) as compared with their predecessors banned in 1977.[96]

Given the relentless pressure to reform education, it can be anticipated that educational concerns will continue to occupy a central place in the calculations of reformist strategists; and indeed, the great priority they attach to educational reform is continually attested to. Prominent representatives of capital urge an all-out attack on educational problems,[97] the PFP demands a 'defence-like' educational budget,[98] while the Urban Foundation busily lobbies support for the implementation of the HSRC Report.[99]

There is also evidence that education is one sphere in which a more favourably disposed Reagan Administration in the United States, as well as those multi-national corporations doing business in South Africa, are seeking to nudge the South African state in a more reformist direction as a means of brushing up its tarnished international image. In a much-quoted position paper on South Africa, Chester Crocker (Assistant Secretary of State for African Affairs) insisted that within the planning process to establish guidelines for a policy of 'constructive engagement' with South Africa,

> the case for education as a priority concern is powerful because it brings a capacity for participation, self-help, communication, and management.[100]

In addition to the involvement of US capital in PACE, a top-

level delegation of the United States Agency for International
Development made a visit to South Africa in 1981 to study
aspects of black education. This is seen as a prelude to major US
involvement (by both state and capital) in South Africa aimed at
overcoming black 'educational disadvantage'.[101] Crocker has
confirmed US commitment to the education of the 'disadvantaged'
as a means of forestalling revolutionary change.[102] Undoubtedly
the lessons learnt from the success of US educational reforms
(aimed ostensibly at the 'disadvantaged') in co-opting a hitherto
radical black petit bourgeoisie will be brought to bear on the
problem in South Africa by US experts.

For capital, however, the immediate problems still are how to
encourage the state to be more sensitive in the educational sphere
to capital's developing labour requirements, and how to lead the
state out of its 'Bantu Education' mentality into more 'creative'
avenues of control. The stumbling-blocks to the successful
implementation of reformist designs remain formidable. Firstly,
there is the state's inherent fear that those 'better' educated blacks
will be even more militant in their demands for change. Secondly,
there is continuing resistance to reformism by white reactionaries,
including influential Afrikaans-speaking teachers' and educational
organisations, who voiced opposition to the co-optive aspects
of the HSRC Report.[103] It remains in doubt at this stage to what
extent the state will be able to overcome its own inhibitions and
the political constraints on its activity.

What is possibly of even greater significance is that the cause of
educational reformism may already have been lost. Judging by
its widespread expression, the anger among black youngsters is
deep-seated. It is extremely unlikely that an educational system
modelled on the lines of the HSRC Report could buy the
acquiescence of the mass of black youth, even if it could deliver
sufficient educational opportunities to the favoured few to win
over a proportion of their 'hearts and minds'. The truth of the
matter is that since no modernised educational system imposed
from above could possibly accommodate the demands of the black
majority for equal and integrated education, the rejection of a
possible future educational dispensation seems well nigh inevitable.

FOOTNOTES

1. For details, see Stanley Greenberg, *Race and State in Capitalist Develop-
    ment,* (Johannesburg: 1980), pp 202-5.
2. Robert Davies, 'Capital Restructuring and the Modification of the

Racial Division of Labour in South Africa', *Journal of Southern African Studies*, 5 (2) April 1979, pp 181-98.

3. Charles Meth, 'Trade Unions, Skill Shortages and Private Enterprise', *South African Labour Bulletin*, 5 (3) October 1979, p 82.

4. Personal Communication, 5 January 1981.

5. Robert Davies, 'Capital Restructuring', pp 190-1.

6. See also other papers in this collection, for example Kallaway and Molteno.

7. See Herman Giliomee, 'The Challenge Facing the Business Elite', *Rand Daily Mail*, 4 April 1981.

8. For further details see South African Institute of Race Relations, *A Survey of Race Relations in South Africa, 1979*, Johannesburg: SAIRR, 1980 (henceforth cited as *A Survey 1979*).

9. CEA/CEDIMO, 'Background on the South African general election 29 April 1981: Crisis of Total Strategy', quoted in *Social Review*, No 14, June 1981, pp 7-8.

10. For critiques of 'Bantu Education', see, for example. Muriel Horrell. *Bantu Education to 1968*, (Johannesburg: South African Institute of Race Relations, 1968), and Freda Troup, *Forbidden Pastures: Education under Apartheid*, (London: International Defence and Aid Fund, 1976).

11. For two of many accounts of these events see, Baruch Hirson, *Year of Fire, Year of Ash, the Soweto Revolt: Roots of a Revolution*, (London: 1979), and John Kane-Berman, *Soweto: Black Revolt, White Reaction*, (Johannesburg: 1978).

12. *The Star*, 22 June 1979.

13. *The Economics of Bantu Education in South Africa*, (Johannesburg: SAIRR, 1964).

14. The 1961 Education Panel, *Education and the South African Economy, Second Report*, (Johannesburg: 1966).

15. *Ibid*, pp 124-126.

16. E G Malherbe, *Education in South Africa. Vol 2*, (Cape Town: 1977).

17. *Ibid*. p 658.

18. *Ibid*.

19. See Kane-Berman, (1978) pp 24-5.

20. Hirson, (1979) pp 282-307; A Mafeje, 'Soweto and its Aftermath', *Review of African Political Economy*, Jan/April 1978, pp 17-30.

21. See below.

22. Darcy du Toit, *Capital and Labour in South Africa: Class Struggle in the 1970s*, (London: 1981), pp 336-8.

23. Kane Berman, (1978) p 151.

24. P Frankel, 'The Dynamics of a Political Renaissance: The Soweto Students' Representative Council', *Journal of African Studies*, 7 (3) Fall 1980, p 179.

25. *Race Relations News*, 41, 2, February 1979, p 2.

26.   *A Survey 1979*, p 489.
27.   *The Star*, 22 June 1979.
28.   *Race Relations News*, 41, 2, February 1979, p 3.
29.   *The Star*, 15 June 1978.
30.   Progressive Federal Party, National Advisory Committee on Education, *Education Cuttings and Comments*, No 30, September 1978, p 6.
31.   *A Survey 1979*, p 491.
32.   Hirson, (1979) p 96.
33.   *Financial Mail*, 11 March 1977.
34.   *The Star* (International Edition), 7 March 1981.
35.   *Financial Mail*, 11 March, 1977.
36.   Quoted in Thamsanga Madiba, '*A Guide to the Urban Foundation*', *Social Review*, 4, April 1979, p 18.
37.   As for example: J H Steyn, 'The Free Enterprise System: The Vehicle for the Fulfilment of Black Aspirations'. Address given to the Graduation Ceremony, University of Fort Hare, 29 April 1978, (Fort Hare University Press, 1978).
38.   'Urban Foundation', *Work in Progress*, 2, November 1977, p 74. My conception of the objectives of the Urban Foundation owes much both to this article and to that by Thamsanga Madiba referred to above.
39.   *A Survey 1979*, p 67.
40.   Kane-Berman, (1978) p 158.
41.   Tom Christoffel, et al, *Up Against the American Myth*, (Toronto: 1970), p 361.
42.   'Extract from Prime Minister's Speech in Parliament: Friday 13 June 1980'. Johannesburg: SAIRR Archives, Brief 9, 8.
43.   Nicholas Oppenheimer, 'Some Thoughts on the Educational Role of Private Enterprise in South Africa', Johannesburg: SAIRR Archives, Box 26A.
44.   Barbara Creecy, 'Riekert, A Preliminary Investigation', *Work in Progress*, 9 August 1979, p 9.
45.   *Rand Daily Mail*, 3 December 1980.
46.   *Rand Daily Mail*, 14 January 1981.
47.   *Rand Daily Mail*, 25 September 1980.
48.   Quoted in Pat Tucker, 'Cillie Commission', *Reality*, May 1980, p11.
49.   *National*, November 1980.
50.   Quoted in 'Black Education and Resistance', *Work in Progress*, 13, July 1980, p 73.
51.   *Rand Daily Mail*, 17 January 1981.
52.   *The Sunday Tribune*, 11 Janury 1981.
53.   *Rand Daily Mail*, 14 January 1981.
54.   *Rand Daily Mail*, 17 January 1981.
55.   *Rand Daily Mail*, 14 January 1981.
56.   *The Star*, 10 July 1980.
57.   *Rand Daily Mail*, 27 November 1980.

58. *A Survey 1980*, p 521.
59. *Ibid.*
60. Nicholas Oppenheimer, 'Some Thoughts on the Educational Role of Private Enterprise', pp 1-4.
61. Quoted in F Van Zyl Slabbert and Jeff Opland (eds), *South Africa: Dilemmas of Evolutionary Change*, (Grahamstown: Institute of Social and Economic Research, Rhodes University, 1980), p 12.
62. See *The Star*, 29 January 1981, *Rand Daily Mail*, 30 January 1981, *Sunday Express*, 1 February 1981, and *Sunday Times*, 1 February 1981.
63. *Newsweek*, 12 January 1981.
64. NEUSA, 'Comment on the Investigation by the Human Sciences Research Council into Education', (Johannesburg: Southern Transvaal Assocation of the National Education Union of South Africa, 22 November 1980).
65. *Sunday Tribune*, 14 December 1980.
66. Report of the Main Committee of the HSRC Investigation into Education, *Provisions of Education in the RSA*, (Pretoria: Human Sciences Research Council, July 1981).
67. *The Star*, 9 October 1981.
68. *Rand Daily Mail*, 10 October 1981.
69. *The Star*, 9 October 1981.
70. *The Sunday Times*, 11 October 1981.
71. *Rand Daily Mail*, 21 December 1981.
72. *The Star* (International Edition), 30 January 1982.
73. *HSRC Report*, pp 205-6.
74. *Ibid*, p 28.
75. *Ibid*, pp 102-3.
76. *Ibid*, p 29.
77. *Ibid*, p 32.
78. *Ibid*, p 31.
79. *Ibid*, p 46.
80. *Ibid*, p 95.
81. Tony Morphet and Clive Millar, 'Adult Education Now', Kenton-at-Glencairn Conference, 1981 (Mimeo).
82. *HSRC Report*, p 15.
83. *Ibid*, p 71.
84. See *Rand Daily Mail*, 9 October 1981 and *The Star* (International edition), 10 October 1981.
85. *Ibid.*
86. *HSRC Report*, pp 17, 203.
87. For details see *The Sowetan*, 12 October 1981 and *The Star*, 10 November 1981.
88. See *The Star*, 10 October 1981, *The Sunday Times*, 11 October 1981, and *Financial Mail*, 16 October 1981.

89. *The Star*, 8 October 1981 and *Financial Mail*, 12 February 1982.
90. See *Rand Daily Mail*, 13 November 1981 and *The Star*, 14 November 1981.
91. *Rand Daily Mail*, 17 February 1982.
92. *Cape Times*, 19 September 1981, *Rand Daily Mail*, 26 January 1982, and *Rand Daily Mail*, 1 February 1982.
93. *The Star*, 8 October 1981.
94. *The Economist*, 19 September 1981.
95. NZPA-Reuter, Cape Town. Quoted in *The Press* (Christchurch), 15 May 1982.
96. *The Sunday Times*, 10 January 1982.
97. *Rand Daily Mail*, 26 January 1982 and 1 February 1982.
98. *The Star* (International Edition), 24 October 1981.
99. Morphet and Millar, 'Adult Education Now', p 3.
100. Chester Crocker, 'South Africa: Strategy for Change', *Foreign Affairs*, 59 (2) Winter 1980/81, p 347.
101. *The Star*, 3 December 1981.
102. *The Star*, 18 December 1981.
103. *The Star*, (International Edition), 27 March 1982.

Technicism and de Lange: Reflections on the Process of the HSRC Investigation

Peter Buckland

While acknowledging the necessity for a critical analysis of the more explicit ideological assumptions underlying the Report of the HSRC Investigation into Education (the de Lange Report) — reflected in the relationship it assumes between schooling and the workplace, its anxieties about schooling and the social order, the factory model of the school that it advances or its essentially reformist approach — this article argues that another less visible set of assumptions underlies the whole investigation. They are reflected in the technological mode of rationality which is the basis of the Report and which appears to have escaped critical comment because as a way of thinking and as a mode of knowing, it has attained virtual hegemonic status among South African educationists and academics.

In seeking to understand the ideological functioning of the technicist assumptions so deeply embedded in the de Lange Report, this article examines the process of the whole investigation in its socio-historical context. This is done in an effort to understand how this process has served the interests of maintaining the status quo, and why it has so successfully evaded critical comment. The method adopted is to shift the focus of critique away from the Report as *product,* and instead to examine the whole *process*[1] of the investigation, including its context, its methodology and the responses to the Report.

Technicism

Manfred Stanley defines technicism thus:

Essentially technicism is a state of mind that rests on an act of conceptual misuse, reflected in myriad linguistic ways, of scientific and technological modes of reasoning. This misuse results in the illegitimate extension of scientific and technological reasoning to the point of imperial dominance over all other interpretations of human existence.[2]

The important point is not that the technological mode of rationality is 'wrong' in itself, but simply that its application to social and education issues *to the exclusion of all other modes of knowing* means that it tends to act as a set of lenses which focus only on certain issues and avoid others. Henry Giroux makes the point that *all* modes of rationality contain a 'problematic' which he defines as 'a "definite theoretical structure" characterised by a dialectical interplay of structuring concepts that serve to raise some questions while suppressing others.'[3] This process operates as an ideology when it serves the interests of a power group.

It remains to establish the key features of technological rationality, how they are reflected in the HSRC Investigation into Education, and how they serve the power interests in the South African socio-historical process.

A key assumption of the technicist mode of rationality is that the deductive-nomological model of explanation, the model most closely associated with the natural sciences, with its interest in explanation, prediction and technical control, is seen as vastly superior to the hermeneutic principles underlying 'speculative' social theory. The positivism implicit in this involves the assumption that social science theory can and ought to be objective, that the relationship between theory and practice in the domain of socal science is primarily a technical one in that social science theory can be used to predict how a course of action can best be realised, and, finally, that the procedures of verification and falsification must rely upon scientific techniques and 'hard data', the results of which are seen as value-free and intersubjectively applicable.[4]

A corollary of these assumptions is the dichotomy between 'facts' and values, and a tendency towards what C A Bowers[5] refers to as 'context-free thinking' as well as an ahistorical approach to social issues which views them in terms of 'problems' to be 'solved' by technical means. When applied to education these assumptions lead to the emergence of an instrumentalist tradition in which progress is seen in terms of technological 'growth' and learning is reduced to the mastery of skills and the solving of practical problems.

Technicism in education frequently assumes the form of systems thinking, perhaps the most extreme example of technological consciousness. The assumptions underlying the systems approach to education management include, as Michael Apple[6] points out, the advocacy of consensus and the negation of intellectual and valuative conflict and a limited perspective of scientific method which is more reminiscent of nineteenth century positivism than of current scientific and philosophical discourse. This tends to lead to a shift in focus from moral and ethical questions towards a focus on questions of efficiency and control. Implicit in the systems approach, too, is a tendency to name and classify segments or components of reality, and an artificial dichotomy between theory and experience, with a hierarchy of knowledge which views abstract thought as inherently superior to experience and thereby defines and elevates the status of the 'expert'.

The essence of all this is that technological rationality is basically a categorical mode of reasoning which ignores the fundamentally dialectical nature of the social world. C A Bowers comments:

> The categorical mode of thought which characterises technicism in education is expressed in the view that theory is inherently superior to commonsense experience, that the future can be anticipated in terms of technological innovation, that the perfection of human nature is essentially a problem in engineering more adequate social environments, that quality rather than equity is the basic moral problem and that it can be solved through a legalistic (expert knowledge) approach, and that communities are simply social systems or collectives that can be redesigned by well intentioned theorists. As a categorical mode of thought, it ignores the complexity of experience.[7]

Socio-historical Context

To attempt to explore the implications of the de Lange Report without locating it in its context within the South African socio-historical process would be a profoundly technicist act. That most of the discussion around the de Lange Report so far has tended to abstract the document from its social and historical context is indicative of the extent of the technicist hegemony in South African education. As I have discussed at length the historical location of the Report elsewhere,[8] I will confine myself here to reiterating the major themes of that analysis.

First, the elements of continuity of the 1981 HSRC Investigation into Education with a long line of previous commissions of inquiry are reflected in the fact that virtually all the major recommendations of the de Lange Report simply reiterate similar recommendations in previous reports: calls for industrial training, vocational education, compulsory school attendance, increased worker efficiency, stress on language skills, and for recognition of 'cultural difference', even the 'single Ministry model' and increased financial support — all of these have been posited in previous 'investigations', and none has yet been effectively implemented.

Second, important as it is to recognise the elements of historical continuity in the HSRC Report, it is also essential to be aware of the discontinuities, the features which make this investigation different from those which preceded it. First, the scope of the de Lange investigation, and the scale on which it was launched, make it stand out as the most comprehensive investigation in South African educational history, covering all levels of education, formal and non-formal, for all inhabitants of the country. A second discontinuity of this investigation is the rhetoric of 'science' used, which has been used to differentiate it from previous commissions. A third feature is the commitment in the terms of reference to 'education of equal quality for all population groups', although it appears that this is to be interpreted in its most limited sense by the authorities.

A third theme to emerge from the analysis of the socio-historical context was that the whole investigation appeared to be dominated, like many of its precursors, by two underlying anxieties arising out of an alleged 'skilled manpower shortage' and 'social unrest', in this case indicated by the 1980 school boycotts and the industrial action of workers in the Eastern Cape. The historical context of each of these elements was traced to its location in the dynamics of the economic and political structures of the society, and it was argued that while the relationship between schooling and the 'manpower crisis' was more complex than conventional wisdom held, the anxiety about social disorder and social control was clearly a powerful force underlying the whole Investigation. The schooling system was not producing workers with 'realistic aspirations' and 'appropriate value systems' required by industry, and the results of this 'inadequate harmonisation' put society 'at great risk' on 'a road to disaster'.[9]

This study of technicism in the de Lange Report also requires an examination of the ideological shifts of the ruling elite in this country to accommodate changes in the social structure, such that the rationality of the technocrat gained acceptance in a political context formerly dominated by nationalist ideologies whose original stance was resistance to modernisation. The National Party, when it finally came to power in 1948, represented basically the alliance between white workers and domestic agricultural, manufacturing and finance capital. The 1960s saw the emergence of the 'politics of security' as the emphasis of the ideology shifted from Afrikaner nationalism to white nationalism. But the really significant shifts in Nationalist ideology have their origins in developments in the social structure other than merely white parliamentary politics. The decade of the 1970s with its international economic turmoil and insecurity, combined with the emergence of more concentrated corporate production, contributed to a rise to prominence of international capital, as well as to a heightened anxiety over labour relations and social security precipitated by the unrest in schools in 1976 and 1980, and the industrial unrest signalled by the Natal strikes of 1973 and the Eastern Cape strikes in 1980. Anxiety over labour relations and social security led to the recognition of two new power factors in the white state — the businessmen and the military. The policy of Total Strategy represents a move toward a tentative alliance with these new forces.

A more instrumental approach to the policy of separate development began to emerge during the period 1974-1977, described by Giliomee as the 'watershed period (when) they began to see separate development as an instrument rather than a goal'.[10] Kurt Danziger sees this in terms of

> . . . a clear shift from a justification of existing institutions in terms of intrinsic value to their justification in terms of their instrumental utility of effectiveness. Secondly, we observe a shift from cultural to political and finally to economic institutions as the main focus for legitimating ideas.[11]

It became more clear with the coming to power of P W Botha and his introduction of the policy of 'rationalisation' of the bureaucracy that a fundamental tension in the ruling party existed between modernisation and nationalism. Economic, political and social pressures had resulted in a shift away from orthodox Christian Nationalism and Afrikaner Nationalism toward a more instrumental approach to social policy. The new breed of Afrikaner which emerged to challenge the ideology of the Verwoerdian era had been through the modern schooling system, which, despite its apparent ideological affiliations to Christian National Education, was rapidly reflecting the technocratic ideals of a modernising society. The transformation of schooling from its origins in Christian National Education, one of the fundamental pillars of conservative Nationalist ideology, into a powerful force for modernisation was achieved through the infusion into the education bureaucracy and education policy of a technicist ideology which tended to elevate goals of efficiency, management and control to primacy over the previous explicit goal of preservation of Afrikaner identity. Such a transformation required the institution of powerful centralised control over education departments, and powerful departmental control over teachers.

The past two decades have seen a battery of legislation to establish such control, an early and crucial example of which was the National Education Policy Act of 1967. Its commitment to education of a 'Christian' and 'broad national character' served primarily to centralise control of the provincial schooling system in order to implement a modern differentiated curriculum calculated to meet the 'needs' of a modernising economy. In the event, the provisions for differentiated curriculums were not implemented for several years and the HSRC was commissioned to investigate the matter.

The Report of this investigation, published in 1972[12] attempted to outline the details of a technically reasoned, functionally oriented, differentiated education programme backed by a powerful guidance service to channel white youths into schooling appropriate to the maintenance of white economic and political dominance. Control of teachers was increased through the institution of 'scientific management' procedures, implemented in part through the South African Teachers Council for Whites Act of 1976 and the introduction of 'accountability' programmes such as the merit award system.

The 'twin crises' in education in 1980 suggested that 'differentiated' education, which was slowly being implemented in various forms in all education departments, was not operating efficiently enough. Total strategy, and the accompanying rhetoric of reform, demanded a wide-ranging revision of the entire education system in a way that would involve 'private enterprise' more actively in the process of schooling. The technicist values of efficiency and control implicit in 'scientific' research, 'scientific management' and 'differentiated education' provided the legitimating ideology expressed in terms of 'equality', modernisation, 'harmonising' of educational 'needs' with 'the needs of society', and 'optimal returns on investment in education'. Wrapped in the rhetoric of 'science' and 'reform' this proved a powerful medium for the control required to implement this modernisation which is likely to encounter some resistance both within the National Party and in the broader society. Considering the concealed manner in which this process operates in American curriculum design, Michael Apple comments:

> . . . the real issue is not that systems techniques yield information and feedback that may be used *by* systems for social control. They themselves *are* systems of control. What is of equal importance is that the belief system underlying them and a major portion of the curriculum field stems from and functions as a technocratic ideology which can often seem to legitimate the existing distribution of power and privilege

in our society.[13]

The point of this brief overview of the socio-historical context is to indicate the shifts in the social and economic order which have facilitated the evolution of a ruling class ideology. It incorporates fundamental technicist assumptions, and these assumptions are embedded in the very context which gave rise to the de Lange Investigation. The danger of these assumptions is their very embeddedness in the modernising ethos which pervades the 'developing' country. The technological mode of rationality does not provide the vocabulary or conceptual tools for a critique which could expose the way in which such assumptions serve the power interests of the ruling elite.

Technicism and HSRC Investigation

One of the widely acclaimed features of the entire investigation was the assertion that this project, under the auspices of the HSRC was to be 'scientific and co-ordinated investigation' rather than the 'opinion' of a commission, as had been the case previously. The entire project was planned in accordance with the HSRC master-plan for educational research, the South African Plan for Research in the Human Sciences, which is explicitly calculated to achieve the 'balanced development' of the human sciences in the RSA, to isolate 'national problem areas' and to 'stimulate, co-ordinate, finance and control' research into such areas.[14] The document outlining the SAPRHS serves as a classic illustration of the way in which technicist assumptions work in the interests of order and control:

> Taken as a whole the proposals that follow represent an attempt to seek consensus regarding the working method that will be adopted in the implementation of the SAPRHS — a working method that will be sufficiently flexible to accommodate the wide range of subjects, approaches, problem areas, ideological orientations, etc., that exist in the human sciences.[15]

The call for consensus and the search for a neutral methodology is followed by an outline of the approach to be used. The national problem areas are selected by a committee of experts and placed in order of priority on the basis of a 'scientific survey'. A Main Committee for each 'problem area' is appointed, and their first task is to divide the topic into a number of smaller areas, for each of which a Working Committee is constituted to conduct 'research'.

A report from each Working Committee is then submitted to the Main Committee which then synthesises the various reports to produce a final document. In the case of the de Lange Committee, this involved the 'synthesising' of some 20 000 pages of 'research' into a two hundred page final report. Heavy stress was placed by the Main Committee on consensus, with the result that any vestiges of scientific inquiry method were sacrificed; the final report represents an account of the issues that the members of the committee were able to agree on, or were able to couch in such ambiguous language that their conflict was submerged beneath a layer of benign circumlocution. On the basis of this it seems extraordinary that the final report should still be regarded as evidence of scientific inquiry, yet the rhetoric of science is constantly used to attach a value-free image to the Investigation. The Report of the Main Committee is, on its own admission,

> . . . not merely an account of the findings and recommendations of the different work committees, but rather an interpretation of these findings and recommendations viewed as a whole. An attempt was therefore made to synthesise the wealth of information.[16]

The tendency to deny or eliminate conflict, or to redefine it and search for consensus, is frequently defended by the argument that this constitutes an attempt to be scientific about problems. Herein, argues Michael Apple, lies the basic difficulty, since this perspective of science is notably inaccurate:

> To link scientific rationality with consensus, however, is to do a disservice to science and shows a profound misunderstanding of the history of scientific disciplines . . . the very normative structure of scientific communities tends towards scepticism and not necessarily toward intellectual consensus. The call for consensus, thus, is not a call for science.[17]

Apple goes on to argue that while the advocates of systems procedures seek to enhance the scientific status of their work, the systems thought they have borrowed is not from the scientific branch of systems logic:

> Rather, they have chosen to appropriate the models of operation of the business community . . . . One has to wonder if their models are indeed appropriate for dealing with students. The issue is made more potent when one realises that systems management was created originally to enhance the ability of owners to *control* labour more effectively, thereby increasing profits and weakening the burgeoning union

movements early in this century.[18]

The language of science attached to the de Lange Investigation, then, serves a rhetorical function. But it is a powerful rhetoric in a rapidly modernising technological society which widely regards 'science' as 'value-free' and apolitical. Although the illusion of strict scientific method cannot really be maintained with regard to the Report of the Main Committee, some of the implicit assumptions of the positivist approach to the social world none-theless survive in the structuring of the Report. Key among these is the assumption that the problems of education are essentially technical ones that can be solved by technical solutions. The basic pattern of the Report reflects the sort of 'examination, diagnosis, prognosis and prescription' approach which Karabel and Halsey describe:

> Theoretically informed exchanges between social scientists and the government may well reveal that there are 'social problems' that cannot be formulated adequately in terms approximating those of medical problems in which the social scientist is defined, by analogy, as a skilled diagnostician. Such a model, apart from assuming that there is a social science theory to be applied in the same way that doctors apply medical theory, also takes it for granted that there is agreement about social ends just as there is consensus about the nature and desirability of good health.[19]

On looking at which interests are served by such an approach, they go on:

> It is in the interests of established government to define the social sciences as apolitical and organised social sciences, as, in effect, an extension of the civil service. On such a view problems are essentially technical and the role of the social scientist is that of hand-maiden. Research strategies and priorities, from this perspective, are finally left in the hands of the government.[20]

A consequence of this is that the investigation is dominated by essentially reformist ideologies which tend to focus on such questions as 'How can we make it work better?' rather than on more fundamental questions such as 'How does it work?' and 'Who benefits?' A certain amount of excitement was generated by the statement in the Report which acknowledges the essentially political nature of schooling, but it soon emerges that questions of efficiency and control are regarded as crucial, and the political element of schooling is reduced to a question of 'user participation':

Various criteria can be applied to evaluate education management and a variety of factors exercise a determinative influence on these criteria (for example the development level of the country and its people, homogeneity in respect of the composition of the population and political philosophy). However, in the final instance, structures for education management should be based on educational considerations . . . . Systems of education are part of the social, economic and political structure of a country. Acceptance by, and involvement of, the 'user' are essential. [21]

Giroux, however, points out that

. . . acknowledging the social and cultural basis of the character of different modes of pedagogy is important but incomplete. This approach must be supplemented by analysing the assumptions embedded in a given educational paradigm against larger social and political interests. Questions which arise out of this type of analysis might take the following form: What interests do these assumptions serve? What are their latent consequences? What are the material and intellectual forces that sustain these assumptions and their corresponding paradigm? [22]

It is just such questions which the HSRC Main Committee Report does not ask. The technicist assumption implicit in the method-ology of the Report is the dialectical interplay between knowledge, power and ideology. Giroux argues that this results in a confusion of objectivity with objectivism. The former he describes as a scrupulous attempt to minimise biases and false beliefs. The latter, 'objectivism',

. . . refers to an orientation that is atemporal and ahistorical in nature. In this orientation 'fact' becomes the foundation for all forms of knowledge, and values and intentionality lose their political potency by being abstracted from the notion of meaning. [23]

Despite the 'principles for the Provision of Education' which were supposed to guide the investigation and which acknowledged in the vaguest possible terms the importance of such values as 'equality', 'recognition of commonality and diversity' and 'freedom of choice', the subtle framework of the methodological assump-tions, the ahistorical approach and the call for consensus served to guide the Main Committee away from considering the fundamental implications of these values towards consideration of technical issues.

This process is reflected in the recommendations of the Main Committee which, in pursuit of consensus in such ideologically sensitive areas as language medium and curriculum, resorts to a concern with 'means' rather than 'ends'. After 13 months of 'research', Recommendation 30 reads:

> The principle of the use of mother-tongue speakers in language instruction also merits attention. The provision of support material on cassette from a central resource centre is recommended. [24]

The first sentence represents a classic example of what Michael Young has called 'the politics of non-decision making'. [25] An even more crucial process is evident in the second sentence, which recommends the use of technology. The point is that while the committee was unable to reach agreement on ends, it was quite prepared to make recommendations regarding the means — technology. The use of such technology is apparently regarded as non-problematic, and this assumption underlies a great many of the recommendations of the Report.

Perhaps the most powerful evidence of a technicist mentality is contained in the following statement from the Report:

> South Africa is a developing country that is changing more rapidly than most developed countries. Modern science, technology and management skills, which are the most powerful resources that man has ever had at his disposal to enable him to change his environment, are not yet the cultural assets of significant sectors of our population. [26]

Progress is seen in terms of technological growth, modernisation and 'development', which itself is defined, somewhat tautologically, in terms of economic development:

> . . . the aim of development, namely provision of skilled manpower with the value system, insight and skills necessary to contribute to the development of a country. [27]

Moreover, 'modern science, technology and management skills' are together seen as 'the most powerful resources that man has ever had at his disposal to enable him to change his environment' and are seen as 'cultural assets' which it is assumed must be acquired by 'significant sectors of our population'. The modernising society is taken uncritically as the status quo to which man must adapt, just as the modern school is regarded as a given for which a child must be made 'ready':

> Pre-primary education offers the child a wonderful opportunity to move over easily (from an affective — social point of view) to the

formal education of the primary school; in doing this it achieves more than school readiness and provides a wider readiness for life.[28]

Systems management and a systems approach to educational problems emerge as the basic 'neutral' ground on which all members of the Main Committee were able to reach consensus:

Educational technology enhances and enriches the quality of education in the classroom. It brings the outside world of education into the classroom thus enriching learning activities. The use of the systems approach which aims at establishing specific goals and using the most appropriate media, enables accurate evaluation to be carried out. The accent therefore shifts from the teacher as the only source of information, to the teacher as manager in the teaching-learning situation.[29]

The primacy of the technicist mind-set is reflected strongly in the language used; an extended technological metaphor is used to describe the new 'education structure':

Canalisation mechanisms are means by which the 'inlet', 'flow' and 'outlet' of learners are regulated in the education structure. These mechanisms can be built into, as well as added to the eduational structure. However, the essence of the matter is that the mechanisms function between two points, namely inlet and outlet, and can be used in various ways to the advantage of the individual and the manpower needs of the country.[30]

Another important technicist feature is the subtle way in which a hierarchy of knowledge is implied in the recommendations. First, the committee itself is composed largely of 'experts'. When all else fails, recommendations are passed for the use of more experts:

. . . it is recommended that a committee or committees of expert teachers and/or educational planners representative of all educational services together with other interested parties be appointed to work out the aims and objectives for English and Afrikaans.[31]

Despite a passage regretting the fact that 'the abstract world of ideas' is valued over the practical world (and this is offered as a reason why there is often a tendency to look down on manual work and practical skills), the proposed education structure by which pupils are systematically 'canalised' into industrial training implies a none too subtle hierarchy of knowledge in that only those pupils who remain in Grade 0 and Grade I 'grades of difficulty' are retained in the schools.

The treatment of social issues as technical problems open to technical solutions, the componential thinking implicit in the division of education into eighteen separate areas, the ahistorical approach and the orientation to the future all serve to rule out consideration of how schooling has been used to further political and economic ends. Knowledge is seen in terms of skills, with an 'appropriate value system' serving to legitimate the differentiated acquisition of such skills.

The technicist features of the Report reflect an ideology that is deeply embedded in western cultural patterns; many of the 'structuralist' criticisms of the western model of schooling also rest on technicist assumptions, particularly those which ignore the dialectical nature of the social process and talk in terms of domination/submission, of 'doer' and 'done to'. Likewise, much of the praise and criticism of the Report itself rest on a futile attempt to evaluate the document 'on its own merits', abstracting it from its socio-historical context.

The technicism in the Report operates as an ideology because it serves to buttress the status quo by undermining the dialectic of human potential and will, thereby denying the possibility that human beings can construct their own reality and can alter that reality in the face of domination. For this reason technological rationality has been incorporated into the ideology of those elements of the ruling elite which, in the face of the realities of the 'politics of survival', have chosen to seek to modernise and stream-line apartheid. This is not meant to suggest a conscious conspiracy to adopt technicism as a new instrument of oppression; rather it is argued that the technicist features of the western mind-set which underline the technological revolution and the ethos of modernisation so serve the power interests of significant sectors of the dominant groups that they are accepted uncritically as 'rational' or logical.

What is perhaps more difficult to understand is the way in which technicism remains unseen or is accepted uncritically by those whose interests are apparently *not* served by it. Crucial to an appreciation of this is an understanding of the way technological rationality has become the prevailing hegemony. The language of modernisation and the logic of technology constitute a powerful psychological and material force. The daily routine of our lives is already structured to some extent by the demands of the technological revolution. But above all the language of technology and the categorical mode of thinking inherent in it serve to deny the vocabulary and the conceptual tools, such as historical consciousness, with which to critique the prevailing belief systems.

There is inherent in this argument the danger of an over-deterministic view of hegemony, which could leave us with a feeling of helplessness and despair in the face of the extraordinarily powerful forces of technology and modernisation. Such despair itself reflects a categorical mode of thinking which ignores the dialectical nature of the social process. Wherever there is a hegemony, there is the possibility of a counterhegemony. Hegemony as a mode of control is not simply a question of projecting the ideas of a dominant elite into the minds of the oppressed. Moreover, it has to be constantly reinforced and adapted to accommodate changing historical circumstances and new forms of resistance.

The technicism which the de Lange Report reflects can and must be countered. But it cannot be critiqued with the language and conceptual tools of the technological mode of reasoning. What is urgently needed is an abandonment of the categorical mode of thinking that cannot tolerate ambiguity and avoids or conceals conflicts in the search for consensus. A vital element of this process is the raising of awareness of the role of language and metaphor in the process of social control, and the provision of the necessary vocabulary with which to critique the manifestations of the technicist mind-set. Equally important is the need to develop historical consciousness and to re-learn our history. This may enable the de-reification of the structures which have come to wield such influence over our lives. Only when their human authorship is acknowledged can their vulnerability to change be recognised. We must reaffirm the potency of experience in relation to theoretical or abstract knowledge so that the status of the 'expert' can be seen in perspective.

Above all we must seek to raise the status of ethical and moral debate so that it holds at least equal status with technical and efficiency 'talk'. Until we as educators tackle these challenges, documents such as the de Lange Report, despite the rhetoric of 'reform' and 'change', will continue to constitute powerful instruments for the maintenance of the status quo.

FOOTNOTES

1. I am aware that the dichotomy between process and product is a false one which itself reflects the categorical mode of reasoning against which I am arguing. The device is used here merely to deflect the reader away from a consideration of the Report in isolation, towards a more realistic view of it as part of an historical process.

2. Manfred Stanley, *The Technological Conscience: Survival and Dignity*

in an Age of Expertise, (New York, 1978).

3. Henry A Giroux, *Ideology, Culture and the Process of Schooling,* (London: 1981) p 9.

4. See Henry A Giroux, 'Schooling and the Culture of Positivism: Notes on the Death of History' in *Educational Theory* 29(4) Fall 1979, p 275.

5. Bowers, C A 'Curriculum as Cultural Reproduction: an Examination of Metaphor as a Carrier of Ideology' in *Teacher's College Record* 82(2), Winter 1980, pp 267-289.

6. Michael Apple, *Ideology and Curriculum* (London, 1979) pp 107-9.

7. Bowers, C A 'Ideological Continuities in Technicism, Liberalism and Education', Mimeo: Centre for Education Policy and Management, University of Oregon, 1979.

8. Peter Buckland, 'The HSRC Investigation: Another Brick in the Wall?' paper presented at the Kenton-at-Glencairn Conference, 7 November 1981. Published in *Proceedings of the Kenton-at-Glencairn Conference 1981,* Cape Town.

9. *Ibid.*

10. Giliomee, H 'The Nationalist Party and the Afrikaner Broederbond' in R M Price & R I Rotberg (eds) *The Apartheid Regime: Political Power and Racial Domination.* (Cape Town, 1980) p 33.

11. Kurt Danziger, 'Modernisation and the legitimation of social power' in H Adam (ed) *South Africa: Sociological Perspectives,* (London, 1971) p 285.

12. HSRC, *Report of the committees for differentiated education and guidance in connection with a national system of education at primary and secondary level with reference to school guidance as an integrated service of the system of education for the Republic of South Africa and South West Africa.* Part One, Report 0-1 of 1972, Pretoria, HSRC.

13. Apple, M (1979) pp 111-112.

14. HSRC *South African Plan for Research in the Human Sciences* (Pretoria, HSRC, 1980) p 1.

15. *Ibid.*

16. HSRC *Provision of Education in the RSA: Report of the Main Committee of the HSRC Committee into Education* (Pretoria, HSRC, 1981) p 7.

17. Apple, M (1979) p 119.

18. *Ibid,* p 114.

19. Karabel, J and A H Halsey (eds) *Power and Ideology in Education* (New York, 1979) p 6.

20. *Ibid,* p 6.

21. HSRC (1981) p 87.

22. Giroux, H (1979) p 267.

23. *Ibid.*

24. HSRC (1981) p 32.

25. Michael F D Young, *Knowledge and Control: New Directions in the Sociology of Knowledge* (London, 1971).
26. HSRC, (1981).
27. *Ibid*, p 109.
28. *Ibid*, p 28.
29. *Ibid*, p 50.
30. *Ibid*, p 127.
31. *Ibid*, p 145.

Redefining Skills: Black Education in South Africa in the 1980s
Linda Chisholm

The South African education and training apparatus is clearly in a process of transition. Both the schooling and training of the black working class, in schools and on the factory floor, is receiving renewed attention. In 1980, four years after the Soweto uprising and in the midst of schools boycotts throughout the country the state appointed a Human Sciences Research Council Commission of Inquiry into Education, which produced what is commonly known as the de Lange report. Through de Lange new forms of educational control and provision were explored and a full-blown attempt was made to renegotiate the racial component of state ideology in education.[1] The report itself has evoked intense conflict between sectors of the dominant classes on a future education system for South Africa.[2] At the same time, the period between 1977 and 1982 saw a great expansion of technical and vocational education. Here the extent of capital's intervention represents a departure unprecedented in South African education history. A dominant theme in the discourse surrounding these reformist initiatives has been that of 'skill shortages.'

These developments closely follow a deepening economic, political and ideological crisis. Since the mid-1970s the South African economy has been sliding into recession. A brief boom in 1980/81 did not alter this trend. It has faced mounting balance of payments difficulties, growing inflation, the limits of a white consumer market and high structural unemployment of blacks. In 1977 inflation ran at 14 percent and showed little sign of abating by 1983. The real growth rate, which averaged 5-7 percent annually during the 1960s, was zero in 1977. Falling output in manufacturing and declining private sector investment have been marked, while black unemployment rose from 11,8 percent in 1970 to 21,1 percent in 1981 to about 24 percent in 1982,[3] accompanied by a steep rise in retrenchments of employed workers during 1982 and 1983. Black worker struggles also reached new levels of organised militance. Since 1973 strikes and work stoppages have become frequent and commonplace. The number of strikes, according to official figures, rose from 76 in 1970, involving 4 146 workers, to 274 in 1975 involving 23 396 workers and climbed to 394 in 1982 involving 141 571 workers.[4]

At the same time the state has faced mounting challenges from the urban black population. This was most vividly demonstrated in education in the 1976 uprising and the school boycotts of 1980 which spread to every major and even some smaller towns throughout South Africa. The collapse of colonial rule in Mozambique and Angola and settler rule in Rhodesia, and increased levels of urban guerilla warfare by the African National Congress also compounded the threat to the stability of the South African state.

The 'transformation of the National Party from a populist movement into a party of the bourgeoisie'[5] has meant that the reformist trajectory embarked upon in 1977 with the appointment of the Wiehahn and Riekert Commissions of Inquiry into labour relations and influx control respectively, has seen the revival of a strategy rejected in the 1940s, namely the fostering of a partially settled, stabilised labour force as opposed to a purely migrant one. This involves an attempt to privilege and thereby win over a small number of blacks to the 'free enterprise' system through selective reforms while at the same time driving a deeper wedge between urban and rural workers, tightening controls over labour and continuing the vicious repression of those who resist.

Educational reform is crucial to the strategy of limited incorporation of small numbers of blacks. Education is a particularly sensitive and fertile area of state intervention since the desire for education and frustration at its denial have been long-standing causes of bitterness. Reforms which appear to be real concessions could defuse significant areas of opposition, at least in the short term. The process, however, is not without its ambiguities or contradictions. These apparent reforms are not mere 'cosmetic' changes, but they are implemented in a manner that leaves the roots of inequality in South Africa untouched.

The Human Sciences Research Council (HSRC) Commission of Inquiry

Appointed by the state in 1980 at the height of nation-wide school boycotts, the Commission reported in June 1981. The report proposed reforms designed to streamline and rationalise the existing education system. It also articulated a new meritocratic, 'non-racial', technicist educational ideology. With a brief to provide recommendations for an education system which would meet the manpower needs of South Africa and provide education of 'equal quality' for all population groups, the Commission recommended a system of formal (academic) education running parallel and 'interfacing' with a non-formal (vocational) education structure. The formal structure was to be composed of three tiers: pre-basic, basic and post-basic education. The non-formal and formal education structures were recommended to fall within a single education department as opposed to the racially divided departments of the present system.

Many of the recommendations concerning the structure of education as divided into formal and non-formal education were based on the recommendations of the Technical and Vocational Education Subcommittee which advised as follows:

> The present general academic [sic] type of high school (for blacks: LC) should therefore in time develop into separate Secondary Academic High Schools or Secondary Vocational Schools, the latter being comprehensive and technical schools.[6]
>
> The majority of pupils require vocational training at school to enable them to enter the world of work. The minority of pupils require the development of academic skills with a view to continuing their academic training at tertiary level . . . 50-80 percent of children in standards 5-8 receiving vocational education in future is in line with the manpower needs of South Africa.[7]

Significantly, this does not depart from earlier government policy statements on the nature of black education. It would seem that the majority of blacks are still destined to receive an inadequate education.

The financial provisions reinforce these aims. Whilst basic education (up to approximately age 12) is to be free, post-basic education is not. That is, at the point at which scholars are channelled either into academic or vocational schooling, the financing of education becomes dependent on the social class of the parents. The cost of formal (academic) secondary schooling is shifted onto parents while that of vocational education is to be borne primarily by capital. Capital will also bear some responsibility for the provision of vocational education. The obvious implication of this is that working class students will be channelled into vocational/technical education. Vocational education, moreover, can be undergone either in schools or on-the-job where it would be cheaper for capital to train workers. Thus vocational education remains relatively free, while academic education does not.

The implications of these provisions are as follows. Instead of being denied academic schooling, as was largely the case in the Bantu Education system, blacks now have the possibility of academic schooling as long as they can afford it. This is allowed for in the principle of 'parental free choice' specified in the report which could allow parents to send students to expensive multi-racial private schools. The vocationalisation of schooling, however, would apply equally to black and white working class students. On the one hand, then, white working class scholars would no longer be protected by free secondary academic schooling, although they would still attend schools in 'white' areas. (This has clearly been recognised by the right wing of the National Party). On the other hand, an escape route is provided for some black students. The majority remain where they were while an ideology of upward mobility and equality of opportunity, made possible by easing restrictions on the training of blacks, disguises the continuities between Bantu Education and present initiatives. Crucially, it also potentially removes at least some of the grounds for antagonism in the older system of Bantu Education.

Thus class location and internal mechanisms within schooling itself, such as elaborate streaming processes ('canalisation' in the jargon of the report), are provided to propel the majority of black students into vocational and technical schooling and to provide the opportunity of academic schooling for a few. In this way the de Lange report, in tandem with the Wiehahn and Riekert Commissions of Inquiry, represents a part of the strategy adopted by the state in conjunction with monopoly capital to 'deracialise' aspects of the industrial process and state structures through co-option of a small black middle class and increasing controls over the working class. Despite the uproar that ensued when it appeared that the government had rejected a report which the 'liberal' press claimed was a 'revolutionary breakthrough' in educational provision in South Africa, many aspects of the Committee's recommendations are being implemented. In particular, its recommendations concerning technical and vocational education have not been ignored. These will be examined below.

The HSRC Commission reported its findings against a chorus of voices lamenting the shortage of skills in South Africa. The Commission itself saw one of its main purposes as addressing this question. The extent of the skills shortage was so great, it was claimed, that it could not be met by the white population which was already 'fully absorbed' in employment, nor by white immigration, which was not of a scale to keep pace with the demand. For economic growth to be maintained, it was intoned, education would have to be revamped to enable the necessary education and training of some categories of blacks. A mass of statistics about the precise number of shortages in each sector and the shortfall in black educational qualifications was produced, flooding popular consciousness with its urgency. In the space thus created, plans for the restructuring of education were floated via de Lange, the provision of technical education was accelerated and industrial training programmes were expanded. All these, it was claimed, would provide a 'higher' level of skill designed to meet the manpower requirements of South Africa.

Major interpretations of the crisis faced by the South African state and capital have also placed this skills shortage near the centre of their argument. Among the most important of these are Saul and Gelb (1981), Davies (1979) and Sharp and Hartwig (1983).[8] An attempt will be made to isolate the major tenets of a thesis that has emerged as conventional wisdom within the last few years.

Sharp and Hartwig have argued that skilled labour shortages arose in South Africa during the 1960s largely as a result of 'the trend towards a rising organic composition of capital through mechanisation, reorganisation and rationalisation of the labour process to thereby enhance capital's national and international competitiveness'.[9] Changes in the labour process involved the 'progressive deskilling and increasing subordination of manual labour, on the one hand, (and) . . . the creation of a minority of specialised supervisory and mental wage-earning places on the other'. Skilled wage-earning places have historically been occupied by whites and unskilled manual places by blacks; 'such a division of labour broadly accorded with the value and technical require-ments of capitalist production', argues Davies, 'and with the political interests of the bourgeoisie or of particular bourgeois fractions'.[10] These shortages were exacerbated, it is argued, both by a shortage of whites and a racist education system which prohibited the production of adequately skilled blacks.

The 'potentially adverse effects' of shortages were, however, countered during the 1960s in the boom conditions that pre-vailed. Shortages of technicians, supervisors and artisans in production were met by floating the colour bar; shortages of clerical, administrative and sales personnel were mitigated by the 'availability of large amounts of foreign investment capital'.[11] At the same time, to reproduce skilled labour power, the state began to place a major stress on vocational and technical education for whites as well as on white immigration.[12]

In the 1970s, 'conditions . . . changed abruptly'. Declining profitability, due in part to reduced levels of foreign capital inflow and intensified worker struggles, led to conditions which made it imperative for capital to seek modification of the racial division of labour. Shortages became acute. The previous means of coping were no longer possible. While the crisis of profitability forced capital to introduce new technology repeatedly to raise product-ivity, thus constantly exacerbating shortages of skilled labour power, the political and ideological dimensions of the crisis necessitated reforming at least some aspects of the reproduction of labour power.

In this context, so the argument runs, 'removing some of the more obvious at least of the various forms of discrimination and oppression affecting the black petit bourgeoisie (including job reservation and overtly racist barriers to 'upward mobility') has become a major political imperative for the bourgeoisie . . . (as well as) a major element in restoring the previous levels of capital inflow'.[13] The only solution, argue Sharp and Hartwig, to solving the problem of shortages of skilled labour power, ' . . . lay in upgrading the qualifications of significant sections of the black population'.[14]

While not denying that skill shortages of specific kinds might exist at particular levels at different points in time or that there is a distinct strategy on the part of the state and sectors of capital to build a black middle class committed to 'free enterprise', this article will seek to cast some light on a dimension of reformist strategies in education unaccounted for in the literature mentioned above. It will emphasise certain of the ideological dimensions of 'skill shortages' as employed in the South African context. The nature of the skills said to be 'required' is considered in greater detail and the *social* nature of the skills demanded is highlighted.[15] The skills needed by certain sectors of monopoly capital, it will be argued here, are concerned as much with the 'moral and ideological preparation of new strata', with labour discipline and with the inculcation of the values of 'free enterprise' as with increasing technical requirements. As the Centre for Contemporary Cultural Studies has written for England, in words equally apt for South Africa, ' "good" worker attitudes are more important to employers than particular skill competencies, even though the latter may be in short supply'.[16]

In South Africa 'good' worker attitudes have become imperative in the context of two factors of major importance. The first is that the reorganisation of capitalist production at a higher organic composition of capital has led not only to job-fragmentation, the emergence of technical and supervisory positions and increasing structural unemployment; it has also involved the 'reorganisation of the production process so as to ensure a real and extended control over the direct producer'.[17]

South Africa's particular pattern of dependent industrialisation, involving the importation of capital-intensive foreign technology, has both increased its dependence on the outside world, and necessitated raising the productivity of labour. Changes in the labour process are of some significance here. The use of capital-intensive technology has led, as mentioned above, to processes of job-fragmentation, deskilling and reskilling. A considerable body of literature and debate has developed in South Africa drawing on Braverman's work emphasising the degradation and not the upgrading of skill under capitalism. The entire notion of 'skill' has thus become a contested one. For example, as Stanley Trapido has written, 'For over seventy years South African gold mines have employed skilled and semi-skilled African workers, though these have been categorised as unskilled, paid unskilled wages and employed as migrant labourers.'[18]

As a consequence some reasearch has been undertaken to investigate the nature of the skills shortage in South Africa. Charles Meth, for example, has argued that there is no crippling shortage of craft skills, or indeed in any of the areas claimed by the state, except for certain categories of technical and engineering workers. He has argued that the apparent extent of the skills shortage is but a 'smokescreen' for the attempt to co-opt a black petty bourgeoisie.[19] While Meth's argument is suggestive, it raises the question of why training is being undertaken on the scale that it is.

Also drawing on Braverman's thesis that capitalism deskills and dequalifies the majority and hyperqualifies a minority of technical workers required to perform a function of control, Webster has argued that the threat of a skills shortage by employers 'conceals an attempt to increase the productivity of labour'.[20] His research into the metal industry has shown how a skills shortage has been used to undercut white craft unions, by introducing black labour into technical and supervisory positions at lower wage rates than those paid to whites. Mechanisation, Webster has argued, has displaced a particular kind of skill and has led to a ' . . . process of cheapening of labour'.[21] Webster goes further than Meth in suggesting that while there is no shortage of craft skills, new skills are required corresponding to the reskilling of a minority of technical workers required to monitor and understand new forms of technology, and that initiatives by the state and capital in training can be explained by reference to these shortages. Formal training is required for the reskilling of these categories of workers.

Accelerating technological change and corresponding deskilling and retrenchments mean that machine operatives and technicians are required to be both technically skilled and 'flexible': flexible enough to adapt to different machines — or to accept their lot if retrenched. Along with the emphasis on a stable, flexible workforce is the importance attached to the mobility of workers.

The need to raise productivity and extend control over labour has occurred in the context of the creation of

> conditions under which the 'indiscipline' of the working class . . . began to manifest itself in organised form, for the introduction of new technology meant changes in the imposition of the rule of capital at the point of production, on the one hand, and the creation of redundancies on a considerable scale on the other.[22]

Increasing worker organisation and militance, as Davies points out, makes it increasingly difficult to extract surplus value through measures such as lengthening the working day. In this context, and given rising wages, other ways of extracting surplus value have to be devised: the nature of the worker's application to the job becomes of paramount importance. S/he has to be motivated, efficient and stable. Here the assertion of ideological control by capital over workers becomes critical. It is this tension between the need to maintain profitability and the need for different ideological controls over a changing kind of labour force that seems to be of crucial importance.

The second major factor of importance concerns the fact that schools in South Africa have failed to create ideologically acceptable school-leavers. Black schools and universities, after a decade of near-silence, became key sites of resistance from 1969 with the emergence of the South Africa Students' Organisation (SASO) and the black consciousness movement. While Bantu Education might thus have produced manual and semi-skilled workers in sufficient numbers for capital, it was also generating people with 'dispositions out of keeping with requirements' for a quiescent labour force.

From 1976 to 1981, with but brief intervals in between, black students mounted a sustained attack on Bantu Education, on apartheid and, more explicitly, in 1980 at least, on capitalism. On each occcasion, albeit in different ways, they forged or attempted to forge links with workers. In 1976 the Soweto Students' Representative Council asked workers to support stay-aways, boycotts of consumer goods over the Christmas season and similar actions. In 1980 students in Cape Town allied themselves with workers' struggles under the slogan, 'The workers are strong; our parents the workers are strong; it is only by supporting them that our struggle will be won'.[23]

The significance of this is not to be underestimated. The 1970s, as mentioned above, had seen an escalation of independent workers' organisation and militance, of strikes and stoppages, unprecedented in their number and scale. To their number, it was clear, would be added politically aware and highly militant school-leavers.

These issues, as much as a real technical shortage of skills, have shaped the manner in which the notion of 'skills' has been constructed. They have influenced the nature of some of the courses available in skills training, and have drawn into sharp focus the 'subjectivity' and hence the subjection of workers and students.

State Initiatives in Technical Education:

It might be argued that the extent of skill shortages can be gauged by the extent to which the state is providing technical training and in the greatly expanded role of capital in the provision of education and training at all levels of production. A close link can be drawn between initiatives of the state and capital in education and changes in the labour process which have led to the emergence of a need for a small group of technically qualified workers. Many of the changes in education are in the direction of expanding facilities in technical education.

Indeed, technical education is receiving a great deal of attention. The Department of Education and Training (so-called in 1979 through an Act of Parliament which replaced the Bantu Education Act of 1954 in virtually nothing but name) has, within the past three years in urban areas, assigned a high priority to the provision of technical education for blacks. While this is not an entirely new departure, the scale certainly is.

Until 1980 the majority of technical schools for blacks were in the bantustans. There were 36 for boys and 9 for girls, compared with none in the urban areas. In 1980, South Africa's first black urban technical high school, Jabulani Technical High School, was built. At the end of 1982 a massive programme for transforming existing Bantu Education schools into technical and commercial high schools acting as feeders for technical colleges was introduced. While subjects such as history, a highly contentious subject in black schools, are being phased out in some schools, the rise of technical subjects in many others is noticeable. A National Technical Certificate now also runs alongside the standard Junior Certificate and Matriculation Certificate.

Courses at these technical high schools, designed to train black operatives and provide basic machine-orientation for technicians, include electrical work, motor mechanics, welding and metal work, fitting and machining and other trades. Schools existing specifically for girls provide gender-specific vocational training, preparing them 'for their future task as home-makers and also . . . as workers, particularly in the textile and clothing industries'.[24] In 1981, 197 women students were enrolled in dressmaking, home management and secretarial courses at such schools.[25]

Where the schools do not yet offer technical courses, departmental training centres have been established to 'provide technical orientation to pupils in standards 5-8 as an extension of the normal school programme'.[26] At present there are 14 such centres in urban areas and 16 more are being planned.

The recent growth of technikons for blacks is also a new development. By 1981 there were four in South Africa. It is envisaged that technical workers and black middle management, so-called High Level Manpower, be trained here.[27] Courses are offered in electrical, civil, mechanical and electrical engineering, 'focusing more on the "practical" than the "theoretical" aspects of engineering'. In-service training of already qualified personnel in labour relations is also seen as a vital task of technikons.[28]

Adequate teacher training is also encouraged, but perhaps not being realised, through upgrading black teacher qualifications and through offering new technical teaching diplomas. In 1981 the Department of Education and Training (DET) took 135 male and female primary school teachers, put them through an intensive one-year training course at Soweto's Molapo Technikon and placed them in eleven secondary schools in 1982.[29] The private sector is also engaged in upgrading teacher qualifications. In 1982 the Urban Foundation, for example, built a R4-million Teachers' Centre in Soweto.[30]

It would be folly, however, to see the education system as responding unproblematically to the 'needs of capital'. Its capacity to resolve contradictions stemming from a crisis much deeper than that manifest in education is likely to be limited. In the first place, the training of scientists, technicians and engineers is undertaken in tertiary educational institutions, but access to such education is restricted. Not only are these facilities limited, but they are also racially segregated. While in some cases they are well-equipped many such institutions are notoriously poorly staffed. Selection processes inside and outside of schools also ensure that only about one percent, or less, of the population receive tertiary education. The total enrolment for advanced technical training in 1981 among Africans, for example, was 547 (372 in the first year, 78 in the second, 62 in the third and 35 in the fourth.)[31]

Secondly, unemployment increasingly includes larger numbers

of black school-leavers. After another year of frequent cries for the training of skilled labour, the *Star* newspaper reported at the end of 1982 that 60 000 black matric pupils 'face poor job prospects'.

Thirdly, while student resistance since then has not taken on the dimensions or forms of 1976 and 1980, many of the more pressing grievances they responded to then remain unaddressed even now: overcrowded schools, authoritarian and hierarchical systems of control, mass failures of Junior and Senior Certificate examinees at the end of every school year, unexplained dismissals of 'political' teachers, inadequate curriculums, etc. Continuing student organisation around these areas indicates that, thus far, the state has not made much headway in its aims.

Capital Initiatives in Training:

Far more significant, however, than the DET's involvement is the greater intervention in educational provision by monopoly capital. Education and training have become, within the last ten years, a major private sector undertaking. So important is the range of these initiatives in education that the Anglo American Chairman's Fund was recently called 'South Africa's Other Government'.[32] More money from this fund is ploughed into education than any other areas of its operations which include research, charity, and 'cultural and social development'. According to the same newspaper report, the fund's committee 'considers that shortcomings in black education strain South Africa's social fabric more than any other factor'.

Unable, in part due to its fiscal crisis, and perhaps unwilling to provide the necessary educational facilities, though having an interest in the ideological control of workers, the state offers tax rebates to employers to undertake training programmes. The importance of this socialisation for the state is indicated by the fact that training tax concessions are costing the country between R100-150 million per annum.[33] Although mining capital is excluded from tax concessions on training, its programmes cost millions, and include literacy and numeracy training generally not undertaken by other sectors since these are not tax-deductible. In taking over a domain that traditionally belongs to the state, intervention by capital represents an entirely new phenomenon in South African educational history.

Kallaway[34] has indicated three forms that private sector involvement in education have taken. Firstly, there are those educational projects established and administered by independent trusts. These are initiated or directly assisted by private enterprise, in particular the large multi-nationals or mining groups or they are funded through the 'home' governments of those multi-nationals, eg USA, West Germany, Switzerland, United Kingdom. These programmes usually involve upgrading of various kinds, training in semi-skilled work, bursaries for blacks to study overseas, and the funding of commercial schools such as PACE College in Soweto. The pupose, as expressed by PACE's vice-principal, poet Oswald Mtshali, 'is the creation of a highly qualified, motivated and employable student'.[35]

The second kind of private sector involvement which Kallaway identified is represented by joint ventures with the DET. These include the running of technical high schools and teacher training colleges. Private enterprise usually provides the funds for buildings and equipment; the DET provides the staffing and often the curriculums, as at the Soweto Teachers' Training College, opened in 1980.

The third form is that of in-service training. These usually involve schools in border industry areas, private in-service industrial training schemes and public in-service industrial training centres. Here the DET provides financial aid and tax concessions of various kinds, while the industrialists provide the buildings, equipment and material.

Restrictions on in-service training of black workers have also been eased quite considerably. Starting from about 1971, barriers to apprenticeship of 'coloureds' and Asians were lifted and training opportunities for all blacks became marginally more available. In 1973 the government started establishing pre-service and in-service industrial training centres in urban African residential areas. By 1977/78 pre-service industrial centres were in operation providing more than 7 000 students with basic manual skills in woodwork, metalwork, welding and other trades. By early 1977/78 in-service training centres had also come into operation and had trained 1 622 workers. In addition, there were 20 registered private ad hoc border industry schools for the training of factory operators.[36] In 1979 the Wiehahn Commission of Inquiry into Labour recommended that restrictions on apprenticeship training for blacks be lifted. This recommendation was accepted by the government.

Although the number of black apprentices remains miniscule,[37] the present scale of in-service training of black workers can be assessed by the fact that 150 000 workers had been 'trained' through 3 722 'approved' in-house courses run by small and large . firms during the first nine months of 1982. Besides schemes run by employers for their own needs, private in-service training centres to which several employers send trainees ran 1 522 courses for more than 77 000 workers in 1982.[38]

This quantitative increase in training facilities for black workers in South Africa is matched by an emphasis on the training of blacks at all levels in industry. A survey undertaken by the University of the Witwatersrand's Division of Adult Education in 1982 revealed that the mining industry, the chemical, clothing, furniture, timber, paper, iron and steel industries and the Chamber of Commerce were engaged in training blacks at all levels. The survey showed a general pattern of in-service training for management, supervisors, technical and artisanal workers and operatives. Apart from courses designed for each category there are also 'specialist' courses. For example, Anglo American trains black workers for blasting certificates; other specialist courses include adult basic education in literacy and numeracy and industrial relations training.

Given this staggering quantitative increase and expansion of technical and on-the-job training and the greater intervention into education by the state and capital, it would appear that the skills shortage is confined to technical skills.

A closer examination will reveal, however, that the 'skills' demanded by employers and the state are defined in terms of social dispositions as much as in terms of technical competence. The Wits survey cited earlier has indicated that industry sees a range of objectives being fulfilled by training. Most frequently cited were the need 'to improve productivity', 'to develop social skills especially in areas of communication', 'to assist in training personnel to perform better and to develop to fill higher positions'.

The importance of characteristics other than technical skills and qualifications was highlighted by the National Manpower Commission (NMC) on High Level Manpower (HLM), 1980. Citing research by the Human Sciences Research Council, the NMC noted that

the HLM of the country should not only have enough qualifications and knowledge, but should combine these with certain important personality traits such as a sense of responsibility, enthusiasm, initiative, tenacity and especially boldness.[39]

The NMC stresses that this area suffers from a 'quality deficiency' and not a 'qualification deficiency', and that this 'leader group should be strengthened by training developments.'[40]

Recruiting blacks into management thus relies on their socialisation into leadership positions. The report continued:

> Economic development in an economically under-developed community awaits the emergence of NEW MEN [sic] of bold imagination and energy who have graduated out of their traditional society and are imbued with a spirit of enterprise, which they wish to apply in the economic field, preferably to build economic empires. For the rest, these men will have a strong urge to achieve, will work harder and learn faster than other people and are prepared to take risks.[41]

It is this 'leader group's' internalisation of the values, the principles and practices of 'free enterprise' that is the greatest concern here. It is a far cry from the conceptions which underlay Verwoerdian discourse in the 1950s and 1960s when it was argued that 'there is no place for him (the black) in the European community above the level of certain forms of labour'.[42]

The strategic necessity for a class of black middlemen in industrial relations was emphasised at the Technical and Vocational Education Conference by the Timber Manpower Services Representative:

> What we need is the appointment of educated and experienced blacks in management positions. They should be in a position to communicate with black workers — not only to convey the policy of management to them, but also to convey the attitudes, opinions and feelings of black workers to management.[43]

Identification with the aims of management — whatever these might be — and a commitment to resolving issues by negotiation rather than strikes or work-stoppages are required. The comment reveals two important points. The first is the clear evidence of a 'breakdown in communication' between management and workers or, more directly, of increased management-worker conflict and heightened worker consciousness. The second is the manner in which management is attempting to regulate this conflict. By introducing blacks to personnel management and supervisory positions in order to 'monitor' workers, elements of black nationalist ideology are exploited and utilised in attempting to neutralise worker discontent. At the same time greater class differentiation amongst blacks is promoted.

That partially politicised blacks ('educated and experienced') are appointed to such positions is also perhaps not accidental. It is these who need to be 'won over' to 'free enterprise' and whose insights into worker grievances are often perceived as more telling than those whose subjugation to, or identification with, management is complete.

The research capacities of a range of companies and consortiums have been harnessed to develop courses inculcating capitalist principles and values. The National Institute for Personnel Research of the Council for Scientific and Industrial Research has developed a particularly interesting and highly popular programme for supervisors and overseers called the '6M Simulation Training Course'. The 6Ms are: men, money, machines, materials, management, markets. According to Rautenbach, writing for the de Lange report,

> it uses models and artificial money to stimulate in a concrete way the establishment and operation of a business in a free enterprise system. Its purpose is to give black overseers a concrete insight into the working of a component of a private enterprise system they are working in, since this experience and knowledge are not yet part of their culture or school curriculum.[44]

Courses such as these are clearly linked to the overall strategy of ideological incorporation. Others, such as those run by the Manpower and Management Foundation of South Africa (MMF), can be seen in a similar way.

The MMF runs about 50 courses covering supervisory and industrial relations, instructional training, communication and management skills. The latter include 'Functions of the Supervisor' and 'Understanding and Motivating the Black Worker'. The significance of these courses and subjects, in terms of the argument of this article, is that the 'skills' that are taught are far from neutral. This contrasts quite sharply with the images conjured up by the 'noise' of a skills shortage. The latter, and the way in which skills are dealt with by Davies and by Sharp and Hartwig, imply that the skills being taught and learnt are purely technical. In practice, however, as can be seen from the above examples, the 'skills' that are being trained also amount to political dispositions. Certain forms of skills training are thus doing little more than socialising blacks with values which schools are patently failing to instil.

As far as operatives and technical industrial workers are concerned, it appears that curriculums are being designed to produce technically skilled workers who are simultaneously 'stable' and 'flexible'. 'Basic vocational skills' are provided for in the 'basic' phase of education defined by de Lange as the necessary period of schooling for potential workers. These skills would include literacy, numeracy and basic technical/vocational skills which can be extended outside schools through vocational education. Technical vocational skills are seen to replace the training in manual work in Bantu Education syllabuses. Further machine-orientations are provided either in vocational schools (technical schools or technical centres) or in in-service technical training where, as mentioned above, skills such as welding and metal work, fitting and machining and electrical work, motor mechanics and repair work are taught. The 'career code' imbuing this form of training differs markedly from that for the 'NEW MEN'. Here the classic values of 'diligence, accuracy, punctuality, etc' — the values by which work-discipline is engendered — become applicable.[45]

No wider education is provided. No overall understanding of the work to be done, the industry of which it is a product, the society of which it is a part, is developed — whether this be 'capitalist' in orientation or not. The skills that are taught here are narrow and limited to enabling the worker to relearn skills or competencies associated with maintaining machines. Thus a semi-skilled or skilled 'flexible' worker is trained.

What emerges quite clearly from the above is that the skills that are demanded are not technical alone. What employers seem to be demanding and training, by contrast, can in practice be defined in terms of the long-term needs of capital as a whole, reflecting and repeating a pattern occurring in advanced capitalist social formations elsewhere.[46] Training is directed at the creation, on the one hand, of a workforce committed to 'free enterprise' and, on the other, one that is both technically and professionally skilled and flexible, motivated and habituated to the machine. In short, it appears that what Frith has written for the English context is equally germane in South Africa.

> Employers are looking for a quality of 'steadiness' that is not the same thing as skill but may be achieved by a process of 'training'. There has always been evidence that jobs with training made for more stable workers than jobs without and it now seems that employers are 'skilling' jobs, adding 'training' programmes as a form of work-discipline.[47]

The attempt to wed workers to the 'free enterprise' system in a disciplined fashion occurs through both the form and content of training. However, it goes deeper than this. By means of the Adopt-A-School Programme launched in mid-1982 through the *Star* newspaper, various companies and other interested bodies have been encouraged to project themselves as foster parents. By the beginning of September 1982, twenty schools in Soweto had been 'adopted', and a few had been taken up in the rural areas. 'Foster companies' involve themselves by funding, repairing buildings, providing libraries; in short, by becoming an active presence in the school. A *Star* editorial noted that:

The programme is not just one of signing cheques. It is involvement and caring. It is also caring and concern. It is not paternalism, but vital partnership.[48]

The purpose of the project, it was claimed, is to develop 'aggressive moderation':

We hope that it will become a campaign for upgrading the entire quality of life, for creating just that opportunity on which our future security and well-being depends.[49]

There is a recommendation by the Technical and Vocational Education Subcommittee of the HSRC Commission of Inquiry into education which sounds remarkably similar to this project:

The most practical solution (to the expense by the state of training skilled workers) appears to be the establishment of a private educational organisation(s) . . . . The purpose of this body would be to funnel the contributions from industry to establish 'model' vocational schools in different communities who want these schools. The schools would be planned to meet the urgent needs of industry.[50]

Thus capital comes to be perceived as a beneficient agency, not antagonistic to the needs of the people; schools are tied more closely to the interest of particular industries, and the process of co-option is begun.

Worker on-the-job training plays much the same role. Even when it is not 'industrial relations' per se that is taught, but, for example, grading systems and how they should be evaluated, workers are 'involved' with a management hierarchical ethos.

While these efforts represent an outcome and partial resolution of the conflicts of the 1970s, they do not, however, represent an overhaul of the education apparatus nor do they signify that the battle for the 'hearts and minds' of the people, whether they be 'target groups' or not, has been won. Educational reform always takes place within a given balance of class and national forces and constantly shifting class alliances. In South Africa new state-capital projects which propose strategies for the incorporation and stabilisation of specific sectors of the black community represent a major challenge to the class alliance which has historically constituted the National Party since 1948. In particular, both the white working class and sections of the petty bourgeoisie appear to be re-aligning in the face of what is considered to be an attack on their interests.

The effects of a combined strategy by the state and capital to train blacks for 'skilled' positions do represent a major attack on white working class organisation which has managed to secure and define for itself certain areas of competence-knowledge. The white working class, holding a monopoly of skills which has gradually been eroded by fragmentation and the introduction of blacks to new positions at reduced wage rates, has responded in different ways. Webster has shown how three engineering unions in the metal industry have opened their membership to Africans. The organisation of black workers has thus been an outcome to some extent of restructuring of the racial division of labour. On the other hand there has been a significant shift of white working class support to the Conservative Party and Herstigte Nasionale Party opposing the National Party on the grounds of its 'liberalism'.

Equally important is the response of the petit bourgeoisie, especially teachers and academics. One section appears to be particularly threatened by loss of control over the educational apparatus. This was most clearly demonstrated during 1982 at the Afrikaner *Volkskongres* on education. Organised by Afrikaner clergy and academics, it provided a forum for the response of the Afrikaans 'new' petty bourgeoisie to the reforms proposed by de Lange. The rhetoric of the *kongres* clearly rejected proposed changes and reasserted a Christian National Education discourse over that of the modernising de Lange report. Nonetheless, significant proposals were passed which indicated acceptance. This appears to have been the result of sophisticated stage-management by the organisers of the conference, for shortly thereafter some Afrikaans teachers began to organise an alternative power base through the Christian National Parent Teacher Association.[51]

On the other hand, English-speaking teacher organisations have accepted de Lange's proposals, while the non-racial National Education Union of South Africa (NEUSA), formed in 1980, has not only rejected it but has also begun to organise teachers around conditions of work and the need for 'a democratic education in a democratic South Africa'. The position of official black teacher organisations has been unclear. While some officials participated in and welcomed the recommendations of the HSRC Inquiry, they continue to voice opposition to apartheid and the inequality of opportunities between black and white. Student organisations, on the other hand, have seen de Lange as part of the current dispensation, as a mixed package of reform and repression, and as not substantially removing any of the causes of inequality in South African education.

Clearly an analysis and description of the purposes of ruling class strategies in education can give no indication of their out-comes. Indeed, these are mediated by a host of other factors.

As far as schools are concerned, some of these have been suggested, although by no means all. Where factories are concerned the success of management training programmes is often mediated by the strength of independent unions in particular areas. Where these unions are active, they have initiated education programmes with purposes often diametrically opposed to those of management. Where unions are strong, it also appears that they regard management training programmes with caution and sometimes suspicion. Similarly, the existence of popular oppositional ideologies within black communities could act as a counter-weight to the attempts of employers to win their allegiance.

Conclusion

Reform in education is a crucial means of winning the 'hearts and minds' of blacks. Through it, limited upward mobility, facilitated by the restructuring of the racial division of labour, comes to be seen as a possibility, if not a reality. Through the same process, belief in the apparent benefits of 'free enterprise' is fostered. Failure to succeed in such a system, where education and training are made available to worker and personnel manager alike, must be seen to lie in the individual and not the system. Expanding educational provision and promoting an awareness of the extent of new initiatives in education is vital in pulling the carpet from under the feet of opponents whose critique of apartheid rests on its denial of equal opportunities alone, and especially of education as a means of achieving these. The old shibboleth of the incompatibility of capitalism and apartheid is perpetuated.

The skills shortage, irrespective of whether there is an actual shortage or not, plays a powerful part in negotiating the discourse of legitimation. It appears to be used as a rationale for bringing about changes which cannot be brought about directly since various class interests are thereby threatened. These changes are nevertheless essential in securing the support of certain categories of blacks and in legitimating continued exploitation of workers, albeit under different conditions. They partly involve the recruitment through education and training into management and middle level supervisory, technical and maintenance jobs of small numbers of blacks and the training of technical industrial workers into work-discipline. Inequality at the workplace and outside remains, as does inequality in both the provision and access to schooling of different classes and races. An egalitarian appearance, however, is created through an emphasis on quantitative changes, apparently necessitated by skill shortages.

The skills shortage is thus partly a metaphor through which consent to restructuring is won. It is part of a sophisticated attempt to negotiate a new 'common sense' about education, one which renders obsolete the discourse of Bantu Education and makes possible the ideological incorporation of sectors of the black population. It is used to rally all forces, right and left, to the 'national interest' which is, again, support for 'free enterprise' as against those who attempt to 'destroy' it.

It has also been suggested that while a link can be made between the need by capital for a technically qualified stratum of workers and new initiatives in education, there is also an ideological dimension to the skills apparently required. An essential component of the 'skill' which capital is demanding is social and ideological. The purpose appears to be as much to intensify ideological controls over workers and wed them more firmly to capitalist values as to provide for South Africa's manpower needs.

It has also been argued that while there might be specific needs of capital which can be fulfilled by education (that there is a relationship between the needs of capital and the state and education) these are not translated automatically or unproblematically. Neither are the outcomes or purposes of education and training programmes guaranteed or predictable. These are mediated by too many factors specific and internal to education as well as factors outside it for this to be so.

An explanation which attempts to understand restructuring in South African education through recourse to a simple understanding of skill shortages fails to come to grips with the challenge posed to capital by workers and students, specifically during the 1970s. In particular, technicist interpretations underestimate ways in which the political and ideological conditions necessary for continued capital accumulation are reconstituted along with economic and political reforms; in short, how processes of legitimation for altered conditions of exploitation change, and how this renegotiated legitimation takes place and is modified in the context of already existing class and national struggles.

For an elaboration of some of the issues dealt with in this article, see the chapter by Chisholm, Linda and Pam Christie in SARS (eds), *South African Review 1*: (Ravan Press, Johannesburg 1983).
My thanks to Kelwyn Sole, Joe Muller and especially Pam Christie for reading and commenting on the numerous drafts preceding this article.

FOOTNOTES

1. See Buckland, P 'Technicism and de Lange: Reflections on the Process of the HSRC Investigation', and Chisholm, Linda 'Training for Capital: the de Lange Report', *Perspectives in Education*, May, 1982. Special Issue on The HSRC Education Report (the Buckland article is also reproduced above); Kallaway, Peter (1983) (above), see also the paper by Davies in this volume; National Education Union of South Africa (NEUSA) *De Lange: Marching to the Same Order* (Johannesburg, 1982).

2. In particular, the response of the Afrikaans community through the *Volkskongres* is analysed by Joe Muller, 'How a Community Responds: De Lange and the Afrikaner *Volkskongres*', *Perspectives in Education* May 1982. Special Issue, The HSRC Education Report; the response of English-speaking liberal capital and allied teacher organisations with official representation can be found in *The de Lange Report: Assessment and Implementation: The Future of Education in South Africa.* Proceedings of the National Education Conference, Grahamstown, 1820 Foundation (4-6 February 1982).

3. South African Institute of Race Relations (SAIRR) *Annual Survey*, 1982 (Johannesburg, 1981) p 73-74.

4. *Ibid*, p 183.

5. Saul, J S and S Gelb *The Crisis in South Africa: Class Defence, Class Revolution* (New York, 1981) p 36, referring to Moss, G, 'Total Strategy' in *Work in Progress* No 11 (Johannesburg, February 1980).

6. Report of the Work Committee: on Technical and Vocational Education Human Sciences Research Council, Investigation into Education (Pretoria, 1981) p 29.

7. *Ibid*, p 95.

8. Saul and Gelb, (1981); Davies, Robert 'Capital Restructuring and the Modification of the Racial Division of Labour in South Africa' in *Journal of Southern African Studies*, 5 (April 1979); Sharp, R and M Hartwig 'The State and the Reproduction of Labour Power in South Africa' (above).

9. Sharp and Hartwig.

10. Davies (1979) p 182.

11. *Ibid*, p 185.

12. Sharp and Hartwig, p 310 above.

13. Davies (1979) p 191.

14. Sharp and Hartwig.

15. See Moos, M 'Government Youth Training Policy and Its Impact on Further Education' Stencilled Occasional Paper, General Series: SP No 57, Centre for Contemporary Cultural Studies, Birmingham, December 1979, for a particularly illuminating analysis of skills and education in England. Also see Centre for Contemporary Cultural

Studies Education Group (1981) *Unpopular Education: Schooling and Social Democracy in England since 1944* (London, 1981).

16.   *Unpopular Education* (1981) p 228.

17.   Bloch, G *A History of Manufacturing in South Africa* (Ravan Press, Johannesburg, forthcoming).

18.   Trapido, Stanley 'South Africa in a Comparative Study of Industrialisation', *Journal of Development Studies*, 7 (3) (1971).

19.   Meth, C 'Trade Unions, Skill Shortages and Private Enterprise', *South African Labour Bulletin*, 5 (3) October, 1979 and Meth, C 'Shortages of Skilled Labour Power and Capital Reconstruction in South Africa' (Unpublished paper, African Studies Institute Seminar, University of the Witwatersrand, 1981).

20.   Webster, E A 'The Labour Process and Forms of Workplace Organisation in South African Foundries' (PhD University of the Witwatersrand, 1983) ch 6, p 199.

21.   *Ibid*, p 210.

22.   Clarke, S, quoted in Legassick, M and D Innes 'Capital Restructuring and Apartheid: A Critique of Constructive Engagement' *African Affairs*, 76 (305) 1977, p 47.

23.   Pamphlet, Committee of 81, Cape Town, 1980.

24.   South African *Official Year Book* (1982), p 675.

25.   SAIRR (1982) *Annual Survey*, p 499.

26.   *Ibid*, p 499.

27.   Meyer, Dr Piet, Director-General of Department of National Education quoted in *The Star*, 5 July 1982.

28.   *Weekend Post*, 22 May 1982.

29.   *The Star*, 25 February 1982; also see Peter Kallaway's introduction where he touches on essentially similar details.

30.   *The Star*, 17 March 1982.

31.   SAIRR, *op cit*, p 500; also see *Unpopular Education*, *op cit*, for discussion of such contradictions in manpower planning and education in England.

32.   *The Star*, 28 October 1982.

33.   *Sunday Times*, Business Times, 17 October 1982.

34.   Kallaway, P (above).

35.   Mtshali, O M 'PACE Commercial College' in Proctor-Sims, R (ed) *Technical and Vocational Education in South Africa*, Proceedings 1981 Conference of Technical and Vocational Education Foundation of South Africa (Johannesburg, 1981) p 140.

36.   Maree, J 'The Dimensions and Causes of Unemployment and Underployment in South Africa' in *South African Labour Bulletin* 4 (4) 1978, p 75.

37.   Meth, C 'Black Advancement: Some Critical Thoughts' in SARS (1983).

38.   Department of Manpower quoted in *The Star*, 22 September 1982.

39.   National Manpower Commission, Report on High Level Manpower,

1980 (2.4).

40. *Ibid,* (2.2).

41. *Ibid,* (2.3.3).

42. House of Assembly, 17 September 1953, *HANSARD* 10 cols 3576/3585; Verwoerd.

43. Proctor-Sims (1981) p 196.

44. Report of the Work Committee: Teaching of the natural sciences, mathematics and technical subjects: Technical and Vocational Education, HSRC investigation into education. (1981) p 14.

45. *Ibid.*

46. This is not completely accidental. De Lange has spent some time in England studying the Manpower Services Commission's training programmes, especially that of Further Education (FE).

47. Frith, S (1978) quoted in *Unpopular Education* (1981) p 234.

48. *The Star,* 2 September 1982.

49. *Ibid.*

50. Technical and Vocational Education, HSRC (1981) p 110.

51. I am grateful to Joe Muller for raising these points.

Part Five: Bibliography:
The Education of Black South Africans
by Peter and Jackie Kallaway

This bibliography is intended as a tool for scholars. It is regretted that it is not more comprehensive, and that the limits of time did not allow for the essential addition of a subject index. A project to produce a more comprehensive bibliography with a subject index is already under way.

This bibliography excludes references to :

- psychological aspects of education, e.g. black vs white intelligence, psychological testing, etc. For references in this area see the excellent bibliography by Andor,L.E., Aptitudes and Abilities of the Black Man in Sub-Saharan Africa 1784-1963, (Johannesburg, NIPR, 1966).

- Syllabi regulations, teaching of specific subjects, booklists, except where they seemed important in the light of our general focus.

- Basutoland/Lesotho, Swaziland, Bechuanaland/Botswana, South West Africa/Namibia, Mozambique/Angola (though in this case there is a good argument for the inclusion of such material, limits of space and time did not make this possible).

Abbreviations :

UB	University of Bophuthatswana	UP	University of Pretoria
UCT	University of Cape Town	U.Potch.	University of Potchefstroom
UDW	University of Durban-Westville	UR	Rhodes University, Grahamstown
UFH	University of Fort Hare		
UN	University of the North - Turfloop	US	University of Stellenbosch
		UT	University of the Transkei
UND	University of Natal - Durban	UW	University of the Witwatersrand
UNISA	University of South Africa		
UNP	University of Natal - Pietermaritzburg	UWC	University of the Western Cape
UOFS	University of the Orange Free State	UZ	University of Zululand - Ngoya

BIBLIOGRAPHIES RELEVANT TO THE STUDY AND RESEARCH
OF EDUCATION IN SOUTH AFRICA

Adler,T. "Select bibliography on South African political economy", in
T. Adler (ed.) Perspectives on South Africa: a collection of
working papers. (Johannesburg, UW, 1977).

Alman,S.B. (compiler). A select bibliography of SA native life and problems:
modern status and conditions, 1964-70. (Cape Town, UCT, 1973). 40p.
(Continuation of Schapera,I., Select Bibliography, (see below)).

Andor,L.E. Aptitudes and Abilities of the Black Man in Sub-Saharan Africa,
1784-1963: an annotated bibliography. (Johannesburg, National
Institute for Personnel Research, SA Council for Scientific and
Industrial Research, 1966) 174p.

Brembeck,C.S. and John,P.K. (compiler). Education in emerging Africa: a
select and annotated bibliography. (College of Education, in
co-operation with Int. programs and African language and area center,
Michigan State Univ. Education in Africa series, 1, 1962).

Brownlee,M. The Lives and Work of South African Missionaries - bibliography
(Cape Town, UCT, 1964) 320p.

Bulletin of the South African Public Library. 1946- (Quarterly).

Bullen,P. (compiler). The education and training of land surveyors: a
bibliography. (Johannesburg, UW, 1968) 16p.

Cape Town - Library of Parliament. Europeans and coloured races. Guide
to publications in the library ... dealing with relations between
Europeans and coloured backward races. (Cape Town, 1927) 36pp.

Coetzee,J. Annotated bibliography of Research in education Part I-IV.
(Pretoria, HSRC, 1970 (parts I & II), Pretoria, HSRC, 1973 (parts III
& IV), Pretoria, HSRC, 1976 (part V). (I & II Ph.D. & D.Eds. 1924-56,
III Ph.D. & D.Eds. 1957-63, IV M.A. 1922-37, V M.A. 1936-1949.)

Coetzee,J.C. (ed.) Onderwys in Suid Afrika. (Pretoria, 1963) Afdeling G.
Onderwys vir Die Blankes, bl.381-451.

Colditz,J.M. (compiler). Educational Planning - A Bibliography with Special
Emphasis on Developing Countries. (Covers period 1970-77 - subject
index, list of authors.) (Bloemfontein, UOFS, 1981) 391p.

Cowie,M.J. "The L.M.S. in South Africa: a bibliography". (Cape Town, UCT,
1969) p.81.

Current Bibliography on African Affairs. (See section on Education.)

Currie,J.C. A bibliography of material published during the period 1946-
1956 on the Indian Question in SA. (Cape Town, UCT, 1957).

Dolan,E.F. (compiler). Higher education in Africa South of the Sahara:
Selected bibliography. 1945-1961. (Washington: Am. Assoc. of
University Women Educational Foundation, 1961.)

Doyle,H.G. Education and its environment in the US and overseas.
(Washington, Int. Co-operation Admin., 1959) -Section on African
Education.

Drake,H. A bibliography of African Education South of the Sahara.
(Aberdeen, Aberdeen Univ. Press, 1942) 97p.

Dubow,R. The status of women in SA: select bibliography. (Cape Town,UCT,1976).

Evalds,U.K. "The 'Bantu Education' system: a bibliographical essay". Current Bibliography on African Affairs 10(3) 1977-78 pp.219-242.

Faerber,D.J. (compiler). The development of educational aids for industrial training of adult Africans; a bibliography. (Johannesburg,UW,1971) 34p.

Freer and Varley. Bibliography of African bibliographies. See Robinson,A.M.L. (ed.) (below).

Giffen,R. (compiler). A select bibliography of SA native life and problems: modern status and conditions 1950-1958. A supplement ... to I. Schapera (see below). (Cape Town, UCT, 1958). 40p.

Ginsberg,E.S. & Schwarts,M. Medical Research on the Bantu in SA 1920-1952 (Cape Town, UCT, 1952)

Greenstein,L.J. (compiler). Education in Natal; a bibliography. (Cape Town, UCT, 1959).

Greshoff,N.M. Some English Writings by South African Bantu. (Cape Town, UCT, 1943, mimeo.)

Greyling,J.J.C. & Miskin,J. Bibliography on Indians in South Africa. (Durban, Institute for Social and Economic Research, Univ. of Durban-Westville, 1976) 51pp.

Hanson,J.W. & Gibson,G.W. African Education and development since 1960. (East Lansing, Michigan State Univ., Inst. for Int. Studies in Education and African Studies Center, 1966) 327p.

Holden,M.A. & Jacoby,A. Supplement to I. Schapera bibliography (see below). (Cape Town, UCT, 1950) 32p.

Journal of Negro Education. Special issue of the Journal of Negro Education (v.3 No.1, 1934) - on the education of under-privileged and subject peoples. (Section on Black Education in SA.)

Kalley,J.A. Bophuthatswana politics and the economy: a select and annotated bibliography. (Johannesburg, SAIRR, 1978). 39p.

Kalley,J.A. The Transkei Region of Southern Africa 1877-1978: An annotated bibliography. (Boston, G.K.Hall & Co. 1980) (First published as : Transkeian bibliography 1945-1946. (Johannesburg, SAIRR, 1976) 67p.)

Kotze,D.A. Bibliography of official publications of the South African homelands. (Pretoria, UNISA, 1979) 80p.

Lewin,E. Select bibliography of recent publications in the Royal Colonial Institute illustrating the relations between European and Coloured races. (London, RCI, 1926). 62p.

Lewin,E. Subject catalogue of the Library of the Royal Empire Soc. Vol. 1. (London, 1930).

Library of Parliament. Annual list of Africana received, 1938-.

Macdonald,A.M. (compiler). A contribution to a bibliography on university apartheid. (Mimeo.) (Cape Town, UCT, 1959). 30p.

Malan,S.I. Union catalogue of theses and dissertations of the SA universities 1942-48. (Potchefstroom,U.Potch.,1959) (Annual supps.)

Marais,J.M. European Education in South Africa 1946-1955 - a select
    bibliography. (Cape Town, UCT, 1956).

Morris,G.R. A bibliography of the Indian in S.A. (Cape Town,UCT,1946).

Muller,C.F.J. & others. A select bibliography of SA history: a guide for
    historical research. (Pretoria 1966. Supp. 1974. Addit. Supps 1-5
    Kleio VI (i) May 1974 - VIII (1 & 2) June 1976).

Muller,C.F.J. & others (eds.) South African history and histories: a
    bibliography. (Pretoria, UNISA, 1979) (Documenta 21).

Musiker,R. & N. Guide to Cape of Good Hope official publications:
    1854-1910. (Boston, G.K.Hall, 1976). 466p.

Musiker,R. South Africa bibliographies: a survey of bibliographies and
    bibliographical works: supplement 1970-1976. (Johannesburg,UW,1977) 34p.

Newenham,E.A. A bibliography of printed catalogues of the libraries of
    Southern Africa: 1820-1920 (Johannesburg, 1967).

Nussbaum,M. A select bibliography for literacy teachers. (Hartford Kennedy
    School of Missions. Hartford Seminary Found. 1958) Special reference
    to Africa.

Parker,F. (compiler). African education: a bibliography of 121 USA
    doctoral dissertations,etc. (Washington D.C., WCTOP, 1965).

Pollak,O.B. & Pollak,K. Theses and Dissertations on Southern Africa: An
    International Bibliography. (Boston, Mass., G.K.Hall & Co. 1976) pp.236.

Potgieter,L. (compiler). A bibliography of Bantu education in the Union of
    South Africa: 1949-59. (Cape Town, UCT, 1959) 24p.

Potgieter,P.J.J.S. Index to literature on race relations in South Africa,
    1910-1955. (Boston, G.K.Hall, 1979) 555p.

"Reports and documents of the Special Committee against Apartheid, April,
    1963-Dec.1975". Notes and Documents,(special issue) June 1976, 46p.

Roberts,E.S. A bibliography of the South African College 1829-1918.
    (Cape Town, UCT, 1947).

Robins,C. A bibliography of African Education 1941-1949. (Cape Town,
    UCT, 1951) 17p.

Robinson,A.M.L. (ed.) Catalogue of theses and dissertations accepted for
    degrees by SA universities 1918-1941. (Cape Town, UCT, 1943).

Robinson,A.M.L. (ed.) A bibliography of African bibliographies covering
    territories south of the Sahara. Comp. by P.Freer and D.H.Varley,
    4th rev. ed. (Cape Town, 1961).

Rodger,D.J. (compiler). The University College of Fort Hare 1905-1959.
    (Cape Town, UCT, 1960). 27p.

Rousseau,M.H. (compiler). A bibliography of African education in the
    Federation of Rhodesia and Nyasaland,1890-1958. (Cape Town,UCT,1958)35p.

SAIRR (Jan H. Hofmeyr Library). A select bibliography on education in SA:
    (as at July, 1970). (Johannesburg, SAIRR, 1970).

SAIRR, (Jan H. Hofmeyr Library). A select list on education in SA.
(Jan. 1976 - June 1978). (Johannesburg, SAIRR, 1978)

SAIRR. 1. Bibliography of Education (as at 31st March, 1981).
(Johannesburg, SAIRR, 1981).

Sales,D. The African homelands of South Africa, July 1975 - June 1978:
A supplementary list of the material held by the Jan. H. Hofmeyr
Library, SAIRR. (Johannesburg, SAIRR, 1978). 21p.

SANB: (South African national bibliography)-Quarterly with annual cumulation.

Schapera,I. (compiler). Select bibliography of SA native life and problems:
compiled for the Inter University Committee for African Studies.
(London, OUP, 1941) 249p. (Reprint 1969).

Scheven,Y. (compiler). Bibliographies for African Studies 1976-1979.
(Massachusetts: African Studies Assn., 1980).

Schmidt,N.J. Children's Books on Africa: and their authors: an annotated
bibliography. (New·York and London - Africana Pub. Co., 1975)
(and supplementary volume published 1979).

Scholtz,P.L., Bredekamp,H.C. & Hesse,H.F. A select bibliography on race
relations at the Cape 1652-1795: a guide for historical research.
(Bellville, UWC, 1976) 132p.

Scott,P.E. List of South African official commissions 1910-1973.
(Pretoria, Division of Library Services, 1979).

Shandling,E.R. Vocational Guidance in SA 1920-1965. (Cape Town,UCT,1967).

Smith,A.H. (ed.) Catalogue of Bantu, Khoisan and Malagasy in the Strange
Collection of Africana. (Johannesburg, JPL, 1942). 232p.

Solomon,C. (compiler). A select bibliography of SA native life and problems:
1958-63: a supplement to I.Schapera (see above). (Cape Town, UCT,
1963) 51p. typescript.

State Library. SA Nat. Bibliography: publications received in terms of
Copyright Act No. 9 of 1916. Continuation of 1938-1958. Copyright
additions 1959-.

Taylor,C.J. Coloured Education: a bibliography. (Cape Town, UCT, 1966/70)

US Education Bureau of: The education of native and minority groups: a
bibliog. 1923-32, by K.M. Cook and F.E. Reynolds. (Washington,
Govt. Pr. Off., 1933). Africa p. 7-10.

Wessels,E. Education in Africa: Works available in the Africa Institute
reference library. (Pretoria, Africa Institute, 1980). 46p.

Willetts,R.J. The Urbanization of the Native in South Africa 1910-1952.
(Cape Town, UCT, 1952) pp.44.

Work,M.N. Bibliography of the negro in Africa and America. (New York,1928).

GENERAL BIBLIOGRAPHY

A.,T. "Making of a chief", SA Outlook, 74: S. 1944, p.122-24.

Abraham,J.H. "What real education means", Bantu Education J., 12(9): Nov. 1966, p.34-7.

Adam,H. Modernizing Racial Domination (Berkley, 1971).

Adam,H. (ed.) South Africa: Sociological Perspectives (London, 1971).

Adam,H. "The rise of Black Consciousness in South Africa", Race XV(2), Oct. 1973, p. 149-65.

Adam,K. "Dialectic of Higher Education for the Colonized: The Case of Non-White Universities in SA", in Adam,H. (ed.) South Africa: Sociological Perspective (London, 1971).

Adler,T. "Bantu Education - a socialization machine" FUNDA 3(1) 1974 p.1-13.

Africa Bureau. Education for Africans in South Africa (Fact sheet No. 10) (Pretoria, 1971).

African Education Commission (1st) - 1920-21. Education in Africa: a study of West, South and Equatorial Africa ... under the auspices of the Phelps-Stokes fund and Foreign Mission Societies of North America and Europe. (New York, Phelps-Stokes Fund, 1922).

African Education Commission (2nd) 1923-24. Education in East Africa - Report prepared by Thomas Jesse Jones (London, 1925), (p.268-283 - Basutoland, Swaziland; p.82-83 Union of South Africa).

African Township Committee. Memorandum on Recreational and Educational Requirements of the Africans of Johannesburg. (Johannesburg,SAIRR,1941).

Aitken,R.P. 'Who is my Neighbour?' (The story of a mission hospital in SA - Donald Fraser Hospital in N. Tvl.) (pam. Lovedale, 1944). Ch. Xiii 'Teachers and Scholars'.

Aldham and Aldham. Lovedale Missionary institution, S.A., photographic views by Aldham and Aldham (Grahamstown, Lovedale, 1884).

Alexander,F. "Australians and Academic Apartheid in South Africa", Australian Quarterly, 29(4) 1957, pp.41-50.

Amor,A. "What the church has done for native education". (no place & date of publication).

Anthony,A. "Indian education in the Province of the Transvaal", mimeo (Johannesburg, SAIRR, 1961).

Arendse,A.J. "Die 'Tergende Onsekerheid': Sal daar vir my kind plek wees by die skool?", Alpha 16(9 and 10), Nov.-Dec. 1978, p.3-6.

Arnett,P.M. "The schooling facilities of the Ndabakazi Location, Butterworth District, Transkei". National Union of South African Students Research Journal, 1951 p.21-25.

Arnold,N. "Die Christelik-nationale onderwysbeweging in S.A. gedurende die tydperk 1907-1920" (M.Ed., U.Potch, 1954) 150p.

Ashby,E. Apartheid in the South African Universities (Congress for Cultural Freedom, 1959).

Ashby,E. & Anderson,M. Universities, BS, Indian, African: A Study in the ecology of higher education (London, 1966) biblio. p.527-540.

Ashley,M.J. "Education and Attitudes in South Africa". Journal of Education 2(1) 1970 pp.25-36.

Ashley,M.J. "Education for White Elites in SA", Comp. Educ. 7: Ag.1971, (bibliog.) p.32-45.

Ashley,M.J. "African education and society in the 19th Century Eastern Cape" in C. Saunders and R. Derricount (ed.) Beyond the Cape Frontier (London, 1974) pp.119-211.

Ashley,M.J. "The Features of Modernity: Missionaries and Education in South Africa 1850-1900", Journal of Theology for Southern Africa 38 (March 1982) pp.49-58.

Ashley,M.J. "Universities in collision: Xhosa, Missionaries and Education in 19th Century South Africa", Journal of Theology for Southern Africa 32 (Sept. 1980) pp.28-38.

Association of European Teachers in Native Educational Institutions. Annual conference, Umtata, 1925. Annual conference of European Teachers in Native Educational Institutions, Umtata, June 22nd to 24th, 1925. (East London, 1925) 7p.

Atkins,W.C. 'The Cash value of native education'. SA Outlook, 54: S. 1924, p.200-203 or S.A. Jour. Sci. 20 (1923) pp.527-540.

Atkinson,N. Teaching South Africans: A History of Educational Policy in SA. (Salisbury, 1978).

Atkinson,T. 'Industrial Training' SA Outlook 69: (1939), p.64-67.

Auerbach,F.E. "Come to visit Mayibuye" (Night school for adult natives) Tvl. Educ. News. 46(9) Oct. 1950 Illus. p.19.

Auerbach,F.E. The Power of Prejudice in SA education. (Cape Town, 1966).

Auerbach,F.E. Race, Prejudice and Education (Johannesburg, SAIRR, 1968).

Auerbach,F.E. Freedom and authority in education: talk given in "Our Western Heritage" series (Johannesburg, SAIRR, 1968).

Auerbach,F.E. School curricula in relation to community needs, etc. (Johannesburg, SAIRR, 1969).

Auerbach,F.E. 'Three Million are Illiterate", Race Relations News 32(10), 1970, p.1.

Auerbach,F.E. "How many young Africans are literate" Tvl. Educ. News 57(4), Ap. 1970, bibl. p.11-12.

Auerbach,F.E. "Bantoe-onderwys in S.A." Buurman 3(1): S.1972 port p.6-7.

Auerbach,F.E. Education 1961-1971: a balance sheet (Johannesburg SAIRR,1972).

Auerbach,F.E. The Spro-cas education report: one year later, etc. (Johannesburg, Christian Inst. of Southern Africa, 1972).

Auerbach,F.E. "South African school enrolment patterns (1920-1970) and problems of early leaving in African, Coloured and Indian Schools", (Ph.D. UNP 1977) 233p. biblio.

Auerbach,F.E. 'Discrimination in Education' (Cape Town, 1978) 26p.

Auerbach,F, & Welsh,D. "Education" in Sheila van der Horst (ed.) A review of Race Discrimination in South Africa. (Cape Town, 1981) pp.66-89.

Back,T. Recent progress of education in the Union of South Africa (Washington, Dept. of the Interior Bureau of Education, Govt. Print. off. bulletin No. 49, 1919).

Badenhorst,D.C. "Some thoughts on the curriculum for the training of black teachers, part I." Paidonomia 5(1) 1977, p.17-22.

Badenhorst,D.C. Die Opleiding van Onderwysers vir ontwikkelende volke. Deel II: Die Kurrikulum van die skool in kultuurperspektief. J. of Racial Affairs 28(3) 1977, p.89-100.

Badenhorst,D.C. 'Die opleiding van onderwysers vir 'n ontwikkelende gemeenskap', (Deel III, Die Onderwyser in kultuur-perspektief) J. of Racial Affairs 28(4) Oct. 1977, p.137-44.

Baer,G.F. "Crux of native education". Tvl.Educ.News 41(3): Mr.1945, p.12+.

Baer,G.F.A. "Some problems in the education of the Mpondo", (M.Ed. UW, 1946)

Ballinger,M. "Some problems of the control of native education", Tvl. Educ.News, 35 (4) 1939 p.15-17.

Ballinger,M. "Mass illiteracy and our industrial future", S.Afr. Industr. & Trade 42(7) Ap.1946, p.85+.

Ballinger,M. From Union to Apartheid (New York, 1969) Part III, Ch.II - "Cultural Apartheid: Educational Insulation".

Bantu Education, Dept. of. Annual Reports and 'Bantu Education' etc. see also periodicals.

Bantu Education Journal or Educamus (see various).

Bantu Education. "Policy for the Immediate Future". (Statement by Hon.H.F. Verwoerd, Dept. of Native Affairs, Pub. 1954).

Bantu Education: Oppression or Opportunity? (Pretoria, SABRA, 1955).

Bantu Education Dept./SA Government. Education for Success. (SA Embassy/ Official Pub. Pretoria, 1965).

Bantu Education Dept. Education and Careers for the Bantu People in the RSA 1972/3. (Johannesburg) Also called 'Bantu Education in RSA'. Also First edition: 1969/70, 2nd edition 1971, 3rd edition 1972-3.

Bantu - European Student Christian Conf. "A report ... Christian Students and modern S. Afr." (Fort Hare, 1930).

Bantu Juvenile Delinquency Conf., Findings of: SA Outlook LXVIII 1938 p.266-71.

Bantu Schools for Tomorrow, Handbook for Student Teachers. (No author given). (Cape Town, 1950).

Bantu Youth League. Constitution and suggested activities of the Bantu Youth League. (In Zulu and English) (Durban, no date). 8p.

Bantu Welfare Trust. Annual Report 1936-7.

Barnett,P.A. "Problems and perils of education in SA." Paper read to meeting of the Royal Colonial Institute - on Tuesday, Feb. 14th, 1905. Proceedings of the RCI,... 36, 1904-5. (London, 1905) p.130-155.

Barton.F, 'The school that wouldn't die.' Drum 135, June 1952, p.55-59.

Basson,M.A. "Die Britse invloed in die Transvaal se onderwys 1836-1907". Archives Year Book, 19, II, 1956.

Batson,H.E. A Socio-Educational Survey of School-Going Coloured Children in the Cape Province. (Reprinted from the Report of the Coloured Educ. Comm., 1956) (Cape Town, 1957).

Baudert,S. "Die Kaffernschuler d Hernhuter Mission", Evang.Miss.Mag., 1930, p.201-7.

Bavinck,J.H. "Probleem van het Bantoeonderwijs", Koers, 21: 0.1953 p.90-95.

Beard,P.N.G. & Morrow,W.E. (eds.) Problems of Pedagogics: Pedagogics and the Study of education in South Africa. (Durban, 1981).

Beard,T.V.R. 'Background to student activities at the University College of Fort Hare' in H.W. van der Merwe and D. Welsh (eds.) Student Perspectives on South Africa. (Cape Town, 1972).

Behr,A.L. Three Centuries of Coloured Education: Historical and Comparative Studies of the Education of the Coloured People in the Cape and Transvaal 1652-1952. (Ph.D. thesis, U.Potch, 1952).

Behr,A.L. "Onderwys aan Nie-blankes", J.Chris Coetzee (ed.) Onderwys in Suid Afrika 1652-1956. (Pretoria, 1958).

Behr,A.L. & Macmillan,R.G. Education in South Africa. (Pretoria,1966 & 1971).

Behr,A.L. University Colleges for Non-Whites: retrospect and prospects. (Johannesburg, SAIRR, Memo No. 7/69, 1969).

Behr,A.L. "Some aspects of Education in SA for the 'Seventies with special reference to the Indian Community". (An address delivered to the Stanger Branch of the SAITA on Satuday, 16 May, 1970) (Unpub.).

Behr,A.L. "Historical perspectives to the Education of Indians in South Africa." (Unpubl. Report) (Faculty of Educ., UDW, no date).

Behr,A.L. New Perspectives in South African Education, a blueprint for the last quarter of the 20th century. (Part II - Africans, Coloureds and Indians) (Durban, 1978).

Beit,A. "Education services for Africans", Race Relat.16: 1949, p.26-31.

Bennett,W.H. Education department directory ... 1909 etc. See Natal (Colony) Educ. Dept. Natal (Province) Educ. Dept. (Pietermaritzburg 1909).

Bennie,W.G. "The Education of the Native". S.Afr.Jour.Sc. 21 (1924) pp.108-119.

Bennie,W.G. "A National system of native education: observations on Dr. Loram's paper". S.Afr.Jour.Sc. XXVI, Dec. 1929, p.928-33.

Bennie.W.G. Native education in relation to the franchise ... an address delivered to a public meeting in Cape Town on ... 1 May 1930. (Cape Town, Non-racial franchise association, 1930). 16p.

Bergins,W.J. "Beroepsgerigte en beroepsonderwys as aspekte van die onderwysprogram in die ontwikkelende Kleurlingsgemeenskap: 'n sosiopedagogiese verkenning". (D.Ed. proefskrif, Bellville, UW, 1975).

Berman,E.H. "Education in Africa and America: A History of the Phelps-Stokes Fund, 1911-1945". (Unpub. Ed.D. dissertation, Columbia University, New York, 1970).

Berman,E.H. "American Influence on African Education: The Role of the Phelps-Stokes Fund's Educational Commissions". Comp. Educ. Rev., XV, (2), June 1971.

Berman,E.H. "Tuskegee-In-Africa". J. of Negro Education 41(2) 1972,p.99-112.

Berman,E.H. "African Responses to Christian Mission education". African Studies Review, XVII (3) Dec. 1974, p.527-40; (or in Kellheer,C.M. (ed.) Political Military Systems, (Beverley Hills, 1974) p.527-40).

Berman,E.H. (ed.) African reactions to missionary education (New York'75)p.231.

Berman,M. "The African Education Movement". (Typescripts SOAS Libr). c.1959.

Bernstein,R. "An Inquiry into Literacy among Adult Africans". Race Relations Jour. 10 (3 & 4) 1943.

Berry,L.L. A century of missions of the African Methodist Episcopal Church, 1840-1940. (New York 1942) 400p.

Bester,F.A. "'n Histories-kritiese studie oor die Naturelle- en Kleurling-onderwys in die Oranje Vrystaat". (M.Ed. UNISA 1946) 374pp.

Beyer,G. "Die handarbeitschule in Südafrika: spezial unter den Sotho in Nordwest-Transvaal". Zeit f Ethral 1926. No. 3-4: 249-61.

Beyers,M.S.B. "Onderwys in die Kaapprovinsie gedurende die eerste sewe jaar die bestuur van dr. Thomas Muir as Superintendent-generaal van onderwys, 1892-1899". (M.Ed., US, 1936, 143p. bibliog.)

Biesheuvel,S. African Intelligence (SAIRR, Johannesburg, 1943) 225p. (Originally a Ph.D. Edinburgh, 1943).

Biesheuvel,S. 'The Study of African ability', African Studies, 11(2-3) 1952.

Biesheuvel,S. Personal selection tests for Africans. (Johannesburg, 1952).

Biesheuvel,S. "Race, Culture and Personality". (Johannesburg, SAIRR, Hoernle Mem. Lect., 1959).

Biko,S. I Write What I Like. (London, 1978) 216p.

Bird,W. State of the Cape of Good Hope in 1822. (orig. pub. London, 1923, reprint, Cape Town, 1966) Ch. VIII p.153, 'Education'.

Birley,R. "African Education": a talk given to the Cape Western Region ... (Johannesburg, SAIRR, 1966, RR135/66).

Birley,R. "African Education in SA". African Affairs 67, (267), Ap. 1968, p.152-158.

Black Community Programmes. See Black Review.

Black Review. (Black Community Programmes) (Pub.Durban). 1972, Khoapa,B.A.(ed.) 1973, Gwala,M.P. (ed.), 1974-5 Mbanjiva,Thabo (ed.), 1975-6 Rambally,A.(ed.)

Black Review. 1972 p.16-30 Black Educational and Cultural Groups; p.144-161 Education for Blacks: Primary and Secondary; p.162-168 Education for Blacks: Teacher Training, Vocational and Technical; p.169-180 Education for Blacks: Higher Education; p.181-189 Youth and Student Organizations.

Black Review. 1973 p.51-57 Education for Blacks: Primary and Secondary; p.58-61 Education for Blacks: Teacher Training, Vocational and Technical; p.62-68 Youth and Student Organizations.

Black Review 1974/5. p.140 Education for Blacks: Primary and Secondary;
p.158 Education for Blacks: Teacher Training Vocational and Technical;
p.162 Education for Blacks: Higher Education.

Blamires,N. "South Africa: the Bantu education act, 1953". Int. Rev. of Miss.
44, (173), Jan. 1955. pp.99-101.

Blignaut,S. Statistics on education in South Africa 1968-79. (Johannesburg,
SAIRR, 1981) 90p.

Bloom,L., de Crespigny,A.R.C. & Spence,J.E. "An Interdisciplinary Study of
Social, Moral and Political Attitudes of White and Non-White South
African University Students". Jour. of Social Psychology 54, (1961).

Blume,F. 'The education of Coloured children in the urban area of Kimberley'.
(B.Ed. thesis, UCT, 1942).

Blythswood Missionary Institution. Brochure. Pub. Blythswood Miss. Instit.
(East London, Daily Despatch, 1948).

Bokwe,J.K. Reflections on the Lovedale Jubilee ... (1891). (see Lovedale
Missionary Institute - Appendix to Jubilee Report) (1891).

Boner,K. "The Irish Dominicans and education in the Western Cape (1863-
1892)" (M.A., UNISA, 1976).

Borman,M.M. "Die Opvoedkundige werk en bydrae van dr. Andrew Murray"
(B.Ed., UCT, 1959).

Boshoff,J.Z. "The Universities for Non-Whites". Symposium 1972/73, p.60-62.

Bosman,J.D. "'n Ondersoek na die gesindhede van Transvaalse Kleurlingonderwysers en studente ten opsigte van onderwys en opvoedkundige
vraagstukke". (M.Ed. thesis, UP, 1959).

Bot,A.K. A Century of Education in the Transvaal 1836-1936. (Pretoria,
1936) Ch. XXIII - The Development of Non-European education in the Tvl.

Bot,A.K. The development of education in the Transvaal 1836-1951. (Pretoria,
1951) Ch. 27 - Coloured and Indian Educ. Ch.29 - p.154-171 by
G.H. Franz - the history of Bantu education in the Transvaal.

Botha,M.C. Chairman of: Report of the Coloured Education Commission
1953-1956. (Parow, 1956).

Botha,M.C. "Bantu Education". SA Outlook 96: N. 1966, Abstr. p.175.

Botha,M.C. "Bantoeonderwys". Bantoe-Onderwysbl., 12(9): No. 1967 port. p.8-10.

Botha,M.C. "New structure for Bantu education", Bantu Education J. 18(10):
D. 1972 p.22-3 ... Also in Afrikaans 18(10) D. 1972 p.22-3.

Botha,M.C. 'Compulsory Education for black children' Bantu 24(2) 1977, p.2-3.

Botha,M.C. "Don't be misled by false slogans", Bantu Education J. 24(1):
F. 1978, port. p.22 ... (Also in Afrikaans).

Bothma,J.P. "Die geskiedenis van die onderwys in Griekwaland-Wes 1800-
1940", (D.Ed., US, 1947) 413p. Bibliog. ((non-whites) coloureds,
blacks, Educ. of: p.177-210, p.341-71.)

Bothsabelo Training Institution. Magazines 1938, 1939, 1940, etc.

Boucher,M. "The University of the Cape of Good Hope and the University of
South Africa: 1873-1946". (D.Litt. thesis, UNISA, 1970) in Archives
Yearbook for South African History, 35, v.I (Pretoria 1974) p.332 (1972).

Boucher,M. Spes in arduis: a history of the University of South Africa. (Pretoria, 1973).

Bozzoli,B. The Political Nature of a ruling class: capital and ideology in SA, 1890-1933. (London, 1981).

Bozzoli,G.R. Education is the key to change in South Africa. (Hoernlé Memorial Lecture, 1977) (Johannesburg, SAIRR, 1977) p.14.

Brand,F.J.C. 'Historiese oorsig van die Kleurling - upvoeding aan die Kaap'. (B.Ed. thesis, US, 1921).

Branford,W. "Official languages in the Transkei", Theoria, 21, 0.1963 p.8-21.

Brazelle,R.R. Die onderwysstelsel van Bophuthatswana: 'n situasie- en behoefte bepaling. (Bloemfontein, UOVS, 1978). (M.Ed. diss.).

Brazelle,R.R. et al. Education in Qwaqwa: planning report 1980 (Bloemfontein, UOFS, Research Unit for Education System Planning, 1980).

Brazelle,R.R. The implications of forecasts of primary and secondary school enrolment in Lebowa, 1980-1984 for the provision of teachers and classrooms and for government expenditure. (Bloemfontein, UOFS, Research Unit for Education System Planning, 1980).

Brebner,J. Memoir of the Life and Work of: (Supt. of Educ. in OFS) (Edinburgh, 1903).

Breutz,P.L. "The Social System of the Sotho-Tswana". (Unpub. MSS). (Education, p.85- p.94-115 'Political Educ. - Initiation'.p.120-1,p.193).

Breytenbach,W.J. "Perspective on the new black education policy". Bantu 24(2), 1977, p.1-2.

Brink,C.B. Die finansiering van naturelle-onderwys. (SABRA 5th Congress, 1954, mimeo.).

British Parliamentary Papers. Cape of Good Hope. Further papers relative to the state of the Kaffir tribes ... Despatch from Sir George Grey to the colonial secretary ... 22 November, 1854.

British Parliamentary Papers. Further papers relative to the state of the Kaffir tribes ... Despatch from Lt. Governor Sir George Cathcart to the Duke of Newcastle ... March 14th, 1854.

British Parliamentary Papers. Cape of Good Hope. Further papers relative to the state of the Kaffir tribes ... Governor Sir George Grey's address to the Legislative Council and House of Assembly ... March 1855.

Brock,S. 'James Steward and Lovedale: a Reappraisal of Missionary Attitudes and African Responses in the Eastern Cape, South Africa'. (Ph.D. University of Edinburgh, 1974-5).

Brooks,A. & Brickhill,J. Whirlwind before the Storm: The Origins and development of the uprising in SOWETO and the rest of South Africa from June to December, 1976. (London, 1980).

Brookes,E.H. "The economic aspects of the native problem". S.Afr.J.Sc. 21, 1924, pp.651-663.

Brookes,A.H. The History of Native Policy in SA from 1830 to the present. (Cape Town, 1924). 531p. (Pretoria, 1927) Ch. XX "Education" p.449-481. (originally D. Litt., Pretoria, 1923).

Brookes,E.H. 'Native Education in relation to National Policy'. (British Assn: proceedings of 1929, p.407).

Brookes,E.H. Native education in South Africa. (Pretoria, 1930) 138p.

Brookes,E.H. The Bantu in South African Life. (Johannesburg, SAIRR, 1943), 60p. Education, pp.38-43.

Brookes,E. "Africa on the march: ... revolutionary proposal for Bantu advancement". Forum 7(1): Ap. 1, 1944 port. p.25-26.

Brookes,E. "Progress of the SA native: impressive increases in educational opportunities". Afr. World 16-17, Jul. 1946 illus.

Brookes,E.H. Reprint of Hansard Report of speech by senator Dr. the Hon. E.H. Brookes, in the senate, on the report of the native education commission. (Johannesburg, SAIRR, 1952) (RR.55-52).

Brookes,E.H. and others. 'The idea of Non-European education: A symposium'. Theoria 5 (1953) pp.9-28.

Brookes,E.H. Apartheid: a documentary study of modern South Africa. (London 1968). Part IV: 'Bantu Education', pp.41-60; Part V: 'University Education', pp.61-71.

Bryant,A.T. Roman legion on Libyan fields: or The Story of the Trappist Missionaries among the Zulus in Natal, SA: The establishment of their monestery at Mariannhill and the past and present condition and prosperity of their missions. By Sihlobosami (Pseud.) (Mariannhill, Natal Trappist Abbey, 1887).

Buckland,F.P. 'The Restructuring of Education Policy Discourse: The de Lange, Buthelezi Commission and Syncom Education Reports'. (Mimeo., Education Policy Unit, UCT, 1982).

Buckland,F.P. "Technicism and de Lange: Reflections on the Process of the HSRC Investigation". Perspectives in Education, July 1982.

Bull,O.B. Training Africans for Trades: A report of a visit to the USA and Canada under the auspices of the Carnegie Corp. Visitors' Grants Comm. (Pretoria, The Carnegie Visitors: Grants Committee, 1935) 75p .

Bunting,B. The Rise of the South Africa Reich. (Harmondsworth, 1964). Ch. 11 - 'Indoctrinating the Young', pp.193-222. Ch. 12 - 'The Control of Ideas', pp.223-251.

Bunting,B. Education for Apartheid. (London, 1971) 34p.

Burchell,D.E. "African higher educ. and the establishment of the South African Native College, Fort Hare", S.A.Hist.J. 8, Nov.1976, p.60-83.

Bureau for Economic Research re Bantu Development. Bophuthatswana Economic Revue (Pretoria 1975) (BENBO 2575); Ciskei Economic Revue (Pretoria, 1975) (BENBO 2075); Gazankulu Economic Revue (Pretoria 1976); Kangware Economic Revue (Pretoria 1978); Kwazulu Economic Revue (Pretoria 1978) (BENBO 20375); Lebowa Economic Revue (Pretoria 1976) (BENBO 20675); Qwaqwa Economic Revue (Pretoria 1978); Transkei Economic Revue (BENBO 20175).

Burger,A.J. "Vordering van die Bantoevolke op onderwysgebied en die betekenis daarvan vir die Blankes", T Rasse-Aangeleent, 23: 0. 1972, pp.164-70.

Burger,J. See Leo Marquard.

Burrows,H.S. and others. A Short pictorial history of the U. College of Fort Hare 1916-1959. (Lovedale, 1961).

Buxton,T.F.V. "Education of the African" J.Afr.Soc. (17) 1918 pp.212-22.

C.,D.A. "Problems in the Religious education of Africans". SA Outlook 77, 1947, p.135-137; 157-159.

Calderwood,H. Caffres and Caffre Missions. (London, 1877).

Callinicos,A. "The Soweto Uprising" (Radical Education Dossier, London, Oct. 1976).

Callinicos,A. & Rogers,J. Southern Africa after Soweto. (London 1977).

Calpin,G.H. (ed.) The SA way of life: values and ideals of a multi-racial society. (London 1953). Ch. VII - 'Education in SA' by Dr. O.D. Wollheim.

Cameron,D. "The case for native education", Spectator, 7 Jul. 1939. (Summarised in SA Outlook 69: 1939, p.193-4).

Campbell,L.J. Rambles in South Africa: the Cape, Natal and Transvaal. (London 1891) Ch. XI 'Education in Natal'.

Cape Colony - Official. (Cape - Official. Native Education).

Cape Government Gazettes (Index to): Education.

Cape Colony - Official. Particulars of Missionary Institutions in the Colony (1849).

Cape Colony - Official. Report on Progress of Native Industrial Institutions(1855)

Cape Colony - Official. Report upon the Progress of the Native Industrial Institutions at Lovedale, Salem and Healdtown (G7 - 1856).

Cape Colony - Official. Lovedale Native Industrial Institution G12 - 58 Report, 1857; G10 - 59 Report 1858; G6 -60 Report 1859; G4 - 61 Report 1860; G4 - 62 Report 1862- etc.

Cape Colony - Official. Bishops Court Kafir Ind. Instit. Report (G.15-59).

Cape Colony - Official. Superintendent-General of Education. Annual Reports 1854-, including Inspector's Reports 1873-, (Cape Town, various).

Cape Colony - Official. Church Mission Schools in Kaffraria which receive aid from the Colonial Revenue (G51 - 60).

Cape Colony - Official. Native Industrial Institutions at Salem, Healdtown, Lesseyton and Durban. Report 1859 G5 -60; Report 1860, G9 - 61; Report 1860 G22 - 61; Report 1861 G7 - 62.

Cape Colony - Official. Commission on the Government Education System: Report (Cape Papers) (Cape Town, 1863) (Watermeyer Commission).

Cape Colony - Official. Superintendent-General of Education report on Industrial Schools reserved for aborigines, 1863.

Cape Colony - Official. Report of Superintendent-General of Education on Industrial Institutions and Schools (1864 C).

Cape Colony - Official. Report of Select Committee on Lovedale Institution Bill. (A7 - 1876).

Cape Colony - Official. Education Commission 1877 (de Villiers Commission).

Cape Colony - Official. Report of the Commission appointed to enquire into the working of the Education Acts in force in this ... 1879. (Proceedings, Minutes of Evidence, and Apprentices 1880) (G75 - 1880).

Cape Colony - Official. Ross,D. Prelim. report on the state of education in the colony of the Cape, 71pp. (G12 - 1883) (Cape Town, 1883, Native education p.44-54.)

Cape Colony - Official. Supt. of Education. The Education manual 1883-4, for the guidance of managers and teachers of schools. (34, 5p., Cape Town, 1883) (Another 46pp. Cape Town, 1885).

Cape Colony - Official. Return showing extent to which Natives trained in Industrial Institutions are engaged in Industrial Pursuits amongst their own people or elsewhere (1886 C).

Cape Colony - Official. Nature of Employment after leaving Institutions of Native Pupils (C1 - 1887).

Cape Colony - Official. Education Commission for Cape Colony. 2nd Report, 3rd Report (G3 - '92) (President: Sir Jacob Dirk Barry) (The Barry Report).

Cape Colony - Official. Sir J.J. Juta. Education Acts and the regulations thereunto (Cape Papers) 61pp. 1898.

Cape Colony - Official. Education Act of 1865 and regulations (G97 - 1904).

Cape Colony - Official. S.A. Native Affairs Commission Report (5 vols) (Cape Town, 1906).

Cape Colony - Official. Select Committee on Native Education (A1 - 1908) Report xii + 632 + xxxvi pp. 1908 (Cape Town) 632p.

Cape Province - Official.

Cape Province - Official. Cape Superintendent-General of Education: Annual Reports. 1910 to the present. (Cape Town).

Cape Province - Official. Cape Education Commission 1910-12. (CP - 6 - 1912) (Freemantle Commission) (Cape Times, 1912).

Cape Province - Official. Report of the Commission on Native Education. (CP4 - 1920) (Viljoen Report). (Cape Town, Cape Times, 1920) 48p.

Cape Province - Official (Dept. of Public Education). Educational statistics 1922 - ?, 1923 - 6, 1929 - 30, 1932, 1935, 1938 - 9, etc. (Cape Town).

Cape Province - Official. (Coloured Education Commission) Report of the Commission on Coloured Education, 1925-26. (Cape Province 1 - 1927). (Cape Town, 1927).

Cape Province - Official. Centenary of the Education Dept. Educ. Gazette, Cape of Good Hope v.38, pp.456-67, 1939.

Cape Province - Official. (Dept. of Public Education). Training colleges, high and secondary schools for European, Coloured and Native Students. (Cape Town, 1946).

Cape Province - Official. (Dept. of Public Educ.) The management of native mission schools (published for the information and guidance of manager) 1953. (Cape Town, the Dept. 1953) 24p.

Cape Province - Official. Report of the Coloured Education Commission, 1953-6, (Botha Commission) (Cape Town, 1956) 67p.

Cape African Teachers' Association (C.A.T.A.) "Verwoerd Speaks Out". (Cape Town, 1954).

Cape African Teachers' Association. "Verwoerd on fundamental education for Africans". (Queenstown, 1954) 2p. cyclostyled.

Cape African Teachers' Association and Teachers League of SA. Second Joint Conference sitting, East London, June 1954, Conference theme: Education for citizenship. Official minutes. (Lansdowne, Cape, Cape Teachers Federal Council, 1954) 12p.

Cape African Teachers' Association. (2 pamphlets, Umtata, the Association, 1955). (in Xhosa).

Cape African Teachers' Association. "It is ordered ... " (Bantu school boards on trial: a brief analysis of the issued and the judgements in the C.A.T.A. cases). (Umtata, C.A.T.A. 1957) 8p.

Cape African Teachers' Association. Cape of Good Hope. The defeat of the NAD and the school boards (the tasks and obligations this imposes on teachers). (Queenstown, Umtata, the Association, 1957) 7p.

Cape Native Education Advisory Board. Draft of evidence to be given on behalf of the CNEAB, to the Inter departmental Committee to enquire into native education. (Johannesburg,SAIRR,1935) (RR 69/1935 mimeo.)

Cape Town Corporation. An Official Guide to the Educational Institutions of the Cape Peninsular. (Cape Town, 2nd Edit. 1914) 139p. (3rd Edit. 1924).

Carnegie Corporation of New York. "Village Education in Africa: report of the inter-territorial "Jeanes" Conference, Salisbury, S. Rhodesia", May 27th - June 6th, 1935. (Lovedale, 1935) 428pp.

Carr,G.L. "Coloured Education, Recreation and Culture in the Transvaal". (Paper given at a conference of the Transvaal Coloured community, convened by the SAIRR) (Johannesburg, RR, 57/1960).

Carter,F.E. "The native question, especially in relation to Christianity and education" - a paper on the recent report of the Native Commission on Native Affairs, read at the Grahamstown Br. of the English Churchmen's Soc., Sept. 20th, 1905. (Grahamstown, 1905) 8p. (Reprinted from Eastern Prov. Illustrated).

Carter,G.M. The Politics of Inequality: SA since 1948. (London, 1959). see Index on: Bantu Education, Christian National Education.

Catholic African Schools. Brochure published by the RCC, pub. S.A. Catholic Bishops' Conference. (No place of publication, 1958).

Catholic Church. Misc. material on the campaign in South Africa to raise money to maintain mission schools and seminaries, 1955.

Centlivres,A.v.d.S. Blundering into university apartheid. (No place of publication, 1959).

Centlivres,A.v.d.S. "Incompatible state policies: tribalism and university education for Africans." Forum 8(4): Jul. 1959, p.4-6.

Centre for Intergroup Studies, Cape Town. Onderwys: 'n oorsig van rassediskriminasie en huidige tendense in die onderwys in SA. (Cape Town, C-15, 1978).

Charton,N.C.J. "The importance of and challenges in regard to education training and human skills in development: some thoughts on the Transkeian experience." (Durban, 1972) 10p.

Charton,N. (ed.) Ciskei: Economics and Politics of Dependence in a South African Homeland. (London, 1980).

Chase,J.C. The Cape of Good Hope. (First printed London, 1863) (Reprinted, Cape Town, 1967) SectionIV 'Education and Schools' pp.142-145.

Christian Express. "Does Education diminish industry". p.61-2. Leader "Industrial Education" p.65. The Chr. Express, 1 Apr. 1887.

Church of England, Johannesburg. "Our mission schools: we close our doors". (Johannesburg, 195?).

Cilliers,A.C. The State and the Universities (1910-1943) (Cape Town, 1944).

Cillie,G.G. Chairman of: Report of the Commission of inquiry into school feeding. (Pretoria, Govt. Printer, 1951).

Cilliers,S.P. The Coloureds of South Africa: a factual survey. (Cape Town, 1963) Ch. V - Education.

Cilliers,S.P. Coloured People: Education and Status. (Johannesburg, SAIRR, 1971) pp.28.

Ciskeian Miss. Council. "Finance of native educ." in SA Outlook 61: 1931, p. 225-8.

Clarke,F. "Essays in the politics of education". (Cape Town and Johannesburg: 1923) p.98-115. The Juvenile and Colour.

Clarke,W.E.C. (Inspector of Native Education in the Transvaal Colony). Transvaal Education Dept. - Report for 1903, Report for 1904, etc.

Clarke,W.E.C. and others. Papers on Cape Education, read before the British Assn.... (Cape Town, 1905) 32p.

Clinton,D.K. 'The London Missionary Society in SA during the years 1798 - 1836'. (B.Litt., Univ. of Oxford, 1935).

Cloete,D. 'On Education' in Education and Development. (Cape Town, NUSAS, 1979) p.203.

Coan,J.R. 'The expansion of missions of the African Methodist Episcopal Church in South Africa, 1896 - 1908'. (Ph.D., Hartford Seminary Foundation, Hartford, Conn. 1961) pp.522.

Cock,J. Maids and Madams. (Johannesburg, 1980). Ch. 8 "Education for Domesticity", pp.265-306.

Coetzee,J.C. Onderwys in die Transvaal 1938-1937. (Pretoria,1941) 219p. (Bibliog. incl. sections on Education for Blacks).

Coetzee,J.C. Courses of Training for Native Teachers. (Cape of Good Hope Dept. of Public Educ. Stell. 1950).

Coetzee,J.C. et al. (P.S. du Toit, M.C.E. van Schoor, B.R. Buys, A.L. Behr).
   - Onderwys in Suid Afrika 1652 - 1956. (Pretoria, 1958, 1st Edit., 455p.)
     Afdeling G. 'Onderwys vir Nie Blankes'. bl.381-454 - Bibliography.
   - Onderwys in Suid Afrika 1652 - 1960. (Pretoria, 1963, 2nd Edition).
     pp.403-484. Onderwys vir Nie Blankes, Ch. VII 'Die opleiding van Kleurlingonderwysers in SA'.

Coetzee,J.H. "Wet of Bantoe-onderwys, 1953", Koers 21; Feb. 1954, p.173-79.

Coleman,K.G. Indian education is making steady progress. (Pretoria, 1946).

Coleman,K.G. Mission Schools play an important role in educating South African natives. (Pretoria, S.A. State Information Office, 1949). 2p.

Collins,C.B. Catholic Bantu Education. (Pretoria, 1957). 35p.

Collins,C.B. "Black Schooling in South Africa: Notes towards a reinterpretation of the schooling of indigenous peoples in South Africa". Africa Perspective 17, Spring 1980, pp.4-16.

Collins,D.P. "The Origins and Formation of the Zulu Congregational Church, 1869 - 1908". (M.A., UND, 1978).

Coloured Advisory Council. Annual Reports, 1943-.

Coloured Affairs Dept. Reports, 1954-.

Coloured Affairs, Commissioner for. Reports 1952 - 1954.

Colquhoun,A.R. "The White Man's Burden. Ethiopian Movement: The Education Difficulty". Morning Post, 7 Dec. 1904.

Committee of Ten. Violence at UDW: The facts. (Durban, 1980) 4p.

Conference on Bantu Education 1969. See SAIRR.

Conference of representatives of the money guarantee towards the founding of the inter-state native college (Kingwilliamstown, 1907), Minutes, Chamber of Commerce KWT. 2-4 Oct. 1907. (Lovedale, 1907).

Conference of the Moravian Missionaries in the E. Province and native territories (Genadendal, 19?) (Proposal for a new system of native educ.)

Conference on Urban Juvenile Native Delinquents held in Johannesburg Oct. 1938.

Cook,P.A.W. "The Education of Rural Bantu Peoples in South Africa". Journal of Negro Education 3(1), 1934, p.98-104.

Cook,P.A.W. "Tribal education". S.Afr.J.Sci., XXVI, Dec. 1929, pp.937-944.

Cook,P.A.W. The Education of a South African tribe. (Cape Town, 1934) 94p.

Cook,P.A.W. "Education of rural Bantu peoples in SA". J. Neg. Ed., III, 1934, p.98-104.

Cook,P.A.W. The Native Standard VI Pupil - a socio-educational survey of Std. VI pupils in native schools in the Union of S.A. (1935) (Pretoria, SACESR, 1939, Research Series 10).

Cook,P.A.W. The Transvaal Native teacher; a socio-educational survey. (Pretoria, SACESR, 1939) 138pp. (Research Series No. 11).

Cook.P.A.W. "Intelligence test for native schools". Tvl. Nat. Educ. Quart. 2: Ja. 1940, p.29-33.

Cook.P.A.W. The Native student teacher; (a socio-educational survey). (Pretoria, 1940) 69p.

Cook,P.A.W. "Non-European Education", in Hellman,E. (ed.), Handbook on Race Relations in SA (Cape Town, 1949) Ch. XV, pp.348-386.

Cooppan,S. "The education of the Indian in Natal, 1860-1947", (Ph.D., UCT, 1948) 2v. bibliog.

Cooppan,S. et al. Four essays on Education (Teachers Educ. and Professional Assn. - pamphlet No. 3) (1957) 57p. (a) Cooppan,S. "Educ. policies in a multi racial society" p.3. (b) Pitje.G.M. "The Implications of the Tomlinson Report on African Education" p.19. (c) v.d. Ross,R.E. "Basic Educational Issues in SA", p.38. (d) v.d. Ross,R.E. "Die Opvoeding van die Kleurling en Toekoms van SA. p.49.

Cooppan,S. The entry of Durban Indian youth into the labour market. (Durban, 1962).

Corke,M.A.S. "Bantu Education: an Evaluation". (mimeo. Johannesburg, 1977).

Corke,M.A.S. The allocation of Educational Resources in SA. (mimeo.1978) 11p.

Corke,M.A.S. "A School System for South Africa", Social Dynamics 5(1), 1979, p.38-42.

Cornevin,M. Apartheid Power and Historical Falsification. (Paris, UNESCO, 1980).

Council of Education, Witwatersrand. See Horton,J.W., Richards,M.W.

Counter Information Service. Black South Africa Explodes. (London, 1977) 90p.

Counter Information Service. Buying Time in South Africa. (London, 1978).

Cragg,E.L. Fort Hare and other memories. (Somerset West, 1973) 61p.

Crehan,K. "Ideology and Practice, A Missionary Case: The London Missionary Society and the Cape Frontier 1799 - 1850". In A. Akeroyd and L.R. Hill (ed.) South African Research in Progress, Collected Papers 4 (York,1979).

Crewe,C.P. "Lovedale, Fort Hare and the Native: impressions of a recent tour". Daily Despatch, 11 Jul. 1924.

Cullis,F.C. "The Story of Zonnebloem - Centenary broadcast 2 Mar. 1958,etc." (No place of publisher, 1958) mimeo 3p.

Curry,R.F. "The Church of the Province and Christian National Education". (Cape Town: CPSA Publications Board occ. Paper No. 3, 1963).

Dag Hammerskjold Foundation. "Educational Alternatives for S. Africa". Papers from the conference in Maputo, April 1978. Pub. in abbreviated form in Development Dialogue 2, 1978.

Dale,L. "The Cape and its People: Education", in Noble,R. (ed.) The Cape and its People. (Cape Town, 1869) p.1-20.

Dale,L. "Technical instruction and industrial training; a necessary supplement to the colonial system of public education". (Cape Town, 1875). 24p. (or Lovedale, 1892).

Daleboudt,H.M. "Sir Thomas Muir en die onderwys in Kaapland tydens sy bestuur as superintendent-generaal van onderwys 1892-1915". (D.Ed. thesis, US, 1942) 475p. (pp.402-426 re Non-White Educ.; 451-457 re Bibliography).

Daniels,J.C. 'Radical Resistance to Minority Rule in SA; 1906-1965". (Ph.D. Graduate School,State University of New York, Buffalo, 1974-5) (Xerox, Univ. Microfilm - Ann Arbor, Michigan 48106).

Daniel,J. "Radical Resistance in SA", in I. Robertson and P. Whitten (eds.) Race and Politics in South Africa (New Brunswick, 1978) pp.55-77.

David,P. "No Wind of Change in Black Universities". THES. 21/12/79, 28/12/79. (Report on the Commission of Inquiry into Universities 1974, van Wyk de Vries Commission).

Davids,J.J. 'The history and development of the education of the Coloured
people in the George-Knysna area up to 1952'. (B.Ed. thesis, UCT, 1960).

Davie,T.B. Education and race relations in South Africa: the interaction of
colonial policies and race relations in SA. (Johannesburg, SAIRR, 1955).
31p. Hoernlé Memorial Lecture.

Davies,H. & Shepherd,R.H.W. SA Missions 1800 - 1950. (London, 1954) 232p.

Davies,J.L. 'Christian National Education in SA: A study in the influence of
Calvinism and Nationalism on Educational Policy'. (Ph.D. diss., Univ.
of Wisconsin, Madison, 1978) 392p.

Davies,R. "Capital Restructuring and the Modification of the Racial Division
of Labour in South Africa", JSAS 5(2), Apr. 1979, p.181-98.

Davis,A. The Native Problem. (London, 1903).

Davis,R. Hunt, Jr. 'Nineteenth Century African Education in the Cape Colony:
A Historical Analysis. (Ph.D. Diss. Univ. of Wisconsin, 1969) pp.346.

Davis,R. Hunt, Jr. Bantu Education and the Education of Africans in SA.
(Athens, Ohio, 1972) p.53.

Davis,R. Hunt, Jr. "1855-1863: a dividing point in the early development of
African education in South Africa". In: The Societies of Southern
Africa in the 19th and 20th Centuries. Vol. 5 (1973-4). pp.1-15.
(Univ. of London, Institute of Commonwealth Studies, London) or
"1855-1863: A watershed era in the early development of African
Education in South Africa". (Paper presented at African History
Workshop, Gaborones, Sept. 1973).

Davis,R. Hunt,Jr. "Penn School as a model for African Education in South
Africa". (Paper presented at the 41st Annual Meeting of the Southern
Historical Association, Washington,D.C., November 1975).

Davis,R. Hunt,Jr. "John L. Dube: A South African Exponent of Booker T.
Washington". J. of Af. Studies 2(4), 1975/6.

Davis,R. Hunt,Jr. "The Black American component in Southern Africa:
Responses to Colonialism in SA: ca 1890-1914", J. of SA Affairs III,
1 Jan. '78, p.65-84.

Davis,R. Hunt,Jr. "School vs. Blanket and Settler: Elijah Makiwane and the
Leadership of the Cape School Community". African Affairs 78 (310),
Jan. 1979. pp.12-31.

Davis,R. Hunt,Jr. "The Administration and Financing of African Education in
South Africa 1910-1953". (Unpubl.paper, 1980).

De Jager,J. "Naturel en sy onderwys." Onderwysbl., 55(620) Jun. 1951, p.17-18.

"Delta". 'The University and colleges of the Cape of Good Hope', Cape Mon.
Mag. 8 (44), Feb. 1874, p.65-71.

Dent,C.P. "Native education: an interpretation for Europeans". Native
Teachers' Journal 21: Ja. 1942, p.55-68.

Dent,G.R. "African education". Native Teachers' J.27: O. 1947, p.18-23.

De Vaal,J.B. "Trade and technical education - its scope and objectives",
Bantu Educ. J. 11(10): D. 1965 illus. p.7-12.

De Vaal,J.B. Trade and Technical Education for the Bantu in the RSA. Tegnikon, Special Edition, March 1967, p.61-67.

De Vaal,J.B. "Vryhedise opleiding- en hoërskool". Bantoe-onderwysbl. 15(4); M. 1969 illus. p.14-15.

De Villiers Commission. Report of the Commission on Technical and Vocational Education, 1945-48. (UG 65 - 1948) (Pretoria, 1948).

De Villiers,F.J. "The Nyanga and Freemantle School Farms". SA Outlook 70, 1940, p.26-30.

De Villiers,F.J. "What Bantu education has already achieved". Bantu Educ. J. 3(3), Ap. 1957, p.107-9.

De Villiers,F.J. "Bantu Educ.: where the money comes from - and where it goes", an address on the financing of B.E. at the annual council of SAIRR, 18 Jan. 1961. (Pretoria, Info. services of the Dept. of Bantu Educ. 1961 16p) (Reprint from Bantu, March 1961).

De Villiers,F.J. The Financing of Bantu Education. (Johannesburg,SAIRR,1964).

De Villiers,G.v.N. 'n Onderwysstelsel vir Qwaqwa: 'n studie betreffende onderwys stelselplanning. (Bloemfontein, UOFS, 1977) (M.Ed. verhandeling).

De Villiers,S.J. "Fundamental arithmetic in Native Schools of the Transkei", (M.Ed. UNISA 1948, 143pp.)

De Vos,D.W. 'Mmadikote tegniese kollege'. Bantoe-onderwysblad 17(6), 1971, bl. 16-19.

De Wet,J.J. "The Effect of the Policy of apartheid on Education: a review article". Journal of Racial Affairs 20(3) 1969, p.131-44.

De Wet-Nel,M.D.C. (Chairman). Report of the commission on the separate universities education bill. (Parow, Cape Times, 1958) (UG. 32 - '58).

Dick,M.G. "The establishment of a mission, being the work of the American Board of Commissioners for Foreign Missions among the Zulus of South Eastern Natal, 1934-1960". (M.A., Columbia Univ., New York, 1934).

Dickie-Clark,H.F. 'The Dilemma of Education in a Plural Society: The S.A. Case'. In: H.Adam (ed.) South Africa, Sociological Perspectives, (London, 1971) pp.214-227.

Dilla,S. 'The nationalisation of Indian education in the Transvaal'. (Unpublished M.E. thesis, Pretoria, UNISA).

Dinnerstein,M. 'American Board Missions to the Zulu, 1935-1900'. (Ph.D. Columbia Univ., New York, 1972).

Dodd,A.D. "Native vocational training in the Cape Province". (M.Ed., UNISA, 1935) 129p. Bibliog.

Dodd,A.D. "Native vocational training: a study of conditions in South Africa, 1652-1936". (Lovedale, 1938). pp.58.

Doke,C.M. "Vernacular Text books in South African native schools". Africa v.8 (1935) pp.183-209.

Dovey,K. "De-Mystifying Christian national education: a programme for teacher training courses". Journal of Education 11, 1979, p.27-35.

Drerup,S. "Black education - a dangerous situation". SASH 20(1) 1978, p.13-14.

Dreyer,J.H. et al. 'Why reject Bantu Education?' Results of a panel discussion. In Paidonomia 6(2), Nov. 1978, p.15-34.

Dube,J.L. In the Clash of Colour, papers read before the Natal Missionary Conference, 7 July 1926, on the subject: "The Relations between the White and black Races in SA, and means for their improvement". Paper by Ven. Archdeacon Lee as representing the European viewpoint. Paper by Rev. J.L. Dube as representing the Native viewpoint. (Durban 1926) 11p.

Dube,J.L. "The Realignment of Native Social and Religious Life through Education". In General Missionary Conference of SA. Being a reprint of a conference on: The Realignment of Native Life on a Christian Basis. (Lovedale, 1928) p.42-47.

Duffy,P.S. "Government Control of Education in South Africa". Catholic Education Review, Feb. 1969.

Dugard,J.H. Address given to the conference of the Cape Bantu Teachers' Union held at Uitenhage, July 1957. In Bantu Educ.J. III(7) Sept. 1957.

Dugard,J.H. "Supervision in secondary schools". Bantu Educ.J. 5: Ap. 1959, port. p.119-23.

Dugard,J.H. "Post-primary education for the Bantu". Bantu Educ.J. 7; 3 Sept. 1961, port. p.348-51.

Dugmore,D. 'Hope for Bantu Education'. Christian Recorder 18(9) Mr.1969, p.5.

Duminy,P.A. "The Educability of the Bantu ...", address to the Rotary Club of East London 7/10/66. (Fort Hare, 1966).

Duminy,P.A. "Some Problems in education". SA Outlook 96, N. 1966, p.181-88; Discussion SA Outlook 97. (1155) Ag. 1967, p.127-8.

Duminy,P.A. (ed.) Trends and Challenges in the Education of the South African Bantu. (Cape Town, 1967) 212p.

Duminy,P.A. African Pupils and Teaching Them. (Pretoria, 1968) 137p.

Duminy,P.A. How Bantu High School pupils see their teachers (Intro. paper) (1969 Conf. on Bantu Educ.) (Johannesburg, SAIRR, 1969 RR 141/68).

Duminy,P.A. "Aspects of the Confrontation between Western School Education and African Indigenous Education, with ref. to recent Educ. developments in the Ciskei". The Ciskei, 1971, p.145-169.

Duminy,P.A. 'School education and the tides of change', a paper read at the South African Pedagogical Society at Fort Hare, on the 26th May 1975.

Duncan,J.H. "Native Sunday Schools", in SA Outlook, 61: 1931, p.188-9.

Dunston,J.T. "Retarded and Defective Children: Native Mentality and Mental Testing". S.A. Journal of Sc. (1923) p.148-156.

Du Plessis,H. "Christianseering van die Bantoelewe met Behoud van sy Bantoiteit", Koers, II (4), Feb. 1935, p.11-18; "Assimilasie of Algehele Segregasie - Die Eenigste Alternatiewe vir Oplossing van die Naturelle probleem", Koers II (6), June 1935, p.32-41; "'n Eie Opvoeding sisteem vir die Bantoes in SA", Koers III (4) Feb. 1936, p.17-25.

Du Plessis,J.H. (Chairman). Minority report of the commission of inquiry into school feeding. (Pretoria, 1951).

Du Plessis,J. "Some interesting statistical facts about Bantu Education". Bantu Educ. J. 16(2) Mr. 1970; 16(4-7) May - Sept. 1970; 16(9-10) Nov. - Dec. 1970; 17(1-2) Feb. - Mr. 1971; 17(4-10) May - Dec. 1971; 15(5) June 1971, p.20-21.

Du Plessis,J.H. "Pupils in secondary and technical secondary schools according to subjects taken: 1970. (Transkei not included) Statistics". Bantu Educ. J. 17(7) Sept. 1971, p.20-21.

Du Plessis,J.H. "Number of pupils in post-primary schools, 1970. (Transkei excluded). Statistical facts". Bantu Educ. J. 17(10) Dec. 1971, p.20.

Du Plessis,J.H. "Some interesting statistical facts about education". Bantu Educ. J. 17(5) 1971, p.20-21.

Du Plessis,J. A History of Christian Missions in South Africa. (Cape Town, 1965) (originally pub. London, 1911).

Du Plessis,J. The Life of Andrew Murray of South Africa. (London, 1920).

Du Plessis, J. Evangelization of Pagan Africa: A history of Christian Missions to the pagan tribes of central Africa. (Cape Town and Johannesburg 1930).

Du Plessis,J. "Missions as a sociological factor", S.Afr.J.Sci. XXIX,1932,p.84-97.

Du Plessis,L.J. 'Separate University Education'. Tydskrif vir Rasse-Aangeleenthede 9(2) 1958, p.64-74.

Du Preez,J.N. The educational system of Transkei: a system description and needs assessment. (Bloemfontein, UOFS, Research Unit for Education System Planning, 1980).

Dutch Reformed Church: Federal Council of the: "Europeans and Bantu": being papers and addresses read at the Conference on Native Affairs, held under the auspices of the Fed. Council of the DRC at Johannesburg on 27-29 Sept. 1923. (Cape Town, 1923) 56p.

Dutch Reformed Church mission. Dr. Aggrey. (Mkhoma Mission Press for DRC, 1939) 52p.

Du Toit,A.E. The earliest British document on education for the Coloured Races. (Communications of UNISA, Pretoria, 1962). C.34 40pp.

Du Toit,A.E. The earliest South African documents on the education and civilization of the Bantu. (Communications of the UNISA, C.47, Pretoria, 1963). pam. 91pp.

Du Toit, P.S. Onderwys aan die Kaap onder die Bataafse Republiek 1803-1806. (Pretoria, 1944) Ch. IX - "Onderwys aan Nie-Blankes".

Du Toit,P.S. Onderwys aan die Kaap onder die Kompanjie 1652-1795; 'n Kultuur-Historiese studie. (Cape Town 1957). pp.327. Biblio. - non-European education, pp.39-50, 180-7; Ch.III - Die vroegste onderwys aan Nie-Blankes; Ch. XIV - Onderwys aan Nie-Blankes 1914-1782; Slawe onderwys, pp.253-254.

Du Toit,P.S. Onderwys in Kaapland 1652-1795; 'n Historiese Oorsig. (Pretoria, 1970) 165p. (first pub. in 1940).

Dyasi,H.M. "The History of the Problems of Bantu Urban Secondary Education in the Eastern Cape, 1937-1954. (Ciskei Region)". (M.Ed. UNISA, 1962).

Dzumba,S.S. 'The Training of Teachers: a comparative study of practice in England and South Africa: (Bantu Schools), with special ref. to problems of training for secondary schools" (Associateship Reports, Institute of Education, London University, 1968).

E,.J.H. "Native training school courses". SA Outlook 74: F.1944, p.22-24.

Edelstein,M.L. "An attitude survey of urban Bantu matric pupils in Soweto with special reference to stereotyping and social distance: a sociological study". (M.A. dissertation, UP, 1971) 150p.

Edelstein,M.L. What do Young Africans Think? (Johannesburg, SAIRR, 1972).

Educational Technology Symposium. Instructa '78: a collection of papers read at the symposium. (Johannesburg, July 1978, Durban, c.1979).

Education Commission of the South African Institute of Race Relations: Report of the: (Johannesburg, SAIRR, 1979) pp.12.

Education Commission of the SAIRR. "Education for a New Era". Social Dynamics 5(1) 1979, p.43-47.

Education Council for Coloured Persons: Annual Reports.

Education Draft Ordinance. "Education for Coloureds: Ten Year Plan for Province). Cape Times, June 9th, 1945. (Cape Town, 1945).

Education Information Centre. Register of bursary funds available to non-white scholars and students. (Johannesburg, the EIC, 1970). 25p.

Education League. Tweede dorsland trek: kommentaar op die "Christelike-Nasionale onderwysbeleid" van die Instituut vir Christelik-Nasionale onderwys - F.A.K. (Johannesburg Opvoedingsbord, 1949) 19p.

Education League. Blueprint for blackout: a commentary of the education policy of the Instituut vir Christelik-nasionale onderwys with an abridged translation of the recent pamphlet in which the policy is stated. Drawn up by C. van Heyningen of the Education League Committee. (Johannesburg, 1947).

Education League. Newsletter on native education. (Johannesburg, 1951) 1p.

Education League. Our dwindling educational freedom; protect your children ... C.N.O. is gaining ground rapidly. (Johannesburg, 1952).

Education League. Freedom of conscience; what do they really mean? (Johannesburg, 1952).

Education League. The background to the Bantu Education Bill and the future of Bantu education. (Johannesburg, Educ. League, 1953) 10p.

Education League. "The indivisibility of education"; address by Trevor Huddleston to annual meeting of Educ. League, 5 June 1953. (Johannesburg, The League, 1953). 4p. mimeo.

Education League. The Tvl. education draft ordinance. (Johannesburg, 1953).

Education League. The Advance of C.N.O. and the setback to education. (Johannesburg, 1954).

Education League. Bantu Education. (Johannesburg, 1954).

Education League. Blackout: a commentary on the education policy of the Instituut vir Christelike-nasionale onderwys, with an abridged translation of the pamplet in which the policy is stated. (Johannesburg, 1959) 35p.

Education Panel, 1961. First Report, Education for South Africa. (Johannesburg, 1963).

Education Panel, 1961. Second Report: Education and the SA Economy. (Johannesburg, 1966).

Education Vigilance Committee, Johannesburg. a) Education Charter for the children of SA. (Johannesburg, 1962) 4p. b) Have Parents rights? (Johannesburg, 1962) 7p.

Eiselen,W.W.M. Die Naturelle-Vraagstuk. (Cape Town, 1929).

Eiselen,W.W.M. Stamskole in Suid Afrika - 'n ondersoek oor die funksie daarvan in die lewe van die Suid-Afrikaanse stamme met 'n kort opsomming in Engels. (Pretoria, 1929) 134p.

Eiselen,W.W.M. (Chairman) Report of. Commission on Native Education 1945-51. (UG.53 - 1951) (Pretoria, 1951).

Eiselen,W.W.M. "Co-ordination of Bantu education and Bantu development". (Opening address 1954 delivered by the Secretary for Nat. Affairs). Bantu 1(2): May 1954, p.11-21.

Eiselen,W.W.M. The Bantu Education Act, Bantu Educ. J. 1(7) Jun. 1955, p.224-6.

Eiselen,W.W.M. "Bantoe-onderwys". T. Wetenskap Kuns 15(2): O. 1955, p.89-97.

Eiselen,W.W.M. Opening address at the 1968 Education Conference of the SAIRR ... on Bantu Education in SA. (Johannesburg, SAIRR,1969) 19p. RR 12/69.

Eiselen,W.W.M. "Standard of English and Afrikaans in our Bantu schools", Bantu Educ. J. 17(5), Jun. 1971, p.4-7. port. bibl. Abstr.

Eisenberg,P.S. "Bantu education in the Union of South Africa". (Unpubl. B. Litt., Univ. of Oxford, 1957-8).

Eisenberg,P. 'Education in South Africa', in H. Kitchen(ed.) The Educated African. (London, 1962).

Elder,J.H. "The School and the community". SA Outlook 75: S. 1945, p.134-5.

Elliot,J. "Black education and economic growth". Development S. Afr. 3: 1976, illus. p.6-9.

Ellsworth,M. "The Rejection of Bantu Education". SA Outlook 106, 1976.p.124-5.

Ellsworth,M. 'African education in the Cape'. (Notes from a talk). Z., I (2), Oct. 1976.

Emanuelson,O.E. "A history of native education in Natal between 1835 and 1927". (M.Ed. Natal, 1927). 334p. biblio.

Engelbrecht,G.C. "Kort oorsig oor die geskiedenis van Bantoe-onderwys in die O.V.S. vanaf 1823 tot 1960". Bantu Educ. J. 6: May 1960, illus. p.210-216+.

Engelbrecht,I.Z. "Apartheid en die Toepassing van die beginsel daarvan in die skoolopvoeding in SA 1652-1956". (D.Ed., U.Potch,1959) 334p. Bibliog.

Engelbrecht,J.D.A. "Die ontwikkeling en beheer van Tegniese en beroeps-onderwys vir Kleurlinge in Kaapland sedert 1925". (M.Ed. verhandeling, Stellenbosch, 1974).

Engelbrecht,M.A.H. "Bantoe-onderwys en ontwikkeling". Bantoe-onderwysbl. 8: Jun. 1962, p.225-27.

Engelbrecht,M.A.H. "Beheer oor ons skoolfondse van Bantoe-gemeenskapskole". Bantoe-Onderwysblad 5; Ap. 1959, port. p.116-118+.

Ennes,W. History of the civilization and Christianization of SA. (New York 1833).

Etheredge,D.A. 'Why Adult Education?' (Johannesburg, Johannesburg Council for Adult Education, 1972) 13p.

Etherington,N.A. "The Rise of the Kholwa (amakholwa or believers) in Southeast Africa: African Christian Communities in Natal, Pondoland and Zululand: 1835-1880". (Ph.D. Yale Univ., New Haven, Conn.,1971) pp.394.

Etherington,N. "Mission Station Melting Pot as a factor in the Rise of SA Black Nationalism". Int. J. of Afr. Hist. Stud. IX(4) 1976, pp.592-605.

Evans,I.L. Native Policy in Southern Africa - An Outline. (Cambride 1934) 177p.

Evans,M.L. "Education among the Bantu of S.E. Africa". Southern Workman XLI (6), June 1912, p.363-8.

Evans,M.S. "Future of national education". Chr. Exp. June 1914, pp.85-6. July 1914, pp.99-100,107.

Eybers,E. "Educational Developments at the Cape of Good Hope, 1952-1839, with special reference to the period of transition from Dutch to British Rule, 1803 - 1839". (Ph.D. New York, Columbia, 1917).

Faku Training Instn., Emfundisweni, Pondoland. Rules,(Palmerton, Mission Pr.1922).

Fannin,D.G. a) "Some problems of Native education"; paper presented at 3rd annual congress of the Chartered Instit. of Secretaries (SA branch) May 1952. (16 leaves mimeo.) b) "Some problems of Native Educ. in Natal". The Secretary 49, (1952) pp.458-464.

Faris,J.T. 'James Stewart of Lovedale'. Miss. Rev. 33: Ja. 1910, p.46-9.

Faure Verbeteringskool vir Kleurlingdogters. - Annual Reports of: (Cape Town, various).

Faure Verbeteringskool vir Kleurlingseuns. - Annual Reports of: (Cape Town, no date) p.11 + (CAD).

Federal Committee for African Adult Education. Memo. to be submitted to the Adult education commission by the Federal Committee for African adult educ. (No place or date of pub. (194?) 12p. mimeo.)

Federal Conference on Education, London 1907. Official report ... convened by the League of the Empire, May 24 - June 1, 1907, Caxton Hall. (London, 1908) 384p. "... the first conference on Educ. between the different Countries and Crown Colonies of the Br. Emp." Refs to ed. in SA: p.54, p.154, 222-3, 261, etc.

Federal Theological Seminary of Southern Africa. Constitution and by-laws. (Grahamstown, 1961) 10p.

Federal Council of African Teachers Associations. Memo to the Dept. of Native Affairs, (Bantu Education), Pretoria, on important educational issues and developments. (mimeo, April, 1956) 14p.

Federal Council of African Teachers' Associations. Memo on the higher primary school course (as set out in the Bantu Education J., July 1955) mimeo SAIRR - RR 151/56. (Marked Confidential). Memo subsequent to the interview of the 21st March 1955, with the Division of Bantu Education, Native Affairs Dept., Pretoria, (mimeo. SAIRR, RR 152/56) (Marked Confid).

Federal Council of the Medical Association of SA. Medical Services for
    Rural Areas, with special reference to Native Areas and the Training
    of Native Medical Practitioners. J. of Medical Assn. of SA, 24 0. 1931.

Federal Theological Seminary of SA. Training for the Christian ministry.
    (Alice, Cape Province, 1965) 12p.

Federal Theological Seminary of SA.: Stubbs,A. The planting of the Federal
    Theological Seminary in SA. (Lovedale, 1972) 18p.

Federasie van Afrikaanse Kultuurvereniginge: Instituut vir Christelike-
    nasionale onderwys. Christelike Nasionale Onderwysbeleid (Johannesburg,
    1948) 29p.

Feit,E. South Africa: The Dynamics of the African National Congress. (Oxford 1962)

Feit,E. "Conflict and Communication: An Analysis of the "Western Areas" and
    "Bantu Education" Campaigns of the African National Congress of South
    Africa: Based on Communication and Conflict Theories". (Ph.D. Diss.,
    Univ. of Michigan, 1965) 242p. (Ann Arbour, Univ. Microfilms 1965).

Feit,E. "The Conception and Planning of the Bantu Education Campaign" in
    African Opposition in South Africa: the failure of passive resistance.
    (Stanford, 1967) 223p.

Fick,M.L.M. The Educability of the SA Native. (Pretoria, 1939).

Fick,M.L. An individual scale of general intelligence for SA. (Pretoria, 1939).

Fihla,P.M. The development of Bantu Education at the St. Matthews Mission,
    Keiskamma Hoek 1853-1959: an historical survey. (Fort Hare, 1962) 234p.
    (based on M.Ed. thesis UNISA, 1963).

First,R. "After Soweto: A Response". Review of African Political Economy 11,
    1978, p.93-100.

Forest,L.M. "Polela Institution" (Bulwer), Nat. Teachers J. 1926, p.6-8.

Fort Hare. Coming of Age and Grad. Ceremony, 26-30 March, 1936.
    (Lovedale, Brochure and Program, 1936).

Fort Hare (University College of): Commission of Enquiry, July 1955.
    Chairman: Prof. J.P. Duminy (Pretoria, 1955) 42p.

Fort Hare (University College of). Golden Jubilee 1916-1966. (Fort Hare 1966)29p.

Fort Hare (University College of). University of Fort Hare: autonomy. (Fort
    Hare 1970) 80p.

Fort Hare (University College of). Report of a commission of inquiry appointed
    by the Council of the University of Fort Hare to enquire into the student
    unrest at Fort Hare in May 1972. (Lovedale 1973).

Fourie,H.C.M. "Christelike Nationale opvoeding van die Naturel", Koers in
    die Krisis, Vol. II. (Stellenbosch 1940).

Franck,J.M.L. "Onderwys in die Paarl gedurende die 19de Eeu 1804-1905".
    (Ph.D., US, 1964). (Hoofstuk IV. 'Onderwys aan Nie Blankes 1804-39'.
    p.105-119; Sendingskole van die Engelse Kerk. 1854-59, p.184-191).

Frankel,P. "The Dynamics of a Political Renaissance: The Soweto Students'
    Representative Council". J. of African Studies 7(3) Fall, 1980.

Frankel,P. 'The Politics of Poverty: Political Competition in Soweto'.
Can. J. of Afr. Stud., 14(2), 1980.

Franz,G.H. "The Organization of the Education of the Bantu". Address to
SABRA by the Chief Inspector of Native Education, Tvl. (Pretoria 1954).

Franz,G.H. 'The history of Bantu education in the Tvl.' in Bot.,A.K. The
Development of education in the Transvaal 1936-1951. (Pretoria 1951).

Franz,G.H. "Why the Bantu Education Act?" Bantu 3(5) May 1955, p.36-45.

Fraser,A.G. "Aims of African Education - The avoidance of denationalization".
Int. Rev. Missions 14. (1925) pp.514-22.

Fredericks,L. 'One of the first Coloured schools' (beginning of the
Trafalgar High School). Alpha 1(6): Aug. 1963, p.30+.

Friedling,M. "The Jeanes Plan and its application to Coloured education".
(B.Ed. thesis, UCT, 1940).

Garbers,J.G. Pedi adolescence: the educational situation and image of
adolescence of the Pedi school child. (Port Elizabeth 1971).

Gardner,C.G. "St. Matthews College, Keiskamma, Ciskei", in SA Outlook,
1 June 1962.

Geber,B.A. & Newman,S.P. Soweto's Children: The Development of Attitudes.
(London 1980).

Geere,C.F.C. 'Die Ontwikkeling van Bantoe-onderwys 1910-1960'. Bantu
Educ. J. 6(4) May 1960. p.189-94.

General Missionary Conference, 7th, Lovedale, 1928 Report - Realignment of
native life on a Christian basis. (Lovedale 1928).

Gerhart,G. Black Power in South Africa: the evolution of an ideology.
(Berkley 1978) 364pp.

Gevers,G. "Die Kulturarbeit der deutschen evangelischen Missionen in Süd
Afrika. Das Eingebornen-schulwesen d. dt. evangel. Mission in der
Südafrikanischen Union. (Phil. F. Diss., Univ. of Göttingen, Germany,
1929 pp.79. Bonna-Leipzig, R. Noske, 1929).

Gibbins,C.W.M. School orgainization in theory and practice: a textbook for
Bantu teachers in SA. (Cape Town 1959) 126p.

Gibson,J.L. "A Critical study of the report of the De Villiers Commission
on technical and vocational educ." (M.Ed., Natal Univ., 1968).

Giniewski,P. Bantustans: A Trek Towards the Future. (Cape Town 1961).
257p. - 'Bantu Education' pp.98-113.

Glass,H.G.L. Apartheidsgedagte: Apartheid Cultural Hegemony. (Ph.D. diss.
Washington Univ., 1980) 436p.

Godlo,R.H. "Native secondary education". SA Outlook 71: M.1941, p.106-8.

Goedhals,M.M. "Anglican Missionary Policy in the diocese of Grahamstown under
the first two bishops 1853-1871". (M.A. thesis, Grahamstown,RU, 1979).

Gopaulsingh,R. 'An analysis of the home conditions in relationship to poor a
academic achievement of Indian students in a Natal high school'.
(Unpub. M.Ed. thesis, Durban, UND, 1960).

Grahamstown Area Distress Relief Assoc. (GADRA). Non-European School Feeding Scheme. (Misc. Paragraphs, 1964).

Grant,A.C. "The realignment of native social and religious life through education". In General Missionary Conference. The Realignment of Native Life on a Christian Basis. (Lovedale 1928) p.35-42. (Report of a conference held in June 1928).

Grant,E.W. "Bantu men's night school". SA Outlook LX 2/6/1930, p.112-13.

Grant,E.W. "Lovedale Bible School: the first five years". SA Outlook 67, 1937, p.162-4.

Grant,G.C. Adams College: 1853-1951. (Pietermaritzburg, Natal Witness,195?)9p.

Grant,G.C. The Liquidation of Adams College. (Ibadan 1957) 54p.

Grant,G.C. Jack Grant's story - educator, cricketer, missionary, 1907-1978. (London 1980) 198p.

Great Britain - Commission of Inquiry upon the Hottentot Population of the Cape of Good Hope. Report upon the Hottentot population of the Cape of Good Hope and of the missionary institutions. (Cape Town 1830).

Great Britain - Board of Education. Special reports on the system of education in Cape Colony and Natal. (Sectional reprint from Vol. V of "Special reports on educational subjects") London, HMSO, 1901) (ii) 210 IXp. (Vol. V of the Special Reports was published as Cd 417 of 1900).

Great Britain - Colonial Office. Report on native education in SA, Part III, Educ. in the Protectorates by E.B. Sargant. (London 1908).

Great Britain - Colonial Office. Educational expenditure (colonies). Return ... dated 29 July 1908. (HMSO, London, 1909).

Great Britain - Board of Education. Special reports on educational subjects Vol. 25. Universities in the Overseas Dominions. (London, HMSO,1912); Universities in SA, p.179-204.

Great Britain. Memorandum on the education of African communities. (London, HMSO, 1935). (Col. No. 108).

Great Britain - Colonial Office. Advisory Committee on Education in the colonies. Mass education in African society. (London 1944) (Colonial No. 168).

Great Britain - Board of Education. Special reports on educational subjects v. 13 educ. systems in the chief Crown Colonies and possessions of the Br. Empire. Inc. reports on the training of the native races, Pt. II, W. Africa, Basutoland, S. Rhodesia, E. Africa, Uganda, Mauritius, Seychelles. (London 1968) (Reprint of 1905 (ed.) pub. HMSO, London).

Greenberg,S. Race and State in Capitalist Development in South Africa. (Johannesburg 1980).

Greswell,W.H.P. "Education of the S. African tribes". Proc. of Roy. Col.Inst. XV 1883-4, pp.68-104.

Grieveson,E.T. "Educational needs of urbanised natives in SA". Afr. Soc. XXXVI 1937, pp.321-36.

Grossert,J.W. "Arts and crafts in education". Native Teachers' J. 29 (sic 28) Jul. 1949, pp.246-53.

Grossert,J.W. Art and Craft for Africans: a manual for art and craft
    teachers. (Pietermaritzburg, 1953) 150p.

Grossert,J.W. Art education and Zulu crafts: A critical review of the
    development of art and crafts in Bantu schools in Natal with particular
    reference to the period 1948-1962. (Pietermaritzburg 1968) 2 vol. illus.
    (from Ph.D. thesis, US, 1969).

Gunn,H. Education in South Africa. (London 1910) 30p. (Reprinted from The
    Times 5 Nov. 1910).

Gunther,M. "'Tribal colleges' will fail". Forum 8(1) Ap. 1959, p.7-8.

Gwala,M.P. editor of Black Review 1973, See Black Review.

Gwalla,N.R. "A Proposed Model for Preparing Teachers of Black Trainable
    Mentally Retarded in South Africa". (Ph.D. Southern Illinois Univ.,
    at Carbondale 1980) 129p.

Haarhoff,D. Report on pre-school situation in Port Elizabeth and Uitenhage's
    African townships: A research project commissioned by the Urban
    Foundation Eastern Cape Region, (Port Elizabeth, Urban Foundation 1979)47p.

Hallowes,Fr. "Report on the working of the Bantu Education Act". Church News
    XXII (10) 17 Oct., 1956, p.426.

Hartshorne,K.B. The position of the official languages in the education of
    the Bantu. (Mimeo, n.d.) 14p.

Hartshorne,K.B. "Education for Non-Europeans in S.Afr. (Comment on an article
    by W. Eiselen)". Tvl. Educ. News 46(8) S. 1950, p.7-8.

Hartshorne,K.B. "The Background to education in the urban areas of SA".
    Oversea Education 22(1) Oct. 1950.

Hartshorne,K.B. "Report of the Native education commission 1949-51".
    Tvl. Educ. News 48(6) Jun-Jul 1952, p.5-8.

Hartshorne,K.B. "Native Education in S. Afr." Bluestocking 20(2) N.1952,p.15-18.

Hartshorne,K.B. "Native Education in the Union of SA: A summary of the report
    of the commission on native education in SA UG53 - 1951". (Johannesburg 1953)62p.

Hartshorne,K.B. "Trends in policy in African education South of the Sahara".
    Symposium Sept. 1960, p.35-38.

Hartshorne,K.B. "Why many Bantu fail 'Matric'". Jewish Affairs 17(4) Ap.1962,
    p.10-13.

Hartshorne,K.E.B. "The Bantu at School", Rotary Club - Roodepoort-Maraisburg,
    Symposium on South Africa, June 1962, pp.D1-D4.

Hartshorne,K.B. "Literature across cultures: English literature in Bantu
    Schools". Engl. Stud. Afr. 13: Mr. 1970, bibl., p.67-79.

Hartshorne,K.B. "Es gibt viele probleme" (Bantu-Erziehung). Afrika-Post 20:
    N. 1973, p.433-35.

Hartshorne,K.B. "Education's role in economic growth". Development S.Afr. 4:
    1974 illus., p.34-36.

Hartshorne,K.B. "Bantu education". S.Afr.Med.J. 48: D.11.1974, p.2517-9.

Hartshorne,K.B. 'The In Service training of African teachers in SA'. In
    Hirschmann,D. and Rose,B. (eds.) Education for Development in Southern
    Africa. (Johannesburg SAIIA 1974) p.171-7.

Hartshorne,K.B. "Education and training of the Black Worker". S.Afr. J. African Affairs 4(2): 1974 p.1-7. (... Also S. Afr. Mech. Engr. 25: 63-67, Mr. 1975. ... Also Civ. Engr. S. Afr. 17: 115-18 M. 1975 ... Also Trans S. Afr. Inst. Elect. Engrs. 66: 124-28 Jun. 1975).

Hartshorne,K.B. "Changing attitudes to Black education". Development S. Afr. 2: 1975 illus., p.12-15.

Hartshorne,K.B. "Notes on black education". N.C.W. News 41(10) May 1976. p.21-27. (National Council of Women).

Hartshorne,K.B. "Reconciliation: Facing the future together". Symposium 1976-77, p.88-91.

Hartshorne,K.B. "Some notes on topical issues in Black education", Tvl. Educ. News 74(1): Ja. 1977, p.9-10+.

Hartshorne,K.B. "Black Education". SA Foundation News 3(3) 1977, p.3.

Hartshorne,K.B. 'Black Education and future needs', in Council of Education Proceedings of the Syndic ... 1977 and Proceedings of the Annual General Meeting ... 1978. (Johannesburg Council of Educ. p.9-18).

Hartshorne,K.B. Black Education in Perspective. (Durban SAIRR, Information Sheet NR/22/78) 6p.

Hartshorne,K.B. "The Unfinished Business: Education for South Africa's Black People". Optima 30(1) 1981, p.16-35.

Hawarden,E. "Strategy of African progress ". Forum 5(45): F.6,1943, p.5-6.

Hawarden,E. "Ten year blitz on ignorance". Forum 5(47): F.20, 1943, p.5-6.

Hawarden,E. Prejudice in the classroom. (Johannesburg 1965).

Hawkins,F.C.W. "Education in the '70s". Fiat Lux 6(7) Sept. 1971, p.2-5.

Healdtown Missionary Institution. A brief account of the jubilee celebrations in connection with the Normal Training Institution, Healdtown, June 1906. (Cape Town 1906) 39p.

Healdtown Missionary Institution. Healdtown 1955-1955. Centenary brochure of: (Healdtown 1955) 38p.

Healdtown Bantu Training School. Instructional pamphlets: Nos. 1-3 compiled by K.S. Kelly and M.I. Floweday. (Healdtown 1958) No. 1 Environment study Std. I. No. 2 Environment study Std. II. No. 3 Health Topics.

Healdtown Bantu Training School. Suggested methods for primary school (ed.). J.L. Omord (Healdtown 1951) 425p.

Heath,A.E. "The Story of Tiger Kloof Native Institution". SA Congregational Magazine, Oct. 1906.

Heaton Nicholls,G. "The Report of the Native Affairs Commission 1936: A Reply". SA Outlook 68, 1938, p.30-35. Section on Native Education.

Heese,J.A. "Onderwys in Namakwaland 1750-1940". (D.Ed., US, 1942).

Hellman,E. "Early school-leaving and occupations by Native juveniles in Johannesburg". (D. Phil., UW, 1939) pp.238.

Hellman,E. Problems of urban Bantu youth: report of an enquiry into the causes of early school-leaving and occupational opportunities amongst Bantu youth in Johannesburg. (Johannesburg, SAIRR, 1940).

Hellman,E. "Needs of native education". Tvl. Educ. News 39(10): 0.1943,p.7-8.

Hellman,E. "Native education - a condition of progress". Tvl. Educ. News 42(4) Ap. 1946, p-12-17.

Hellman,E. "Progress in Native Education". Race Relations 13(3 & 4), 1946, pp.99-104.

Hellman,E. (ed.) Handbook on race relations in SA. (Cape Town 1949).

Hellman,E. "Some comments on Bantu education". Race Relations J. 28(3): Jul-S. 1961, p.35-49 ... Errata 28(4): 2 D. 1961, or (Johannesburg, SAIRR, 206/60 1961).

Hellman,E. Soweto - Johannesburg's African City. (Johannesburg 1968).

Henderson,J. 'Industrial training in Africa: the situation in SA with special reference to Lovedale'. Int. R. Missions 3: F. 1914, p.336-43.

Henderson,J. Whole number devoted to Dr. J. Henderson, principal of Lovedale, on his death. SA Outlook 60, 1930, p.166-183.

Hennessy,R.W. "Bishop Gray's Educational Work". (B.Ed. thesis, US, 1950).

Herbstein,D. White Man, We Want to Talk to You. (London 1978) Ch. 4. "Education for Slavery" pp.83-109.

Hewton,L.A. Healdtown 1855-1955: centenary brochure. (Lovedale 1955).

Hewson,L.A. "Healdtown: A Study of a Methodist Experiment in African Education". (Ph.D., RU, 1959).

Hey,P.D. "African aspirations for education in rural Natal". Comp. Educ. Rev. 5: (1961) p.112-117.

Hey,P.D. "The Rural Zulu Teacher in Natal". Comp. Educ. Rev. 5: (1961)p.54-8.

Heyman,R.D. "The Role of the Carnegie Corporation in Africa Education, 1925-1960". (Ed.D. Dissertation, Columbia Univ., New York, 1970).

Heyman,R.D. "C.T. Loram: A South African Liberal in Race Relations". Int. J. of African Hist. Stud. V.1. (1972) pp.41-50.

Heystek,J.L.K. 'Transkeian Education', in Hirschmann,D. and Rose,B. (eds.) Education for Development in Southern Africa. (Johannesburg 1974). pp.97-104.

Hinchcliff,P. The Church in SA. (London, SPCK, 1968) 116p.

Hirschmann,D. & Rose,B. (eds.). Education for Development in Southern Africa. (Johannesburg 1974) 195p.

Hirson,B. Year of Fire, Year of Ash: The Soweto Revolt: Roots of a Revolution. (London 1979).

Hirson,B. "Books of the 1976 revolt". RAPE 11 (1979) p.101-8.

Hirson,B. "Language in Control and Resistance in South Africa. African Affairs 80 (319) April 1981, pp.219-237.

Hoddinott,D. Educating a nation, etc. (London, SA Foundation, 1963) 24p.

Hoernlé,A.W. & Hellman,E. "An Analysis of social change and its bearing on (Bantu culture and) education". Race Relat. J. 20(4): 1953, p.10-14; p.33-44.

Hoernlé,A.W. & Hellman,E. Report of the Working of the Bantu Education Act. (Johannesburg, SAIRR, 1955) (RR 19/1955; RR 20/1955).

Hoernlé,R.F.A. and others. "Educability of the Bantu", in E.G. Malherbe (ed.), Educational adaptations in a changing society. (Johannesburg, 1937) pp.445-66.

Hoernlé,R.F.A. "Native Education at the crossroads in SA". Africa v.11, (1938) pp.389-411.

Hoernlé,R.F.A. South African Native Policy and the Liberal Spirit. (Being the Phelps-Stokes Lectures, UCT, May 1939). (Lovedale, 1939, Johannesburg 1945). Lecture I "Technique of Domination"; Lecture II, 'Education' pp.10-20 and pp.84-89.

Hoernlé,R.F.A. "Native secondary education in S. Afr." Int. Inst. Teachers' Coll. Col. Univ. Ed. Ybk. 1939, pp.303-14.

Hoernlé,R.F.A. "S. Afr.: education and democratic ideals". Yearbook of Education (1940) p.392-9.

Hoernlé,R.F.A. "Native education in post-war SA". Educ. 52: Ag.1942,p.119-21.

Hoernlé, R.F.A. Race and reason: being mainly a selection of contributions to the race problem in SA with a memoir by Prof. I.D. MacCrone. (Johannesburg, 1945); Ch. 10 'Native Education at the Crossroads in SA'. p.123-144.

Hofmeyr,J.H. "The Education of the South African Native". Afr. Soc. 37, (1938) pp.147-55. (Graduation address delivered at S.A. Nat. Coll. Fort Hare). Also in SA Outlook LX (7), p.112-5, 1937.

Hofmeyr,J.H. "Native Education". Forum Dec. 17, 1938.

Holmes,H. "Five Years on: English teaching in black schools". Symposium 1978, p.50-54.

Holmes,M. "Training for Growth". ENERGOS 2, 1980. 8p.

Horrell,M. "Standards of Education at Present attained by the Union's African Population". (Johannesburg, SAIRR, RR 86/1953).

Horrell,M. African Education: Some Origins and Development until 1953. (Johannesburg, SAIRR, 1963) 80p.

Horrell,M. A Decade of Bantu Education. (Johannesburg, SAIRR, 1964) 187p.

Horrell,M. Facts on African education. The Word 2(2) 1967, p.2-7.

Horrell,M. (ed.) Bantu education to 1968. (Johannesburg, SAIRR, 1968) 170p.

Horrell,M. "Bantu school education 1955-1968 - a review and assessment - theme paper, etc." (Johannesburg, SAIRR, 1969).

Horrell,M. (comp.) The Education of the Coloured Community in South Africa 1652-1970. (Johannesburg, SAIRR, 1970) 190p. and bibliog.

Horrell,M. Action, Reaction and Counteraction: a Review of Non-White Opposition to the Apartheid Policy. (Johannesburg, SAIRR, 1971).

Horrell,M. "Education in Apartheid Society", in N.J. Rhoodie (ed.) South African Dialogue: contrasts in SA thinking on basic race issues. (Johannesburg 1972) p.611.

Horton,J.W. The First Seventy Years 1895-1965. (Johannesburg 1968). (Work of the Council of Education on the Witwatersrand).

Hotz,L. 'Church gives up schools' re (South Africa). Times Educ. Supp. 3013: F. 23, '73, p.16.

Houghton,K.A.H. "The Problem of Bantu education in South Africa" - a paper read before the annual meeting of the SA Association for the Advancement of Science, Grahamstown, 1908. (Lovedale 1908) 21p. (Also published in East and West Review VIII, 1910, p.63-75 and S. Afr. J. Sci. 1908, p.334-340).

Houghton,K.A.H. "Agricultural training of natives". SA Afr. Ass. Sci. Rep, 6: 1909, p.230-233.

Houghton,K.A.H. "The Proposed S. Afr. Native College". Afr. Soc. XI, 1911, p.35-46.

Houghton,K.A.H. "The Proposed S. Afr. College". East and West, Oct. 1911, p.425-32.

Houghton,K.A.H. "Report of the Inter-State Nat. Coll. Convention". Chr. Exp. 1 Feb. 1913, p.23-4.

Houghton,D.H. & Walton,E.M. (eds.) The Economy of a Native Reserve: The Keiskammahoek Rural Survey. (Pietermaritzburg 1952).

Houghton,D.H. The Tomlinson Report: Summary. (Johannesburg 1956). 106p. (Education pp.86-9).

Houghton,D.H. The South African Economy. (Cape Town 1964, 1967).

Howell,L. & Howell,D. "How to establish a farm school for natives". Farmer's Weekly 97: July 8, 1959 illus., p.28.

HSRC (Institute of Statistical Research) (van Rensburg,F.A.J.) Trends in Bantu Educ. in the RSA. (Pretoria, the Council, n.d. 94(3)p). (Report No. WS-10).

HSRC (Info. & Special Services, Dept. of:). Stimie,C.M. Education in the RSA. (Pretoria 1970) 92p. Report No. IN13.

HSRC. Provision of Education in the RSA (the de Lange Report). (Pretoria 1981), and reports of various Work Committees on specific topics.

Hubback,J.C. "Native women teachers in SA". United Empire 22, 1931, p.612-3.

Hubbard,M. & Qunta,V. Education for under employment - employment positions and opportunities of educated Africans in Cape Town, a survey of Langa. (Cape Town, SAIRR, pref. 1975) mimeo. 26p.

Huddleston,T. "The indivisibility of education", address by ... at annual meeting of the Education League 5/6/53. (Johannesburg 1953) 4p.

Huddleston,T. Death of a School. (St. Peters, Rosettenville). (Johannesburg, 1954) 4p.

Hudson,E.H. "Die geskiedenis van die onderwys in die gebied Zoutpansberg met verwysing na die maatskaplike verband". (D.Ed., UP, 1948) 386p. Bibliog.

Hudson,J. Bantu Education. (Summary of the findings from facts and figures derived from a questionnaire submitted to all branches of the NCW in anticipation of the Conference on the Bantu Education Act. NCW News 28(3) Sept. 1962.

Hughes,H. "Black Mission in South Africa: Religion and Education in the African Methodist Episcopal Church in South Africa. 1892-1953". (B.A. (Hons.) Dissertation, UW, 1976) (M.A. diss. SOAS 1978?).

Hughes,J. "Language problem in native education". SA Outlook 62: 1932,p.35.

Hunt Davis,R. Jr. See Davis.

Hunter,A.P. "The Reorientation of educational policy in South Africa since 1948". (Ed.D., Univ. of California, L.A., 1963) pp.276.

International Defence and Aid. Children Under Apartheid. (London 1980).

Inter-territorial Jeanes Conf., Salisbury, 1935. Findings (Lovedale 1935).

Ireland,R.R. "Current Status of Non-White Education in South Africa". School and Society 97: Oct.'69, p.381-386.

Ireland,R.R. "Bantu Primary and Secondary Education in the RSA". Social Studies 61: Apr. 1970, p.150-7.

Ireland,R.R. "Transkei: the significance of education for the development of the Republic of South Africa's first 'Bantustan'". Plural Societies 3, Spring 1972, p.39-58.

Ireland,R.R. "Education for What? A Comparison of the Education of Black South Africans and Black Americans". J. of Negro Education 41(3), 1972, pp-227-240.

Ireland,R.R. 'Specialized Educational Facilities for the Bantu in SA'. Intellect 102: Ja. 1974, p.265-9.

Ireland,R.R. 'Apartheid and the education of the coloureds in RSA'. Plural Soc. Summer 1974, pp.9-23.

Ireland,R.R. 'Apartheid and the education of the Indian community in the RSA'. Plural Societies Summer 1975, p.3-17.

Isaacs,H. 'Education in South Africa'. Inkwezi (7) Dec. 1977, p.29-33.

Jabavu,D.D.T. The Native Teacher out of school. (Pietermaritzburg, Natal Educ. Dept. 1918) 8p. (Paper read at Natal Native Teachers Conf. 1918. Bibliographical footnotes).

Jabavu,D.D.T. The Black Problem. (Lovedale 1920).

Jabavu,D.D.T. The Life of John Tengo Jabavu. (Lovedale 1922). See pp.69-109 "Education".

Jabavu,D.D.T. "Higher education and the professional training of the Bantu". S. Afr. J. Sci. XXVI, 1929, p.934-46.

Jabavu,D.D.T. "European teachers in Bantu schools". SA Outlook 70: F.1940, p.39-40. (A response to the article by J.W. Macquarrie in prev. edition).

Jabavu,D.D.T. and others. "The African child and what the school makes of him", in E.G. Malherbe (ed.) Educational Adaptations in a Changing World (1937) pp.432-44.

Jacobs,G.F. 'Testing Native aptitudes for mining'. Optima 7(2) June 1957,

Jacobs,G.F. 'Is education in SA geared for growth?' Business Alert 24, Oct. 1980, p.6-17.

Jacobs,S.V. 'The Development of post-primary education for the coloured child in the Cape Province from 1900 onward'. (UCT, B.Ed., 1946); 'The development of post-primary education for the Coloured Child in the Cape Province, Union of SA'. (M.A., Syracuse Univ., New York,1949)98p.

Jansen,I.D. "Die opvoeding van die Naturel". Die Kerkbode, XLV (24)
June 12, 1940, pp.1037-1038.

Janson,P. "Bantoe tegniese opleiding". S. Afr. Build. 53(11) N. 1975,p.16-17.

Jeffrey,R.M. "The Bantu Education Act and its effects". East and West
Review (1959) 25 (4) 1959, p.101-9.

Jenkins,E.R. "Bantu education". New Nation, 12-14, N. 1974.

Jerome,G. "To make good citizens of native youth". Farmer 35(52) D.27,'46,p.10.

Jiya,Y. "Problems in black education". NCW News 46(5) Nov. 1980, p.5-6.

Johannesburg (City) Non-European housing and native admin. dept.:
Anthropology and Social Welfare Branch. Survey of Bantu education
in Johannesburg. (Johannesburg 1938).

Johannesburg (City). Secondary school bursaries. (Johannesburg 1965).

Johannesburg council for adult education. Circular (misc.) 1949. 1
- Correspondence, 1944-1969, 5 boxes. (Johannesburg Public Library).

Johannesburg committee on non-European adult education. (a) Draft constitution
to be submitted to meeting of constituent bodies. (Johannesburg 1948)
5p. mimeo. (b) Pamphlet concerning adult educ. for non-Europeans in
Johannesburg. (Johannesburg 1947) mimeo. (c) "What's on? Johannesburg"
v.1. No.2, Feb. 1951.

Johannesburg Joint Council of Europeans and Africans. Provincial Memo. on
Native Education. (Johannesburg 1938).

Johannesburg Municipality (Non-European and Native Affairs Dept.). Report on
Bantu Schools in the Johannesburg area, including Alexandra Township.
(August 1938).

Johannesburg Municipality (Native Affairs Dept.) Education of native juvenile
delinquents passing through the probation office June 1937 - June 1938,
860 recorded cases. mimeo. 1938 2p. presented at Conference on Urban
Juvenile Native Delinquents held Johannesburg Oct. 1938.

Johannesburg Municipality, Non-European Housing and native admin. dept.
Anthropology and Social Welfare Branch. Survey of Bantu education in
Johannesburg. (Johannesburg 1938) 50p.

Johannesburg Municipality Library Dept. Municipal reference library.
Education Organizations (Johannesburg MRC 1941) 1p.

Johannesburg Municipality (Non-European Affairs Dept.) Schools in the
Bantu locations/villages, 30 June 1965. (Johannesburg 1965) 4p.

Johannesburg Municipality, Dept. of Non-European Affairs. Types of schools
by ethnic group and numbers of pupils as at 30 June 1971.
(Johannesburg, NEAD, 1971) 1p.

Johnson,K.C. "Non-European libraries in South Africa" - a paper prepared for
the S. African Library Assn. 25 June 1941. (Johannesburg, 1941) 63p.

Johnson,R.W. How Long Will South Africa Survive? (London, 1977) pp.197-201.
"The Road to Soweto".

Jones,B. "Educational Institutions: Pholela High School". Bantu Teachers J.
January 1956, p.83-91.

Jones,E.B. Memo. on the finances of native education for Council of SAIRR. (Johannesburg, SAIRR, 1943) RR 8/43.

Jones,E.B. A ten year plan? (Johannesburg SAIRR 1949) RR 183/49.

Jones,R.C. 'The development of attitudes leading to the nationalist apartheid philosphy of Bantu education in the RSA'. (Ph.D. diss., Oklahoma, Univ. of Oklahoma, 1966) 183p.

Jones,R.C. 'The Education of the Bantu in South Africa', in Rose,B. (ed.) Education in Southern Africa. (Johannesburg 1970) pp.38-89.

Jones,T.J. Educ. in Africa: a study of West, South and Central Africa by the African Education Committee under the auspices of the Phelps-Stokes Fund and foreign missionary societies of N. America and Europe. (New York, Phelps-Stokes Fund, 1922) (XXVIII 323pp. illus.)

Jones,T.J. Education in East Africa: a study of East, Central and S.A. by the second African Education Commission under the auspices of the Phelps-Stokes Fund, in co-op with the International Education Board. (New York, Phelps-Stokes Fund, 1924) (Reprinted, New York, Negro University Press, 1970).

Joorst,A. Compulsory education as a state obligation, etc. (Wynberg, TEPA, 1958). (TEPA pamphlet No. 2).

Joshua,F.P. 'The Coloured child: an analysis of the social, economic and educational background of the Coloured school children in the Cape Peninsula'. (B.Ed. thesis, UCT, n.d.).

Joubert,D.H. 'Report on an experiment made in teaching practice at St. Matthew's Training School in 1969'. Bantu Educ. J. 16(5) 1970, p.38-40.

Joubert,R.J.O. 'Onderwys en Ekonomiese Groei in Suid Afrika'. SAJE 47 (1979), pp.136-155.

Jowitt,H. "African education - a view of recent trends". SA Outlook 76: Mr. 1946, p.38-40.

Junod,H.A. "Native Education: what should be the place of the native language in native education?" - paper read at Johannesburg Missionary Conference, etc. (Morija, 1905) 17p. (Also see papers of General Missionary Conference 1905, p.63-80).

Junod,H.A. 'The Native Language and Native Education'. J. of the African Society 17, 1905, p.1-14.

Junod,H.A. "Native educ. and native literature" : address delivered at Bloemfontein Gen. Miss. Cong. 1909. (Lovedale 1909).

Kabane,M.L. & Rousseau,H.J. "Report of the interdepartmental committee on native education: the official and home languages in native schools: a discussion". SA Outlook 66: 1936, p.253-60.

Kabe,S.I. "Must educ. lead to detribalization?" Overseas Educ. XII, 1941,p.60-64.

Kahn,S. Sam Kahn speaks: the parliamentary record of SA's first communist M.P. (Cape Town 1949) p.21-28. Educ. Hist.

Kambule,T.W. 'Negotiations Futile'. Wits Student 21 Feb. 1977, p.6.

Kambule,T.W. 'Comments on Black Education'. Reality 10(5) S.1978, p.16-17.

Kamfer,L. 'Die probleem van skool verlating by Kleurlingkinders'.
     (M.A. thesis, US, 1954).

Kane-Berman,J. 'The Soweto upheavals: 16-22 June; a sociological and political
     analysis'. (Johannesburg, ASI, UW, Unpublished seminar paper, 1976).

Kane-Berman,J. Soweto: Black Revolt White Reaction. (Johannesburg 1978).
     (or The Method in the Madness) (London 1979).

Kannemeyer,H.D. 'A Critical Survey of Indian Education in Natal, 1860-1937'.
     (unpublished M.Ed., UW, 1943).

Kanya,C. The Training of African primary school teachers. NUSAS Research J.
     (Transkei Survey) n.d.

Karis,T. & Carter,G. (ed.) From Protest to Challenge: A Documentary History
     of African Politics in South Africa 1882-1964 (5 volumes) (Stanford 1972).

Katiya,N. The development of Bantu rural secondary education in the Ciskei,
     1941-1968, a historical survey. (Fort Hare 1973) (Based on M.Ed.
     thesis, Univ. of Fort Hare, bibliography p.98-101).

Kearney,P. "Success and failure of 'Sobululeka': Bishop Colenso and African
     education". Theoria 43: D. 1974, biblio. p.29-38.

Keegan,T.J. "African Responses to the Implementation of the Glen Grey
     Policy". (UCT Hons. diss., 1975) p.53,63-4 re Education; see p.53.

Keenan,J.H. "Open Minds and Closed Systems, Comments on the Functions and
     Future of the "Urban 'English-Speaking' University in South Africa".
     Social Dynamics 6(2) 1981, p.36-47.

Keller,B.B. "The Origins of Modernism and Conservatism among the Cape Nguni".
     (Ph.D., UCLA, Berkeley, 1970).

Kempen,P.D. "Rol van die pedagogiese institusie in die ontwikkelingsproses
     van Bantoetuislande met besondere verwysing na die Herscheldistrik in
     die Ciskei". T. Rasse-Aangeleent. 24: Ja. 1973 bibl. p.24-34.

Kendall,E. The End of an Era: Africa and the Missionary. (London 1978).

Kerr,A. "Need for a native higher education". SA Outlook LXII, 1932,p.130-3.

Kerr,A. "Native education: evidence laid before the Prov. Comm. - Aug.1933".
     SA Outlook LXIII, 1933, p.195-6.

Kerr,A. "Church's place in native educ." SA Outlook 69: 1939, p.162-3.

Kerr,A. "Report on the progress of native education".(to Christian Council
     of SA). SA Outlook 77: Jul. 1947, p.105-6.

Kerr,A. "Bantu Education Act". SA Outlook 84: June 1954, p.86-88.

Kerr,A. 'University Apartheid'. SA Outlook 87: 1957, p.53-56.

Kerr,A. Fort Hare, 1915-1948. The evolution of an African College.
     (London, 1968) 290p.

Keto,C.T. 'Black American involvement in South Africa's race issue'.
     Issue 3, 1 (1973) p.6-11.

Keto,C.T. "Race Relations, Land and the Changing Missionary Role in South
     Africa: A Case Study of the American Zulu Mission, 1850-1910".
     Int. J. of Afr. Hist. Stud. X(4) (1976) pp.600-627.

Keyter,J.de W. "Die algemene beginsels van die verslag van die kommissie insake naturelle-onderwys". (mimeo, SABRA, 1954).

Keyter,J.de W. 'Die geestesontwikkeling van die Bantoe, met spesiale verwysing na onderwys'. J. of Racial Affairs 11(4) July, 1960.

Kgware,W.M. "Part played by missionary churches in Bantu education in the province of the O.F.S." Student 5(6): 1952, p.23-25.

Kgware,W.M. "Bantu Education in the Province of the OFS during the 20th Century: 1900-1953: an historical study". (M.Ed., UNISA, 1955) (Summary, Heilbron, 1955).

Kgware,W.M. "Christian missions and Bantu education in the Free State". SA Outlook 85: Ja. 1955, p.8-11.

Kgware,W.M. "In search of an educational system: a critical appraisal of the past and present administrationoof Bantu educ." Inaugural address, Univ. of the North, 1961) 37p.

Kgware,W.M. "Education in a Bantu community". Bantu Educ. J. 8: S. 1962, port., p.363-65.

Kgware,W.M. "Present revolution in Bantu education in SA and its implications for the future". SA Outlook 96: N. 1966, p.176.

Kgware,W.M. "Bantu teacher-training schools in the OFS 1900-1960, with special attention to their admin. and control". (D.Ed., UNISA, 1969).

Kgware,W.M. ... "Primary and secondary schools in African education in SA" - introductory paper, etc. (Johannesburg, SAIRR, 1969) 21p. RR41/69.

Kgware,W.M. "Education for Africans" : address delivered at Bantu Education conference, Johannesburg, 1969. (Johannesburg, SAIRR, 1969) p.14.

Kgware,W.M. "Bildungsmöglichkeiten für die Bantu - Jugend sind gut - und werden jeds Jahr besser". Afrika-Post, 20: N. 1973, illus., p.430-1.

Kgware,W.M. "Education and the changing scene in black SA". Tvl. Educ. News 70(9): O. 1973, p.14-18.

Kgware,W.M. "Educational needs in relation to education for development". Paper given to the National colloquium; Man and His Environment in the Northern Homelands, held in Oct. 1973 at the Univ. of the North. 12p.

Kgware,W.M. "Education of the Africans in S. Afr." S. Afr. Intern., 5: O. 1974, biblio. p.75-86.

Kgware,W.M. "The Role of Black Universities in SA", in van der Merwe,H.W. and Welsh,D. (ed.) The Future of the University in Southern Africa. (Cape Town 1977).

Khoapa,B.A. Editor of Black Review 1972. See Black Review.

Khotseng,B. "A study of the development of technical education in a Black Community in SA with special reference to Qwaqwa". (M.Ed., U.Natal,1977).

Kidd,D. Kafir socialism and the dawn of individualism: an intro. to the study of the native problem. (London 1908) 286p. Ch.IV 'The Educ. of the Kafir'.

King,E. "An educational way ahead for South Africa". International Review of Education 25, 1979, p.481-500.

King,K.J. "Africa and the Southern States of the USA: Notes on J.H.Oldham and American Negro Education for Africans". JAH X(4) 1969 pp.659-677.

King,K.J. "James E. Aggrey: collaborator, nationalist, Pan African". Canadian J. of African Studies, III (1970).

King,K.J. "African students in the American Negro colleges: some notes on the 'good African'". Phylon 31 (Spring 1970) p.16-30.

King,K.J. Pan Africanism and Education. (Oxford, 1971).

Kingon,J.R.L. "Native education in the Transkei". S.A. J. Sc. 13 (1916) p.447-94. (Also printed as a pamphlet by the SA Association for the Advancement of Science, (Cape Town 1917) 48pp.)

Kleinschmidt,H. "Black Parents' Association". (Johannesburg 1976) mimeo.

Kloss,H. Problems of Language policy in SA. Ethnos 16, 1978, 68p.

Kobe,D., van Rooyen,I. and Verwey,C.T. 'n Statistiese oorsig van die skolestelsel in Lebowa. (Bloemfontein, UOVS Navorsingseenheid van Onderwysstelselbeplanning, 1980).

Kolege ya Bana ba Afrika. Univ. for non-Europeans in the Tvl. (Pretoria: The Temporary Committee, 1946) 39p. ill.

Krause "Die neue Entwicklung d Eingeborenen-schulwesers in Transvaal u. ihre Bedentung für unsere Arbeit". Miss u. Unterricht XVI, 1928,p.108-15.

Krige,E.J. "Some aspects of the educational pattern of the Bantu". Theoria 5: 1953, p.29-35.

Kumalo,C. "Education and ideology in SA, a sociological case study of African education". (M.Soc. Sc., U. Natal, 1954).

Kumalo,C. "Ideological and Institutional factors in the Debates on African Educ. in Kenya and South Africa". (Ph.D., Boston, 1959) 197p. bibliog.

Kumalo,M.B. "Swartonderwys en sy probleme". Buurman 6(4) p16-19 Jun. 1976.port.

Kuper,L. The college brew: a satire. (Durban 1960?).

Kuper,L. An African Bourgeoisie. Race, Class and Politics in SA. (New Haven and London 1965). esp. Ch. 13 'Teachers'.

Kuper,L. "African Nationalism in South Africa 1910-1964", in Wilson,M. and Thompson,L.M. (ed.) Oxford History of SA II (Oxford 1971) pp.424-476.

Kuppusami,C. "Indian Education in Natal, 1860-1946". (Unpub.M.Ed. UNISA 1946).

Kuppusami,C. & Pillay,M.G. Pioneer footprints: growth of Indian Education in SA 1860-1977. (Bloemfontein 1978) 119p.

Kuschke,H.F.G. "Naturelleonderwys is ons Plig". Die Basuin, I (6) (January 1931) pp.10-15.

Kuschke,H.F.G. "Native Education", in National European-Bantu Conference,5th, Bloemfontein, 1933, Report pp.145-55.

Kwazulu. Dept. of Education and Culture. Annual Reports 197- (Ulundi, 197-).

Lacey,M. Working for Boroko: The Origins of a Coercive Labour System in South Africa. (Johannesburg 1981) pp.422. (Based on "Land, Labour and Africa Affairs 1924-34" (M.A., UR, Grahamstown, 1979).)

Lanham,L.W. Teaching English in Bantu primary schools: a final report on research in Johannesburg schools. (Johannesburg, Engl. Academy of SA,1967).

Laubscher,J.M. "Die Koranasending en die ontwikkeling van onderwys in Gordonia (1871-1900". (M.Ed., US, 1946) v. 135.

Laurence,J.C. Race, Propaganda and SA. (London 1979) 215p.

Lautenschlager,G.M.P. Die sozialen Ondnungen bei den Zulu und die Mariaunhiller Mission 1882-1909. (Munster 1963) 395p. (Thesis diss.)

Lawson,L. "People's College: A South African experience in Mass Media Education", in Education and Development (NUSAS 1979) p.85.

Lee,R. "Evaluating an intensive educational programme" (SACHED) Tvl.Educ. News 73(11): N. 1976, p.10-13.

Leftwich,A. "Bantu education - what price indoctrination?" (Cape Town, NUSAS, 1961) (Paper delivered before the Western Cape branch of the SAIRR).

Legassick,M. NUSAS: ethnic cleavage and ethnic integration in the universities. (Los Angeles, U.C. 1967). (African Studies Centre, Occ. pap. No. 4).

Lekhela,E.P. "The Development of Bantu Education in the North-Western Cape 1840-1947. (A Historical Survey)". (M.Ed. diss., UNISA, 1958).

Lekhela,E.P. "The Origin, development and role of missionary teacher-training institutions for the Africans of the north-western Cape: an historical critical survey of the period 1850-1954". 2 v. (D.Ed UNISA 1970).

Lekhela,E.P. Tendencies in the history of Bantu Education in SA: Inaugural lecture, Sept. 1972. (Pietersburg, UN, Sovenga, 1972) 28p.

Lekhela,E.P. A survey of the development of education among the Botswana of Bophuthatswana. (Mafeking, 1972) 51p.

Lemana Training Institution, N. Tvl. Lemana Training Institution (Johannesburg, 1938?) 8p. (Founded by the Swiss Mission in 1906 to train Native Teachers).

Lennox,J. et al. Lovedale, SA. (Edinburgh, United Free Chruch of Scotland 1903).

Lennox,J. The story of our missions: South Africa. (Edinburgh: Foreign Mission Committee, United Free Church of Scotland, 1911).

Lennox,J. "What becomes of Fort Hare students?" SA Outlook LXIV 1934, p.90.

Lenyae,S.M. "A Comparative study of some problems encountered in teacher education in Bophuthatswana and Botswana". (M.Ed. diss., UN, Pietersburg, 1977).

Leipoldt,C.L. "Medical Training of Natives". J. of the Medical Association of SA, 22 Dec. 1928.

Leonard,L.D. "Apartheid and Education in the Republic of South Africa since 1948". (Ed.D. M.A.(?) diss. Utah State Univ. 1970) 225p.

Leonie,A. "The development of Bantu education in SA: 1652 to 1954". (Ph.D., Montana State Univ., Bozeman, 1965) biblio. pp.217. (Ann Arbor, 1967).

Le Roy,A.E. "The educated native: facts vs theory", a paper read before the SA General Missionary Conference (Johannesburg, 9 July 1906) 15p. or Dundee, Natal, Church of Sweden Mission, n.d. or pamphlet of the American Zulu Mission 1966/7 Reviewed in Chronicle of the LMS, July 1907, p.127.

Le Roy,A.E. "Does it pay to educate the native?" S. Afr. J. Sc. 15: 1919, pp.339-56.

Leshoai,B. "Education for what?" The Voice 4(3) 23-9 Jan., 1980 p.6; "How blacks were conned by the whites" The Voice 30 Ja. - 5 Feb. 1980, p.6.

Lesolang,S.J.J. "Hungry teachers can't teach hungry children". Tvl. Educ. News 40(6) Jun. - Jul. 1944, p.8.

Lestrade,G.P. "Die Plek van die Naturelle-taal in die Naturelle-onderwys". Die Basuin I, (3) July 1930, pp.3-6.

Levin,R. (spelt Lewin by mistake in AP 17). "Black Education, Class struggle and the Dynamics of Change in South Africa since 1946". Africa Perspective 17 (Spring 1980) pp.17-41.

Lewin,J. "Shall we cheat their children?" (Discussion of Eiselen report). Forum 2(5): Aug. 1953 p.13-14.

Lewin,J. "Education to make men free!" Africa Today IV (6) Nov. Dec. 1957 (Special Issue).

Lewis,L.J. Equipping Africa: educational development in Br. Colonial Africa, Etc. (London 1948).

Liebenberg,B.A. "Vroeë pogings om die Hottentotte op te voed (1795-1814)". (M.Ed. diss., US, 1943) 180p. bibliog.

Liebenberg,J.J. "Die Gesichte des Berufs - und Fach-schulwesens in Südafrika". (Phil, F., Diss., Univ. of Munich, Germany 1933) pp171.

Liston,J.A.M. "An Examination of the rationale and implications of TEACH". (B.Ed. diss., UW, 1978).

Lloyd,B.W. "Native Education (primary) in the Union of S. Africa". Overseas Education (1932) v.3 pp.164-72.

London Missionary Society. South African Council. "The future of Tiger Kloof": (a paper read before the South African Council of the London Missionary Society at their meetings held at Tiger Kloof, March 1911). (Tiger Kloof, C.P., Tiger Kloof Native Institution, 1911, 8p.).

Loram,C.T. "Dissertation on the education of the SA native". Teach Col. Rec. 17: (1916) pp.268-73.

Loram,C.T. The Education of the South African Native. (London 1917, 1927).

Loram,C.T. "Education of the S. African Native", in Chr. Exp. Aug. 1917, pp.118-21, Sept. 1917, pp.135-6.

Loram,C.T. Three Lectures on the New Education ... 1918, Durban Technical College. (Durban 1918) (Lectures by Campbell,S.G., Narbeth,B.N. and Loram,C.T.).

Loram,C.T. "Suggestions towards a better provision for the medical needs of the Natives". S. Afr. Ass. Sci. Rep. 15: 1918, p.319-24.

Loram,C.T. "The Phelps-Stokes Education Commission in South Africa". Int. Rev. Missions X, Oct. 1921, pp.496-508.

Loram,C.T. "The Claims of the Native Question upon Scientists". S. Afr. J. Sci., 1921 pp.99-109.

Loram,C.T. "South Africa", in Educational Yearbook of the Int. Inst. of Teachers College. (New York, Columbia Univ., 1924-1925) p.387-429.

Loram,C.T. "What is wrong with Native education?" Native Teachers J.4: Ja. 1925, p.192-3.

Loram,C.T. "Adaptation of the Penn School Methods to Education in South Africa". (New York, Phelps-Stokes Fund, 1927).

Loram,C.T. "National system of Native education in SA". S. Afr. J. Sci. 26: 1929, p.921-27.

Loram,C.T. "Education in the Union". (typescript of a paper) (1980) (Loram Papers, Yale University).

Loram,C.T. "Native education in SA: the community outlook". School and Soc., XXXIII 69-73, 1931. (Original typescript in Loram Papers Folder CT, Yale University dated 1930).

Loram,C.T. (C.T. Loram) Native Teachers J. 10: Jul.1931, p.165-66.

Loram,C.T. "Native progress and improvement in race relations in SA", twenty year report of the Phelps-Stokes Fund 1911-1931. (New York, Phelps-Stokes, 1932, pp.84-92).

Loram,C.T. "Missionary education and social questions", in Int. Inst. Teachers' Coll. Univ. Ed. Yearbook, 1933, pp.259-98.

Loram,C.T. "Natives going to U.S.A. to study for degrees". SA Outlook 70: Sept. 1940, p.165.

Louw,J.F. "Onderwys" in Theron,E. Die Kleurlingbevolking van Suid Afrika, (SABRA Verslag). (Stellenbosch 1964) p.140-156. (Ook in Alpha 2(1) Jan. 1964, p.2-4).

Louw,W. "Bantu education: facts and figures in review". J. Racial Affairs 13: Jun. 1962, p.151-61, bibliog.

Louw,W. "Bantoe-Onderwys in perspektief". SABRA - News Letter 50 (15 May 1963) p.1-8.

Louw,W.J. Paper on Coloured Education given at a symposium convened by the National Council of Women of SA. (Johannesburg, June 1966).

Lovedale Education Board. "Is our native education on right lines?": an experimental inquiry into the results of education of native scholars in the higher standards of the Cape Provincial School Code, contributed by a member of the Lovedale Educ. Board. (Lovedale 1924 (1930?)) 24p.

Lovedale Missionary Institution. Lovedale past and present: a register of 2000 names ... (of ex-students) by J. Stewart. (Lovedale 1887)xxiii 642p.

Lovedale Missionary Institution. Lovedale, Past and Present: a Statement. (Cape Town, 1884) 12p.

Lovedale Missionary Institution. The jubilee of Lovedale Missionary Institution 21-22 July 1891. (Lovedale 1891) 48p.

Lovedale Missionary Institution. Lovedale, South Africa: fifty views from photographs. J. Stewart (ed.) (Edinburgh, 1894) 110p.

Lovedale Missionary Institution. Lovedale appeal: issued by authority of the governing council. (Cape Town 1926) 28p.

Lovedale Missionary Institution. Lovedale Centenary: a record of the celebrations 19-21 July 1941. (Lovedale 1941) 118p.

Lovedale Missionary Institution. Memo submitted to the Inter Departmental Committee of enquiry into Native Education, 15 Nov. 1935 (mimeo.).

Lovedale Missionary Institution. Handbook of information for parents and guardians. (Lovedale 1950).

Lovedale - Native Convention 1905. Proceedings of Native Convention held at Lovedale : (Inter-State Native College Scheme) 28-29 Dec. 1905. (Lovedale, 1906) 23p.

Lovell,O.E. "Missionary Education and the South African problem". (M.A., Univ. of Chicago, Ill., 1919) 100p.

Lovett,R. The history of the London Missionary Society, 1795-1895. 2 vols. (London 1899).

Low,V.N. "Education for the Bantu: a South African dilemma". Comparative Educ. Rev. 2(2), Oct. 1958, p.21-27.

Lubbe,A.N.P. "Some interesting statistical facts about Bantu education". (title varies). Bantu Educ. J. 12(3) Ap.-Dec. 1966; 13(1) F.-D. 1967, p.10; 14(2) Mr.-D. 1968, p.10.
   - Some interesting statistical facts about Bantu education: the matriculation results, Bantu Educ. J. 15(2) Mar. 1969, p.10-13.
   - Some interesting statistical facts about Bantu education: the number of schools ... in 1968. Bantu Educ. J. 15(4) May 1969, p.16-19.
   - Some interesting statistical facts about Bantu education: teachers. Bantu Educ. J. 15(5) June 1969, p.8-10.

Lubbe,A.N.P. "First national convention for Bantu teachers of science and mathematics". Bantu Educ. J. 15(7), Sept. 1969, p.8-9 illus.

Lubbe,A.N.P. "Some interesting statistical facts about Bantu education". Bantu Educ. J. 15(1), Feb. 1970, p.18-19.

Lubbe,A.N.P. (comp.) Bantu Education in the RSA. (Johannesburg, 1971). (various editions for 1969, 70, 71, etc.) + 100p.

Lubbe,A.N.P. Education and Careers for the Bantu Peoples of the RSA. (Johannesburg 1973) 118p.

Luthuli,A.J. "Vernacular as a medium of instruction". Native Teachers' J. 14, 1934, p.30-4.

Luthuli,A. Let My People Go. (London 1962) re Bantu Educ. Act - pp.40,47-52, 146-8,157,192,195.

Luthuli,P.C. The Philosophical foundation of Black Education in South Africa. (Durban 1981).

Luthuli,P.C. An Introduction to Black-Orientated Education in SA. (Durban 1982).

Lynch,I.R. "The Financing of state education in the Union of S. Afr. 1910-1935". (M.Ed., Pretoria, 1935) 74p. bibl. p.48-58 native education.

Lyons,C. To Wash an Aethiop White: British Ideas about Black African Educability. (New York 1975) Educ. in SA pp.134-143. See Index.

M.,J.G. "Verslag van die Naturelleonderwyskommissie". Unie 47, Apr.1952,p.233-5.

MacCrone,I.D. "Race Attitudes in South Africa; historical, experimental and psychological attitudes. (Oxford, 1937).

MacDonald,O.A. "Groei en ontwikkeling van Bantoe-onderwys in die N. Transvaalse streek". Bantoe-Onderwys bl. 9, Mr. 1963, p.74-77 illus.

MacDonald,M.A. "The science education project in the Ciskei: Materials, training, context and outcomes. (Johannesburg 1980) 75p.

MacDonald,M.A. & Gilmour,J.D. Teacher reaction to innovation. The reaction
    of Ciskei teachers to the Science Education Project. (Johannesburg,
    UW, the Project, 1980).

MacIntyre,A.S. "A Technical School for Natives". S.Afr. J. Sci. v. 32,
    1935, pp.671-79.

Mackenzie,J. "The Moffat Institution". The Christian Express XIII, 1 May
    1883, p.7o-71.

Macmillan,R.G., Hey,R.D. & Macquarrie,J.W. (eds.) "Education and our
    Expanding Horizons". (National Conference on Education, Durban,1960)
    (Durban 1962).

Macmillan,R.G. "Education and legislation in South Africa". Comparative
    Educ. Review 6(1) June 1962.

Macmillan,R.G. & Behr,A.L.   See Behr,A.L. (1966).

Macmillan,W.M. "The Importance of the Educated African". J. of the Africa
    Society 33 (CXXXI) 1934, p.137-142.

MacQuarrie,J.W. "Native Economic Commission report: Native education".
    SA Outlook LXII 1932, p.190-193.

MacQuarrie,J.W. "The New education and the natives". SA Outlook LXIV,
    1934, pp.181-105, 201-205.

MacQuarrie,J.W. "Native, educ. and the Provincial Finance Comm." SA Outlook
    LXIV, 1934, p.28-32.

MacQuarrie,J.W. "Cape and Native Education". SA Outlook LXV, 1935, p.249-252.

MacQuarrie,J.W. "Native Education Committee". SA Outlook LXV, 1935,p.230-2.

MacQuarrie,J.W. "Some needs of native education". SA Outlook LXVII, 1937,
    p.180-184.

MacQuarrie,J.W. "Education at the Cape in 1938". SA Outlook 70, 1940,p.9-10.

MacQuarrie,J.W. "European Teachers in Bantu Schools". SA Outlook 70, 1940,
    p.19-20. (See also response to this article by D.D.T. Jabavu and
    Z.K. Matthews in following edition).

MacQuarrie,J.W. "Has missionary education failed?" SA Outlook 84, Oct. 1954,
    p.149-51.

MacQuarrie,J.W. "New order in Bantu education". Afr. South 1(1), Oct.-Dec.
    1956, p.32-42.

MacQuarrie,J.W. ... The implementation of the Bantu Education Act.
    (Johannesburg, SAIRR, 1957?).

MacQuarrie,J.W. "Race and education in SA". Phi Delta Kappan 41(4),
    Jan. 1960, pp.169-173.

MacQuarrie,J.W. "The African in the City: his education". (Johannesburg,
    SAIRR, 1960) RR 130/60.

MacQuarrie,J.W. "Race and Language in South African Education", in MacMillan,
    R.G. et al. (1962) p.200-222.

MacQuarrie,J.W. "The Main needs for the future in Bantu Education". (Theme
    Paper) (1969 conference on Bantu Educ.) (Johannesburg,SAIRR,1969)RR 2/69.

McConkey,W.G. "Future of Indian education". Theoria 15: 1960, p.28-37.

McConkey,W.G. Memorandum submitted at the request of the S.A. Institute of
    Race Relations, of the Commission of Inquiry into the Educational Standard
    of the Official Languages in the Transkei. (Johannesburg, SAIRR, 1962).
    6p. (RR 134/62).

McConkey,W.G. Twilight in Education. (Durban, SAIRR, 1962) NR 47/1962.
    (Reproduced from articles published in the Natal Mercury 10-13 Apr. 1962).

McConkey,W.G. The failure of Bantu Education. (Cape Town 1970) 15p.

McConkey,W.G. "Bantu education: a critical survey". Theoria 38, May 1972,
    p.1-43, bibliog.

McKenzie,P. Report on disturbances in African schools by regional secretary,
    S. Tvl. Region. (Johannesburg,SAIRR,1964) 3p. (RR 19/64).

McKerron,M.E. A History of Education in South Africa 1652-1932. (Pretoria,
    1934) 182p. Ch. 7, p.154-180 'Non-European Education'.

McLarty,M. Education in South Africa: what has been done and what remains
    to be done. (Johannesburg: Soc. of the Friends of Africa, 1946).
    (S. African Affairs Pamphlet No. 12, 2nd series).

Malcolm,D.McK. Corporation native aided night schools. (Rules for the conduct
    of native night schools). (n.p. 1925).

Mafeje,A. "Soweto and its aftermath". RAPE 11 (1979) p.17-36. ("After Soweto -
    a Response". (ibid.) p.93-100) (R. First).

Mahabir,B. Indian education in South Africa after nationalisation: a meta-
    pedagogical perspective. (M.Ed. diss., UNISA, 1977).

Maharaj,S.R. "Secondary education for Indians in Natal". (Unpub. Ph.D.
    thesis, UND, 1961).

Maharaj,S.R. An investigation into the status of the vernacular languages
    in Natal. (Pretoria, HSRC, 1974).

Maharaj.S.R. "Education for South Africa's people", in Stepping into the
    Future part III. (Johannesburg 1975).

Maimane,H.M. "African education and religious instruction". SA Outlook 74,
    May 1944, p.67-8.

Majeke,N. (Dora Taylor). The Role of the Missionary in Conquest. (Cape
    Town, 1952).

Makanya,U.S. "Problem of the Zulu girl". Native Teachers' J. (Natal) X,
    1931, p.116-120.

Makapan,H.R.M. "Onderwys uit die volk, vir die volk". Lantern 4: Jun. 1955,
    p.353-55 illus.

Malherbe,E.G. "Education in South Africa 1652-1922". (Ph.D. Teachers College,
    Columbia, 1924).

Malherbe,E.G. Education in South Africa. (Vol. I 1652-1922) (Cape Town,
    1925) (Reprinted 1975).

Malherbe,E.G. Education in South Africa. (Vol. II 1923-1973) (Cape Town 1976).

Malherbe,E.G. "Native Education in the Union of South Africa". The Yearbook
    of Education 1933, pp.601-24.

Malherbe,E.D. (ed.) Handbook on Education and Social Work in SA. (The New
    Education Fellowship (SA) Secretariat: National Bureau of Education
    and Social Research, Pretoria, 1934).

Malherbe,E.G. "Cultural and Economic Forces in SA Education". The Yearbook
    of Education 1936, pp.644-672.

Malherbe,E.G. (ed.) Educational Adaptations in a Changing Society. (Report
    of 1934, SA Educ. Conference) (New Education Fellowship) (Cape Town
    1937) - Part II Educ. in a Changing Afr. Society, pp.403-520.

Malherbe,E.G. Educational and social research in South Africa. (Pretoria,
    SACESR, 1939 Research Series No. 6).

Malherbe,E.G. Race Attitudes and Education. (Hoernlé Memorial Lecture).
    (Johannesburg, SAIRR, 1946) 29p.

Malherbe,E.G. "Higher education for Non-Europeans in S. Afr." Afr. World
    Nov. 1947, p.9-10.

Malherbe,E.G. "Higher Education of Non-Europeans in South Africa". Optima
    6(1) 1956, p.1-9. (Reprinted in SA Outlook 2/7/56).

Malherbe,E.G. Education for leadership in Africa. (Durban 1961) 25p.

Malherbe,E.G. Manpower Training: educational requirements for economic
    expansion. (Durban, SAIRR, 1965) (RR 5/65).

Malherbe,E.G. "Education and the Development of South Africa's human resources":
    paper delivered to the 1966 National Congress of the Progressive Party
    of SA. (Athlone, 1966) 66p.

Malherbe,E.G. "Bantu Manpower and Education": a theme paper delivered on
    Jan. 17th at the 1969 conf. on Bantu Education. (Johannesburg, SAIRR,
    1969) p.38.

Malherbe,E.G. "Conflict and Progress in education", in Hellman,E. and Lever,H.
    (eds.) Conflict and Progress: 50 Years of Race Relations in SA.
    (Johannesburg, SAIRR, 1979) 278p. Ch. 7.

Malinga,B.J. "Environmental influences on the education of Zulu children in
    Natal Native primary schools". (M.Ed., UNISA, 1946) 54pp.

Malinowski,B. "Native Education and Culture Contact", (address Cape Town 1934).

Manganyi,N.C. Being Black in the World. (Johannesburg, SPROCAS, 1973).

Mangope,L.M. "Development significance of technical education". Development
    4, 1977, p.11.

Marable,M. "A Black School in South Africa". Negro History Bulletin,
    1974, pp.258-61.

Marais,J.C. "Die socio-ekonomiese agtergrond as faktor by die druiping van
    skoolgaande Kleurlingkinders op die platteland van die Kaapprovinsie".
    (M.A. thesis, US, 1955).

Marais,N.J. "Die voorsiering en administrasie van Kleurlingonderwys in
    Kaapland, veral sedert 1910". (M.Ed. thesis, US, 1955).

Maree,L. "What shall we tell the Blacks?" Bantu Educ. in SA: its problems
    and possibilities". (Unpub. MA, London Univ., Goldsmith College, 1976).

Maree,W.A. "Opening address ... to discuss draft regulations for an advisory
    board for Bantu education ...". Bantu Educ. J. 9: Mr. 1963, p.106-8, port.

Marianhill Mission Press. The Student Teachers' Handbook on Organization and Management of African Schools. (Marianhill, 1939) 176p.

Marks,S. "The Ambiguities of Dependence: John L. Dale of Natal". JSAS 1(2) April 1975, pp.162-180.

Marquard,L. & Standing,R.G. The Southern Bantu. (London 1939).

Marquard,L. (pseud. Burger,John). The Black Man's Burden. (Washington, New York, 1943, Reissue, 1973). Ch. XI Education p.166-180.

Marquard,L. The Native in South Africa. (Johannesburg 1944).

Marquard,L. The People and Policies of South Africa. (Cape Town 1960, 1962). - Ch.8 - 'Education' pp.177-203; pp.220-221, Coloured and Asian Educ.; pp.221-232, University Education.

Martin,J.P. "Education for the Zulu: the experience of the American Board in Natal, 1860-1880". (M.A. Teachers' College, Columbia Univ., New York, 1968-8).

Mashologu,B. "Prospects for the natives of SA after completing a college course, re work and service among his own people". SA Outlook LXI,1931, p.97.

Mason,F. The Native policy in Natal, past and future. (Durban 1906) 36p.

Mathie,M.P.C. "Education in the Cape Province from 1929-1945". (B.Ed. diss., UCT, 1947).

Matseke,S.K. "High School Education for Africans", in Tunmer,R. and Muir,R.K. (eds.) Some Aspects of Education in South Africa. (African Studies Programme, UW, Johannesburg, 1968) Occasional Paper No. 4, pp.48-58.

Matshoba,M. "Soweto sceptical about the coming of compulsory education". Race Relations News 43(1) Jan./Feb. 1981.

Matthews,Z.K. "The Native Economic Commission and native education". SA Outlook LXII, 1932, p.213-4.

Matthews,Z.K. "Educational needs of the Bantu", in National European-Bantu Conference. (5th, Bloemfontein, 1933) p.139-44.

Matthews,Z.K. "Certain considerations regarding Native Education in South Africa". May, 1934, typescript, Karis & Carter microfilm, Reel 18A, 2: XM66: 83/1; and "The Educated Native in South Africa", typescript K & C. Reel 18A, 2: XM 66: 77/17.

Matthews,Z.K. "Who should control native education?" Teaching in Africa III (1) 1939, p.1-4.

Matthews,Z.K. "European teachers in Bantu schools". SA Outlook LXX 1940,p.39-40.

Matthews,Z.K. "Native education in SA during the last 25 years". SA Outlook 76, Sept. 1946, pp.138-141.

Matthews,Z.K. & M'Timkulu,D.G.S. "The future in the light of the Tomlinson Report", in Race Relations J. 24 (1-2) Jan.-June, 1957, p.12-19.

Matthews,Z.K. "Ethnic Universities". Africa South I(4) July-Sept.1957,p.40-48.

Matthews,Z.K. "The University College of Fort Hare". SA Outlook 87, 1957, I p.57-64; II p.74-77.

Matthews,Z.K. "The education of the African", in Spottiswoode,H. (ed.) South Africa: The Road Ahead. (Cape Town 1960) 248p.

Matthews,Z.K. "African awakening and the universities ...", the Third T.B. Davie Memorial Lecture delivered at UCT on 15 Aug., 1961. (Cape Town, 1961) 20p.

Matthews,Z.K. Freedom for my people: The autobiography of Z.K. Matthews: Southern Africa 1901-1968. Memoir by Wilson,M. (Cape Town 1981) 253p.

Maurice,E.L. "The History and Administration of the Education of the Coloured Peoples of the Cape 1652-1910". (B.Ed. thesis,UCT, 1946) 2 vols. (Ch. I-V, Educ. of Slaves; Ch. VI-VII, Educ. of Hottentots; Ch. VIII, Educ. of Coloureds).

Maurice,E.L. & Kies,B.M. Education Ordinance No. 20, 1956 with annotations. (Cape Town and Johannesburg 1957) 313p.

Maurice,E.L. The Colour Bar in Education. (The Teachers' League of SA, The A.J. Abrahamse Memorial Lecture) (Cape Town 1957) 47p.

Maurice,E.L. "The Development of policy in regard to the education of coloured pupils at the Cape, 1880-1940". (Ph.D., UCT, 1966).

Maurice,E. "What did you learn in School today? 80 Years of Educational Protest", (background to 'Coloured education' and the coloured community protest against the inferior system) SASH 23(4) Feb. 1981, pp.2-10.

Mayhew,A. Education in the Colonial Empire. (London 1938).

Maytham,Y.M. Conflicting Views on the National Advisory Education Council: as reflected in the proceedings of a Select Committee. (Johannesburg, SAIRR, 1963) p.13.

Mazibuko,F. "Bantu Education. An Obstacle to Development", in Education and Development (NUSAS 1979) p.51.

Mbanjwa,T. Editor of Black Review 1974-5. See Black Review.

Mbatha,M.B. "African Education in South Africa", in Macmillan,R.G. et al. (1962) p.226-227.

M'Belle,B.I. Kafir Scholar's Campanion. (Lovedale 1903).

Mbere,A.M. "An Analysis of the Association between Bantu Education and Christian Nationalism: A study of the role of ideology in Education". (Ed.D. Harvard, 1979).

Mdhluli,S.V.H. The development of the African. (Marianhill, 1933) 64p. (Reprint in 1968, State Library, Pretoria, No. 20) 64p. - Ch. IX, 'Educ. Progress'.

Mdedle,B.B. "Cape African Teachers in Conference". SA Outlook XII, 1932,p.181-2.

Mdedle,B.B. "Recent trends of native education in the Cape". SA Outlook 80: Dec. 1950, p.182-3.

Mdluli,S.B. A description of the educational system of Kwazulu with emphasis on pupil repetition. (Bloemfontein, UOFS Research Unit for Education System Planning, 1980).

Mears,W.G. "The Educated Native in Bantu Communal life", in Schapera,I. (ed.) Western Civilization and the Natives of South Africa. (London 1934) P.85-101.

Medlicott,P. "Black Education in South Africa". New Society (1.5.75) pp.261-64.

Meer,F. "Education in a multi-racial South Africa". Reality Sept. 1974, p.7-11.

Mehlape,P. "Wat wil die kinders van Soweto?" Buurman 8(1): S. .1977,p.27-28 illus.

Meiring,J.G. "Naturelle-onderwys", in Die Naturellevraagstuk. (Salira, n.d.).

Mentz,J.C.N. "Compulsory education for the Bantu of SA". J. Racial Affairs 19(3) Jul. 1968, p.35-44 bibliog.

Methodist Church. The story of Indaleni. (Pietermaritzburg, 192?).

Methodist Church. Shawbury: the Story of a Mission 1843-1943 (ed.) by D. Wilson (Lovedale 1943).

Methodist Church of S.A. (Conference Programme Committee). Programme of education in race relations: notes and suggested outlines of procedure for districts and regional conferences, circuit study groups, etc. Bibliog. p.9-11, 11p. (n.d.)

Meyer,L.E. "Oppression or Opportunity?: Inside the Black Universities of South Africa". The J. of Negro Studies XLV (4) 1976, p.365-382.

Mfeka,R. "Educated African after 25 years". New Nation 6(11) Jun. 1973, p.11-13, port.

Mhlongo,S. "Classes in South Africa". Race and Class 16(3) 1975 p.259-94.

Millar,C. "An Adventurous Cinderella", (non-formal education for blacks seen as both an individual opportunity and a political constraint). SASH 23(4) Feb. 1981, p.11-13.

Mills,W.G. "The Role of African Clergy in the Reorientation of Xhosa Society to the Plural Society of the Cape Colony, 1850-1915". (Ph.D.,UCLA,1975).

Mjamba,H. "The United Transkeian Territories African Teachers Assoication". SA Outlook 71 (839) 1 March 1941, p.60. (Report of the annual conf.).

Mkize,I.M.D. "The Cape African Teacher". (M.Ed., UNISA, 1941).

Mlahleki,M.I. Little Known Facts about Kilnerton Institution. (n.p., the author, 1967).

Mncube,F.C.M. Bantu school boards and school committees. (Johannesburg, NCW, 1962) 2p.

Mncube,F.C.M. The School and the Community. (Johannesburg, SAIRR, 1969).

"Mnguni". A History of South Africa. (Cape Town 1952).

Mnguni,E.E. "Youth work (among natives)". Native Teachers' J. 29: Ap. 1950, p.164-7.

Mocke,H.A. "Die Geskiedenis van die onderwys vir Bantoedowes in SA". (D.Ph8l., UP., 1971).

Moeketse,J. "Mnr. O. Venter en Bantoe-onderwys". Bantoe-Onderwysbl. 5: Oct. 1959 port. p.439-40.

Moerane,M.T. "The road ahead for African urban youth". Paper delivered at the J.C.C. Symposium "Conference and the urban Bantu", Nov.1971. (Mimeo,4p.)

Mohanoe,P.F. "Psycho-cultural considerations in the learning of the black pupil: a didactical reflection". Inaugural lecture, UN, 5 Sept. 1974. (Sovenga, UN, 1976) bibliog. p.19-20-

Möhr,L.V. Present facilities and future plans in Coloured Education: A survey. (Johannesburg, SAIRR, 1971).

Möhr,L.V. Education for Progress. (from a survey "Present facilities and future plans in Coloured education). Alpha 9 1972 (4,5,9); 10 1972 (1,2,3).

Mokgeledi,L. African educ. in the Tvl.: are teachers in the Tvl. getting a square deal? (Johannesburg, African Orthodox Church Pub. Dept. 1933, 4p.) - "An African Teachers Defence Fund appeal". (No place or date).

Mokgokong,P.C. "Language, homeland and social background and their significance on education". Discussion 1965/6, p.12-13.

Molema,S.M. The Bantu past and present: an ethnographical and historical study of the native races of SA. (Edinburgh, 1920). (Part III: The Present p.202-219 'Missionaries and Missions'; p.226-237 'Education of the Bantu').

Molope,N.J.K. "Now that idol had feet of clay, whither do we go?". The Voice 25 Nov. 1978, p.13.

Moloto,E.S. "Bemerkungen eines Bantu-Erziehungsplanners". Afrika-Post 20: Nov. 1973 illus. p.431-33.

Moloto,E.S. (ed.) A survey of the development of education among the Botswana of Bophuthatswana, by E.P. Lekhela and others (Mafeking 1973?) Bibl. p.51.

Moloto,E.S. Vooruitsigte van die Tswana op onderwysgebied. (Pretoria,SABRA,1969).

Molteno,F. "The Uprisings of 16th June: A Review of the Literature". Social Dynamics 5(1) 1979, p.54-76.

Moodley,K. "The Politization of Ethnic Universities", in P. van den Berghe (ed.) The Liberal Dilemma in SA. (London 1979).

Mooki,E. "Education for African Children at Primary Level", in Tunmer,R. and Muir,R.K. (ed.) Some Aspects of Education in SA. (African Studies Programme (UW, 1968) Occasional Paper No. 4) pp.42-47.

Motapanyane,T. "How the June 16 demo was planned". Sechaba 11(2) 1977.

Motlana,N. "Crisis in education - a black man's view". Reality 11(2) Mr.'79,p.8.

Mphahlele,M.C.T. "The Methodist Venture in Education at Kilnerton 1886-1962: An Historical-Critical Survey". (M.Ed., UN., 1972).

Msomi,J.E.B. "The Development of African Education in SA, 1954-1977". (Unpublished Ph.D. Syracuse Univ., 1978) 255p.

Msomi,J.E.B. "The development of African education in SA before 1958". Paidonomia 8(1) June 1980, p.25-35.

M'Timkulu,D.G.S. "The African and education". Race Relations J. 16(3) 1949, p.56-63.

M'Timkulu,D.G.S. "Ohlange Institute: Its History and Development". Bantu Teachers J. Jan. 1950, p.21-24.

Mtimkulu,D.G.S. "Teaching of English in Bantu schools". SA Outlook 88: Aug. 1958, p.123-5.

Mtoba,L.S. Speech by Mr. Mtoba: (Advisory board for Bantu education). Bantu Education J. 18(9) Nov. 1972, p.30-31.

Muhlbauer,P. "Native education in Natal". Natal Teachers J. VII, 1927, p.56-8.

Muir,R.K. & Tunmer,R. "The African's desire for education in South Africa". Comparative Education 9(3) Oct. 1965.

Muir,T. Diaries of the S.G.E.'s tours 1909-12. Contents: (1) Transkeian Tour 1909, etc. (Mss. South African Public Library, Cape Town).

Mulder,P.W.A. Die Ontwikkeling en beheer van Tegniese en beroepsonderwys onder provinsiale bestuur in SA van 1910-1924. (D.Ed., UPotch, 1963).

Mulira,E.M.K. The vernacular in African education. (London 1951).

Mumford,W.R. "The Conference on Native Education in Johannesburg". (New Education Fellowship). J. of the African Society 33 (CXXXIII) 1934 p.411-413.

Munro,D. "Environment and the intellectual growth of pre-school urban African children". Bull. Inst. Social Res. 1: 1966 p.31-36, bibliog.

Murphree,M.W. Education, Development and Change in Africa. (Hoernlé Memorial Lecture) (Johannesburg, SAIRR, 1976).

Murphy,E.J. "Bantu Education in South Africa: its compatability with the contrasting objectives of African self-development and white domination". (Ph.D., Univ. of Connecticut, Storrs, 1973, pp.268).

Murray,A.V. The school in the bush: study of the theory and practice of native education in Africa. (London 1929 and 1938).

Murray,A.V. "Native education in the Union of South Africa". Overseas Education VIII, 1937, p.126-30.

Musi,O. "A million kids on the streets". Drum Jan. 1977, p.35-36.

Muso,T. "African advancement foundation". Zonk 11(9): S. 1959, p.35-37, port.

Muthiora,J. "Education and Apartheid in South Africa". (Ph.D., George Washington Univ., Washington, D.C. 1971).

Mvemve,E. "On appreciating the child's point of view". Native Teachers' J. 29 (sic. 28) Jul. 1949, p.261-63.

Myers,D. U.S. Business in S.A. (Bloomington and London, 1980) - ('Education Under Apartheid', p.20-3; 'Training Opportunities for Blacks, p.24-26).

Naidoo,K.P. "Post primary education for Indians in Natal, 1927-1952". (Unpub. M.Ed. thesis, UNISA, 1953).

Naidoo,M.S. "A study of truancy among the pupils in the Indian school in the Clairwood area". (Unpub. M.Ed. thesis, UND, 1957).

Naidoo,R.S. "The Indian Community and Education". Race Relations News 38(11) 1976, p.2.; "Evaluation of education(Indian)" Race Relations News 38(12) 1976 p.6.

Narseth,B.M. Annual Report on Indian Technical education, 1938-1939. (Publisher, place of publ. and date not available).

Nash,J.O. A South African comment on the school question.(London 1925) 24p.

Natal Colony. A Project for the promotion of educ. in general as well as for the European as for the native races of Natal, by J. Stuart. (Pietermaritzburg, 1859).

Natal Colony - Official. Coolie Commission 1872. Report of the Coolie Commission appointed to enquire into the conditions of the Indian immigrants in the Colony of Natal; the mode of their employment and also complaints made by returned immigrants to the Protector of Immigrants at Calcutta. (Pietermaritzburg, 1872).

Natal Colony - Official. Commission to enquire into the subject of education, includes Report on Native population (1874) 23pp.

Natal Colony - Official. Report of the Natal Native Commission 1881-2. (Pietermaritzburg, 1882).

Natal Colony - Official. Annual Reports of Supt. of Educ. 1880-1900; Native Dept. Rep. 1901-6-7. (Pietermaritzburg, 1881-1910) (First issued as reports of Supt. Insp. of Schools. There is a separate report of the Supt. of Native Education).

Natal Colony - Official. Technical Education Commission Report, 1905.

Natal Province - Official. Dept. of Education. Director of Education. Annual Reports - 1920 to the present. (Pietermaritzburg: The Dept.)

Natal Province - Official. Dept. of Education. Vacation course for European teachers in Native schools. (n.p. of pub., 1919).

Natal Province - Official. Education Dept. Second Winter School for native teachers ... at Marianhill Training College, Natal 7-17 July, 1919. (Durban, 1919) p.41.

Natal Province - Official. Education Dept. Summer School for Native teachers ... at Centocow Mission Station, Natal, 15-29 January, 1920. (Pietermaritzburg, 1920) 32p.

Natal Province Official. Education Dept. Syllabus of fourth winter school at Marianhill Training College, 4-16 July, 1921. (Dundee 1921) 41p.

Natal Province - Official. Dept. of Education. Primary syllabus for use in Government and Government-Aided schools. (n.p. of pub., 1928).

Natal Province - Official. Education Dept. Summer School for Native Teachers ... at Kwa Mondi Mission Station, Eshowe, Zululand 22-30 January, 1930. (Durban, 1930) 44p.

Natal Provincial - Official. Broome Commission: Report of the Education Commission, 1937. (Pietermaritzburg, 1937).

Natal Province - Official. Natal Education Commission 1937. (Summary of the section on Coloured Education (Johannesburg,SAIRR,1938) RR 35/1938).

Natal Province - Official. Education Dept. Report of a Committee to enquire into the present facilities and future policy for higher education for Indians in Natal. (Pretoria 1942) 6p.

Natal Province - Official. Report of the Natal Prov. Educ. Committee 1946. (Wilks Committee) (NP 2 - 1946) (Pietermaritzburg 1946) 271pp.

Natal Province - Official. Provincial Committee on Native Education 1944 - 1946. (Thomas Report) (NP 5 - 1946) (Pietermaritzburg 1946).

Natal Province - Official. Education Dept. Natal Education Then and Now 1849-1949, illus. (Durban 1949) Native Education p.39-45.

Natal African Teachers Union. "African education at the dawn of a new era", by A.J. Thembela (an address delivered at the 55th Annual Conference of the Natal African Teachers Union on the 29th June 1973 at Vuleka).

Natal Indian Association. Memorandum submitted at the Indian Technical and University Enquiry Commission. (Durban 1942).

Natal Indian Congress. Memo. submitted to the Indian Education Enquiry Committee. (Durban, n.d.).

Natal Indian Congress. We want schools for 37,000 children; the N.I.C. policy on education. (Durban 1953).

Natal Indian Teachers' Society. Silver Jubilee 1925-1950. (Durban 1950).

Natal Native Education Advisory Board (Minutes of Meetings, 1945) <u>Native Teachers J.</u> 24: 97-99; 25: 52-54 Jul. 1945; Ja. 1946 ... (1946) 25: 135-36; 26: 28-29 Jul., Oct., 1946.

Natal University, Medical School. The Durban Medical School, a response to the challenge of Africa. (Durban, Natal Univ., 1954?) 40p.

Natal University, Projects Comm. Pupils Protest Education. (Natal, SRC Press, 1980) 4p.

National Bureau of Educational and Social Research: (various and listed by author).

National Bureau of Educational and Social Research. Tests for the Bantu Population. (Note on Psychological and scholastic achievement tests for school pupils) (Pretoria 1966) 1p.

National Conference on Education, UND, 1960. Education and our Expanding Horizons: (proceedings) (edit.) R.G. Macmillan, P.D. Rey, J.W. Macquarrie. (Pietermaritzburg 1962) 534p.

Naude,P.S. "Indiër Onderwys in Suid Afrika". (Unpub. M.Ed. thesis, UPotch,1933).

Naude,P.S. "Indiër en Indiër-onderwys in Natal en Transvaal; 'n historiese en kritiese studie: 1860-1940". (Unpub. D.Ed. thesis, UNISA, 1950).

Ncwana,S.M.B. Black outlook for natives: a comprehensive appeal to the Govt., Native local councils and location advisory boards on the expansion of Native education. (Queenstown 1931) 19p.

Ndaba,E.P. "Need for a spiritual regeneration for our education". <u>Bantu Educ. J.</u> 18(1): Feb. 1972, p.26-33+ bibliog.

Ndaba,E. "The psycho-pedagogical study of differentiated secondary education and its significance in KwaZulu". (Unpub. D.Ed. thesis, UZ, 1975).

Ndaba,E.P. Current trends and practices in KwaZulu education. (Durban,SAAAE,1977).

Ndaba,E.P. "The necessity for guidance and counselling in black schools". <u>Paidonomia</u> 6(2) Nov. 1978, p.35-48.

Ndamse,C.M.C. "Bantu Education in South Africa". (M.A., Kennedy School of Missions, Hartford, Conn., 1956).

Nel,A. "Some reflections on the possibility of formulating a philosophy of education for black nations in Southern Africa". <u>Humanitas</u> 6(4) 1980,p.393-402.

Nel,B.F. "Inleidende Opmerkings tot: Die Afrikaner en Naturelle-opvoeding en -onderwys". <u>Koers</u> VIII (2) Oct. 1940, pp.65-73; "Die Huidige Stelsel van Opvoeding en Onderwys van die Naturel onder Oënskou". <u>Koers</u> VIII (4) Feb. 1941, pp.150-157.

Nel,B.F. "Die Afrikaners en naturelle opvoeding en onderwys: die huidige stelsel van opvoeding en onderwys van die naturel onder oënskou". <u>Koers</u> 8, 1941, p.150-157.

Nel,B.F. Naturelle-Opvoeding en -Onderwys. (2 vols.) (Bloemfontein 1942) (Tweedetrek-Reeks Nos. 19 en 20) pp.152 and 111. (vol. I: Standpunt en Beskoning insake Huidige Stelsel. Vol. II: 'n Christelike-Nasionale Stelsel).

Nel.B.F. Aspekte van die onderwysontwikkeling in Suid-Afrika. (Kaapstad 1959) 224p. (Ch. VI 'Die ontwikkeling en reëlings van Bantoe-onderwys as deel van die pedagogiese kultuurpatroon in SA'. - Ch. VII 'Beskouinge oor die geestestruktuur van "Primitiewe" volkere met spesiale verwysing na die geestestruktuur van die Suid Afrikaanse naturellekind'.)

Nel,C.F.B. "Gedagtes rondom die begrip van swart onderwys". J. of Racial Affairs 30(2) April 1979, p.48-60.

Nel,P.R.T. (RSA - Official). Report on Education for Indians in South Africa to the Minister of Indian Affairs, Durban. (Unpublished, 1964).

Nel,P.R.T. 'Toekomstige onderwysvraagstukke'. Saipa 11: D. 1976, p.153-60.

Nettleton,C. 'Racial cleavage on the student left' in H.W. v.d. Merwe and D. Welsh, Student Perspectives on South Africa. (Cape Town 1972) 229p.

NEUSA 'Comment on the Investigation by the Human Sciences Research Council into Education'. (Johannesburg: Southern Transvaal Association of the National Educational Union of S.A., 22 Nov., 1980).

Ngcobo,S.B. 'Natal Bantu Teachers' Union silver jubilee'. Native Teachers' J. 23: Ja. 1944, p.32-34.

Hghihulitua,I.G. 'Vooruitgang van skole in die Ukuanjama-stamgebied'. Bantoe-Onderwysbl. 8: Nov. 1962, p.459.

Ngakane,W.H. Syllabuses for Bantu Education. (Johannesburg, SAIRR, 1955).

Ngubane,J.K. An African Explores Apartheid. (New York, 1963).

Ngubeni,N. 'A Review of Bantu Education in Northern Transvaal'. Bantu Educ.J. 12(5) 1966, p.40-42.

Nicol,W. 'The Dutch Reformed Church and Native education'. SA Outlook LXVI, 1936, pp.111-113.

NIPR (National Institute of Personnel Research) - Retief,T. (comp.) NIPR Symposium: Instructa 80. Development and Training of Black Employees in industry. (Johannesburg, CSIR, NIPR, 1981). Parts 1,2,3 and 4.

Niven,J. "Educational planning and the supply of teachers in a diverse society with reference to South Africa". J. of Education 10 (1978) p.41-48.

Nkabinde,J.J. 'Progress and obstacles in Native education'. Native Teachers J. 19: Jul. 1940, p.186-188.

N'Lanbala,P. 'The Abyss of Bantu Education'. Africa South 4(2) 1960, p.42-47.

Nkomo,W.F. 'Problems of Local school administration' - introductory paper. (Johannesburg, SAIRR, 1969).

Nkondo,G.M. (ed.) Turfloop Testimony: the Dilemma of a Black University in South Africa. (Johannesburg 1976) 93p.

Nkuhlu,W.L. "Problems of bridging the education gap for blacks". Paper delivered at a Symposium for the extension of professional development to all racial groups, Nov. 1980. (Johannesburg, SA Institute of Chartered Accountants, 1980) 31p.

Noel,R. 'Native education from an economic point of view'. SA J. Sci.14, 1917, pp.88-100.

Nolte,D.J.C. Educational needs of the coloured people in the Tvl.: Report of 1st National Coloured-European Conf. (Cape Town, 1934) pp.74-77. (See also National Coloured-European Conference).

North,J. 'Student Boycott Defies Racial Barriers'. In These Times June 4-17,1980.

Norton,B. & Colley,A. 'The Obstacle Course of Black Education'. Wits Student 14 June, 1976, p.7-9.

Norton,F.V. "An Overview of Industrial Education curriculum at Technical Colleges in SA with proposals for Manpower Development through course offerings". (M.A. Michigan State Univ., 1979).

Norton,V. 'Preliminary chronology of events in Cape Town in the unrest following the Soweto riots'. (Cape Town, mimeo., 1976).

Ntantala,P. "Abyss of Bantu education". Africa South 4(2) Ja-Mr 1960, p.42-47.

Ntloedibe,E.L. 'Plek van Afrikaans in Bantoe-skole'. Huis 40(1762) D. 26, 1955, p.11.

Ntusi,D.M. Education and economic development of the Transkei. In: Backer,W. (ed.) The economic development of the Transkei: papers read during a symposium presented by the Fort Hare Economic Society at the University of Fort Hare, on 14-15 August 1969. (Alice, UFH, 1970) p.38-55.

NUSAS (National Union of South African Students). Journal 1947-8. (Cape Town 1948).

NUSAS. National Union of SA Students in 1950. (Cape Town 1950).

NUSAS. A NUSAS handbook on the problems of higher education in SA (written for NUSAS by the Pres. P. Tobias) (Cape Town 1951) 40p. illus.

NUSAS. The African in the universities: a survey of the facilities for education for non-European students in SA, with an examination of the system of university segregation and non-segregation by M. O'Dowd. (Cape Town, 1955) p.44.

NUSAS. Prospect and retrospect: being a series of lectures delivered at the Winter School of NUSAS, UCT, 1960, (ed.) A. Dashwood. (Cape Town,NUSAS,1960).

NUSAS. ... Memo. on higher education for non-whites in SA consequent upon the enactment of the extension of univ. education and Fort Hare Univ. College transfer legislation. (Cape Town, 17-20, Jan. 1961).

NUSAS. Report on South African Education. (Cape Town, NUSAS, 1966) 20p.

NUSAS. 'Bantu Education - What price indoctrination?'. (mimeo, n.d.)

NUSAS. Education and Development: A collection of papers presented at the Education and Development Conference held at the University of Cape Town, 16-20 July 1979. (Cape Town 1979).

Nutt,P.W. 'Bantu education policy: a plan to serve the community'. Bantu 4(12) p.73-88.

Nxumalo,D.E.H. Black Education and the quest for true humanity. (Paper given at Black Theology Seminar, Mimeo., 1971) 6p.

Nxumalo,O.E-H.M. 'Adult Education'. (An address delivered at the Univ. of Zululand African Staff Association Symposium on the 5th April 1975).

Nyati,H.B. "African Education on the East Rand". South African Sentinel 3(1) Feb. 1948.

Nzimande,A.M. 'Bantoe-onderwys binne die raamwerk van die S. Afr. situasie'. Bantoe-Onderwysbl. 16(2) Mr. 1970 port. p.25-27.

O'Dowd,M.C. The African and the Universities. (Cape Town, NUSAS, 1954) 44p. (Also see NUSAS publications).

O'Dowd,T. 'The Potato Harvest'. Africa South Oct-Dec 1959, p.50-2.

Olckers,P.J. Education in South Africa: How the Union provides for a multi-racial population. (Pretoria, State Information Office, 1953) mimeo.

Oldham,J.H. & Gibson,B.D. The Remaking of man in Africa. (Oxford, 1931).

Olivier,S.P. 'Die Universiteitskollege vir Indieërs: Durban'. Tydskrif vir Rasseaangeleenthede 14(1): (1962) p.57-69.

Olivier,T. 'Culture chasm: Bantu education and the use of English'. Theoria 39: Oct. 1972, p.49-60, bibliog.

O'Meara,J. 'Night school for natives'. Tvl. Educ. News 36: Ag. 1940, p.4-5.

Oosthuizen,G.C. Shepherd of Lovedale. (Johannesburg 1970) 247p.

Orange Free State - Dept. of Education - Official. Report of Director of Education. (Bloemfontein, The Dept. 1910,1911,1912-).

Orange Free State Province - Education Dept. - Official. Annual Reports, 1920 to the present.

Orange Free State Province - Official. (Dept. of Education). Report of the Provincial Education Commission of Enquiry, 1951. Ch. XXIII - Coloured Ed.

Oscroft,L.E. 'Zulu National Training Institution, Nonqoma'. Natal Teachers J. VII 1928, p.89-91.

Osler,S.G. 'A Layman's Guide to Education in SA'. (Pretoria 1964).

Osman,E. 'Education and the Indian Girl'. Fiat Lux 10(3) Apr. 1975, p.4-8.

Ottery Nywerkeidskool, Cape. Annual Report of:

Parker,F. 'Separate Schools and Separate People of South Africa'. Journal of Negro Education 41(3) 1972 p.266-275.

Parnett,P.A. 'Problems and perils of education in SA'. Roy. Col. Inst. Proc. 36: 1904-5, pp.130-55.

Petterson,S. Colour and culture in SA: a study of the status of the Cape Coloured people within the social structure of the Union of SA. (London 1953) pp.90-105: Education.

Pauw,B.A. Religion in a Tswana Chiefdom. (London 1960) 258p. See index re 'Education' and 'Schools'.

Pauw,B.A. The Second Generation: A study of the family among urbanized Bantu in East London. (London 1973). See Education - p.37-8.

Pells,E.G. The Story of Education in South Africa: European, Coloured and Native 1952-1938. (Cape Town and Johannesburg 1938). (Revised version reprinted in 1954 as '300 Years of Education in SA'.).

Pells,E.G. Three Hundred Years of Education in SA. (Cape Town 1954) 152pp.

Pelzer,A.N. (ed.) Verwoerd Speaks: Speeches 1948-1966. (Johannesburg 1966).

Perry,A.R. African secondary school leavers: employment experiences and attitudes to employment in Durban. (Johannesburg, SAIRR, 1975) 94p.

Peteni,R.L. 'Tomorrow's education'. Educ. J. 88(2) Sept. 1978, p.11-15.

Peteni,R.L. Towards Tomorrow: The Story of the African Teachers' Association of South Africa. (Algonac, Michigan, 1980).

Peters,F.K.A. Some problems in the training of students for science
   professions. (Kwa Dlangezwe, University College of Zululand, 1966) 24p.

Peters,F.K. ... Mathematics and the sciences in Bantu education. (Johannesburg,
   SAIRR, 1969). (RR 13/69) 8p.

Peters,L.E. 'A critical and comparative study of the preparation of science
   teachers at institutions for the education of Indian teachers in Natal'.
   (Unpub. M.Ed. thesis, UDW, 1975).

Phahle,R. "We Don't Want No Education". Solidarity 4 Oct. 1980, p.9-35.

Phatudi,C.N.M. 'Nursery school facilities for African children on the
   W. Rand and some suggestions'. (B.Ed. thesis, UW, 1960).

Phatudi,C.N. 'Education and Family Life'. Paper given at a conference on
   African family life, organized by SAIRR, Tvl. Region and the Witwatersrand
   Christian Council, 1967. (Johannesburg, Mimeo., 1967) 6p.

Phelps Stokes Fund. Report on: Education in Africa. (New York, 1922).
   See Also: Jones,T.J.

Phelps Stokes Report on Education, Native Welfare and Race Relations in East
   and South Africa. (New York 1934).

Philip,T.D. 'Education with Tools', a lecture. (Lovedale, 1892) 14p.

Phillips,C.J. 'Protestant America and the pagan world: the first half century
   of the American Board of Commissioners for Foreign Missions, 1810-1860'.
   (Ph.D. Harvard Univ., Camb. Mass., 1954) 360p.

Phillips,R.E. The Bantu are Coming. (London 1930).

Phillips,R.E. 'Meeting the needs of Bantu Youth'. World Youth X, 1935,p.324-30.

Phillips,R.E. 'The Bantu in the City: A Study of Cultural Adjustments on the
   Witwatersrand. (Lovedale 1938) Ch. IV: Education.

Pienaar,P.T. "Breakthrough in Beginning Reading through 'Breakthrough to
   Literacy'". Journal of Education 6(1) 1974, p.9-24.

Pieterse,C.G.L. 'The Training of Coloured Teachers in the Cape since 1865'.
   (B.Ed. diss., UCT, 1952).

Pollak,H.P. (comp.) Education for progress: being a report of the Proc. at the
   1971 Conf. on Education with Special reference to the needs of the Coloured
   community, together with the findings and recommendation, etc.
   (Johannesburg, SAIRR, 1971).

Pont,D. Bantoe-onderwijs. (Amsterdam, 1965) 12p.

Pope,M. 'Universities'. Africa South Oct-Dec 1959, p.41-9.

Porschka,D.C. 'Bantu in Schüle und Aüsbildüng'. Afrika Post 20: N. 1973,p.427-9.

Potgieter,C.J. "Steady growth in Natal region". Bantu Educ. J. 9: Jun. 1963,
   p.244-47 illus.

Potgieter,E.F. "Part that the university plays in the community development
   of the Bantu"; with discussion. Inst. Adm. Non-European Affairs 15:
   1967, p.109-18.

Pretorius,A.M. "So sal die Bantoe in die Blanke gebiede opgelei word".
   Volkshandel 35(1): 1974, p.74-77 port.

Price,R. & Rosberg,C. (eds.) The Apartheid Regime. (Cape Town 1980).

Proctor-Sims,R. (ed.) Technical and Vocational Education in Southern Africa.
    (Grant Park, 1981) 320p.

Prozesky,M. "After Fifty Years" : address by P. - then Regional Director of
    Bantu Education for the Southern Tvl. Bantu Sept. 1956. (An Address
    delivered ... at the Golden Jubilee Conference of the T.A.T.A. at
    Kilnerton institution on 28 June 1956).

Prozesky,M. Education for the Bantu in operation. (Pretoria 1962) 19p.

Prozesky,M. "... Positive aspects of Bantu Education". Bantu Educ. J. 8:
    May 1962, p.203-5 port.

Pupils Representatives and Parents Action Committee. Joint Statement (re
    Indian and Coloured education). (No place of pub., mimeo., 1980) 2p.

Raath,M.H. "Opvoeding Nodig vir die Naturel". Die Basuin II (4) Sept.
    1931, p.2-14.

Rajbansi,A. "The more or less boss - who controls Indian schools?".
    Drum 8 March 1976, p.53.

Ramaila,H.S. "Christian education endeavours in a culturally changing
    South Africa". (M.A., Columbia Univ., New York, 1955) 59p.

Rambiritch,B. "An investigation into some aspects of the education of Indian
    girls in Natal". (M.Ed. thesis, UND, 1959).

Rambiritch,B. "A study of the philosophy and practice in the education of
    the South African Hindu". (Ph.D. thesis, UND, 1959).

Rambiritch,B. A brief Review of Indian Education, 1860-1961. (Durban 1962).

Rambiritch,B. "Higher education: key to Indian progress". The Indian South
    African 14 Oct., 1966, pp.37-54.

Rambally,A. Editor of Black Review, 1975-6, see Black Review.

Ramphal,C. "A study of three current problems of Indian Education".
    (Ph.D. thesis, UND, 1961).

Rand Afrikaans University. A framework for development planning in Venda,
    Vol. I: Planning proposals for Venda. (Johannesburg, Institute of
    Development Studies, RAU, 1979).

Randall,P. "Towards Equality in Education". Pro Veritate (15 August 1973).

Randall,P. Education beyond apartheid; Spro-Cas Education Commission 1971.
    (Johannesburg, Christian Institute of Southern Africa, Sprocas Occ.
    Pub. No. 5, 1971).

Randall,P. Little England on the Veld: A study of the Private Protestant
    Schools in South Africa. (Johannesburg, 1982).

Rao,L. & Somniso,O.P. "Is the educated African pulling his weight?"
    Race Relations J. 22(1) 1955, p.29-30.

Rathbone,R. "Students and Politics in South Africa". Journal of Commonwealth
    and Comparative Politics (July 1977), p.103-11.

Rathbone,R. "The People of Soweto". (Review Article) JSAS 6(1) 0. 1979,p.124-131.

Raubenheimer,A.M. "Naturelle-onderwys in die Tvl". (M.Ed., UNISA,1944) 86p.Bibl.

Raum,J.W. "Das Bantu Schulwesen in der Südafrikanischen Union". (Ph.D., Univ.
    of Munich, Fed. Rep.of Germany, 1963).

Raum,O.F. "Problems of Non-European University Education in SA", in The Yearbook of Education (London, 1959).

Raum,O.F. "Imbalances of educational development in Southern Africa". S. Afr. J. African Affairs 1: 1971, p.8-30, bibliog.

Rautenbach,C.H. Open discussion on closed universities. (Turfloop, Univ. College of the North, 1963) 16p.

Rautenbach,C.H. "Geskeie universitêre ontwikkeling - imperatief van die geskiedenis in wording". Tydskrif vir Rasse-Aangeleent. 16: Ja 1965 p.24-49.

Rawlins,G.E. The Contribution of the Anglican Church to Education at the Cape. (M.Ed., UR, 1961).

"Rebusoajoang" (pseud.) "Education and Social Control in South Africa". African Affairs 78(311) 1979, p.228-239.

Reeves,(R) A. (bp. of Johannesburg). "Anglican Church and the Bantu education act". Forum 3(9): D. 1954, p.29-30.

Reeves,R.A. (bp. of Johannesburg). "Bantu education and the Tomlinson report". Forum 5(3): Jun.1956, p.11-15.

Rheinallt-Jones,E.G. "Rural education". Race Relations 2: D. 1934 - Ja. 1935, p.122-3.

Rheinallt-Jones,E.G. "Crisis in Native Education: A ten-year plan". Race Relat. 10(3) 1943, p.40-45.

Rheinallt-Jones,J.D. "The need of a scientific basis for S. African native policy". S. Afr. J. Sc. 23 (1926) pp.79-91.

Rheinallt-Jones,J.D. "The School and the Community". Mimeo., 1931.

Rheinallt-Jones,J.D. The finance of native education. (Johannesburg, SAIRR, 1932) (RR 14/1932).

Rheinallt-Jones,J.D. & Saffery,A.L. The Social and Economic Conditions of Native Life in the Union of SA (being a summary of the findings of the Native Economic Commission 1930-32) (Johannesburg,SAIRR,1932) : "Native Education" p.61.

Rheinallt-Jones,J.D. Education and the African. (mimeo.) (article for The New Era in Education) (Johannesburg, SAIRR, 1934) (RR 24/1934) 4p.

Rheinallt-Jones,J.D. "Education and race attitudes". Race Relations III, 1936, p.38-45.

Rheinallt-Jones,J.D. "The crisis in native education in SA". Int. Rev. of Miss. 28 (1939) p.191-204.

Rhoodie,N.J. & Venter,H.J. Apartheid: A Socio-Historical Exposition of the Origin and Development of the Apartheid Idea. (Cape Town 1960) 268p.

Rich,P. "Ideology in a Plural Society: The Case of South African Segregation". Social Dynamics 1(2) 1975, p.167-80.

Rich,P. "The South African Institute of Race Relations and the Debate on 'Race Relations', 1929-1958", The Societies of Southern Africa in the 19th and 20th Centuries, vol. 12. (University of London, Institute of Commonwealth Studies, 1981) pp.77-90.

Richards,M.W. Council of Education: Witwatersrand: the next decade 1965-1975. (Johannesburg, 1975) 14p.

Ritner,S. "The Dutch Reformed Church and Apartheid". J. of Contemporary History 2(4) 1967 pp.17-37.

Ritner,S.R. Salvation through Separation: The Role of the Dutch Reformed Church in SA in the formulation of Afrikaner Race Ideology. (Ph.D. diss., Columbia Univ., 1971) 302p.

Robbins,F. "The Dismal state of African education". Reality May 1971,p.14-15.

Roberts,N. Native education from an economic point of view. (Cape Town, 1917/8) 13p. (Reprint from S.Afr.J.Sci. 14(2) (1917) p.88-100).

Robertson,I.A. "Education in South Africa: A Study on the influence of Ideology on Educational Practice". (Ph.D. Harvard Univ., Cambridge, Mass., 1973).

Robertson,I. "South African Education", in Robertson,I. and Whitten,P. (eds.) Race and Politics in South Africa. (New Brunswick, 1978) p.103-126.

Robertson,N.L. & Robertson,B.L. Education in South Africa. (Bloomington: Phi Delta Kappan Educational Foundation c. 1977).

Rogan,J.M. "Planning for effective science training". Bantu Educ. J. 17(8) 1971, p.10-11.

Rogers,H. Native Administration in the Union of South Africa. (Johannesburg, 1933) - 2nd edit. 1949 revised. (Pretoria, Government Printer) - Ch. X Native Education pp.253-258.

Rogers,M.L. "The higher education available to non-Europeans in the Union of SA". (M.A., Univ. of California, Berkeley, 1957). 226p.

Rose,B.W. "Bantu Education as a facet of South African policy". Comparative Education Review 9(2) June 1965, p.208-12.

Rose,B. (ed.) Education in Southern Africa. (Johannesburg 1970).

Rose,B. "Economic Problems in African Education", in Rose,B. (ed.) Education in Southern Africa. (Johannesburg, 1970) p.3-11.

Rose,B. & Tunmer,R. (eds.) Documents in South African Education. (Johannesburg, 1975).

Roseveare,E.H. "The Christian Contribution to Native Education - How are we to defend it?". SA Outlook 68, 1938, p.60-63.

Ross,D. Preliminary Report on the state of education in the Colony of the Cape. (Cape Town 1883) 71p.

Ross,J.J. " 'n Merkwaardige Besluit oor Naturelle-opvoeding in Afrika". Die Basuin II (3) (July 1931) p.8-9.

Ross,J.J. et al. "Fort Hare se taak ten opsigte van die Transkei en Ciskei". (S.A. Bureau of Racial Affairs, Pretoria, n.d.) 20p.

Ross,J.J. "Nie-blanke universiteitskolleges word selfstandig". Unisa 1970, p.12-13 port.

Rousseau,G.J. "Beplanning van die onderwysstelsel vir Bantoes in Suid Afrika", in UOVS Instituut vir Eietydse Geskiedenis, Seminaarreeks (n.d.). (Onderwysplanning huidige toestande en toekomsbehoeftes pp.37-75.)

Rousseau,H.J. "Realism in African education". SA Outlook LXVII, 1937,p.30-35.

Rousseau,H.J. "Educating adult Africa. 1. How to start continuation classes". SA Outlook 74: D 1944, p.165.

Rousseau,H.J. "Learn to live by living". SA Outlook 75: 88-89; 110; 141-42; 157-58; 190-91 Jun. Jul. S. D. 1945. (Articles on practical reform in Native education).

Rousseau,H.J. "To learn to live better". SA Outlook 77: Mr. 1947 p.42-43.

Rousseau,H.J. "Education for a multi-racial country". Symposium S. 1960 p.67-8.

Roussouw,C. "Coloured education". SASH 17(2) Aug. 1974, p.16-19.

Roux,E. Education through reading. (Johannesburg, SAIRR, 1942) 12p.

Roux,E. Time Longer than Rope. (London, 1949).

Roux,E. Rebel Pity. (London, 1970).

Runge,C.H.S. The finance and control of native education for the stimulation and fuller recognition of non-government participation in native education. (Johannesburg, SAIRR, 1939) (RR 60/39).

Ruperti,R.M. Die Onderwysstelsel in Suid Afrika. (Pretoria 1974).

Ruperti,R.M. " 'n Evalueering van primere en sekondere Bantoe-onderwys". Woord en Daad 16(165) June 1976, p.13-14.

Rurik,G. "The School System needs overhauling". The Star   July 1978.

Russell,A.G. Colour, Race and Empire. (London 1944).

Russell,P.H. "The riot police and the suppression of truth". (Mimeo., Cape Town, 1977).

Russel,M. "Intellectual and Academic Apartheid 1950-1965", in P. v.d. Berghe (ed.) The Liberal Dilemma in South Africa. (London 1979).

Russel,R. Report on System of Education in Natal, Vol. V. (English Bd. of Ed. Special Report, 1899).

S.,E.B. "The Lovedale Mission". (Reprint from The Scotsman, 30 Sept. 1905).

St. Francis College, Mariannhill, Natal. The Student Teacher's Handbook on organisation and management of African Schools. (3rd Edit. Mariannhill, 1946) 183p.

St. Peter's and St. Agnes' Schools, Rosettenville. Prospectus 1932. (St. Peter's hostel: a school for native boys.)

St. Peter's Secondary School, Johannesburg. Annual Speech Day, 27 Nov. 1954 programme, 1954.

SABRA - Suid-Afrikaanse Buro vir Rasse-Aangeleenthede. South African Bureau of Racial Affairs.

SABRA. "Fort Hare se taak ten opsigte van die Transkei en Ciskei", by J.J. Roos et al. (Pretoria, SABRA, n.d.) 20p.

SABRA. Samevatting van die Verslag van die Naturelle Onderwyskommissie 1949-1951. (Stellenbosch, SABRA, 1951) p.25; "The Commission on Native Educ. (1949-1951): Summary of Finding and Recommendations". J. of Racial Affairs April 1952 (+ Reprint).

SABRA - Du Plessis,I.D. "The Coloured people of SA: some aspects of their present position". (Stellenbosch, SABRA, 1955) pp.19-21 - Education.

SABRA. Bantu Education: Oppression or Opportunity? (Stellenbosch,SABRA,1955)48p.

SABRA. Die jeug se aandeel in rasse-en-volks verhoudinge. (Pretoria, SABRA, 1970). Jaarboek, 1962-9, No. 4-5, 156p.

SABRA. Proposed scheme for the reorganization of Bantu Education. (Mimeo,n.d.)

Sached Trust. Annual Reports. (Johannesburg, 1978, 1979, 1980).

Sadler,M.J. "On teaching English to Africans". Forum 2(3): Jun. 1953,p.28-30.

SAIRR. Transvaal Native Education Advisory Board. (The Native Education Board on the subject of native education). (Johannesburg, SAIRR, 1931) (RR 15/1931).

SAIRR. Native Education. (Johannesburg, SAIRR, 1932) (RR 33/1932).

SAIRR. Rural Education: (The application to native education of the findings of the conference on rural education convened by the Union Minister of Education, Feb. 1934) (Johannesburg, SAIRR, 1935) (RR 86/35).

SAIRR. Native Education. (Evidence as presented on behalf of the Transvaal Missionary Association and the Johannesburg Joint Council of Europeans and Africans to the Commission on Native Education). (mimeo., Johannesburg, SAIRR, 1935) (RR 83/1935).

SAIRR. Draft of evidence to be given on behalf of the Cape Native Education Advisory Board, to the Inter-Departmental Committee into Native Education. (Johannesburg, SAIRR, 1935) (RR 69/35).

SAIRR. Recommendations of the Inter-Departmental Committee on Native Education 1935-6. (Johannesburg, SAIRR, 1936) (RR 54/46).

SAIRR. Indian Education: summary of the section on Indian Education of the report of the Natal Education Commission, 1937. (Johannesburg, SAIRR, 1938) (Memo. RR. 37/38).

SAIRR. Native Education: Summary of the section on Native Educ. of the Report of the Natal Educ. Commission. (Johannesburg,SAIRR,1938) (RR 34/38).

SAIRR. Control of Native Education. (Johannesburg,SAIRR,1939) (RR 62/39).

SAIRR. Finance of Native Education. (Johannesburg,SAIRR,1939) (RR 61/39).

SAIRR. Finance of Native Education. (Johannesburg,SAIRR,1940).

SAIRR. Night Schools for Adult Africans. (Johannesburg,SAIRR,1941)14p.

SAIRR. Education. (Johannesburg,SAIRR,1942) (RR 2/42).

SAIRR. Native Education. (Johannesburg,SAIRR,1943) (RR 90/43; RR 119/43).

SAIRR. The Control of Native Education: Report of the Conference convened for 2 Feb. 1944 by the Minister of Native Affairs. (Johannesburg,SAIRR,1944) (RR 29/44).

SAIRR. Collection of pamphlets on adult education for non-Europeans. (Cape Town, SAIRR, 1947).

SAIRR. Conference on Adult Education for Non-Europeans. (Cape Town, 1947). (Material issued in connection with the conference).

SAIRR. Handbook of Race Relations in SA, ed. by E. Hellman. (Cape Town 1949). pp.348-386 'Non European education'.

SAIRR. Findings of the Institute's Council on Fundamental Education. (Johannesburg, SAIRR) (RR 34/1949).

SAIRR. Evidence submitted by the SAIRR to the Commission on Native Education. (Johannesburg, SAIRR, 1949) (RR 185/1949).

SAIRR. Careers for Africans - A Survey conducted by the SAIRR. (Johannesburg, 1951) 28p.

SAIRR. Report of the Proceedings of a National Conference convened by the SAIRR to study the report of the Commission on Native Education at Johannesburg, July 1952. (The Eiselen Commission) (Johannesburg,SAIRR,1952)32p.

SAIRR. Memorandum on the draft education ordinance, 1952 (Tvl.) (Johannesburg, SAIRR, 1952) (RR 131/52).

SAIRR. Evidence to the Coloured Education Commission. (SAIRR, Johannesburg) (RR 193/1953).

SAIRR. Memorandum on the Bantu Education Bill. (Johannesburg,SAIRR,1953) mimeo.

SAIRR. "Proposals under the Bantu Education Act". (Extract: State Information Office Newsletter dated 1954) (Johannesburg,SAIRR,1954) (RR 15/54).

SAIRR. "The idea of the university" - a symposium of addresses delivered by Dr. T.B. Davie, Prof. E.E. Harris at a conference called by the SAIRR, together with an account of the discussions at the conference, and the evidence presented by the SAIRR to the Commission of enquiry into separate university education. (Johannesburg, 1954) 36p.

SAIRR. Teachers in Bantu schools. (Johannesburg,SAIRR,1955).

SAIRR (S. Tvl. Region) Notes on African Education: African School Libraries Scheme. (Johannesburg, June 1961) (RR 136/61).

SAIRR. African education: some origins and development 1953. Comp. by M. Horrell, etc. (Johannesburg,SAIRR,1963).

SAIRR. A decade of Bantu Education by M. Horrell. (Johannesburg,SAIRR,1964)186p.

SAIRR. F.L. de Villiers. "The Financing of Bantu Educ." (Johannesburg,SAIRR,1964).

SAIRR. Some educational statistics by M. Horrell. (Johannesburg,SAIRR,1965).

SAIRR. ... Secondary education for Africans, etc. (Johannesburg,SAIRR,1965).

SAIRR. Salary scales for teachers by M. Horrell. (Johannesburg,SAIRR,1965).

SAIRR. "Apartheid hampered by Bantu Education". (Johannesburg,SAIRR,1965). (RR 122/65 3p. also Race Relations News Aug. 1965).

SAIRR. Some facts and figures on primary and secondary education - White and Indian pupils - Natal. (SAIRR, Natal Region Information Sheet No. 2/67 Memo. NR 7/67 (1967)).

SAIRR. ... "Race, prejudice and education": address - AGM S. Tvl. region. (2 Nov. 1968 by F.E. Auerbach. (Johannesburg, SAIRR, 1968).

SAIRR. Bantu Education to 1968, comp. by M. Horrell. (Johannesburg,SAIRR,1968)168p.

SAIRR. Conference on Bantu Education, Johannesburg, 16-18 Jan. 1969, Report of: (Johannesburg, SAIRR, 1969) 28p. (The factual background to the conference is the book by M. Horrell pub. 1968).

SAIRR. The Education of the coloured community in SA 1652-1970. Comp. by M. Horrell, etc. (Johannesburg, SAIRR, 1970).

SAIRR. Notes on the ages and educational standards of the White, Coloured and Asian people of the Republic, 1970, by M. Horrell. (Johannesburg, SAIRR, 1972) Fact Sheet. 4p. (RR 18/72).

SAIRR. ... "Education for progress with special reference to the needs of the Coloured community" : papers given at a conference organised by the South African Institute of Race Relations, in Cape Town, January 1971. (Johannesburg, SAIRR (1971?)) At head of title: Conference papers. Mimeographed S 855,286.

SAIRR. ... Education for progress, etc. Contents: Malherbe,E.G. Conference opening address; O'Dowd,M.C. Priorities in education; Cilliers,S.P. Socio-economic status of the coloured community and implications for education; Lighton,F.K. Socio-economic status of the coloured community and implications for education - lead-in paper; Möhr,L.V. Present facilities and future plans in coloured education: a survey; Forbes,J. Present facilities and future plans - lead-in paper; Ulster,D.R. Status and conditions of service - lead-in paper; Bergins,W.J. Compulsory education and wastage of scholars - lead-in paper; Rampono,D.L.J. Teacher training - lead - in paper; Ashley,M. Special services in education - lead - in paper. Desai,A. The curriculum, syllabi and examinations - lead - in paper; Small,A. University education - lead - in paper; Nel,G.J. Technical and vocation training - lead - in paper. Davids,A. The school and the community - lead - in paper; Auerbach,F.E. Summing up.

SAIRR. Report on discussions between representatives of the Directorate of Education, Administration of Coloured Affairs, and of the SAIRR, 3 August 1971. (Johannesburg, SAIRR, 1971) (RR 04/71).

SAIRR. Archives. Organizations: Bantu Education Campaign, 1954. (typed 1975-8)2p.

SAIRR. Turmoil at Turfloop: a summary of the reports of the Snyman and Jackson Commissions of Inquiry into the University of the North; comp. by J.G.E. Wolfson. (Johannesburg, 1976).

SAIRR. South African Travail: The Disturbances of 1976-77 (Evidence presented to the Cillie Commission by the Institute of RR). (Pietermaritzburg, SAIRR, 1978).

SAIRR. Comment on the draft Education and Training Bill published in the Government Gazette 6213, 10 Nov. 1978. (Johannesburg, SAIRR, 1978) 3p. (RR 168/78).

SAIRR. Statistics on education in South Africa 1968-79 by S. Blignaut. (Johannesburg, SAIRR, 1981) 90p.

Saayman,R.B. "Native education", in National European-Bantu Conf., 5th, Bloemfontein, 1933, pp.125-38. (See National European-Bantu Conference).

Saayman,R.B. "Naturelle Opvoeding", Race Relations J. I(2) 1934, pp.19-25.

Sabelo,N.B.J. "Advice to young teachers". Native Teachers' J. 19: Jul. 1940, p.182-4.

Sabili,L. "Bantu Education and the African Teacher". Africa South Dec. 1956, pp.42-51.

Sales,J.M. "The mission station as an agency of civilization: the development of a Christian coloured community in the eastern Cape,S.A., 1800-1859". (Ph.D., University of Chicago, Ill., 1972).

Sangaran,L.F. "A historical evaluation of Indian education in the Transvaal covering the period 1900-1968". (M.Ed. thesis, UW, 1969).

Sangarin,L.F. A historical evaluation of Indian education in the Transvaal. (Johannesburg, 1967) 14p.

Sargant,E.B. Report on Native Education in SA. Part I and II. (Mafeking,
     1904) 273p. 2v. in 1.
     (pt. 1, Education and Law; pt. 2, Agencies for the change of law and the
     education of natives; pt. 3, Education in the Protectorates).

Sargant,E.B. The Lovedale Mission. (no place, no pub., 1905?) (Reprint
     from The Scotsman, Sept. 30, 1905).

Sargant,E.B. (Education Adviser to the High Commissioner of South Africa).
     Report on Native Education in SA. (London, 1908) 74p.

Saunders,A.H. "Training of girls in missionary schools". SA Outlook LVI,
     1926, p.232-4.

Saunders,C.C. "The new African elite in the Eastern Cape and some later 19th
     Century origins of African Nationalism". Societies of S. Africa in 19th
     and 20th Centuries, University of London ICS Vol. I (1969-70) pp.44-55.

Schapera,I. "The aspirations of Native school children". Critic II (3)
     (March 1934) pp.152-162.

Schimlek,F. Mariannhill: a study in Bantu life and Missionary effort.
     (Mariannhill, 1953) 352p. illus.

Schlemmer,L. Employment opportunity and Race in SA. (Denver, Univ. of
     Denver, 1973) 60p.

Schmidt,R. Terugblik: Op het begin en de voortgang van het werk in de School
     te Genadendal 1737-1818: Tot het Honderdjarige Jubelfest van de School
     te Genadendal, 15 Julie 1814 - 15 Julie 1941. (Genadendal, Zending van
     de Moraviese Broederkerk, 1914) 16p.

Schmidt,W.H.O. "School and the community". Native Teachers' J. 29: April
     1950, p.143-48.

Schrotenboer,P.G. Conflict and hope in SA. (Hamilton, Ontario, 1968) 134p.
     "Bantu Education in SA" pp.37-44.

Schwartz,L.J. "Johannesburg's night schools for natives, 1938-1947".
     Bluestocking 17(2): N. 1948, p.26-30.

Seatlholo,K.S. "A Soweto student speaks". (Press release for SSRC)
     Pro Veritate Nov. 1976.

Seaton,W.H. One-teacher kraal school: a study in adaptation. (Cape Town 1932)36pp.

Seboni,M.O.M. "The South African Native Collebe, Fort Hare, 1903-1954: A
     Historical-Critical Survey". (D.Ed. thesis, UNISA, 1958 1959?) 478p. Biblio.

Semple,D.W. Emgwali Girl's Institution 1861-1961 - A Century's Appraisment.
     (Lovedale, 1961) 18p.

Seshibe,N.R.M. "Education Planning for South Africa's Refugees". (Ed.D. diss.,
     Univ. of Massachusetts, 1979) 190p.

Shaw,D.A. "Industrial Training of Natives in Natal". Afr. Month 5 (1909)
     pp.359-67.

Shaw,M.A. "Training of adolescent girls". SA Outlook LVI 1926 p.12-15.

Shepherd,R.H.W. "The missionary attitude to the new Bantu intelligensia":
     address to the General Missionary Conference of SA held at Lovedale,
     28 June 1928. (Lovedale 1928) 8p.

Shepherd,R.H.W. The Bantu. (Edinburgh, United Free Church of Scotland 192?)
     95p. Ch. V 'Educational and Industrial Work', p.65-72.

Shepherd,R.H.W. "Religious and moral instruction in native schools".
SA Outlook 61, 1931, p.48-51.

Shepherd,R.H.W. Lovedale, South Africa: the story of a century, 1841-1941.
(Lovedale, 1940) 531pp.

Shepherd,R.H.W. "Native Secondary Education". SA Outlook LXXI, 1941, p.78-9.

Shepherd,R.H.W. "Churches and the future of native education". SA Outlook
73: D. 1943, p.165-8.

Shepherd,R.H.W. The Churches and the future of native education: an individual
viewpoint. (Lovedale 1944) (Christian Council Study Series No. 7) 11p.

Shepherd,R.H.W. "The Riot at Lovedale". SA Outlook 76, 1946, p.141-2.

Shepherd,R.H.W. "Progress in African education: some facts and figures".
SA Outlook 82: Ag. 1952 p.118.

Shepherd,R.H.W. "New education plan for the Bantu: South African commissions
for reaching recommendations". African World Apr. 1952, p.15-16.

Shepherd,R.H.W. "Role of the educated African". Forum 2(8) N. 1953, p.50-52.

Shepherd,R.H.W. "The SA Bantu Educ. Act". African Affairs 54 (215) 1955.

Shepherd,R.H.W. "Education and Poverty". SA Outlook 56 Dec. 1956, p.272-273.

Shepherd,R.H.W. Lovedale South Africa 1924-1955. (Lovedale 1971) 163p.

Shingler,J.D. "Education and Political Order in South Africa 1902-61".
(Ph.D. Yale Univ., 1973).

Shutte,D.S. "Student Protest at the University of the Witwatersrand 1955-1959".
(B.A. Hons. Diss., UW, 1981) 67pp.

Sibisi,J.S. "Juvenile Delinquency" in Macmillan,R.G. et al. (1962) p.210-212.

Sibisi,J.S. "Teacher Training with a focus on Kwazulu". Paidonomia 3(2)
1975, p.38-55.

Sihlali,L.L. "Bantu education and the African teacher". Afr. South 1(1)
O-D 1956, p.42-51.

Sikakane,J. A Window on Soweto. (London, Int. Defence and Aid Fund, 1977).

Simkins,C. & Clarke,D. Structural Unemployment in Southern Africa.
(Pietermaritzburg, UNP, 1978) 82p.

Simons,H.J. & R.E. Class and Colour in SA: 1850-1950. (Harmondsworth, 1969).

Skinner,J. (collated by). Bantu Education: 1949-50. A Summary of developments
in the field of African primary and secondary education and teacher
training over a ten year period. (Johannesburg,SAIRR,1960) (RR 150/60).

Slabbert,M. & Thomas,W.H. Pre-School facilities for coloured and black
children in greater Cape Town. (Bellville, Inst. for Social Development,
UWC, 1976?).

Smith,E.W. Aggrey of Africa: a study in black and white. (London, Student
Christian Movement, 1929).

Smith,E.W. "Indigenous education in Africa" in W.E. Evans Pritchard and others,
Essays presented to C.G. Seligman. (London, 1934) 385p.

Smith,P.E.S. "Opvoedkundige, sosiale en geestelike ontwikkeling van die
Transkei". J. of Racial Affairs 14(2) March 1963, p.83-102.

Smithen,J.M. "Departmental education agencies at work in the Transkeian Territories and the problem of better co-ordination of native school education with them". (M.Ed. thesis, UNISA, 1953) 117p.

Sneesby,G. "The Vernacular in Bantu Education in SA". Overseas Education V 33 1961, pp.75-83.

Snyman,J.H. (Chairman). Report of the Commission of Inquiry into certain matters relating to the Univ. of the North. (Pretoria, Govt. Printer 1975)243p.

Sonn,F.A. "Coloured Education". ASPACTS 19 Sept. 1977, p.4.

South Africa - Official - Publications relating to Black Education.
   a) Government Commission Reports
   b) Annual Reports
   c) Statistical Publications
   d) Occasional Official Publications relating to "Native Education" for the period 1910-1948.
   e) Publications of the Bantu Education Dept/Dept. of Information/D.E.T.

a) Government Commission Reports relating to Black Education.

South Africa: Official. Reports of the South African Native Affairs Commission 1903-1905. (Cape Town, 1905-6).

South Africa: Official. Report of the Select Committee on Native Affairs (S.C.3 - 1910).

South Africa: Official. Fourth Report, Second - Sixth Reports of the Select Committee on Native Affairs (SC 6a - 1917).

South Africa: Official. Report of Committee on Industrial Education, 1916. (UG.9 - 1917) (Pretoria, Govt. Printer, 1917).

South Africa: Official. Interim Report of the Asiatic Enquiry Commission, appointed by H.E. the Governor General to enquire into certain aspects concerning the Asiatic Community. (Chairman: J.H. Lange) (UG.4 - 1921) (Pretoria, 1921).

South Africa: Official. Report of the Commission on Education Administration (Hofmeyer Commission) (UG.19 - 1924) (Pretoria, 1924).

South Africa: Official. Report of the Commission on Agricultural Education (UG.26 - 1926) (Pretoria, 1926).

South Africa: Official. Cape Province: Commission on Coloured Education, Report 1925-1926. (Cape Town 1927) 24pp.

South Africa: Official. Report of the Committee appointed to inquire into the Training of Natives in Medicine and Public Health. (UG.35 - 1928) .(Chairman: C.T. Loram) (Pretoria, Govt. Printer) pp.36.

South Africa: Official. Native Economic Commission. (Holloway Commission). (UG.22 - 1932) (Pretoria 1932).

South Africa: Official. Report of the Provincial Finance Commission appointed in 1933. (UG.46 - 1934) (Pretoria, Govt. Printer).

South Africa: Official. Report of the Committee of Enquiry into subsidies to universities, university colleges and technical colleges. (UG.8 - 1934) (Pretoria, Govt. Printer, 1934).

South Africa: Official. Interdepartmental Committee on Native Education. 1935-1936 (Welsh Report) (UG.29 - 1936) (Pretoria, 1936).

South Africa: Official. Native Representative Council: Reports of the
    Proceedings of ... (1937 - 1951).

South Africa: Official. Report of the Commission of Inquiry regarding the
    Cape Coloured Population of the Union (Wilcocks Commission) (UG 54/1937)
    (Pretoria 1937) Ch. IX - Education. (Appendix 48, pp.326-342 - Cruse,H.P.
    'An historical survey of Coloured education'.)

South Africa: Official. Report of the Committee to enquire into present
    facilities and future policy for higher education for Indians in Natal.
    (Chairman: F.D. Hugo) (UG.39 - 1941) (UG.27 - 1942) (Pretoria 1942)

South Africa: Official. Report of the Inter-Departmental Committee on the
    Social, Health and economic conditions of Urban Natives. (The Smit Report)
    (Pretoria, Govt. Printers) (1942).

South Africa: Official. Interim Report of the Commission of Enquiry into
    matters affecting the Indian population of the province of Natal.
    (Chairman: F.C. Broome) (UG.22 - 1945) (Pretoria 1945).

South Africa: Official. The Committee on Adult Education (Chairman: Eybers)
    (UG.35 - 1945) (Pretoria, Govt. Printer, 1945) 186p.

South Africa: Official. Report of the Commission on Technical and Vocational
    Education (de Villiers Commission) (UG.65 - 1948) (Pretoria, 1948).

South Africa: Official. (Dept. of Education) Native School Feeding Scheme,
    Report of the Committee of Enquiry. (Pretoria 1949) mimeo. 142p.

South Africa: Official. Commission on Native Education, Report of:
    (Chairman: W.W.M. Eiselen) (UG.53 - 1951) (Pretoria, Govt. Printer, 1952).

South Africa: Official. Report of the Commission on the Implications of
    Providing Separate Training Facilities for Non-Europeans at Universities.
    Report, 1953 - 1954 (Holloway Commission) (Pretoria, Govt. Printer, 1954)66p.

South Africa: Official. Report of the Commission of Enquiry into the Socio-
    Economic Development of the Bantu Areas within the Union of South Africa.
    (The Tomlinson Commission) (UG.61 - 1955) (Pretoria, Govt. Printer, 1955).

South Africa: Official. Report of the Fort Hare Commission. (Pretoria 1955) 42p.

South Africa: Official. Interdepartmental Fact-Finding Committee on the
    Financial Implications in connection with the Establishment of Separate
    University Colleges for Non-Europeans. (Pretoria 1957).

South Africa: Official. Report of the commission on the separate universities
    Education Bill. (Chairman: M.D.C. de Wet Nel) (UG.32 - 1958) (Parow/
    Pretoria, 1958) 76p.

South Africa: Official (Dept. of Coloured Affairs). Interim Report of the
    commission of Enquiry into the Financial Relations between the Central
    Government and the Provinces, dealing with the financial implications
    of a possible transfer of Coloured Education from the Provinces to the
    Central Government. (Schumann Commission) (UG.62) (Cape Town 1962).
    (Duplicated by Cape Prov. Library Service).

South Africa: Official (Dept. of Bantu Educ.) Report of a Commission of
    inquiry into the teaching of the official languages and the use of the
    mother tongue as a medium of instruction in Transkeian primary schools.
    (Report: Oct. 1962) (RP.22 - 1963) (Pretoria, Govt. Printer, 1963) 32p.

South Africa: Official. Report on Education for Indians in South Africa, to the Minister of Indian Affairs, Durban. (Unpub. 1964).

South Africa: Official (Dept. of National Education). Report of the committee of inquiry into the treatment, education and care of autistic children. (Pretoria, Govt. Printer, 1971) (RP.26 - 1972).

South Africa: Official. Report of the Commission of Inquiry into the Universities. (De Vries Commission) (RP.25 - 1974) (Pretoria 1974).

South Africa: Official. Commission on enquiry into the riots at Soweto and elsewhere from the 16 June 1976 to the 28 Feb. 1977. Vol. I and II. (Cillie Commission) (RP.55 - 1980) (Pretoria, Govt. Printer, 1980).

b) Annual Reports or Publications related to Black Education.

South Africa: Official. Hansard - Senate Debates; - House of Assembly Debates.

South Africa: Official. Official year book of the Union of SA 1910-20. (Containing statistics for the period 1910-81) (Pretoria, Govt. Printer, 1921) XX 1007p. - Education p.254-300.

South Africa: Official (Native Affairs Dept.) Annual Reports (Pretoria, 1911?)

South Africa: Official. Education Dept.: Annual Reports 1920-1948.

South Africa: Official. Provincial Education Departments: Annual Reports. Cape 1920 - 19- ; Natal 1920 - 19- ; Tvl. 1920 - 19- ; OFS 1920 - 19-.

South Africa: Official. Native Affairs Commission Annual Reports: 1921,22,23,etc.

South Africa: Official. Coloured Advisory Council. Annual Reports: 1943-

South Africa: Official. Union Advisory Board on Native Education: Annual Reports: 1946, '47, '48 ... (various) (Pretoria, Govt. Printer).

South Africa: Official. Coloured Affairs: Commissioner for. Reports: 1952 - '54.

South Africa: Official. Department of Coloured Affairs: Reports, 1954-

South Africa: Official. Regulations governing the approval of State-aided schools and conditions under which grants-in-aid may be made. (No. 119, 21 Jan. 1955).

South Africa: Official. Department of Bantu Education: Annual Report, 1955-

South Africa: Official. Bulletin: statistics and other information about Bantu Education for 1959. (Pretoria, Govt. Printer, 1959).

South Africa: Official. Dept. of Bantu Education (later DET) Annual Reports 1961- (Pretoria, Govt. Printer).

South Africa: Official. National Advisory Education Council Reports: Annual Reports (RP 1963-68) (Pretoria, Govt. Printer).

South Africa: Official. Reports of the Education Council for Coloureds. (1964 - 1970).

South Africa: Official. National Education Council Reports (RP 1969 - 1973).

South Africa: Official. Dept of National Education. Annual Report for the period ... (various) (Pretoria, Govt. Printer, 1970-).

South Africa: Official. Department of Education, Arts and Science: Annual Reports 1948 - 1968.

South Africa: Official. Department of Education, Arts and Science: Annual Reports: 1955-1964.

South Africa: Official. Department of Higher Education: Annual Reports 1968-1970?.

South Africa: Official. Education Council for Coloureds ... Report for the financial year ... (various) (Pretoria, Govt. Printer).

c) Statistical Publications relating to Black Education.

South Africa: Official. Department of Census and Statistics. - Official Yearbooks: 1920 - 1963; Statistical Yearbooks: 1964 - 1966; South African Statistics: 1966 - 1974; Quarterly Bulletin of Statistics: 1960 - 1974 (? to the present).

South Africa: Official. National Bureau of Educational and Social Research). Bulletin of Educational Statistics for the Union of South Africa: Annual - 1939 - 1947 (Pretoria, Govt. Printer) (various).

South Africa: Official (State of SA) Economic, financial and statistical yearbook for the RSA (Johannesburg, 1963) etc.

South Africa: Official. Bureau of Statistics Report 08-04-01: Education: Coloured and Asiatics 1957-1963.

South Africa: Official. Bureau of Census and Statistics. Union Statistics for Fifty Years 1910 - 1960 (Jubilee Issue) (Pretoria 1961).

d) Occasional Official Publications relating to Native Education for the period 1910 - 1948.

South Africa: Official. (Department of Native Affairs). Prospectus of the Zulu National Training Institution for Sons of Chiefs and Headmen, Nongoma, Zululand. (Pretoria, Govt. Printer, 1932) 8p.

South Africa: Official. Union Department of Education. Report of Conference on Rural Education, 1934. (Pretoria, Govt. Printer, 1934).

South Africa: Official. Council of Social and Economic Planning. Report No. 13: The economic and social condition of the racial groups in SA: 1948. Ch. VII - Education.

e) Official Publications of the Bantu Education Department (or DET from 1979) or related to the question of Black Education.

South Africa: Official. (Dept. of Bantu Education). Bulletin 1957 (in continuation) (Pretoria, Govt. Printer).

South Africa: Official. The Progress of the Bantu people towards nationhood. (SA Govt. Inf. Services, n.d., vol. 2, n.d., vol. 5).

South Africa: Official. Bantu Schools for Tomorrow: handbook for student teachers. (Cape Town, 1950) 290pp. illus.

South Africa: Official. Educational Facilities for the Bantu in S. Africa. Native Affairs. Paper XV., Dept. of Educ., Arts and Science, Jan. 1950. (Pretoria, State Info. Office, 1950).

South Africa: Official. (Dept. of Finance) UG/RP reports. Estimates of the expenditure to be defrayed from revenue and Bantu educ. accounts ... 1955/6. (Cape Town, 1955).

South Africa: Official. (Native Affairs: Dept. of Bantu Educ.) The higher primary school course, 1956; The lower primary school course, 1956. (Pretoria, Govt. Printer) 191p.

South Africa: Official. (Dept. of Native Affairs). Bantu education: Handbook of regulations and instructions. (Pretoria 1957).

State Information Office. Bantu Education Policy: A plan to serve the community. (Fact Paper No. 39) (Pretoria, Aug. 1957).

South Africa: Official. (Native Affairs Dept./Bantu Educ.) Draft syllabus for Junior Certificate, 1957. (Pretoria, Govt. Printer, 1957) 118p.

South Africa: Official (Dept. of Native Affairs). Bantu Education: 1. Syllabuses for the Bantu Teachers' Diploma, 1958. 2. Syllabuses for the Higher Primary Teachers' Course, 1956 (Pretoria).

South Africa: Official (Dept. of Bantu Educ.) Bulletin: statistics and other information about Bantu Education for 1959. (Pretoria, Govt. Printers, 1959) 208p.

South Africa: Official (Dept. of Native Affairs). Report of the Dept. of Native Affairs for period 1/7/54 - 31/12/57. (Pretoria, Govt. Printer, 1959). (p.16-28 deals with the development of Bantu Education as authorised by legislation).

South Africa: Official. Graduation trends in SA Universities 1918-1957. (Pretoria 1960) 119p.

South Africa: Official (SA Info Service/Dept. of Information). The progress of the Bantu people towards nationhood: self development (Series 1-5) (Pretoria, Inf. Service 1961 - issued in parts) (New edit. pub. Dept. of Info. 1965) 149p.

South Africa: Official. Education in South Africa. (Pretoria 1961) 59p.

South Africa: Official (State Information Office). The Truth about the transfer of coloured education. Pamphlet issued with the fornightly Digest of South African Affairs 25 June 1962.

South Africa: Official. Administration of Coloured Affairs. Education for Progress: Present facilities and future plans for the education of the Coloured peoples. (Pretoria, Govt. Printer, n.d.) 28p.

South Africa: Official. Regulations issued in terms of the Coloured Person's Education Act of 1963. (Government Notive R. 1968 of 21 November 1963 as amended).

South Africa: Official (Dept. of Bantu Education). Native Farm Schools. (Departmental Circular No. 18 of 1963) (mimeo. Eng. and Afr.) 6p.

South Africa: Official. (National Bureau of Education and Social Research, Dept. of Education, Arts and Science). Education in South Africa. (Pretoria, 1964).

South Africa: Official. Education for success. (London, SA Embassy, 1965) 32p.

South Africa: Official (Dept. of Info.) Stepping into the future: Education for SA's developing nations. (Pretoria, Govt. Printer, 1969) 40p.

South Africa: Official. (State Information Office). Education - for more and more Bantu. (Fact Paper No. 88) (Pretoria, n.d.)

South Africa: Official. (Dept. of Statistics). Education: principal statistics, 1968. (Pretoria, Govt. Printer, 1969) Report No. 08-07-02. N.B. Also Provincial Education Statistics Public.

South Africa: Official. (Dept. of Education, Transkei) Report for the period ... (various) (Umtata, Elata Printers, 1970).

South Africa: Official. (Dept. of Education and Training). Information on trade training, technical training, advanced technical training, industrial training, etc. (Pretoria, 197-).

South Africa: Official (Dept. of Bantu Education). Provision of more funds by the Government for the education of all races in the Republic and the extension of facilities for elementary and technical education. (Copy of a letter to TUCSA) March 1972.

South Africa: Official (Bantu Education Dept.) Instructions for requisitions and control of equipment and consumable requisites for Bantu schools. (Pretoria, Govt. Printer, 1972).

South Africa: Official. (Dept. of Bantu Education). Lists of schools, addresses and statistics 1973 (17 vols) (Pretoria, 1973).

South Africa: Official. (Dept. of Information). Stepping into the future: Education for SA's Black, Coloured and Indian peoples. Ed. Chris van Rensburg, Contributions A.J. Arendse et al. (Pretoria, 1974).

South Africa: Official. Bureau of national and international communication. Education (Pretoria, The Bureau, 1978) 46p.

South Africa: Official. (Human Sciences Research Council). Report of the HSRC Investigation into Education: Provision of Education in the RSA. (HSRC, Pretoria, 1981) 22Up.

South African Association for the Advancement of Education. Tertiary Education: the subject of the 11th Congress held in Pretoria, 1973. (Durban, SAAAE, 1973).

South African Association for the Advancement of Education. Educational planning for the future: papers delivered. ... at the 13th Congress of the SAAAE. (Ed. B.F. Nel) (Pretoria/Durban?, the Association,1975)223p.

South African Association for the Advancement of Education. Congress, 15th. Bloemfontein. Recurrent education ... papers read, Feb., 1977. (Pretoria, the Association, 1977) 202p.

South African Association for the Advancement of Knowledge and Culture (SAAAKC). "Education for the Bantu of South Africa". (Pretoria, The Association, 1961?) 32p. (being a reprint from Lantern XI (1) Sept. 1961, pp.64-96).

South African Congress of Democrats. Educating for Ignorance: the SA Congress of Democrats view of the Bantu Education Act. (Johannesburg, SACOD,1954)12p.

South Africa Foundation. Educating a Nation. (Pretoria/London ?1967) 24p.

South African General Missionary Conference. Memorandum on Native Education, October 26th, 1932.

South African Native Races Committee. The Natives of S. Afr.: their economic and social condition (London, 1901); S. Afr. natives: their progress and present condition. (London, 1908).

South African Native Races Committee. The S. African Native College: a statement by the SANR Comm. (London, 1911) 16p.

South African Native College (Fort Hare). Annual calendars, brochures and publications for graduation ceremonies (various).

South African Native College. SA Outlook 53: J. 1923 p.12-13; 54: J. 1924, p. 129-35.

South African Native College. Second graduation. SA Outlook 55: J. 1925, p.129-35.

The South African Native Races Committee. The South African Natives: Their Progress and Present Condition. (London 1908). (Educ. Ch. VI. pp.136-191, p.231).

South Africa: 1980 School Boycott Briefing Paper No. 1, March 1981 (IDAFSA) 4p.

South African Vacation Course on Native Education. Native Education: first SA vacation course. (Mariannhill, July 1928) 20p. bibliog.

Soweto Lay Ecumenical Association. Conference on the causes of student unrest, 13 Jul. 1974. (Johannesburg, The Association, 1974).

Spokes,S.L. "Technical education" (Coloured) Alpha 1(4) June 1963, p.14-15.

Spokes,S.L. The Training of Coloured Persons by the Peninsula Technical College (Pub. by the National Development and Management Foundation of SA, Cape Western Region, Nov. 1969).

Spro-Cas. Education beyond apartheid: Report of the Education Commission on Christianity in Apartheid Society. (Johannesburg, Christian Institute of SA, 1971) (SPROCAS Publication No. 5).

Spruyt,O.W. "Training of African Teachers" in Educational adaptations in a changing society, ed. E.G. Malherbe. (Cape Town, 1937).

Stadler,A.W. "From Lisbon to Soweto". SASH 18(8) 1977, p.5-7.

Stadler,A.W. "Educational Reform and Political Change". J. of Education 11, 1979, p.3-10.

Stauffer,M. (ed.) Thinking with Africa. (Chapters by a group of Nationals Interpreting the Christian Movement). (New York, Student Volunteer Movement for Foreign Missions, 1927) 184p. Includes contributions by C.T. Loram, T. Jesse Jones, R.V. Selope Thema, W.B. Rubusana, J.D. Rheinallt Jones, W. Hoernlé, D.D.T. Jabavu, Z.R. Mahabane, etc.

Stewart,J. - "The educated kaffir: an apology"; - "Industrial education: a sequel" (to the above) (address to the Lovedale Literary Society, 1880) (Lovedale, 1880) 16p.

Stewart,J. "The experiment of native education", an address delivered by J. Stewart to the Lovedale Literary Society. (Lovedale 1884) 31p.

Stewart,J. Lovedale: past and present: a register of 2 000 names. A record written in black and white, but more in white than black. (Lovedale 1887).

Stewart,J. (ed.) Lovedale, South Africa, illustrated by 50 views from photographs with introduction by author. (Edinburgh, 1894) 110p. illus.

Stewart,J. "Experiment of native education". SA Outlook 70: Jul.1940 p.136-9.

Steytler,P.M.V.A. Die Geskiedenis en ontwikkeling van Naturelle-onderwys in die O.V.S. 1823-1912. (B.Ed., US, 1941).

Stimie,C.M. Education in the RSA. (Pretoria, HSRC, Institute of Information and Special Services, 1970).

Stimie,C.M. & Geggus,C. University Education in the RSA. (Pretoria, HSRC, 1972).

Stokes, A. Phelps. Report of Rev. Anson Phelps Stokes on education, native welfare and race relations in East and South Africa. (New York, 1934) 59p.

Store,J. "Black Nationalism and Apartheid: Two Variations on a Separate
    Theme". Social Dynamics 2(1) June, 1965, p.19-30.

Stone,P. "The need for agriculturalists trained for the self-governing
    territories". Bantu Educ. J. 24(1) 1978, p.36-7.

Stormont,D.D. On the unemployment of native teachers. (Blythswood, 1923).

Strauss,F.J. "Die Londen se Sendinggenootskap en hulle onderwys aan
    nie-Blankes in Suidelike Afrika, 1799-1836". (B.Ed., US, 1950).

Strydom,G.C. & Strydom,A.E. Technical education for Indians. (Pretoria,
    HSRC: Institute for Educational Research, 1980).

Stuart,J. A Project for the promotion of Education in General for the
    European as for the Native Races of the Colony of Natal, SA.
    (Pietermartizburg, 1859).

Students African Movement et al. Dossier on Education. (Johannesburg, SAM,
    1978?) mimeo. 20p.

Swanepoel,C.B. " 'n Histories-pedagogiese evalueering van die Bantoegemeenskap-
    skool in Suid Afrika". (M.Ed. verhandeling, Pretoria, UP, 1966).

Symington,F.C. "Onderwys in Transvaal gedurende die Kroonkolonieperiod, 1900-
    1907". (D.Ed., UP, 1948) "Native Education 1903-7" - p.215-223.

Tabata,I.B. Education for Barbarism: Bantu (Apartheid) Education in SA.
    (Durban, 1959; London, 1960; United Movement of South Africa,
    reprint 1980) (Preface by Patrick Ncube).

Taberer,C. Special appeal for the S.P.G. Missionary and Industrial
    Institution of St. Matthew's, Keiskamma Hoek. (no place of pub. 1885) 14pp.

Tabor,G.W. "Technical Education for Africans" in Tunmer,R. and Muir,R.K. (eds.)
    Some Aspects of Education in South Africa. (African Studies Programme,
    UW, Johannesburg, 1968) Occasional Paper No. 4, pp.59-69.

Tabor,G.W. Vocational and technical education for the Bantu. (Johannesburg,
    SAIRR, 1969).

Tatham,F.S. The race conflict in South Africa: an enquiry into the general
    question of native education. (Pietermaritzburg, 1894) 28p.

Taylor,J.D. (ed.) Christianity and the natives of SA : A Yearbook of SA
    Missions. (Lovedale 1928).

Taylor,J.D. One hundred years of the American Board Mission in South Africa
    1835-1935. (n.p., n.d., 1935?).

Teachers' Educational and Professional Association (by P. v.d. Ross).
    The control of education of Coloured children (Cape Town 1957) 10p.
    (pamphlet No. 1).

Teachers' Educational and Professional Association. Compulsory Education as a
    state obligation (by R. Joorst) (Cape Town, 1958) 18p. (pamphlet No. 2).

Teachers' Educational and Professional Association. Four essays on education
    by S. Cooppan et al. (Cape Town, n.d.) (pamphlet No. 3).

Teachers' League of South Africa (TLSA). Port Elizabeth conference, 1953.
    A manifesto to the Cape Coloured people: the Coloured Education commission,
    the threat to the education of our children ... (Lansdowne, C.P., the
    League, 1953).

Teachers League of SA. The Colour Bar in Education (by E.L. Maurice) (Cape Town, 1957).

Thembela,A.J. "African education at the dawn of a new era", an address delivered at the 55th Annual Conference of the Natal African Teachers' Union on the 29th June 1973 at Vuleka. (no place of publication).

Thembela,A.J. "The problem of the medium of instruction in African schools". (Paper read at the South African Pedagogical Society Congress, Univ. of Zululand, 1974).

Thembela,A.J. "A socio-pedagogic description of some factors which influence the quality of the didactic situation in urban and rural African schools in Natal: a comparative study". (Unpub. M.Ed. diss, UZ, 1975).

Thembela,A.J. "Teaching the African child (curriculum adaptation): an evaluation of the present curriculum in the light of the needs and aspirations of the African society in SA". Paidonomia 3(2) 1975, p.7-16.

Thembela,A.J. "A consideration of the idea of compulsory education with a view to planning for its introduction in the 'State of KwaZulu'". (A paper read at the Univ. of Zululand on the 17th Sept. 1975).

Thoahlane,T. Black Renaissance: Papers from the Black Renaissance Convention. (Johannesburg, 1975).

Thomas,D.R.O. "Adult Education for the native in SA". J. of Adult Educ. 6(2) Apr. 1933, p.164-175. (also reprint edit.).

Tiffen,B.W. "English versus African Languages as a Medium of Education in African Primary Schools", in G.N. Brown (ed.) Conflict and Harmony in Education in Tropical Africa. (London 1975) pp.319-35.

Tillema,R.G. "Apartheid in South African Education". (Thesis, Ph.D., Univ. of Wisconsin, 1974) 300p. biblio.

Tiro,O.R. "Bantu education". SA Outlook 102: Jun. Jul. 1972, p.99+.

Tiryakian,E.A. "Apartheid and education in the Union of SA". Harvard Educational Review 25 (1955) pp.242-259.

Tladi,W. "Black White education: birth of an anomaly". People Profits 5(10): 32 Ap. 1978, p.32-34.

Tobias,P. "Africans at our universities". SA Outlook 80: Ja. 1950, p.14-15.

Tobias,P. "Education in Danger". (Speech given at the opening of the 1972 National Conference of the Black Sash at UW). SASH 16(3) N. 1972,p.10-16.

Tobias,R. "Squatting and Education in Cape Town". SA Outlook Ag.1975,p.127-192.

Transkei - Official Publications.

Transkei - Official. Commission of Inquiry into the Standard of Education in the Transkei. (Chairman: G.L. Kakana). Report (Umtata: Dept. of Educ. 1973) 133p.

Transkeian Teachers' Library. List of books. (n.p., n.pub., 193-?) 15p. A catalogue of the Library's holdings.

Transvaal - Official Publications - ZAR - Crown Colony - Province.

Transvaal Province - Official. (Transvaal Education Department). Annual Reports of the Director of Education: Sections on Native Education. (Pretoria, TED) (various).

Transvaal Province - Official. Tvl. Educ. Dept. Report 1910/11 to the present. (Pretoria, Govt. Printer, 1912-).

Transvaal Province - Official. Tvl. Educ. Dept. Third Report of the Council of Education dealing with native education. (T.P. 1-'15(1915)).

Transvaal Province - Official. (Tvl. Educ. Dept.) Handbook of Regulations and Instructions for the guidance of Superintendents of Native Schools and Teachers. (Pretoria, Govt. Printer, 1938).

Transvaal Province - Official. (Dept. of Education). Report of the Provincial Education Commission, 1937-1939. (TP. 5 - '39) Ch. XIV - Education of Coloured and Indian children.

Transvaal Province - Official. (Dept. of Education). Verslag van die departementele komitee insake ondersoek na Kleurling en Indieëronderwys in die Transvaal. (Pretoria, the Dept., 1951).

Transvaal Province - Official. (Dept. of Education). 'n Ondersoek na die bekwaamheid van Kleurlingonderwysers in die Transvaal. (Pretoria, 1957).

Transvaal Indian Congress. Statement submitted to the Tvl. Educ. Enquiry Commission 24 Nov. 1937. (Johannesburg, the Congress, 1937).

Transvaal Workers' Educational Association - Western Native Township, BC. Report of the working committee, 1941).

Trevor,T.G. "Native education from an employer's point of view". NADA 5: 1927, p.97-99.

Trotter,G.J. "The Economic Rationale for Educational Planninq". SAJE 44(4) 1976, pp.343-377.

Trotter,G.J. "Education and Income Distribution". SAJE 45, 1977, p.335-361.

Troup,F. Forbidden Pastures: education under apartheid. (London, Int. Def. and Aid Fund 1976/1977) 72pp.

Tucker,F.N. "On Native Education": being a copy of a letter which appeared in the Natal Witness of 24 April 1895. (Pietermaritzburg, 1895) 6p.

Tucker,P. "Cillie Commission". Reality May 1980, p.11.

Tucsa. Memo to the Permanent Interdepartmental Committee on the co-ordination of Education for all races. (Johannesburg, TUCSA, 1968) 34p.

Tunmer,R. & Muir,R.K. "African desire for Education in South Africa". Comp. Educ. 9(3) October 1965.

Tunmer,R. Race and Education. (Johannesburg, Inst. for the Study of Man in Africa, 1967) 26p.

Tunmer,R. "Education in South Africa", in Tunmer,R. and Muir,R.K. (eds.) Some Aspects of Education in South Africa. (African Studies Programme, UW, Johannesburg, 1968) Occasional Paper No. 4, pp.1-15.

Tunmer,R. ... African attitudes toward education. (Johannesburg, SAIRR, 1969). (RR 10/69).

Tunmer,R. "The Education of Coloured and Indians in South Africa", in Rose,B. (ed.) Education in Southern Africa. (Johannesburg 1970) pp.90-117.

Tunmer,R. (Rose,B. and ...) Documents in South African education. (Johannesburg, 1975) incl. section on African education.

Turner,H.W. "African Independent churches and educ." JMAS 13(2) 1975 p.295-308.

United Nations Security Council. United Nations programmes for the education and training of South Africans in pursuance of Security Council Resolutions S/5773 of the 18th June 1864. Report by the Secretary General. (New York, UNO, 1965).

United Nations Organization. "The United Nations Educational and Training Programme for Southern Africa", (UNETPSA) in Notes and Documents. (Centre Against Apartheid, UN, New York, NY 10016).

UNESCO. Apartheid - its effects on education, science, culture and information. (Paris, UNESCO, 1967).

Universiteit van die Oranje-Vrystaat. Instituut vir Sosiale en Ekonomiese Navorsing. Die Onderwysstelsel van Qwaqwa: 'n situasiebepaling in ontwikkelingsriglyne. (Bloemfontein, 1977) (Ontwikkeling van Qwaqwa No. 10).

University of the Orange Free State. (Research Unit for Education System Planning). Research Unit for Education System Planning. (Bloemfontein, UOFS, 1978).

University of the Orange Free State. Multi-Purpose Centre: Soweto. (Bloemfontein, Reasearch Unit for Education System Planning, 1979).

Urban Foundation - Natal Region. Report on the education and training of teachers in teacher training institutions in KwaZulu. (Durban 1979).

V.,E.O. "Native education (Cape Province)". Educ. 55: 0. 1945, p.131-33.

Van Aswegan,G.J. "Naturelle-onderwys". Skoolblad 38(1): Ja. 1950, p.3-4.

Van den Berg,C.G. "A comparative study of European, Indian and Zulu children in Natal as regards intelligence and learning and memory". (M.Ed., UNISA, 1938) 84p. bibliog.

Van den Berg,D.J. "Black education: a new perspective on developing the potentialities of the black pupil". Humanitas 6(2) 1980, p.97-110.

Van der Horst,S.T. (ed.) Race Discrimination in South Africa: A Review. (Cape Town 1981) 247p. - Section on Education by F. Auerbach and D. Welsh pp.66-89.

Van der Merwe,B.de V. "The new era in education for the Blacks". (A paper read at the South African Pedagogical Society Congress at Fort Hare on the 26th May 1975).

Van der Merwe,H. & Welsh,D. Student perspectives on SA. (Cape Town 1972).

Van der Merwe,I.V. " 'n Opvoedkundige beskouing van die finansiering van primêre en sekondêre Bantoe onderwys in Suid Afrika". (M.Ed. verhand., UNISA, 1973).

Van der Merwe,I.V. Die beplanning van 'n skole netwerk vir Bophuthatswana met spesiale verwysing na die streek Taung. (Bloemfontein, UOFS, Navorsingseenheid vir Onderwysstelselbeplanning, 1978).

Van der Merwe,L.S. "Die N.G. Kerk en Kleurlingonderwys". (M.Ed. thesis, US, 1941).

Van der Merwe,P.J. "The obligations of our Government towards the education of the lower races". (M.A., UW, 1924) 52p.

Van der Merwe,P. "Die verhouding van ons Kerk teenoor Naturelle Opvoeding". (two parts) Die Basuin II (2) (May 1931) pp.11-14; II (3) (July 1931) pp.9-11.

Van der Merwe,W. "Die Britse beleid t.o.v. Bantoeonderwys en sending in die Transvaal gedurende die tydperk 1902-1906". (M.A., UP, 1970).

Van der Merwe,W. "Britse beleid t.o.v. Bantoeonderwys en sending in die Transvaal in die periode 1902-1906". Humanitas 1: 1972, p.253-55.

Van der Mescht,A.J.B. "Bantoe-Onderwys sedert die wet op Bantoe-Onderwys 1953". (M.Ed., US, 1965) 382pp.

Van der Poel,J. "Education and the Native". pam. SA Teachers' Association address. (Cape Town June 1934) 24p.

Van der Poel,J. "Educ. of the Native in SA". Bluestocking 1(3) Ap. 1931. p.11-14; in J. of the Royal Africa Society 34 (1935) p.313-31.

Van der Poel,J. "The Present Position of Coloured Education in the Cape Province", pub. in the J. of the SAIRR 9(1) 1942.

Van der Ross,R. "The Control and Education of Coloured Children". TEPA pamphlet No. 1. (Cape Town Teachers' Educational and Professional Association, 1957).

Van der Ross,R.E. "Education of Coloured children", in "Education for Isolation": a special issue of The Black Sash, Sept.-Nov. 1960.

Van der Ross,R.E. "Education for Equal Opportunity: issues, attitudes and action among the Coloured people". Symposium 1976/7, p.17-25.

Van der Walt,N. "Education of Coloured children in the Transvaal". Tvl. Educ. Bulletin 2: March 1957, p.31-35.

Van Deventer,T.J. " 'n Ondersoek na die verband tussen onderwyspeil, werkgeleenthede en inkome onder die Bantoevolksgroepe van Suid Afrika". (M.Com. verhandeling, UP, 1974).

Van Dyk,D.F. "The Education of the Griquas, Coloureds and Bantu in E. Griqualand - a historical survey, 1863-1892". (D.Ed. thesis,UOFS,1964) 647p.

Van Dyk,D.F. "The Contact between the early tribal African Education and the Westernized system of missionary education". (Inaugural lecture, 1967, pub. Fort Hare). (Published in Educare 3(1) 1974 p.1-14, biblio.)

Van Dyk,J.H. "Bantoe-onderwys vanuit die oogpunt van 'n inspekteur van skole". Bantoe-onderwysbl. 9: Ag. 1963, port., p.339-43.

Van Dyk,J.H. " ... Groei van Bontoe-onderwys". Bantoe-Onderwysbl. 9: N. 1963, p.495-97, port.

Van Dyk,J.H. (Sec. for Bantu Education). Opening of the first meeting of the Advisory Board for Bantu Education, 5 Aug. 1964. (Pretoria, Dept, of Info., 5.8.64) 1964.

Van Dyk,J.H. "Whither Bantu Education". J. of Racial Affairs 17: Ja. 1966, p.4-9. (Originally an address delivered at a graduation ceremony 14 May 1965. Kwa-Dlangezwa, Univ. of Zululand, 1965). (Pub. Univ. of Zululand, Series II (1)) 9p.

Van Heerden,P.W. "Nie-blanke vraagstuk en die onderwys". Onderwysbl.53(604) F. 1950, p.15-17.

van Heerden,P.W. "Ontwikkeling in the Soutpansberggebied". Bantoe-onderwysbl. 9: Sept. 1963, p.375.

Van Huyssteen,R.J. "An Investigation into the educational position of
the Coloured children in a rural district (Worcester, C.P.)".
(Ph.D., Cape Town, 1935).

Van Lill,G.J. "Die Beheer en administrasie van Bantoe-Onderwys in SA: met
spesiale verwysing na die tydperk sedert Unie, 1910". (M.Ed.,US,1955) 164pp.

Van Niekerk,C. "Some Aspects of Correspondence tuition in South Africa".
Humanitas I (1) 1971, p.31-38.

Van Rensburg,C. (ed.) Stepping into the future: education for South africa's
Black, Coloured and Indian peoples. (Johannesburg, 1975).

Van Rensburg,F.A.J. Trends in Bantu Education in the RSA. (Pretoria, HSRC,
1975) 74p.

Van Rensburg,F.A.J. Trends in education for Coloureds in the RSA. (Pretoria,
HSRC, 1976) Report WS-17, 87p.

Van Rensburg,J.I.J. "Die Lewe en werk van Sir Langham Dale 1859-1892".
(D.Ed., US, 1943) 814p.

Van Rooyen,G.P. "Sir John Ernest Adamson as Direkteur van Onderwys, 1905-24:
'n verhandeling oor sy bydraes tot die praktyk van die onderwys en die
opvoeding gedurende sy ampstermyn as direkteur van onderwys in Tvl".
(D.Ed., U. Potch, 1951): XIII p.398-420, Education of blacks.

Van Rooyen,I. Vooruitskattings in die primêre en sekondêre skool bevolking
van Qwaqwa 1979-1983 met implekasies vir die onderwyserstelsel.
(Bloemfontein, UOVS, Navorsingseenheid vir Onderwysstelsel-beplanning 1978).

Van Wyk,F.J. The Bantu Education Act: A Brief analysis of the act and some
comments on it. (Johannesburg, SAIRR, 1954) (RR 107/54).

Van Wyk,F.J. The Bantu Education Bill. (summary by F.J. van Wyk)
(Johannesburg, SAIRR, 1953) (RR 152/53).

Van Zyl,H. "Bantu Education" in N.J. Rhoodie (ed.) South African Dialogue:
contrasts in South African thinking on basic race issues.
(Johannesburg, 1972) 611p.

Van Zyl,H.J. A practical guide for Bantu teachers (Johannesburg 1951)
(List of Books for use in Bantu schools, p.133-147).

Van Zyl,H.J. "Gedagtes oor 'n nuwe rigting: Bantoeonderwys en die opleiding
van hoofmanne en raadsmanne". Bantu 2(3) Mar. 1955, p.10-20.

Venter,H.J. & Retief,G.M. Bantoe-Jeug misdaad - 'n Krimineel-Sosiologiese
Ondersoek van 'n groep Naturelle jeugoortreders in die Boksburgse
Landdrosdistrik. (Cape Town, 1960).

Venter,I.S.J. Die Anglikaanse Kerk en die Onderwys in die Oranje Vrystaat
1854-1900. (Pretoria, 1959) 268pp.

Venter,J.D. Die rehabilitasie van Bantoejeugoortreders: 'n opvolgstudie van
'n groep onder leerlings van die Diepkloofverbeteringskool 1937-1950.
(Pretoria, Dept. van Onderwys, Kuns en Wetenskap, 1960) 58p.

Venter,J.K. "Educational Activities of the Johannesburg Municipal Social
Welfare Department". (M.Ed., UNISA, 1948) 206pp.

Venter,P. "Die groei van onderwysaangeleenthede, Johannesburg, 1886-1920".
(D.Ed., U.Potch, 1950) 587p. Bibliog. - incl. black education.

Verloren van Themaat,R. "Legal education for the Bantu of SA". Comp. Intern. Law J. S. Afr. 2, Mr. 1969, p.73-86, bibliog.

Vermaak,D. "Education and development in Qwaqwa". Paper presented at a ... conference on the development of Qwaqwa, Phuthoditjhoba, 26-7 Sept. 1979. (Bloemfontein, UOFS, Research Unit for Educ. System Planning, 1979).

Vermaak,D. "Education for Development in Transkei: some statistical considerations". (Paper presented at the conference on education for development, Umtata 21-3 May 1979). (Bloemfontein, UOFS, Research Unit for Education System Planning, 1979).

Vermaak,D. "Education and work: problems and challenges". (East London, Ciskeian Conference on Education, June 1980).

Verster,T.L. "Aspekte van die provinsiale en uniale Bantoe-onderwysbeleid en beheer in Transvaal tussen die jare 1910 en 1967: 'n histories-pedagogiese deurskouing". (M.Ed., UNISA, 1970).

Verwoerd,H.F. Bantu Education (Policy pursued by Minister of Native Affairs). Hansard, Senate, 7 June 1954, col. 2595-2622. Also see (Durban, SAIRR, 1960) (NR 141/1960).

Verwoerd,H.F. "Bantu education: policy for the immediate future; with discussion". Institute of Administrators of Non-European Affairs 1954 pp.77-93. (Statement by the Hon. Dr. H.F. Verwoerd Min. of Nat. Affairs in the Senate of the Parliament of U.S. Afr. 7/6/54). (Pretoria, Inf. Service, Dept. of Native Aff., 1954).

Verwoerd,H.F. "Development and progress in Bantu communities: statement of policy in the Senate of the Parliament of the Union of SA. 20/6/55. (Pretoria, Dept. of Native Affairs, 1955)

Victor,O. "Native Education in South Africa". East and West Review 3 (1937-8?) pp.274-78.

Viljoen,C.J. "The development of education among Coloured people of the Cape Province". (B.Ed. thesis, UCT, 1931).

Visagie,J.H.H. 'n Historiese-Kritiese Studie van die ontwikkeling van die Onderwys in die Kaapse Skiereiland en omgewing 1839-1915. (Die Raad van Geestewetenskaplike navorsing, Publikasie reeks, No. 2. (Durban 1970).

Vegter,M.C.E. "Intellectual development of the Bantu since 1910". Bantu Educ. J. 6: M. 1960, p.195-209 illus.

Vos,A.J. "Some factors that determined the planning of trade training in the educational system of Africans in South Africa during the period 1867-1948". Paidonomia 2(2) 1974 p.25-31.

Vos,A.J. "Education for Development - some African Experiences". J. of Racial Affairs 29(2) 1978 p.15-7, or Paidonomia 8(2) 1980 p.1-7.

Vos,A.J. "Verantwoorde beplanning van Kwazulu se onderwysstelsel op grond van sekere riglyne: moontlikhede en probleme". Tydskrif van rasse-aangeleenthede 30(2) 1979 p.61-71.

W.,M. "Literacy for Africans". SA Outlook 77: Jun. 1947, p.87-89.

Walshe,P. The Rise of African Nationalism in South Africa, The ANC 1912-1952. (London 1970) - various refs in index under Education.

Walshe,P. Black Nationalism in South Africa: a short history. (Johannesburg, Spro-cas 1973) 40p.

Walshe,P. "Mission in a Repressive Society: The Christian Institute of Southern Africa". The Societies of Southern Africa in the 19th and 20th Centuries Vol. 12. (Univ. of London, Inst. of Commonwealth Studies, 1981) pp.91-99.

Walton,J. Craftwork for African Schools, etc. (Cape Town, 194?)

Watkinson,E.J. "A decade of progress in Native secondary education in the Cape Province, 1933-1942". (M.Ed., UNISA, 1942).

Watson,G. Passing for White: A study of racial assimilation in a SA school. (Preface by J. Simons) (London 1970) 130p.

Watts,H.L. Urbanization and Education in Durban. (Durban, SAIRR Natal Region) (Info. Sheet No. 7/70 Memo, NR 59/70) 1970).

Webb,M. "Education and social opportunities for non-Europeans". S. Afr. J. Sci. 33: 1937 p.1093-9.

Webster,E. "Servants of Apartheid? A Survey of Social Research into Industry in South Africa". Africa Perspective 14 (Summer 1980) pp.1-33.

Wells,J. Stewart of Lovedale: the life of James Stewart. (London 1909).

Welsh Report - Union of SA - Official. Report of the Interdepartmental Committee on Native Education, 1935-6. (Pretoria, 1936).

Welsh,A. "A tax on poverty". Africa South (Jan.-Mr. 1959) 7pp.

Welsh,D.J. The Roots of Segregation: Native Policy in Natal, 1945-1910. (Cape Town, 1971) re Education.

Welsh,D. "The Cultural dimension of Apartheid". African Affairs 71 (282) Jan. 1972, p.35-53.

Welsh,G.H. "Training of native teachers for village schools". SA Outlook 65 (1935) pp.186-91.

Welsh,G.H. "European Teachers in Bantu schools". SA Outlook 69 (1939) p.237-8. (and response by D.D.T. Jabavu and Z.K. Matthews on p.267).

Welsh,H.E. "Report of the Chief Inspector for Native Education, Cape". Blythswood Review VIII, 1931, p.77-8, 89-90, 101-2, 114.

Wentzel,E.M. "NUSAS and the government's education policy". The Forum 5(9) Dec. 1956.

Weslyan Mission, Tembuland (Transkei). Clarkebury Mission, Tembuland: centenary souvenir 1830-1930. (East London, the Church, 1931) 64p. - Cover title: "The Deathless Years" - Register of student 1875-1929, p.53-64.

Wessels,A.J.J. "Bantoe-onderwys moet aanpas by nywerheidsontwikkeling". Volkshandel 29(1) Mr. 1968 port. p.11+.

Westermann,D. "The Place and function of the vernacular in African Education". Int. Rev. Missions 14 (1925) pp.25-36.

Wheeler,J.H. "Apartheid implemented by education in South Africa". J. of Negro History 30(3) Summer 1961.

Whiteside,J. History of the Wesleyan methodist church of South Africa. (London 1906) 479p.

Whyte,M. Fundamental Education in SA. (Johannesburg, SAIRR, RR 34/1949).

Whyte,Q. "We must educate our millions of illiterates". Outspan 42 (1074)
S. 26th 1947, p.57+.

Whyte,Q. Native School feeding: summary of the report of the native school
feeding committee published 1949. (Johannesburg,SAIRR,1949) 26p.

Whyte,Q. Native educ. and the budget. (Johannesburg,SAIRR,1954) (RR 49/54).

Wilkie,A.W. "The Phelps Stokes Fund and Dr. Thomas Jesse Jones: a Tribute".
SA Outlook 69, 1939 p.32-33.

Williams,D. When Races Meet. (Johannesburg, 1967).

Willoughby,W.C. Tiger Kloof: the L.M.S.'s native institution in South Africa.
(London, LMS, 1921) 119p. photos, (see also Tiger Kloof).

Willoughby,W.C. "Tiger Kloof Native Institution". The Southern Workman
Dec. 1919, p.618.

Willoughby,W.C. The Soul of the Bantu. (London 1928).

Wilson,D. "Native education in the Free State". SA Outlook LXI 1931, p.193-4.

Wilson,D. (ed.) The Methodist Church of SA: Shawbury: the story of a mission
1843-1943. (Lovedale Press/printers 1943) 62pp.

Wilson,D. "Teaching the African". Lantern 1: Jun. 1951 p.229-30.

Wilson,F. & Perrot,D. (ed.) Outlook on a Century. (Lovedale 1972).

Wilson,L. "Cape township riots - some African accounts". SA Outlook 106,
1976, p.121-2.

Wilson,M. (Hunter,M.) Reaction to conquest. (London, OUP, 1936) 582p.

Wilson,M. et al. "Social Structure" in Keiskammahoek Rural Survey.
(Pietermaritzburg, 1952) Part III.

Wilson,M. "Church and School" pp.72-84, in "The Growth of Peasant Communities".
Ch. 2 of M. Wilson and L. Thompson (ed.) The Oxford Histroy of South
Africa II. (Oxford, 1971).

Wilson,M. "Missionaries: conquerors or servants of God?" An address given
on the official opening of the S.A. Missionary museum, 30/1/76, King
William's Town, S.A. 1976, 11p.

Winter,F.A. "Native education in the Transvaal". Tvl. Educ. News 37:
S. 1941, p.5-6.

Witwatersrand Council of Education. Report of the Syndic ... 1903; Annual
Reports ... 1903 to the present.

Wolfson,J. "Medium of Instruction as an ideological issue in South African
Black Schools". J. of Education 8, 1976, p.3-16.

Wolfson,J.G.E. (comp.) Turmoil at Turfloop. (Johannesburg,SAIRR,1976) 99p.

Wolfson,J.G.E. "Black Education 1976: student opinion". Race Relations News
39(1) 1977, p.3. - "Prospects for unitary education in SA". Race
Relations News 39(9) 1977, p.4.

Wollheim,O.D. Crisis in native education: The present position". Race
Relations 10(2) 1943, p.37-40.

Wollheim,O.D. "Education in S.A.", in Calpin,G.H. (ed.) The South African way of life ... (London, 1953) Ch. VII.

Woudstra-Van Riessen,M.W. "Jong Bantoe-slagoffer en sleutelfiguur". Bull. S. Afr. Ver Christelike Wet 39: D. 1973, bibliog. p.26-31.

Xuma,A.B. "Bridging the gap between white and black in South Africa". Paper read before the conference of European and Bantu Christian Students Associations held at Fort Hare 27 June - 3 July 1930. (Lovedale 1930) 20p.

Xuma,A.B. Bantu schools under Bantu Education. (Cape Town, SAIRR, 1961) (RR 11/61).

Young,R. African waste reclaimed: illustrated in the story of the Lovedale Mission. (Lovedale and London, 1902) pp.268.

Zulu National Training Institution. Prospects of the: ... for sons of chiefs and headmen. (Dept. of Native Affairs, Pretoria, 1932).

Zunga,Y. "The Education of Africans in South Africa". J. of Negro Educ. 46(3) 1977, pp.202-218.

Zwarenstien,D. "Night schools for natives". Tvl. Educ. News 41(10): N.-D. 1945, p.7-8.